TOLSTOY

ALSO BY ROSAMUND BARTLETT

Wagner and Russia (1995)
Chekhov: Scenes from a Life (2004)

CO-AUTHORED

Literary Russia: A Guide (1997)

EDITED AND CO-EDITED

Shostakovich in Context (2000)
Victory over the Sun: the World's First Futurist Opera (forthcoming)

TRANSLATED AND EDITED

Anton Chekhov, *About Love and Other Stories* (2004)
Anton Chekhov, *A Life in Letters* (co-translated with A. Phillips, 2004)
Anton Chekhov, *The Exclamation Mark* (2008)
Leo Tolstoy, *Anna Karenina* (forthcoming)

TOLSTOY

· A RUSSIAN LIFE ·

Rosamund Bartlett

P
PROFILE BOOKS

First published in Great Britain in 2010 by
PROFILE BOOKS LTD
3A Exmouth House
Pine Street
London ECIR OJH
www.profilebooks.com

Copyright © Rosamund Bartlett, 2010

1 3 5 7 9 10 8 6 4 2

Typeset in Caslon by MacGuru Ltd
info@macguru.org.uk
Designed by Sue Lamble

Printed and bound in Great Britain by
T. J. International

The moral right of the author has been asserted.

A CIP catalogue record for this book is available from the British Library.

ISBN 978 1 84668 138 7
eISBN 978 1 84765 283 6

Mixed Sources
Product group from well-managed
forests and other controlled sources
www.fsc.org Cert no. SGS-COC-2482
© 1996 Forest Stewardship Council
FSC

for Lucy

CONTENTS

The Western Russian Empire in the reign of Nicholas I

NORWAY

SWEDEN

Barents Sea

URAL MOUNTAINS

500 kilometres

300 miles

Solovetsky Islands

White Sea

•Arkhangelsk

Gulf of Bothnia

FINLAND

Helsingfors

Gulf of Finland

Revel

St Petersburg

Tsarskoe Selo

Dorpat

•Pskov

•Riga

•Vologda

RUSSIAN EMPIRE

Volga

Volga

Kama

Tver

Suzdal

Nizhny Novgorod

Cheboksary

Trinity St Sergius Monastery

Vilna•

Vitebsk•

Moscow

Kazan

Mozhaysk

Moscow

Arzamas

Sura

Minsk•

Optina Pustyn Monastery

Ryazan

Oka

Tula

Samara

Buzuluk

PRUSSIA

Oryol

Astapovo

Penza•

Gavrilovka•

Orenburg

Yasnaya Polyana

•Lipetsk

Volga

AUSTRIAN EMPIRE

•Chernigov

•Kursk

•Voronezh

Saratov•

Ural'sk

Kiev•

Kharkov

Lizinovka

Ural

Poltava

Dnieper

Don

Dniester

Kishinyov

MOLDAVIA

Odessa

Tsaritsyn

Volga

WALLACHIA

•Rostov

Astrakhan

•Bucharest

Danube

CRIMEA

Alma

Sebastopol

Starogladkovskaya

Caspian Sea

Silistria

Balaclava

Simferopol

Zheleznovodsk

Pyatigorsk

Kizlyar

Oltenita

Inkerman

Yalta

Kislovodsk•

Stary Yurt

Black Sea

Groznaya

Terek

OTTOMAN EMPIRE

Georgian Military Highway

•Vladikavkaz

•Istanbul

Tiflis•

CHRONOLOGY

1828 Born at Yasnaya Polyana, Tula Province

1830 Death of Tolstoy's mother

1837 Father dies shortly after family moves to Moscow

1841 The five Tolstoy children move to Kazan

1844 Becomes a student at Kazan University

1847 Starts writing a diary and returns to Yasnaya Polyana without finishing his degree when he comes into his inheritance

1851 Travels to the Caucasus with his brother Nikolay and joins the army

1852 *Childhood* is published

1854 Receives his commission and transfers to Bucharest, then the Crimea

1855 *Sebastopol in December* greeted with wide acclaim; arrives in St Petersburg and meets Turgenev and other writers for the first time

1856 Death of brother Dmitry; retires from the army

1857 First visit to Western Europe

1859 Opens school at Yasnaya Polyana for the peasants

1860 Second visit to Western Europe, to study pedagogy; death of brother Nikolay

1861 Appointed Justice of the Peace after serfs are emancipated; opens more schools and founds an educational journal

1862 Yasnaya Polyana raided by the secret police while Tolstoy is in Samara; marries Sofya Bers

1863 Starts writing *War and Peace* (completed 1869); birth of first child – son Sergey

1871 Buys an estate in Samara province

1872 Publishes *ABC* book and re-opens Yasnaya Polyana school briefly

1873 Starts writing *Anna Karenina* (completed 1877)

1875 Publication of the *New ABC*

1877 Becomes devout – visits Optina Pustyn Monastery

1878 Reconciliation with Turgenev; meetings with sectarians in Samara

1879 Renounces the Orthodox faith

1880 *Confession* (circulates in samizdat in 1882)

1881 Appeals to Tsar to exercise clemency after the assassination of Alexander II
Union and Translation of the Four Gospels
Family moves to Moscow for the winter months

1882 *Investigation of Dogmatic Theology* (published in 1891)
What I Believe (circulates in samizdate in 1884)

1883 Meets Vladimir Chertkov; *Gospel in Brief* published in France

1885 Sonya takes over the publication of Tolstoy's earlier fiction
First English translations of *Confession*, *What I Believe*

1886 *What Then Must We Do?*; *The Death of Ivan Ilych*; *The Powers of Darkness*
First English translations of *War and Peace* and *Anna Karenina*

1887 *On Life* (first publication in French in 1889)

1888 The Tolstoys' last child, Ivan, is born
First grandchild is born (to Ilya and his wife Sofya)

1889 *The Kreutzer Sonata* – circulates immediately in samizdat
Tolstoy's sister Masha becomes a nun

1890 Sonya obtains permission to publish *The Kreutzer Sonata* after an audience with Alexander III; Tolstoy is anathematised

1891 Renounces copyright and divides property among his wife and children. By now vegetarian, teetotal; no longer smokes or hunts

1892 Famine relief in Ryazan province

1893 *The Kingdom of God is Within You* – immediately published in translation

1894 Death of first Tolstoyan 'martyr'; meets first Dukhobors

1895 Death of Ivan Tolstoy before his seventh birthday; Tolstoy takes up cycling

1896 First Tolstoyan colony established in England

1897 Chertkov exiled to England; founds press to publish Tolstoy's writings

1898 *What is Art?*

1899 *Resurrection* – royalties pay for Dukhobors to emigrate to Canada

1901 Excommunicated

1902 Recovers from serious illness in the Crimea

1904 Death of brother Sergey

1906 Chertkov allowed to return from exile

1908 'I Cannot Be Silent!'

1910 Death at Astapovo railway station

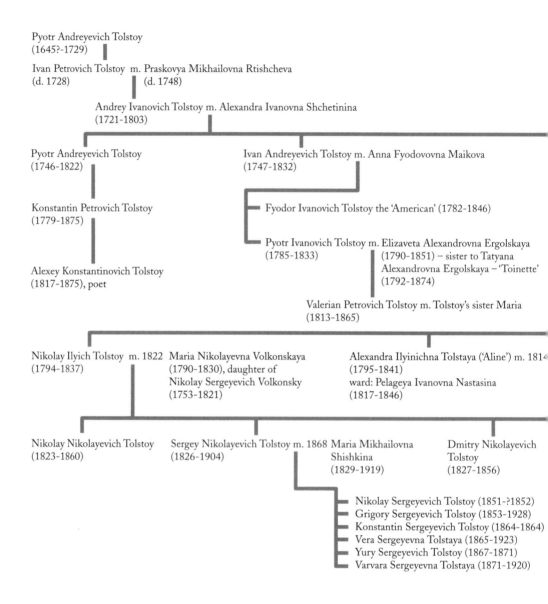

Pyotr Andreyevich Tolstoy
(1645?-1729)

Ivan Petrovich Tolstoy m. Praskovya Mikhailovna Rtishcheva
(d. 1728)   (d. 1748)

Andrey Ivanovich Tolstoy m. Alexandra Ivanovna Shchetinina
(1721-1803)

Pyotr Andreyevich Tolstoy   Ivan Andreyevich Tolstoy m. Anna Fyodovovna Maikova
(1746-1822)   (1747-1832)

Konstantin Petrovich Tolstoy   Fyodor Ivanovich Tolstoy the 'American' (1782-1846)
(1779-1875)

                                             Pyotr Ivanovich Tolstoy m. Elizaveta Alexandrovna Ergolskaya
                                             (1785-1833)   (1790-1851) – sister to Tatyana
Alexey Konstantinovich Tolstoy   Alexandrovna Ergolskaya – 'Toinette'
(1817-1875), poet   (1792-1874)

                                             Valerian Petrovich Tolstoy m. Tolstoy's sister Maria
                                             (1813-1865)

Nikolay Ilyich Tolstoy m. 1822 Maria Nikolayevna Volkonskaya   Alexandra Ilyinichna Tolstaya ('Aline') m. 181⁴
(1794-1837)   (1790-1830), daughter of   (1795-1841)
                                Nikolay Sergeyevich Volkonsky   ward: Pelageya Ivanovna Nastasina
                                (1753-1821)   (1817-1846)

Nikolay Nikolayevich Tolstoy   Sergey Nikolayevich Tolstoy m. 1868 Maria Mikhailovna   Dmitry Nikolayevich
(1823-1860)   (1826-1904)   Shishkina   Tolstoy
                                                            (1829-1919)   (1827-1856)

                                             Nikolay Sergeyevich Tolstoy (1851-?1852)
                                             Grigory Sergeyevich Tolstoy (1853-1928)
                                             Konstantin Sergeyevich Tolstoy (1864-1864)
                                             Vera Sergeyevna Tolstaya (1865-1923)
                                             Yury Sergeyevich Tolstoy (1867-1871)
                                             Varvara Sergeyevna Tolstaya (1871-1920)

Note: *The Tolstoy and Bers family trees reproduced here are principally designed to clarify the genealogies of Tolstoy and his wife Sonya and are not comprehensive.*

TOLSTOY FAMILY TREE

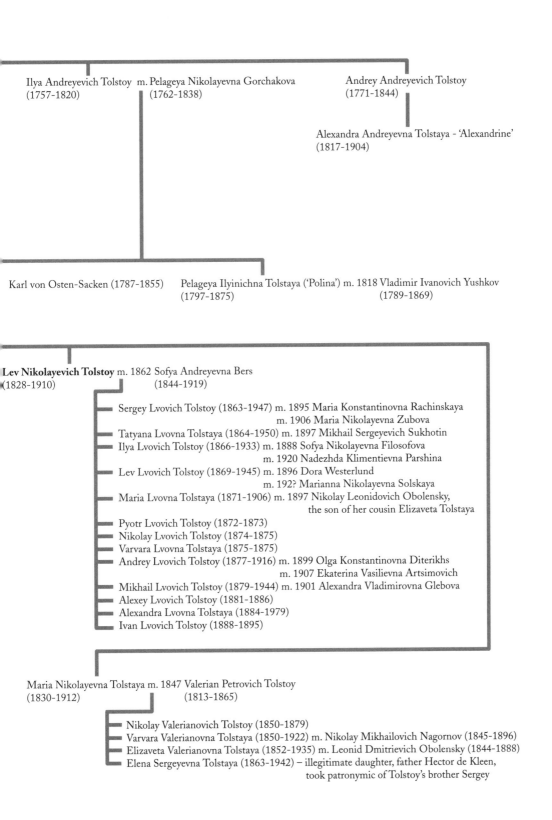

Ilya Andreyevich Tolstoy m. Pelageya Nikolayevna Gorchakova
(1757-1820)   (1762-1838)

Andrey Andreyevich Tolstoy
(1771-1844)

Alexandra Andreyevna Tolstaya - 'Alexandrine'
(1817-1904)

Karl von Osten-Sacken (1787-1855)   Pelageya Ilyinichna Tolstaya ('Polina') m. 1818 Vladimir Ivanovich Yushkov
                                    (1797-1875)   (1789-1869)

Lev Nikolayevich Tolstoy m. 1862 Sofya Andreyevna Bers
(1828-1910)   (1844-1919)

Sergey Lvovich Tolstoy (1863-1947) m. 1895 Maria Konstantinovna Rachinskaya
                                   m. 1906 Maria Nikolayevna Zubova
Tatyana Lvovna Tolstaya (1864-1950) m. 1897 Mikhail Sergeyevich Sukhotin
Ilya Lvovich Tolstoy (1866-1933) m. 1888 Sofya Nikolayevna Filosofova
                                 m. 1920 Nadezhda Klimentievna Parshina
Lev Lvovich Tolstoy (1869-1945) m. 1896 Dora Westerlund
                                m. 192? Marianna Nikolayevna Solskaya
Maria Lvovna Tolstaya (1871-1906) m. 1897 Nikolay Leonidovich Obolensky,
                                  the son of her cousin Elizaveta Tolstaya
Pyotr Lvovich Tolstoy (1872-1873)
Nikolay Lvovich Tolstoy (1874-1875)
Varvara Lvovna Tolstaya (1875-1875)
Andrey Lvovich Tolstoy (1877-1916) m. 1899 Olga Konstantinovna Diterikhs
                                   m. 1907 Ekaterina Vasilievna Artsimovich
Mikhail Lvovich Tolstoy (1879-1944) m. 1901 Alexandra Vladimirovna Glebova
Alexey Lvovich Tolstoy (1881-1886)
Alexandra Lvovna Tolstaya (1884-1979)
Ivan Lvovich Tolstoy (1888-1895)

Maria Nikolayevna Tolstaya m. 1847 Valerian Petrovich Tolstoy
(1830-1912)   (1813-1865)

Nikolay Valerianovich Tolstoy (1850-1879)
Varvara Valerianovna Tolstaya (1850-1922) m. Nikolay Mikhailovich Nagornov (1845-1896)
Elizaveta Valerianovna Tolstaya (1852-1935) m. Leonid Dmitrievich Obolensky (1844-1888)
Elena Sergeyevna Tolstaya (1863-1942) – illegitimate daughter, father Hector de Kleen,
                                  took patronymic of Tolstoy's brother Sergey

BERS FAMILY TREE

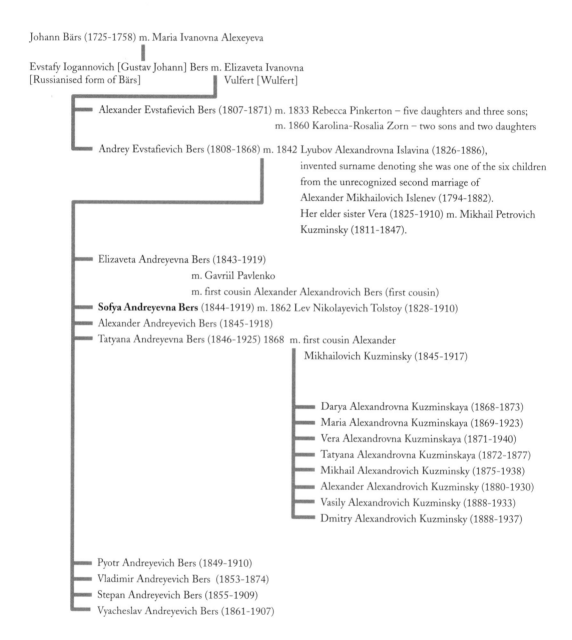

Johann Bärs (1725-1758) m. Maria Ivanovna Alexeyeva

Evstafy Iogannovich [Gustav Johann] Bers m. Elizaveta Ivanovna
[Russianised form of Bärs]   Vulfert [Wulfert]

Alexander Evstafievich Bers (1807-1871) m. 1833 Rebecca Pinkerton – five daughters and three sons;
m. 1860 Karolina-Rosalia Zorn – two sons and two daughters

Andrey Evstafievich Bers (1808-1868) m. 1842 Lyubov Alexandrovna Islavina (1826-1886),
invented surname denoting she was one of the six children
from the unrecognized second marriage of
Alexander Mikhailovich Islenev (1794-1882).
Her elder sister Vera (1825-1910) m. Mikhail Petrovich
Kuzminsky (1811-1847).

Elizaveta Andreyevna Bers (1843-1919)
m. Gavriil Pavlenko
m. first cousin Alexander Alexandrovich Bers (first cousin)

Sofya Andreyevna Bers (1844-1919) m. 1862 Lev Nikolayevich Tolstoy (1828-1910)

Alexander Andreyevich Bers (1845-1918)

Tatyana Andreyevna Bers (1846-1925) 1868 m. first cousin Alexander
Mikhailovich Kuzminsky (1845-1917)

Darya Alexandrovna Kuzminskaya (1868-1873)
Maria Alexandrovna Kuzminskaya (1869-1923)
Vera Alexandrovna Kuzminskaya (1871-1940)
Tatyana Alexandrovna Kuzminskaya (1872-1877)
Mikhail Alexandrovich Kuzminsky (1875-1938)
Alexander Alexandrovich Kuzminsky (1880-1930)
Vasily Alexandrovich Kuzminsky (1888-1933)
Dmitry Alexandrovich Kuzminsky (1888-1937)

Pyotr Andreyevich Bers (1849-1910)
Vladimir Andreyevich Bers (1853-1874)
Stepan Andreyevich Bers (1855-1909)
Vyacheslav Andreyevich Bers (1861-1907)

NOTE ON CONVENTIONS

A simplified transliteration system has been used in the body of the text (e.g. 'Pyotr Andreyevich Tolstoy'), but a more accurate one in the notes and bibliography (e.g. 'Petr Andreevich Tolstoi'). Exceptions are made in the case of accepted spellings such as 'Potemkin' (pronounced 'Potyomkin'), 'Tchaikovsky' and 'Bolshoi Theatre'.

Russian dates before 1918 are given according to the Julian calendar, which was twelve days behind the Gregorian calendar in the nineteenth century, and thirteen days behind in the twentieth century.

ЛЕВЪ ТОЛСТОЙ

INTRODUCTION

IN JANUARY 1895, deep in the heart of the Russian winter, Lev Nikolayev-ich Tolstoy left Moscow to go and spend a few days with some old friends at their country estate. He had just experienced another fracas with his wife over the publication of a new story, he felt suffocated in the city, and he wanted to clear his head by putting on his old leather coat and fur hat and going for some long walks in the clear, frosty air, far away from people and buildings. His hosts had taken care to clear the paths on their property, but Tolstoy did not like walking on well-ordered paths. Even in his late sixties he preferred tramping in the wilds, so he invariably ventured out past the garden fence and strode off into the deep snow, in whichever direction his gaze took him. Some of the younger members of the household had the idea of following in his footsteps one evening, but they soon had to give up when they saw how great was the distance between the holes left in the soft snow by his felt boots.[1]

The sensation of not being able to keep up was one commonly felt by Tolstoy's contemporaries, as he left giant footprints in every area of his life. After racking up enormous gambling debts as a young man, during which time he conceived and failed to live up to wildly ambitious ideals, he turned to writing extremely long novels and fathering a large number of children. When he went out riding with his sons, he habitually went at such a fast pace they could barely keep up with him. Then he became moral leader to the nation, and one of the world's most famous and influential men. A tendency towards the grand scale has been a markedly Russian characteristic ever since the times of Ivan the Terrible, who created an enormous multi-ethnic empire by conquering three Mongol Khanates in the sixteenth century. Peter the Great cemented the tradition by making space the defining feature of his new capital of St Petersburg which arose in record time out of the Finnish marshes. By the time Catherine the Great died at the end of the eighteenth century, Russia had also become immensely wealthy. Its aristocrats were able to build lavish palaces and assemble extravagant art collections far grander than their Western counterparts, with lifestyles to match. But Russia's poverty was also on a grand scale, perpetuated by an inhumane caste system in which a tiny minority of Westernised nobility ruled over a fettered serf population made to live in degrading conditions. Tolstoy was both a product of this culture and perhaps its most vivid expression.

Many people who knew Tolstoy noticed his hyper-sensitivity. He was like litmus paper in his acute receptivity to minute gradations of physical and emotional experience, and it was his unparalleled ability to observe and articulate these ever-changing details of human behaviour in his creative works that makes his prose so thrilling to read. The consciousness of his characters is at once particular and universal. Tolstoy was also hyper-sensitive in another way, for he embodied at different times of his life a myriad Russian archetypes, from the 'repentant nobleman' to the 'holy fool'. Only Russia could have produced a writer like Tolstoy, but only Tolstoy could be likened in almost the same breath to both a tsar and a peasant. From the time that he was born into the aristocratic Tolstoy family in the idyllic surroundings of his ancestral home at Yasnaya Polyana to the day that he left it for the last time at the age of eighty-two, Tolstoy lived a profoundly Russian life. He began to be identified with his country soon after he published his national epic *War and Peace* when he was in still his thirties. Later on, he was equated with Ilya Muromets, the most famous Russian *bogatyr* – a semi-mythical medieval warrior who lay at home on the brick stove until he was thirty-three – then went on to perform great feats defending the realm. Ilya Muromets is Russia's traditional symbol of physical and spiritual strength. Tolstoy was also synonymous with Russia in the eyes of many of his foreign admirers. 'He is as much part of Russia, as significant of Russian character, as prophetic of Russian development, as the Kremlin itself,' wrote the liberal British politician Sir Henry Norman soon after visiting Tolstoy in 1901.[2] For the Austrian writer Stefan

Zweig, meanwhile, Tolstoy had 'no face of his own; he possesses the face of the Russian people, because in him the whole of Russia lives and breathes'.[3]

Tolstoy lived a Russian life, and he lived many more lives than most other Russians, exhibiting both the 'natural dionysism' and 'Christian asceticism' which the philosopher Nikolay Berdyaev defines as characteristic of the Russian people.[4] First of all he lived the life of his privileged class, educated by private foreign tutors and waited on by serfs. He became a wealthy landowner at the age of nineteen, and immediately began exhibiting Russian 'maximalist' tendencies by squandering his inheritance on gypsy singers and gambling. Whole villages were sold off to pay his debts, followed by his house. Tolstoy also lived up to the reputation of the depraved Russian landowner by taking advantage of his serf girls, then assumed another classic identity of the Russian noble: he became an army officer. For most of his comrades-in-arms the next step was retirement to the country estate, but Tolstoy became a writer – the most promising young writer of his generation. It was at this point that he started showing signs of latent anarchism: he did not want to belong to any particular literary fraternity, and soon alienated most of his fellow writers with his eccentric views and combative nature. Turgenev disappointed him by failing to take writing as seriously as he did, and for being too enslaved to western Europe. Turgenev's creative work was as deeply bound up with Russia as Tolstoy's was, but he lived in Paris. Tolstoy made two visits abroad during his lifetime, but he was tied to Russia body and soul.

As he matured under the influence of the writers and philosophers who shaped his ideas, Tolstoy inevitably became a member of the intelligentsia, the peculiarly Russian class of people united by their education and usually critical stance towards their government. The deep guilt he now felt before the Russian peasantry, furthermore, made him a repentant nobleman, ashamed at his complicity in the immoral institution of serfdom. Like the Populists, Tolstoy began to see the peasants as Russia's best class, and her future, and around the time that serfdom was finally abolished he threw himself into teaching village children how to read and write. But he was mercurial, and a year later abandoned his growing network of unconventional schools to get married and start a family. The emotional stability provided by his devoted wife Sofya ('Sonya') Bers enabled him next to become Russia's Homer: *War and Peace* was written at the happiest time in his life.

Tolstoy's overactive conscience would not allow him to continue along the path of great novelist, and in the first half of the 1870s he went back to education. This time he devised his own system for teaching Russian children from all backgrounds how to read and write, by putting together an *ABC* and several reading primers. He taught himself Greek, then produced his own simplified translations of Aesop's fables, as well as stories of his own, a compilation of tales about Russian bogatyrs and extracts from sacred readings. The Yasnaya Polyana school was reopened, with some of the elder Tolstoy children as teachers. Tolstoy was more of a father during these years than at any other time, and he took his family off to his newly acquired estate on the Samaran steppe for an unorthodox summer holiday amongst Bashkirs and horses. He revelled in the raw, primitive lifestyle, even if his wife did not.

In the second half of the 1870s everything began to unravel. In 1873, the year in which he began *Anna Karenina*, Tolstoy first spoke out on behalf of the impoverished peasantry by appealing nationwide for help in the face of impending famine. *Anna Karenina*, set in contemporary Russia, reflects Tolstoy's own search for meaning in the face of depression and thoughts of death. Initially, he found meaning in religious faith and became one of the millions of pilgrims criss-crossing the Russian land on their way to visit its hallowed monasteries. Like many fellow intellectuals, Tolstoy was drawn to the Elders of the Optina Pustyn Monastery – monks who had distanced themselves from the official ecclesiastical hierarchy by resurrecting the ascetic traditions of the early Church Fathers, and who were revered for their spiritual wisdom. He found it was the peasants who had more wisdom to impart, however, and the next time he went to Optina Pustyn, he walked there, dressed in peasant clothes and bast shoes like a *Strannik* ('wanderer'). The Stranniks were a sect who spent their lives walking in pilgrimage from one monastery to another, living on alms. The nomadic spirit runs deep in Russia, and Tolstoy increasingly hankered as time went on to join their ranks. He had long ago started dressing like a peasant, but he soon wanted to dispense with money and private property altogether.

From extreme piety Tolstoy went to extreme nihilism. At the end of the 1870s he began to see the light, and he set down his spiritual journey in a work which came to be known as his *Confession*. He also undertook a critical investigation of Russian Orthodox theology, and produced a 'new, improved' translation of the Gospels. Over the course of the 1880s he became an apostle for the Christian teaching which emerged from his root-and-branch review of the original sources, and at the same time his newfound faith compelled him to speak out against the immorality he now saw in all state institutions, from the monarchy downwards. Home life now became very strained, particularly after Tolstoy renounced the copyright on all his new writings and gave away all his property to his family. He discovered kindred spirits amongst the unofficial sectarian faiths which proliferated across Russia, whose followers were mostly peasants, and gradually became the leader of a new sectarian faith, although his followers were mostly conscience-stricken gentry like himself. These 'Tolstoyans' sometimes vied with each other to lead the most morally pure life, giving up money and property, living by the sweat of their brow and treating everyone as their 'brother'. Thus one zealous Tolstoyan even gave up his kaftan, hat and bast shoes one summer, glad to be no longer a slave to his personal possessions.[5]

By the 1890s Tolstoy had become the most famous man in Russia, celebrated for a number of compellingly written and explosive tracts setting out his views on Christianity, the Orthodox Church and the Russian government, which were read all the more avidly for having been banned: they circulated very successfully in samizdat. It was when Tolstoy spearheaded the relief effort during the widespread famine of 1892 that his position as Russia's greatest moral authority became unassailable. The result was a constant stream of visitors at his front door in Moscow, many of whom simply wanted to shake his hand. One of them was the twenty-three-year-old Sergey Diaghilev, who with characteristic chutzpah turned up one day with his cousin, and immediately noticed the incongruity of Tolstoy's peasant dress and 'gentlemanly way of behaving and speaking'. Tolstoy had come for a rest from the famine-relief work he had been doing in Ryazan province, and talked to the sophisticated young aesthetes from St Petersburg about soup kitchens. Diaghilev shared his impressions with his stepmother:

When we got out into the street, our first words were exclamations: 'But he's a saint, he's really a saint!' We were so moved we almost wept. There was something inexpressibly sincere, touching and holy in the whole person of the great man. It's funny that we could smell his beard for a long time, which we had touched as we embraced him ...[6]

Tolstoy received thousands of visitors in the last decades of his life, and he had a reputation for rarely turning anyone away. Before long, he became known as the 'Elder of Yasnaya Polyana'.

Tolstoy received over 50,000 letters during his lifetime, 9,000 of which came from abroad. With the help of the eminence grise of the Tolstoyan movement, Vladimir Chertkov, who found him secretaries, he did his best to answer as many as he could (there are 8,500 letters printed in his *Collected Works*, and there must have been many more).[7] Chertkov was the scion of a distinguished noble family who became Tolstoy's trusted friend, and the chief publisher of his late writings. Tolstoy's family often felt neglected. It was his wife Sonya who bore the brunt of domestic duties, almost as a single parent of their eight children, some of whom were very unruly. She also had the demanding job of publishing her husband's old writings, which guaranteed the family some income, even if her profitable enterprise caused him pain. It was not easy being a member of Tolstoy's family. Sonya wrote to her husband in 1892: 'Tanya told someone in Moscow, "I'm so tired of being the daughter of a famous father". And I'm tired of being the wife of a famous husband, I can tell you!'[8]

Tolstoy's fame increased further when he published his last novel *Resurrection* in order to aid the members of the Dukhobor sect to emigrate to Canada, where they could practise their beliefs freely and without persecution. Finally exasperated by Tolstoy's blistering satire of a mass in one of its chapters, the Russian Orthodox Church excommunicated him, and so Tolstoy joined the illustrious ranks of Russian apostates – rebels like Stenka Razin and Emelyan Pugachev. Because of his fame, Tolstoy was able to do what few others in Russia could: speak out. The government was powerless to stop him, as it knew there would be international outrage if he was either arrested or exiled. Tolstoy took advantage of the situation by behaving like a 'holy fool' so that he could speak frankly to the Tsar about his failure as a national leader. There was a widespread feeling in Russia in the last decade of Tolstoy's life that he was the 'real' Tsar.

Tolstoy lived many lives in the course of his eighty-two years, but there are some noticeable exceptions from the roster of Russian archetypes. He had a longstanding aversion to merchants, for example, who formed a separate class in Russian society, and had a similarly aristocratic disdain for the *chinovnik*, that representative of the imperial bureaucracy, and the *raznochinets*, the 'mixed class' members of the intelligentsia who came from lowly backgrounds and were often radical 'Westernisers', anxious to fight for social reform. Tolstoy was also no 'Oblomov' – the Russian bear who is Goucharov's most famous fictional character, and who takes several chapters to get out of bed. Despite all his efforts, Tolstoy failed to acquire that cardinal Russian virtue of humility which Oblomov so effortlessly manifests. And yet there is one life we might add albeit not a Russian one: Tolstoy is seen almost as an honorary Chechen. The small Tolstoy Museum in Starogladkovskaya, the Russian military base where Tolstoy was billeted in the 1850s, was the only museum on Chechen territory not to close during the more recent war with Russia, while the national museum in Grozny was desecrated. The statue of Tolstoy in front of the museum also remained unscathed.

The Chechens admire Tolstoy for making friends with them during his time in the Caucasus (this was indeed highly unusual for Russian officers, who tended to treat the natives with contempt), and for writing about them in a positive light. According to Tolstoy's great-great-grandson Vladimir Ilych, who became director at the Yasnaya Polyana Museum in 1994, 'The Chechen people think that Tolstoy wrote most truthfully of the events that happened then and the character of the mountain peoples, their striving to be independent, for freedom, and their religious, ethnic and other particularities'. Salavdi Zagibov, who succeeded his father as director of the Starogladkovskaya Tolstoy Museum in 2008, has also noted the similarities between the pacifist teachings of Tolstoy and the nineteenth-century Sufi leader Sheikh Kunta Khadji, a Chechen shepherd.[9] The Starogladkovskaya Museum was reopened in December 2009 after renovation, which was funded by the personal foundation of Ramzan Kadyrov, President of Chechnya.

While Tolstoy is universally regarded as one of the world's great writers, he remains a controversial and contradictory figure. His marriage had already gone into a steep decline by the time he met Vladimir Chertkov, but it was his submission to his devoted friend which caused a bad situation to disintegrate entirely in the last year of his life. Chertkov's influence over Tolstoy's estate meant that his version of events initially prevailed over dissenting voices, chiefly that of the writer's grieving widow, whom he had displaced in her husband's affections. The publication in 2006 of a collection of scholarly articles dedicated to her memory, and in 2010 of the first Russian biography of Sofya Tolstaya, is witness to the sea-change in attitudes that swiftly took place after the collapse of the Soviet Union.[10]

Sonya can be forgiven for becoming paranoid and hysterical in the last year of her husband's life. She can be forgiven a lot, as her husband treated her very badly, by any account. His strengths were also his weaknesses, and his attitude towards the female gender is in general not admirable. Sonya did not, like him and their daughters, become vegetarian, nor did she want to dispense with money and private property; she just wanted to maintain the comfortable lifestyle she was used to. Sonya was a talented woman who selflessly put aside whatever interests she might have developed in order to go on bearing the children her husband wanted, and help him as his copyist. For long years she supported a man whose ego often blinded him to the needs of his family, and it was unfair of him to expect her to follow him meekly on his quest to lead a more spiritually enlightened, ascetic life just because he decided it was time to change. She also had her faults, however, and her rigidity stopped her from seeing that she could be just as controlling as Chertkov.

Tolstoy has had his share of detractors. One of the most eloquent and witty is Alexander Boot, an admirer of Tolstoy the artist, but also the author of an effective hatchet job on Tolstoy the thinker:

> He wished to be more than a novelist, even one of genius. He wished to be more than a seer or a soothsayer, although that would have been a good start. He wished to be God … He wanted to correct God's mistakes in having allowed the world to become imperfect and sinful. He, Count Tolstoy … set out to usurp God's job. But the job was already taken, and the deity stubbornly hung on to it. Therefore Tolstoy declared war on God and fought it with every means at his disposal. Alas, though he tried many lines of attack, each disguised by the camouflage of pseudo-Christian verbiage, Tolstoy came off a poor second. By way of revenge, he came, in effect, to deny God the Father, ignore God the Son and dismiss God the Holy Spirit. No one was allowed to defeat Tolstoy and get away with it.[11]

Boot concedes Tolstoy's enormous impact on many of the movements of the modern age, such as vegetarianism, anti-capitalism and animal rights, and his arguments are persuasive, yet they need to be squared with the fact that Tolstoy's philosophy of non-violence was revered by Gandhi, Wittgenstein and Martin Luther King. To see Tolstoy principally in terms of artist versus thinker, moreover, is to overlook his important humanitarian work.

It is perhaps Tolstoy's impact on Russian life while he was still alive which is his greatest legacy beyond his great fictional works. If for nothing else, Tolstoy should be hailed for trying to improve literacy in a country where only a tiny percentage of the population could read and write at the end of the nineteenth century, for doing something about the national disaster threatened by famine, and for having the courage to speak some home truths to a complacent and corrupt regime which was indifferent to the poverty of its subjects. Numerous people approached Tolstoy with scepticism, but came away, like Diaghilev, convinced of his sincerity. Even if some of his sons did their best to practise the opposite of what he preached, his daughters were devoted to him. And there is something touching about his untiring zest for life, however wrong-headed his ideas were.

The greatest task facing the biographer of Tolstoy is the challenge of making sense of a man who was truly larger than life. It was a task he himself took on the moment he started writing a diary in his late adolescence, and one he never abandoned, particularly in his last years. Tolstoy never stopped trying to make sense of himself in his writing, whether it was through the public medium of his fictional characters or the quasi-private one of his diary entries. Indeed, as the scholar Irina Paperno has suggested, he even seems to have wanted to extend the extraordinary feat he achieved in his fiction of articulating latent as well as overt psychological processes by 'turning himself into a book' in his diaries.[12] If encompassing and describing his conscious-ness as it evolved was a project doomed to failure, like so many Russian utopian dreams, its very lack of finitude nevertheless reassures us of Tolstoy's humanity.

The task of charting his artistic and intellectual journey has also proved a daunting one for Russia's great Tolstoy scholars. It is indicative that the mammoth multi-volume biography which Tolstoy's former secretary Nikolay Gusev embarked on in the 1950s is modestly titled *Materials for a Biogra-phy*. It remained unfinished at his death at the age of eighty-five in 1967, when his pupil Lidiya Gromova-Opulskaya took up the baton. Although she added a further two volumes to Gusev's four, she also died before the project could be completed, leaving the last eighteen years of Tolstoy's life still to be covered (before this distinguished scholar's death in 2003 she launched the new definitive hundred-volume edition of Tolstoy's *Complete Collected Works*).[13] While there is a paucity of sources concerning Tolstoy's early life, necessitating reliance on the sometimes erratic and incomplete memoirs the writer compiled in old age, the sheer abundance of sources on his last years create problems for the biographer of a different kind. Such was his fame that many episodes in the 'hagiography' of Lev Tolstoy were set down while he was not just still alive, but comparatively young: the first biography was published when he was in his early sixties, in German moreover. The innumerable cliches which cling to Tolstoy's *vita* – 'great writer of the Russian land', 'the Elder of Yasnaya Polyana' – can also be inhibiting, as can be the many contradictions with which his personality bristles. Tolstoy's life is rich and fascinating but also deeply mythologised, and he himself contributed to the process of mythologisation.

In the early years of his marriage, while he was writing *War and Peace*, Tolstoy would insist that his young wife was present, and so Sonya would usually curl up by his feet on the bearskin rug next to his desk – a trophy from one of his hunting expeditions.[14] Later on he worked in seclusion, but all through their married life, the Tolstoys read each other's diaries, which meant their confessions could never really be private. In Sonya's case, it was in the letters she wrote to her sister Tanya that she wrote most frankly; her diary was often written with a high degree of self-consciousness. For Tolstoy, however, who was always deeply connected to the land and those who worked it, there was from the beginning that very Russian yearning for oneness, to the extent that the borders between public and private eventually became blurred. His was a Russian life.

ANCESTORS: THE TOLSTOYS AND THE VOLKONSKYS

[T]he extraordinary beauty of spring this year in the countryside would wake the dead. The warm breeze at night making the young leaves on the trees rustle, the moonlight and the shadows, the nightingales below, above, further off and nearby, the frogs in the distance, the silence, and the fragrant, balmy air – all this happening suddenly, not at the usual time, is very strange and good. In the morning there is again the play of light and shade in the tall, already dark-green grass from the big, thickly covered birch trees on the avenue, as well as forget-me-nots and dense nettles, and everything – above all the swaying of the birch trees on the avenue – is just the same as it was when I first noticed and started to love its beauty sixty years ago.

Letter to Sofya Tolstaya, Yasnaya Polyana, 3 May 1897[1]

'BY HIS BIRTH, by his upbringing and by his manners, father was a real aristocrat. Despite the worker's blouse he invariably wore, despite his complete contempt for all the nobility's prejudices, he was a gentleman, and he remained a gentleman until the end of his days.'[2] Thus Tolstoy's son Ilya summed up perhaps the greatest contradiction in the personality of a man whose whole life was a bundle of contradictions. For most of his life, Tolstoy never questioned his status as a *barin* (a landowning gentleman), and he was proud of his noble heritage. He continued to behave like an aristocrat long after he dropped his title and started wearing peasant clothes, because it was in his blood. 'Although he wore the dress of a peasant, he had neither the aspect nor the bearing of a peasant. No *muzhik* [peasant] ever had his piercing eyes or his air of composure and mastery,' wrote the economist James Mavor when reflecting on his meeting with the seventy-one-year-old writer in 1899.[3] Whether it was someone seeing a weather-beaten peasant walking along a country road and noticing there was something about him which was 'out of keeping with his garb', as his American translator Isabel Hapgood commented,[4] or the way in which Tolstoy invariably used the polite form of address when speaking to people, something defiantly aristocratic remained about his bearing.

Tolstoy certainly shared his family's deep reverence for their ancestors. He loved the myths that surrounded them, and the feeling of being connected to them through the generations. According to one Russian Tolstoy specialist, he was even convinced 'that he existed before he was born, that he was the product of all his ancestors who lived long before him'.[5] That sense of being part of a continuum was indeed profoundly important for a writer whose life was so deeply bound up with his country's history. Tolstoy also loved the fact that he was constantly reminded of his family's past by the physical environment of Yasnaya Polyana, the country estate where he spent the greater part of his life, and which, as his son Lev was to comment, he regarded as 'an organic part of himself'.[6] His beloved home had been in his family for generations, it was where he was born, it was where he spent his early childhood, surrounded by family portraits, furniture and heirlooms, and it was really the only place where he was happy. It was fitting that he himself ultimately became an organic part of Yasnaya Polyana by being buried in the middle of its grounds. 'It is difficult for me to imagine Russia and my attitude to it without my Yasnaya Polyana', Tolstoy wrote in 1858, at the beginning of a projected essay about the summer he had spent the previous year on his estate. He explained that without Yasnaya Polyana he might understand certain general laws about Russia, but he would not love it with such a passion, and that this was the only form of love for the motherland that he knew.[7]

Tolstoy's cult of his ancestors may have been a badge of pride, and fundamental to his own sense of identity, but it also furnished the inspiration for his great novels. His abiding interest in the generation of the 1825 Decembrist Uprising, for example, which was the inspiration behind *War and Peace*, was in part fuelled by his being distantly related to Sergey Volkonsky, who had been one of its leaders and a hero of the war with Napoleon. Tolstoy actually met Volkonsky in Florence in 1860. Volkonsky had recently returned from thirty years' exile in Siberia, having been amnestied by Alexander II and was by then an old man. Once Tolstoy began writing *War and Peace* three years later, it was his ancestors who became the indispensable prototypes of many of its memorable central characters. For this reason alone it is worth extending our view of Tolstoy's life back several generations.

Tolstoy was committed to truth in his fiction, but for some reason he never submitted his family history to the razor-edged rational analysis he applied to most other things. Thus he continued to believe into his dotage that his family was descended from a German immigrant called Dick. Amongst the books in his library were four volumes tracing the genealogies of Russia's most important aristocratic families,[8] and Tolstoy believed what he read there – that his earliest ancestor came to Russia in the Middle Ages, and that his surname was simply a translation of *dick*, which means 'fat' in German.[9] This is what Tolstoy often told foreign visitors who were curious to know about his family's history,[10] and this is what was reproduced in the earliest biographies of the great writer. Evgeny Solovyov, for example (whose biography went on sale for twenty-five kopecks in 1894, when Tolstoy was sixty-six), explained that *tolsty*, the Russian word for 'fat' (stressed on the first syllable) had given rise to *Tolstye* – 'the Tolstoys'. From *Tolstye* had then come Tolstoy, with a stress on the second syllable.[11]

There is not a scrap of evidence to suggest this putative German immigrant who founded the Tolstoy dynasty ever existed, nor indeed was it ever accepted practice to translate foreign surnames into Russian in old Muscovy. The Tolstoy family's belief in its German provenance certainly ran deep, however. In the 1840s, 'Der Dicke' was what Nicholas I reputedly called General Count Pyotr Alexandrovich Tolstoy, a distant relative of Lev Niko-layevich who served as ambassador to Paris in the crucial years before the Napoleonic invasion. Maybe the Tsar was hoping to pay the Tolstoy family a compliment by alluding to its German origins, being himself a Germano-phile. But perhaps it was just because the venerable count was rather portly.[12]

In another family legend it was supposedly a German called Indros who launched the Tolstoy dynasty. According to Russian annals of genealogy dating back to the seventeenth century, this Indros migrated from the Holy Roman Empire with two sons and 3,000 men in 1352, settled in Chernigov, changed his name to Leonty and converted to Russian Orthodoxy. Tolstoy's former secretary Nikolay Gusev wondered with good reason, however, how this feudal lord and his enormous retinue could have managed safely to cover hundreds of miles and cross several states usually at war with each other. Why did they attempt such a journey in the first place, and why should they have chosen the politically insignificant Chernigov as their destination? There is also the inconvenient fact that bubonic plague was raging in Rus in the mid-fourteenth century, as elsewhere in Europe, which was hardly an incentive to the pioneering spirit.[13] Tolstoy's grandson Sergey Mikhailovich, who also subscribed to the peculiarly resilient family myth about its German origins, complicated the issue by suggesting Indris was actually a Flemish count called Henri de Mons who set off for Russia after an unsuccessful expedition to Cyprus.[14] It does at least seem probable, however, that the Tolstoys could trace their lineage to this fabled progenitor's great grandson Andrey Kharitonovich, who brought the family to Moscow in the early fifteenth century and whose corpulence earned him the nickname which in time gave rise to the family's illustrious surname.

In 1682, when the old feudal hierarchical system was abolished, Russian noble families rushed to register their genealogy with the state in order to legitimise their claim to noble status. Another fact which casts doubt on the theory that the Tolstoys were descended from German immigrants is that nearly all the families who registered their genealogy claimed foreign ancestry (most of which was completely spurious), in the hope of enhancing their position, and also their standing with the Tsar.[15] One of the six signatories who submitted the Tolstoys' early family history to the Russian heraldry office in Moscow in 1686 was the court servant Pyotr Andreyevich, who a few decades later would become the first Count Tolstoy. Pyotr Andreyevich was an exceptional individual, and the first Tolstoy to enter the history books, and he clearly also had creative talent, as he probably invented the story about his earliest ancestors, in which case the family talent for writing fiction can also be traced back several centuries.

Pyotr Andreyevich Tolstoy (1645–1729) led a remarkable life. A man of immense energy, with a brilliant mind, he was also known to be treacherous, switching his political allegiance to the young Peter the Great soon after the latter wrested power from his half-sister Sofia in 1689. Pyotr Andreyevich played his cards skilfully. By 1697, at the age of fifty-two, and already a grandfather, he had demonstrated sufficient loyalty to be sent by Tsar Peter to Italy to study navigation and ship-building, along with many other scions of noble families. One of them was his near contemporary Boris Petrovich Sheremetev, who was rather higher up on the social ladder and travelled with an enormous retinue, including a scribe. Pyotr Tolstoy, by contrast, was accompanied by one soldier and one servant, and he wrote his own diary, which provides a far more interesting and informative account of Italian life seen through Russian eyes.

During his year and four months away, Pyotr Andreyevich travelled the length and breadth of Italy from Venice to Bari, and was able to study Italian life and social customs in some detail. Since he had come from 'Holy Mother Moscow', where secular culture was thin on the ground, it is not surprising to find a great deal of attention in his diary devoted to the Church. Pyotr Andreyevich came back to Moscow erudite and beardless, however, and the sight of a Russian Orthodox Christian without a beard probably shocked many of his contemporaries (the foundation of St Petersburg was still a few years off). Pyotr Tolstoy was one of the first Russians to don Western dress in the last years of old Muscovy. Years before Peter the Great began the wholesale import of Western culture into Russia, he could boast an impressive knowledge of European letters, as well as exquisite manners.[16]

In 1701, seeing his brilliant diplomatic potential, Peter appointed Pyotr Andreyevich as Russia's first ambassador to Constantinople. It was a tall order to hope to improve relations with the Sublime Porte, which fought three wars against Russia during the reign of Peter the Great alone, and Pyotr Tolstoy spent the last years of his posting languishing in the Yedikule ('Seven Towers') Fortress – the dungeon where foreign ambassadors whose countries were at war with the Ottoman Empire were traditionally incarcerated. But Tolstoy was clearly a restless man who needed to be engaged on something. Either before or after Sultan Ahmed III declared war in 1710, he drew on the knowledge of Latin he had acquired during his time in Italy to produce the first Russian translation of Ovid's *Metamorphoses*.

By the time Pyotr Tolstoy returned to Russia in 1714, Peter the Great had not only founded St Petersburg, but made it his new capital. Tolstoy accompanied the Tsar on further foreign trips, and then in 1717 was entrusted with the most delicate and challenging of missions. He was to go to Naples and persuade Peter's errant son Alexey, the heir to the throne, to return to Russia. Hostile to his father's reforms, Alexey had sought refuge in Vienna with his brother-in-law Emperor Charles VI, who stationed him out of harm's way in Naples in order to avert a diplomatic crisis. Pyotr Andreyevich had to resort to nefarious means, employing guile and cunning, and a great deal of disinformation, but his mission was successful. Upon his return to Russia the *tsarevich* Alexey was immediately thrown into the dungeon of the St Peter and Paul Fortress and interrogated for treason; he died soon afterwards.

Pyotr Tolstoy also took part in the interrogation. He did not endear himself to the Russian population at large, but was showered with riches by the grateful Tsar, who decorated him, appointed him senator and gave him extensive lands. By the time he was made a count, on the day of the coronation of Peter's wife Catherine I as Empress in 1724, the year before the Tsar's death, Pyotr Andreyevich was one of the most powerful men in Russia. But his machinations to ensure that Catherine's daughter Elizabeth succeeded her were to be his undoing. Following Catherine's death in 1727, Tolstoy's rival Menshikov had him arrested and imprisoned in the Peter and Paul Fortress. At the age of eighty-two, Pyotr Andreyevich was sentenced to death and summarily shorn of his title, his decorations and his lands. Shortly before his execution, Tolstoy's sentence was commuted to life exile in the Solovetsky Monastery prison, which was located on an island near the Arctic Circle. It was a month's journey away, and he was escorted there, as befitted his rank, by some 100 soldiers, first by land up to the port of Arkhangelsk, and then across the freezing waters of the White Sea. Here Tolstoy was kept in solitary confinement, forbidden to engage in correspondence, and only allowed out, in irons, to attend church services.

The Solovetsky Monastery in the White Sea had been founded in the fifteenth century by two Stakhanovite monks who regarded life in a normal cloister too easy an option. They had sought instead a life of the utmost physical privation in emulation of the desert ascetics of early Christianity and found it on 'Solovki', the remote Solovetsky islands, where there is no daylight in deepest winter. The piety of the monastery's founding forefathers stood in stark contrast to the barbarity of Ivan the Terrible, who saw nothing untoward in establishing a prison in its sacred grounds. With its harsh climate, it was a particularly bleak place to serve a sentence. Pyotr Andreyevich's son Ivan, who accompanied him into exile, died the year after they arrived. Within eight months, Pyotr Andreyevich was also dead.

A century and a half later, in the 1870s, their descendant Lev Tolstoy became fascinated by this chapter of his family history while planning a novel set in the times of Peter the Great. Writing to his friend and relative Alexandra Andreyevna Tolstaya in June 1879, when he was making notes on the case in the Moscow archive of the Ministry of Justice, he declared that the exile of Pyotr and Ivan was the 'darkest episode' in the lives of their ancestors. For him, the time of Peter the Great was the 'beginning of everything', and he became so interested in Pyotr Andreyevich's fate that he thought seriously for a while about visiting his place of exile that summer, in the hope of finding out more about him.[17] By this time the monastery had become one of the most sacred places in Russia (and was attracting around 20,000 pilgrims each year),[18] but in the 1870s it was still not an easy place to get to. Tolstoy heard more about Solovki at this time from a peasant storyteller from northern Russia who shared with him the popular legend of the Three Elders.

In 1886, as part of his mission to provide the masses with high-quality reading matter, Tolstoy reworked the story for a popular weekly journal. It is a typically subversive work, in keeping with the ideas he had begun to develop at the time. The story is about the events which take place during a journey to the monastery on one of the boats ferrying pilgrims to the islands from Arkhangelsk. A bishop asks to be set down on an island inhabited by three legendary 'holy men' whom he wants to meet. To his consternation, their modest, unconventional and practical Christianity proves to contain more holiness than the 'official' Church dogma he tries to inculcate them with. The bishop is humbled by his meeting with the Three Elders. Such provocative ideas caused Tolstoy to become the Russian government's greatest threat. He was so determined to expose the lies and hypocrisy he saw embedded in the fabric of the tsarist system that he positively hoped he could emulate his ancestor Pyotr Andreyevich, but the government refused to allow him to become a martyr. Alexander III once famously remarked, 'Tolstoy wants me to exile him to Solovki, but I am not going to give him the publicity.'[19] After the 1917 Revolution Solovki became one of the Soviet Union's most notorious concentration camps, and it is grimly ironic that some of Tolstoy's followers ended up there in 1930 simply for refusing to give up their beliefs about non-resistance to violence and the abolition of private property.[20]

Fourteen children were born to Tolstoy and his wife Sonya during their long marriage, but Lev Nikolayevich was not the first Tolstoy to have so many offspring. Pyotr Andreyevich's eldest son Ivan had five sons and five daughters before he died in the Solovetsky prison at the age of forty-three in 1728, and the second son was Andrey Ivanovich (1721–1803). This was Tolstoy's great-grandfather, about whom not much is known beyond the fact that he was christened 'Big Nest' because he had twenty-three children, twelve of whom reached adulthood.[21] Tolstoy's aunt once told him that Andrey Ivanovich had married at such a young age that he apparently burst into tears when his equally young wife Alexandra went to a ball one evening without saying goodbye to him.[22]

In 1741 Catherine I's daughter Elizabeth finally became Empress, as Pyotr Andreyevich had hoped, and at some point in her reign, she returned one of the Tolstoy family estates to his son Ivan Petrovich's widow. In 1760 the remaining properties and Pyotr Andreyevich's title were finally restored.[23] It would have been at this time that the Tolstoy family crest was designed, consisting of a shield supported by two borzoi dogs, signifying loyalty and swiftness in attaining results. The shield, divided into seven segments, features at its centre a crossed gold sword and a silver arrow running through a golden key, as a symbol of the family's long history. In the top left-hand corner is half of the Russian imperial eagle, and next to it on a silver background is the blue St Andrew Cross which Pyotr Andreyevich was awarded in 1722. In the bottom right-hand corner the seven towers topped with crescents recall Pyotr Andreyevich's incarceration in Constantinople's Yedikule Fortress, and his role in securing Russian victory over the Turks.[24]

Count Andrey Ivanovich Tolstoy, as he now became at the age of thirty-nine, was a loyal servant of the state. He was also clearly fiscally astute, as by the time of his death in 1803 the family's fortunes had begun to improve. The profligate and sybaritic ways of Tolstoy's grandfather, Ilya Andreyevich (1757–1820), however, ensured the family was soon impecunious again. Ilya Andreyevich followed the conventional career path at this time for Russian noblemen, who were still required to serve: he went into the army. After retiring in his thirties, he got married, and he married well: he and his wife Pelageya Nikolayevna (1762–1838) had at their disposal not only a Moscow mansion, but also extensive properties in Tula province. They chose to make their home in their 5,500-acre Polyany estate, which came with hundreds of serfs, an aviary and orchards. The couple lived in some style: the sterlet served at their table came fresh from the White Sea via Arkhangelsk, the oysters were imported from Holland, while asparagus and pineapples were grown in the huge greenhouses they built on their lands. According to one family legend, the count even despatched his linen to Amsterdam to be laundered. Tolstoy describes their life as one long succession of 'parties, theatres, balls, dinners, excursions'.[25]

Ilya Andreyevich was hospitable and generous, but not terribly well educated: when he parted from his wife for the first time in twenty years in 1813, he wrote her a letter riddled with spelling mistakes, and almost totally lacking in punctuation. A brief extract might be rendered in English thus: 'Sadd very sadd my dear friend Countess Pelageya Nikolayevna to congratulate you on your absent name-day for the first time in my life but whatcanbe done friend of my heart but necesery to submit to reason.'[26] Pelageya, for her part, spoke better French than Russian, and that was the limit of her education according to her grandson, who bucked the family tradition by acquiring 22,000 volumes for his personal library.[27]

Throughout his writing career, Tolstoy pillaged his family history for creative material to use in developing his fictional characters, and it is not hard to see shades of Ilya Andreyevich and Pelageya Nikolayevna behind the august figures of Count and Countess Rostov in *War and Peace*. Tolstoy actually named his grandfather in his early drafts, referring to him as 'kind and stupid'. His subsequent notes for the character of Count Ilya Rostov also correspond very closely to Ilya Andreyevich, who was also a stalwart of the English Club in Moscow. Tolstoy's account of the lavish dinner Count Rostov hosts there in *War and Peace* is based on sources describing the dinner for 300 which Ilya Andreyevich hosted in 1806 in honour of Bagration's defeat of Napoleon at Schöngraben. Ilya Andreyevich was certainly somewhat larger than life. As Tolstoy has recorded, his penchant for placing large bets at games of whist and ombre without being actually able to play, his readiness to give money to anyone who asked him for a loan, and his extravagant lifestyle eventually led to him becoming mired in debt, and in 1815 he was forced to take a job.

The card-playing, and consequently the debts, continued during the five undistinguished years that Ilya Andreyevich served as governor of Kazan, and a succession of poor business deals further increased his debt to 500,000 roubles by 1819. In February 1820 he was dismissed from his post on charges of corruption (which were probably trumped-up – it seems to have been his wife who secretly took bribes). Ilya Andreyevich never recovered from this blow, and he died within the month. Tolstoy inherited his grandfather's gambling habit, and his habit of staking and losing large sums, but he was fortunately able to curb both by the time he got married.

Tolstoy's father, Nikolay Ilyich, born in 1794, was the eldest of Ilya Andreyevich's and Pelageya Nikolayevna's four sons, and very different. When surveying his dismal financial prospects, Ilya Andreyevich realised his son would probably have to work for his living, and so he enrolled Nikolay in the civil service when he was six years old. This meant that when he reached sixteen, he automatically received the rank of collegiate registrar, which placed him on the bottom rung of the civil service ladder. In keeping with his kindly character, Ilya Andreyevich did not beat his children, which was highly unusual, as even the children of the imperial family were subject to corporal punishment at this time. Otherwise, Tolstoy's father had a fairly conventional upbringing for a Russian nobleman in early nineteeth-century Russia. When he was fifteen his aunt gave him Afanasy Petrov to be his personal servant, and the following year his parents gave him a peasant girl for his 'health', as it was euphemistically put at the time. This resulted in the birth of Mishenka, Tolstoy's illegitimate brother, who was trained to work in the postal service, but later apparently 'lost his way'. Tolstoy later found it disconcerting to encounter this poverty-stricken elder brother who was more like their father than any of them.[28] He too would later have an illegitimate son, whom his children felt resembled him more closely than they did.

When Napoleon invaded Russia in 1812, Nikolay Ilyich Tolstoy naturally transferred from the civil service to the army, fighting with distinction before being taken captive by the French. He was unable to afford to serve long in the prestigious and costly Cavalry Guards regiment to which he was transferred when he returned to St Petersburg in 1814, however, and then a combination of disillusionment with the military, ill-health and his father's parlous financial situation led him to resign his commission. Since civil servants could not be sent to debtors' prison, Nikolay Ilyich was obliged to take a job, and this became particularly necessary after the death of his father in 1820 left him as the sole provider for his sybaritic, spoiled mother, unmarried sister and cousin. After all the debts had been paid off, the family could afford only to rent a small flat in Moscow. When Tolstoy describes the position Nikolay Rostov finds himself in after the death of the old count in *War and Peace*, he is essentially telling the story of his father, who in 1821 took up a very minor appointment in Moscow's military bureaucracy. The magic solution for Tolstoy's father, as for Nikolay Rostov, was a rich bride. In the novel she appears as Princess Maria Bolkonskaya; in real life she was Princess Maria Volkonskaya. It was through Maria Volkonskaya that Nikolay Ilyich's family came to be connected with Yasnaya Polyana, the country estate which would be irrevocably linked to Tolstoy's name.

Tolstoy's family pedigree meant a great deal to him. The passage in Part Two of *Anna Karenina* in which the old-world Russian noble Levin scoffs at nouveau riche aristocrats like Vronsky, who lack breeding and cannot point back to three or four generations, expresses a fair degree of his own snobbery. Also very telling is Levin's contempt for the merchants he has to deal with – the up-and-coming Russian middle class. The aristocratic Tolstoy also had no time for merchants, and the fact that he invariably chose nobles or peasants to be his artistic heroes says a lot about his prejudices – he regarded the peasantry as the 'best class' in Russia. Compared to the Volkonskys, who were descended from the legendary Scandinavian settler Ryurik, the ninth-century founder of Russia, the Tolstoys were actually mere parvenus as a noble family. Tolstoy's maternal ancestors came from some of the most venerable and distinguished families in Russia, but his paternal lineage did not actually go back all that far when compared with some of the great families of western Europe. As a Tolstoy, he was a count, but this was a title imported from Germany by Peter the Great in the eighteenth century, along with that of baron, as part of his Europeanisation programme. These titles, which were a reward for service, furthermore kept their original German names, *Graf* and *Baron*. The Russian tradition of each child inheriting the family title, rather than just the eldest son, meant that there were soon hundreds of counts and barons mingling with the old-world Russian princes and princesses.

Tolstoy's mother Princess Maria Volkonskaya could trace her roots back at least to the thirteenth century, when one of her early ancestors was involved in altercations with the Mongol overlords of old Rus. A century later the family took its surname from the Volkona river in the area near Kaluga and Tula where they had lands. In 1763, when he retired from the army, Tolstoy's maternal great-grandfather Major General Sergey Volkonsky bought a share of the Yasnaya Polyana property, south of Tula. Later he bought out the other five part-owners. Yasnaya Polyana, meaning 'Clear Glade', received its name for a very specific reason. In the sixteenth century, when the Muscovite state needed to stave off attacks from nomadic invaders such as the Crimean Tatars, it was able to make the most of a series of natural fortifications along its southern borders in the form of forests and rivers. Vulnerable border areas were strengthened by cutting down trees to form a solid barricade, known as a *zaseka*. The Kozlova Zaseka (named after a military leader called Kozlov) ran for several hundred miles, with clearings at various points which had gateways and access roads. Yasnaya Polyana was located in one of these clearings. It was originally called 'Yasennaya Polyana', because ash trees (*yaseni*) once grew there.[29]

Tolstoy's grandfather Nikolay Sergeyevich Volkonsky (1753–1821) inherited Yasnaya Polyana in 1784, and it was he who transformed it from a fairly ordinary piece of land into a carefully landscaped estate, complete with ponds, gardens, paths and imposing manor house when he retired from the army in 1799. Until the age of forty-six, Nikolay Sergeyevich had served in the army, having been signed up for military service when he was six. He was a guards captain in Catherine the Great's retinue when she met Emperor Joseph II at Mogilev in 1780, and fought in the two victorious Russo-Turkish Wars which took place during her reign. After serving briefly as Russian ambassador in Berlin, he accompanied his victorious sovereign on her triumphant tour of the Crimea in 1787 and he was promoted to brigadier and then general-in-chief. In 1794 he was suddenly sent on compulsory leave for two years. According to Tolstoy family lore, this was because Volkonsky had refused to marry Varvara von Engelgardt, the niece and mistress of Prince Potemkin, the great favourite of Catherine the Great. Volkonsky's brilliant career now came to a sudden halt, and he was more or less sent into exile by being appointed military governor in distant Arkhangelsk. Tolstoy greatly admired his grandfather's feistiness, and he clearly enjoyed reproducing Nikolay Sergeyevich's alleged reaction to Potemkin's plan in his memoirs ('Why does he think I am going to marry his wh …'). It was a story he loved to recount to his guests, and he even upbraided two early biographers for omitting it from their manuscripts.[30] The truth was, as usual, far more prosaic, as Potemkin had died in 1791 and Volkonsky was not posted to Arkhangelsk until 1798,

1. Portrait of Tolstoy's maternal grandfather, Nikolay Sergeyevich Volkonsky

by which time Catherine had been succeeded by her son Paul I. At some point in the late 1780s (information is sparse), Nikolay Sergeyevich appears to have married Princess Ekaterina Trubetskaya (1749–1792) in a marriage of convenience. His wife died at the age of forty-three, leaving a two-year-old daughter, Maria Nikolayevna. This was Tolstoy's mother.

It was Paul I's notoriously difficult temperament and constant fault-finding which ultimately prompted Volkonsky to resign permanently from the army in 1799 and retire to his country estate. He never remarried. For the remaining two decades of his life he devoted himself to the upbringing of his beloved daughter Maria, and to creating the idyllic surroundings for them to live in at Yasnaya Polyana which would in turn become instrumental to his grandson's creativity. Volkonsky left one reminder of his military posting in the far north: he built a summer cottage on the banks of the Voronka river, near to Yasnaya Polyana, and named it 'Grumant'. This was the Russian name at that time for Spitsbergen. Volkonsky was governor of Arkhangelsk, the gateway to the Arctic, and also of Spitsbergen, which had originally been discovered by fishermen and hunters from the area near Arkhangelsk. A village grew up around Volkonsky's cottage which was also called Grumant, but the local peasants, for whom this was a very odd-sounding name, renamed it Ugryumy ('Gloomy'). Tolstoy came here as a boy to fish in the pond.[31]

The early nineteenth century was the golden age of the Russian country estate, and Nikolay Volkonsky was not alone in wanting to retreat from the official world associated with St Petersburg and the court, and go back to nature. Russian aristocrats had been rediscovering their roots ever since the 1760s, when the nobility began to be progressively freed from the compulsory state service that Peter the Great had introduced in order to drive through his ambitious programme of reform and Europeanisation. With vast swathes of property now in private hands, manor houses began springing up all over the Russian countryside, some of them grand classical mansions, others more humble wooden affairs. The house in which Tolstoy was born was somewhere between the two. The Yasnaya Polyana estate was not quite a tabula rasa when Nikolay Volkonsky took up permanent residence there. In the early eighteenth century, guided by the vogue for straight lines and geometrical precision which characterised the new city of St Petersburg, previous owners had established the main part of the estate in its northeastern corner, and had constructed two rows of wooden dwellings and a formal garden with lime trees. They had also built a long straight avenue leading from the main house to the entrance of the property, near the main road to Tula.

Volkonsky had grand plans for Yasnaya Polyana, but he needed to find a good architect first, and principal construction work began only after 1810. He decided the main manor house should be at the highest point of the property, facing the south-east. It would be flanked by two identical, two-storey wings, each containing ten rooms. These were built first, with wooden decking leading to the main house. Only the first floor of the manor house was completed in Volkonsky's lifetime. The second storey, which was built in wood to save costs, was added by Tolstoy's father in 1824. It was a house in the classical empire style so beloved in Russia in the early nineteenth century, with thirty-two rooms and a façade graced by an eight-column central portico.

Over time, another nineteen buildings appeared in the grounds, a few of which were built in brick, such as the ice house and a threshing barn, but most in wood. They joined a classically proportioned building already standing, which had been used to house a small carpet factory. Later it accommodated the family's servants, and became known as the 'Volkonsky House'. Nikolay Sergeyevich was kept busy. Apart from the main family house he built stables, a coach-house, further living quarters for the servants, a bath-house and a summer-house. He also built two orangeries, linked by a gallery, in which to grow exotic fruits for his table such as melons and peaches. This gallery (which burned down in 1867) was a favourite haunt for Tolstoy when he was growing up. To judge from an evocative passage in his early work *Youth*, on summer nights he liked to come and sleep in the gallery, from where he could see the lights in the main house gradually being extinguished, listen to the sounds of the night and feel he was part of nature.

Nikolay Sergeyevich seems to have had a finely tuned aesthetic sense. Tolstoy records proudly in his memoirs that what he built was not 'only solid and comfortable but extremely elegant'.[32] Volkonsky also brought his taste and discernment to bear on the landscaping of the property. First of all he built a ha-ha running round its perimeter, then some iron gates at the front entrance positioned between two large round white towers.[33] These were hollow so that the watchman could seek shelter during inclement weather. Then, as now, the gates opened on to an avenue lined with birch trees leading up to the manor house, which was wide enough for a troika or a coach and four. This was the famous 'Preshpekt', and a similar driveway is mentioned in *War and Peace* in the description of the Bolkonsky estate Bald Hills, which bears many similarities to Yasnaya Polyana.

Volkonsky laid a lawn in front of the main house, which he edged with two tree-lined paths running parallel to the main avenue, but he kept the French-style miniature park of pollarded lime trees. The paths traversing it in what Tolstoy called a 'square and star' formation created the wedges which gave the park its name. Soon the natural song of nightingales and orioles who liked to cluster in the branches of the park's densely planted trees was augmented by music performed by Volkonsky's serfs, who had been specially trained for the purpose. According to Tolstoy, Volkonsky loathed hunting, but he loved plants, flowers and music, and kept a small orchestra for his and his daughter's entertainment. By the standards of someone like Prince Sheremetev, who maintained a company of singers, dancers and musicians, and staged full-scale theatrical performances of the latest French operas, or Prince Naryshkin, who had enough serfs to play in a forty-piece horn band, with each playing only one note, Volkonsky's artistic ambitions were quite modest. It was nevertheless common for Russian landowners to train their more talented serfs to perform for them.[34] One day, long after his grandfather's death, Tolstoy found some wooden benches and stands arranged round an enormous elm tree in the park: this was where Volkonsky liked to stroll in the early morning to the accompaniment of music *en plein air*. As soon as the prince left the park, the orchestra would fall silent, and the musicians would go back to their normal duties digging the garden or feeding the pigs. In one of the drafts for *War and Peace* Tolstoy describes eight bewigged serfs in jackets and stockings standing on the gravel in the middle of the park, surrounded by lilac and rose bushes, tuning their instruments at seven in the morning, ready to burst into a Haydn symphony the minute they receive word that their master is awake.

As the nineteenth century wore on, the passion amongst aristocratic Russian landowners for the regularity of formal gardens in the style of Louis XIV was superseded by an enthusiasm for more 'natural' English landscaping. Nikolay Sergeyevich shared this enthusiasm. His next project was to create a much wilder 'English park' from the sloping contours of the lower part of the estate by the entrance towers. Volkonsky also created a cascade of ponds, whose banks were planted with rose bushes. Tolstoy enjoyed walking in this part of Yasnaya Polyana because it was where his mother most liked to spend her time. It was in her memory in 1898 that he restored the little gazebo on stilts from where she used to watch the traffic passing on the road outside. Later on, she would sit there waiting for her husband to come home. It was Maria Volkonskaya who planted the silver poplars round the edge of the Middle Pond, and the shrubs and fir trees lower down. On the other side of the entrance towers was the Big Pond, half of which was traditionally given over for use by the local peasants.

One thing missing from the traditional estate ensemble at Yasnaya Polyana was a church. Possibly this was because Nikolay Sergeyevich believed his family could rely on the church down the road, where his ashes were transferred in 1928. As a student of Voltaire, however, and a child of his time, it is more likely that he simply had no interest in building a church. This did not prevent him having dozens of theological books in his library, not to mention a twenty-volume edition of the Bible and accompanying exegesis. They sat next to works by Racine, Virgil, Montaigne, Rousseau, Homer, Plutarch and Vasari, to mention just some of the authors collected by Nikolay Sergeyevich. There were also plenty of books which he bought for the education of his daughter.[35]

The Russian country estate was many things – family seat, arena for artistic performance, rural retreat – but it was also a centre of agricultural production. As such, it reinforced the patriarchal ways which impeded Russia's modernisation, since the arcadian idyll of the country estate was made possible by the peasants who sustained it. In terms of his wealth in human beings, that is to say, serfs, Volkonsky was a middle-ranking aristocrat, since he only had 159 'souls' at Yasnaya Polyana, but he was in the majority. In early nineteenth-century Russia only three per cent of the nearly 900,000 members of the nobility owned more than 500 serfs. Nevertheless, it was free labour, and the peasants got a very raw deal, particularly after 1762, when the nobility were 'emancipated' from state service. The serfs had to wait another hundred years before they were emancipated in 1861. Until then, they were unable to own property, and could not marry without the permission of their owner, who had the right to subject them to corporal punishment or exile them to Siberia at whim.

There were some Russian landowners who abused their unlimited powers, and treated their serfs with unimaginable cruelty. Nikolay Volkonsky was not one of those. Like other landowners, he treated Yasnaya Polyana as his own private kingdom but was, it seems, only mildly despotic. He may have forced his musicians to double up as swineherds, but he did not beat them. He may have had a succession of children with his servant Alexandra, whom he sent off to the orphanage, but he did not keep a harem as some landowners did. Volkonsky's relationship with his serfs features heavily in Tolstoy's memoir of his grandfather, whom he clearly idolised. He recalls, for example, how his grandfather built fine accommodation for his servants, and ensured they were not only well fed and dressed but also entertained. 'My grandfather was considered a very strict master,' he wrote, on the basis of his conversations with some of the older Yasnaya Polyana peasants, 'but I never heard any stories of his cruel behaviour or punishments, so usual at that time.'[36] At the same time he admitted that his grandfather probably did overstep the mark on occasion. Later on in his memoirs, he recalls Nikolay Sergeyevich's particular fondness for Praskovya Isayevna, the housekeeper, who represented the 'mysterious old world' of Yasnaya Polyana. If Tolstoy based old Natalya Savishna in *Childhood* on her as faithfully he claims in his memoirs, then at a much earlier stage of her life, when she had been halfway along her career path from maid to housekeeper and was working as a nanny, Praskovya was banished by Nikolay Volkonsky to work in a cowshed in a distant estate in the steppes. Her crime had been to fall in love with one of Prince Volkonsky's footmen, and to have asked Nikolay Sergeyevich's permission to marry him. She proved so irreplaceable, however, that within six months, she was brought back and installed in her former position, at which she apparently fell at Prince Volkonsky's feet and begged for forgiveness.

Maria Volkonskaya was seven when her father took her to live in Yasnaya Polyana, and it would be her home for the rest of her life. Until then, she had barely known her father, who had been away in the army, but he devoted a great deal of time to her during the lonely years of his retirement, and paid particular attention to her education. Four handwritten textbooks containing materials written out by a scribe for Maria Nikolayevna when she was in her teens indicate what her father's priorities were – and also his expectations. She studied mathematics and astronomy (the authorities here being Pythagoras, Plato, Ptolemy and the ancient Babylonians), forms of government (including despotic, monarchical and democratic), classics (the letters of Pliny the Younger were a major source), and agriculture.[37] Tolstoy's mother also took a keen interest in the natural world. In 1821, when she was thirty-one, she compiled a detailed 'description of the orchard' at Yasnaya Polyana, naming each of the sixteen varieties of apple growing there. Another time she described what was blooming at Yasnaya Polyana in July: poppies, sweet william, stock, marigold and delphinium.[38]

Maria Nikolayevna had a good knowledge of five languages, including Russian, which was not all that common amongst upper-class Russian women at that time, for whom French was their first language. In his memoirs Tolstoy also records that his mother was an accomplished pianist, artistically sensitive, and a born storyteller. Apparently her tales were so compelling that the friends who gathered round at balls preferred listening to her to dancing. She wrote many of them down, as well as poems, odes and elegies. One unfinished story is called 'The Russian Pamela, or There are No Rules Without Exceptions'. Inspired by Samuel Richardson's famous 1740 novel about a maid whose virtue is rewarded with marriage to her late mistress's son, Maria's Russian version incorporates a young serf girl being given her freedom before she can marry her noble suitor, Prince Razumin. The character of Prince Razumin (whose name means 'Reason') is clearly a thinly disguised portrait of her father. He is described as a man with an excellent mind and noble in spirit, who imposes very strict rules but has a kind, sensitive heart. He is a man who knows his own worth, demands respect and obedience from his subordinates and high standards from his children, considers himself superior to others and is proud of his high birth. A similar portrait would emerge when Tolstoy sat down to describe the character of old Prince Bolkonsky in *War and Peace*, although there were some important fundamental differences – Maria Nikolayevna was a devoted daughter like Princess Maria Bolkonskaya, but did not live in a state of discord with her father, as far as can be ascertained from her diary and other sources.[39]

Very little is known about Maria Nikolayevna's childhood and adolescence, and next to nothing is known about her early adulthood. Nikolay Volkonsky took his daughter for a six-week stay in St Petersburg when she was twenty, so she could be presented in society. She kept a diary, recording her impressions of the Romanov tombs in the St Peter and Paul Cathedral, the paintings by Raphael and Rubens in the galleries of the Hermitage, and the ballet, but there is otherwise scant information about her life at this time. The Volkonskys stayed in the capital with the recently widowed Princess Varvara Golitsyna, with whose family Sergey Nikolayevich had become very friendly. Portraits were exchanged as Maria Nikolayevna had been betrothed from childhood to one of the Golitsyns' ten sons, but he died of fever before the wedding. Tolstoy believed his mother experienced a profound sense of loss when her fiancé died. (Supposedly, his name was Lev and Tolstoy was named after him, but this is just another family legend that Tolstoy subscribed to, for there was no Lev Golitsyn.)

The second most important emotional attachment formed by Tolstoy's mother seems to have been with her French companion Louise Henissiènne, who lived at Yasnaya Polyana from 1819 to 1822. Maria Nikolayevna had already shown a desire for social justice unusual for her time by writing a story about a serf who is given her freedom, and she also befriended a young peasant girl at Yasnaya Polyana. Very soon after her father's death in 1821 she proceeded to cause a scandal in Moscow by selling one of her estates and putting the proceeds in Louise Henissiènne's name. The 'ugly old maid' with the 'heavy eyebrows', as malicious tongues referred to Maria Nikolayevna in letters, then created further scandal by arranging for her cousin Mikhail Volkonsky to marry Marie, the sister of her French companion. The following year she almost gave away her Oryol estate to Marie, finally giving her husband 75,000 roubles instead.[40] Maria Nikolayevna's relatives found this wilful, headstrong behaviour shocking. Her youngest son Lev would have heartily approved, however. In due course, he would give away all his property.

Tolstoy was bewitched his whole life by thoughts of the mother he never knew, and was almost glad no portrait of her survived, as it meant he could concentrate his mind on her 'spiritual image'. Her old maid Tatyana Filippovna told him when he was growing up that his mother had been self-possessed and reserved, but also hot-tempered. He treasured the idea of her blushing and shedding tears before uttering a rude word, although did not believe she even knew any rude words. And he was convinced that his eldest brother Nikolay probably inherited her best qualities – an unwillingness to judge, and extreme modesty. At the age of thirty-two, Maria Nikolayevna probably thought she would never marry, but she was then introduced by relatives to Nikolay Tolstoy, who was four years her junior and a distant relative (her great-grandmother Praskovya was his great-aunt). She was wealthy; he was in need of money. They were not in love, but they married in June 1822.

· 2 ·

ARISTOCRATIC CHILDHOOD

Levin could barely remember his mother. His idea of her was a sacred
memory for him.

Anna Karenina, Part One, Chapter 27[1]

WHEN, TOWARDS THE END OF HIS LIFE, visitors to Yasnaya Polyana
asked Tolstoy where exactly he was born, he sometimes pointed to the tip of
a tall larch growing amongst a clump of trees next to his house. He was not
suffering from dementia, nor was he born at the top of a tree, but indicating
precisely the former location of his mother's bedroom on the first floor of
the columned mansion built by his grandfather Nikolay Volkonsky, where
he spent his early childhood.[2] Despite this being the happiest period in his
life, and despite his almost fetishistic reverence of his ancestors, particularly
his maternal grandfather, Tolstoy sold off his ancestral home in 1854 after
heavy gambling losses. The main house did not completely disappear: the
neighbouring landowner who bought it dismantled it brick by brick and then
rebuilt it on his property about twenty miles down the road. When Tolstoy
came back to live permanently at Yasnaya Polyana in the late 1850s, he moved

into one of the two wings Volkonsky had built on either side of the house and planted some maples and larches in the gaping space between them. Many decades later Tolstoy's children developed a passionate desire to return their father's house to its original location between the two wings. It was a hare-brained scheme that came to nothing, but in 1897, when he was sixty-nine, Tolstoy rode over to look at the house again, and seeing it brought back a flood of memories. He walked through its dilapidated rooms and came to a halt in one of the bedrooms. 'This is where I was born,' he said, thinking about his mother and the blissful days of his early childhood.[3]

Tolstoy could not remember his mother, who died before he was two years old, but her idealised image was a constant presence throughout his life, right up until his last years. He openly admitted to one of his early biographers in 1906 that he had a *culte* of his mother, and as an old man was still thinking about her when he went on his solitary morning walks round the estate.[4] In the memoirs he wrote when he was in his seventies, Tolstoy confesses he had often prayed to her soul to help him at moments of temptation when he was younger. Even in his eighties he could not talk about her without crying. On days when he felt particularly melancholy at the end of his life, he still had an intense longing to curl up and be comforted by his mother, who represented for him a 'supreme image of pure love'.[5]

By the time Tolstoy was born in 1828, Yasnaya Polyana was getting quite crowded. Maria Nikolayevna had led a mostly secluded and solitary life on the estate while her father was alive. After her marriage to Nikolay Tolstoy in 1822, however, her husband brought various members of his family to live with them. Apart from his venerable mother Pelageya Nikolayevna, by then sixty, there was his younger sister Alexandra Ilyinichna ('Aline'), who was twenty-seven, and so five years younger than Maria Nikolayevna. Aline came with a ward, Pashenka, who was then about five years old. There was also 'Toinette', his distant 'aunt' Tatyana Alexandrovna Ergolskaya (pronounced 'Yorgelskaya'). Her father had been Tolstoy's grandmother's cousin, and she was thirty – three years younger than Maria Nikolayevna. All these women were to be important figures in Tolstoy's life, particularly Aunt Toinette, who lived at Yasnaya Polyana after he inherited the estate. She died when he was in his late forties, and represented a precious link to the parents he lost when he was very young. Three other members of the family also took up residence at Yasnaya Polyana before Tolstoy was born: his elder brothers

Nikolay, Sergey and Dmitry, born in 1823, 1826 and 1827, respectively.

Nikolay occupied a special place in his mother's affections as her first-born. Anxious to inculcate her son with obedience and the right moral qualities, she kept a detailed diary of his behaviour from the age of four, and expressed displeasure at the first sign he showed of cowardice or laziness. She also deplored manifestations of sentimentality, such as when Nikolay shed tears after reading about a bird being shot, or when he was frightened by a beetle. Maria Nikolayevna wanted her son to be brave, stoic and patriotic, and she allowed him to wear a sabre as a reward for good behaviour. She also discouraged vanity. Turgenev, with whom Nikolay was friendly many years later, would remark that unlike his youngest brother Lev he indeed completely lacked the abundance of vanity necessary for anyone wishing to become a writer.[6]

When Lev was born on 28 August 1828, the youngest of four sons, he replaced Nikolay as the chief and final object of his mother's affections according to Aunt Toinette.[7] His mother's nickname for him was 'mon petit Benjamin', but he was christened Lev, the Russian form of Leo. Unlike her father, Maria Nikolayevna was deeply religious, and thought carefully about the names of her children. After her fifth (and final) child was born, she commissioned a small icon featuring images of their five namesakes, and St Leo the Great is depicted in the bottom right-hand corner. Tolstoy's Christian name certainly seems to have been well chosen: he shared with the fifth-century St Leo (only one of two Popes to be called 'The Great') not only noble birth but an astonishing fearlessness. Pope Leo is known to have ridden out to the gates of Rome to confront Attila the Hun, whom he persuaded to abandon his idea of invading Europe. Tolstoy fought with bravery while he was in the army, and once wrestled with a bear while he was out hunting. He also shared literary distinction with his illustrious namesake: St Leo founded what would become an influential prose style called *cursus leonicus*.

Maria Nikolayevna may also have had in mind the exclusively Orthodox St Leo of Catania when she named her last son, and Lev proved to have even more in common with him. This St Leo is sometimes confused with the other St Leo, but seems to have been a more familiar figure in Russian folklore. It was well known, for example, that one should not look at shooting stars on St Leo's day – peasants associated *Lev katanskii* with the verb *katat'*, meaning to roll (along).[8] St Leo of Catania was a bishop who originally came from a noble family in Ravenna. He chose to turn his back on his wealthy background to devote his life to preaching Christianity and serving the poor, and was particularly known for his kindness to pilgrims and beggars. Tolstoy's life followed a similar pattern, and like Bishop Leo, he came into direct conflict with his government during his lifetime. If St Leo was persecuted by the ecclesiastical authorities of the Byzantine Empire for vehemently opposing the destruction of holy images during the iconoclast controversy in the eighth century, however, Lev Tolstoy was the scourge of the Russian Empire for being himself an iconoclast and respecting no authority, including, most famously, the Orthodox Church. Curiously, both St Leo of Catania and Lev Tolstoy were opposed at the end of their lives by apostates called Heliodoros (Iliodor in Russian), who were the cause of great scandals. St Leo's adversary tried to lure Christians away with the help of the occult, while the renegade Russian monk Iliodor saw Tolstoy as the devil in human form, and only later came to repent. It is curious that Tolstoy began a story called 'Father Iliodor' in 1909, at the very end of his life, just when the monk Iliodor was causing his greatest scandals.[9]

Tolstoy was born in 1828, on the twenty-eighth day of the eighth month in the year, and twenty-eight became his lucky number. He had become so superstitious by the time he reached adulthood, in fact, that in 1863 he ordered his wife to hold on until after midnight so that their first child Sergey could be born in the early hours of 28 June. He was also pleased to discover that the number twenty-eight was particularly significant in mathematics as the second 'perfect' number (it is also one of seven 'magic' numbers in physics). He would open books of poetry on the twenty-eighth page and wind his watch twenty-eight times. He even wove the number twenty-eight into his fiction: it is a symbolically important number in his last novel *Resurrection*, which concludes on chapter twenty-eight of its third part. Before making any decision, Tolstoy would toss a coin on to the parquet floor at Yasnaya Polyana, seeing a good or bad omen in whether it rolled over an odd or even number of the wooden squares.[10] It was also no coincidence that Tolstoy left Yasnaya Polyana for the last time near the end of his life on 28 October (he was eighty-two when he died). He probably inherited his superstitious nature from his grandmother Pelageya Nikolayevna, but it is a surprising trait to discover in someone who prided himself on the rationality of his thought.

Tolstoy was also superstitious about objects, such as the old leather couch on which he was born. Made by one of old Prince Volkonsky's serfs, it was ritually taken from Nikolay Ilyich's study and carried upstairs to Maria Niko-layevna's bedroom in the corner of the house for the birth of each of their five children. Eleven of Tolstoy's own children were born on it, not to mention two of his grandchildren (after five stillbirths, his eldest daughter Tanya gave birth to his favourite granddaughter Tanya on it in 1905).[11] Along with his desk, the couch was a permanent piece of furniture in each of the four rooms Tolstoy used as his study at Yasnaya Polyana at different times of his life, and it also makes an appearance in his novels. A very similar-sounding couch is brought out of Prince Andrey's study for the birth of his son in *War and Peace*, and in one of the drafts of *Anna Karenina* it is also mentioned as a Levin family heirloom with a similar function.

Tolstoy's earliest memories were of being tightly swaddled as a baby, and screaming at being unable to stretch out his arms. 'I feel the injustice and cruelty, not from people, as they pity me, but of fate, and of pity for myself,' he wrote in the autobiography he began when he was fifty. He was uncertain as to whether this memory – of the complexity and contradictoriness of his feelings rather than of his cries and suffering – was not, in fact, a composite of many impressions, but he was sure this was the 'first and strongest impression' of his life. Tolstoy also claimed (rather improbably) to have recalled his 'tiny body' being bathed in a wooden tub by his wet-nurse Avdotya Nikiforovna, a peasant engaged from the village. His next memories date from when he was four, and lying in a cot next to his younger sister Maria. By this time, his mother had already died. We can only regret that 'My Life', as it was provisionally called, petered out after the first few vivid pages of his earliest recollections. The same happened with the memoirs he began a quarter of a century later, which cover only his early childhood.[12]

Maria Nikolayevna died in 1830 not long after the birth of her only daugh-ter, also christened Maria. She had been married for eight years, and had led a very quiet life at Yasnaya Polyana. As Tolstoy records in his memoirs, it was nevertheless a peaceful and happy time, her days taken up with raising her family, and her evenings devoted to reading aloud to her mother-in-law. The one member of her family she did not see so much of was her husband, who was embroiled in endless court cases concerning his late father's disas-trous financial affairs, and often away. This was not easy for her, and she would sit for hours watching for his return in the gazebo in the corner of the estate. Her husband was obliged to write her letters reassuring her he had not forgotten her. 'My sweet friend,' he wrote to her in June 1824, 'you finish your last letter by asking me not to forget you; you are going mad: can I forget that which constitutes the most noble part of myself?' ('Ma douce amie, tu finis ta dernière lettre avec une recommendation de non pas t'oublier; tu deviens folle: puis-je oublier ce qui fait la partie la plus élevé de moi même …')[13] Even when Nikolay Ilyich was at home, he was often out hunting, or according to one salacious claim, secretly pursuing other women.[14] There was certainly some kind of romantic entanglement with a neighbour after his wife's death, but Nikolay Ilyich was by all accounts an attentive husband, and he became a conscientious father as a single parent, devoted to his five children.

Tolstoy remembered his father well, even though he too died young. His father was by far the most important person in his life during his early years, and as Tolstoy himself was later to acknowledge, he did not realise quite how much he had loved him until after his death. Tolstoy describes him being of average height, well built, with pleasant features and a ruddy complexion, but with eyes which were always sad. The Tolstoy children loved their father for the funny stories he told, and the enchanting pictures he drew for them. He was clearly a charismatic man in many ways, but what Tolstoy later claimed to have particularly loved and admired about his father was his independent spirit and clear sense of his own dignity.[15]

Nikolay Ilyich was quite a gentle man, and he was certainly more lenient with his serfs than the previous master of Yasnaya Polyana, Prince Volkonsky. He also rarely resorted to corporal punishment, unlike many sadistic Russian nobles at that time. Nikolay Ilyich was a keen reader: he added substantially to the library his youngest son would one day inherit by purchasing quantities of French classics and works about natural history. Tolstoy was later informed by his aunts that his father never bought new books until he had read the ones he already owned, but he doubted whether his father really had waded through all those dusty French tomes on the history of the Crusades.[16] Nikolay Ilyich was also artistically gifted, and produced many fine watercolours of idyllic rural landscapes and pen-and-ink drawings, including a sensitively drawn sketch of a spirited Bashkirian horseman in native costume with bow and arrow.[17]

Tolstoy cherished his memories of his father cracking jokes at the dinner table, and of being allowed to come and sit beside him on the fabled leather sofa in his study while he smoked his pipe. There was one occasion when Nikolay Ilyich was particularly impressed with the pathos with which his youngest son Lev read aloud Pushkin's poem 'To the Sea', which he had learned by heart.[18] The poem was written in 1824, when Pushkin was taking leave of the south after his period of exile, and by the time the young Tolstoy came to recite its lines a decade later, the fateful duel which killed the young poet in 1837 was only a few years away. The ocean was probably the one element which would never hold any attraction for Tolstoy. He lived in the heartland of Russia for nearly all his long life, far from any salt water, so may not later have identified with the sentiments in Pushkin's last stanza, in which the poet speaks of carrying into the 'woods and silent wildernesses' of Russia the sea's cliffs and coves, and the sound of its waves. But as if to compensate, Tolstoy was moved to shed an ocean of salty tears over his lifetime by music or stories of suffering. The emotional sensitivity his father noticed in him as a young boy rendered him very susceptible to crying: it was not for nothing that one of his nicknames as a child was Lyova-Ryova – 'Lyova the howler'.

As a small boy, Tolstoy liked to see his father elegantly dressed in frock-coat and close-fitting breeches in preparation for trips into town, but his most vivid memories of his father were connected with hunting. Nikolay Tolstoy loved hunting – both riding to hounds and shooting – and he had a particular affection for two servants, the brothers Petrusha and Matyusha, who usually accompanied him. Like many of his class, Nikolay Tolstoy considered hunting second only to warfare as an arena for showing courage and bravado, and so Tolstoy and his brothers were thus trained to hunt from a young age.[19] Nikolay Ilyich thought it important for his sons to start learning to be real men as early as possible and they were each given ponies. In old age Tolstoy cherished memories of walking with his father through the long grass of the meadows with his beloved borzoi puppies running circles round them.[20] Tolstoy himself would become a passionate huntsman (the hunting scenes in *War and Peace* are amongst the most lovingly written in the novel), and it took him a long time in later life to relinquish an activity which clearly contravened the moral and religious principles he embraced after his spiritual crisis. Tolstoy never abandoned horseriding, however, and his love of horses can be seen both in the exquisite detail of his description of Vronsky's horse Frou-Frou in *Anna Karenina*, and in 'Kholstomer' ('Strider'), the remarkable story he began in the 1860s and later revised, which is told from a horse's point of view.

Tolstoy's most vivid memories of his father may have been connected with hunting, but his fondest ones were of seeing him sitting next to his grandmother on the sofa, and helping her lay out the cards for patience while she occasionally took snuff from her gold snuffbox. His aunts would be in armchairs nearby, one of them reading aloud, while in another armchair his father's favourite borzoi Milka would be curled up asleep, or gazing at everyone with her beautiful black eyes (she appears in *War and Peace* as herself). In his memoirs, Tolstoy recollects a particular evening when his father stopped whichever aunt was reading aloud and pointed to the mirror on the wall. Tikhon the manservant could be seen stealing furtively on tiptoes into his study and stealing tobacco from his leather pouch. Tolstoy's father found this very amusing.[21]

Nikolay Ilyich had a busy life, and he worked hard to restore the family fortunes. He certainly proved to have greater business acumen than his hapless father, and he left his children a legacy that amounted to far more than his late wife's dowry. In 1832 he owned 793 male and 800 female serfs, including 219 'souls' at Yasnaya Polyana and the surrounding villages. He was particularly pleased to be able to re-acquire Nikolskoye-Vyazemskoye, one of his mother's estates that had previously been mortgaged. Tolstoy later inherited it when his brother Nikolay died. In 1837 Tolstoy's father was also able to buy Pirogovo, a large estate not far from Yasnaya Polyana, which came with 472 serfs, and was later inherited by Tolstoy's brother Sergey and his sister Maria.

When he was at home at Yasnaya Polyana, Tolstoy's father had his hands full with managing the estate, which he continued to run on the patriarchal lines established by Prince Volkonsky. Now that his family was so numerous, Nikolay Ilyich's most pressing task was to finish building the main family residence. A couple of thousand roubles thus went on building a second, rather more modestly appointed storey in oak over the elegant ground floor. At its centre were rooms with parquet flooring and high ceilings, while the side rooms had a mezzanine floor, which gave the house the appearance of having three storeys. When everything was complete, there was finally enough room for Nikolay Ilyich and his five children, his mother, the two aunts and his sister's ward Pashenka, the children's tutor Fyodor Ivanovich, and the last permanent additions to the household: Evdokiya (Dunechka) Temyasheva, the illegitimate, freckled daughter of a neighbouring landowner and his serf mistress, and her tall, elderly nanny Evpraksiya. Dunechka was five years old when she arrived at Yasnaya Polyana in 1833 (the same age as Tolstoy), and she was brought up with the rest of the family as part of the complex property dealings over the Pirogovo estate. Tolstoy later described Dunechka as a nice, straightforward, not very bright girl who was a big cry-baby, but she got on very well with the rest of the family.[22]

In his early childhood, Tolstoy was never alone. Among the grown-ups living at Yasnaya Polyana, his grandmother and the two aunts were important figures in his early life. Tolstoy's *babushka* Pelageya Nikolayevna had lived a life of luxury and was not inclined to give it up, despite the family's straitened circumstances. After being spoiled first by her father, then her husband and finally her son, she became rather tyrannical and capricious in her old age. Since everyone in the household went out of their way to please her in deference to her senior position, she made the most of being able to torment her maid, Agafya Mikhailovna, who put up with it as she was proud to be called a 'lady-in-waiting'. Agafya Mikhailovna remained a beloved member of Tolstoy's household when his own children were growing up, and he notes with amusement in his memoirs that his grandmother's ways must have rubbed off on her, as she later became just as demanding and capricious herself.

Tolstoy remembered his grandmother well. She had never particularly warmed to Maria Nikolayevna, whom she considered unworthy of the son she idolised, but she was very fond of their children, and found them very amusing. Tolstoy retained only a few memories of his grandmother dating from his earliest childhood, but they were vivid ones. First of all he remembered the enormous soap bubbles she produced when washing in the morning. He and his siblings found them so captivating they were sometimes brought into their grandmother's room just to watch her perform her ablutions. A picture of her white blouse, white skirt, elderly white arms and white shining face imprinted itself forever in Tolstoy's memory. He himself also acquired the nickname of 'Levka the bubble' as he was so rotund as a little boy.

Tolstoy also remembered a magical excursion on a hot day, when the family went into the woods to collect hazelnuts. His grandmother was transported in a yellow cabriolet pulled not by horses, but by his father's servants Petrusha and Matyusha, who bent down the branches for her so she could gather the nuts.²³ That yellow carriage with the tall springs was also later used for summer outings to the little wooden house with shutters built by Sergey Volkonsky in Grumant, where there was a picturesque view of the River Voronka winding its way through the meadows to one side, and forests on the other. Nearby was a grove with a spring, which was the source of the fresh water used by the Tolstoy family; great quantities of it would be taken over to Yasnaya Polyana every day. There was also a deep pond full of tench, bream, carp, perch and sterlet, where the boys and their tutor could fish. *Babushka* Pelageya Nikolayevna, who had no great desire to be entertained by Matryona the cattlewoman in her shabby dress, did not join the children on these trips. But the children loved their afternoons with Matryona, her daughter and the peasant children, when they would be treated to chunks of black bread, and milk that had come straight from the cows. They liked being surrounded by cattle and hens, and the assortment of village dogs which congregated round Bertha, their tutor's setter.²⁴

Tolstoy's strongest memories of his grandmother were connected with the treat of spending the night in her bedroom with Lev Stepanych, her blind storyteller. In pre-emancipation Russia it was quite common for serfs to become professional storytellers, who could be bought and sold at will by the nobility like pieces of furniture. Lev Stepanych had been purchased for Pelageya Nikolayevna by her late husband, and so he was brought along to Yasnaya Polyana along with the rest of her retinue. He was totally blind, so he had developed an exceptional memory, and was able to recall any story that had been read to him a couple of times word for word.

Tolstoy recalled that Lev Stepanych lived somewhere in the main house, but only appeared in the evening, when he would go upstairs to his grandmother's bedroom in preparation for the evening's storytelling. He would sit in his long blue frock-coat with puffy sleeves on a low windowsill there, and some supper would be brought to him while he waited for Pelageya Nikolayevna to retire. Since he was blind, she undressed in front of him without qualms, and then she and whichever grandchild was with her would climb into bed to get comfortable for that night's story. Tolstoy vividly recalled the moment when the candle was extinguished in his grandmother's bedroom, leaving the flickering light of the small lamp burning beneath the icons in the corner. He would see the dim profile of his grandmother tucked up in bed on a mound of pillows, again a vision all in white, this time with a nightcap on her head. At her command, Lev Stepanych's quiet, steady voice would then launch into a captivating tale – Tolstoy particularly remembered him telling one of Scheherazade's stories from *The Arabian Nights*. The story went over the young Lev's head, but he was transfixed by the sight of the shadow of his grandmother's profile quivering on the wall.[25]

Tolstoy's aunt Aline could not have been more different from her mother Pelageya Nikolayevna, who continued to behave like the grande dame she had once been well into her dotage. Refined and graceful, with dreamy blue eyes and a fair complexion, Aline was fond of reading and she played the harp.[26] She scored a great success in Petersburg high society when she came out, and at the age of nineteen, in 1814, she was married off to Karl von Osten-Sacken, son of the Saxon ambassador to Russia, in what was thought to be a brilliant match. The young couple repaired to the family's Baltic estate, but within a year of the wedding Aline's husband was showing signs of serious mental illness. Tolstoy tells a gripping story in his memoirs of one incident when the deranged Count von Osten-Sacken shot at his pregnant wife at point-blank range before being permanently committed to an asylum.

Aline recovered (many years later she showed her nephew the scar left by the bullet), but the traumatic experience marked her. She moved back to St Petersburg, but gave birth to a still-born baby. Fearing the effect this would have on her, her family arranged to have her own child replaced with the newly born daughter of a servant they knew about, who was the wife of a court chef. This was Pashenka – Pelageya Ivanovna Nastasina, whom Aunt Aline brought up as her own child. Tolstoy reproduces this story in Part Two of *Anna Karenina*: Kitty makes friends at the German spa with a Russian girl Varenka, whose background is remarkably similar. Pashenka was about ten years older than Tolstoy, and sickly (she later died of tuberculosis). Neither Tolstoy, who described her as 'pale, quiet and meek', nor his siblings seem to have felt she was really their cousin, but she appears in the list he compiled in his memoirs of people he particularly loved in his childhood.

Aline was thirty-three when Tolstoy was born, and by this time she had become exceptionally pious. If it came naturally to Tolstoy later in his life to want to devote his money and energy to helping others, it may have been partly because he grew up with an aunt who practised the Christian principles she preached. She not only spent her time praying, observing the fasts, reading the lives of saints and visiting monasteries, but, like Princess

Maria in *War and Peace*, sought out the company of monks, nuns, religious wanderers, beggars and holy fools. Some of these people came on visits to Yasnaya Polyana, but others virtually lived on the estate, including Marya Gerasimovna, a holy fool. She had spent her youth wandering through Russia in men's clothes under the guise of 'Ivan the Fool', a familiar character from Russian fairy tales. When Tolstoy's mother was about to give birth for the fifth time, she had asked Marya Gerasimovna to pray that she would finally have a girl. After his sister Masha was born, Marya Gerasimovna became her godmother, and a familiar figure in the Tolstoy household. The touching, naïve faith of their gardener Akim led the Tolstoys to see him as almost another holy fool who lived at Yasnaya Polyana. The children would come across him praying in the main room of the summer house which stood between the two orangeries. Akim talked aloud to God, his 'healer', as if he was standing right there in front of him.[27]

Foreshadowing the path later taken by her nephew, Aline consistently gave her money away to the poor, maintained the simplest of diets and paid no attention to her external appearance, to the point of looking extremely unkempt; her nephew was clearly pained in his memoirs to have to comment on the rancid smell he remembered her exuding. At the same time he recalled her radiant expression and good-natured laughter, and his childhood memory of how uniformly kind she was to people, whatever their background, must have sunk deep into his consciousness. Aunt Aline may have had a far greater impact on her nephew's character than he realised.

Aline was an important person in Tolstoy's life, but he was not as close to her as he was to his aunt Toinette, who had been taken in as an orphaned child by Tolstoy's grandparents. Tolstoy supposed she must have been very attractive as a young girl with her mass of curly dark hair tied severely into a thick braid, agate-black eyes and a vivacious expression. He never stopped to ponder whether she was beautiful or not when he was a boy, but simply loved everything about her – her eyes, her smile, her slender hands and her warm personality. Toinette spoke better French than Russian, was a fine pianist and, like Aunt Aline, kind to everyone around her, including the servants. She may never have stopped to consider questions of social justice, according to Tolstoy, and she accepted the existence of serfdom as a fact of life, but he emphasises in his memoirs that she used her position of privilege only to serve people. She was also adamantly opposed to the family's serfs receiving corporal punishment of any kind. Tolstoy could not indeed remember her uttering even one harsh word in all the thirty years he knew her. She was a strong-willed and selfless person, he recollected in his memoirs, but her most important defining feature was love. Her whole life was love, Tolstoy wrote, but for just one person – his father. Despite wishing otherwise, Tolstoy was aware that she loved him and his siblings because of his father, and her affection for everyone else came also as a natural consequence of loving him.

Toinette was two years older than Nikolay Ilyich, with whom she had grown up, and she remained devoted to him, but like Sonya in *War and Peace*, she stepped aside so he could find a bride with a large dowry and thus have some hope of settling his father's enormous debts. Just as selflessly, Toinette became good friends with Maria Nikolayevna after his marriage. Six years after his wife died, perhaps prompted by fears for his health, Nikolay Ilyich proposed marriage to Toinette, but she declined, apparently not wanting to ruin what Tolstoy describes as her 'pure, poetic' relations with the family. She never spoke about this proposal, but she did accept Nikolay Ilyich's second request: to become a mother to his children and never leave them. Tolstoy declares in his memoirs that it was his aunt Toinette who taught him the 'spiritual pleasure' of love. She never imparted instruction on how to live, or on the reading of morally edifying literature, nor did she ever talk about religion or how to pray. It was not words but Toinette's 'whole being' which infected Tolstoy with love as a boy. Her moral and spiritual life was something which was completely internalised, and which manifested itself outwardly only in the supremely serene, unhurried and humble way in which she lived from day to day. This was something Tolstoy regarded as one of the greatest influences on his life.[28]

Tolstoy can be forgiven for not remembering everybody in his early childhood. With all the Tolstoys and their dependants, not to mention the large number of servants who also had to be accommodated, the Yasnaya Polyana house must have been quite a warren in the early 1830s. Not until well into his memoirs does Tolstoy remember another person who joined their family at some point in his early childhood – a girl called Lyubov Sergeyevna, another illegitimate child born out of wedlock who was taken in out of pity. Like Pashenka and Dunechka, she did not have an easy life, but the Tolstoys did their best for her, even attempting, but failing, to matchmake between her and Fyodor Ivanovich, the children's German tutor.[29] Fyodor Ivanovich was another person who always seemed to be there in Tolstoy's childhood. He arrived in the summer of 1829 to take charge of Nikolay, who was then already six years old.

Foreign tutors were a fixture in Russian noble households, particularly in the first half of the nineteenth century, before serfdom was abolished. The offspring of aristocratic families did not, by and large, go to school, nor indeed was it feasible when so many of them grew up on remote country estates. Instead, tutors and governesses were imported, chiefly from France, Germany and England, and occupied a sometimes uneasy position in their new households between their employers and the domestic staff. Thus it was in the Tolstoy family. Fyodor Ivanovich was the Russian name the Tolstoys gave to Friedrich Rössel when he began his employment at Yasnaya Polyana. Tolstoy does not say much about him in his memoirs, but points instead to the fact that his portrait of the German tutor Karl Ivanovich in *Childhood* was very true to life (and once even referred to Fyodor Ivanovich as Karl Ivanovich in one of his letters). He was a very kind and decent man, and beloved by the Tolstoy children, to whom he was devoted, but rather naïve, and not particularly well educated. The Tolstoy children all learned to speak good German – but with a distinct Saxon accent.[30]

The other important people in Tolstoy's early life, of course, were the servants – the nannies, butlers, valets, chefs, waiters, wine stewards and coachmen who were part of every Russian noble household during the years of serfdom. Some of them lived in the main family house; others in the grounds of the estate. As a baby, Lev was looked after first by old Annushka, who had been his brother Nikolay's nanny. He remembered her having very dark eyes and one tooth, and the Tolstoy children were both thrilled and scared when they were told she was 100 years old. For Tolstoy, old Anna Ivanovna and the venerable family housekeeper Praskovya Isayevna had a special aura, having worked under his grandfather, Nikolay Volkonsky. Praskovya Isayevna was later immortalised by Tolstoy in *Childhood*, and he later declared that the portrait of Natalya Savishna was true to life.[31]

The small, dark-skinned Tatyana Filippovna took over from Annushka as nanny to the Tolstoy children. She returned to Yasnaya Polyana after helping to raise Tolstoy's sister's daughters, and helped care for his first-born, Sergey. She later died in the house at Yasnaya Polyana, in the very room where Tolstoy sat writing his memoirs as an old man. He describes Tatyana Filippovna as a simple soul who was completely devoted to his family and was continually exploited by her own family: her good-for-nothing husband and son saw her as a source of ready money. Her brother Nikolay Filippovich was the coachman at Yasnaya Polyana, and he was also loved and respected by the Tolstoy children, who liked the fact that he smelled pleasantly of manure, and had a gentle, melodious voice.

Every Russian landowner had his favourites amongst their servants, and Tolstoy commented that this was particularly true of people like his father, who were passionate about hunting. The preferential treatment Nikolay Ilyich gave the two brothers Petrusha and Matyusha, who were invaluable in the field and doubled up by serving at table at home, meant they were not so popular with other servants, who resented the gifts and other privileges given to them. As was quite common in such cases, when they were given their freedom the brothers did not cope well with the sudden change from their former state of slavery, and never seemed to be satisfied with what they had been given. Neither of them ever married. As a young boy, Tolstoy simply admired them as strong, handsome men, always neatly turned out.

Along with Petrusha and Matyusha, the diminutive, grey-eyed Tikhon (the one who stole Nikolay Ilyich's tobacco on the quiet) also waited at the Tolstoy family table, but he was quite different. He had been a flautist in Nikolay Volkonsky's orchestra, and his second job was to sweep the reception rooms in the house every morning, after which he would sit in the front hall knitting socks. He was a born comic, and very popular with the Tolstoy children when he stood behind their father or grandmother at table and pulled funny faces. He would immediately become motionless again, plate held tight against his chest, as soon as an adult turned round. The mild-mannered, kind Vasily Trubetskoy, the wine steward with the crooked smile, was also remembered with affection, and he was very fond of all the children: he used to delight the Tolstoy boys when they were very small by putting them on a tray and carrying them round the pantry. Tolstoy tells us in his memoirs that as a six-year-old boy he was thunderstruck when he learned that Vasily had been appointed to manage an estate inherited by the family. He later claimed that the moment when Vasily came to kiss the Tolstoy children on the shoulder that Christmas, after learning of this promotion, was when he first experienced the anguish of confronting change.[32]

Christmas was the one time of year when the Tolstoy children traditionally mingled with the serfs on the estate. Extending for the whole twelve days until Epiphany, Yuletide in Russia was a particularly jolly time, when the rules of normal life were temporarily suspended, and mummers dressed in colourful and outlandish costumes would go on wild troika rides, or walk from house to house singing carols, and be treated in return to festive food and drink. It was also the custom for serfs to visit their owners. Every Christmas about thirty peasants belonging to the Tolstoy family would come up to the main house in fancy dress (there was always a bear and a goat), or dressed up as the opposite sex. The Tolstoy children also dressed up, giving themselves black moustaches with the aid of a burnt cork, and old Grigory, the former violinist in Nikolay Volkonsky's serf orchestra, would make his annual visit to Yasnaya Polyana to accompany the singing and dancing.[33] Happy memories of these festivities, which were continued while Tolstoy's own children were growing up at Yasnaya Polyana, later inspired the enchanting scene in *War and Peace* when the young Rostovs, Natasha, Sonya and Nikolay, get dressed up one evening and travel by sleigh to visit their neighbours.

Foka Demidych, the family butler, had played second violin in the orchestra, but his performances in the 1830s, when Tolstoy was growing up, were restricted to announcing in his blue frock-coat every day at two o'clock that lunch was served, with as much ceremony as possible. The Tolstoys actually lived quite austerely compared with many noble families – apart from a pair of fine gilt-framed mirrors, some Voltaire armchairs and some mahogany tables, the house was decorated in a fairly spartan fashion, with furniture and table linen produced by their own carpenters and weavers. But in other respects the old patriarchal traditions of the Russian aristocracy were studiously maintained. Tolstoy comments proudly in his memoirs that his father did not have to undergo the indignity of having to become a civil servant in Nicholas I's government, and indeed he could not remember ever having even seen an official during his childhood and youth.[34]

The Tolstoys had various rituals which were faithfully observed. Each day began and ended with members of the family kissing each other's hands, and every Sunday they would troop off to the village church (where the children would try to copy their father, who bowed so low his right hand touched the ground).[35] But it was lunch which was the most ritualised occasion in the Tolstoys' daily life. The entire family, including the children and their tutor, would gather in the drawing room to wait for Nikolay Ilyich to emerge from his study, and at the appointed time he would offer his hand to his mother to escort her into the dining room. Servants holding plates against their chests with their left hands would be stationed behind each family member's chair, while guests would be attended to by their own servants. At the end of each meal, Tolstoy's father would be handed his pipe and he would retire to his study; *babushka* would proceed to the drawing room and the children would go downstairs with Fyodor Ivanovich and draw pictures.

Tolstoy was the first to acknowledge how idyllic and privileged his early childhood was. Like so many Russian country estates at that time, Yasnaya Polyana was an almost self-sufficient kingdom, with its own population of serfs to till the fields, milk the cows, chop wood, weave carpets, cobble shoes, groom the horses, breed hounds for hunting, clear paths, complete the accounts, prepare meals, fetch water and do the laundry. It was also a whole world which Tolstoy never had to leave. Yasnaya Polyana provided a sheltered environment for him to grow up in, surrounded by his relatives and an extensive second family of household servants. It was also an elite school where he began his education with a private tutor, and an enormous playground whose woods, ponds, winding paths and streams promised the possibility of endless enticing adventures. Finally, it was a physically beautiful landscape of tree-lined avenues, elegant gardens and tranquil ponds. Tolstoy remained cocooned in this rural paradise for the first eight years of his life; indeed, the most significant journey he made during this period was downstairs, when he left the nursery at the age of five to join his elder brothers and come under the charge of his German tutor.

There are precious few third-person accounts of Tolstoy as a little boy, but his mischievousness stands out even in those few sources. In a letter Aline wrote to Toinette when he was around six, for example, she made a point of saying that it was some time since 'little Lev' had been dismissed from the dinner table, suggesting this had hitherto been a regular occurrence. Tolstoy's 'originality' was also noticed from an early age: his relatives remembered their amusement when the young boy took it into his head one day to come into the drawing room, turn round and bow to everybody present with his backside, throwing his head back, instead of inclining it, and clicking his heels.[36]

When he came to write to his memoirs near the end of his life, Tolstoy refused to recount all his happy childhood memories, both because they were 'endless' and also because he feared it would be impossible to convey adequately to others the memories he cherished which were so important to him.[37] He could recall very few specific events from his early childhood beyond his father coming and going, and the riveting stories he told about the adventures encountered on his hunting expeditions. He remembered only three occasions when something really made an impression on him, but two of these impressions are intriguing. One was when his mother's cousin, one of the Prince Volkonskys, a hussar, came to visit when he was very small and sat him on his knee. In his memoirs Tolstoy writes that the experience of feeling constricted compelled him to try to break loose while the young officer talked over his head to the other adults. This resulted in the hussar holding the young Lev even tighter. The feeling of captivity, of not being free, he writes in his memoirs, so incensed him that he started howling and trying to escape.[38] Tolstoy would spend his life asserting his independence and resisting people's attempts to make him conform.

The other notable impression, made by another relative who visited Yasnaya Polyana, 'the famous American', Count Fyodor Ivanovich Tolstoy, his uncle-once-removed, was far more positive, and is connected to what Tolstoy defined as the cardinal family trait: *dikost*. This is a word with many meanings, as so often encountered in the Russian language. *Dikost* literally means 'wildness', but it can also convey unsociableness or shyness. In other contexts it can mean weirdness, eccentricity, or absurdity. Tolstoy liked further to define *dikost*, when applying this word to members of his family, as the quality of possessing passion and daring. It was not a noun with negative connotations in his book. For him it denoted originality and independence of thought, as well as the propensity to do the opposite of everyone else. Tolstoy himself certainly went against the grain in almost everything he did as an adult, and even used *dikost* in this vein to describe the radical ideas he wished to apply to education when launching his pedagogical journal in 1862.[39] Tolstoy perceived *dikost* not only in many of his illustrious ancestors, but also in some of his contemporary relatives – even his very prim and proper distant relative, who was a spirited but nevertheless very poised lady-in-waiting at the imperial court. 'You've got the Tolstoyan *dikost* that we all have,' he wrote to Alexandra Andreyevna in 1865. 'It was not for nothing that Fyodor Ivanovich got himself tattooed.'[40] Count Fyodor Ivanovich Tolstoy was indeed the wildest Tolstoy of them all: while visiting a Polynesian island in the South Pacific as a young man, he decided to emulate the natives by having his body completely covered in tattoos. Alexandra Andreyevna in turn called her younger relative Lev Nikolayevich 'the roaring lion'[41] (the word *Lev* in Russian meaning both Leo and lion).

Tolstoy also invested one of his most autobiographical characters with *dikost*. 'All you Levins are *diky*,' says the sophisticated bon viveur Stiva Oblonsky to his socially awkward but ardent, truth-seeking friend Konstantin Levin in *Anna Karenina*; 'you always do what no one else does.'[42] This is precisely how Tolstoy was perceived by his contemporaries. In 1868 Eugene Schuyler, the newly appointed American consul to Moscow, was discouraged but not deterred from meeting Tolstoy by a society hostess who characterised Tolstoy as 'very shy and very wild'.[43] If it was from his early ancestor Count Pyotr Andreyevich that Tolstoy inherited his capacity for erudition, it was probably from Fyodor Ivanovich, the 'wild' Tolstoy who got himself tattooed all over, that he inherited his independent spirit and physical strength. Young Lev Tolstoy hardly needed fairy tales when there was a relative in his own family whose life story read like an adventure novel – and his own son Sergey was later so captivated that he published a short biography of Fyodor Tolstoy in 1926.[44]

Fyodor Tolstoy (1782–1846) earned a reputation for wildness at a young age, fighting his first duel at the age of seventeen soon after being commissioned as an officer in the elite Preobrazhensky Guards regiment in St Petersburg. In 1803, four years later, he escaped the confines of military life by securing, against all odds, a berth on Adam von Krusenstern's three-masted British-built sloop *Nadezhda*. The mission was to complete the first Russian round-the-world expedition, along with a sister ship, the *Neva*.[45] After stops in Copenhagen, Falmouth and the Canary Islands, the *Nadezhda* set sail for Cape Horn, and thence for the Marquesas Islands in the South Pacific, where Fyodor Tolstoy acquired his famous tattoos. By this time, Captain Krusenstern was heartily fed up with the young officer. Unlike the naturalist, the astronomer, the artist and the doctor on board, Fyodor Ivanovich had nothing much to do, and so amused himself by provoking arguments with the crew, just for the sheer hell of it, and carrying out outrageous pranks, such as apparently letting loose an orang-utan (or was it a monkey?) in the captain's cabin. He also got the ship's priest paralytically drunk one day and then glued his beard to the deck with sealing wax. When the *Nadezhda* arrived at the Kamchatka peninsula on the eastern edge of the Russian Empire, before sailing on to Japan, Captain Krusenstern ordered Tolstoy to leave the ship.

Fyodor Tolstoy's life became so shrouded in legend and prurient gossip that it is difficult to establish the veracity of the many stories which circulated about him, or even the facts of his departure from the *Nadezhda*. One story maintained that he had been abandoned on the Aleutian Islands in the North Pacific between Kamchatka and Alaska, together with a monkey (or was it an orang-utan?), which he was later forced to eat out of hunger. The monograph of Fyodor Ivanovich which Tolstoy's son Sergey published in 1926 refutes this. Sergey Tolstoy notes that he once had his hair pulled at the age of nine by a monkey when visiting Fyodor Tolstoy's ageing daughter in Moscow in 1872: she always had a monkey as a pet in memory of the original one her father had kept. In his book, Sergey Tolstoy concludes that Fyodor Ivanovich was certainly put ashore, and definitely spent some time with native tribes on Sitka Island in southern Alaska, which was then part of the colony called 'Russian America'. This is how Fyodor Ivanovich came to acquire his nickname of 'Tolstoy the American'.[46]

In August 1805, two years after leaving St Petersburg, Fyodor Tolstoy arrived back in the Russian capital, having made his way back across Siberia overland. He was promptly arrested and sent to serve for three years in a remote fortress in current-day Savonlinna, 150 miles north of St Petersburg. By risking his life in the Finnish War, against Sweden (Finland was formally annexed by Russia in 1809), Tolstoy was allowed to rejoin the Preobrazhensky Guards, but his nefarious exploits led to more duels and in 1811 he was dismissed from the army. Nevertheless, his swashbuckling spirit led him to volunteer when Napoleon invaded Russia and his bravery during the Battle of Borodino, during which he was wounded, resulted in him being restored to the ranks and decorated. It is not surprising that Fyodor Ivanovich came to Tolstoy's mind when he was writing *War and Peace*. His relative provided him with the initial inspiration for the character of the desperate, fast-living Dolokhov, who shares his name and patronymic, as well his passion for cards.

In keeping with Tolstoyan *dikost*, Fyodor Ivanovich continued to be full of surprises after finally retiring to Moscow post-1812. He gave up fighting duels and gambling, and calmed down. In 1821 married a gypsy singer (after which he was promptly ostracised by many in Moscow society) and had twelve children, only one of whom lived to adulthood. Tolstoy got to know Fyodor's widow Avdotya and daughter Praskovya in Moscow in the 1840s and 1850s. Fyodor Tolstoy became very pious as he got older, and those who asked to see his tattoos would see him first remove the large icon of St Spiridon, the patron saint of the Tolstoy family, which he wore round his neck, before showing off the brightly coloured bird in the middle of his chest, surrounded by red and blue patterns, and serpents on his arms.

Fyodor Ivanovich had led a colourful life, and it clearly meant a great deal to Tolstoy to have met his notorious ancestor when he was a child. In his memoirs he declares there is much he would have liked to say about this 'extraordinary, lawless, and attractive man', whose handsome, tanned face with thick sideboards extending to the corners of his mouth clearly left an unusually vivid impression on him as a young boy.[47] Fyodor Ivanovich had mellowed by the time he visited Yasnaya Polyana in the early 1830s, when he was in his fifties, but he was still eccentric, producing two embroidered lawn handkerchiefs which he claimed would magnetically cure the toothache suffered by Tolstoy's elder brother Sergey.

When Fyodor Ivanovich visited Yasnaya Polyana, Tolstoy was around seven years old. His earliest extant manuscript dates from around this time. The two notebook pages preserved in his archive were his contribution to a journal co-produced with his brothers:

Children's Amusements

Section One
Natural History

Written by C[ount]. L[ev]. N. To[lstoy]: 1835

1. The Eagle
The eagle is king of the birds. They say that a boy started to tease him once, and he grew angry with him and pecked him to death.

2. The Falcon
The falcon is a very useful bird, it catches gazelles. The gazelle is an animal which runs very fast, so dogs cannot catch it; the falcon will swoop down and kill it.

3. The Owl
The owl is a very strong bird, and it cannot see in sunlight. An eagle owl is also an owl. The eagle owl only differs through its tufts.

4. The Parrot
The parrot is a very beautiful bird, its beak hangs down or is like a hook, and it is taught to speak.

5. The Peacock
The peacock is also beautiful, it has blue patches, and its tail is bigger than it is itself.

6. The Humming Bird
The humming bird is a very small little bird, it has a golden beak, it can be white.

7. The Rooster
The rooster is a beautiful bird, its brightly coloured tail hangs downwards, its throat is red, blue and all colours, and its wattle is red. When the Indian rooster sings, it lowers its tail and its throat, which is red, black and all colours, puffs up. The Indian rooster has a different tail to the rooster, the Indian rooster has a tail which is loose.

We know very little else about 'Children's Amusements', and equally little about other literary ventures that the Tolstoy brothers engaged in during the 1830s. When he wrote his memoirs, Tolstoy had only a few distinct early childhood memories of his brothers, who were his first playmates, but there was one event which he remembered his whole life, and which was one of the most important and most cherished of all his memories. When he was about five years old, his beloved eldest brother Nikolay, then about eleven, announced that the secret to human happiness was written on a little green stick which was buried in the woods a short walk from their house. When the secret was revealed, he told his brothers, people would not only be happy, but they would also cease to be ill, and would no longer be angry with each other. At that point everybody would become 'ant brothers' (*muraveinye bratya*). Tolstoy explains in his memoirs that Nikolay must have read something about the Moravian Brethren (the *moravskie bratya*).

As the eldest, Nikolay Tolstoy was revered by his brothers, who all used the polite *vy* form of address with him (rather than *ty*). Young Lev admired Nikolay most of all, and describes him in his memoirs as a 'remarkable boy with a keen artistic sensitivity, a vibrant imagination, and a highly developed moral sense, who was kind and good-natured without ever being smug'. The Tolstoy boys were enthralled by the elaborate games and rituals thought up by Nikolay, who one day promised to take them to the mythical 'Fanfaronov mountain' if they carried out to the letter the conditions he set. These included standing in the corner and trying not to think about the white bear, and avoiding seeing a hare for a whole year. In their childhood, the Tolstoy brothers also played at being 'ant brothers' by huddling together in a den created from two chairs, a couple of boxes and some shawls. In his adulthood, Tolstoy would continue to believe fervently in the possibility of the ant brothers' ideal, but writ large, so as to encompass the whole of humanity. In memory of his brother Nikolay, and his aspirations to love and kindness, which he had sought to emulate, Tolstoy requested towards the end of his life to be buried at the spot where the little green stick was supposedly hidden, and this was indeed where he would be laid to rest in November 1910.[48]

The religious impulse which inspired Tolstoy in the 1880s was strangely not so distant from that which gave rise to the Moravian Brethren. The Moravian Church, which continues to flourish today, dates back to the rebellion against Roman Catholicism mounted by Jan Hus in the late fourteenth century, more than 100 years before Luther and the Protestant Reformation. Hus and his other Czech-speaking followers were based in Bohemia and Moravia, whose Slav populations had been the first to be converted to Eastern Orthodoxy by the Byzantine missionaries Saints Cyril and Methodius in the ninth century. The 'Hussites' were keen to revive those traditions, as well as rejecting the contemporary practice of indulgences ministered by the Catholic Church, to which the local populations had been forcibly converted when they became subjects of the Austrian Empire. The idea of personal salvation based on the individual's relationship with God was and remains central to the doctrine of the Moravian Church, and Tolstoy would preach something similar many centuries later, when he rebelled against what he perceived as the Orthodox Church's dependence on ritual and superstition. The early Protestants of Bohemia and Moravia were inevitably persecuted during the Counter Reformation, and in the years which followed, their church went underground. Many of their number eventually emigrated to parts of Europe hospitable to Lutheranism, with whose doctrines they had much in common.

It is intriguing that Tolstoy also has something in common with the founder of the revived Moravian Church, the eccentric Count Nikolaus

Ludwig von Zinzendorf, whose commitment to serving the poor led him to allow a group of Brethren to form a community on his land in the 1720s. Zinzendorf ended up leaving his position with the Saxon royal court in Dresden, and turning his back on his title and aristocratic lifestyle to live a simple life and devote himself to serving God. It was he who brought unity to the new village established by the immigrants, which led to them adopting a 'Brotherly Agreement', and he was key to the Brothers one day experiencing a spiritual transformation which led them to love one another. Tolstoy, of course, never believed he was starting a new church and he also dispensed with all sacraments. But in his appeal to ecumenical ideas of fellowship, and in his preaching of the merits of a simple life of service, he aligned himself with the ideals of the Moravian Brotherhood. As a pioneer ant brother, he would, moreover, definitely have approved of their motto: 'In essentials, unity; in non-essentials, liberty; and in all things, love'.

· 3 ·

ORPHANHOOD

I congratulate you, my dear Lyova, and also your brothers and sister, I wish you good health and diligence in your studies, so that you never cause any unpleasantness for dear Auntie Tatyana Alexandrovna, who works so hard for us. Mitya and Lyova, we went on a wonderful walk the other day, we all went to Sparrow Hills, and drank tea there. Since the weather is so good, I imagine you were in Grumant. I hope you have lots of fun. I send love to my dear Masha …

Letter from Nikolay Tolstoy in Moscow to Lev, Dmitry and Masha Tolstoy in Yasnaya Polyana, on the occasion of Lev's tenth birthday, August 1838[1]

LOOKING BACK OVER HIS LIFE when he was in his seventies, Tolstoy described the 'innocent, joyful, poetic period' of his childhood as lasting until he was fourteen.[2] Only the first seven of those fourteen years were truly cloudless, however. In the second seven, Tolstoy lost his father, his grandmother and his aunt, was temporarily separated from his elder brothers, and moved three times. The last upheaval resulted in a relocation several hundred miles from home. In a very real sense, the most idyllic part of Tolstoy's childhood began its decline with the first of those relocations, when the reassuring bucolic surroundings of Yasnaya Polyana were exchanged for the intimidating new world of metropolitan Moscow. It is these years, and the ones immediately following, which are amongst the least documented in what is generally an over-documented life. With a few exceptions, Tolstoy's memoirs essentially come to a halt with the family's departure from Yasnaya Polyana, although his trilogy *Childhood, Boyhood, Youth* is also a wonderful source of atmospheric detail about his early years, since it is clearly rooted in his own experience, despite it being a work of fiction.

Tolstoy's father moved his family to Moscow in January 1837 for the sake of the elder boys' education. Lev was only eight years old, but his eldest brother Nikolay was now fourteen, and already preparing for his university entrance. The relocation was a major undertaking, since the family was numerous, comprising the five Tolstoy children, two wards, two aunts, Nikolay Ilyich and his mother, and was accompanied by a full complement of thirty servants.[3] The journey north lasted two days, and involved a caravan of seven carriages, plus a special closed sleigh for grandmother Pelageya Nikolayevna. To make her feel safe, she was chaperoned by two of the family's manservants, who were forced to endure freezing temperatures and stand on the runners all the way.[4] The children took it in turns to sit with their father, and when they finally drove into Moscow, it was Lev who was lucky enough to be sitting next to him as he proudly pointed out the churches and prominent buildings they could see through the carriage windows.[5]

Arriving from the south, the Tolstoys would have driven through the colourful merchants' quarter, the Zamoskvorechie ('Beyond the Moscow river') and so would have first seen a profusion of onion-domed churches. The merchants were traditionally the most pious section of the Russian population, and the Zamoskvorechie had the greatest concentration of churches in Moscow, which was already a city renowned for its large number of churches. Nikolay Ilyich had rented a handsome house with a mezzanine set back from the street in a spacious courtyard, and after driving through the Zamoskvorechie, the Tolstoy family caravan would have turned west and arrived in a quiet residential area near to the Moscow river. It was to this part of Moscow that Tolstoy returned when his own family moved to the city in the 1880s.

In old age, Tolstoy had only dim memories of these first few months in the old capital. The city had by now fully recovered from the traumatic events of 1812, following an intense period of reconstruction, and the new urban

2. The house in Plyushchikha Street, Moscow, to which Nikolay Ilych Tolstoy brought his mother, sister and five children in 1837

surroundings would have seemed overwhelming for a boy used to a tranquil rural environment; he now found himself in the midst of buildings and strangers, and no longer the centre of attention. Nikolay was busy preparing for the university, and the Tolstoy children rarely saw their father, who had engaged as many as twelve tutors (including a dancing teacher) to keep his children busy, at an imposing annual cost of 83,000 roubles.[6] Meanwhile Nikolay Ilyich had become embroiled in a lawsuit over his purchase of the estate of Pirogovo from Alexander Temyashev, the man who had begged him to bring up his illegitimate daughter Dunechka. Temyashev was stricken with paralysis shortly after the contract was signed, and his relatives wanted the deeds declared null and void. As far as Tolstoy's father was concerned, however, he was now its legitimate owner. Nikolay Ilyich's health had been frail ever since his gruelling time in the army during and after the Napoleonic invasion. The stress of having to pick up the pieces and take responsibility after his father's bankruptcy, dismissal from the governorship of Kazan and untimely death had not helped. Tolstoy's father also had a tendency to drink too much. In 1836 he had written to a friend to tell him he was on a strict diet and taking medicines after experiencing the shock of coughing up a lot of blood.[7]

In June, a few months after arriving in Moscow, Nikolay Ilyich was obliged to go urgently to Tula to try to deal with the crisis which had blown up over his purchase of Pirogovo. Taking only his faithful servants Petrusha and Matyusha, he covered the distance in half the time it had taken his family to travel to Moscow earlier that year. That also had a deleterious effect on his health.[8] The following evening, shortly before his forty-third birthday, he suffered a massive lung haemorrhage and stroke while walking down the street in Tula, and died that same day. Rumours flew about that he had been poisoned by his servants, since all his money appeared to have been stolen, but Tolstoy was later not inclined to believe this story.[9]

Nikolay Ilyich's unexpected death was understandably a huge shock to his family. His sister Aline and his eldest son Nikolay travelled down from Moscow, and they buried him next to his wife Maria Nikolayevna in the village cemetery next to Yasnaya Polyana. For young Lev, his father's death was the most significant event of his childhood, and for a long time he kept expecting to see him one day on the streets of Moscow.[10] *Babushka* Pelageya Nikolayevna, who had doted on her son Nikolay, never really recovered, and the loss was also acutely felt by his sister Aline, and perhaps above all by his distant cousin Toinette, for whom he had been the centre of her world.

It was Aline who now became guardian to the five Tolstoy children, with assistance from one of her late brother's friends, Sergey Yazykov, who had an estate in Tula province. Sergey Yazykov was also Lev's godfather, but his involvement was fairly minimal from the start, and even that decreased over time. As well as assuming responsibility for the children's education, Aline now had to occupy herself with the crude practicalities of selling cattle and organising harvests, since she was now in charge of the considerable income that came from the five disparate properties the Tolstoy children had inherited. Each estate came with a farm, and each farm had complicated accounts that needed to be carefully checked, obliging Aline to deal with uncouth stewards and bookkeepers who could often be truculent and dishonest. Aline was also now responsible for the welfare of the hundreds of serfs who belonged to the Tolstoy family. It was their toil, after all, which enabled the Tolstoys to maintain a comfortable lifestyle. All in all, it was a job for which someone so naïve and otherworldly was ill-qualified, to say the least, as Aline's chief interests, after all, were spiritual, not material. Nikolay Ilyich had done some intricate and crafty manoeuvring in order to enable his family to live in the manner to which it had become accustomed in Moscow as well as in the country, but he left his financial affairs in a perilous state at the time of his death. All Aline could see were debts.[11] And then there was the still-unresolved lawsuit, which would drag on for several more years before finally being resolved in the Tolstoys' favour.

The Tolstoy children remained in Moscow throughout the hot summer months following their father's death, when otherwise they would probably have returned to Yasnaya Polyana. Aline was fortunate to be assisted by Aunt Toinette in caring for them. It was Toinette, for example, who took the children to the Bolshoi Theatre for the first time later that autumn. They sat in a box, and as an old man Tolstoy remembered that he had not immediately realised that he should not be looking straight across to the boxes opposite but sideways, down to the stage.[12] Even the children's redoubtable grandmother now took a hand in their upbringing. Prospère Saint-Thomas had been engaged as French tutor for the elder boys, and three days after her son's death Pelageya Nikolayevna decided to invite the fair-haired Frenchman from Grenoble to become resident governor to her grandchildren, replacing their kindly but not terribly competent German tutor Fyodor Ivanovich, who was consequently demoted. Being impressed by all things French, Pelageya Nikolayevna imagined Saint-Thomas would become the male authority figure that the children needed. The small, wiry Frenchman was certainly dynamic, but Tolstoy bridled at his self-importance and vanity, and he was also not impressed by his grandiloquent rhetorical flourishes.[13] Saint-Thomas was also a harsh disciplinarian who forced his pupils to beg forgiveness for misdemeanours on their knees. Worst of all was the moment when he locked the young Lev up and threatened to punish him with the rod. In terms of its significance, the incident was certainly not on a par with his father's death, but it nevertheless left a very deep impression on Tolstoy – so much so that some sixty years later he recalled in his diary the humiliation and misery of overhearing his family's laughter and merriment while he was locked up 'in prison'. In his memoirs, he went so far as to date his lifelong horror of violence back to this ordeal.[14] It is telling that Tolstoy should have dwelled on this incident. In 1908 Lenin would famously characterise the 'tearing off of masks' as a hallmark of Tolstoy's fiction and it seems that, at nine years old, Tolstoy was already capable of seeing through his French tutor's pretentious veneer. Even though it was precisely at this point that he began to enjoy studying, his already obstinate and headstrong nature made him resent moreover submitting to the authority of a person he did not respect.[15] Later on, he would resent submitting to any authority.

The friction in Tolstoy's relationship with Saint-Thomas may have been caused by an awareness at some level that he possessed a superior intellect, but his mental acuity was not always on show, and certainly not on the day he tried to fly. It was more probably Tolstoyan *dikost* which impelled him to go up to the classroom on the mezzanine floor one day and take a running jump out of the window. He claimed afterwards that he had wanted to do something unusual and surprise everybody. Since everybody was at table, however, wondering where he was, they remained oblivious – until the mystery of young Lev's absence was solved by the cook, who had seen him hurtling towards the ground through the kitchen window. As it turned out, Tolstoy was blessed with a strong constitution. He lost consciousness briefly and suffered some concussion, but was fully restored to health after sleeping solidly for eighteen hours.[16]

Just before the first anniversary of Nikolay Ilyich's death in May 1838, *babushka* Pelageya Nikolayevna died after a long and painful illness. She was seventy-six. This death Tolstoy experienced fully, as he had to endure being taken with his siblings to kiss the lifeless white hand that lay on top of the mound of white linen on their grandmother's high bed, and say goodbye to her before she breathed her last. He also had to confront the sight of her stern, hook-nosed face in the open coffin lying on the table before she was taken off to be buried, and put on a newly sewn black mourning jacket.[17] Unable to contemplate any change to her formerly grand aristocratic lifestyle, Grandmother Pelageya had insisted on maintaining the family's highly ritualised and formal dining habits after her son's death, but now everything fell apart. Even the impractical Aunt Aline could see that the sums did not add up. After subtracting the money needed to pay various wages, bribes and dues, the income from the family's five estates barely covered the rental of their Moscow house and the salaries of all the tutors who had been engaged, let alone any of their other expenses.

Some drastic decisions had to be taken, which resulted in the family being split up, with Aline remaining in Moscow with Saint-Thomas, her ward Pashenka and the two eldest boys. They now moved to a smaller and much cheaper flat, but were glad to leave behind the big house 'which had seen so many tears'. The two youngest boys, their sister Masha and Dunechka accompanied Aunt Toinette and Fyodor Ivanovich back to Yasnaya Polyana.[18]

One casualty of the downsizing was the Tolstoys' faithful coachman Mitka Kopylov, whom the family could no longer afford to keep on. His strength and agility, combined with his diminutive size, had also made him an irreplaceable and valued postilion, and the rewards for his good service and his pride in his work were reflected in the silk shirts and velvet coats he wore. There were plenty of Moscow merchants ready to give such a smartly turned-out coachman a wage, but when Mitka's brother was conscripted into the army due to the quota system that was in operation, he was forced to go back to work as a labourer at Yasnaya Polyana. Conscription always represented a major loss for peasant families, even after the term of service was reduced to twenty years, as soldiers in the infantry were not able to return home while serving. It was particularly difficult in this case. Mitka's elderly father now needed his other son to come back and work in the fields, and within a few months the debonair new Muscovite had gone back to being a drably dressed peasant in bast shoes. As a serf, he had no choice, and Tolstoy later explained that Mitka's quiet acceptance of his lot, and the uncomplaining way he surrendered a job he loved for heavy agricultural work, were highly influential on his nascent feelings of affection and respect for the Russian peasantry.[19]

Although he had partly enjoyed the experience of living in Moscow, and the chance to make new friends, Tolstoy must have been relieved to escape from his tutor and go back home to Yasnaya Polyana after his grandmother's death. He and Dmitry were now able to go and visit the new estate at Pirogovo, which had a fine stud farm, and they each received their own pony. It would be two years before the brothers were all reunited at Yasnaya Polyana, but in the meantime they started writing to each other. At this stage their correspondence was not terribly exciting. A week after Dmitry and Lev left Moscow, Sergey wrote to tell them that all was well in their new home, and that the cactus was about to start flowering. Lev wrote back to tell Sergey and Nikolay about his new pony. Sometimes Nikolay wrote, sometimes the letters were in French, and sometimes the elder brothers deigned to include their sister Masha as an addressee.[20] Occasionally Dunechka also got a mention in their letters, but she left the family in March 1839 to go to a boarding school in Moscow, and Tolstoy now became closer to Masha for the first time as a result.[21]

In August 1839 the cadet branch of the family enjoyed a leisurely journey back to Moscow for a visit. Since they were travelling in the summer months, and since Tolstoy was now eleven, and curious about everything, it was a great adventure for him. Most exciting of all, however, was the prospect of seeing the Tsar lay the cornerstone of the Cathedral of Christ the Saviour. This was the Cathedral Alexander I had pledged to build back in 1812 when Napoleon retreated from Moscow, 'to preserve the eternal memory of that unprecedented zeal, loyalty for the Faith and the Fatherland with which the Russian people exalted itself in these difficult days, and to mark Our gratitude to God's Providence, by saving Russia from the ruin threatening her'.[22] Five years after Napoleon had been driven from Moscow, the cornerstone had been laid in 1817 at a magnificent ceremony attended by 400 members of the Russian Orthodox clergy, 50,000 guards officers, the Tsar and his family and hundreds of thousands of their loyal subjects. But despite the injection of 16 million roubles from the state treasury, and the labour of some 20,000 serfs specially drafted in for the purpose, construction had not gone according to plan. Officially it came to a halt because the foundations were insufficiently secure. In reality, the money was embezzled, creating a huge scandal whose duration was long enough to provide inspiration for Gogol's classic play about Russian corruption, *The Government Inspector*, in 1836.[23]

After becoming tsar in 1825, Nicholas moved the cathedral's location from the Sparrow Hills, the highest point in Moscow, to a site by the river nearer to the Kremlin. He also exchanged the original neoclassical blueprint for a new Russian-Byzantine design modelled on Justinian's Cathedral of St Sophia in Constantinople, which was much more in keeping with his tastes, not to mention his vision of the Russian Empire. Nicholas I's arrival in Moscow to lay the new cornerstone of the cathedral in September 1839 was a national event, and the Tolstoys were there to witness it. As friends of Alexey Milyutin, who headed the Commission for the Construction of the Cathedral, they were able to watch the ceremony from the windows of his house, which looked out right on to the site. They thus had a thrilling bird's-eye view not only of the Tsar, but of the elite Preobrazhensky Guards in their formal dress uniforms, who had travelled specially from St Petersburg along with Nicholas I to take part in the military parades.[24] After a special liturgy in the Assumption Cathedral in the Kremlin, the Tsar led a procession on foot to the building site, followed by veterans of 1812, church dignitaries, twenty infantry battalions and six cavalry troops, accompanied by constant cannon fire and the ringing of the bells in all of Moscow's churches. Thus was the great victory over Napoleon celebrated again.[25]

A quarter of a century later, the construction of the enormous cathedral's exterior would be complete, and Tolstoy would be hard at work writing the vast novel which would commemorate the events of 1812, his patriotic feelings still intact. But he had no desire to be anywhere near the cathedral when it was finally consecrated amidst great pomp in May 1883, after the completion of its sumptuous interior decoration. Indeed, he was hundreds of miles away drinking fermented mare's milk (koumiss) on his farm in the steppe, having by this time renounced his Orthodox faith, his fiction and any lingering patriotic feelings. He had, however, been casting his mind back to that visit to Moscow in 1839 at that time, for he was eleven years old when he consciously began to question his faith. On the first page of his *Confession*, which he tried to publish in 1882, he describes how excited he and his brothers had been when Alexey Milyutin's son Vladimir came to see them one day that autumn and told them of his discovery that there was no God.[26] Along with the pain of being locked up by his French tutor, this event was also etched deeply into Tolstoy's memory.

Other memories from this period of Tolstoy's childhood are few and far between, but the isolated incidents recalled in his memoirs for that reason resonate all the more. It was only after his father's death, for example, that the young Tolstoy was brought face to face with the corporal punishment that was occasionally practised at Yasnaya Polyana, where the regime was generally far more humane than on other noble estates. One day, as they returned with their tutor from a walk and were walking past the threshing barn, the children encountered Andrey Ilyin, the overweight steward of the estate, followed by the family's assistant coachman Kuzma, whose mournful expression astonished them. Upon enquiring where they were going, Andrey calmly replied that he was taking Kuzma to the threshing barn to flog him. 'I cannot describe the terrible feeling these words and the sight of the kind and dejected Kuzma produced in me,' Tolstoy wrote in his memoirs, pointing out that Kuzma by this time was a married man, and no longer young. When that evening he told Aunt Toinette about it, she reproached the children angrily for not stopping Andrey, although they clearly did not realise they had the power to intervene. Toinette loathed corporal punishment, and she not only would not countenance the Tolstoy children receiving it, but she did her best to prevent it being meted out to the serfs whenever she could.[27] Tolstoy would later also recall this incident in an incendiary article he wrote in 1895 entitled 'Shameful', in which he railed about peasants having to submit to humiliating corporal punishment for any small misdemeanour.[28]

Tolstoy never forgot the time his French governor threatened to thrash him, but the rancour he felt towards him evaporated, particularly when Saint-Thomas wrote him a congratulatory and encouraging letter about a touching poem of gratitude he had written on the occasion of his aunt Aline's name-day in January 1840, when all the Tolstoys gathered at Yasnaya Polyana. The family were so taken with it that Aunt Aline took a fair copy back to Moscow to show Saint-Thomas, who clearly was not so much of a martinet that he could not recognise signs of talent.[29] That summer, friendly relations were established on a firmer footing when Saint-Thomas visited Yasnaya Polyana for the first time, and went hunting with the Tolstoy boys. His verdict on Lev was that he was 'un petit Molière'.[30]

Lev meanwhile continued to resist having to learn lessons by rote, whether from the seminarian engaged to teach the younger boys at Yasnaya Polyana, or from old Fyodor Ivanovich Rössel, who was dismissed for drunkenness in 1840.[31] Adam Fyodorovich Meyer, the German who replaced him, proved to be even worse, and in the end Fyodor Ivanovich was allowed to return to Yasnaya Polyana, where he remained, living on as a pensioner until the middle of the 1840s. Tolstoy may not have been the most diligent pupil, and that situation did not change during his adolescence, but he clearly enjoyed reading, which did not involve submitting to any kind of coercive authority. Many years later, when he was in his sixties, Tolstoy revealed the books that had made the most impression on him as a small boy.[32] First of all there were the books which made a 'great' impression on him: *A Thousand and One Nights*, some of whose tales he had heard from his grandmother's blind storyteller, and Pushkin's 1821 poem 'Napoleon', which sparked off an interest that would later produce spectacular literary results. Then there was Anton Pogorelsky's story 'The Black Hen or The Underground Residents', which made a 'very great' impression on Tolstoy, perhaps partly because when he was a very young boy he kept hens and chicks himself.[33]

Written in 1829 for the author's twelve-year-old nephew Alyosha Tolstoy (a distant cousin who was later to become a distinguished writer himself),[34] it is about a young boy (also named Alyosha), who saves a favourite hen from being served up for dinner one day. The hen, it turns out, is also a minister in a secret underground kingdom of miniature people, whose king rewards Alyosha with a magic kernel of corn enabling him to come top of the class without studying. One day, however, things start to go wrong, and Alyosha loses his magic powers, only to rediscover the importance of hard work and humility. Along with fantasy, this classic story incorporates certain biographical details, and was the first work for and about children in Russian literature. Admittedly, Pogorelsky (1787–1836) was a minor writer, and this story was written for children; all the same, the common view that Tolstoy's first published work, his autobiographical trilogy *Childhood, Boyhood, Youth*, was the first work in Russian literature to have a child as the central character is not quite accurate.[35] Tolstoy himself clearly never forgot 'The Black Hen', and later in his life he himself turned to writing simple stories for a popular audience, also combining a degree of fantasy with a moral. Since there was still very little children's literature available when he became an adult, particularly for peasant children, he also sought to fill this gap; the 629 works he produced during his lifetime comprise tales, fables, legends and sketches.

The works which Tolstoy recorded in 1891 as having made an 'enormous' impression on him as a child were the story of Joseph from the Bible, Russian fairy tales, and the popular folk epics (*byliny*) about the semi-historical, legendary heroes (bogatyrs) of old Rus. Tolstoy mentions three names in particular: the Kievan boyar Dobrinya Nikitich, a diplomat and dragon slayer; the priest's son Alyosha Popovich, who uses cunning to outwit his enemies; and Ilya of Murom, the greatest hero of them all, who is still the most powerful literary personification of the Russian people. Ilya of Murom is a peasant's son, who lies at home on the brick stove until he is thirty-three years old, apparently unable to move. After some wandering beggars give him strength, he then sets out on his horse to perform mighty feats, defeating whole armies single-handedly, and always drawing his super-human power from the Russian land. Ilya of Murom was a warrior who combined strength with meekness, patience and stamina, not wanting to kill, but passionate about defending his nation. The only bogatyr ever made into an Orthodox saint, and an ascetic who refuses to marry, Ilya of Murom has always also been a symbol of spiritual power.[36]

The only Russian who ever came close to bearing comparison with the mighty Ilya of Murom was Tolstoy, who was just as devoted to his native land, and was similarly identified with it by Russians and foreigners alike ('when you read Tolstoy's works, it is impossible not to feel the Russian soul in them' is a familiar refrain).[37] Tolstoy was thirty-five when he found his feet, as it were, and began writing *War and Peace*, his own epic, one of the longest and greatest works of fiction ever written (which he never regarded as a novel in the conventional sense). He was renowned for his physical strength and stamina, spending long periods in the saddle and fighting with bravery while serving with the Russian army. He had enormous wealth and a huge family, and was later to give it all up to live humbly and work on behalf of the peasantry, fighting against injustices of every kind and becoming the most influential spiritual leader in Russia, even proclaiming chastity. He was frequently portrayed in cartoons as a giant amongst the pygmies of contemporary Russian literature, or towering physically over his fellow writers, with one cartoonist actually portraying him as Ilya of Murom astride his mighty steed in a parody of Vasnetsov's famous 1898 painting of the three bogatyrs (with Korolenko as Dobrinya Nikitich and Chekhov as Alyosha Popovich).[38] It is not surprising, then, that many visitors making the pilgrimage to visit the great sage of Yasnaya Polyana, and expecting to encounter a giant, were disconcerted to discover that Tolstoy was actually quite small.[39]

After the deaths of their father and grandmother in 1837 and 1838, it took time for the young Tolstoys to settle down, and there was to be one more major upheaval for the family. In August 1841, on Tolstoy's thirteenth birthday, his pious aunt Aline died during a prolonged stay at the Optina Pustyn Monastery, her already fragile health undermined by the strict fasting required of devout Orthodox believers. It was the deep spiritual wisdom of Optina's elders which had drawn Tolstoy's aunt Aline. After her death, guardianship of her three nephews and niece Masha, who legally were still minors (only Nikolay, the eldest had reached the age of eighteen), passed to her younger sister Pelageya, who had been named after their mother but was known in the family as Polina. The young Tolstoys barely knew their other aunt as she had remained in Kazan after their grandfather's death. In 1818, when she was twenty, she had married a retired colonel from the Hussars, Vladimir Yushkov. Nikolay Tolstoy now wrote to Vladimir Ivanovich on behalf of his siblings in polished French:

> We all ask our auntie – I, my brothers and my sister – not to leave us in

our grief, and to become our guardian. You have to imagine, Uncle, the full horror of our situation. Please, Uncle, don't refuse us, we ask you in the name of God and the departed [Aunt Aline]. You and Auntie are our only support in the world.[40]

Because her husband had at one time nurtured romantic feelings for Toinette, and because she still harboured a grudge against her, Polina decided her brother's children should relocate to Kazan. It would have been much more natural for Aunt Toinette to continue in loco parentis, but as a very distant relative, she was obliged to acquiesce with Polina's wishes. None of the children wanted to go, nor did they want leave their beloved Aunt Toinette, who now went to live with her sister Elizaveta. In November 1841 the Tolstoys started packing up their belongings once again.

· 4 ·

YOUTH

'I have read all of Rousseau, all twenty volumes, including the *Dictionary of Music*. I did more than admire him – I worshipped him. When I was fifteen, I wore next to my skin a medallion with his portrait rather than a cross. Many of his pages are so close to me that it feels like I wrote them myself.'

Tolstoy in conversation with Paul Boyer, 1901[1]

THE MOVE TO KAZAN spelled the end of Tolstoy's innocence. When he was fourteen, he lost his virginity, and he would later define the subsequent twenty years as a period of 'crude dissolute living in the service of ambition, vanity, and, above all, lust'.[2] The five and half years Tolstoy spent in Kazan were certainly not the happiest in his life, and few of his memories of this time were fond ones. Nevertheless, it was during his adolescence that he embarked on the intense self-analysis which culminated in the writing of his first fictional masterpieces. From the outset, Tolstoy conducted his self-analysis on the page. At the age of eighteen, shortly before he left Kazan to return home to Yasnaya Polyana, he began to keep a diary. It was with his first diary entries in March 1847 that his turbulent creative journey began, rather than with the completion of his first piece of fiction in 1851, or the publication of his first work a year later. This diary, which was to become the engine-room of his writing and which he kept on and off for the rest of his life, became increasingly voluminous in his last decade and fills fourteen volumes of his collected works.

As with the move to Moscow in 1837, the Tolstoys' relocation to Kazan in November 1841 was a major undertaking, even without accompanying adults. The smallest and most remote of the Tolstoy properties was sold to pay outstanding debts, and then the family's belongings were loaded on to a number of barges to make their slow way down to Kazan via the Oka and Volga rivers. The family's belongings, of course, included numerous serfs, including tailors, decorators, carpenters and cooks, on whom they would depend for their well-being in their new home. The four brothers and their sister set off later, and travelled overland by sleigh, via Moscow, Nizhny Novgorod and the Chuvash capital of Cheboksary, one of the ports on the Volga. They settled upon arrival in Kazan into the ground and mezzanine floors of a centrally located house; their landlords occupied the top floor. It was not far from the river and one of the city's monasteries, but its windows looked out on to the prison. The Tolstoys' servants had separate lodgings.[3]

Kazan was not like other Russian cities, as would have been immediately apparent to the new arrivals, for there were minarets alongside the domes of its many churches. Until 1552 Kazan had been the centre of a powerful Tatar khanate which had gradually adopted Islam as its state religion. After Kazan was conquered by Ivan the Terrible (who celebrated his first great victory over former Mongol lands by building the oriental-looking St Basil's in Moscow's Red Square), the city was populated by Russians, and its small remaining Tatar population would henceforth become a persecuted minority. The miraculous survival, after one of the city's many fires, of the venerated icon of Our Lady of Kazan in 1579 is testament to the vigour with which the new Russianisation policy was pursued in this former Islamic kingdom. And the fact that it was to Our Lady of Kazan that the Russian army's commander-in-chief Mikhail Suvorov appealed for help after Napoleon's invasion of Russia in 1812, meanwhile, is testament to the esteem in which this icon came to be held. In 1813 Suvorov was for this reason buried in the Kazan Cathedral in St Petersburg; it was here that a precious copy of the original icon was kept, and it now became the chief memorial to Russia's victory over Napoleon in the city.

Kazan never lost its Tatar character entirely. Catherine the Great had permitted mosques to be built again in Kazan towards the end of the eighteenth century, and the university founded in the city in 1804 rapidly became a major centre for oriental studies. The very foundation of Kazan University, where all the Tolstoy boys became students, speaks volumes about the city's importance nationally. Until Alexander I's famous 1804 statute, the only universities in the Russian Empire were located in Moscow, Dorpat and Vilna, the last two of which provided an education delivered in German and primarily for the benefit of their elite Baltic German populations. In 1804, these three were joined by two new universities in European Russia (St Petersburg and the Ukrainian city of Kharkov), and a third in the distinctly Asian setting of Kazan, some 750 miles south-east of St Petersburg. It was also in Kazan that the first state lycée was founded outside Moscow and St Petersburg, but as the Russian nobility preferred to educate their offspring at home, the younger male Tolstoys continued to be privately taught after moving to Kazan.

Kazan was a provincial city, but by the standards of provincial Russian cities at the time it was exceptional, and its university was a major reason behind the Tolstoys' relocation there. Soon after they arrived in November 1841, Nikolay became a second-year mathematics student, having failed the exam to transfer to the third year at Moscow University.[4] He graduated in 1844, then joined the army, and was soon transferred to the Caucasus. His younger brothers, meanwhile, started to prepare for their entrance examinations with tutors. Sergey and Dmitry both entered Kazan University in August 1843 to study mathematics like Nikolay, and Lev followed in 1844. Their sister Maria had a German governess, then was educated at the newly founded Rodionov Institute for girls in Kazan.[5]

By all accounts Aunt Polina had very little impact on the upbringing of the young Tolstoys, nor was she in any serious way involved with it. Radically different from her reclusive and abstemious late sister Aline, she was a social butterfly for whom good taste was everything. According to her nephew Lev's subsequent reminiscences, she was a kind and pious woman, but rather frivolous. She was also vain, and clearly flattered by the chance now given to her to step into the role of saviour to the orphaned Tolstoys, but she was too busy socialising to exert any moral authority over her young charges, who now had the chance to go wild. Polina's marriage was unhappy, and her husband was frequently unfaithful, so she seems to have drowned her sorrows in parties: the Yushkovs had a reputation for entertaining in style, and boasted one of the best chefs in town. Polina's main contribution to the Tolstoy boys' upbringing was to give each of her nephews their own personal serf, in the hope that each of them would become in time a faithful and devoted servant.[6] Dmitry was given Vanyusha, whom he mistreated, according to his younger brother. Tolstoy could not remember Dmitry actually hitting Vanyusha, but he did have clear memories of him begging contritely for forgiveness.[7] Dmitry soon radically changed his ways and became a fervent Christian, although he never lost his irascible temperament.

Dmitry is a shady figure in Tolstoy's life – he was the first of the brothers to die, at the age of twenty-nine, and does not appear ever to have been close to his siblings – but he looms large in Tolstoy's memoirs of their life in Kazan. It was really only in Kazan, in fact, that Tolstoy's real memories of Dmitry began. Unlike his brother Lev, just one year younger than him, who confessed to preening and being conscious of his appearance even before they moved to Kazan, Dmitry never had any aspirations to being *comme il faut*. With rare exceptions he was serious and quiet, particularly after he started to attend church regularly and observe all the fasts, like Aunt Aline before him. As the youngest, Lev had a tendency to envy all his elder brothers, and what he envied in 'Mitenka' was his indifference to other people's opinions about him, which he believed was a trait inherited from their mother.[8] Indeed it was only because of Mitenka's unkempt appearance that he came to the attention of his far more image-conscious siblings, who were embarrassed by him. Dmitry had no interest in dancing or attending social events, nor did he spend much time with his family, and he stuck rigidly to his student's uniform. Tolstoy retained a strong memory of Dmitry's tall, thin frame, his sad, large, brown, almond-shaped eyes, and the nervous tic he developed during his first serious bout of fasting, when he would jerk his head, as if his tie was too tight. Tolstoy would draw heavily on this and other aspects of Dmitry's life when he came to create the character of Levin's brother Nikolay in *Anna Karenina*.

As the grandchildren of the former governor of Kazan, the Tolstoys were invited to all the best households in town, and they thoroughly enjoyed becoming acquainted with the local aristocracy – all except Dmitry, who only ever befriended one poor, bedraggled student who went by the unfortunate name of Poluboyarinov (apart from simply sounding clumsy, the name implies someone who is only 'half-noble'). Otherwise Dmitry preferred to spend his time in church. Rather than go to the fashionable university church, he went to the one attached to the prison opposite their house, and at Easter probably spent more time there than at home. It is the custom for excerpts from the four Gospels concerning Christ's Passion to be read out on Good Friday, but this church's very strict priest unusually insisted on all four Gospels being read out in their entirety. Since the Orthodox Church requires its parishioners to stand for services, the congregation would have been on its feet for a very long time indeed, but this was probably welcomed by Dmitry, who had a tendency to apply himself with almost masochistic zeal to anything he cared passionately about.[9]

When casting his mind back to his years in Kazan, Tolstoy readily acknowledged that he and his siblings were far too 'obtuse' to appreciate the unusual moral purity of their brother as adolescents. Like their fashionable friends in Kazan, they instead 'continually subjected him to ridicule', as Tolstoy recounts in *Confession*, even nicknaming him Noah.[10] Dmitry's remarkable altruism was perhaps best observed in his relationship with Lyubov Sergeyevna, the illegitimate child taken in at some point by the Tolstoy family out of pity. In Kazan, Lyubov Sergeyevna was taken in by Aunt Polina, and Tolstoy's memories of her date from this time. They were not very affectionate memories. Lyubov Sergeyevna was a 'strange and pathetic creature', he later recorded, who suffered from some ailment which made her face puff up as if stung by bees. During the summer months she was insensitive to the numerous flies that settled on her face, which made her even more unpleasant to look at. In Tolstoy's recollection she had only a few strands of black hair and no eyebrows, and found it physically difficult to speak, probably as a result of a tumour. He also recalled that she also always smelled bad, and lived in a suffocating and equally malodorous room whose windows were never opened. When Tolstoy became aware of Lyubov Sergeyevna she was 'not only pitiful but repellent', and most of the family did little to conceal their feelings of revulsion. Dmitry, however, went out of his way to listen and talk to her, and become her friend, not giving the slightest sign that he regarded what he was doing as philanthropy. Impervious to his family's opinion of him, he just did what he thought right. Nor was his selfless behaviour a fad. He remained close to Lyubov Sergeyevna until her death in August 1844, when he completed his first year at university.[11]

Like their father, Dmitry was artistically gifted. When playing games many years earlier, Nikolay had promised his younger brothers that their wishes would be fulfilled if they carried out all the conditions he imposed on them. It was characteristic that Sergey declared his desire to mould horses and chickens out of wax, while Dmitry wanted to draw big pictures like an artist: the Tolstoy museum in Moscow stores in its archive many pencil drawings he executed of rural landscapes which are impressive for a ten-year-old.[12] (Lev, meanwhile, could think of nothing he wanted back then except the ability to draw small pictures.)

There are no biographical events at all listed for 1842 and 1843 in the official chronicle of Tolstoy's life and works. Careful sleuthing, however, has established that after Tolstoy turned fourteen in August 1842 his brothers Nikolay and Sergey took him for the first time to a brothel. Many, many years later, his wife castigated him for writing a seduction scene in his last novel *Resurrection*, believing that as an old man (he was then seventy) he ought to be ashamed of writing such 'filth'. This unpleasant altercation induced Tolstoy to confess to a friend that after committing the 'act' for the first time that fateful day in Kazan, he had stood by the woman's bed and wept. And he was deeply shaken when an acquaintance later told him that he had once been a novice at the Monastery of the Cyzicus Martyrs, located on the outskirts of Kazan. Tolstoy responded quietly that it had been in that part of town that he had had his 'first fall'.[13] Perhaps his feeling of guilt was heightened by his awareness that his grandfather was buried in the monastery's cemetery along with other dignitaries (the only grave from that period that has survived to the present day).

Tolstoy later regretted the absence of moral guidance in his early teenage years in Kazan. On 1 January 1900 he confided to his diary that he had done a lot of bad things when he was young out of a desire to copy his elders, who drank, smoked and led debauched lives.[14] Dmitry, of course, whom their brother Nikolay characterised as an extreme 'eccentric', was not included in their number: he practised complete abstention until the age of twenty-five, which in those days, according to Tolstoy, was a great rarity, particularly as far as relations with women were concerned.[15] This was certainly not true of Sergey, however, who was Dmitry's polar opposite, and a major influence on their youngest brother Lev's waywardness. Of all the brothers, Sergey was the most talented and good-looking, and if Tolstoy loved and 'respected' Nikolay, and was on 'comradely' terms with Dmitry, he 'admired and copied' Sergey. Indeed, as he famously puts it at one point in his memoirs, he actually 'wanted to be him'.[16] Sergey had a reputation for being gregarious and good-humoured, and for singing continually. Where Tolstoy was painfully shy and acutely self-conscious, which interfered with his enjoyment of life, Sergey was an extrovert whose egotism made him supremely oblivious of whether his behaviour and appearance aroused approval or disapproval. For this reason he was all the more attractive to his younger brother, for whom he was a mysterious and unfathomable exotic species. Tolstoy started copying Sergey in early childhood, first by rearing different kinds of speckled and tufted hens and painting pictures of them.[17] During his adolescence in Kazan, it was Sergey who led Tolstoy into debauchery.[18]

In May 1844, when he was sixteen, Tolstoy formally applied to the rector of Kazan University, Nikolay Lobachevsky (a mathematician famous for developing non-Euclidean geometry) for permission to take the various entrance exams. Tolstoy's letter of application launches the twenty-five volumes of his letters in his *Collected Works*. As ever, Tolstoy wanted to be different, and instead of applying to study mathematics like his brothers, he elected to join the Faculty of Oriental Languages, whose scholarly achievements were already renowned. It was a smart move. By 1828, the year of Tolstoy's birth, the faculty had professorships in Persian, Arabic and Turkish, and by the time he became a student, chairs in Mongolian, Mandarin Chinese, Armenian and Sanskrit had been added. Thanks to Lobachevsky's active support, the teaching of oriental languages at Kazan University was of a quality unsurpassed anywhere in Europe.[19] Tolstoy was thinking of his future career in making this choice: his plan at this stage was to join the diplomatic service (although when one bears in mind the direction his life took, a less suitable spokesman for Russian imperial policy is hard to imagine).[20] First, however, he had to pass several exams. Tolstoy excelled in his French exam, and did well in German, English, Arabic and Turkish (though he later claimed to have no memory of the last three). He also received good results for mathematics, logic, Russian literature and religious studies, which, like most people of his background, he did not take seriously at all. Much later, in an early draft of *Confession*, he wrote that the whole edifice of theology collapsed for him as soon as he took an interest in philosophy when he was sixteen, and began to see that the cat-echism was a 'lie'.[21] Tolstoy did poorly in his Latin exam, having been unable to translate even two lines of an ode by Horace, and even worse in statistics and geography, his superlative command of the French language clearly not accompanied by even a basic familiarity with the country where it was the mother tongue. His performance in history was also execrable, and he later added the comment in the manuscript of Pavel Biryukov's biography: 'I knew nothing.'[22] As a result, he was forced to resit these last two exams, and had to spend the summer in Kazan rather than Yasnaya Polyana, where he would much rather have been. In September 1844, however, just after his brother Nikolay graduated, he was admitted as a student.

Tolstoy's university career was not distinguished. He had never before attended an educational institution, so mingling with other students in lecture halls was a novelty at first. It clearly soon wore off, though, despite Tolstoy having the chance to study with the distinguished orientalist Profes-sor Mirza Kazem-Bek, whose scholarship was world-renowned. He ended up failing his first-year exams, which meant having to repeat the year. Rather than face this indignity, he decided to transfer to the less distinguished Law Faculty, but of course had to start from scratch again as a first-year student. He justified this change of direction in a letter he wrote to Aunt Toinette in August 1845, just before the start of the academic year, by maintaining that law was a more practical choice in view of its application in daily life ('je trouve que l'application de cette science est plus facile et plus naturelle que toute autre à notre vie privée').[23]

If Tolstoy did not respond well to the demands placed on him by his tutors at Kazan University, it was because he wanted to be in control of his own educational curriculum. He had already began to read seriously on his own. Occasionally there are references to novels he enjoyed in the scant lit-erature documenting his Kazan years, such as *The Three Musketeers* and *The Count of Monte-Cristo*, two contemporary 'best-sellers' by Alexandre Dumas which had just been published in France for the first time, and were also popular in Russia.[24] Dumas's earlier novel *The Fencing Teacher*, meanwhile, had been banned in Russia by Nicholas I for describing the events of the Decembrist Uprising, and the subsequent exile to Siberia of its leaders, as was its author (Dumas was unable to visit Russia until 1858, during the reign of Alexander II). The Russian novel was still in its infancy at this time, but when

Tolstoy stumbled upon Pushkin's *Eugene Onegin* at a friend's house during these years, he was so entranced that he sat up all night reading it, and started immediately reading it a second time when he got to the end.[25]

Tolstoy later drew up a list of the books which had the greatest influence on him between the ages of fourteen and twenty. The most influential Russian works included *Eugene Onegin*, Lermontov's *A Hero of Our Time*, Gogol's *Dead Souls* and Turgenev's *A Hunter's Notes*. Amongst the foreign volumes we find Schiller's *The Robbers* and Sterne's *Sentimental Journey*. Others that made a 'huge' impression on him were Dickens's *David Copperfield*, the 'Sermon on the Mount' in the Gospel according to St Matthew, and Rousseau's *Confessions* and *Emile*.[26] Tolstoy was sometimes inaccurate about dates, and certainly in this case, as *David Copperfield* was first published in 1850, but it is nevertheless interesting to see the early appearance of Rousseau on his literary horizon.

It was philosophy which most excited the young Tolstoy during his student years, and it was Jean-Jacques Rousseau (1712–1778) who probably exercised more influence on Tolstoy than any other thinker over the course of his lifetime. This influence can be seen in Tolstoy's later condemnation of human civilisation for its corruption of human behaviour and distortion of man's true nature (*Discours sur les sciences et les arts*, 1750, and *Discours sur l'origine de l'inégalité*, 1755), in his promotion of a radical child-centred education in a natural environment and his rejection of organised religion in favour of belief based on personal conscience (*Émile, ou de l'éducation*, 1762), in his fictional exploration of marital relations and family life (*Julie, ou la Nouvelle Héloïse*, 1761) and in his advocacy of greater social equality (*Du contrat social*, 1762). Tolstoy also took a page out of Rousseau's posthumously published *Les Confessions* (1781–1788) when writing his own autobiographical works, emulating the candour and rigour of the French-Swiss thinker's unsparing self-analysis, not to mention the egocentric belief that the truth he discovered about himself had universal application. It is no wonder that Tolstoy saw himself in Rousseau, who also lost his mother at a young age, and followed a number of different paths in his life before finding his metier. Both figures are united by soaring genius, overweening vanity, a dogged, noble but often misguided sincerity, and a lamentable lack of a sense of humour, the latter being the single thing which sometimes makes the study of Tolstoy's life and works slightly hard-going.

Both Tolstoy and Rousseau were thin-skinned and highly emotional people which led to frequently turbulent relations with their contemporaries. They shared a huge energy and ambition which led them into diverse areas of intellectual and artistic endeavour, and a complete lack of fear in the face of controversy. Their most incisive works were deemed so subversive they were banned by the authorities, and yet neither Rousseau nor Tolstoy, despite their devotion to the Enlightenment ideals of liberty, equality and fraternity, sought revolution, retaining little faith in the efficacy of political activity. Rousseau died shortly before the French Revolution and Tolstoy shortly before the Russian Revolution, events they both inspired and were blamed for. As Robert Wokler writes, Rousseau had a greater impact on his age than almost anyone else in the eighteeenth century:

> No other eighteeenth-century thinker contributed more major writings in so wide a range of subjects and forms, nor wrote with such sustained passion and eloquence. No one else managed through both his works and his life to excite or disturb public imagination so deeply. Almost alone among the seminal figures of the Enlightenment, he subjected the main currents of the world he inhabited to censure, even while channelling their direction …[27]

One could say that Tolstoy almost picked up where Rousseau left off, for the above achievements are also associated with his prodigious legacy.

After his rather dismal first year at university, Tolstoy spent the summer of 1845 at Yasnaya Polyana, during which time he did a lot of reading and thinking. He became interested in the ethical ideas of the pre-Christian Cynics – Greek philosophers who preached, amongst other things, the virtues of a life without material possessions.[28] For Aunt Toinette, her nephew Lev now became an 'incomprehensible creature' obsessed with plumbing the depths of human existence, and only happy when he met someone prepared to listen to him hold forth passionately about his ideas.[29] Tolstoy's inborn eccentricity had certainly begun to exhibit itself in various ways. Under the influence of Rousseau and the philosophical ideas of Diogenes, one of the chief Cynics, he tried to simplify his life. In the fourth century BC Diogenes chose to live an ascetic and self-sufficient life, jettisoning the idea of marriage and family and rejecting laws and conventional social institutions as corrupt and hypocritical. He was famous for sleeping in a tub on the street. Tolstoy made a start by trying to simplify his own life. Apart from giving up wearing socks, he invented a utilitarian one-piece garment which was buttoned up from the inside, serving him as both daytime clothing and bed-linen-cum-blanket. A party of lady visitors to Yasnaya Polyana were slightly nonplussed when they encountered him in this strange garb. Nor was Aunt Toinette entirely convinced by this Russian Diogenes, though had she been alive during the last decades of his life she might well have thought otherwise.

While he was walking incognito in this garment one day, Tolstoy was able to listen in on unguarded conversations amongst his peasants. This was how he first discovered how hated the nobility were by the peasants, and how little respect the peasants accorded their owners.[30] It came as a shock for him to hear such sentiments from his own serfs. More shocking to him, though, was the contempt generally shown by the Russian ruling class for the well-being of their serfs, particularly since it was the peasants who habitually had to bail their masters out – literally, in Tolstoy's case. One warm day during a visit to the Yushkovs' country estate on the banks of the Volga, Tolstoy took it into his head to impress the young ladies amongst the guests by throwing himself head-first into the large pond near the house, fully dressed, intending to swim to the island in the middle. He had to be rescued from drowning by peasant women who had been gathering hay nearby: they hauled him out of the water with their rakes.[31] Tolstoy's social conscience was beginning to awaken, but it would be a long time yet before he would renounce his aristocratic birthright and become a fully fledged 'repentant nobleman'.

Tolstoy went to great lengths to try to make a good impression on his contemporaries during his student years, and he also tried enhancing his physical appearance. He was never happy with his looks, but his attempts to improve them did not always meet with very successful results. He once conceived the idea of shaving his eyebrows to make them grow back more bushy, and ended up almost shaving them off completely.[32] Shy and lacking in self-confidence, he never quite cut the dashing figure on the dance floor who lived in his imagination, and he was too absent-minded and ungainly to succeed in emulating his suave and debonair brother Sergey. But he nevertheless enjoyed being part of the uppermost echelon of Kazan society, made a few good friends, and even wrote a waltz with one of them.[33]

Tolstoy had promised Aunt Toinette in the summer of 1845 that he would work hard in his second year at university, and in his leisure time study music, art and languages. 'I won't go into society at all,' he vowed in a letter ('Je n'irai pas en société du tout').[34] That autumn, however, he went to all the most prestigious social events, including a grand ball held in October 1845 in honour of the visit of Nicholas I's son-in-law Maximilian, the Duke of Leuchtenberg. And in January 1846 he had to spend a few days in the university jail for persistently failing to attend lectures.[35] This oscillation between the setting of unrealistic, puritanical goals for a future life of purity and self-denial and the self-mortification which followed his actual pursuit and enjoyment in the present of a hedonistic social life, is the leitmotif of Tolstoy's first diary entry, which he famously began in the university's venereal diseases clinic in March 1847. In fact, one could say that the battle between these two opposing sides of Tolstoy's personality was the main theme of his entire life as an adult, and certainly fundamental to his creative processes. Simultaneous possession of these two warring impulses was not unique to Tolstoy, but may be seen as the mark of a quintessentially Russian nature. The early-twentieth-century philosophical thinker Nikolay Berdyaev certainly thought along these lines. As he wrote in his book *The Origin of Russian Communism*, 'In the typical Russian two elements are always in opposition – the primitive natural paganism of boundless Russia, and an Orthodox asceticism received from Byzantium, a reaching out towards the other world.'[36]

In January 1847, when he was eighteen, Tolstoy started compiling a 'Journal of Daily Activities', listing on the left-hand side of the page a strict timetable for each day under the heading 'The Future'. Here he set out exactly which hours he would devote to his coursework, when he would have lunch, when he would study English, go for a walk or play chess. On the right-hand side, marked 'The Past', he entered comments on his performance. Thus on good days, when he maintained his self-discipline, he could write that he had kept to his regime, while on others he was forced to admit that he did 'nothing', 'almost nothing', did things 'badly', 'read Gogol' or 'overslept'.[37] This journal was maintained until June. At the same time Tolstoy started compiling rules for developing his willpower. These included getting up at five and going to bed no later than ten, with two hours permissible for sleeping during the day. He resolved to eat moderately, and nothing sweet, to walk for an hour every day, to carry out everything he prescribed for himself and visit a brothel only twice a month. In the second tier of his rules he vowed to disregard luxuries and all public opinion not based on reason, and to love those to whom he could be of service. The rules in the third and last tier called on him to do only one thing at a time, and not allow flights of imagination unless necessary.[38]

In February 1847 Tolstoy had felt a compulsion to compile some new rules, this time more general ones, concerning his relationship to God, other people and himself, but broke off before setting out exactly what they were.[39] In March he started again, delineating forty-seven different rules under twenty headings. He told himself, for example, to never to show his emotions, to stop caring about other people's opinion of himself, and to do good inconspicuously. He ordered himself to keep away from women, suppress his feelings of lust by working hard and help those more unfortunate than him.[40] At times Tolstoy's rules remind one in spirit of the *Domostroi*, the notoriously cheerless and minutely detailed 'housekeeping' rules produced in the pious times of Ivan the Terrible, where we read, for example:

> A man cannot be healed if he is insolent and disorderly; does not fear God
> or comply with His will; does not keep Christian law and the tradition
> of the Fathers on the Church and on Church singing, on reading from
> the holy books before communion, on prayer; if he is not concerned with
> praising God; if he eats and drinks to excess and fills himself with food and
> wine when it is not fitting to do so; does not honour Sunday, Wednesday,
> and Friday, the holy days, the great Lent, the Lent of the Mother of God;
> if he fornicates with no restraint, at improper times …[41]

It has to be said, Tolstoy does not come across as a particularly attractive person at this point, his self-absorption and sanctimoniousness detracting somewhat from his worthy aspirations and self-deprecation.

On 17 March, six days after entering the university clinic, where he was being treated for gonorrhoea, Tolstoy began writing a proper diary. He welcomed this period of complete solitude, with no servant nearby, since it enabled him perceive that the dissolute life led by the majority of his class during their youth was the consequence of 'an early corruption of the soul'. He was talking about himself, of course. In condemning his way of life, however, he was already cognisant that it was easier to read ten tomes of philosophy than to put one principle into practice.[42] The following day, in the absence of anything better to do (he spent almost a month in the clinic), Tolstoy started to tackle an assignment given to second-year law students, in which they were asked to compare Catherine the Great's *Nakaz* (or *Instruction*), first drafted in 1765, with Montesquieu's 1749 *De l'esprit des lois*. Although he failed to complete the assignment, rather to his surprise he became engrossed in Catherine's proposals for a new code of laws, and ended up spending over a week dissecting them at great length on the pages of his diary.[43] Tolstoy criticises autocratic rule as despotic, since laws provide no protection in a state where they are applied at whim by the sovereign. And he challenges Catherine's insistence that the autocrat's limitless powers are, in fact, limited by the sovereign's conscience, by pointing out that the assertion of limitless powers is predicated on an absence of conscience.[44] There was also a limit to Tolstoy's republican tendencies, however. As Count Tolstoy, the scion of a distinguished noble family, he argues that the aristocracy, guided by honour, are the essential ballast needed to limit a monarch's powers. The views he puts forward here about the moral duties of the Russian aristocracy were to reach their fullest expression, of course, in *War and Peace*. Since he was preoccupied with the moral relationship between landowners and peasants, there is little in Tolstoy's analysis of the *Nakaz* which relates to the fundamental injustice of serfdom. He comments that serfdom impedes the development of trade, but never raises the idea that it should be abolished, since, as he would later record in his memoirs, that simply never occurred to anyone from his milieu in the 1840s.[45]

Meanwhile, on 11 April 1847, the legal document setting out the division of the Tolstoy family property was drawn up, having been the subject of negotiations for many months. The very next day Tolstoy requested permission to leave Kazan University for 'health' and 'domestic' reasons. The study of the *Nakaz* had fired him with a desire to continue his studies independently, and he felt his university curriculum would actually now hinder them. Also, both Dmitry and Sergey were about to graduate, while Masha had already left Kazan, and was living at Yasnaya Polyana. Unwilling to remain in Kazan on his own, and fulfil university requirements he found tedious, Tolstoy left without taking a degree, having completed only the first two years of his law course.

Under Russian law in the 1840s, daughters were entitled to inherit one-eighth of their late parents' property and a fourteenth share of everything else, but the Tolstoy brothers voted to share their inheritance equally with their sister. Nikolay was assigned the Nikolskoye estate in Tula province, together with 317 male serfs (the only ones considered worth counting), and a large piece of land. As a great horse-lover, Sergey inherited the Pirogovo estate, also in Tula province, together with its stud farm and 316 male serfs. Maria received land in the same village, a flour mill, and a large sum of money. Dmitry received Shcherbachevka, the family estate in Kursk province, and over 300 serfs, while Lev inherited Yasnaya Polyana and its neighbouring villages, and also some 300 serfs. There were also sums of money given and received to even everything out.[46] The legal document was signed by all parties on 11 July 1847 in Tula, after which they departed for their new properties. That November Masha, who throughout the previous few years had lived rather apart from her brothers, married their distant cousin Valerian Petrovich, who was a nephew of Fyodor Tolstoy, the famous 'American' (and indeed of Aunt Toinette). She was seventeen; he was thirty-four. In August 1847 Tolstoy turned nineteen, and now had the freedom to do as he wanted.

· 5 ·

LANDOWNER, GAMBLER, OFFICER, WRITER

Call things by their name.

Diary entry, 21 February 1851[1]

TOLSTOY HAD GRAND PLANS for his new life as a member of Russia's landowning nobility. He wanted to use his time wisely, and for a noble and worthwhile purpose, so on 17 April 1847 he set out in his diary what he planned to do over the next two years as the owner of Yasnaya Polyana. He would study French, German, English, Italian, Russian and Latin as well as acquire a 'moderate degree of perfection' in music and painting. He would devote himself to history, geography, statistics, mathematics and natural sciences, practical and theoretical medicine, and farming in all its aspects. He would complete his course of study in law, so that he could take his final exam and graduate. He would write a dissertation. He would write essays on all the subjects he was going to study. And he would write down rules. But all those good intentions came to nothing. The very next day he admitted somewhat sheepishly to himself that he was not actually capable of meeting his own expectations, and so he scaled everything back, deciding he would stick to following just one rule at a time. The first rule he resolved to follow was to carry out whatever task he set himself – except that he failed at the first hurdle. On 19 April he admitted in his diary that he had got up very late, and only decided what he would do that day at two o'clock in the afternoon. There was an easy way out: on 20 April he stopped writing his diary. There were a further three entries in June, then it completely petered out. After the entry on 16 June, in which he lambasted women for emasculating men, and resolved to avoid them as far as possible, came a three-year silence.[2]

The period from June 1847 to October 1848 is almost a complete blank page in Tolstoy's biography: there are not even any letters from him which could shed light on what he did when he was not adhering to his rules. Presumably he threw himself into the farming at Yasnaya Polyana, and discovered it was very hard work. Not only had he never worked on the land, and knew nothing about agriculture, but he had no experience in managing the serfs he owned. When his brother Dmitry wrote to ask him in September 1847 whether he had grown bored of running the estate at Yasnaya Polyana yet, we can assume the answer was affirmative.[3] Tolstoy seems to have been a very fickle youth at this time. Some indication of his volatility comes from the fact that in the early autumn of 1847 he apparently decided on a whim to accompany his future brother-in-law to Siberia, and jumped into his carriage as he was setting off, thinking twice about it only when he realised he did not have a hat. In the end Valerian Petrovich set off alone to tie up his business in Tobolsk, in advance of marrying Tolstoy's sister Maria.[4]

If Tolstoy's siblings seemed more settled than he was, it was because none of them nurtured such huge aspirations. As a female member of the provincial nobility, nothing was really expected of Maria except decorum. She and Valerian set up home at his Pokrovskoye estate in the Tula region, a day's travel by carriage from Yasnaya Polyana, and they soon launched themselves into family life. Nikolay was serving in the Caucasus, having joined the army as a volunteer after leaving university in 1844. He had received his commission eighteen months later, and was now an ensign with the 20th Artillery Brigade, but his was by no means a brilliant army career, not least because he lacked ambition.[5] The gifted, dashing Sergey would also join the army a few years later, and was expected to excel, but he lasted all of a year, due to his unwillingness to submit to authority and a similar lack of drive and ambition. The Pirogovo stud farm and large kennels he inherited were enough to keep him busy. Like Tolstoy, Sergey was passionate about hunting – he had soon shot so many wolves that he had enough bones to make an original fence along one of the paths on his estate.[6] Otherwise his main passion in life was a gypsy girl in Tula.

Dmitry had ensconced himself on his Shcherbachevka estate in Kursk province. Like most of his class, he did not question the institution of serfdom, but he did feel morally obliged to show concern for his serfs. He also felt it was his duty as a Russian nobleman to serve, a conviction which was perhaps a vestige of Peter the Great's rule, when lifelong service was imposed on the gentry in return for the privileges of noble status. The length of compulsory service to the state had been progressively reduced over the course of the eighteenth century until it became merely a matter of honour under Catherine the Great, but the idea of serving clearly lingered for high-minded young men like Dmitry Tolstoy. Accordingly, he set off for St Petersburg, where he naively presented himself to one of the Ministry of Justice's mandarins and declared that he wished to be useful. Since he failed to specify what exactly he wanted to do, however, he was despatched to copy Chancellery documents, and was soon living the life of Akaky Akakievich in Gogol's immortal story 'The Overcoat' (1842). In this merciless satire of the St Petersburg bureaucracy, the lowly copyist Akaky Akakievich, a man who is oblivious to his threadbare clothes, is eventually compelled to buy a new overcoat. In order to save enough money to pay his tailor, he practises extreme self-denial, and then the coat is stolen from him on the first day he wears it. Dmitry Tolstoy similarly paid no thought to his clothes, and merely dressed to cover his body, but his coat, ironically, was practically all he had. According to Tolstoy's memoirs, his brother one day decided to visit a family acquaintance in the hope that he might help him find a better job. After arriving at Dmitry Obolensky's dacha, and being invited to take off his coat and join the other guests, it turned out, to the embarrassment of all present, he was wearing nothing underneath, having decided a shirt was unnecessary.[7] Apart from being actually quite well off, Dmitry differed from the hapless Akaky Akakievich in one other important respect: he became rapidly disillusioned at becoming another faceless cog in Nicholas I's vast bureaucratic machine, and he soon retreated back to his estate, sending Obolensky a valedictory letter which made Tolstoy and Sergey wince (whatever Dmitry had written, Sergey told Tolstoy that it made him break out in a sweat, go red in the face and start pacing about the room in excruciating embarrassment).[8]

'The Overcoat' was naturally one of the masterpieces of Russian literature which Tolstoy devoured in the 1840s, along with many other works by Gogol, including the novel *Dead Souls*, published in 1842. Perhaps because he did not need to tell himself to read, it was an activity he enjoyed, and it was fundamental to his intellectual and artistic development in the years immediately following his departure from Kazan. He read voraciously. Tolstoy came of age at a very bleak time in Russia's history, which was something he became aware of only gradually. Nicholas I had begun his reign in 1825 by suppressing the Decembrist Uprising, and his regime had grown more repressive and reactionary as time went on. Foreign visitors were shocked. In the book the Marquis de Custine wrote following his visit to Russia in 1839,[9] he described the country as a police state ruled by a despot. De Custine's condemnation of the Russian nobility as 'regimented Tatars' who confused splendour with elegance, and luxury with refinement, touched a raw nerve. Not surprisingly, his book was banned when it was published in 1843 (as it would be by Stalin in the twentieth century, in view of its alarmingly accurate prophetic qualities).[10] When the spectre of revolution raised its head again in Europe in the late 1840s, Nicholas responded by increasing censorship, yet in this suffocating atmosphere, or perhaps because of it, literature managed to flourish. Indeed, writers were now expected to provide moral leadership as well as entertainment and aesthetic pleasure.

By the end of the 1840s many works of Russian literature had made a deep impression on Tolstoy. Pushkin's *Eugene Onegin* (1833), Lermontov's *A Hero of Our Time* (1840) and Gogol's *Dead Souls* (1842) were Russia's first 'proper' novels, but their form was already highly idiosyncratic: *Eugene Onegin* is a novel in verse, *A Hero of Our Time* is a collation of interlinked stories and *Dead Souls* is sub-titled 'A Poem'. Tolstoy would later proudly uphold the Russian refusal to conform to the European model by asserting the sui generis form of *War and Peace*, which he adamantly insisted was not a novel. From the beginning Tolstoy was drawn to prose rather than poetry, whose 'Golden Age' had in any case given way at the end of the 1830s to an era of realist fiction. He regarded 'Taman', one of the constituent stories in *A Hero of Our Time*, as a paragon of artistic perfection (a view Chekhov would later share).[11]

Talented new writers emerged in the 1840s to assume the mantle of

Pushkin and Gogol, who had dominated the literary scene in the previous decade, and chief amongst them was Turgenev, who published the first of the stories which make up his *A Hunter's Notes* in 1847, the year in which Tolstoy took up residence again at Yasnaya Polyana. Turgenev's stories about contemporary rural life created a furore, not so much for their form as for their content, since they were the first works of Russian literature to depict peasants as three-dimensional human beings. As a liberal-minded Westerniser who abhorred the institution of serfdom, Turgenev consciously set out in his fiction to endow the peasants with a natural dignity, and as worthy of as much respect and artistic attention as the gentlemen who owned them. His oblique criticism of serfdom was all the more powerful for its subtlety, and forced his readers, including the future Alexander II, to confront the evil which had engendered such an iniquitous system. The embarrassment, indignation and then disgust which Turgenev declared he felt with respect to his own land-owning noble class would eventually lead him to move abroad.[12] Tolstoy, by contrast, did not yet subscribe to the view that serfdom should be abolished. In this he was no different from most of the landowning nobility, and he was later frank about it in his memoirs, where he points out that treating the serfs justly was already a sign of enlightened ownership. But Turgenev's *A Hunter's Notes*, a collection whose political importance was equal to its artistic merit, could not but make Tolstoy think as he came into his inheritance.

There were also numerous other foreign authors who stimulated Tolstoy's imagination during these formative years. He could justly be proud of acquiring a sufficient command of English to read writers like Dickens in the original (one rule he appears to have managed to abide by). *David Copperfield* (1850) was the Dickens novel Tolstoy most enjoyed as a young man, and he also greatly admired Laurence Sterne's *Sentimental Journey* (1768). Both Dickens and Sterne were powerful influences on Tolstoy when he first embarked on writing fiction. He was still quite eclectic in his tastes however, enjoying William Prescott's epic *History of the Conquest of Mexico* (1843) and Schiller's play *The Robbers* (1781).[13] It was Rousseau who still captivated him most, however. The *Confessions, Emile* and *The New Héloïse* were instrumental in his moral education.[14] Beyond some of the books on his reading list, we know little else about Tolstoy's life in the late 1840s, but we do know that he brought his beloved Aunt Toinette back to live at Yasnaya Polyana. For a while her sister Elizaveta lived at Yasnaya Polyana too, otherwise she was based with her son Valerian Petrovich and new daughter-in-law Maria. Elizaveta's place at Yasnaya Polyana was permanently taken by Natalya Petrovna, an impoverished widow who became Toinette's companion (no Russian estate was complete without its meek and deferential *prizhivaltsy*, who were always acutely conscious of their status as dependants). It is difficult to overestimate the importance of Aunt Toinette to Tolstoy during his early twenties. She was his rock, and the most frequent recipient of his letters when he was away. It was she who kept him on an even keel, and she was also the one to entreat him to take up writing. She believed in his talent.

In October 1848 Tolstoy suddenly upped sticks and moved to Moscow, ostensibly to prepare for his law examinations, which he had finally decided to take. He rented the annexe of a building occupied by some friends in the Arbat area, not far from where he had lived as a boy. Having not been in the city since his childhood, he was excited to be back, but he never went anywhere near his law books. Instead, he was lured by the bright lights of the city into experiencing Moscow high society. He was twenty years old and well educated, he was the owner of a handsome country estate, he had a title and an income – in short, he was an eligible bachelor, welcomed in all the best drawing rooms in the city. It was all very flattering to the ego, although Tolstoy's vanity was checked by shyness and an acute self-consciousness about his looks which caused him to feel awkward in polite society. Without the inconvenience of a job, or even any real obligation to study, Tolstoy led a completely hedonistic life that winter, during which time he developed a passion for playing cards, or rather for gambling. It was a passion which would last for well over a decade, and was an expensive habit which brought some serious personal consequences in its wake.

Tolstoy was far from the first Russian nobleman to acquire a gambling addiction – he had some illustrious forebears here, not least amongst his own family. The deeply ingrained recklessness of Russian gamblers (which led some foreign visitors to assume that betting was a national pastime) may have been attributable to the need to assert a degree of independence in Russia's repressive and rigidly hierarchical society, where even private life was subject to state surveillance. Russian writers seemed particularly susceptible to gambling, and many made it a theme of their work.[15] Pushkin, author of the quintessential gambling story 'The Queen of Spades' (1834), staked money on his own poetry and ended up having to surrender precious manuscripts.[16]

'The Fatalist', one of the stories in Lermontov's *A Hero of Our Time*, is devoted to a game of Russian roulette, while the principal characters of Gogol's play *The Gamblers* (1836) are two incorrigible card sharps. Turgenev grew up with a father who gambled, and there was a room at their family estate which his mother called the 'casino'. Along with Gogol, he was a rare example of a Russian writer able to resist the lure of the betting tables in German casinos. Dostoyevsky, author of the classic novella *The Gambler* (1867), had an addiction to excitement which led him on one occasion to gamble everything he had, leaving him with nothing but the shirt on his back.

Gambling certainly ran in Tolstoy's family. While his none-too-bright paternal grandfather was one of the most incompetent gamblers who ever lived, stories of the outrageous stunts pulled by his notorious 'American' cousin Fyodor Ivanovich were still circulating in Moscow years after his death in 1846. Tolstoy's gambling compulsion was not helped by another deeply rooted Russian trait amongst the educated classes: an indifference to money which bordered on contempt. He soon ran up large debts and was left feeling very dissatisfied with himself. As he wrote to Aunt Toinette in December 1848, his life of excess had left him world-weary, and longing for the country air again: 'I have been completely corrupted in this social world, all that annoys me terribly at the moment, and I am dreaming again of my life in the country which I hope to resume soon' ('Je me suis tout à fait débauché dans cette vie du monde, à présent tout cela m'embête affreusement et je rêve de nouveau à ma vie de campagne que je compte reprendre bientôt.')[17] Instead of returning to Yasnaya Polyana, however, Tolstoy decided on a whim to go to St Petersburg in January 1849, just because some friends were going there.

The impressionable young Tolstoy had never been to the Russian capital, which was a far more sophisticated and aristocratic city than provincial Moscow, and he straight away decided he wanted to settle there. He took a room in the Hotel Napoleon, on the corner of Malaya Morskaya and Vosnesensky Streets (it is now the Angleterre Hotel). If he was lucky, he would have been given a room facing the largest church in Russia – construction of the neoclassical St Isaac's Cathedral was then nearing completion. When he was settled, Tolstoy sat down to write a long letter to his brother Sergey, telling him St Petersburg was having a good effect on him. Everyone was always busy doing things, he wrote, and their industry was rubbing off on him: he was finally planning to take his law exams at the university. Afterwards, he continued in his letter, he planned to take up a job in the civil service. If necessary, he told Sergey, he was prepared to start at the bottom of the Table of Ranks if he failed his exams. No one in the nobility could avoid being hierarchically classified in the table of fourteen ranks that Peter the Great had originally instituted for the court, the civil service and the armed forces. It had led to an obsession with official status which was subjected to magnificent ridicule by Gogol in his story 'The Nose' (1836). Tolstoy went on to say that he was aware his brother would greet his assurances that he had changed with some scepticism, having heard the same story twenty times before. He hastened to tell him that this time he really *had* changed in quite a different way from the way he had changed on previous occasions, and it was no longer just a question of good intentions. For the first time, he declared, he had understood that he could not live on philosophy alone, and needed to undertake practical activities. He did need some money so that he could pay off his gambling debts, however – 1,200 roubles, to be precise – and he asked Sergey to sell off a birch forest at Yasnaya Polyana.[18] Selling off bits of his inheritance would become a regular occurrence over the next few years.

Sergey was indeed sceptical of his brother's protestations, and rightly so. He was particularly worried that his younger brother would start gambling again in St Petersburg, where he stood to lose spectacularly large sums to unscrupulous players. Sergey repeatedly implored Tolstoy in letters he sent him that spring to start work, and on no account to play cards. He was generally concerned about Tolstoy's lack of discipline at this time, as well as that of his brother's servant Fyodor, who had stolen money from him, pawned some silver spoons and then spent all the money his master had given him to redeem them on drink.[19] Actually, none of the Tolstoy brothers seemed to be coping well with suddenly coming into money: Dmitry's gardener had stolen 7,000 roubles which he had foolishly left in the estate office at Shcherbachevka, and Sergey was himself spending considerable sums in pursuit of Maria (Masha) Shishkina, a girl in the famous Tula gypsy choir, with whom he was madly in love.[20] But that was small fry compared to his brother Lev's recidivism. On 1 May 1849, Tolstoy sent Sergey a letter which he instructed him to read alone:

> Seryozha.
> I imagine you are already saying that *I am the most empty-headed fellow*
> [Sergey's pet phrase for Tolstoy], and you will be telling the truth. God
> knows what I have gone and done! I set off for no reason to Petersburg,
> did nothing worthwhile there, just spent a heap of money and got into
> debt. It's stupid. It's unbelievably stupid. You won't believe how much it's
> tormenting me. The main thing are the debts which I *have* to pay, and *as*
> *soon as possible*, because if I don't pay them soon, I will lose my reputation
> on top of the money. Do this, I beg you: without telling the aunts and
> Andrey [Sobolev, the estate manager] why and what for, sell [the village
> of] Vorotinka to either Uvarov or Seleznev …[21]

Since he had arrived in St Petersburg, Tolstoy had taken two law exams, but
then had got bored and given up. His latest half-baked scheme was to join
the army as a volunteer.

As soon as the news had reached St Petersburg from France in March
1848 that King Louis Philippe had been overthrown and a republic had been
proclaimed, an alarmed Nicholas I had started mobilising his troops. The
1848 French Revolution launched a wave of insurrections across Europe, and
Nicholas I was particularly alarmed when revolution broke out in areas of
the Habsburg Empire such as Hungary (which shared a border with Russia).
The dreaded 'Gendarme of Europe' was thus only too happy to accept the
invitation of the Austrian government to help restore order in Hungary by
despatching four infantry regiments and an artillery brigade in May 1849, not
least because there were two Poles in charge of the Hungarian troops who
had been in exile since their own failed uprising against Russian rule in 1831.
The solipsistic and rash Tolstoy was oblivious to all the politics, however. He
was dreaming of military glory. He now set his sights on joining the Horse
Guards, and perhaps even receiving his commission as an officer before completing the standard two-year period of service.[22] It was another plan that was
not thought through.

Just over a week later Tolstoy wrote again to Sergey to tell him he was, in
fact, not going to join the army now, and had gone back to his previous plan
of taking his law exams. He also asked Sergey about the possibility of his serf
Alexey Petukhov working for him, offering to take care of his family and pay
him ten roubles a month (a sum which puts into perspective the thousands of

roubles he sometimes lost at cards).[23] Sergey had been dutifully biting his lip and helping his brother out over the previous months, and he did not bother giving him any advice now, knowing in advance that it would not be heeded. But he did exhort Tolstoy to come back home and sort himself out. 'You say that stupid things only happen once in one's life, and if only that were so!' he wrote, warning him that he was in danger of squandering his entire assets.[24] To Aunt Toinette, before whom he felt ashamed, Tolstoy wrote that he had dropped his earlier idea of working for the Ministry of Foreign Affairs and was intending to come back and prepare for his exams at Yasnaya Polyana. Sometime either at the end of May or the beginning of June in 1849, just as the northern capital's famed 'white nights' were about to reach their peak, he set out to travel home, first to Moscow and then on towards Tula. He was leaving behind a number of creditors, and his unpaid debts would gnaw at his conscience over the next few years.

One person who saw nothing of the white nights that summer was Fyodor Dostoyevsky, the talented but impoverished young writer who had published a story bearing the name 'White Nights' the previous year. He was languishing in a jail cell that barely let in any light at all. The week before Tolstoy sent his grovelling letter to Sergey, the tsarist secret police had descended on Dostoyevsky's flat to arrest him. In a coincidence worthy of his later masterpieces, he had been living in the building which faced the Hotel Napoleon on the other side of the street. Dostoyevsky was one of twenty-four members of the left-wing intelligentsia group called the Petrashevsky Circle who were all engaged to varying degrees in the struggle for political freedoms and civil rights. Their crime was to have met on Friday evenings to discuss such incendiary topics as socialism, the abolition of serfdom and censorship. In the suffocating, paranoid climate of Nicholas I's Russia, even discussing such topics was tantamount to conspiracy, particularly in the wake of the 1848 Revolutions. At the Circle's last meeting, on 15 April 1849, someone had read out the celebrated letter to Gogol composed by the radical critic Vissarion Belinsky. This was an outspoken and fearless document, written on the eve Belinsky's untimely death, in which he castigated the writer for his seemingly spineless defence of Russian absolutism and all it stood for. Belinsky had written the letter in Germany in 1847, while dying of tuberculosis, and handwritten samizdat copies had spread like wildfire amongst the progressive intelligentsia after being smuggled into Russia.

Dostoyevsky and his comrades were imprisoned in the Peter and Paul Fortress, the notorious, dank prison where Peter the Great's son, Tolstoy's ancestor Pyotr Andreyevich and the Decembrists had all been held. While Tolstoy was still strutting about St Petersburg in suits made by the city's best tailor, and dining at its finest restaurants (it is no surprise who his creditors were), Dostoyevsky was communing with fleas, lice, cockroaches and rats in a damp, dark cell. At the end of 1849 he was clamped in irons and sentenced to four years of hard labour in Siberia.[25] The two giants of Russian literature would spend their lives coming close to each other but never meeting, either physically or ideologically. For one thing Dostoyevsky was socially Tolstoy's inferior, and for another, he was his main rival, but they would also come to espouse radically different worldviews.

Tolstoy brought a German pianist back to Yasnaya Polyana when he returned from Petersburg in June 1849, and he spent much of the summer learning the rudiments of music from him. This was to be a good investment, as music became an important part of his life. When he was not teaching Tolstoy, Rudolf the pianist retreated to the greenhouse to compose, or engaged in inebriated music sessions with all the old servants who had played in Count Volkonsky's serf orchestra. One of those musicians was the former second violinist Foka Demidych, who had been the family's butler while Tolstoy's father was alive. That autumn, Tolstoy co-opted him to become the teacher at the first school he started for the Yasnaya Polyana peasant children – twenty little boys who were given lessons in arithmetic and scripture along with being taught how to read and write.[26] It seems to have been a short-lived experiment, about which there is next to no documentation, but it is one of the first signs of Tolstoy's awakening social conscience. Over the course of the next two decades popular education would become a cause very close to his heart.

Tolstoy resumed his diary for one week in June 1850, but this was otherwise another year about which we have little information beyond knowing that he stayed put at Yasnaya Polyana. He became a proud uncle and godfather in January 1850 when his sister Masha gave birth to a little girl, Varvara (Varya). This was not Masha's first child: her first son Pyotr died soon after being born in 1849, but Varya survived (as did Nikolay and Liza, born one and two years later, respectively).[27] After the birth of Varya, Tolstoy immediately travelled to Pokrovskoye to attend her christening (it was about fifty miles away from Yasnaya Polyana), but this seems to have been the longest journey he undertook until the end of the year. Most of the travelling he did in 1850 was to nearby Tula. At the end of 1849 Tolstoy had taken a modest civil-service post in the Tula local government (which placed him on the bottom rung of the Table of Ranks as a collegiate registrar), but it was very undemanding, and gave him a good excuse to spend much of that winter socialising with the city's local nobility and consorting with the gypsies.

Tolstoy had his favourites amongst the gypsy girls, but he was chiefly drawn to the gypsies for their sultry, melancholic music and wild dancing. Gypsies had appeared in the Russian Empire in the early eighteenth century. Some settled, while others continued to lead a semi-nomadic life, lodging with Russian peasants during the winter months and earning their living by bartering horses in the summer. From the beginning they had also given professional performances of Russian songs as a way of earning money. The first Russian gypsy choir was formed in the 1770s by Count Orlov-Chesmensky, who brought together some of his gypsy-serfs from the family of Ivan Sokolov to perform at his estate outside Moscow. They were given their freedom in 1807, but their reputation only began to soar after the war with Napoleon was over, and they began to be invited to perform late into the night at Moscow's restaurants and taverns. Soon choirs began to spring up in other Russian cities, launching great singing dynasties who performed a cappella, or to the accompaniment of violins and the Russian seven-stringed guitar. The gypsy choirs appealed to both the ends of the social spectrum – the merchantry and the nobility (particularly army officers), and they filled a gap. There were no other professional musicians in Russia at that time except for foreign virtuosi, and the chief virtue of the gypsy choirs was that they performed Russian songs, tinged with elements of their own distinct and exotic traditions. Perhaps uniquely, gypsies were not discriminated against in Russia, at least by the people amongst whom they lived. The gypsy choirs reached the peak of their popularity in the 1840s, and the one in Tula was reputed to be one of the best in Russia. Sergey's inamorata Masha Shishkina (herself from one of the great gypsy musical dynasties) was its greatest songbird.[28] Hearing gypsy choirs perform in Moscow and Nizhny Novgorod was certainly a highlight of the Marquis de Custine's Russian tour in 1839. He was struck by their differences to other gypsies he had encountered:

Their wild and impassioned song has some distant resemblance to that of the Spanish gitanos. The melodies of the north are less lively, less voluptuous, than those of Andalusia, but they produce a more profoundly pensive impression … it was nearly midnight, but this house was still full of people, noise, and light. The women struck me as being very handsome; their costume, although in appearance the same as that of other Russian females, takes a foreign character when worn by them: there is magic in their glances, and their features and attitudes are graceful, and at the same time imposing. In short, they resemble the sibyls of Michael Angelo.[29]

It was the gypsies who first spurred Tolstoy to think about writing a story, and they feature in one of his early unfinished pieces of fiction from 1853, in which the clearly autobiographical narrator laments that their art has already become debased. 'There was a time when people loved gypsy music more than any other; when the gypsies sang the good old songs,' the narrator writes, going on to maintain that gypsy music in Russia was the 'only way for us to cross from popular to serious music', unapologetic that his love for gypsy music had made him digress.[30]

Tolstoy combined his love of popular Russian song with a serious enthusiasm for the classical European repertoire (particularly Beethoven, such as his Piano Trios, Op. 70), with which he largely became acquainted at the keyboard. He was still hell-bent on living up to the absurd standard he kept setting himself, but to judge from his week of diary entries in June 1850, he generally failed to follow his strict daily timetable for swimming, managing his serfs, reading and writing, and playing the piano that summer. Even if he chastised himself when he did not manage to play all twenty-four scales and arpeggios in two octaves every day, however, he could not help but attain a respectable level of proficiency of musicianship. He would continue to play the piano into his old age, sometimes playing duets with his wife Sonya or his sister Masha.

Another source of Tolstoy's dissatisfaction with himself in the summer of 1850 came from his inability to suppress the physical attraction he felt towards the pretty peasant girls on his estate. Like so many Russian landowners during this period, Tolstoy abused the nobleman's 'privilege' of owning serfs and exercised his *droit de seigneur* with peasant girls on a regular basis when he was a young man. He confessed to his diary on 19 June 1850 that he was incapable of controlling himself, and that what made it worse was that seducing girls had become a habit.[31] There was one particular innocent young girl who tempted him that summer: Toinette's servant Gasha Trubetskaya, who went on to work for his sister Masha and accompanied her abroad in 1859. Tolstoy's conscience was later sorely troubled by his exploitative behaviour, and in the 1890s he made an attempt at atonement by fictionalising and condemning his moral failings through the experiences of the central characters in his story 'The Devil' and his last novel *Resurrection*. As he was writing the latter in 1898, he confessed to his wife Sonya that he was recycling details from his own life. She had seen Gasha as an old lady, and was disgusted both by the idea of her husband's taking advantage of a peasant girl and by him recalling lascivious details in his old age.[32] (This is what prompted Tolstoy to confess to a friend about his first experience with a prostitute.) At the end of his life Tolstoy also confessed to having had amorous feelings for Avdotya (Dunyasha) Bannikova, the daughter of the servant who was his first tutor, Nikolay Dmitrievich. Dunyasha later married Tolstoy's servant Alexey Orekhov, and worked as a maid at Yasnaya Polyana, but he was adamant he had not laid a finger on her.[33] Tolstoy was generally quite predatory as a young man – he also began to develop a passion for hunting with borzois at this time.

Despite all his good intentions, by autumn 1850 Tolstoy had once again succumbed to drinking, gambling and spending time with the gypsies in Tula. There were some huge losses at cards this time: 4,000 roubles on one occasion.[34] Another change of routine was called for, so in December 1850 he again departed for Moscow, where he got out his diary and started compiling rules once more. Some of them were unrealistic ('play the piano for four hours every day'), some were practical ('do exercise every day', 'say as little as you can about yourself', 'speak loudly and clearly'), some were idealistic ('don't have women'), some were quite odd ('before a ball do a lot of thinking and writing'), and some were just plain silly ('don't read novels').[35] Tolstoy also drew up elaborate rules for card playing – this time he intended to play cards seriously, and gamble only with people richer than him.[36] He went to a lot of balls that winter (there were rules about dancing too), as he wanted to mingle with the *haut monde* of Moscow society and find a wife. It would in fact be a long time before he found the right person to marry, but his socialising meant he was up to date with all the latest intrigues, and so was able to send Aunt Toinette long letters telling her all the gossip doing the rounds of the Moscow salons – such as the scandal surrounding the evidence which implicated Alexander Sukhovo-Kobylin's aristocratic Russian mistress in the notorious murder of her French rival.[37]

Toinette greatly enjoyed the letters she received from her favourite nephew. On 27 January 1851 she told him in one of her replies that he wrote so engagingly, and so naturally, that it was if he was standing there before her. But she was concerned about the aimlessness of his life, and his worrying gambling habit. She reminded him reproachfully that he had come back to join his family for Christmas, but had preferred to play cards all night in Tula rather than spend time with his brother Nikolay, who was back 'in Russia', as he put it, on leave from the Caucasus for the first time in nearly four years. Aunt Toinette also despaired of Sergey ('If he had a job which occupied him seriously, he would not have given into that mad passion for the gypsy girl'), and she hoped Lev would find some purpose in his life, and not enter into a marriage of convenience just to pay off his debts.[38] She beseeched Tolstoy to take himself in hand.[39] He was beginning to. He was already painfully aware of the emptiness of Moscow society, and he had begun to think seriously about writing fiction. It was in December 1850 that he declared in his diary that he wanted to write a story about the gypsies.[40]

From the very beginning, Tolstoy's ability to hold up a mirror to his blemishes (looking in the mirror too frequently was another habit he faulted himself for at this time) would be fundamental to his powers of psychological analysis. On 8 March 1851 he began keeping a 'Franklin Journal' as a way of monitoring his moral lapses. Benjamin Franklin had described his technique of drawing up a table of virtues, and marking those he had failed to demonstrate each day, in his autobiography *Mémoires de la vie privée*, which was published in Paris in 1791.[41] Whether he had finally found his resolve, or whether the arrival of spring simply fired him with new energy, Tolstoy now became rigorous about writing in his own diary every day, convinced that acknowledging his moral failings was half the battle to eliminating them. He was quite successful at keeping up regular gymnastics and fencing lessons, but his behaviour rarely passed muster: the words 'laziness', 'cowardice', 'gluttony', 'false modesty' and 'self-deception' punctuate his diary entries during these months as a regular admonishment of his lack of moral fibre.

As he began experimenting with fiction for the first time, Tolstoy became more reclusive, and he also started to spend even more time reading. Earlier in the year he had been working his way through Montesquieu; now he read Lamartine's newly published *Histoire des Girondins* (1847), Bernardin de Saint-Pierre's *Paul et Virginie* (1787), Goethe's *The Sorrows of Young Werther* (1774), and Sterne's *Tristram Shandy* (1759–1769). During the spring of 1851 he began to be more observant not only of the turbulent emotional and intellectual processes going on inside his head, but of life around him. What Tolstoy had in mind when he embarked on the first draft of *Childhood*, which would become his first published work, was an original kind of *Bildungsroman* in four parts, to be entitled *Four Epochs of Development*. Under the clear influence of *David Copperfield*,[42] and also Laurence Sterne, amongst many other influences, Tolstoy's goal was to explore the psychological experiences of a young boy growing to adulthood. As with almost every work of fiction he ever published, Tolstoy drew on his own life as raw material for the evocation of particular scenes from two days in his character Nikolenka's childhood. It is important to recognise that his own life was the means and not the end, but as the Tolstoy scholar Richard Gustafson has put it, 'this distortion of personal experience conceals only to reveal',[43] since sincerity and emotional truth were always Tolstoy's ultimate goal. *Childhood* is deceptively simple. In order for it to work, Tolstoy had to come up with a convincing narrative voice, thus one of the first problems he wrestled with was whether to have an adult narrator, and risk his story seeming like a memoir, or have the child Nikolenka himself tell the story of his life, which posed dilemmas of a different kind.[44] Tolstoy's artistic techniques were already sophisticated. The fact that he wrote to a friend in Petersburg that spring to ask if he might help negotiate the literary censor was a sign that he was taking his writing seriously.[45]

Nikolay came to visit him in Moscow that March. The end of his furlough was fast approaching, and he suggested that his brother accompany him back to the Caucasus. Tolstoy immediately agreed, and at the beginning of April he left Moscow and returned to Yasnaya Polyana. The Caucasus offered Tolstoy the opportunity to start from a clean slate. It was a chance to leave behind his debts and his bad habits, and embrace a life of danger and adventure on the most dangerous frontier of the Russian Empire. The famous daguerreotype taken of the two brothers that spring shows the future writer clean-shaven, sitting tensely in rather scruffy clothes, his hands resting on a cane, fixing the viewer with a penetrating stare, while the more relaxed, phlegmatic Nikolay sits beside him in his army uniform, nonchalantly resting his elbow on the back of his brother's chair. By the end of the month the brothers were on the road, deciding to take a scenic route via Kazan, to catch up with family and friends. They took along two Yasnaya Polyana serfs as their personal servants: Alexey Orekhov and Ivan Suvorov (Alyoshka and Vanyushka).

After a pleasant week in Kazan, during which time Tolstoy's head was turned by the demure and pretty Zinaida Molostvova, the brothers headed south. On 30 May, after a glorious week sailing down the Volga from Saratov to Astrakhan and a further week on horses, they finally arrived in Starogladkovskaya, in present-day Chechnya. That same evening Tolstoy got out his diary. 'How did I end up here?' he asked himself. 'I don't know. And why am I here? Also I don't know.'[46] As it turned out, Starogladkovskaya was to be Tolstoy's base for the next two and a half years, and the time he spent there was to be the making of him. By the time he left the Caucasus he would be a commissioned officer in the imperial army and a published writer. His first-hand experience of warfare in the Caucasus, furthermore, would prove to be invaluable when he later came to write the battle scenes in *War and Peace*.

It was Catherine the Great who had brought Russia into the Caucasus, when she graciously came to the aid of the struggling Orthodox Christians in the Kingdom of Georgia. In truth, she really wanted to keep Persia and the Ottoman Empire at bay, with the ulterior motive of moving closer to realising her 'Greek Project'. She dreamed of defeating the Turks, and placing a Russian ruler on the throne of a newly restored Christian Constantinople. Her *annus mirabilis* was 1783, when she not only conquered the Crimea but signed the Treaty of Georgievsk, thus making Georgia a protectorate of Russia. Aggression by a newly resurgent Persia then played into Russia's hands. In 1795, the last year of Catherine's reign, Russia offered no assistance when the Persians invaded the capital of Tiflis, and Alexander I then violated the Treaty of Georgievsk in 1801 by simply annexing Georgia and abolishing its monarchy. Subsequent wars with the Ottoman Empire and Persia over the next decade resulted in the Russian Empire adding other small Caucasian nations to its territories.[47]

A town quickly grew up around the fortress at the foothill of the mountains which had been established in 1784 to become Russia's main military base in the area. It was optimistically named Vladikavkaz ('Ruler of the Caucasus'), but it took more than building the Georgian Military Highway between Vladikavkaz and Tiflis for the Russians to conquer the Caucasus. Although the Georgians largely surrendered peacefully to the Great White Tsar, with many of their aristocracy later distinguishing themselves in the war with Napoleon, there were many north Caucasian peoples who strongly resisted the Russian presence, chief amongst them the Chechens and Avars in the mountainous east (close to the Caspian Sea), and the Circassians in the west (near to the Black Sea). Russia soon found itself fighting a protracted war against a tenacious resistance movement. General Alexey Ermolov, the first commander-in-chief appointed to run operations in the Caucasus, was notorious for his brutal methods, but the Chechens (whom he saw as primeval savages) often outwitted him, and he was replaced in 1827 by Ivan Paskevich. Other strategies were deployed by subsequent commanders-in-chief until the war finally came to an end in the east in 1859, and in the west in 1864.

Tolstoy's experiences in the Caucasus were restricted to Chechnya in the eastern theatre of war, which had entered its last decade by the time he arrived in 1851. That was also the year in which Russia scored a minor victory. Since the 1830s, the disparate Muslim tribes of the northern Caucasus had been united by the Avar leader Imam Shamil who ruled the peoples of Chechnya and Daghestan. Shamil saw the war with Russia as a holy war, but he did not always enjoy full support from the highlanders. In 1851 he had fallen out with his commander Hadji Murat, a fellow Avar who went over to the Russian side. The following year, Hadji Murat tried to rejoin Shamil, but was murdered by Russian forces. Proof that Tolstoy's involvement in the protracted struggle with the Caucasian highlanders made a deep impression on him is provided by the fact that he decided to turn this litany of betrayals into fiction at the very end of his life. *Hadji Murat* was written at a time when his priorities were more religious than literary, but it is one of his greatest works of fiction.

Before Tolstoy met any Avar or Chechen rebels, he met Cossacks. Starogladkovskaya was one of five Cossack settlements which extended over a distance of about fifty miles along the northern bank of the River Terek. Named after Gladkov, one of the local *atamans*, the settlement was founded in the 1720s and its population contributed to the thousand or so Cossack troops who fought for the Russians in the Caucasian War. They were descendants of the original sixteenth-century Mountain or Terek Cossacks (*Grebenskie* or *Terskie kazaki*) who had settled along the Terek, some of whom had been part of autonomous military units and some of whom had originally fled central Russia to avoid enserfment.[48] The Cossacks' desire to maintain their traditional lifestyle of independence and freedom ultimately brought them into (sometimes very violent) conflict with the tsarist authorities, particularly under Catherine the Great. By the end of the eighteenth century they were forced into a position of accommodation, whereby they were granted special status in return for acting as border guards along the edge of the empire, particularly its threatened southern frontier. Although they were subjects of the Russian Empire, and were usually Christian, the Terek Cossacks had their own language and looked very like their Chechen neighbours on the other side of the river, with whom they had peacefully co-existed for centuries.[49] The men wore tall fur hats and the same long tunics with strings of cartridges worn across their chest.

Tolstoy was initially quite disappointed by the rather flat landscape where his brother's regiment was stationed – it was not until he started travelling in the Caucasus that he began to see the magnificent mountain scenery which had inspired visiting Russian poets to flights of rhetoric. The Cossack lifestyle was certainly an eye-opener for him, however. It was completely different from what he knew back home in Russia. The men had a cult of machismo, and left heavy work to their wives, but the women, far from being downtrodden, were often smarter, and usually far more attractive. They had a dignity which came from centuries of defiant independence (no Cossack had ever been a serf), and their standard of living was far higher than that of the average Russian muzhik. They also lived close to nature. Tolstoy would draw deeply on his knowledge of the Terek Cossacks for his fiction. In 1863, just before he embarked on *War and Peace*, he finally finished a novella called *The Cossacks* which he had begun when he was still living in the Caucasus. As a civilian with not much to do while his brother was out on manoeuvres, Tolstoy began to befriend the Cossacks in Starogladkovskaya, and learn their language. He became particularly close to Epifan (Epishka) Sekhin, a tall old Cossack with a big beard, then apparently in his late eighties, who became his first landlord and who was immortalised with great precision as Eroshka in *The Cossacks*.[50] Epishka took his young Russian friend with him on hunting trips, played the balalaika and regaled him with stories of old Cossack life.

Tolstoy's first experience of Chechens came a month after his arrival in the Caucasus. In June he followed his brother's regiment to the fortress at

Stary Yurt, some thirty miles away, and took part as a volunteer in a raid. By chance, General Prince Alexander Baryatinsky, who was in charge of the army's operations in the eastern Caucasus, happened to be present, and Nikolay relayed to his brother that he had been impressed by the young volunteer. Flattered by the attention of one of the most important Russian soldiers in the Caucasus (in 1856 he would be appointed commander-in-chief of the Caucasian army, and viceroy in the region), and encouraged by his brother, Tolstoy decided to join up. First, however, he had to obtain a letter from the Tula local government giving him leave to resign from the post he still nominally held.

Meanwhile, since he had a lot of time on his hands, he carried on with reading and writing: he was now working on his second draft of *Childhood*. He also played a lot of card games with Russian officers. On 13 June he lost 850 roubles in one sitting, which meant asking his brother-in-law to sell off another of his villages.[51] Tolstoy found it very hard to renounce gambling, but it did at least give him the opportunity to teach a Chechen how to count. Not all Chechens were hostile, and he became friends with a hot-headed young man called Sado Miserbiyev who was often cheated by the Russian officers with whom he played cards. Tolstoy took him under his wing and was rewarded with undying loyalty and a Chechen sword. He was also later bailed out by his devoted *kunak* (a Caucasian term for friend) when he suffered another terrible gambling loss.

That first autumn Tolstoy began to travel further afield, including to the Russian fortress at Groznaya (current-day Grozny), a new outpost built in 1818 by General Alexey Ermolov. The forbiddingly named Groznaya (which means 'threatening') was one of a number of new forts he built and named with the intention of terrorising the locals, such as Vnezapnaya ('Sudden') and Burnaya ('Stormy'). It was also Ermolov who in 1817 had completed major improvements to the 126-mile-long Georgian Military Highway which served as a vital artery for Russian troops over the mountains. It was the only passable road crossing the Caucasian range, and one of the highest in the world – higher than the Simplon Pass. When Pushkin had shared his impressions of the Highway in his *Journey to Erzerum* (1829) it was still extremely dangerous: travellers had to go with a convoy of 500 soldiers and a cannon, and sometimes covered only ten miles a day. By Tolstoy's time it had become both safer and faster.[52] He travelled along it for the first time with his brother when they went to Tiflis in October 1851, and now he was finally rewarded with the spectacular views of the snow-capped peaks which Pushkin and Lermontov had found so exhilarating before him.

Resigning his civil-service post and joining the army proved to be a lengthy bureaucratic procedure, and Tolstoy was forced to remain in Tiflis for over two months, where he also lost all his money at billiards and fell ill. During that solitary time, when he carried on working on *Childhood* and tried to stop himself womanising, he wrote fond, homesick letters to Aunt Toinette, who was his only regular correspondent. He told her how glad he was to be able to play the piano again, as it was the only thing he missed in his new life at the Starogladkovskaya camp (around this time he also decided to give his grand piano at Yasnaya Polyana to his sister Masha, knowing he would not soon return home). Tolstoy was also able to hear some music at the Tiflis Opera House which had just opened. For that, and for the city's new tree-lined streets and its first Russian newspaper, Tolstoy had Prince Mikhail Vorontsov to thank. Commander-in-chief of the Caucasian army from 1844 to 1854, and the first imperial viceroy in the region, the British-educated Vorontsov was a moderniser who had previously transformed Odessa, and he had now brought his enlightened city-planning ideas to Tiflis.[53]

Following his formal application to join the artillery regiment in which his brother served, Tolstoy need to sit an exam. Passing it entitled him to call himself a cadet, or, to use the Russian term, a *yunker* (a corruption of the German 'Jung Herr', the rank for junior under-officers from the nobility). On 3 January 1852 Tolstoy was appointed *Feierverker* (Bombardier), 4th class, in the 4th Battery of the Russian Army's 20th Artillery Brigade – though his appointment would not become official until his resignation from the Tula government was formalised. Two weeks later he was back in Starogladkovskaya, but left again immediately to take part in a month of raids against the Chechens for the first time as a full-time soldier, often side by side with his brother. It was relentless, intense and very dangerous, but after decades of successful guerrilla warfare from the Chechens and other mountain tribes, the Russians were beginning to gain the upper hand.

To begin with, Russian military strategy in the Caucasus was designed with a conventional European army in mind as the enemy, but this was no ordinary theatre of war. The Russians were not fighting large numbers of conventional troops with bayonets on a plateau, but small, heterogeneous bands of rebels on heavily wooded mountain slopes. Their enemies knew every inch of the land and were adept at knowing how to take cover. Eventually the Russian army changed its tactics. Under Vorontsov, who was as ruthless as Ermolov, the new strategy was to cut back forests and decimate villages so as to undermine the Chechen defence system.[54] It began to produce results. Tolstoy relished the opportunity to prove his mettle in his first raids against the Chechens, and his valour should have been rewarded with the St George Cross, but since his papers had not come through from Tula, he was still technically a volunteer, and so not officially eligible. He was bitterly disappointed. His papers finally arrived at the end of March.[55]

Tolstoy took part in several forest-clearing expeditions that spring, and the following year he would start distilling his experiences into the story 'The Wood-Felling', but his first priority was to complete *Childhood*, and when he came back to Starogladkovskaya in March he began working on his third draft. It was ironically just at the time that he joined the army that he began distancing himself from his rowdy fellow officers, who found his aloofness arrogant. Nikolay was happy to sit up all night drinking, but not Lev, who now began to prefer chess and fencing, and sitting with a book. His army duties were fairly light. In April he travelled a little way east to Kizlyar where he consulted a doctor about his poor health, and May found him undertaking a much longer journey, a few hundred miles west this time, to Pyatigorsk in the foothills of the north Caucasus, where he would undertake treatment. He would not return to Starogladkovskaya until August, by which time he had not only finished and submitted *Childhood*, but learned that it was accepted for publication.

Pyatigorsk ('Five Mountains'), so-called because it is overlooked by the five peaks of Mount Beshtau (a Turkish name meaning 'five mountains'), was founded as a Russian fortification in 1780. Following the discovery of its mineral springs it was developed as a health spa by imperial decree, and had become a thriving and fashionable resort embellished by Italian architects by the time Tolstoy arrived in 1852. It was, in fact, the most fashionable Russian spa throughout the nineteenth century. Pyatigorsk had also seen its fair share of drama: Lermontov was shot in a duel near the town's cemetery in 1841, and there was still a very real threat of raids by marauding Circassians, which gave an edge to otherwise peaceful rest cures. Tolstoy knew Pyatigorsk in his mind before he arrived because he had read *A Hero of Our Time*: it provides the setting for the longest of its stories. He followed the recommended treatment of bathing in Pyatigorsk's sulphurous springs for six weeks, and then travelled on to the springs of Zheleznovodsk ('Iron Waters'), situated a little way to the north, for three weeks of treatment there.

Tolstoy rented a little house on the outskirts of Pyatigorsk which had a garden and a beehive and a view of the snowcapped peak of Mount Elbrus, and rolled up his sleeves to get down to work. He did a lot of reading during his cure, particularly of Rousseau, whom he read and re-read, but he also did a lot of writing. On 27 May he finished the third draft of *Childhood*, and four days later he started on the final draft. In early July, finally happy with his manuscript, he resolved to send it to the editor of *The Contemporary*, Russia's most prestigious literary journal, without revealing his identity beyond the initials 'L.N.'.[56] *The Contemporary* was a St Petersburg-based journal which had been founded by Pushkin in 1836. Since 1847 it had been edited by the poet Nikolay Nekrasov, who had cemented its reputation as the platform of the progressive, liberal-minded intelligentsia by publishing the work of leading Westernisers such as Herzen and Turgenev, and inviting the collaboration of prominent critics like Vissarion Belinsky.

On 29 August, three weeks after arriving back in Starogladkovskaya, Tolstoy received a reply from Nekrasov, informing him that he had been impressed by *Childhood* and would be printing it in the next issue. Tolstoy was over the moon – until he finally received the September issue of the journal at the end of October. He was incensed to see that his text had been mutilated by the censor and, furthermore, was now called *A History of My Childhood*.[57] He had expressly not set out to write the story of *his* childhood, he remonstrated in the angry letter he drafted to Nekrasov, which he ultimately (and wisely) decided not to send. Tolstoy was also crestfallen not to be paid a royalty. He was desperately short of money, and unaware of the practice of Russian literary journals not to pay fledgling authors for their first publication. He had no option but to acquiesce, and at least had the enviable consolation of having an editor who wanted to publish more of his writing. Tolstoy had a very warm reception for his first published work. Critics particularly praised the gifts of psychological analysis which brought *Childhood* to life. The Russian reading public were also full of praise for the mysterious but extremely promising new author. The members of the author's own family, who had not been forewarned, reacted with delighted surprise when they discovered his identity.[58]

That autumn Tolstoy carried on writing. He was teeming with new ideas, and he began to think about resigning from the army: the success of *Childhood* showed him where his future lay, and it was not with the military. He now began to work on several things at once. First of all he resolved to add to *Childhood* by writing *Boyhood*. At the same time, as he became increasingly occupied by religious ideas, he began to conceive a novel about a Russian landowner wanting to improve the life of his peasantry. Finally, he was keen to publish stories about the Caucasus. This was the project he brought to completion first. He had already started writing stories inspired by his own experiences with the army, and in late December he sent Nekrasov the manuscript of 'The Raid – A Volunteer's Story'. It was published the following March, again with cuts dictated by the censor. With 'The Raid', Tolstoy turned a new page in the history of Russian writing about the Caucasus. Thanks to Pushkin and Lermontov, readers were used to a romantic and mythologised view of the Caucasus and its peoples. The story Tolstoy made of his memories of the first sortie against the Chechens which he had observed close-hand the previous year was highly realistic. Just beneath the surface we can also detect a nascent anti-militaristic stance.

The spring of 1853 was both the high point and the low point of Tolstoy's time in the Caucasus. He took part in further skirmishes with Chechen rebels, and was commended for his bravery. After being obliged to cede the St George Cross he deserved to an old soldier who stood to receive a decent pension as a result, he was promoted to ensign instead, but then ended up being arrested when a particularly riveting game of chess led him to miss parade. His promotion was therefore cancelled (and he had to wait until 1854 for it to be reinstated). Tolstoy was bitterly disappointed to miss the St George Cross again and there were other disappointments. His brother Nikolay had decided to resign from the army the previous autumn, having served in the army for eight years,[59] and in February 1853 his papers came through, permitting him to retire at the rank of staff-captain. Tolstoy was already quite lonely in the Caucasus and he felt Nikolay's absence keenly. His financial affairs were also still in a dire state. In April his brother-in-law sold another village on his estate to provide him with funds, which meant losing another 350 acres, plus twenty-six serfs and their families.[60] Even his writing suffered: the story he began about a young man in Moscow who goes to a high-society ball, then to a tavern to hear the gypsies was suddenly dropped and never picked up again.

Because fortune had not yet smiled on Tolstoy's military career, he had initially delayed tendering his resignation, thinking it would be just too humiliating for him to return to civilian life as a retired cadet. In the end, however, he decided he would go ahead anyway, and he submitted his resignation request on 30 May 1853.[61] Yet again he was unlucky. Russia had just broken off diplomatic relations with Turkey, and after its invasion of the Romanian principalities of Moldavia and Wallachia in June, no officer was permitted to apply for leave or resign. In July Tolstoy returned to Pyatigorsk, where he joined Nikolay and also his sister Masha, whom he had not seen for two years. She had come to spend the summer taking the waters at Pyatigorsk with her husband. It was not a particularly happy time for Tolstoy, who was feeling irritable and restless, and it was made no better by the realisation that he would have to sell the main Yasnaya Polyana mansion to rectify his financial affairs, something he had previously vowed would be an absolute last resort.[62] He buried his sorrows in his writing. As well as starting the first draft of what would become his novella *The Cossacks*, and working further on his sequel to *Childhood*, he also wrote another completely different story which he started and finished in four days. 'Notes of a Billiard Marker', the only work Tolstoy sent off to Nekrasov that summer, is more strongly autobiographical than most of Tolstoy's stories. It is a bleak tale of a young aristocrat's moral disintegration, inspired by the gambling disaster which had befallen Tolstoy in Tiflis. Close reading of Rousseau's *Confessions* helped to keep Tolstoy on an even keel at this time, and reminded him that he could only be happy doing good works.[63] He was beginning to develop a strong social conscience.

Tolstoy was by this point bored with regimental life in the Caucasus, dissatisfied with himself and longing for a change of scenery, so before he returned to Starogladkovskaya in October, he applied to be transferred to active duty in the war against Turkey. In January 1854, when his request was granted and he was finally promoted to full officer class as an ensign, he decided to travel to his new regiment in Bucharest via Yasnaya Polyana, a detour of over 600 miles. February was an ecstatic month for Tolstoy. He was overjoyed to see Yasnaya Polyana again, and be reunited with his beloved Aunt Toinette. He went to see his sister Masha at Pokrovskoye, and his brother Dmitry at Shcherbachevka, and in Moscow the four Tolstoy brothers posed for a photograph. It was the last time they would ever be together. The visit was over all too soon. On 3 March Tolstoy set off to join his new artillery brigade, travelling via Kursk, Poltava and Kishinyov before finally arriving in Bucharest ten days later, shortly before France and Britain declared war on Russia.

The Crimean War ostensibly blew up over access to the holy sites in Palestine, but was really about Russia's expansionist ambitions, and the threat that they represented to French and British interests. After the annexation of Georgia in 1801, and Bessarabia in 1812, Russia proceeded to defeat the Ottoman Empire in 1829, thus acquiring new powers and new territories (including part of Armenia). For the allies, it was only a matter of time before Nicholas I gained full access to the eastern Mediterranean. Hostilities between Turkey and Russia began in October 1853, most of them taking place around the mouth of the Danube. When France and Britain became involved in March 1854, and Russia was forced to withdraw from Moldavia and Wallachia, wrongly counting on Austrian support (in return for having sent in troops to quash the rebellion in Hungary in 1850), the Crimean peninsula became the main theatre of war. So Tolstoy was out of luck again, as three months after he arrived in Bucharest the main action was transferred elsewhere.

Tolstoy was pleasantly surprised by the elegance of Bucharest, and enjoyed going to the Italian opera and the French theatre when he first arrived.[64] Once he was settled, he carried on with his writing. He concentrated on revising and completing *Boyhood*, and then at the end of March he was posted for two weeks to Oltenița, just north of the Danube, which had been the site of a battle with the Turks the previous November. Then came an attachment to the artillery commander General Serzhputovsky, which meant going on patrol to different parts of Moldavia, Wallachia and Bessarabia. In May Tolstoy observed the last days of the Russian siege of the Ottoman fortress town of Silistra, situated on the south side of the Danube in present-day Bulgaria. Russia needed to take Silistra in order to advance further, and huge numbers of Russian troops had been moved into the area in April when the siege had begun. Tolstoy was not actively involved in the bombardment of the town, but since he was working as an orderly, and for a sadistic superior, he often ended up in the trenches and found himself exposed to mortal danger on more than one occasion. Writing home to Aunt Toinette, he described the strangely magnificent spectacle of watching people killing each other every morning and evening. When he was not relaying orders he was stationed in the Russian camp, located in gardens belonging to Silistra's governor, Mustafa-Pasha, which afforded grand views of the Danube and of the besieged town (particularly during the night-time bombardments). A date in June was set for the final storming of Silistra, but at two in the morning, an hour before it was due to commence, Field Marshal Pashkevich sent word that the Tsar, under pressure from Austria, had ordered a retreat. Tolstoy, along with the entire company on the Russian side, was extremely disappointed.[65]

The Russian forces now began their retreat towards the Russian border, and Tolstoy initially returned to Bucharest, taking with him positive impressions of the Bulgarians he had met in Silistra. It was in Bucharest that a letter sent to him by Nekrasov back in July finally caught up with Tolstoy. Nekrasov was full of praise for the manuscript of *Boyhood*, which greatly raised his spirits, but in August he lost another 3,000 roubles gambling.[66] In early September Tolstoy also headed back to Russia, learning on the way that he was to be promoted to sub-lieutenant. He was stationed at the army's new headquarters in Kishinyov, capital of Bessarabia, where once again he had plenty of time for reading and for music: he had a nice flat with a piano.[67] At this point he was reading George Sand and *Uncle Tom's Cabin* in German translation. He also had time to put together a proposal with some of his fellow officers to launch a weekly forces newspaper. He was greatly excited by this project, and as soon as he heard his brother-in-law had sold the Yasnaya Polyana house that autumn, he wrote to ask him for 1,500 roubles so he could invest in taking the project further.[68] The Yasnaya Polyana house had been sold for 5,000 roubles to a local landowner who dismantled it and rebuilt it on his own estate. Tolstoy's brother-in-law rightly had grave misgivings about releasing the funds.[69] Meanwhile, the proposal for the forces newspaper was taken to St Petersburg for Nicholas I to consider.

Russia had suffered heavy losses in the war with the allied forces that autumn. The allies had won major battles at Alma, and in September 1854 besieged Sebastopol, Russia's main naval base on the Black Sea. While the Russians started scuttling some of their ships and using the cannons of others to back up their artillery, the allies built trenches and gun redoubts in the south of the city, and were ready for the battle by the middle of October. On the first day of bombardment, on 17 October, a British attack set off the ammunition store on the Malakoff redoubt and killed Admiral Kornilov, but Russian artillery also destroyed a French magazine. Four days earlier, at the end of the Battle of Balaclava, Raglan's Light Brigade had charged into the 'valley of death', and the Russians saw their capture of the British redoubts as a victory. The Battle of Inkerman on 24 October crushed Russian hopes, however, and made it clear that the rest of the war would be fought at Sebastopol.

In Kishinyov, meanwhile, balls were being thrown for two visiting grand dukes, which left a bad taste in Tolstoy's mouth. He began petitioning to be transferred to Sebastopol. First of all he wanted to see the action for himself, but mostly he was driven by his feelings of patriotism, particularly when he learned that the 12th Artillery Brigade he had served with briefly had taken part in the Battle of Balaclava. The Russian military headquarters in St Petersburg finally began sending reinforcements down to the Crimea, and Tolstoy arrived around the same time as the 10th and 11th divisions. By early November he was in Odessa, and a week later he was in the Crimea. He might have arrived earlier, but kissing a pretty young Ukrainian girl through a window in a town south of Kherson led him to spending the night with her.[70] When he arrived in Sebastopol, Tolstoy was assigned to the 3rd Battery of the 14th Light Artillery Brigade.[71] He was not mobilised to be on active duty at this point, but he remained in the besieged city for nine days, during which time he was able to assess for himself exactly what was going on, by visiting the Russian fortifications and talking to soldiers and officers. He wrote to tell Sergey the harrowing stories he had heard from a wounded soldier who told him about how the taking of a French battery at Inkerman had come to nought, as reinforcements never arrived, and how 160 men in one brigade had valiantly remained at the front, even though they were wounded. Then there were the sailors who had withstood thirty days of constant bombing, and refused to be relieved from their duties. He saw priests with crosses walking along the bastions and saying prayers under fire, and heard about displays of heroism greater than in ancient Greece when Vice Admiral Kornilov had asked the Russian forces if they were prepared to die.[72] There were some 35,000 Russian troops stationed in Sebastopol at this point; 13,000 of them would not return home (French and British losses were almost as heavy).[73]

Tolstoy was greatly moved by the fighting spirit of the troops, but he now could not help seeing why the Russian army was faring so badly. A week after leaving Sebastopol on 15 November and moving north to the Tatar village outside Simferopol where his battery was stationed, he noted in his diary that he had become more convinced than ever before that Russia either needed fundamental reform, or would collapse.[74] He had talked to allied prisoners of war in Sebastopol, and was struck by their high self-esteem, and their pride in the contribution they were making to the war effort, confident it was valued. There was none of that in the Russian army, where the military leadership clearly regarded its seemingly inexhaustible supply of infantry as cannon-fodder. Tolstoy also noticed that the artillery used by his brigade was out-dated compared to that deployed by the allies, and he started putting together a plan in which he set out a number of detailed reforms.[75] Tolstoy had come to see that Russia's military tactics were woefully out of date. He could not fail to be aware that communications between Russia and the Crimea were abysmal, with primitive roads which were often impassable because of mud, and a minuscule railway network. Conditions for rank and file soldiers were also appalling, with military service still set at twenty years and five years in the reserves. Nicholas I's emphasis on drills and parades had meant his troops were not even properly trained.

The Tsar turned down the proposal for a forces newspaper in late November, on the grounds that it was not in the government's interests.[76] He suggested instead that Tolstoy and his comrades publish articles in *Russian Veteran*, the official newspaper patronised by the Ministry of War, which of course they already were entitled to do. The news angered Tolstoy when it reached him, but after collecting more raw impressions from a sortie to Sebastopol in early December with his platoon, he began sketching out an article with which he hoped to respond. This was the first draft of 'Sebastopol in December', his first piece of war reportage, which would bring him national celebrity. On 11 January Tolstoy wrote to Nekrasov with the proposal that he send him articles on the war which he promised would be of a quality not inferior to anything else published in *The Contemporary*. Nekrasov wrote back by return of post giving Tolstoy carte blanche. It was now that Tolstoy learned that his story 'Notes of a Billiard Marker' had been published in the January issue for 1855, and that *Boyhood* had appeared in the journal back in October. The censor had once again objected to several passages, such as the one where the narrator regrets that some people are poor while his family are rich, and all references to the Church and its rituals, which were at that time prohibited in secular publications (they include the passage about the boy's father making the sign of the cross over the window of the carriage his family is to travel in, and the horse's nickname of 'Deacon').[77]

Tolstoy was stationed in the quiet Tatar village of Eski-Orda for one and a half months, so he had plenty of time again at his disposal, and enjoyed hunting wild goats, playing duets and dancing with young ladies.[78] But in the middle of January 1855 he was transferred to the 3rd Battery of the 11th Artillery Brigade, which was stationed on the Balbek river, six miles outside Sebastopol. On the way, he stopped in the city and picked up money sent him by his brother-in-law from the sale of his house at Yasnaya Polyana. Tolstoy earned a reputation amongst his new battalion for his physical strength – one day he impressed his comrades by lying on the floor and lifting a twelve-stone man with his bare hands. The officers in his battalion did not impress *him*, however; he felt very alienated in this new posting. He was miserable during that cold winter. He had no books, and no one to talk to. It was not a situation conducive to writing either, and the torpor made him vulnerable to his vices. On 3 February he steeled himself to write a difficult letter to his brother Nikolay. He had succumbed once again to his gambling addiction, and over the course of two days and two nights had lost the 1,500 roubles he had just received as seed money for the forces newspaper. Confessing this lapse to Nikolay was Tolstoy's way of doing penance.[79]

When news of Russia's latest defeat at Evpatoria reached the Tsar on 12 February 1855, he had wept like a child, and no longer wanted to hear any more despatches from the front. On 18 February Nicholas I died. He had ruled Russia with an iron fist for thirty years and his death at the age of fifty-eight was completely unexpected. As far as most of the educated population of Russia was concerned, however, the news was more a reason for celebration than for mourning. The relaxation in censorship which followed soon after Alexander's accession would make an immediate impact, and Russians would begin to speak about a 'thaw', just as they would a century later after Stalin's death. Down in the Crimea, Tolstoy clearly now felt emboldened to extend his reforming plans for the military, for in early March he began sketching out a plan for modernising the entire army, not just the artillery's weapons. He did not mince his words. 'We don't have an army,' wrote Tolstoy, 'but a mob of oppressed disciplined slaves who have submitted to robbers and mercenaries.' The Russian soldier, he went on, was someone legally constricted from satisfying even his most basic needs, and he was certainly not given enough to prevent him from suffering from hunger and cold. Tolstoy divided Russian soldiers into the oppressed, the oppressors and the desperate. It was hardly surprising that an oppressed soldier spent the niggardly seventy kopecks he received every quarter (a 'bitter mockery of his poverty') on drink, and that morale was low. Tolstoy had nothing good to say about those in charge: a lot of the officers were crooks devoid of any sense of duty or honour, while the generals were more often appointed for their acceptability to the Tsar rather than for their abilities.[80] Tolstoy abandoned this ambitious project after a few days, no doubt because he realised it would not go anywhere even in the new climate, but it is important to realise that there was a precedent for speaking out when he began railing in public against social and political injustices thirty years later.

At the same time that Tolstoy was preoccupied with military matters, he was also thinking deeply about religious questions. On 4 March 1855 he took communion and made a remarkable declaration in his diary about the founding of a new religion. It is often quoted in view of its prophetic nature:

> Yesterday a conversation about divinity and faith led me to a great and stupendous idea, the realisation of which I feel capable of devoting my whole life to. This idea is the foundation of a new religion corresponding to the development of mankind – the religion of Christ, but purged of dogma and mystery, a practical religion, not promising future bliss but providing bliss on earth. I realise that to bring this idea to fruition will take generations of people working consciously towards this goal. One generation will bequeath this idea to the next, and one day fanaticism or reason will implement it. Working consciously to unite people with religion is the foundation of the idea which I hope will occupy me.[81]

In a sense, all of Tolstoy's future career is here, as he was always a religious writer, concerned with seeking the truth. In his early works this concern was implicit, but it became increasingly explicit as he evolved as an artist. Tolstoy's literary works, in the compelling argument of Richard Gustafson, can even be seen as 'verbal icons' of his religious view. Until the nineteenth century the icon had fulfilled the role of theology in the Russian Orthodox Church. There simply was no written theological tradition in Russia as there was in the Roman Catholic and Protestant Churches, and when the art of icon painting fell into decline in the nineteenth century, after the Orthodox Church was made into a department of state, it was literature which took its place. As Gustafson has commented, people in Russia began instinctively to understand the role of literature as theology: 'the images created by artists were taken seriously as words which reveal the Truth'. Tolstoy's writing is hailed for its realism, but it is a very emblematic, religious kind of realism.[82]

At the end of March 1855 Tolstoy began writing properly again. He started *Youth*, which would end up being the third and last instalment of his projected four-part work. He also began reworking the draft of his article about events at Sebastopol. He did not get very far, however, as he was called into action. After the long winter months, during which time the allies built a railway to speed up the delivery of supply of guns and ammunition, French and British troops were ready to resume their bombardment of Russian defences in Sebastopol. Tolstoy's battery was despatched to the fourth bastion in the south of the city, which was the most dangerous owing to its close proximity to the French position. The new allied bombardment ceased on 7 April, except in the case of the fourth bastion, which continued to be pummelled for another five days. Tolstoy was first on duty between 5 and 6 April, and then in stints of four days, followed by eight days' rest, during which time he retreated to a flat in town and played the piano.[83] On 19 April the allies seized the trenches between the fourth and fifth bastions, and the Russian forces began to doubt that they would prevail.

On 25 April Tolstoy finished 'Sebastopol in December', his first, very patriotic and gripping piece of reportage about the realities of fighting in the besieged city, and he sent it straight away to Petersburg. Together with the two other works he wrote which make up the *Sebastopol Sketches*, it constitutes his most sophisticated writing yet. In this first sketch, the narrator takes the reader on a tour of Sebastopol set in the present tense, so that the experience of hostilities is all the more vivid when it begins, and reminiscent of the experience of watching a film:

> The whistle, close at hand, of a shell or a cannonball, just at the very moment you start to climb the hill, gives you a nasty sensation. Suddenly you realise, in an entirely new way, the true significance of those sounds of gunfire you heard from the town. Some quiet, happy memory suddenly flickers to life in your brain; you start thinking more about yourself and

less about what you observe around you, and are suddenly gripped by an unpleasant sense of indecision ...[84]

Tolstoy, hailed as the first war correspondent, was adept at combining personal impressions, conveyed in a conversational, intimate tone, with the lofty viewpoint of a historian or epic poet able to speak for the nation. Meanwhile he continued his turns of duty on the fourth bastion. The allied bombardment now became fiercer, particularly during a battle beginning on the evening of 10 May, which resulted in heavy casualties (about 2,500 on each side), and further attrition of Russian defences. The experience of living through these events provided Tolstoy with material for his second despatch. On 15 May he was sent to command the guns of a mountain platoon twelve miles out of Sebastopol, and this ended his tour of duty on the fourth bastion.[85]

In June Tolstoy once again had time to write. He turned first to 'The Wood-Felling: A Cadet's Tale'. This was a story he had begun earlier about his army experiences in the Caucasus, which now seemed so distant. He finished the story on 18 June, and sent it off to Nekrasov for publication in *The Contemporary*, where it appeared that September. Meanwhile, 'Sebastopol in December' was published in the June issue, and it created a furore. Russian readers had never been given a true picture of what warfare was like in their literary journals, still less an idea of what it was like for ordinary soldiers while it was still going on. Tolstoy's descriptions of their heroism and suffering were deeply moving, the more so for the calm, unsensational tone in which they were delivered. Tolstoy learned that the Tsar himself had read 'Sebastopol in December', and had ordered it to be translated for publication in the Russian government's French-language journal *Le Nord*.[86] He was flattered, naturally, but his thoughts were now dominated by his longing to retire from the army and concentrate on his writing. The optimism he had expressed in 'Sebastopol in December' was misplaced: the situation was becoming bleaker by the day. On 28 June another of the army's commanders died when Admiral Nakhimov was shot in the head.

On 5 July Tolstoy sent off his second sketch about the siege of Sebastopol to *The Contemporary*. He was well aware the censor would object to much in 'Sebastopol in May', which is a far bleaker work than 'Sebastopol in December' and represents the first strong expression of Tolstoy's views on the futility of war:

Yes, white flags have been raised on the bastion and all along the trench, the flowering valley is filled with stinking corpses, the resplendent sun is descending toward the dark blue sea, and the sea's blue swell is gleaming in the sun's golden rays. Thousands of men are crowding together, studying one another, speaking to one another, smiling at one another. It might be supposed that when these men – Christians, recognising the same great law of love – see what they have done, they will instantly fall to their knees to repent before Him who, when He gave them life, placed in the soul of each, together with the fear of death, a love of the good and the beautiful, and that they will embrace one another with tears of joy and happiness, like brothers. Not a bit of it! The scraps of white cloth will be put away – and once again the engines of death and suffering will start their whistling; once again the blood of the innocent will flow and the air will be filled with their groans and cursing.[87]

On 24 August the allies started their sixth and final bombardment of the Sebastopol fortress. Tolstoy took part in the defence of the Malakov redoubt, but it was seized on 27 August. That night, the Russian army began to abandon its positions on the south side of Sebastopol and crossed the river over to the north side. After a year-long siege, Sebastopol had fallen to the allied forces. Tolstoy cried when he saw the once beautiful city in flames, with French flags flying on all the bastions.[88] He was still there on 28 August to witness the city fall strangely silent. It was his twenty-seventh birthday, and he remembered back to another gloomy birthday in 1841, when his aunt Aline had died. On the same day, Ivan Panayev, co-editor of *The Contemporary*, wrote to Tolstoy to tell him that 'Sebastopol in May' had been massacred by the censor, who had reduced its length by about a third. Panayev had wanted to withdraw it from publication, but the censor insisted it be published exactly as it now stood.[89] The only consolation was that Panayev published it anonymously, as 'A Night in the Spring of 1855 in Sebastopol' to spare Tolstoy's feelings. It appeared in the August issue of *The Contemporary*, coinciding with the fall of Sebastopol.

Tolstoy felt listless throughout the warm days of September. He began his third and final piece about the siege – 'Sebastopol in September' – but his heart was not in it. He was burned out and exhausted, and so surrendered to gambling again. This was a bad sign, and he realised he needed to leave the army sooner rather than later. In early November Tolstoy was sent to St Petersburg as a courier. The next stage of his life was about to begin.

LITERARY DUELLIST AND REPENTANT NOBLEMAN

Measuring myself against my former Yasnaya memories, I can feel how
much I have changed in the liberal sense.

Diary entry, May 1856

NO PERIOD OF TOLSTOY'S LIFE was uneventful, but the years between
the time he left the Crimea in 1855 and married in 1862 were particularly
crucial in terms of his artistic and intellectual formation. Tolstoy had been
away from Russian metropolitan life for four years, and arriving back in the
city was a big shock to the system. He had launched his career from outside
the Russian literary establishment, and his talent had catapulted him right
into its midst. Now he had to contend with it face to face, which meant living
up to expectations – his own, and those of his new colleagues. It also meant
confronting insecurities with regard to more established writers, and discovering where his allegiances lay. But during this time of great social change,
he began to recognise within himself an impulse which ran counter to the
pursuit of an artistic career: a deep moral need to do something about social
inequality in Russia. He had taken jejune steps in this direction when he first

came into his inheritance, but the experience of standing next to common soldiers in the Crimean War had been more than chastening: Sebastopol marked Tolstoy for life. He began this seven-year period as an ambitious twenty-seven-year-old writer anxious to consolidate his early successes, but he ended it as a village schoolteacher.

Tolstoy was rarely at peace with himself during this turbulent time. It was not just that his new writing met with a mixed reception, or that he remained unmarried (it was a matter of great consternation to him that his attempts to find a bride always ended in failure). His family life was also troubled: his brothers Dmitry and Nikolay both died of tuberculosis within a few years of each other, and his sister Masha ended an unhappy marriage. Turgenev now became a major part of Tolstoy's life, but the warm embraces they exchanged when they first met were gradually replaced by fractious disagreements; theirs was a volatile friendship. In 1861 Tolstoy would challenge Turgenev to a duel, and their uneasy reconciliation was followed by a seventeen-year feud. The trajectory of the friendships Tolstoy formed with many other Russian writers followed a similar, albeit less dramatic pattern. It was in the early years following his retirement from the army that Tolstoy had his closest contacts with many of his peers, most of whom were based in St Petersburg. As he shuttled between Yasnaya Polyana, Moscow and the capital, torn by conflicting desires, he discovered that he did not want to be part of the literary community, nor was there any place for him under its rapidly changing agenda. When he returned from his second trip abroad in 1861, he settled in Yasnaya Polyana for good, and made his feelings emphatically clear by not returning to St Petersburg for seventeen years. It was not an outcome he was expecting when he packed his bags in the Crimea, excited at the prospect of the warm reception he was going to receive from his new writer friends.

Tolstoy received his first letter from Turgenev just before leaving Sebastopol in November 1855. The two writers had read each other's work, but never met. Tolstoy was in awe of his elder contemporary, who had been a fixture of the St Petersburg literary scene for almost a decade by the time he made his own debut. A careful re-reading of *A Hunter's Notes* during his second summer in Pyatigorsk had produced the lapidary comment in his diary 'Writing is a bit difficult after him'.[1] For his part, Turgenev had immediately perceived Tolstoy's literary talent, and was deeply flattered that 'The Wood-Felling' was dedicated to him (no other writer would receive a dedication from Tolstoy). When Turgenev wrote his first letter to Tolstoy, he felt he was addressing someone he already almost knew, as he had met (and rather fallen for) his sister Masha the previous autumn.[2] Her husband Valerian Petrovich's Pokrovskoye estate was only twelve miles from Turgenev's ancestral home, and a shared love of hunting had brought the two neighbours into contact. Naturally, when Tolstoy arrived in St Petersburg, the first person he wanted to see was Turgenev. After checking into a hotel and paying a visit to the bath-house, he went straight round to Turgenev's apartment, only to find the writer on his way out – in the hope of finding him. They exchanged hearty kisses, and Turgenev immediately insisted that Tolstoy share his flat on the Fontanka river.[3] It would be Tolstoy's home for the next month as he readjusted to civilian life.

As a celebrated author and officer who had arrived straight from the front line, Tolstoy was welcomed like a conquering hero by the editors of *The Contemporary*. There was also an air of mystery about him. Here was a young man who had submitted an unsolicited manuscript from the Caucasus three years earlier, and no one at *The Contemporary* had actually met him. In fact only a few people even recognised his name, as he had signed all his stories so far with his initials only. Tolstoy was also anxious to meet the new colleagues he had been corresponding with, and he hoped they would be kindred spirits. He had been a callow and impressionable youth when he had last been in St Petersburg, but now he was a published writer, a war hero and a celebrity. On his first day in St Petersburg Turgenev took Tolstoy round to meet Nekrasov (the editorial offices of *The Contemporary* were located in a building on the other side of the river), and they had lunch and talked and played chess until eight in the evening.[4] Nekrasov went into raptures in a letter to a friend, describing Tolstoy as 'better than his writing', a 'falcon', or perhaps even an 'eagle'.[5] There followed meetings with critics and publishers, and dinners with other writers, including the novelist Ivan Goncharov, then working on his masterpiece *Oblomov* (1859), and the poet Fyodor Tyutchev. Soon Tolstoy was personally acquainted with all the leading lights of Russian literature, who fell over themselves to express how delighted they were by this talented young artillery officer.

Tolstoy found it intoxicating to be back in civilised surroundings, where there was plenty of intellectual stimulation, but he also craved the intoxication of gypsy music and card games, in which he could seek oblivion and shake off the stresses of the last few years. The poet Afanasy Fet visited one day for mid-morning tea with Turgenev and was told by his servant Zakhar that the gleaming sabre in the corner of the hall belonged to Count Tolstoy. Fet and Turgenev then had to spend the next hour talking in whispers, as the count was still asleep on the couch in the drawing room, having been up all night carousing. Turgenev, though only ten years Tolstoy's senior, had assumed a kind of paternal role in their relationship and explained that it was the same every night, and that he had long since given up on him.[6] On 11 December Tolstoy spent all the money he had left throwing a party with gypsy singers at the Hotel Napoleon.[7]

Of all the writers Tolstoy met during his sojourn in St Petersburg, only Fet became a lasting friend, but even he would fail to make the cut when Tolstoy emerged from his spiritual crisis in the 1880s. Much as they all liked Tolstoy, the writers in St Petersburg soon realised that it was actually not all that easy to get on with him. He came out with such provocative opinions, and seemed to go out of his way to be contrary. Many of the writers associated with *The Contemporary* were either writing about Shakespeare or translating him, for example, but Tolstoy was simply dismissive of him.[8] And the mild-mannered Turgenev soon found himself having violent arguments with Tolstoy. They were two men from the same patrician background, but Tolstoy did not like compromise, and he instinctively recoiled from Turgenev's refined elegance and spirit of moderation, which were a great disappointment to him. One evening Turgenev read from the manuscript of his first novel, *Rudin*, to an assembled company. In comparison with *A Hunter's Notes*, Tolstoy found it unbelievably contrived, and could not believe how seriously it was received by the other literati present.

Turgenev had not had a particularly easy time. He was a self-confessed Westerniser, so was anxious to see reform and modernisation in Russia along European lines. He had bravely gone against the grain of his upbringing by befriending the radical critic Belinsky, whose reforming zeal stemmed partly from his lowly social origins, and his implicit criticism of serfdom in his *A Hunter's Notes* had made him a very dubious figure in the eyes of the tsarist establishment. Turgenev never shied away from standing up for what he believed was right, or from dealing with political issues in his works. He had defiantly published an obituary of Gogol back in 1852, despite knowing that all mention of a writer who had satirised the Fatherland had been forbidden by the censor (the same censor who disfigured Tolstoy's 'Sebastopol in May'). For daring to call Gogol 'great', Nicholas I had personally ordered Turgenev's arrest and imprisonment for a month, to be followed by permanent exile to his estate. It had only been thanks to the future Alexander II, who had liked *A Hunter's Notes*, that he had been allowed to travel again at the end of 1853. At the time of his meeting with Turgenev, Tolstoy was intent on carving out a career as a novelist himself, but *Rudin* cut no ice with him.

Something else marked Tolstoy out from the progressive writers grouped round *The Contemporary*: his contacts with the St Petersburg aristocracy. Tolstoy came to despise the social conventions of high society, but he made an exception for family, and he would become particularly close to Alexandra Andreyevna Tolstoya, whom he got to know now for the first time. 'Alexandrine' was the daughter of his paternal great uncle, and she and her sister Elizaveta had apartments in the Mariinsky Palace opposite the cathedral in St Isaac's Square, as they were tutors and then ladies-in-waiting to Nicholas I's daughter Grand Duchess Maria Nikolayevna and her daughters Maria and Evgenia. If Tolstoy unconsciously looked to Turgenev as a father figure, he jocularly called Alexandra Andreyevna his *babushka* (grandmother), although, like Turgenev, she was only ten or so years his senior. In the memoir Alexandrine wrote of her relationship with her unruly cousin at the end of her life, she recalled the distinct impression he had made on everyone when he arrived from Sebastopol:

> He himself was very simple, extremely modest [this was early in his career] and so playful that his presence enlivened everybody. He spoke very rarely about himself [one rule he had followed!], but examined each new face with particular attention, and then relayed his impressions, which were nearly always quite extreme, in a most amusing way. The adjective *thin-skinned*, which his wife later applied to him, suited him exactly, so strongly was he affected by the slightest nuance that he caught. His unattractive face, with clever, kind and expressive eyes, replaced with their expression everything he lacked by way of refinement, and, it may be said, was superior to beauty.[9]

Along with Aunt Toinette, Alexandrine was one of the few women in Tolstoy's life whom he really respected. She had not married or had children, and so he did not categorise her as a 'typical' woman, although he was certainly attracted to her. She clearly also felt there was a frisson between them. They were to fall out very badly over religion later on, at a time when Tolstoy burned his boats with nearly everyone he was close to, but they cared for each other deeply. Alexandrine was a tremendously intelligent, no-nonsense woman whose company Tolstoy greatly enjoyed. After Tolstoy became ensconced at Yasnaya Polyana, their contact became more sporadic, but their correspondence was always lively. It was to Alexandrine, of course, that Tolstoy invariably turned to when he needed a direct line to the Tsar, as she was extremely well connected at court. Addressing personal letters to the Tsar would become something of a habit with Tolstoy, and in the early days Alexandrine was a willing intermediary, although rather less so when her cousin became a public liability towards the end of his life by openly going head to head with the Russian government.

At the end of November, Tolstoy wrote an ebullient letter to his sister Masha to tell her how his meeting with Turgenev had gone (and how unscintillating Nekrasov had turned out to be). Just a few days later he received a letter from her, in which she exhorted him to come and visit their brother Dmitry, who was now gravely ill. Since Tolstoy was technically still on active duty with the army, he had to apply for leave, and was unable to get away until 1 January. By that time he had been transferred to a naval munitions unit in St Petersburg, which effectively left him free to pursue his own interests. Dmitry was now living in Oryol, south-west of Tula, and was being cared for by Masha and her husband along with Aunt Toinette and his common-law wife – a former prostitute also called Masha. Tolstoy arrived on 9 January to find Dmitry ravaged by tuberculosis, and in great suffering, his emaciated face dominated by huge staring eyes. Unwilling to accept that he was going to die, Dmitry was convinced he would be healed with the help of a miracle-working icon, to which he prayed constantly. Tolstoy found the experience so distressing he left the next day. Dmitry died in his wife's arms on 22 January 1856.

Tolstoy had not been in touch with Dmitry for over a year, and had not even known his brother was ill. All the Tolstoys had their share of *dikost*, particularly Lev, but Dmitry gave him a good run for his money. They shared the same uncompromising maximalist impulse. After the fiasco Dmitry had suffered in St Petersburg, he had returned to his estate in Kursk province, and taken a minor job in local government. In 1853 he had fallen seriously ill in Moscow, where he grew a huge beard and became very reclusive. When he realised he had not much longer to live, he suddenly relinquished all his ascetic habits and former piety and abandoned himself to a debauched life of drinking, gambling and whoring. He had 'bought out' Masha from her brothel, and then treated her very badly, throwing her out only to call her back.[10] Dmitry, the 'unloved' brother, had written his last letter to Tolstoy from his Shcherbachevka estate in October 1854, telling him he had racked up nearly 7,000 roubles of debts and was sitting at home working in the garden and on the estate. Without telling his brother he was dying, he told him he was sad rather than bored: 'sad because I am alone, and not what I might have been, and finally because *nothing has quite worked out*'.[11] Tolstoy had not approved of Dmitry's sudden change of lifestyle, and did not reply. While he was in Oryol visiting Dmitry, he noted in his diary that all the bad thoughts he had harboured about him 'crumbled to dust' as soon as he saw him, but he still left.[12]

From Dmitry's deathbed, Tolstoy had travelled to Moscow, and it was here that he learned of his brother's death when the former prostitute Masha arrived back in the city. She told Tolstoy that Dmitry had only realised the hopelessness of his situation hours before he passed away, when he had started asking for a priest and a doctor, and pleading to be taken to Yasnaya Polyana so he could die quietly there. It was at Yasnaya Polyana that he was buried. Tolstoy later repented bitterly of being so wrapped up in his own life that he had not noticed the seriousness of his brother's condition earlier. He also felt remorse for the caddish way he had behaved towards him. In *Anna Karenina* he would bring Dmitry back to life again as Levin's brother Nikolay, a character who also has a relationship with a former prostitute. Having missed the real event, Tolstoy took particular care when it came to describing Nikolay's agonising demise in the only chapter in the novel to bear a title ('Death'), by which time he could also draw on the experience of witnessing his brother Nikolay die. Tolstoy also went out of his way at the end of his life to write at length about the real-life Dmitry in his memoirs.

Tolstoy stayed on in Moscow for about a month before returning to St Petersburg, which gave him the opportunity to meet those writers who were based in the old capital, such as Sergey and Konstantin Aksakov. As prominent Slavophiles opposed to to Russia's Westernisation, the Aksakovs would have never dreamed of living in the European-looking St Petersburg. The controversy amongst the Russian intelligentsia between the two warring camps of the Slavophiles and Westernisers had first flared up in the previous decade, and the impassioned public debates about Russia's present and future would continue for the rest of Tolstoy's life. He probably already knew he was not a Westerniser, but he would typically also come to reject Slavophile ideology in time, even though his preoccupation with traditional forms of native rural life would seem to make him a natural ally. When it came down to it, Tolstoy's egotism would simply not allow him to become part of a movement in which he and his ideas did not take centre stage. He returned to Petersburg at the end of January 1856. This time he wisely lived on his own, and stayed in the capital until the middle of May. The last of his war stories was published in *The Contemporary* in the January issue, but this time with a difference: 'Sebastopol in August' was the first of his works to be signed 'Count L. Tolstoy'.[13]

That spring he worked hard on two further stories, which were both published in *The Contemporary*. The first was 'The Snowstorm', which appeared in March, an artistically ambitious and visionary work inspired by the atrocious weather he had encountered during his journey home from the Caucasus in January 1854. 'The Two Hussars' was a gambling tale with a moral which compared two generations of the Russian nobility. It was dedicated to Tolstoy's sister Masha and appeared in May. As far as the editors of *The Contemporary* were concerned, Tolstoy was still their star writer, and at some point that spring he signed a contract with the journal. Along with Turgenev, Ostrovsky and Grigorovich, the journal's three other most valued writers, Tolstoy promised first refusal on new works for the next four years, in return for a share of its profits.[14]

Tolstoy came to regret signing that contract. His headstrong and eccentric views had been met with raised eyebrows and pursed lips during his first meetings with the Petersburg literary fraternity, but after he came back from Moscow in January there were remonstrations and then arguments, some of which became very heated, particularly with Turgenev. Tolstoy took offence easily, but he also gave offence easily. He was younger than his new friends, and sometimes seemed to be contrary just for the sake of it – he liked being outrageous. And then were arguments on subjects he had strong and dogmatic views about, such as the 'woman question'. The first major conflict arose in early February over the prolific French novelist George Sand, whom Turgenev greatly admired for her bravery and independent spirit. Tolstoy believed in the institution of marriage, and was not an adherent of women's emancipation (the 'girls' he visited in Petersburg's brothels were another matter, of course). It was a particularly charged argument, because of the *menage à trois* arrangement maintained by Nekrasov and his co-editor Panayev, whose wife Advotya was Nekrasov's mistress, as Tolstoy well knew. Another altercation with one of Nekrasov's colleagues on 19 March even led Tolstoy to challenge him to a duel. The challenge went unanswered, and for a while Tolstoy considered giving up literature and moving back to the country.[15]

Tolstoy did try to fit in and be part of the collective. At the end of March he arranged for a group photograph to be taken to mark the visit to St Petersburg of Alexander Ostrovsky, a promising new playwright.[16] This was quite an event, as Sergey Levitsky, the pioneer of Russian photography, had only just set up his studio on Nevsky Prospekt. In time he would receive an imperial warrant to photograph the Romanovs, but one of his most famous photographs remained the portrait organised by Tolstoy, the only writer in the shot wearing army uniform. Levitsky had studied in Paris and set up a studio there before returning to Russia, and he was an interesting man in his own right: apart from being Alexander Herzen's cousin, he had taken celebrated photographs of the Caucasus in the late 1840s, and much later on would inadvertently provoke Tolstoy into suddenly taking Orthodox Christianity very seriously. The 1856 photograph of *The Contemporary*'s writers became a permanent fixture on the wall of Tolstoy's study at Yasnaya Polyana.

Tolstoy would get to know Ostrovsky better a few years later, when he rented a house near to where he lived in Moscow. Ostrovsky's father was a Moscow lawyer, and he came from a far less privileged background than Tolstoy and Turgenev. His first play, *Bankruptcy*, had been personally censored in 1850 by Nicholas I, who had been so appalled by its depiction of Russian merchants as dishonest that he had placed the playwright under police surveillance. Ostrovsky's first stage success had come in 1853 with the production of his third play, *Don't Get Into Someone Else's Sleigh*, and he was now about to widen his horizons. In the optimistic climate following Nicholas I's death, the Tsar's liberal-minded younger brother Grand Duke Konstantin, who was in charge of the Marine Ministry, hatched an enlightened plan to send a group of eight young writers, rather than bureaucrats, on an expedition down the Volga to study the lives of those who fished and navigated its waters. Ostrovsky was one of the eight, and he left for the Volga in April 1856, as soon as the police surveillance on him was lifted.

April 1856 was also an important month for Tolstoy. At the end of March Alexander II had given the famous speech in Moscow in which he declared that it was better to abolish serfdom 'from above' than to wait for it to abolish itself 'from below'. The prospect of the Russian peasantry being freed was sensational news, and spread rapidly throughout the country.[17] Tolstoy immediately began to sketch out a project to free his serfs, having by this time joined the distinguished ranks of the Russian gentry whose awakened social conscience caused them to become 'repentant noblemen'. The first had been the eighteenth-century writer Alexander Radishchev, whom Catherine the Great exiled to Siberia in 1790 for exposing the evil of serfdom in his book *A Journey from St Petersburg to Moscow*. As a credulous young man, Radishchev had believed the myth that Catherine was enlightened and just. He had enjoyed an elite education, and so was frequently exposed to the 'richness and splendour' of the Russian court which for the British visitor William Coxe in the 1780s almost surpassed description.[18]

Radishchev was consequently shocked after the opulence of St Petersburg to discover quite how wretched the living conditions of the Russian peasantry really were when he left the city and began his journey to Moscow. He now began to see the immorality of the whole edifice of the tsarist autocracy for the first time, and also the role of the Russian nobility in supporting such an inhumane system, as becomes abundantly clear in the following passage:

> Twice every week all of the Russian Empire is informed that N. N. or B. B. is unable or unwilling to pay what he has borrowed, taken or what is demanded from him. The borrowed money has been gambled away, traveled away, spent away, eaten away, drunk away, given away or has perished in fire and water ... Any case will do for the announcement which reads: At ten o'clock this morning, on order of the county court or city magistrate, the real estate of retired captain T ... consisting of house no. X, in such and such a district, and six male and female souls, will be sold at auction ... Everyone is interested in a bargain. The day and hour of the sale has arrived. Buyers are assembling from all around. In the hall where the sale is to take place, the condemned are standing motionless. An old

man of 75 years, leaning on an elmwood cane, is anxious to find out into whose hands his fate will pass, who will close his eyes. He served with the Master's father in the Crimean campaign under Field Marshal Munnich. At the battle of Frankfurt he carried his wounded master off the field of battle on his shoulders. Returning home, he became the tutor for his young master. In [the Master's] childhood, he had saved the boy from drowning, jumping into the river into which he had fallen while crossing on a ferry, and putting his life at risk, pulled him out. In [the Master's] youth he had bailed him out of prison where he had been confined for his debts incurred while serving as a junior officer …[19]

It was Radishchev's book (republished by Herzen in London in 1858) which launched the birth of Russia's intellectual aristocracy – its intelligentsia. For the most progressive members of this class of Russians defined by their opposition to the state, of whom the editorial staff on *The Contemporary* were amongst their number, the abolition of serfdom was the single burning issue which needed to be addressed. Only writers had dared to broach this and other sensitive topics before the accession of Alexander II, hence their hallowed status in Russia, and the noble tradition of the writer as the moral voice of the nation would in time be continued by Tolstoy.

Tolstoy had become a confirmed opponent of serfdom while he was in Sebastopol, but his views were no doubt further influenced by the conversations he had with Nekrasov and his new colleagues. After many meetings and consultations, including with the historian and liberal thinker Konstantin Kavelin, whose proposal for the emancipation of the serfs had been circulating in samizdat form for the previous year, Tolstoy went to discuss his own emancipation plan with a senior bureaucrat at the Ministry of Internal Affairs. His intention was to give his serfs complete personal freedom, and to sell the land to them over a thirty-year period for 150 roubles for each *desyatina* (2.7 acres). The Ministry was not yet ready to make decisions on such matters at this point, but Tolstoy was firmly resolved.

Although he was promoted in March 1856 to the rank of lieutenant for his bravery in Sebastopol,[20] Tolstoy had little interest in continuing his military career. He immediately put in a petition for an eleven-month leave. The winter months he had spent in Petersburg had been exceptionally busy. He had largely managed to curb his degenerate habits and had worked hard on his writing, but there were a few cultural outings. The flat he had taken on Ofitserskaya Street was close to the city's two main opera houses, and on 4 May he sat in the same box as the composer at the premiere of Dargomyzhsky's *Rusalka* at the Circus-Theatre (home to the Russian opera, and forerunner of the Mariinsky Theatre).[21] Later in the month he took the train out to Pavlovsk, and is bound to have been at the second concert given that season by Johann Strauss Jr and his orchestra. Pavlovsk had become an important concert venue after the opening of the railway link with St Petersburg in 1837 (the first in Russia). The country's first railway station – called, for reasons that are not entirely clear, a *vokzal* after the English 'Vauxhall' – included a spacious and well-appointed pavilion where the performance of light music had turned into regular orchestral concerts during the summer months, and one of the first signs of the liberalisation of Russian society under Alexander II was the invitation to the 'Waltz King' to come to Russia. The arrival in Russia of dance music seemed to augur well for the new reign. On 16 May, the day after he went to Pavlovsk, Tolstoy was finally given permission to go on leave, which meant he could finally head back to Yasnaya Polyana and put his emancipation plans into action. Within two days he had packed his bags and departed.

By the end of May, after stopping in Moscow for a few days, and visiting the Trinity St Sergius Monastery with his aunt Polina, Tolstoy was finally back in Yasnaya Polyana. He had not lived at home for about five years, and he initially found it hard to readjust. First of all he had to get used to the gaping hole where his family home had stood, and it was strange living in one of the house's two identical wings. Secondly, after all the liberal talk in St Petersburg, the very idea of his being a landowner with serfs now seemed utterly repellent to him. He even found it difficult being with dear old ancien régime Aunt Toinette at first, as even she seemed 'unpleasant'.[22] Tolstoy immediately called a meeting with his peasants to propose his scheme for freeing them, but, to his surprise, they were suspicious of his motives, and did not give him a definitive response. The peasants were convinced they would be given their freedom when the new tsar was crowned, and so believed Tolstoy's offer of a contract was just a cunning ruse to swindle them. After several more meetings they refused all his revised offers. It was very frustrating for him, as he had not anticipated such distrust.[23] He resolved to put his emancipation plans to one side.

Tolstoy threw his energies instead into reading (Dickens's *Little Dorrit* was one book he immersed himself in that summer) and writing. Mostly he worked on *Youth*, the third and final volume of the quartet of short novels he had originally planned about the early life of a young noble, and the first draft of what came to be the novella *A Landowner's Morning*, in which he focused on Russian peasants for the first time. During the summer months Tolstoy also went on visits to his sister Masha and her husband, and rode over from their house to visit Turgenev at his estate at Spasskoye. His brother Nikolay by this time was back in the Caucasus. Despite having resigned from the army in 1854, the following summer he had applied to rejoin, and he had been posted back to Starogladkovskaya.[24] Sergey was briefly in the army too at this time, and Tolstoy was reunited with him in July in Mtsensk, where he was serving with the Life-Guards 4th Imperial Family Rifle Regiment (he had joined the army in March 1855, presumably on a wave of patriotic fervour engendered by the Crimean War, but he had already begun to tire of it, and was about to resign).[25]

What claimed most of Tolstoy's attention that summer was romance. His old university friend Dmitry Dyakov had suggested he marry Valeria Arseneva, a twenty-year-old neighbour who had become his ward upon the death of her father in 1854. Her family home was five miles away from Yasnaya Polyana on the road to Tula, and Tolstoy started making frequent visits, and cultivating her as a potential bride. It was an awkward relationship, as Tolstoy was not prepared to accept Valeria as she was – he wanted to mould her according to his ideal of womanhood. He was dreadfully disappointed when she seemed to take too much interest in dresses and dancing, while she seemed to have little idea of what he wanted from her. Reading between the lines of the many entries Tolstoy made in his diary about her, it appears his feelings of affection for Valeria were mostly wishful thinking. He wanted to be in love with her, and sometime he was 'almost' in love with her, but it was all too contrived.[26] All the time that he was courting her that summer, he found it impossible to restrain his guilt-provoking urges to pursue peasant women.[27]

By the onset of autumn 1856 Tolstoy had finished dictating *Youth* to a copyist and received author's copies of his first books: *War Stories* (which brought together his Sebastopol tales together with 'The Raid' and 'The Wood-Felling'), *Childhood* and *Boyhood*. He had also submitted his letter of resignation to the army on the grounds of illness, and by the end of November he was once again a civilian.[28] On 1 November he set off for Moscow, and then on to St Petersburg, still seeing Valeria as his future wife. The poor girl continued all autumn to receive patronising letters instructing her on what her role was to be, which was a mother (*mat'*) but not a queen bee (*matka*), and he asked her whether she understood the difference.[29] Some of the letters were long and very attentive, but some of the de-haut-en-bas directives were jaw-dropping in their self-righteous hypocrisy, when one bears in mind his own record. 'Your chief defect is weakness of character, and all your other minor faults proceed from it,' he wrote in one letter. 'Work on improving your willpower. Take yourself in hand and do battle with your bad habits.'[30] Tolstoy's already lukewarm ardour cooled further that autumn, and at the end of 1856 he wrote her a brusque letter breaking off relations, leaving her understandably feeling hurt and confused. In January he wrote a contrite letter of apology, but even then his admission of guilt before himself came before his admission of guilt before her.[31]

Before Tolstoy had signed his contract with *The Contemporary* he had promised a story to the journal *Notes of the Fatherland*, which was its main rival, and he spent much of his time in Petersburg that autumn working further on the story he had extracted from his unfinished *Novel of a Russian Landowner*, which he had been tinkering with ever since he had been in the Caucasus. In *A Landowner's Morning*, which was published in December, he fictionalised his own experiences in trying to improve the life of his serfs. In its concern to deal seriously with Russian peasants as fictional characters, it was a kind of *A Hunter's Notes* a decade further on, but under the new tsar, so much more could now be said. Importantly, *A Landowner's Morning* met with the approval of *The Contemporary*'s new critic Nikolay Chernyshevsky, who published a lengthy and influential review of Tolstoy's work to date in the journal's December issue.

Tolstoy and Chernyshevsky were the same age, and they both sought the abolition of serfdom, but there was nothing else they had in common. Chernyshevsky came from a new breed of a political radicals whose real goal was revolution. Both he and the younger Alexander Dobrolyubov, who joined *The Contemporary* in 1857, came from the same social and ideological stock as Belinsky, but they were dismissive of the ineffectual idealists of Turgenev's generation. As children of clergy, they were *raznochintsy* – a class which often denoted educated members of the intelligentsia who came from lowly back-grounds, and they were far more dogmatic about the need for art to serve a political purpose than Nekrasov and Panayev. Chernyshevsky had set the new agenda for *The Contemporary* in his 1855 essay *The Aesthetic Relations of Art to Reality*, in which he declared that 'beauty is life', and proclaimed art to be inferior to science.[32] In his review of Tolstoy's work, Chernyshevsky defined his technique in following the development of the evanescent thoughts and feelings of his characters as the 'dialectics of the soul', and compared it to the ability of certain painters 'to capture a flickering reflection of light on rustling leaves' or 'the play of colours in the changing outlines of clouds'.[33] By this he meant that Tolstoy was not so much interested in the end result of a psychological process as in the process itself. It was a deliberately flattering review, but it was clear that Tolstoy would not respond warmly to Cherny-shevsky's utilitarian views about art. As a result of Nekrasov's support of his radical younger colleagues, the left-wing political agenda of *The Contemporary* now started to be prioritised over artistic criteria, and this would lead to the journal losing all its top writers to the *Russian Messenger* in Moscow, Tolstoy included.

Once Tolstoy received his resignation papers from the army at the end of November, he was free to leave St Petersburg for good. He had set himself two goals, and accomplished both. Firstly, he had 'tested' his feelings for Valeria Arseneva, and proved to himself they had no substance, and secondly, he had completed *Youth* and submitted it for publication in January 1857. All he had to do now was obtain a foreign passport so that he could make his first trip abroad. After a month of tedious bureaucratic procedures, he was ready to set off for Moscow to prepare for his trip, and on 9 November (21 November according to the Gregorian calendar used in western Europe), he arrived in Paris at the end of a twelve-day journey. He had decided to travel alone, without a servant. The same evening, after unpacking his bags at the Hôtel Meurice on the rue de Rivoli, he set off to go to the traditional 'Samedi Gras' ball at the Paris Opéra, where he joined Nekrasov and Turgenev.

Tolstoy's six weeks in Paris were coloured by his meetings with Turgenev, whom he saw most days. By and large, they got on. Turgenev was spending more and more time abroad and knew the city extremely well, so would have been a marvellous guide. Tolstoy surrendered himself to sightseeing – the Louvre, Notre Dame, the Musée de Cluny, Napoleon's tomb at the Hôtel des Invalides ('terrible deification'),[34] the Père Lachaise Cemetery, and then trips out to Versailles, to Fontainebleau and further afield to Dijon. He also saw a lot of shows. He went to the Théâtre Français to see Molière and Racine, he heard *Rigoletto*, *Il Barbiere di Siviglia* and *La Fille du régiment* at the Italian Opera, an operetta at the Bouffes Parisiens and watched a farce at the Théâtre des Variétés. He also went to lectures at the Sorbonne. And then early in the morning of 25 March he went to witness a public execution by guillotine, an experience which traumatised him so much that he could no longer stay in Paris. Despite having had plans to go on to London (he had been taking English lessons in Paris), he headed instead for Geneva, for a reunion with Alexandrine and her sister, who were holidaying there along with Grand Duchess Maria Nikolayevna.[35] He told his sister by letter that he had arrived just before the end of Great Lent, and had fasted in order to take communion.[36]

Relieved to have escaped from 'Sodom and Gomorrah', as he referred to Paris, Tolstoy spent the next three and half months restoring his spirits in Switzerland. He also picked up his pen again, and caught up with his reading, which was eclectic, and included Gaskell's *Life of Charlotte Brontë*, De Tocqueville, Proudhon, Balzac, Las Cases' memoirs of Napoleon, and Goethe. Turgenev still found Tolstoy very bemusing. 'He's a strange person,' he confided in a letter to a friend. 'I've never met anyone like him, and don't quite understand him. A mixture of poet, Calvinist, fanatic, nobleman – something reminiscent of Rousseau, but more honest than Rousseau – highly moral and at the same time unattractive.'[37] Turgenev did understand Tolstoy better than most, and, knowing his low boredom threshold, predicted that his friend would soon tire of Lake Geneva. In fact, Tolstoy enjoyed his stay in Switzerland. It is true he did not stay still for very long, but the company of Alexandrine was very congenial. After two weeks they took a ferry across the lake to Clarens, from where he wrote excitedly to Aunt Toinette, telling her it was the same village where Rousseau's Julie had lived in *La Nouvelle Héloïse*. The scenery was ravishing. 'I won't try to describe to you the beauty of this country, particularly at the moment, when everything is in leaf and blossoming' ('Je n'essayerais pas de vous dépeindre la beauté de ce pays surtout à présent quand tout est en feuilles et en fleurs'), he wrote, telling her he found it impossible to detach his gaze from the lake. He spent most of his time going on walks, or just looking out of the window in his room.[38]

From Clarens there were excursions to Lausanne, Vevey, Montreux and Chillon, with walks in the mountains and picnics with other Russian visitors. At the end of May Alexandrine and her sister went back to Geneva and Tolstoy went on a walking tour in the Alps, taking with him for company Sasha Polivanov, the eleven-year-old son of some Russian acquaintances, as well as his diary and a supply of paper in his knapsack. It was the first time he had been in the mountains since being stationed in the Caucasus five years earlier, but the tranquillity of the picture-book Alpine pastures full of narcissi and well-fed cows with bells round their necks was a far cry from Chechnya. When the travellers got to Grindelwald, where Tolstoy went down a glacier, he started writing up his travel notes, thinking they could be published in some form or other in *The Contemporary*. The main focus of Tolstoy's writing in Switzerland, however, was the story which would eventually become *The Cossacks*.

Turgenev was right about Tolstoy being restless. Soon after returning from his eleven-day walking tour he was off again, to Bern and Fribourg. A few days after that he went back to Geneva, then on to Chambéry in Savoie, and many other places which brought the Savoyard vicar from Rousseau's *Emile* to mind. In Turin, Tolstoy met up with his friends the Botkins and Alexander Druzhinin. The return journey to Switzerland took Tolstoy first to Ivrea, followed by two ascents of Monte Rosa. Then came stops in Pont Saint-Martin, Gressoney and Chambave, and a night in the famous hospice founded by St Bernard in 1049, located at the highest point of the Great St Bernard Pass (the oldest in the Alps). Before descending, he looked round the monastery church and inspected the St Bernard dogs, who had been part of the monastery since the seventeenth century, and had saved the lives of hundreds of travellers stuck in avalanches.[39] Then it was back down into Switzerland, via the glorious Pissevache waterfall. The 114 metre-high fall had been visited by Rousseau and, in 1779, inspired Goethe to flights of rhetoric. By this stage, Tolstoy was making only brief notes in his diary, and his own enigmatic verdict on the waterfall was 'tumbling rye'.[40] Down on the lake at Villeneuve, Tolstoy caught a ferry back to Clarens.[41]

In early July Tolstoy travelled via Bern to Lucerne, where he took a room in the Schweizerhof Hotel and was reunited with Alexandrine. The Schweizerhof, built overlooking the lake in the heart of the old town in 1845, was as luxurious then as it is today (it prides itself on being one of the few hotels in Switzerland of 'national significance'). In 1857 it seemed to Tolstoy to be overrun with 'frigid', 'stuffy' English tourists, who seemed to like dining in complete silence. Tolstoy was also struck by the fact that they seemed oblivious to their surroundings, as demonstrated by an incident he later turned into a short story. One evening, after visiting a brothel, he came across a busker singing Tyrolean folksongs and accompanying himself on a guitar.[42] He was rather good, so Tolstoy suggested he go and sing under the windows of the Schweizerhof. There were soon wealthy guests flocking round him and enjoying his songs, but each time he proffered his cap, it remained empty. Tolstoy was astounded, and when the busker started trudging back into town he ran after him, took him back to the hotel and ordered a bottle of Moët. The passionate anger aroused in Tolstoy by the miserliness of the Schweizerhof's wealthy guests was initially expressed in a letter to one of his friends, and then turned into a story. But 'Lucerne' was pointedly not written in the Schweizerhof, as the hotel likes to claim, but in the modest pension he moved into straight afterwards.[43] Indeed, as a symbol of bourgeois Western civilisation, it is the object of the passionate invective unleashed in that story. Tolstoy read it to Nekrasov soon after arriving back in St Petersburg on the steamer he had boarded in the Prussian port of Stettin. 'Lucerne' was published in *The Contemporary* in September 1857 to a mixed response.

From Switzerland Tolstoy travelled to Germany, and on 24 July arrived in Baden-Baden, where his strength of will failed him. He soon lost all his money at the roulette tables, which necessitated humiliating begging letters to Alexandrine, Nekrasov and Turgenev. On 31 July Turgenev arrived in person and gamely bailed his friend out, and for once Tolstoy's customary derogatory diary entries about him changed to 'Vanechka is very nice'. Tolstoy then immediately gambled away all the money Turgenev lent him. His plans to travel to Holland and England now went up in smoke as he was forced to retreat to Russia. He also received a letter from home informing him that his sister Masha had separated from her husband, which was another reason for returning home quickly. None of the Tolstoy brothers had particularly liked Valerian Petrovich, but they had not known quite how depraved he was. It now emerged that when he was not away on hunting expeditions, or continuing to spend periods living with his peasant mistress, who had borne him several children, he had been a cruel and despotic husband. Turgenev described Valerian Petrovich as a 'most disgusting kind of rural Henry

VIII'.[44] The saving grace for Masha, who had stoically put up with her lot for ten years, were her three children. In the summer of 1857, no longer prepared to be the 'chief sultaness' in her husband's harem (Valerian Petrovich had at that point four mistresses, and was openly plotting his next move with one of them should he 'happen' to become a widower), Masha decided to leave him. She moved to her part of the Pirogovo estate and became Sergey's neighbour. Tolstoy went there the day after he arrived home.

Tolstoy was glad to be back at Yasnaya Polyana, but found that the 'crude, mendacious' side of Russian life only stood out in sharper relief after the freedoms taken for granted in other countries.[45] Despite having gravitated towards his fellow countrymen while he had been abroad (a proclivity he shared with many Russian travellers), and despite rejoicing in seeing birch trees again,[46] Tolstoy found the return to his homeland rather depressing. Imperial Russia was no longer the police state it had been under Nicholas I, but it was still a very long way from embracing the kinds of civil liberties that were the bedrock of Western civilisation. Russia was 'horrible, horrible, horrible,' he wrote to Alexandrine, describing to her numerous instances of casual brutality he had witnessed in the course of the first week he had been back. They included seeing a woman beating her servant girl and an official thrashing an old man whom he wrongly believed had tripped him up.[47] Tolstoy buried himself in Beethoven and the *Iliad*. He also renewed his efforts to come to a better arrangement with his serfs. Eventually they all transferred from the old *corvée* system to quit rent (effectively a 'buy-out' payment freeing them from their obligation to serve and enabling them to work the land for themselves), though years later he continued to feel guilty for demanding any kind of financial compensation from his serfs in return for allowing them to take over their own land. On what remained of his own property he now used hired labour, and freed all his house serfs.[48] Much of his experience negotiating with his serfs is reflected in Part Three of *Anna Karenina*, where Tolstoy describes how Levin's goodwill is rebuffed by his mistrustful peasants.

In October 1857 Tolstoy set off with Masha and her children to spend the winter in Moscow, settling in the unfashionable merchant quarter, the Zamoskvorechie, where the playwright Ostrovsky lived. Nikolay joined them there, having retired from army service for a second and final time. Tolstoy made two brief visits to St Petersburg that winter. During the nine days he spent in the capital at the end of October he had meetings with the Minister of State Property about a forestry project he had in mind, and spent time with Alexandrine. He also enjoyed a performance of Verdi's *Trovatore* (the prestigious St Petersburg Italian Opera was at the zenith of its popularity at the time), but otherwise it was a sobering visit. Tolstoy's new work had not been met with the acclaim that had greeted his first publications, and by criticising Western bourgeois civilisation in 'Lucerne' he was throwing down the gauntlet to critics like Chernyshevsky, who were heavily influenced by Western ideologies. Tolstoy had no interest in making contemporary political and social issues the subject of his writing, and he even toyed with the idea of founding a journal to counter these trends.[49] He was alienated by the new militant strain in Russian letters which brandished literature as a weapon for social reform, and dismissed aesthetic concerns as outmoded.

In February 1858 Tolstoy wrote to Nekrasov to tell him he wanted to end his contract with *The Contemporary*,[50] and when he went to St Petersburg for a brief visit in March he handed over the manuscript of his last work to appear in the journal.[51] Like 'Lucerne', the story 'Albert' is about an impoverished musician, and had taken Tolstoy over a year to finish. Notwithstanding the delay caused by the censor, Nekrasov took his time, publishing 'Albert' in the August issue of *The Contemporary*, which was its nearest equivalent to a 'graveyard slot' as the journal no longer wanted to solicit this kind of fiction.[52] 'Albert' is also another *profession de foi* in the sense that it expresses Tolstoy's belief that art should deal with eternal moral truth (*istina*) rather than the ephemeral truth of political ideology (*pravda*). His defiant defence of beauty was his way of responding to the challenge issued by Chernyshevsky, and it is probably not a coincidence that during his visit to St Petersburg in March he went to the Hermitage. One of the few highlights of Nicholas I's cultural policy was his decision to open the Hermitage as a public museum in 1852.[53] Tolstoy was impressed most of all by Ruisdael's landscapes, Rembrandt's *Prodigal Son* and *The Descent from the Cross* by Rubens.

During the winter season Tolstoy took another stand on behalf of the fine arts by helping to organise regular Saturday concerts, and even tried to set up a 'quartet society'.[54] He also was still hunting for a wife, and in December 1857 he had started homing in on the poet Tyutchev's young daughter Ekaterina. He was also slightly attracted to another young woman called Praskovya Shcherbatova, but in the end, despite Turgenev hearing rumours in Rome that his dalliance with Ekaterina Tyutcheva was becoming serious, he married neither of them.[55] Their names came in useful later on, however. Ekaterina Tyutcheva and her sister Darya were known affectionately as Dolly and Kitty, and they had an elder sister called Anna. In *Anna Karenina*, Kitty's surname is Shcherbatskaya, which is not so far off Shcherbatova.[56] In April 1858 Tolstoy headed back to Yasnaya Polyana. He had spent the previous winter participating in conventional social activities, but he was now about to make a break with the life he had led since returning from Sebastopol and settle permanently in the country.

Tolstoy did not stop writing in the summer of 1858, but this was the time of year he now preferred to devote to working on the land. He now threw himself into farming, acquiring the most modern ploughs and the best fertilisers, and reading up on the latest developments in agriculture. He occupied himself with forestry, planting trees in the Yasnaya Polyana park and selling peach, plum and pear trees that had been cultivated in his greenhouses. He worked in the vegetable garden and in the fields, ploughing, sowing and reaping, and also did a lot of physical exercise to keep fit and maintain his strength. As his brother Nikolay commented, he always wanted to 'embrace everything all at once, without leaving anything out, even gymnastics'. Sometimes the steward would come up to Yasnaya Polyana to receive instructions, and be greeted by Tolstoy hanging red-faced upside down from a bar he had installed outside the window of his study.[57]

That summer another side of Tolstoy's physicality manifested itself when he fell in love, more deeply than he had ever been before, with a young peasant girl from a village six miles from Yasnaya Polyana. Aksinya Bazykina had a largely absent husband, and Tolstoy found it hard to resist her charms. Their relationship was a serious one, and lasted for over a year. Later Aksinya gave birth to a son, who was regarded by everyone at Yasnaya Polyana as Tolstoy's illegitimate son (Timofey grew up to be a tall young man with fair hair and grey eyes, and he worked for Tolstoy as a coachman).[58] In his diaries Tolstoy recorded his trysts with 'A.' in the forest, and the times when he waited for her in vain, in one entry admitting to feeling more like a husband than a 'stag'.[59] At the end of his life, he would come to experience feelings of bitter remorse over the affair, which he sublimated in the writing of his late story 'The Devil'.

While Tolstoy enjoyed a euphoric summer of love in 1858, his sister Masha was pining. A tentative romance had sprung up between her and Turgenev since their first meeting in 1854, and now that she was free of her dreadful husband, she was keen for it to blossom. Turgenev had failed to come to back to Russia that year, however, and she was upset and lonely. Tolstoy, who knew all about Turgenev's devotion to the married opera singer Pauline Viardot, whom he followed around Europe, was incensed on Masha's behalf, feeling it very wrong to have made overtures to a young lady he had no intention of marrying.[60] It was a major factor in his rapidly deteriorating relationship with Turgenev.

In the winter, when Tolstoy could not so easily go on the prowl looking for Aksinya, he hunted animals. In late December 1858 he and his brother Nikolay were invited to go bear hunting with some friends – it was traditional to hunt bears in Russia while they were hibernating.[61] On the first day, armed with two rifles and a dagger, Tolstoy killed a bear, but on the second a bear nearly killed him after being frightened by the sound of a gunshot. Tolstoy was left with a permanent scar on his forehead and an anecdote to dine out on for the rest of his life (which he later wrote up as a story for children). Being of stern mettle, he was, of course, undeterred by his injury, and a few weeks later killed the bear which had attacked him.[62] The bearskin ended up as a rug for Yasnaya Polyana. That spring Tolstoy also went wolf and fox hunting. He had not completely abandoned writing since settling at Yasnaya Polyana. In January 1859 he published a story called 'Three Deaths'. A parable of art and morality which compares the deaths of a coachman, a tree and a cantankerous noblewoman, it is of a piece with 'Lucerne' and 'Albert', and also met a cool and uncomprehending reception. A much longer work published that year was the short novel *Family Happiness*, whose plot (older man marries a much younger girl who is his ward) clearly drew on his experiences with Valeria Arseneva. He was later very displeased with this work, which was also not particularly popular with the reading public, but it has many interesting qualities, not the least of which is the fact that it is narrated by a woman. It is also in this work more than any other that Tolstoy seems to be wrestling with the father figure of Turgenev as a writer, in a determined attempt to emerge from his shadow.[63]

Tolstoy's popularity with Russian readers may have dipped slightly, but his fiction was beginning to command princely sums. Tolstoy was paid 1,500 roubles by Mikhail Katkov for *Family Happiness*, which was published in the journal he edited, the *Russian Messenger*. Tolstoy immediately went and blew the lot during a session of Chinese billiards (a game similar to baga-telle, played on a board).[64] He would not publish any more fiction for almost three years, as what really claimed his attention now was popular educa-tion. When Tolstoy had come to the realisation that the peasants had so far resisted his efforts to improve their conditions because were they were simply too uneducated even to understand that he was working in their best interests, he resolved to teach them how to read and write. Less than six per cent of the rural population were literate in the 1850s.[65] There were no state schools in the countryside, even at the primary level, and what little tuition there was on offer from a village priest or a retired soldier (learning to read and write was one of the few benefits of army service) was primitive and had to be paid for. Teachers taught unimaginatively by rote, with the assistance of corporal punishment. Landowners were under no obligation to educate their serfs, and it is not surprising that in a country where the peasants were treated almost as a sub-human species, very few did. Tolstoy did not see the point in introducing railways, telegraphs and other forms of modernisation to Russia while there was no public education.[66]

In October 1859 Tolstoy reopened his school for peasant children at Yasnaya Polyana on a more serious footing than before. The peasants were initially very wary of the enterprise, not least because there was no charge (Tolstoy paid for everything out of his own pocket), but by March 1860 there were fifty pupils enrolled – boys, girls and also some adults. Tolstoy's main mission as an educator was to introduce freedom into the learning experi-ence, so pupils were allowed to come and go as they pleased, and there was no corporal punishment. There was a solid curriculum of twelve subjects, but Tolstoy placed great importance on the need for flexibility, to suit the needs of his pupils rather than those of the teacher. This was highly innovative. It was the Yasnaya Polyana school which gave Tolstoy an inkling of what he felt might be his true calling, as it was only when he undertook practical measures to redeem Russia's enormous debt towards its benighted peasantry that the voice of his conscience was stilled. As time went on, he realised it was going to be his destiny to swim against the current, but he was now starting to feel more comfortable in his own skin.

In May 1860 Tolstoy's brothers Nikolay and Sergey went abroad to Germany. Nikolay was now suffering from tuberculosis, as Dmitry had, and their plan was for him to undertake a cure at the spa town of Soden. Their hypochondriac sister Masha also felt unwell, so she too had decided to go for treatment abroad, taking her three children with her, and Tolstoy elected to accompany them. Classes at the school stopped anyway in the summer, when the children were needed to help in the fields, and he found an excellent deputy in Pyotr Morozov, a former seminary student, to take over from him as teacher at the Yasnaya Polyana school while he was away. He planned now to go to Europe to find out as much as he could about primary education in other countries. He would be away for almost a year.

Four days after leaving St Petersburg, Tolstoy was in Berlin. Masha took, Varya, Nikolay and Liza off to join Nikolay and Sergey in Soden, but Tolstoy went instead to Bad Kissingen, which was about sixty miles away. He was far more interested in finding out about German educational methods than taking the waters. The day after his arrival he set off to inspect the local schools, where he was horrified to observe coerced rote learning and liberal use of corporal punishment. He also started studying and making notes on various theoretical works on pedagogy. Pride of place in his reading list went to the four volumes of Karl Georg von Raumer's recently published *History of Pedagogy from the Revival of Classical Studies to Our Own Time*. In this work Tolstoy was pleased to discover that Martin Luther had been a pioneer of popular education, and also that his own belief in the necessity of freedom in teaching and learning had first been voiced by Montaigne in the sixteenth century.[67] Tolstoy's next step was to talk to teachers in the village schools around Bad Kissingen. He also met the politician nephew of Friedrich Froebel, who had founded the kindergarten system, and Wilhelm Heinrich Riehl, who had begun to publish his *Natural History of the German People as the Foundation of German Social Politics*.

Three months into his stay, Tolstoy received a visit from his sick brother Nikolay, whose condition was now worsening. Nikolay's doctors recommended he repair to somewhere with a warmer climate, so at the end of August, accompanied by Masha and the children, Tolstoy took him down to Hyères in the south of France. On 20 September, two weeks after they arrived, Nikolay died in Tolstoy's arms. Writing to Sergey afterwards, Tolstoy recalled that Nikolay had been a person whom they had loved and respected more than anyone else on earth. Indeed, Tolstoy had regarded Nikolay as his best friend, so his death was an incalculable blow.[68] Nikolay had never quite delivered on his great promise. He published a well-written sketch entitled

'Hunting in the Caucasus' in *The Contemporary* in February 1857, but had not followed it up with anything else. In a haze of grief, Tolstoy took himself off to Marseilles, where he visited eight primary schools and was again dismayed to encounter a narrow, lifeless approach to the education of young minds.

Tolstoy remained in Hyères with Masha and the children until the end of the year, and then in early 1861 travelled on to Nice and Florence, where he was excited to meet the recently amnestied Decembrist Prince Sergey Volkonsky, who was his distant relative and now an old man. From Florence Tolstoy travelled to Livorno, and then to Naples and Rome, where he met the painter Nikolay Ge, with whom he would later become great friends.[69] Tolstoy enjoyed seeing Italy, but his great passion at this time was still for pedagogy. In February he arrived in Paris, where he he set off to visit French schools, armed with a letter of recommendation from the Russian Ministry of Education. He also accumulated large numbers of books on pedagogy which were duly shipped back to Yasnaya Polyana. Then on 1 March he travelled on to London for his first visit to England, where he suffered severe toothache and confirmed his prejudices against the English. There is sadly very little documentation about Tolstoy's only visit to England, but we do know that the well-connected lawyer and journalist Henry Reeve sponsored his honorary membership of the Athenaeum Club in Pall Mall from 5 March to 6 April 1861.[70]

The most important meeting for Tolstoy in London was with the socialist thinker Alexander Herzen, who had emigrated from Russia in 1847. In 1852 Herzen had settled in London, where he first founded the Free Russian Press and then in 1857 the important newspaper *The Bell*, which campaigned for reform in Russia. Tolstoy made the journey to Herzen's handsome detached residence, Orsett House (located on Westbourne Terrace, near Paddington), several times during the sixteen days he spent in England. On 7 March Herzen wrote to Turgenev to tell him he had already quarrelled with Tolstoy, who was in his opinion 'stubborn' and talked 'nonsense', but was nevertheless an 'ingenuous, good person'.[71] On 11 March Tolstoy spent three hours at the Houses of Parliament, where he heard the prime minister, Lord Palmerston, give a speech on naval policy, which he found very boring. Of far greater interest to him was the reading given the following evening at St James's Hall, Piccadilly, by Charles Dickens, who was one of his favourite writers (as he was for many Russians). But his priority was to learn about British education. On 12 March, having been assisted by Matthew Arnold, an inspector of schools who had been appointed Professor of Poetry at Oxford in 1857, Tolstoy visited the Practising School at the College of St Mark in Chelsea, where he asked the boys in Class 3B to write an essay for him. He took their work back home to Russia.[72] Arnold arranged for Tolstoy to visit primary schools in Bethnal Green, Brentford, Spitalfields, Hoxton, Westminster and Stratford, but Tolstoy did not keep a diary during his visit to Britain, and it is not clear whether he visited any of them. We do know, however, that he made several useful visits to the library attached to the South Kensington Museum, which contained many interesting pedagogical materials. The future Victoria and Albert Museum had opened its doors two years earlier.

On 17 March (5 March in Russia), the day that Tolstoy left London, the Emancipation of Serfdom manifesto, which had been signed on 3 March (19 February), on the sixth anniversary of Alexander II's accession to the throne, was finally published.[73] The manifesto had been written by Metropolitan Filaret in a deliberately grandiloquent language suitable to be read in every church and published in every newspaper and Tolstoy was indignant, realising the peasants would never understand it. He was also angered by its tone, which seemed to suggest the manifesto was granting a favour rather than rectifying a grave injustice.[74] He was right to be angry. The peasants were no longer the property of landowners, but the terms by which they were freed left them no better off than before.

Tolstoy's next stop was Brussels, where he met the socialist politician Pierre-Joseph Proudhon,[75] author of *The General Idea of Revolution in the Nineteenth Century* (1851), amongst other works, and the former Polish politician Joachim Lelewel, who had taken part in the 1830 Warsaw Uprising. He also visited Belgian schools and had his photograph taken. The last portrait, taken in St Petersburg, had shown a serious-looking mustachioed officer with short-cropped hair. For his European travels, Tolstoy had dressed to the nines in long frock-coat and top hat, but was now already sporting the beard that would become an intrinsic part of his identity. After Brussels came his last months of travelling – to Antwerp, Frankfurt, Eisenach and Weimar, where there were more schools to inspect. He was hankering to go home at this point, but he wanted to get as much done as he could while he was in Europe, not knowing when he would return. (Never, as it turned out.) There were further stays in Jena, Dresden and Weimar, where he met Gustav Keller, a young mathematics teacher, whom he invited to come and teach at the Yasnaya Polyana school.[76] His final stop was Berlin, where he sought out the writer Berthold Auerbach, whose weighty (and now largely forgotten) novel *A New Life* (1851) had been highly influential on his decision to start his school for the Yasnaya Polyana peasant children in the first place. Tolstoy had clearly identified with its protagonist Eugen Baumann, an aristocrat who becomes a village schoolteacher. Without giving his name, Tolstoy simply marched up to Auerbach and announced 'Ich bin Eugen Baumann'.[77] He was very excited to meet Auerbach, recording the event with fifteen exclamation marks in his diary.[78]

On 13 April Tolstoy finally arrived back in St Petersburg. Before returning home he arranged meetings with the Minister of Education in order to ask formal permission to found a pedagogical journal, which was granted (no one in the ministry had any idea at this point quite how subversive Tolstoy's educational ideas would turn out to be). By May he was back in Yasnaya Polyana and holding classes in the apple orchard, but was restless as usual. At the end of the month, he travelled over to Spasskoye-Lutovinovo to visit Turgenev, who had just finished *Fathers and Sons*, the novel which explores the clash between the radical new 'nihilists' of the 1860s and the old-world generation of the 1840s. Turgenev read it aloud, and Tolstoy found it so boring he fell asleep. Turgenev was mortally offended. A couple of days later an argument flared up between them over a trivial matter when they went to visit Fet at his newly acquired country property. Tolstoy this time felt so insulted that he challenged Turgenev to a duel. He sent for arms from his nearby Nikolskoye estate, which he had inherited from his brother Nikolay, and spent a sleepless night, but the duel was never fought. Neither, though, was the friendship ever fully repaired. There followed a flurry of recriminations, apologies and letters which either failed to arrive at the right place or were read too late, and the situation was exacerbated by rumours of copies of these letters circulating in Moscow. Tolstoy considered Turgenev a coward, despised his liberalism and could not forgive him his lack of passion.[79] They agreed to cease all communication.

Turgenev was not the only person Tolstoy had testy conversations with that spring. Soon after returning home from abroad, he had learned that he had been appointed Justice of the Peace in his district by the liberal Tula governor.[80] The government had decided that arbiters should be elected from amongst the nobility to oversee the implementation of the manifesto and mediate between landowners and peasants. It was not an easy job for any Russian noble, but it was particularly challenging for Tolstoy, who was already loathed by his conservative neighbours for having granted his peasants their freedom ahead of the manifesto. Within a month he had fallen out with all of them. Many of the nobility saw it as their God-given right to have slaves, and so viewed the Emancipation of Serfdom Act as a disaster. In their opinion, Alexander II had robbed them. What on earth was a peasant going to do with his 'personal freedom' they wondered. A free peasant in their view was like a stray dog – not worth giving a crust to, as it would eventually come to grief anyway. It never occurred to Russia's reactionary nobles that the peasants were human beings like themselves, and that they were just as responsible in creating the ignorance and misery which led the peasants to drink as the regime. The reactionary nobility looked to the Justices of the Peace to take care of their interests, and be on their side. Tolstoy, however, had the peasants' interests at heart, and he now viewed most of his fellow nobles as vile parasites.[81] His neighbours had soon filed a barrage of complaints about him, which they sometimes did en masse, but this only made Tolstoy rub his hands with glee. He took relish in exposing the dishonesty and cruelty of the *krepostniki* – the defenders of serfdom – and was not deterred even when he received threatening and abusive letters or was summoned to fight duels.

Tolstoy had also not endeared himself to his neighbours by wanting to educate his peasants. It seemed preposterous to the krepostniks that a count, a retired officer, should become a teacher, while the very idea of a school for peasant children seemed outlandish to these hardened apologists of patriarchal Russia. The Yasnaya Polyana school was flourishing, but it was the only one in the whole district. With 9,000 peasants living in the area, however, Tolstoy wanted to do more. Using his position as Justice of the Peace, he had twenty-one schools up and running locally by the autumn of 1861. The schools were set up in peasant huts. There were no desks or chairs or blackboards, but the walls were usually so dirty that they served very well to write on with chalk. Some of the teachers were the usual priests and ex-soldiers, but Tolstoy also employed former university students who were in need of employment. Widespread demonstrations had erupted the previous October when the government introduced a series of ill-conceived university reforms, including obligatory attendance and fees which many students could not afford, and large numbers of them had been expelled. Each student teacher was paid fifty kopecks per pupil per month, so monthly salaries averaged about ten roubles. Teachers were also paid an honorarium for contributing to the *Yasnaya Polyana* journal.[82]

The first issue of *Yasnaya Polyana* was published in January 1862, and eleven more followed. Although some articles were written by teachers, the journal's editor Tolstoy was also its most prolific contributor. In the first issue he provided an account of the day-to-day life at the school in Yasnaya Polyana:

> No one brings anything with him, neither books nor copybooks. No homework is set them. Not only do they carry nothing in their hands, they have nothing to carry even in their heads. They are not obliged to remember any lesson, nor any of yesterday's work. They are not tormented by the thought of the impending lesson. They bring only themselves, their receptive nature, and an assurance that it will be as jolly in school today as it was yesterday … No one is ever scolded for being late … They sit where they like: on the benches, tables, window-sills, floor or in the armchair … By the timetable there should be four lessons before dinner, but sometimes in practice these become three or two, and may be on quite different subjects … In my opinion this external disorder is useful and necessary, however strange and inconvenient it may seem to the teacher … First this disorder, or free order, only frightens us because we were ourselves educated in and are accustomed to something quite different. Secondly, in this as in many similar cases, coercion is used only from hastiness or lack of respect for human nature …[83]

Tolstoy's child-centred approach, then, was based on there being a complete freedom to learn. In addition to accounts of the activities of his schools, Tolstoy contributed lengthy articles about his teaching methods to the *Yasnaya Polyana* journal, arguing that the much-vaunted European system was fundamentally flawed, and inapplicable to Russia, which had to find its own way.[84] The journal issues were accompanied by supplements of reading matter for children. These contained stories written by the pupils at Tolstoy's schools, or written down by their teachers, and brief articles written in a clear, simplified language on historical topics. Tolstoy invested an enormous amount of effort in his schools, and he loved all his peasant pupils. The feeling was mutual, and was helped by the fact that he had begun to dress like a peasant, and never stood on ceremony. He was a marvellous storyteller, of course, but he also threw himself into other extra-mural activities, such as snowball fights and tobogganing in the winter. For Shrovetide in 1862 Tolstoy invited 100 pupils from different villages to Yasnaya Polyana for *bliny*. At Easter the children received gifts of pencils, mouth-organs and pieces of calico which could be used by their mothers to make shirts for them.[85]

While the Ministry of Education approved of Tolstoy's pedagogical activities, the Ministry of Internal Affairs took a very different view. Along with Tolstoy's adversaries amongst the landowners in his district, the Ministry of Internal Affairs perceived Tolstoy's schools as hotbeds of anarchy and revolution. The arrival of radical students was the last straw, and a secret police file was opened on Tolstoy in January 1862. It detailed Tolstoy's contacts abroad with dangerous figures like Herzen and Lelewel, his employment of politically active students and the trouble that had been caused by his actions as a Justice of the Peace. Tolstoy's landowner neighbours were delighted to supply the police with regular denunciations, including the spurious charge that Tolstoy had set up an underground printing press. A fat file of evidence against Tolstoy started to build up.

In the tense atmosphere that was exacerbated by peasant riots and student unrest around the time of the emancipation, the publication of Turgenev's *Fathers and Sons* in March 1862 was like the explosion of a bomb. In his young university graduate hero, the 'nihilist' Bazarov, Turgenev had created the first fictional *raznochinets*, but both the 'fathers' and the 'sons' felt they had been ridiculed, and the novel created a storm of controversy. As its first English translator commented a few years later, 'passionate criticisms, calumnies, and virulent attacks abounded … Of course the more the book was abused, the more it was read. Its success has been greater than that of any other Russian book.'[86] Tolstoy was probably the only person in Russia who found it boring. His mind was on other matters that spring. The stress caused by other Justices of the Peace obstructing all his initiatives and the mounds of paperwork generated by his job were debilitating, and had started to make him ill. To the rejoicing of all the vindictive landowners who wanted revenge on the man who had ruined their corrupt livelihoods, Tolstoy resigned his post in April 1862. Shortly afterwards he set off for the steppes beyond Samara, taking with him two of his favourite pupils and his servant Alexey. He planned to undergo a koumiss cure, hoping to restore his frayed nerves.[87] Tolstoy's hostile neighbours wreaked their greatest revenge on him later that summer. In July 1862, soon after the government had shut down *The Contemporary*, Chernyshevsky was arrested for spreading revolutionary propaganda and exiled to Siberia. That same month the tsarist secret police descended on Yasnaya Polyana, where they conducted a two-day search of the estate, hoping to find seditious material connected with his schools. Aunt Toinette was so traumatised by the intrusion of the police into the tranquillity of her home that she became ill, and Tolstoy's sister Masha, who was staying at Yasnaya Polyana and sleeping in his study, had to endure tsarist gendarmes rifling through her brother's papers and reading everything he had ever written. The police ransacked the entire house, including the cellars and the water-closet, and placed Tolstoy's twelve student teachers under arrest, but were forced to go away empty-handed.[88] Tolstoy was livid when he discovered what had happened upon his return from Samara at the end of July, and he vented his fury and anguish in a passionate letter to Alexandrine. 'It was my whole life, my monastery, my church, in which I found salvation, and saved myself from all the worries, doubts and temptations of life,' he wrote, describing how important his school work was to him.[89] Fearing that the police action had irreparably damaged his reputation for probity amongst the peasants, he decided he should close his schools down, and by the following spring all the teachers had left (Gustav Keller, the young German mathematics teacher, went to tutor Sergey Tolstoy's son Grisha). But there was another reason why Tolstoy suddenly lost interest in his schools: he had finally found the woman he wanted to marry.

· 7 ·

HUSBAND, BEEKEEPER AND EPIC POET

The epic genre is becoming the only one natural to me.

Diary entry, 3 January 1863[1]

AT SOME POINT in the autumn of 1862 Tolstoy received a surprise visit from the father and grown-up daughter of a large family he had helped to evacuate during the siege of Sebastopol. His visitors were themselves surprised to discover that Tolstoy had married, and they were to encounter a further surprise. When Tolstoy's wife came running into the drawing room to meet the visitors, the beautiful, tall young lady she was introduced to could not help staring at her. 'What, Lev Nikolayevich,' she blurted out, 'this young girl is your wife?' Sofya Andreyevna was indeed very young – she had just turned eighteen, and would have looked even younger, as she was wearing a short brown cotton dress rather than the elegant gown the guests were clearly expecting the new Countess Tolstoy to be wearing. Tolstoy had specially ordered and purchased it for her, on the grounds that he would never be able to find his wife under the steel-hooped crinolines and dresses with long trains fashionable at that time. He also did not believe that such formal attire was suitable in the countryside anyway. Sonya had become pregnant almost immediately after their wedding, and the dress was loose-fitting as well as very plain.[2] Her husband's own preferred attire in the countryside was a baggy grey flannel shirt, belted around the waist, worn loose over trousers tucked into boots.[3]

Tolstoy was embarking on the happiest years of his life, but there was no question of husband and wife ever being equal partners in this marriage. At thirty-four, Tolstoy was acutely conscious of his bride being a child, and he even refers to her as such in his diaries.[4] He was also only two years younger than his mother-in-law, Lyubov Alexandrovna Bers, whom he had known since childhood, their fathers having been good friends. Indeed, his youngest brother-in-law, Vyacheslav, was just one year old when Tolstoy married his sister Sonya. Nevertheless, it suited Tolstoy to have a young girl as his bride. As their son Sergey would later comment, his father was deeply in love with his mother when he married her, but he also wanted someone he could educate and mould according to his own tastes.[5] Sonya, happily, accepted her husband's moral authority from the beginning, and even directly referred to herself in letters to him in the early years of their marriage as his 'eldest daughter'. In one letter she reassures her husband that she has not forgotten his 'parental advice'.[6]

Then there was the difference in social backgrounds. Sergey also notes at the start of his memoirs that his father had not wanted to marry an aristocrat like himself. As the daughter of a doctor descended from a German immigrant and an illegitimate Russian noblewoman, Sonya certainly could not boast such an impressive pedigree. When she married, she took on a title as well all her husband's views, and she liked being Countess Tolstoy. Her husband later renounced his title, but she continued to sign herself 'Grafinya S. A. Tolstaya' (*grafinya* being a Russian form of the original German *Gräfin*). Sonya never had the time to ruminate on the religious and philosophical ideas which inspired her husband's radical change of lifestyle – she was too busy raising their family – so it was all the harder for her to repudiate the values he had so carefully inculcated her with during the first decades of their marriage and suddenly live another kind of life.

Sonya's great-grandfather was Johann Bärs (or Behrs), an officer in the Horse Guards from Saxony, whose coat-of-arms depicted a bear repelling a swarm of bees, as befits a surname derived from the German word for bear.[7] Ivan Bers, as he became known in his Russianised incarnation, was sent to St Petersburg by Empress Maria Theresa in the mid-eighteenth century to assist Empress Elizabeth with Russian military training. Before he was killed in action in 1758 at the Battle of Zorndorf, he married and had a son, Evstafy (Gustav), who grew up in Moscow, became a chemist and married into another Russianised German family. Evstafy Bers lost all his wealth and possessions in the great Moscow fire of 1812, but through his German connections was able to give his two sons a fine education. They both became students at Moscow University in 1822, and trained as doctors at the same time as Russia's most famous nineteenth-century medical practitioner Nikolay Pirogov. One of the two sons was Sonya's father Andrey, born in 1808.

Owing to its low social rank, medicine was not a highly regarded profession in early-nineteenth-century Russia, and certainly never pursued by aristocrats. At the time the Bers brothers qualified, when they were about twenty years old, the most respected doctors were still foreign, but still socially inferior. In the late 1820s Andrey Bers became family doctor to the Turgenevs (when the future writer was still a boy), and accompanied them to Paris. For the next two years he devoted himself to further study, Italian opera, and, it seems, Turgenev's redoubtable and unhappily married mother, who bore him an illegitimate daughter, Varvara, whom she raised as her ward (which makes Sonya Turgenev's half-sister). After he returned to Moscow, Andrey Bers started working as a doctor attached to the Senate, which was located in the Kremlin, and then under Nicholas I he was appointed court physician. This entitled him to a cramped, low-ceilinged state apartment adjacent to the Kremlin Palace, the Tsar's imposing 700-room Moscow residence. This is where Sonya was born in 1844.

The family was never wealthy. They had servants in their Kremlin apartment, of course, but they never owned a country estate or possessed any serfs. Working for the Russian state meant that Dr Bers entered the civil service and the Table of Ranks, thereby gaining greater social respectability. Indeed, by finally attaining the eighth rank of collegiate assessor in 1842, Andrey Estafevich was entitled to acquire hereditary nobility, but he was still considered a very unsuitable match for sixteen-year-old Lyubov Islavina, to whom he proposed after treating her as a patient. Quite apart from the fact that her family were old-world Russian aristocrats, albeit an illegitimate branch, who regarded him as little better than a tradesman, Bers was by this time already thirty-four, and a Lutheran to boot. Nevertheless, the marriage went ahead, and Andrey and Lyubov Bers had eight children. Sonya was the middle of three daughters, who were all educated at home, first by German governesses. When she was sixteen, in 1860, Sonya acquired a private teaching qualification from Moscow University. By this time she had got to know Tolstoy's family quite well, having taken dancing lessons on Saturday afternoons one winter with his sister Masha's three children. Masha had been her mother's friend since childhood, and when the Bers came to visit Varya, Liza and Nikolay at home, their uncles Lev and Nikolay would sometimes be there as well.[8]

When Tolstoy first started to visit the Bers during his trips to Moscow, everyone assumed he was interested in the eldest daughter Elizaveta (Liza). But in the summer of 1862 he turned his attention to Sonya. It was an eventful few months. When the secret police had raided Yasnaya Polyana that summer Tolstoy had been away on the Bashkirian steppe taking his two-month koumiss cure, having been in poor health. He learned of the raid only when he visited the Bers in Moscow on his way back home back to Yasnaya Polyana at the end of July. Days later he had guests. Lyubov Alexandrovna, plus her three daughters and youngest son were on their way to spend a couple of weeks at Ivitsy, her father's estate, which was not far away, and they decided to stay the night with Tolstoy. Lyubov had not been to Yasnaya Polyana since she was a child, and she was shocked by the patch of weeds growing in the gaping empty space where the old house had stood before being dismantled by its new owner. The wing that Tolstoy had settled in had never been intended to be a principal home, and it was quite a squash accommodating everybody. Along with the permanent residents (Tolstoy, Aunt Toinette and her companion Natalya Petrovna), his sister Masha was still staying, and now there were five extra guests. Beds were made up on the blue-and-white striped sofas downstairs for the three girls Liza, Sonya and Tanya, then twenty-seven, eighteen, and sixteen years respectively. A few months later the spartanly furnished room would be where Tolstoy sat down to write the opening chapters of *War and Peace*.[9]

After being shown around, the city-dwelling Bers children were most excited to be taken into the garden to pick raspberries. Tolstoy, meanwhile, was distracted from his preoccupation with the recent disturbing events by the charms of Lyubov Alexandrovna's ingenuous middle daughter. No sooner had the Bers arrived at Ivitsy than 'le Comte', as they called him, came riding over on his white horse to visit them.[10] This is when he started communicating with Sonya by spelling out the first letters of words with a piece of chalk, which he would later immortalise when describing Levin's courtship of Kitty in *Anna Karenina*. One can only marvel at Sonya's ability to understand the words behind the letters 'V. v. s. s. ı. v. n. n. i. v. s. L. Z. m. v. s. v. s. T.', which in English would read: 'In your family there is a false view of me and your sister Liza. You and your sister Tanya must defend me.' A week later Tolstoy decided to accompany the Bers back to Moscow, and he then spent the next two weeks walking almost daily to visit them at their dacha five miles north of the city, and falling more and more in love with 'S', as he refers to her in his diaries.

During this euphoric time Tolstoy tried to concentrate on a pedagogical article he was writing, but not very successfully. He did, however, write a forceful letter to Alexander II in which he complained in the strongest terms about the search of his estate:

> I consider it unworthy to assure Your Majesty that the insult I have suffered is undeserved. All my past, my contacts, my activities in serving people's education, which are open to all, and finally the journal in which my most heartfelt convictions are expressed, could have proved to anyone interested in me, without the deployment of measures which have destroyed people's peace and happiness, that I could not have been a conspirator, an initiator of proclamations, murders or arson. Apart from the insult, suspicion of criminal activities, apart from the opprobrium in the opinion of society and that feeling of eternal threat, under which I am obliged to live and work, as a result of this visit, I have completely plummeted in the opinion of the people, which I have cherished, which I spent years earning, and which was vital for the activity which I had chosen – the foundation of schools for the people.

Alexander II happened to be visiting Moscow, which meant the letter could be hand-delivered. The Tsar did not bother to reply to Tolstoy himself, but Prince Dolgorukov, the head of the secret police, was instructed to send a mealy-mouthed letter of self-justification to the governor of Tula for him to pass on.[11]

Fortunately Tolstoy had other things to occupy him at this time. Rather than return to Yasnaya Polyana, he had stayed on in Moscow when the Bers returned to their Kremlin apartment at the beginning of September, and for once the strength of his romantic feelings stopped him from becoming too self-analytical. The previous year, when he was considering the merits of another woman as a potential bride, his sister Maria had warned: 'For heaven's sake, don't analyse too much, because once you start analysing, you always find some stumbling block in every straightforward issue, and without knowing how to respond to *what and why*, you run away.'[12] He had indeed prevaricated back then, and nothing came of the liaison, but this time he moved swiftly, perhaps realising the dangers of reflection. On Sunday 16 September he proposed to Sonya and, at his insistence, they were married seven days later.

It was not just the fact that the engagement lasted only a week which made their marriage quite unusual, or even that Sonya could only eat pickled cucumbers and black bread in the days leading up to the wedding.[13] Tolstoy offered his fiancée the choice of going back to live with her parents, a honeymoon abroad, or starting their new life straight away in Yasnaya Polyana.[14] Sonya chose the last option; she never went abroad even later in her life. There was no time for Lyubov Alexandrovna to sew her daughter a complete trousseau, but Tolstoy made sure to give Sonya his old diaries to read, not wanting to conceal anything in his past. As an innocent and inexperienced girl who had seen little of life, she was deeply shocked and upset by what she later termed his 'excessive conscientiousness'. The previous month she had given him a thinly disguised autobiographical story to read, it is true, in which she described a young girl being courted by a prince of 'unusually unattractive appearance' and volatile opinions.[15] But this was different. Sonya found it painful to learn about his sexual conquests and romantic liaisons with peasant women, no matter how much he now repented of them.[16] Her father, meanwhile, was seething with anger. Initially opposed to the marriage, he felt deeply for his slighted elder daughter, who should have been the one to marry first, and he was only gradually reconciled. Sonya's mother was also hardly overjoyed by the match, and for a while adopted a patronising tone with Tolstoy, whom she continued to call by his childhood nickname of 'Lyovochka'.[17] Both parents were well aware, however, of Tolstoy's eligibility, and of the unlikelihood of finding similar suitors for their other daughters.

The wedding was scheduled for eight in the evening but was delayed by at least an hour and a half. In the haste of all the packing that had to be done in preparation for the journey to Yasnaya Polyana, which would begin immediately after the ceremony, Tolstoy's servant had forgotten to leave out a clean shirt for him. Thus instead of his best man arriving at the Bers' apartment to announce that the bridegroom was waiting in the church, a sheepish Alexey Stepanovich came to rummage through the packed luggage.[18] The ceremony took place at the Church of the Nativity of Our Lady in the heart of the Kremlin, minutes from the Bers' apartment. Dating back to the late fourteenth century, this small church is the oldest of all the Kremlin buildings, and in the nineteenth century it became part of the Great Palace built by Nicholas I. (All one can see of it nowadays is its single white drum and golden cupola rising above the palace's green rooftop – it has not been returned to the Orthodox Church, nor is it open to the public.) Unlike the grand cathedrals nearby, where state occasions were held, this was a church attended by those who lived and worked in the Kremlin, and on the evening of Tolstoy's wedding it was filled with gatecrashers – curious employees of the court who worked in the palace – as well as the small number of invited guests. None of Tolstoy's own family were present except for his aunt Polina, who accompanied Sonya to the church in the carriage, along with her nine-year-old brother Volodya, who carried the icon of St Sophia the Martyr she had just been blessed with by her mother and uncle. Tolstoy's brother Sergey had been in Moscow, but had departed already so that he could organise a proper welcome party for the couple at Yasnaya Polyana.[19] His sister Masha was in Marseilles.

Late in the evening, after the celebratory champagne, and after observing the Russian custom of sitting down and saying prayers before going on a journey,[20] the newly-weds set off in the brand new *dormeuse* Tolstoy had purchased for the occasion: a particularly well-sprung carriage with extensions so that a bed could be made up for the occupants. It came with six horses, driven by a coachman and postilion. Sonya found it difficult to leave her family, as she had never been parted from them before, nor had she ever travelled in the autumn or winter, let alone at night. The light given off by the streetlamps of Moscow was exchanged for pitch blackness as soon as they left the city. It was also raining heavily. Still unable to pluck up the courage to switch from the *vy* form of address to the more intimate *ty* with her husband, Sonya was also terrified: they had never been alone before. The married couple barely spoke before stopping at the coaching inn in Biryulevo, fifteen miles south of Moscow, where they spent their wedding night. 'She knows everything', 'Her fright', 'Something painful' were amongst the pithy telegraphic comments Tolstoy made in his diary after they finally arrived at Yasnaya Polyana the following evening.[21] A couple of weeks later Sonya was evidently still struggling to come to terms with the 'physical manifestations' of their relationship, which she found appalling, but which she discovered were clearly so important to him.[22]

At the house they were greeted by Sergey, who offered the traditional Russian bread and salt as a sign of welcome, and by Aunt Toinette, holding up the family icon of the Mother of God of the Sign. Sonya bowed deeply before them both, crossed herself, kissed first the icon and then Aunt Toinette. Tolstoy did the same.[23] Over the next few days Sonya met the various members of the household as they came to offer their congratulations to the happy couple. They included Nikolay Mikhailovich the cook, Anna Petrovna the cowherd, accompanied by her daughters Annushka and Dushka, grandmother Pelageya Nikolayevna's old maid Agafya Mikhailovna, always knitting stockings, even while she was walking about,[24] the jolly laundrywoman Aksinya Maximovna and her pretty daughters Polya and Marfa, as well as the coachman, the gardener, the pastry cook and numerous other servants and peasants from the estate and neighbouring villages. Sonya's mother had thoughtfully given her 300 roubles, so she would not have to depend on her husband for money initially, but it nearly all disappeared as gifts to those who came to offer congratulations. Henceforth, Sonya was entirely dependent on her husband in financial matters, and disliked having to ask him for money. He never made her feel she was a penniless bride without a dowry, however, nor that his wealth belonged to him alone, she notes in her autobiography.[25]

Yasnaya Polyana was now also Sonya's domain, and she would barely leave it for the first eighteen years of her marriage. Aunt Toinette put Sonya in charge of running the house straight away, handing her an enormous bunch of keys on a ring, which she later hung from the belt round her waist. Sonya had not grown up in luxury, but she was nevertheless taken aback by the austerity ('almost poverty') of her new surroundings. Her husband was used to sleeping on a grubby dark red leather pillow without a pillowcase,[26] and there was no bath anywhere in the house. Sonya was determined to change that. When her trousseau arrived, her silverware replaced the ancient metal cutlery and a silk eiderdown replaced the cotton one, which, much to her husband's amazement, she lined with a sheet.[27] She embroidered 'L.T.' in red on his underwear.[28] After finding an unpalatable species of vermin in her soup one day, Sonya also tackled the lack of hygiene in the kitchen. White chef's jackets and hats soon materialised, and Sonya took over responsibility for the daily menu. Over time she built up a Yasnaya Polyana cookery book consisting of 162 recipes, for everything from 'Partridge in Herring Sauce' and 'Duck with Mushrooms' to 'How to Cook a Pike'. Then there were recipes for traditional Tolstoy dishes such as almond soufflé, and black bread pudding, or the special Bers recipe for apple pie, and Marusya Maklakova's lemon kvass (comment: 'very good').[29] Sonya came to be very fond of Nikolay Mikhailovich the cook, even if he was too drunk to turn up to work sometimes, and had to be replaced by his breezy wife. He had once played the flute in old Prince Volkonsky's serf orchestra, and had turned to cooking when he lost his embouchure, as he recounted to her with a sad, wry smile.[30]

The first few days and weeks, while Lev and Sonya were setting up house together, were a mixture of wild happiness and the inevitable friction caused by the differing habits and expectations of two people who in reality barely knew each other. Tolstoy wrote to Alexandrine soon after arriving back at Yasnaya Polyana to tell her that he had not known that it was possible to be so happy, and that he loved his wife more than anything else in the world.[31] He also commented on experiencing 'unbelievable joy' in his diary, but just a few days later he recorded having an argument with Sonya, and expressed his sadness at discovering their relationship was no different from that of any other couple.[32] By this time, Sonya had resumed the diary she had started keeping two years earlier, and she now turned to it whenever she began to sense she was losing her husband's affections. She was certainly beginning to lose his attention. Tolstoy could occupy himself with domestic matters and marital bliss up to a point, but after a while the prolonged distraction from intellectual pursuits began to be irksome. Three weeks into their marriage, he confided to his diary: 'All this time I have been busy with matters which are termed practical. But I'm finding this idleness difficult. I cannot respect myself. So I am not satisfied with myself and not clear in my relationships with others ... *I must work* ...'[33]

First of all, Tolstoy was behind with the August and September issues of his journal *Yasnaya Polyana*. His heart was no longer in it, but there were two articles for it that he needed to finish, one of which typically put forward the Tolstoyan idea that the peasant children actually had more to teach their supposed teachers than the other way round. At the end of September Sonya's spurned elder sister Liza sent in the brief article about Luther she had been commissioned to write by Tolstoy. It was conceived as one of the popular historical sketches he hoped would interest peasant children. Whether it was due to her suddenly being elevated to a countess, or just plain jealousy of anything which took her husband away from her, Sonya resented and disliked Tolstoy's involvement with the peasantry. Having grown up in the city, peasants were alien beings to her, and neither then nor later did she understand her husband's deep devotion to them. She certainly never came to share his love of the muzhik, much to his chagrin. But there was an additional reason for her jealous resentment: she had read with horror the entries in his diary about his romantic liaison with the peasant girl Aksinya Bazykina, such as the one in which he claimed that he was in love 'like never before'. Sonya knew she might run into her any day, because Aksinya had not, of course, moved away and was still working on the estate. 'I've been reading the beginnings of his works,' she wrote now in her own diary on 16 December 1862, 'and I'm disgusted and sickened by everywhere where there is love, where there are women, and I'd like to burn absolutely all of it. So that I don't have to be reminded of his past.'[34]

The trouble was, Tolstoy's involvement with the peasantry was also a creative and linguistic one. Fighting in the Crimean War had revealed to him how great was the abyss between the educated classes and the peasantry. Reluctant to continue writing solely for the nobility, he had resolved to try to bridge that abyss, not only by writing fiction in which the protagonists were peasants, but in an unvarnished language and style that was close to peasant speech. His first experiments in this vein had produced several unfinished stories which he returned to in the first few months after he married, and Sonya helped with the completion of one of them by writing out a fair copy to send to the publisher. Thus began what was to be an extraordinarily fruitful partnership, in which Sonya acted as amanuensis to her husband, performing an invaluable service by deciphering the often barely legible handwriting of the amendments which were invariably crammed into the margins of his tortuously composed drafts. 'Polikushka', a parable about the evils of serfdom, was the first story Sonya copied out,[35] and it was published in early 1863.[36] Another of Tolstoy's stories of peasant life was entitled 'Tikhon and Malanya', but at some point in December 1862 he abruptly stopped working on it, most likely for the simple reason that the central female character Malanya was modelled on Aksinya. He never returned to it, and it was published for the first time only after his death.[37]

Marriage diverted Tolstoy from the path taking him closer to the peasantry that he had started out on. He now embarked on the lengthy but productive detour which just happened to result in him writing *War and Peace* and *Anna Karenina*. Tolstoy's changes of direction may no longer have been as frequent as when he was in his twenties, but they were no less violent when they took place. For two and a half years he had turned his back on art while he had thrown himself into his revolutionary educational activities and worked as a Justice of the Peace. Now he was preparing to turn his back on working for the peasantry and leave this life behind to return to the cultural milieu of his class. But before he could proceed, he needed to fulfil his obligation to his publisher Mikhail Katkov, who had lent him 1,000 roubles back in February 1862 to pay a gambling debt. This was the last time Tolstoy gambled. Under the terms of the deal, Katkov was to have the right to publish Tolstoy's 'Caucasus novella' in his journal the *Russian Messenger*. It was nowhere near finished, however. Tolstoy tried vainly to persuade Katkov to allow him to send money now rather than a manuscript, but eventually he knuckled down and pulled his various drafts into shape.

Tolstoy had been working on this novella for ten years – longer than for any work he ever published – and it had undergone many changes as he read and absorbed works such as *The Iliad*.[38] What was ultimately published in the January 1863 issue of the *Russian Messenger* was a novella entitled *The Cossacks*,[39] but because Tolstoy had submitted his manuscript so late, the issue in fact only physically appeared at the end of February. He had planned to write a sequel, and he continued to toy with this idea, but really his mind was on other things. *The Cossacks* is a kind of Rousseau-inspired metaphor of Tolstoy's spiritual journey in the decade before his marriage. It tells the story of Olenin, a young Russian officer from Moscow, who is stationed with some Cossack villagers during his period of service in the Caucasus. He envies them their freedom, perceiving in them a natural grace and nobility, and he falls hopelessly in love with a particularly alluring Cossack girl. Ultimately, however, Olenin realises he cannot overcome his aristocratic, metropolitan background and become one with nature like the Cossacks, and he realises he has to go back to his old life. Something similar happened to Tolstoy when he married, and he openly acknowledged that his views on life had changed when writing to his closest confidante, Alexandrine.[40] He was now ready to go back to writing fiction for an educated audience about members of his own class.

In January 1863 Tolstoy announced in the Moscow press that his journal *Yasnaya Polyana* would cease publication.[41] Later that year his schools would also close, causing the student teachers to disperse. Sonya did not regret their departure, as the dense fumes of tobacco smoke during the meetings she had attended in their small drawing room had made her nauseous while she was pregnant.[42] She came to hate the students' presence on the estate as soon as she began to feel at home at Yasnaya Polyana, inasmuch as the students came from an alien social background, and took her husband away from her.[43] But Tolstoy still had to publish the December 1862 issue of his *Yasnaya Polyana* journal, and he completed his last article for it on 23 February 1863. Two days later Sonya wrote to her sister Tanya to tell her her husband had started a new novel.[44] This was *War and Peace*. Over 5,000 manuscript pages, numerous false starts, several different titles and six years later, it was finished. In the exhilaration which overcame Tolstoy soon after marrying he declared that he wished to have the freedom to work on a long-term project ('*de longue haleine*'),[45] but even he could not have imagined the life he would breathe into this novel would be quite as long drawn-out as this.

Just as it took the newly married couple several months to acclimatise to each other, it took the best part of the year for Tolstoy to find his focus with this new novel, but there was no question that he wanted to harness this new surge of creative energy to the composition of a substantial work of fiction. First he tinkered with an idea for a story he had been given back in 1856, about the fate of an old piebald gelding that had once been renowned for its speed. 'Kholstomer', usually translated as 'Strider', is one of his most remarkable stories. Tolstoy later adopted a third-person narrator, but much of the story is told from the horse's point of view. One summer when he had been visiting Turgenev, and they were returning home from an evening walk, they encountered an emaciated old horse standing in a pasture with strength only to swish its tail at the flies buzzing round it. Tolstoy went up to stroke the horse and commented on what it must have been thinking, prompting Turgenev to tell him he must have been a horse in a former life. Tolstoy was not happy with the story in 1863, so he put it aside, and resumed work on it some twenty years later at the instigation of his wife.[46]

Work on the estate also distracted Tolstoy from his purpose initially, especially with the approach of spring. Filled with new energy, Tolstoy bought cattle, sheep, birds and pigs, and tried vainly to interest Sonya in milking and butter-churning. Apart from being pregnant, she was also a city girl, and she found she could not tolerate the smell of manure in the cattle-sheds.[47] For a while Tolstoy took an interest in a distillery which he built with his neighbouring landowner and friend Alexander Bibikov.[48] Sonya tried to dissuade Tolstoy from pursuing this project on moral grounds, but he argued that he also needed grain for his pig-breeding.[49] In any event, it only operated for about eighteen months. Far more rewarding was the planting of about 1,000 apple trees at the Nikolskoye estate,[50] and an orchard of about 6,500 trees at Yasnaya Polyana. Each spring they produced clouds of exquisite pink and white blossom, which always seemed to Tolstoy to be about to float up into the sky.[51] This was on a much larger scale than Tolstoy's animal husbandry, which was never terribly profitable; indeed, it was believed that the Yasnaya Polyana orchard was the second largest in Europe. By the mid-1870s, Tolstoy had increased its size from ten to forty hectares.[52] Sonya was actually keen to help with tree planting – this was one aspect of farming she did not find too distasteful. That autumn she for the first time experienced the air on the estate filling with the dense, sweet smell of thousands of ripening apples. By May 1863, when she was weeks away from giving birth, it became physically impossible for her to do very much, but that did not stop Tolstoy chastising her for being idle.[53]

Tolstoy also became passionately interested in bees after he got married. He bought some hives from Sonya's grandfather, and installed them in a distant part of the estate, about a mile from the family home in the lime and aspen wood beyond the Voronka river.[54] Sonya tried and failed to share this passion as well. As she later wrote in her autobiography:

> The whole of Lev Nikolayevich's passionate nature was revealed in this enthusiasm. He developed enthusiasms for the most diverse things throughout his life: games, music, [ancient] Greek, schools, Japanese pigs,

pedagogy, horses, hunting – too many in fact to count. And that's not including his intellectual and literary interests: they were most extreme. He was madly passionate about everything at the height of his enthusiasm, and if he could not convince whomever he was talking to of the importance of the activity he was caught up in, he was capable of being even hostile to that person.[55]

In Moscow while she growing up, Sonya had never had time on her own. Now when Tolstoy pursued his enthusiasms, she was left by herself at home, and she became very lonely, as she recorded in her diary. Sometimes during the early summer of 1863, when her husband spent whole days with his bees, she walked through the fields to take him his lunch or a glass of tea in the evening, and would find him with a net over his head arranging the combs in a hive, or capturing a swarm.[56] After sitting there and getting stung, she would face a solitary walk back home. As well as reading about beekeeping, Tolstoy spent hours observing the patterns of behaviour of his bees, assisted by his beekeeper, an old man with a long grey beard. During the summer he was also helped by Nikolka, the gardener's young son.[57] His absorption with the Yasnaya Polyana apiary abated after about two years, but his enthusiasm for beekeeping left its mark in his writing. Firstly, there is the famous epic simile in *War and Peace*, borrowed from Virgil's *Aeneid*, in which Moscow in 1812 is compared to a queenless hive. Conversely, Tolstoy thought of a busy hive when conveying the atmosphere of the ball in *Anna Karenina*, and a little later in the novel he describes bees on their first spring flight after the relocation of their hive for the summer. The precision of his vocabulary, overlooked by most translators, tells us a great deal about the rigour he applied to his study of apiculture.[58]

Apart from the prolonged visit to Yasnaya Polyana of Sonya's sister Tanya and brother Sasha, plus two of their cousins, Tolstoy had one other major distraction from the writing of fiction in the summer of 1863. In the middle of June, husband and wife temporarily stopped writing and reading each other's diaries, and for a short period at least, Sonya was able to claim Tolstoy's full attention: on 28 June their first child was born. In her autobiography Sonya does not describe the birth of Sergey as a joyous event. This was not only because he arrived in the world over a week early, and caught everybody unawares. Lyubov Alexandrovna just managed to arrive in time, but the set of baby clothes she had sent from Moscow did not. The newborn had to be wrapped in one of Tolstoy's nightshirts before being placed in the crude limewood cradle that had been made by the family carpenter. Both the midwife, Maria Ivanovna Abramovich, and Dr Shmigaro, the chief doctor at the Tula armaments factory, were Polish exiles, whose number in Russia had exponentially increased after the government had brutally suppressed the Polish uprising that January. Compared to the thousands of Poles deported to Siberia, the Tolstoys' doctor and midwife had a much easier fate. Over the next twenty-five years Maria Ivanovna would make many journeys from Tula to Yasnaya Polyana – she assisted Sonya at all except one of the births of her thirteen children, five of whom did not live to adulthood.

Tolstoy had not completely abandoned his Populist ways, and now he flatly refused to allow Sonya to take on a wet-nurse, despite mastitis making it impossible for her to breast-feed baby Sergey. Lyubov Alexandrovna found it exasperating that her daughter meekly followed her husband's wishes, and must have been relieved when her own husband weighed in with some common sense. The crusty Dr Bers had already lost patience with his son-in-law's unorthodox ideas on numerous occasions. He had been upset and offended by a pedagogical article Tolstoy had written the previous year con-demning university education, for example, and had written and told him so.[59] In August 1863 he wrote to Lev and Sonya from Moscow to tell them they had both gone mad. 'You can be sure, Lev Nikolayevich, my friend,' he wrote, 'that your nature will never become that of a peasant, just as your wife's nature cannot tolerate that which can be tolerated by the Pelageya who beat up her husband and the innkeeper at a tavern outside Petersburg (see *Moscow Gazette*, issues 165 and 166).' Tolstoy, he remarked tartly, was skilled at writing and talking, but not always so smart when it came to practical things.[60]

It took a while for Tolstoy to acquire paternal feelings for Sergey. He refused to hold him when he was very small,[61] and only began to love his son when he was nearly two years old and very unwell. It was 'a completely new feeling,' he noted in his diary in March 1865.[62] Nevertheless, it was with the birth of Sergey that the happiest years of the Tolstoys' marriage began. Lev and Sonya's relationship became stronger and more stable, leading him to declare in his single diary entry for 1864 that he and Sonya meant more to each other than anyone else in the world.[63] Sonya no longer had time to be bored or lonely, and as a mother she was now fulfilling her husband's idea of womanhood, but she was doing more than that. By sitting up late at night to write out fair copies of her husband's drafts, which gave her a sense of involvement in his creative life, she was also indispensable to his artistic productivity. This profound happiness in Tolstoy's personal life was intimately connected to the extraordinary creative energy which was welling up inside him, and which would be expressed in the writing of *War and Peace*.[64] He wrote about this to Alexandrine in October 1863:

> I've never felt my intellectual and even all my moral energies to be so free and so capable of work. And I've got work going on inside me now. This work is a novel about the period from 1810 to 1820 ... I'm now a writer with *all* the power of my soul, and am writing and thinking as I have never written and thought before. I'm a happy and calm husband and father, with nothing to hide from anybody, and no wish except for everything to go on like this ...[65]

Two autumns later, in September 1865, Tolstoy noted in his diary that his happiness with Sonya was the sort of happiness enjoyed by one couple in a million.[66]

The first parts of *War and Peace* started appearing in 1865 under the title 'The Year 1805'. Turgenev's novel *Fathers and Sons* had been published in its entirety in one journal issue in 1862, but it was a fraction of the length of *War and Peace*. It was more customary for substantial prose works to appear in instalments in the country's top literary journals before appearing in book form. This is how Tolstoy proceeded, but given his propensity for changing tack and carrying out endless revisions, this was a risky venture. True to form, by the time he had published the first parts of *War and Peace*, which he had contracted to the *Russian Messenger*, Tolstoy had completely changed his ideas about where his novel was going. Even when he then started publishing the novel under his own auspices in book form, his thoughts were not fixed, and changes were also made to his text in the 1870s and 1880s, leading inevitably to much confusion. In the 1920s one Tolstoy scholar even felt compelled to write an article about the difficulties in establishing which was the canonical text of the novel.[67]

Tolstoy's impulse to write on the events of 1805 had come from his interest in the Decembrists – the group of army officers who had staged an ill-fated uprising in December 1825 at the time of Nicholas I's accession. Occupying Paris after the defeat of Napoleon in 1814 had opened their eyes to a more enlightened system of government, and they returned to Russia full of hope that the liberal-minded Alexander I might now introduce political reform. When their hopes were dashed, they turned to conspiracy with the revolutionary aim of replacing Russia's autocratic rule with a republic, or at least a constitutional monarchy. The mutiny they staged in St Petersburg's Senate Square after Alexander I's death was a dismal failure, however, and the leading Decembrists were punished with either execution or lifelong exile in Siberia. Fear of revolution marked the whole of Nicholas I's reign. In 1856, as part of Alexander II's liberalisation of Russian society after the death of his father, the new tsar amnestied those Decembrists still serving long sentences of exile in Siberia, and amongst them was Tolstoy's distant relative Prince Sergey Volkonsky. It was Volkonsky, whom he met in Florence in 1860, that Tolstoy had in mind when he first began planning a novel about the Decembrists. He soon discovered, however, that he needed a larger cast of characters, and that he also needed go back in time to 1812 in order to bring their story to life. That in turn led him to the realisation that he really needed to go back to 1805, when Russia first went to war with Napoleon. As he explained in one of the many forewords he drafted, which reflect his changing views of the novel, 'I was ashamed to write about our victory in the struggle with Napoleonic France without writing about our failures and our disgrace.'[68] Tolstoy's initial plan, then, was to capture artistically the history of his nation over a fifty-year period and call it 'Three Ages'. The first 'age' would encompass the events of 1805 to 1812, the second would focus on the 1820s, and in particular on the fateful uprising in 1825, while the third would bring the action into the 1850s, and incorporate the disastrous Crimean War, the unexpected death of Nicholas I and the amnesty of the Decembrists at a time of hope for reform. As we know, Tolstoy eventually ended up concentrating on the events leading up to 1812 and their immediate aftermath, and he never in fact went back to his early fragment about the ageing Decembrist returning to Moscow from Siberia in the 1850s. He had no idea, however, when he was starting out in 1863, of the dimensions his new novel would ultimately assume.

If Tolstoy was able to sustain his concentration for six years and maintain an iron discipline, it was because of the hospitable environment in which he was able to work, living in his beloved ancestral home deep in the heart of the Russian countryside, supported by his devoted wife. For a while he even moved his study downstairs so that he was not distracted by family life. The old vaulted store room where old Prince Volkonsky had once hung his hams on the hooks still hanging from the ceilings, and where Sonya had stayed before their marriage, was also where he wrote the first chapters of *War and Peace*, after trying fifteen different openings. Isolated from the outside world (there was not even a railway connection to nearby Tula until 1867), with weeks and months going by during the winter when there were no visitors, Tolstoy could fully immerse himself in the hundreds of sources he gathered about Russian history during the Napoleonic Wars, and also draw deeply on his powers of imagination. Most of his fiction to date had an element of autobiography, but now he also found inspiration for his most memorable characters amongst his immediate family, with the vivacious and ingenuous Natasha, his most beloved character, reflecting aspects of the personalities of both his wife and his sister-in-law Tanya at different times.[69] Tolstoy also looked further back into his family's past for raw material, projecting his aunt Toinette's love for his father on to the hopeless devotion of Natasha's adopted sister Sonya for her brother Nikolay. His knowledge of the habits of his epicurean grandfather Ilya Andreyevich gave substance to his portrait of Count Rostov, and he breathed life into the story of old Prince Bolkonsky and his daughter Maria at their Bald Hills estate by conjuring up in his imagination the secluded life led by his other grandfather Prince Volkonsky and his unmarried mother at Yasnaya Polyana. A few of his brother Sergey's traits went into Prince Andrey,[70] and the desperate Fyodor Ivanovich Dolokhov was partially inspired by his distant cousin, the swashbuckling Fyodor Ivanovich Tolstoy. Sonya's sister Tanya liked to flatter herself that the character of Natasha was modelled exclusively on her, but the truth is that real-life people merely provided Tolstoy with the necessary spark he needed to create. His canvas was huge, and it is not surprising to find Homer on the list of authors he acknowledged as having made an impact on him at this time, alongside Goethe, Victor Hugo and Stendhal.[71]

Numerous friends, relatives and acquaintances helped Tolstoy with the research for *War and Peace*, including leading historians and his doughty father-in-law Andrey Bers, who shared his personal memories of living through the events of 1812 as a child, and rounded up an army of old Moscow ladies ready to tell their story. Andrey Estafevich also enjoyed the task of tracking down contemporary newspaper cuttings for Tolstoy, as well as the correspondence of people who had lived in Moscow during Russia's war with Napoleon.[72] Tolstoy made regular research trips to Moscow, and profited particularly from a long visit he made in the autumn of 1864 after breaking his arm. He had been riding his horse Masha, accompanied by two of his borzois, and had fallen off while impulsively galloping over a ploughed field in pursuit of a rabbit one of them had spotted.[73] Old Dr Shmigaro did such a poor job of setting the arm in Tula that Tolstoy travelled to Moscow for a further operation, and he spent his convalescence researching early-nineteenth-century Russian history. Sometimes this meant sitting in the Rumyantsev Museum, poring over manuscripts about Russian Freemasons, and sometimes he took himself off to the Chertkov Library to read letters and memoirs and look at portraits of Alexander I's generals.[74] These two public libraries had just opened in Moscow, and without them his task would have been much harder. Tolstoy had actually picked a wonderful time to write a historical novel.

The decade of the 1860s was not only famous as the era of the Great Reforms. This was also a golden age for Russian literature, with Turgenev, Tolstoy and Dostoyevsky all at the height of their powers. It was an important time for music: Tchaikovsky became a student at the Petersburg Conservatoire when it was founded in 1862, and then was immediately appointed to teach at the even newer Moscow Conservatoire when he graduated; they were the first institutions in Russia set up to train professional musicians. The opening of the Mariinsky Theatre in 1860 paved the way for Russian opera and ballet to flourish, and the easing of censorship led to the publication of previously suppressed literary and historical works. These included the autobiography of the Archpriest Avvakum, a persecuted leader of the Old Believer sect, published for the first time in 1861. It had been suppressed for two whole centuries, owing to fears that the spread of sectarianism could lead to popular rebellion. The opening of Moscow's first public libraries was part of this great explosion in Russian cultural and intellectual life, and contributed substantially to it. In 1862 the refurbished Pashkov House, one of the many elegant Moscow mansions damaged in the fire of 1812, opened as the Rumyantsev Museum, home to a research library and important art and archive collections (Tolstoy's own manuscripts were later deposited there for safekeeping).[75] The following year Alexander Chertkov's son Grigory made available to the public for the first time his late father's unique and rich collection of books and primary sources devoted to the history of Russia. The Chertkov Public Library was established in a specially built wing of the family's spacious mansion in the centre of Moscow, and Grigory Chertkov proceeded to increase the holdings to about 20,000 items. The respected historian Pyotr Bartenev became the first librarian at the Chertkov Library, and, also in 1863, founder-editor of its journal *Russian Archive*. The latter performed a valuable service in publishing primary sources about eighteenth- and early-nineteenth-century Russian history, many of which were vital for Tolstoy when he was writing *War and Peace*. Bartenev also went out of his way to help Tolstoy with unpublished historical materials for his new novel.

By the end of 1864, Tolstoy delivered to the Moscow offices of the *Russian Messenger* what he believed would be the first part of his new novel, entitled 'The Year 1805'. The thirty-eight chapters he submitted correspond roughly to the first two parts of what is now volume one of *War and Peace*, and they were published in the January and February 1865 issues of the journal. The day after the February issue appeared (actually in March), Andrey Estafevich wrote to the Tolstoys to let them know he had just been at a reception given by the Military Governor-General, and that Tolstoy's latest instalment had been much talked about. This had been Dr Bers' first social engagement after a long convalescence recovering from a tracheotomy (as a court employee he had to ask the Tsar for special permission to grow a beard).[76] He was obviously pleased to be out and about again, and reported that the subject of Tolstoy's protracted negotiations over his royalties was also hot gossip in Moscow. Feeling he would be better placed to act for his son-in-law, Andrey Estafevich offered his services to Tolstoy, but the deal had already been done.

Tolstoy had driven a hard bargain with his editor Mikhail Katkov. At the beginning of his career, back in 1852, he had been paid fifty roubles per printer's sheet, but he now felt he could ask for more – a lot more. Nikolay Lyubimov, a retired professor of physics at Moscow University and Katkov's closest editorial associate (or favourite donkey as he was referred to disparagingly in some circles), was deputised to act as go-between, and in November 1864 he spent two hours trying to persuade Tolstoy to back down and accept a rate of fifty roubles for his new work.[77] But Tolstoy knew his own worth, insisted on 300 roubles, and got it. This meant Katkov paid his star author 3,000 roubles for the first section of the novel (ten printer's sheets).[78] This was a lot of money. As a concession, he managed to persuade Tolstoy to agree to a separate book publication of all the chapters which made up 'The Year 1805' after they had been published in the *Russian Messenger*, which then had about 3,000 subscribers. They agreed on a print run of 500 copies, with Katkov as the beneficiary, and the book went on sale in June 1866, for a price of two and a half roubles.[79] Working out exactly how much these figures would be at today's values is a difficult and rather fruitless exercise, but one can gain a good sense of relative worth when comparing Tolstoy's honorarium with the average manual worker's wage at the time, which was about ten roubles a month – the eventual price of *War and Peace* when it was finally published as a book. Village teachers earned about twenty-five roubles a month, which was what Tolstoy paid the governesses who came to teach his children, on top of providing them with room and board.[80]

The year 1866 was something of an annus mirabilis for Mikhail Katkov, as he found himself publishing Tolstoy's novel and Dostoyevsky's masterpiece *Crime and Punishment* on the pages of his journal at the same time. Dostoyevsky was not the easiest of authors, but on this occasion far more amenable than Tolstoy. He struggled to meet the deadlines for each of the monthly instalments of *Crime and Punishment*, but he kept to them, and the novel was complete by December 1866. (If Tolstoy read it, which is unlikely, he did not record what he thought about it.) With *War and Peace*, things were altogether trickier. By this point, Tolstoy had come up with a new title: 'All's Well That Ends Well', projecting a happy ending which was different from the one he had initially conceived, and different again from the ending of the final version of the novel. Tolstoy still believed he would finish his new work the following year, and that spring he began lengthy and ultimately disappointing discussions with an artist whom he commissioned to produce illustrations for the projected book publication.[81]

Katkov wanted to continue printing the next sections of Tolstoy's novel in the *Russian Messenger* in 1867, before producing it in book form. Accordingly, a new set of negotiations began in November 1866, but the following spring there was still no agreement, and in June 1867 Tolstoy took matters into his own hands. Deciding against first publishing the rest of the novel as monthly instalments in a journal in the time-honoured Russian fashion, he decided now to publish it in separate volumes as they were completed. He turned for help to Pyotr Bartenev. The eventual form of *War and Peace* changed radically as a result, and the nature of the changes can be roughly gauged by consulting the list of 'distinguishing merits' compiled by a commercial Moscow publisher of the so-called 'first complete edition of the great novel completed in 1866, before Tolstoy reworked it in 1867–1869':

1. Twice as short and five times more interesting.
2. Almost no philosophical digressions.
3. A hundred times easier to read: all the French text is replaced by Russian in the author's own translation.
4. Much more 'peace' and less 'war'.
5. Prince Andrey and Petya Rostov remain alive.[82]

Igor Zakharov, the publisher in question, drew on authoritative editions to compile the version of the novel he published in 2000,[83] but he was pilloried for his popularising efforts on Russian television, and also by literary scholars anxious to preserve the integrity of Tolstoy's masterpiece. Zakharov was certainly disingenuous in claiming he was bringing to readers the 'real Lev Tolstoy' and the 'real *War and Peace*' as Tolstoy translated the French material in the novel into Russian later, for the 1873 edition.[84] Nevertheless this 'edition', which appeared in English translation in 2007,[85] is helpful in throwing into greater relief the impact which Tolstoy's collaboration with Pyotr Bartenev had on the future evolution of *War and Peace*, which has everything to do with the greater number of historical sources he now consulted. Tolstoy once commented that turning to Bartenev with a research query was like turning on the tap of a samovar.[86]

Tolstoy drew up a contract with Bartenev and a Moscow printer to publish his novel in June 1867. He was now at last calling it *War and Peace*, perhaps under the influence of Proudhon's 1861 tract of the same name, which had appeared in Russian translation in 1864. He was perhaps also acting under the influence of Herzen, who had written three articles under this title in 1859.[87] Tolstoy and Bartenev agreed to an initial print run of 4,800 copies of six separate volumes, corresponding to the six parts the novel was then divided into, with a planned price of eight roubles. Fifteen per cent of the proceeds were to go to Bartenev for copy-editing the book and dealing with the censor, and twenty were to go to booksellers.[88] Sonya's father was clearly still keen to be involved, and he turned out to be very useful when Tolstoy experienced unexpected delays in receiving the first proofs. In the summer of 1867 Andrey Estafevich fired off regular bulletins to Yasnaya Polyana to report on what was going on in Moscow, telling Tolstoy when Bartenev was coming back from his dacha, what he said upon his return and so on and so forth. Tolstoy, meanwhile, realised that the first half of volume one was much longer than the second. While he started pruning the first part, which he believed improved it immeasurably, he requested Bartenev to take out as many indentations as possible in the first half and increase them in the second. This created some very long paragraphs.[89]

While Tolstoy was proofreading the early chapters for the publication of this new edition he was, of course, still writing and researching later parts of his novel. In September 1867 he did some research of a different kind. He was getting near to the crucial Battle of Borodino in his narrative, and in order to deepen his understanding of the movements of the 250,000 soldiers who took part in it, he decided to go and inspect the battleground, located near the town of Mozhaysk, about seventy miles west of Moscow. The Battle of Borodino was the decisive confrontation between Napoleon's Grande Armée and the Russian forces led by General Kutuzov in 1812, and accordingly it occupies a pivotal position in Russian history, and indeed in *War and Peace*, coming roughly at the halfway mark in the novel. The battle took place during the course of one long day, but it occupies twenty chapters in Tolstoy's epic narrative, including discursive commentary from the author himself. Combining the lofty perspectives of both the historical figures of Napoleon and Kutuzov with the ground-level viewpoint of fictional characters like Prince Andrey, in charge of a regiment, and Pierre, a civilian who unwittingly becomes caught up in the maelstrom, Tolstoy's artistic tactics are equal to the most sophisticated and effective of military strategies, while his campaign against professional historians no less aggressive.

Napoleon's troops had been marching relentlessly on Moscow since invading Russian territory in June 1812, and the speed of the French army's advance led Alexander I to appoint the venerable Prince Kutuzov as his commander-in-chief just days before the historic battle, replacing General Count Barclay de Tolly. Kutuzov was sixty-seven years old, but greatly revered by all ranks in the Russian army. Unlike Barclay de Tolly, the Lutheran descendant of a Scottish family which had settled in the German Baltic province of Livonia in the seventeenth century, Kutuzov was thoroughly Russian. He established his defence of Moscow in the village of Borodino, and it was here, at dawn on

7 September 1812,[90] that the two armies met for their bloody encounter. The fatalities were enormous, with the Russian army losing as many as 44,000 men, and the French 58,000. Technically the victory was Napoleon's, as he was able to march on to Moscow after Kutuzov withdrew, but his forces were fatally weakened. Tolstoy's conclusion was that the Russians had scored a crucial moral victory at Borodino, the kind which 'convinces the opponent of the moral superiority of his enemy, and of his own impotence'. He was unabashed about including in his novel authorial pronouncements to this effect:

> The direct consequence of the Battle of Borodino was Napoleon's groundless flight from Moscow, his retreat along the old Smolensk road, the defeat of the 500,000-strong invasion, and the defeat of Napoleonic France, on which had been laid for the first time the hand of an opponent whose spirit was stronger.[91]

Half a century later, when he came to visit the battleground, Tolstoy found accommodation in a local convent and spent two days wandering around the village and surrounding fields of Borodino, in the company of his brother-in-law Stepan Bers, then twelve years old, who was thrilled to be taken along. Tolstoy was disappointed not to be able to talk to a recently deceased veteran of the war who had worked as the custodian of the monument to the battle which stood in the middle of the field, but he used his eyes effectively instead. By sketching out a plan of the battlefield, and noting where the troops had been positioned, he was able to work out vital details such as exactly in whose eyes the sun had shone when it came up on that fateful day. Before heading back home, he got up at dawn and completed one last tour of the battlefield. Tolstoy's skewed presentation of history in *War and Peace* has attracted criticism ever since it was published; indeed, some of his accounts of the battles in 1812 left some veterans apoplectic with rage at his manipulation of historical sources to suit his own artistic and ideological ends. There is nevertheless a general consensus on the authenticity of his portrayal of the events at Borodino.[92]

After coming back from Borodino, Tolstoy finished the part of the novel which culminates with Natasha's seduction by Anatole Kuragin. This comes at the halfway mark in the final version of the novel, at the end of volume two. Tolstoy regarded this episode as the crux of the entire work, since it functions as a kind of mirror of Napoleon's 'violation' of Russia, with which it coincides, and he found it extremely difficult to write. This was also perhaps partly because he was reflecting the recent experiences of his sister-in-law Tanya, who had gone through something similar with an inappropriate suitor.[93] At this point, Tolstoy decided it would be best to publish everything he had written so far rather than hold up publication until he had finished the next part (which covers the Battle of Borodino). The three volumes of the first book edition were accordingly published in December 1867, and sold for a price of seven roubles. One critic took exception to having to pay such an 'indecent' price for the three slim volumes with yellow covers which he claimed had a large typeface more suitable for old people and children. Nevertheless the books sold.[94] The next volume went on sale three months later in March 1868, with a cunning advertising ploy: those who bought the first four volumes would receive the fifth free, while those who waited until the edition was complete would have to pay more, since the price would then go up. The books sold so well, however, that a second edition, incorporating certain new revisions, appeared that autumn.[95] The Russian reading public was still relatively small, so this was no mean achievement.

By 1868 Tolstoy was working furiously to finish *War and Peace*. The further he got into the novel, the clearer its shape became to him, and the greater his inspiration and sense of purpose. He was anyway a person of extraordinary sensitivity, and now, in the middle of this enormous creative outpouring, his friend, the poet Afanasy Fet, likened him to a great bell made of the thinnest glass, liable to produce a sound at the slightest touch.[96] It was this sensitivity which compelled him to respond to some of the early carping reviews by publishing in Pyotr Bartenev's journal *Russian Archive* 'A Few Words About the Novel *War and Peace*' in March 1868. Long before he had finished writing his novel, he hoped he could thus anticipate any further misapprehensions, which he knew were inevitable. First he confronted the tricky question of the genre of his novel by offering his own oft-quoted, and not necessarily very helpful definition: 'What is *War and Peace*? It is not a novel, still less a [narrative] poem, and even less an historical chronicle. *War and Peace* is what the author wanted to and could express in the form in which it was expressed.' Justifying his apparent lack of reverence for conventional European literary forms, Tolstoy quite rightly argues that from Gogol's *Dead Souls* to Dostoyevsky's *Notes from the House of the Dead*, 'in the modern period of Russian literature there is not one artistic work in prose, even slightly better than average that could fully fit into the form of a novel, a [narrative] poem or a novella'. He also tackles other potential points of contention, such as the fact that not only the Russians but also the French speak a mixture of French and Russian in the novel. And as well as providing a robust defence of the artist's right to diverge from historical accounts in evoking past events, he explains that his invention of names such as Bolkonsky and Drubetskoy, so similar to the well-known real-life aristocratic surnames of Volkonsky and Trubetskoy, was governed by a desire for his fictitious characters to have names which would sound pleasant and natural to the Russian ear.[97]

When he wrote his 'Few Words' about the novel he had been working on 'continually and exclusively' for the previous five years, Tolstoy openly acknowledged he had been able to take advantage of 'optimal living conditions'. Presumably he had in mind not only his comfortable state of financial independence and all the fresh air and exercise he could want, but also the emotional and practical support provided by his wife. Sonya gave birth to four children during the six years Tolstoy was writing *War and Peace*, and also suffered at least one miscarriage (in October 1867). After the birth of Sergey, Tanya was born in 1864, followed by Ilya in 1866 and Lev in 1869. When she was not looking after their children, Sonya worked willingly as her husband's scribe, and thus became intimately involved in his creative life. This sometimes required a good deal of patience, as she records in her autobiography:

> Sometimes proofs which had been finally corrected and sent off were returned again to Lev Nikolayevich at his request in order to be recorrected and recopied. Or a telegram would be sent to substitute *one* word for another. My whole soul became so immersed in the copying that I began myself to feel when it was not altogether right; for instance, when there were frequent repetitions of the same word, long periods, wrong punctuation, obscurity, etc. I used to point all these things out to Lev Nikolayevich. Sometimes he was glad for my remarks; sometimes he would explain why it ought to remain as it was; he would say that details do not matter, only the general scheme matters.[98]

If her brother Stepan's memoirs are to be believed, Sonya copied out the entire manuscript of *War and Peace* seven times. Unfortunately this supposition appears to have been wishful thinking on his part: Nikolay Gusev dismisses it as a myth in a footnote of his 900-page biographical study of Tolstoy's life and works from 1855 to 1869. Conceding that some of Tolstoy's chapters were indeed reworked and copied many times, he points out that others went straight to press.[99] On the other hand, there were numerous chapters which Tolstoy rewrote endlessly, so Sonya's contribution should not be underestimated. Deciphering his execrable handwriting, and then preparing a legible final draft of the manuscript, was a gargantuan task, and in 1866, during a particularly intense period of the novel's composition, a clerk was also employed to help with the copying.[100]

Tolstoy was wise enough to know he needed sometimes to take a break from his literary activities, and his general custom was to concentrate on his writing from autumn through to spring, and then enjoy outdoor pursuits like shooting and riding during the warm summer months when Sonya's sister Tanya and other friends and relatives would come to stay at Yasnaya Polyana. In 1865 he discovered an enthusiasm for Anthony Trollope, whose novel *The Bertrams* provided welcome light relief and a distraction from his immersion in Russian history.[101] And during a stay in Moscow the following year, he also took up sculpture for a brief period (not surprisingly, it was the figure of a horse which he decided to tackle as his first subject).[102] Tolstoy never lost his readiness to try out new pastimes, even in old age. He also began to use the newfangled mode of railway transport as soon as he had the chance: the construction of an extensive network of Russian railways in the 1860s is also the legacy of the era of the Great Reforms. The Moscow–Kursk railway line was completed in 1867, while Tolstoy was working on *War and Peace*, and it cut his journey times in half.

When, a few decades later, Yasnaya Polyana became a site of pilgrimage for thousands of Tolstoy's devotees, its sheer accessibility had a lot to do with it: the mainline station built in the village of Yasenki, south of Tula, was just four miles down the road from Yasnaya Polyana. A large number of the many Tolstoy followers who made the journey felt it was their duty to publish an account of their visit afterwards, but amongst the mountain of memoirs of personal meetings with Tolstoy, there is one which stands out not only by virtue of the fact that it was written a long time before all the other ones, but also because it happens to be well written. Its author was Eugene Schuyler, an American writer and diplomat who arrived in Moscow in 1868 to take up the post of consul.[103] Schuyler was one of the very first Americans to receive a PhD, and had taken up Russian after meeting crew members of the *Alexander Nevsky*, the imperial navy's last wooden frigate, when it was docked in New York. In 1866 he published the first American translation of Turgenev's *Fathers and Sons*, and on his way to Russia the following year, he met the author in Baden-Baden. Despite the coolness in their relationship at that time, Turgenev gave Schuyler a letter of introduction to Tolstoy. Schuyler's account of his visit to Yasnaya Polyana gives us a vivid glimpse into Tolstoy's life in the autumn of 1868.

At five o'clock in the afternoon on Saturday 14 September, the twenty-eight-year-old Schuyler found himself getting on a train in Moscow, and nine hours later, at two in the morning, he got off at Yasenki to be met by Tolstoy's carriage. Torrential rain meant that it took a further hour and a half to drive the four miles to Yasnaya Polyana. Upon arrival, however, he was relieved to be told that 'late hours were kept' and that the usual time for morning coffee was eleven o'clock. The following day he joined the count and his young wife, plus their three young children, Seryozha, Tanya and Ilya, and their English governess, for breakfast. Tolstoy, he discovered, had in fact been up at dawn, and had gone off into the woods with his dogs and his gun. Schuyler was duly taken hare-hunting himself, and later came to have a particular appreciation for the exquisitely written chapters describing shooting parties in *War and Peace* and *Anna Karenina*. He had before then only ever made botanical excursions into forests, in search of trees and shrubs, and had never held a gun, but he now acquired direct experience of one of Tolstoy's greatest passions:

> It was new to me to sit still and use my ears as well as my eyes; to appreciate the different noises of the wood; to know whether that was a twig or a leaf which fell – for the leaves were just falling … to distinguish between the noises made by the birds; to speculate as to the origin of unknown sounds, and to have one's attention always strained for the patter-patter of the hare.[104]

Tolstoy did little work on *War and Peace* during the week in which he entertained Schuyler, but he got his American guest to help him sort out his ever-expanding library. At the end of his stay, Schuyler was granted permission to translate *The Cossacks*, a project which took a while for him to complete due to his professional commitments. After Moscow, he was posted to St Petersburg for several years, during which he made an intrepid and noteworthy journey to the new cities of Russian Turkestan, then created a storm during a posting in Constantinople by exposing atrocities committed by the Turks against the Bulgarians, thereby helping their nationalist cause. As a result, he was removed from his post in 1878 and appointed as American Consul in Birmingham, which he clearly found boring, as this is where he finally finished his translation of *The Cossacks* (he is game enough to admit in his memoir that Tolstoy did not rate it very highly).[105] Schuyler and Tolstoy shared a great interest in Peter the Great, to whom Tolstoy turned as the possible subject of his next novel after completing *War and Peace*. In 1873, Tolstoy eventually abandoned his Peter the Great project to write *Anna Karenina*, but chapters of Schuyler's study of the Russian tsar finally started appearing in 1886.

After a wonderful week of convivial outings and conversations about literature and education which continued late into the night, Schuyler returned to Moscow, leaving Tolstoy to get back to *War and Peace*. The novel's fifth volume was published in May 1869, and the sixth and final volume appeared in December of that year (it was only when Tolstoy started to revise the novel a third time in 1873, in connection with a new edition of his collected writings, that he reduced the six initial volumes to the current four). It had been a long haul. Tolstoy worked phenomenally hard during the six years it took to write *War and Peace*, and Sonya had to bite her lip on the frequent occasions when he was late for dinner. As she records in her autobiography, she would tell herself on such occasions that being on time for meals was too petty a concern for geniuses like her husband.[106] A great believer in gymnastics and vigorous exercise outdoors, Tolstoy was physically very robust and he certainly had the stamina required to complete such a gargantuan project, but he frequently endured periods of poor health during the writing of *War and Peace*. There were times, particularly towards the end, for example, when he suffered from terrible migraines,[107] and others when he felt generally so unwell that he had to travel to Moscow for a consultation with Grigory Zakharin, one of Moscow's leading clinicians.[108]

War and Peace was wildly popular with the public when it was first published, but it also provoked a storm of controversy.[109] It was clear to everyone that what Tolstoy had produced was something exceptional, and the writer Ivan Goncharov was not exaggerating when he proclaimed that Tolstoy had now become a 'real lion of literature'.[110] Many members of the older generation, however, thought that Tolstoy had distorted Russian history, and felt affronted. Politically motivated younger critics desperate to push Russia further on the road to reform, on the other hand, reviled the conservative family values Tolstoy upholds in the novel, and in particular his celebration of the nobility. Even those with no particular axe to grind found Tolstoy's lengthy digressions disconcerting. Many Russian prose writers, meanwhile, were simply consumed with envy, and dismissed *War and Peace* with a few withering comments.

Amongst the novel's early critics was Turgenev, who had additional personal reasons to be galled by the greater success his younger contemporary seemed so effortlessly to achieve. But Turgenev was at heart a modest and generous man, and by the time the French publisher Hachette brought out the first French translation of *War and Peace* in 1879, their differences had been resolved. He now took every opportunity to promote Tolstoy to the French public, which was almost completely unfamiliar with his works. The appearance of the translation of *War and Peace* completed by 'Une Russe' (Princess Irina Paskevich, born Vorontsova-Dashkova, who was a remarkable Petersburg grande dame in her own right)[111] gave Turgenev a felicitous opportunity to write to Edmond About, editor of the Paris newspaper *Le XIXe Siècle*. In his letter, which was published on 23 January 1880, Turgenev provides French readers with an introduction to the novel and its author which is superlative in its concision and objectivity, and deserves to stand in full as the last word on this chapter of Tolstoy's life:

> Dear Monsieur About,
> You were kind enough to place in the *XIXe Siècle* my letter about the opening of the exhibition of paintings by Vereshchagin. The success I dared to predict for it, and which even exceeded my expectations, has given me the courage to write to you again. I'm writing to you again about the work of an artist, but an artist who creates with a pen in his hand.
> I have in mind the historical novel by my fellow countryman, Count Lev Tolstoy, *War and Peace*, a translation of which has just been published

by Hachette. Lev Tolstoy is the most popular amongst modern Russian writers, and *War and Peace*, if I may be so bold, is one of the most remarkable books of our time. This expansive work is pervaded by an epic spirit; in it the private and public life of Russia in the first years of our century is recreated by a masterly hand. Before the reader passes a whole epoch, rich with great events and major figures (the story begins not long before the Austerlitz defeat and goes up to Borodino); a whole world unfolds with a multitude of characters belonging to all levels of society, taken directly from life. The manner in which Count Tolstoy develops his theme is as new as it is original; this is not Walter Scott, and, it goes without saying, this is also not Alexandre Dumas. Count Tolstoy is a Russian writer to the core of his being; and those French readers not put off by certain longueurs, and the oddity of certain judgements, will be right in telling themselves that *War and Peace* has given them a more direct and faithful representation of the character and temperament of the Russian people, and about Russian life generally, than they would have obtained if they had read hundreds of works of ethnography and history. There are whole chapters here in which nothing needs to be changed; and there are historical figures (like Kutuzov, Rostopchin and others) whose characteristics have been etched for all time; this will never perish.

As you see, dear Monsieur About, I am expressing myself extravagantly, and yet my words do not fully convey my thoughts. It is possible that the deep originality of Count Lev Tolstoy will impede the foreign reader's sympathetic and rapid understanding of his novel by its very power, but I repeat – and I would be happy if people trusted what I say – that this is a great work by a great writer and it is genuine Russia.

Please accept, dear Monsieur About, assurance of my devotion.

Ivan Turgenev.[112]

· 8 ·

STUDENT, TEACHER, FATHER

Poetry is the fire burning in a person's soul. This fire burns, warms and brings light … There are some people who feel the heat, others who feel the warmth, others who just see the light, and others who do not even see the light … But the true poet cannot help burning painfully, and burning others.

That's what it is all about.

Diary entry, 28 October 1870[1]

BY THE MIDDLE OF 1869, nearly the whole of Russia was engrossed in *War and Peace* and avidly awaiting its conclusion, according to a Petersburg newspaper.[2] Tolstoy still had to oversee the publication of the last chapters (which finally went on sale that December), but his mind was racing in all sorts of new directions. In truth, his interest in the novel was already beginning to recede by this time. He spent the following summer immersed in German philosophy, then embarked on an intense study of Russian fairy tales and folk epics, with a view to putting together books to help children learn to read. He read Shakespeare and Molière and started writing a play. He toyed with ideas for a novel about Peter the Great, and at the same time began contemplating another completely different novel about the predicament of a high-society woman in contemporary Russia. He also began learning ancient Greek. But he was happiest when his mind was not racing. In fact, in the weeks and months which followed the completion of *War and Peace*, Tolstoy was happiest when he did not have to think at all. Games of bezique with his aunt were a pleasant diversion on cold winter evenings, and a sign that he was unwinding (he generally switched to playing patience compulsively when he was at the start of a new work), but what he really enjoyed was cross-country skiing out in the woods, and skating on the big pond below his house. He gave lessons to his six-year-old son Sergey, and spent hours mastering complicated manoeuvres on his own.[3] When summer arrived he worked in the garden, digging up nettles and burdock and tidying up the flowerbeds.[4] He also took himself off to the fields to spend whole days mowing with the peasants. 'I cannot describe to you not just the enjoyment but the happiness which I experience in doing this,' he wrote to Sergey Urusov, whom he had met and become friends with during the defence of Sebastopol.[5] He later did describe it, though, when he was writing *Anna Karenina*: the novel's most lyrical passages are devoted to the ecstasies of scything rather than the blossoming of romance. With the return of autumn Tolstoy went hunting as usual, mostly for woodcock and hare, but the following year he shot two wolves while on an expedition with friends.[6]

When he was engaged in physical pursuits, Tolstoy could stave off the dark thoughts that threatened to encroach on him during what he called the 'dead time' between writing projects.[7] It was a time of terrible uncertainty, he wrote in the first letter he sent to the Petersburg-based critic and philosopher Nikolay Strakhov, who was to become one of his closest friends and confidants.[8] A priest's son from the provinces, and a man of formidable intellect, Strakhov had spent the earlier part of his career teaching mathematics and natural science, but was now employed at the St Petersburg Public Library, where he remained until his retirement in 1885.[9] He and Tolstoy, whom he idolised, were exactly the same age. Strakhov had been the first to recognise the magnitude of Tolstoy's achievement in the three review articles he had written about *War and Peace*. After the last of them was published in the new Slavophile journal *The Dawn* in January 1870,[10] he wrote to Tolstoy to invite him to become a contributor. Tolstoy declined, explaining that he was in an awful state, one minute conceiving wildly ambitious plans and the next succumbing to self-doubt. Perhaps this was the necessary prelude to a period of happy, self-confident work like the one which had just ended, he conceded, but perhaps it meant that was never going to write anything ever again.[11]

Tolstoy always found the start of a new work of fiction mentally taxing, as he felt he needed to work out the different trajectories of the characters in his head before he could proceed, as if it were a game of chess. He described this complicated process in a letter he wrote to Afanasy Fet in November 1870:

> I'm moping and not writing anything, and finding work torturous. You can't imagine how difficult I find this preparatory work of thoroughly ploughing the field I *have* to sow. Thinking through and reflecting on everything that could happen to all the future people of my forthcoming work, which is going to be very big, and thinking through millions of possible combinations in order to choose 1/100000 is terribly difficult. And that's what I am busy with.[12]

Far from being able to enjoy a sense of achievement having finished *War and Peace*, Tolstoy was plagued by fears that he himself was finished as a writer. But his anxieties went deeper, as Sonya later recalled. Occasionally his spirits lifted when he had flashes of inspiration, but he was more often morose, and convinced that 'it was all over for him, that it was time for him to die, and so on and so forth'.[13] He was forty-one. As it turned out, he had exactly forty-one more years to live.

While he was carried along by the huge wave of creative inspiration that drove the writing of *War and Peace*, Tolstoy had successfully suppressed his tendencies towards depression, but now he could not help succumbing to melancholy thoughts, and his continuing ill-health also contributed to his low spirits.[14] Two years after he finished *War and Peace*, he still felt so low that he confided in Sergey Urusov that he had no will to live, and had never felt so miserable in all his life.[15] Misreading the symptoms, which at this point her husband himself did not fully understand, Sonya became increasingly anxious for him to start another book. It would be three years before Tolstoy started *Anna Karenina*, however, and writing it would prove to be as arduous as the writing of *War and Peace* had been stimulating. More than any other, *Anna Karenina* is the novel which readers invariably say they cannot put down. Tolstoy, by contrast, had so little desire to finish it that he had to force himself to pick it up. Neither he nor Sonya quite realised it yet, but the happiest years of their marriage were already over.

If Tolstoy was visited by thoughts of his own mortality after finishing *War and Peace*, it was because he had begun to confront death seriously while he was writing it. The first unwelcome confrontation with death had come through his chance involvement in the court-martial of Private Vasily Shabunin in 1866. This isolated incident exerted a far greater impact on him than he was prepared to admit at the time. That summer the Tolstoys had received a visit from a family friend of the Bers, Grigory Kolokoltsov, an officer serving with a Moscow infantry regiment stationed a few miles down the road from Yasnaya Polyana. On subsequent visits to Yasnaya Polyana, he brought his colonel, Pyotr Yunosha, and another officer called Alexander Stasyulevich, and Tolstoy enjoyed going riding with them.[16] One day Kolokoltsov and Stasyulevich came to ask Tolstoy if he would defend one of the regiment's regular soldiers at his forthcoming court-martial: Private Shabunin had struck his superior, and according to Russian law, this was an offence punishable by death. As an opponent of capital punishment ever since he had witnessed a public execution in Paris, Tolstoy agreed.[17]

Despite Tolstoy's plea, Shabunin was convicted and sentenced to be shot by firing squad. Appalled that such a minor infraction could attract such a drastic and inappropriate punishment, Tolstoy immediately appealed to higher channels via his influential cousin Alexandrine in St Petersburg, but to no avail. This was perhaps owing partly to the hysteria at court following the attempt to assassinate Alexander II in St Petersburg a few months earlier. The man wielding the gun, Dmitry Karakozov, who was one of Russia's first revolutionaries, was also sentenced to death. In September, a few weeks later after Shabunin's execution, Tolstoy asked the military band which had been obliged to accompany it to come up to Yasnaya Polyana to play as a surprise for Sonya's name-day party. It was a warm evening, and after dinner on the veranda, at a long table decorated with flowers, the guests had danced into the night – Sonya recorded in her diary that it had been a very jolly evening, and her husband had been in particularly good spirits.[18] Tolstoy then went back to writing *War and Peace*. Stasyulevich's suicide the following year, which apparently struck Tolstoy deeply, was not directly related to Private Shabunin's death, but it was a chilling postscript to an event which, as it turned out later, would gnaw at his conscience.[19]

Then there were personal losses. He had not been particularly close to his father-in-law Andrey Estafevich, or his philandering uncle Vladimir in Kazan, still less his ghastly brother-in-law Valerian Petrovich Tolstoy, who all died in the 1860s, but he was greatly upset by the deaths of Elizaveta, the sister of his distant cousin Alexandrine, and particularly Darya Alexandrovna, known to all as Dolly – the wife of his best friend Dmitry Dyakov, whom he had known since student days.[20] Then, in 1869, Tolstoy's friend Sergey Urusov, already widowed, lost his only daughter Lidia, while another friend Afanasy Fet lost his sister Nadezhda and two brothers-in-law, Nikolay and Vasily Botkin, in quick succession. Tolstoy had himself been friends with Vasily Botkin for well over a decade, and was disturbed to hear that he had died suddenly, in the company of the friends who had gathered at his home to hear a string quartet performed.[21]

In the summer of 1869 Tolstoy had also begun to confront life and death philosophically by reading Schopenhauer (1788–1860), a thinker famed for his pessimistic view of the world. One of the great philosophers of the nineteenth century, Schopenhauer was esteemed by figures as diverse as Nietzsche, Wittgenstein, Freud and Jung, but he also held particular appeal for creative minds in view of the beauty and simplicity of his exposition, his direct engagement with the real-life problem of existence, rather than with abstractions, and the high value occupied in his philosophical system by art. Schopenhauer was one of the first Western philosophers able to undertake a serious study of Indian philosophy through translations which had become available, and the influence of Buddhist ideas on his view of life as suffering is plain to see. As in Buddhism, Schopenhauer identified suffering with attachment to desires, regarded art, along with resignation and compassion, as one of the few means available to man of experiencing a temporary liberation from suffering. Schopenhauer's ideas about the futility of human striving made perfect sense to Tolstoy, and such was his newfound fervour for them that he acquired a portrait of the philosopher and put it up on the wall of his study.[22] Tolstoy was not alone in his veneration of Schopenhauer. There have been many other major artists for whom he has been equally important, including Turgenev, Thomas Mann and Samuel Beckett, not to mention composers such as Richard Wagner, who was engaged while Tolstoy was writing *War and Peace* in composing the *Ring* cycle, its musical equivalent not only in terms of scale and ambition, but also technically through its creative use of repetition.

Somehow Tolstoy's morbid thoughts all came to a head in the autumn of 1869, when he made a trip to Penza province to inspect some land he was thinking of buying. While stopping overnight in the town of Arzamas, he found himself awake at two in the morning, exhausted but unable to sleep. Although physically quite well, he was suddenly gripped by a fear of dying more intense than any he had experienced before, which produced in him a state of existential anguish he found completely terrifying. Many years later he drew on this memory of extreme emotional desolation when he started writing an autobiographical story called 'Notes of a Madman', although he never completed it.

Apart from his fixation with death, another cloud appeared on Tolstoy's horizon after he finished *War and Peace*: marital difficulties. Tolstoy may have treated his wife as a child to begin with, but in many ways he was also like a child with her. Once they started a family, Sonya became a source of maternal protection, and provided him with the emotional stability he needed to concentrate on his writing. There had been a few troubling incidents which had intruded into the serenity of the fundamentally happy years while Tolstoy was writing *War and Peace*, but they were exceptions rather than the rule, and had been dismissed as aberrations. Now it began to be the other way round. In August 1871 Sonya noted in her diary that something in their relationship had 'snapped' the previous winter when they had both been unwell. Tolstoy also later referred to becoming aware of his loneliness after 'a string broke' in their marriage at around this time in his diary.[23] They had squabbled before, of course, but this rift was more serious, and initially arose over their differing views of the woman's role in a marriage. Even though Sonya continued to defer to her husband, she was becoming increasingly confident about asserting her own views, sometimes goaded by sheer physical necessity.

In February 1871 Sonya gave birth to their second daughter and fifth child, who was christened Maria after Tolstoy's sister, and who, like her, immediately became known to everybody as Masha. After an extremely difficult delivery, Sonya contracted puerperal fever and nearly died, which understandably made her unwilling to endure the terror and pain of another bout of life-threatening illness. She began to think it would be best for her not to become pregnant again, but her husband had different ideas. It was not just that Tolstoy could not conceive of marriage without children – he regarded a woman's main vocation as being to bear children, breast-feed and raise them, and was therefore horrified at the thought of his wife avoiding future pregnancies. As a matter of fact, in March 1870 he had set out his ideas on this subject in an unsent letter addressed to Nikolay Strakhov, who had immediately followed up his review of *War and Peace* with an article on 'The Woman Question' in the next issue of *The Dawn*. Even though he never sent this letter, it is revealing that Tolstoy felt moved to respond straight away. In fact, he had begun to draft an article on the subject himself in 1868, describing men as the 'worker bees in the hive of human society' and women as queens who should not be distracted from their primary role to reproduce the species.[24] The 'woman question' exercised him deeply, and would indeed lie at the very heart of *Anna Karenina*.

Tolstoy generally did not like to read or subscribe to newspapers or journals, but there were a few exceptions. In 1870 Theodor Ries, the German from Oldenburg who had been responsible for printing *War and Peace*, became founding editor of the *Moskauer Deutscher Zeitung*. As he started publishing a German translation of *War and Peace* in its inaugural issue,[25] only one month after producing the last volume in Russian, he sent his newspaper to Tolstoy gratis. The Parisian *Revue des deux mondes* was for a long time the only journal the Tolstoys actively read,[26] but later in the 1870s, they arranged to share the cost of several subscriptions with Sergey over in Pirogovo.[27] Tolstoy affected never to read reviews of his work, remembering how the critics had hounded Pushkin during his lifetime.[28] But the truth is, he did read them, and he took criticism very personally, invariably responding to it immediately in writing, although his hurt feelings clearly often soon subsided, as he left most of his ripostes to critics unfinished.[29] If he made an exception for Strakhov, it was because his review was intelligent and highly positive, and also because *The Dawn* was also sent to him gratis – that is how he had come to read Strakhov's article on the topic of women's liberation.

The 'woman question' was a hot topic in Russia at this time, as it was all over Europe, so much so that two Russian translations of John Stuart Mill's seminal essay *The Subjection of Women* were published within months of its original publication in England in 1869, and Strakhov's article followed a few months later, in February 1870. John Stuart Mill, famous for being the first British member of parliament to call for women's suffrage and for his advocacy of women's rights, had plenty of followers in Russia, but as conservatives, Strakhov and Tolstoy were not amongst them. Strakhov, a quiet, scholarly, lifelong bachelor, had celebrated *War and Peace* for being a family chronicle, and he argued in his article that a woman's place was within the family. Tolstoy wholeheartedly agreed, and took issue only over Strakhov's negative view of prostitutes, arguing that they had an important role to play in preserving the institution of the family. 'Imagine London without its 80,000 magdalenes – what would happen to families?' he wrote.[30]

Sonya was only twenty-seven when Masha was born, so must have been filled with dread at the thought of complying with her husband's wishes: the intransigence of his views would lead to her having eight more children, only three of whom survived to adulthood. Quite apart from the health risks, each new pregnancy bound her more tightly to Yasnaya Polyana, and meant she had to postpone yet again her hopes of having a life outside the nursery. 'With every child you have to give up a life for yourself even more, and resign yourself to the burden of cares, worries, illnesses and years,' she noted in her diary in June 1870.[31] Sonya was a devoted mother, and she loved living at Yasnaya Polyana, but she was a young woman who had grown up in a city, and after a while she began to long for a change of scene, some company, and the chance to go to the occasional soirée. She found the solitude depressing.[32] The custom for Russian families from their milieu was to spend the winter in the city, and retreat to the country estate or a dacha during the summer months, but the Tolstoys lived the country life all year round. At the beginning of their marriage Tolstoy had dreamed of having a pied-à-terre in Moscow – a flat on Sivtsev-Vrazhek, a quiet back-street in the heart of the city favoured by the well-to-do, where his cousin Fyodor Ivanovich 'the American' had lived. He confided in Sonya's father that he imagined transferring their Yasnaya Polyana life to Moscow for three or four months each winter, complete 'with the same Alexey, the same nanny, the same samovar', in order to be able to enjoy stimulating conversation with new people, visit libraries and go to the theatre.[33] That plan was stymied by lack of funds, however, and by the time the income from *War and Peace* had made Tolstoy an affluent man, he no longer had the inclination. He became more reclusive as he got older, preferring to be at home for long stretches, when he could work undisturbed. City life soon chafed him, so he was always happy to leave, but he did have the freedom to come and go more or less as he pleased. He did not particularly appreciate hearing operas like Rossini's *Mosè in Egitto* and Gounod's *Faust*, but at least he had the opportunity to go to the theatre while he was writing

War and Peace. Opera was Sonya's great passion – what would she have given to be able to dress up occasionally for a night at the Bolshoi Theatre![34] She went to Moscow a handful of times during these years, but for the most part she was at home in the countryside: the highlight of the year for her was the summer, when her sister Tanya and other relatives came to stay. 'If all my intellectual and emotional capacities were awakened, and most of all my desires, I would be crying until kingdom come,' she wrote to Tanya in November 1871, and a few months later she wrote to her again about the 'lonely, monastic' life at Yasnaya Polyana.[35]

Tolstoy also had the freedom to undertake trips elsewhere. Apart from his nightmare experience in Arzamas, he had enjoyed lifting his gaze to the tops of the tall pine trees as he travelled through the dense forests of the Penza region in the autumn of 1869. After crossing the Sura river, teeming with sterlet, he also relished the region's distinctive pebbled black earth. Like the local population, it reminded him of the mighty ploughman of Russian folklore Mikula Selyaninovich, the traditional peasant symbol of Russian strength and the hero of the medieval epics he had been reading.[36] In the summer of 1871 Tolstoy went further afield and lived like a Bashkirian nomad again out on the steppe east of Samara. The plan was that Sonya would go too the following year, but by autumn she discovered that she was pregnant again. Writing despondently to tell her sister Tanya about it that October, she spoke about the mud and the monotony, and how having a sixth child would mean having to stay put the following summer: 'it will be impossible to go to Samara, it will be impossible to come and visit you, we'll have to take on another nanny, and so on and so forth'.[37] By copying out *War and Peace*, Sonya felt she was involved, and was contributing to her husband's creative work, albeit in a very minor way, so it is understandable that she was keen for him to start writing a new book. But a 700-page ABC book was not exactly what she had in mind.

Tolstoy literally went back to basics for his next book. From sophisticated fiction about Russian aristocrats and lofty philosophising about history, he turned to helping children learn to read: the first of the four volumes of his *ABC* begin with the thirty-five letters of the Cyrillic alphabet in large type. He was never short of new ideas for novels, but what was the point of executing them when the vast majority of the population could not even read? He had been carried along by momentum when he was writing *War and Peace*, but after finishing it he was drawn ineluctably back to the path he had been treading before he had got married. Educating the people once again loomed into Tolstoy's field of vision, and he regarded the *ABC* he published in 1872 as the culmination of thirteen years of working towards this goal.

If Tolstoy's thoughts turned back to questions of teaching and learning in the early 1870s, it was because he certainly still cared deeply about the cause of popular education, but he was also thinking closer to home: his own children. The Tolstoys' eldest son Sergey was seven when Masha was born in 1871, Tanya was six, Ilya was nearly five and Lev approaching two. Tolstoy may have not been very interested in his children when they were babies, and for much of the 1860s he was preoccupied with *War and Peace*, but he naturally had very strong ideas about how he wanted his children to be educated, and as soon as they got to school age, he wanted to be involved. He was adamant that his children were to be home-educated, as he had been, and that both he and his wife would give instruction. This was when he discovered the inadequacies of the textbooks available at the time. Tolstoy believed that texts for children learning to read should be comprehensible, varied and interesting, but too many books, he found, were either insufferably dull or too far removed from life. Naturally, he resolved to write a much better textbook himself, and because he was Tolstoy, the most Russian of all Russians, it became an enormous, ambitious project involving the entire family, aimed not just at the junior Tolstoys but at all Russian children learning to read.

Tolstoy put a great deal of thought into the compilation of his *ABC* (*Azbuka*) and reading primer. He first planned on publishing these separately, but then combined them into one volume, sub-divided into four books of progressive difficulty. Half of each book was given over to stories, fables and scientific explanations. The other half was split between extracts from the Scriptures, the lives of saints and Russian chronicles (in Church Slavonic and in modern Russian) and the rudiments of mathematics, followed by instructions to teachers. He had first jotted down the idea for a 'First Book for Reading and an ABC for Families and Schools with Instructions to the Teacher by Count L. N. Tolstoy' as a diary entry in September 1868, at the time of Eugene Schuyler's visit.[38] While they had been rearranging Tolstoy's library, Schuyler had noticed the top shelf began with the German writer Berthold Auerbach, which had led to a discussion of the latter's weighty novel *A New Life*. Tolstoy took it down from the shelf and told Schuyler to go away and read it, explaining that this was the book which had prompted him to start his Yasnaya Polyana school. When Schuyler happened to meet Auerbach while travelling in Germany after his visit to Yasnaya Polyana, he mentioned this conversation to him, and Auerbach recalled Tolstoy well, saying: 'Yes, I always remember how frightened I was when this strange-looking man announced he was Eugen Baumann, as I feared he was going to threaten me with an action for libel and defamation of character.'[39] Tolstoy's conversations with Schuyler in 1868 had resuscitated his interest in popular education, and when he came to start the practical work of compiling his *ABC* in the autumn of 1871, he consulted a wide variety of textbooks and theoretical works by foreign educationalists such as Johann Heinrich Pestalozzi, as well as several American primers that Schuyler had procured for him.

As it turned out, the years immediately following *War and Peace* were a fallow period only in a manner of speaking, as before Tolstoy got to work on his *ABC*, he reminded himself of the learning process by taking up ancient Greek. This was partly so he could teach his son Sergey, to whom he wanted to give a classical education,[40] but also so he could produce his own translations of Aesop's fables for his *ABC*.[41] Since the Cyrillic alphabet is based on the Greek one, many letters are familiar, which gives Russians a head-start, but the idiosyncrasies of Greek grammar are not for the faint-hearted. Tolstoy was not a typical pupil, however. At the beginning of December 1870 he invited a seminarist from Tula to come up to Yasnaya Polyana and give him some lessons, and by the end of the month he was already spending whole days reading Greek literature in the original. He began with *The Anabasis*, Xenophon's account of the campaign led by Cyrus and his army of 10,000 Greek mercenaries against the Persian ruler Artaxerxes II in the fifth century BC. Tolstoy found it thrilling to be able to read and understand on his own, and Greek became his latest obsession. 'I'm completely living in Athens,' he wrote to his friend Fet. 'I speak in Greek in my dreams.'[42] No sooner had Sonya recovered from puerperal fever in March 1871 than he graduated to Plato and Homer, producing his own translations of parts of *The Iliad*, which he compared to the best-known Russian version completed by Nikolay Gnedich in 1829. A few months later, en route for the steppe that summer, he was reading unprepared texts *à livre ouvert* with Pavel Leontiev, professor of classical philology at Moscow University, whom he even showed up on a few occasions.[43]

While he was living on a diet of fermented mare's milk out on the steppe in a Bashkirian felt tent, the news that Count Tolstoy had learned Greek in three months became the talk of the town in Moscow.[44] Tolstoy was by now reading Herodotus, who had described the Scythians amongst whom he was living, he reported, 'in detail and with great precision'.[45] There was indeed a similarity between the lifestyle of the Bashkirs and the nomadic Scythians, who also lived on mare's milk. As with the beekeeping, Tolstoy's new passion for Greek was for a time all-engulfing, so much so that Sonya and his close friends feared for his mental health (Sergey Urusov wanted him to read the lives of Saints instead).[46] 'Clearly, nothing in the world interests and enraptures him as much as each new Greek word or phrase he learns,' Sonya noted in her diary.[47] But Tolstoy's overactive, mercurial mind was soon on the rampage again. Reading the classics of ancient Greek literature ignited an interest in the 'classics' of Russian literature, which in turn made him dream about writing something on the life of ancient Rus.[48]

Obviously there was nothing in the Russian 'classics' comparable to the epic poems of *The Iliad* and *The Odyssey*, not least because there was no literature in Russia at all before the year 988, when the Christianisation of Russia brought the need for a written language to help spread the Word of God. The huge upsurge of interest in the pre-Petrine past which began in the 1860s as an offshoot of the Great Reforms nevertheless resulted in Russians discovering and valuing their old literature for the first time. The excitement was contagious, and Tolstoy was able to benefit from the proliferation of new editions, collections and studies which now appeared – the Yasnaya Polyana library began to swell.[49] His study of medieval Russian literature was personally rewarding, but it was also a necessary preparation for his *ABC*, since he had decided at the outset to include in his primer a substantial section of religious and historical texts in old Slavonic (the medieval literary language of the Orthodox Church), with parallel translations in modern Russian.

Amongst the sacred works which most inspired Tolstoy was the *Cheti-Menei* ('monthly readings'), a voluminous compendium of religious texts arranged chronologically, and designed to be read on the feast days of the Orthodox saints.[50] The policy of the Byzantine Empire had always been for its missionaries to translate the Gospel for the heathen peoples they converted. After the adoption of the cyrillic alphabet, which had been devised by the two Greek monks Cyril and Methodius, literary activity in Russia had accordingly been exclusively religious in character to begin with, and followed Byzantine practice. But in the sixteenth century, after Metropolitan Makary of Novgorod incorporated texts such as the lives of newly canonised Russian saints, the originally Greek but now Russianised *Cheti–Menei* began to occupy a position of supreme importance in the nation's spiritual and literary life. Another important edition of the *Cheti–Menei* was later produced in the seventeenth century by Dmitry of Rostov (himself later canonised), and the copy of the 1864 edition Tolstoy acquired was soon densely annotated by him.[51] Tolstoy regarded the texts of the *Cheti–Menei* as Russia's 'real poetry'[52] (he famously did not think much of verse written by contemporary poets), and he chose extracts from both collections to include in the reading primer sections of his *ABC* alongside passages from the Bible and the oldest Russian chronicle, dating back to the twelfth century. One was a miraculous episode from Makary's life of St Simeon Stylites the Younger (a hermit who lived on a pillar near Antioch), in which a robber is inspired to repent of his sins. Another was a shortened version of Dmitry's life of St Sergius of Radonezh, the Patron Saint of Russia and founder of the most important monastery in the Russian Orthodox Church, the fourteenth-century Trinity Lavra of St Sergius outside Moscow.

If Tolstoy alighted particularly on Sergius, it may have been because the saint's life resonated with certain of his own aspirations on a subliminal level (although it would not be for another decade that he became fully cognisant of what those aspirations really were). St Sergius, the first great Russian ascetic, had turned his back on his noble background as a boy to seek out a life of poverty and seclusion in the 'desert' in emulation of St Antony of Egypt, the founder of monasticism. The rural wilderness was the Russian equivalent of the 'desert' – a deep forest in the case of St Sergius – and the disciples he attracted later followed his example by deliberately founding more than forty monasteries in parts of Russia that were similarly remote and inhospitable and far away from cities. Sergius's life was a model of humility. He turned down the opportunity to assume the pre-eminent position in the Russian ecclesiastical hierarchy he was offered, preferring instead to continue his life of poverty, engaged in hard physical work. Tolstoy would not forget his study of the *Cheti–Menei*. He would draw on the life of St Sergius in 1890 when he came to write his story 'Father Sergius',[53] which is about the struggles of a monk and former nobleman to overcome his pride and live up to his Christian ideals. Tolstoy's Father Sergius finally finds peace living as a Strannik – that specifically Russian type of religious wanderer dependent on alms, whose asceticism is based on a life of constant pilgrimage without material possessions. It also became Tolstoy's dream to detach himself from the world and become a wanderer, and eventually he would fulfil this dream, but in his own way, like everything else in his life.

Tolstoy was awed by the beauty of the writing in Russian hagiography, and it was aesthetic criteria as much as anything else which guided his selection of texts for the *ABC* – he wanted young children to be brought into contact with poetic language from the very beginning. But it was the secular legacy of the medieval oral epic, the *bylina*, which really bewitched him. Collections of narrative poems chronicling the exploits of Russia's semi-mythological warriors (*bogatyry*) had first been put together in the eighteenth century,[54] but it was not until the 1860s that they began to be made widely available. For Tolstoy, as for many of his contemporaries, they were a thrilling discovery, and even more tantalising was the revelation that this oral tradition had not yet died out. Pavel Rybnikov, an ethnographer who had been exiled to the far north for alleged revolutionary propaganda, found that there were peasants in the region still singing and reciting bylinas. He created a sensation in the 1860s by noting them down and publishing them.[55]

This living link with the past via the Russian language was thrilling for a writer like Tolstoy, who had an enduring passion for native sayings and proverbs. He was one of the founders of a society set up in Moscow in 1870 to study and preserve Russian folksong,[56] and the friendship he later formed with one of the most celebrated of the peasant 'reciters' from the Russian north would have a direct impact on his writing. Tolstoy's enthusiasm even led the author of an 1869 play based on bylinas about the warrior Alyosha Popovich to write an entire book about the structure of old Russian verse.[57] At the same time that the bylina tradition was being uncovered, Alexander Afanasiev was following in the footsteps of the Brothers Grimm to publish the first anthologies of Russian fairy tales. His pioneering collection of 640 tales appeared in eight volumes published between 1855 and 1864.[58] Since the Russian literary language had been created with the express purpose of translating the Bible, the Church had for centuries considered it blasphemous to use it to write down 'heathen' folktales (which first appeared in print in English translation), but now this rich tradition began to be valued too.

Tolstoy was completely captivated by the fairy tales and *byliny* he started reading after completing *War and Peace*, and it is no wonder when travelling through the fertile agricultural lands of the Penza region in 1869 on his property inspection trip that he should have thought of Mikula Selyaninovich. The *bylina* about the ploughman who works so fast the prince can only catch up with him after three days on horseback was one of the first he chose to include in his *ABC*. Tolstoy was also entranced by the tragic legend of the *bogatyr* Danilo Lovchanin. In one version of this *bylina*, Prince Vladimir sends Danilo on a dangerous mission to kill a ferocious lion, hoping to marry his beautiful wife in the certain event of his death, but Vasilisa takes the precaution of sending her husband off with 300 arrows to ensure his mission is successful. Danilo then stabs himself in despair rather than cross swords with the assassins next sent by the determined prince, but the faithful widow Vasilisa takes her own life over her husband's body rather than marry him. Tolstoy dreamed of turning this story (the closest Russian equivalent to *Romeo and Juliet* or *Tristan und Isolde* in terms of the tragic deaths of two lovers) into a play. Naturally the folk hero who most appealed to him, however, was the mighty Ilya of Murom, whose exploits he had read about when he was a boy. He even began thinking of writing a novel or a popular drama in which he would create characters with the traits of the great bogatyrs.[59] Ilya would still be a peasant's son, but instead of defeating armies single-handed after lying on the stove for thirty-three years, Tolstoy wanted to cast him as a clever young university student.[60]

A major goal for Tolstoy was to cultivate in his young readers a love of Russia – its landscape, its history, its way of life, and, of course, its language. One of his favourite pastimes became walking down to the high road which passed close to Yasnaya Polyana in order to collect sayings and proverbs from the many pilgrims and religious wanderers making the journey on foot to the great Caves Monastery at Kiev. Sayings such as 'A crow cannot be a falcon' enabled him to explain the idiosyncrasies of Russian pronunciation in a simple and engaging way to children. Tolstoy also wanted to spark in young readers a curiosity for the workings of science in his *ABC*, but in order to answer questions such as 'Where does the water from the sea go?' and 'What is wind for?' in a way that would be both comprehensible and appealing to children, he felt he needed to have a profound understanding of these phenomena himself. So he threw himself into an intense and wide-ranging study of nearly every branch of science, from zoology to physics. Wherever possible, Tolstoy undertook practical research, which led to him on one occasion spending an entire night in the garden gazing up at the stars, in order to brush up on his astronomy.[61] Understanding and then explaining processes such as galvanism and how crystals form required sustained concentration at his desk indoors, however: his notebooks from this time are littered with references to scientists like Michael Faraday, Humphry Davy and John Tyndall.[62]

Finally, Tolstoy also wanted to nurture in young children an appreciation for truth, honesty, and the value of hard work, but not in a dry didactic way, like all the foreign textbooks and primers he had pored over and made notes on. He was certainly not impressed by the English books he consulted, including Thomas Ewing's *Principles of Elocution*, which was a 'model of pointlessness' in demonstrating 'how to be silent', and *Abbott's Second Reader*, which was far too abstract.[63] Like the available Russian books, everything seemed to be cut off from real life. It was the stories and fables which naturally lay at the heart of Tolstoy's *ABC*. After an enormous amount of reading, as well as months of fastidious work in condensing and simplifying, Tolstoy eventually produced simplified versions of over 600 stories, which he whittled down to 372 for publication. He favoured Aesop over all other authors, including such well-known fables as the 'The Frog and the Lion':

> A lion heard a frog croaking loudly and turned towards the sound, thinking that this must be the sound of some huge beast. After a while, the lion saw the frog come up out of the swamp. He went over to the frog and as he crushed him underfoot, the lion said, 'No one should be worried about a sound before the thing itself has been examined.' *This fable is for a man with a big mouth who talks and talks without accomplishing anything.*[64]

Tolstoy produced his own free translations, subtly changing their meaning, which he then, as a consummate artist, revised endlessly. After he had produced the first draft of his translation of this particular fable, for example, Tolstoy worked on it again, before producing another version, which was then reworked a third and a fourth time.[65] Changes even went into the proofs before Tolstoy was happy:

> A lion heard a frog croaking loudly, and thought it must be a large animal

to be shouting that loudly. He went closer and saw the frog coming out of the swamp. The lion crushed it with his paw and said: 'It's tiny – and to think I was scared.' [66]

While Aesop took pride of place, Tolstoy ranged very widely in terms of authors, including not only more recent writers such as La Fontaine and Grimm, but some really up-to-date ones such as Sofya Tolstaya ('Some Girls Came to See Masha') and Vasily Rumyantsev, a former pupil of the Yasnaya Polyana school ('How a Boy Told About Getting Caught by a Storm When He Was in the Forest'). Tolstoy also fashioned miniature tales from Russian folk anecdotes, and contributed real-life stories about the adventures of his dogs Milton and Bulka in the Caucasus, as well as stories about the lives of birds and animals in the Russian countryside ('Sparrows', 'How Wolves Teach Their Cubs'). Not all the stories and vignettes are set in a world reassuringly familiar to Russian children. Tolstoy carefully juxtaposed stories like 'The Girl and the Mushrooms' with pieces about Eskimos, elephants and silk-worms. He wanted to inculcate Russian children with a respect for foreign cultures along with a love of their native land, so he treated his young readers to excerpts from Herodotus and Plutarch, and exotic stories from countries as far-flung as India, America, France and Turkey. Tolstoy also contributed fiction he had written himself, beginning with very simple tales such as 'The Muzhik and the Cucumbers':

> One day a muzhik went over to a vegetable patch to steal cucumbers. He got to the cucumbers and thought: 'Suppose I carry off a bag of cucumbers and sell them; I can buy a hen with that money. The hen will give me eggs, and when she is broody she will produce lots of chicks. I'll feed the chicks, sell them, and buy a piglet who will grow into a pig; and my pig will bring me lots of piglets. I'll sell the piglets and buy a mare; the mare will have foals. I'll feed the foals and sell them; then I'll buy a house and have a vegetable patch. I'll have a vegetable patch and plant cucumbers, and I won't let them be stolen because I will keep a strict watch on them. I'll hire watchmen, station them by the cucumbers and I will go along myself and shout: "Hey, keep stricter watch!"' And he shouted that out at the top of his voice. The watchmen heard, jumped out and thrashed the muzhik. [67]

For his more advanced young readers, Tolstoy wrote two of his finest works of fiction, 'God Sees the Truth But Waits' and 'Captive of the Caucasus', whose power lies precisely in their carefully wrought simplicity. From the beginning, Tolstoy had intended the artistic level of his *ABC* to be in no way inferior to that of *War and Peace*, and both stories exemplified in fact the devices and the language he declared he would now employ in his adult fiction, as he explained in a letter to Nikolay Strakhov.[68]

Work on the final compilation began in earnest in September 1871, and Tolstoy inveigled not only Sonya, but her uncle Kostya and his niece Varya into helping him as copyists. He was as exacting with his tiny stories for children as he was with his adult fiction, as Sonya commented in a letter to her sister,[69] but finally in December 1871 the first of the four books was ready, and Tolstoy set off for Moscow to find a publisher. This proved difficult, partly because of all the old Church Slavonic in the manuscript, forcing Tolstoy to resort to signing a deal with his old publisher Theodor Ries. But once his *ABC* was finally in press he was clearly excited, and when he wrote to Alexandrine in St Petersburg in January 1872 he told her that if just two generations of all Russian children, from the Romanovs to rural peasants, learned to read with his *ABC*, and had their first contact with art through it, he could die a happy man.[70] He was convinced this was the work he would be remembered for,[71] and rated it higher than *War and Peace*.[72]

There was now an intense period of work to finish the three remaining books of the *ABC*. Typically for Tolstoy, the printing process had begun while he was still writing and adding to his manuscript, but he was an inveterate risk-taker and gambler. At times even he had to admit he was overwhelmed by the dimensions of his task. It was enough work for 100 years, he wrote to Alexandrine again in April: 'You need to know Greek, Indian and Arabic literature for it, as well all the natural sciences, astronomy and physics, and the work on the language is terrible – everything has to be beautiful, concise, simple, and most important of all, clear.'[73] Meanwhile, he was dying to try his *ABC* out, so in January 1872 he reopened the Yasnaya Polyana school to thirty-five local peasant children.

The school was located in the family house this time – in the front hall and in the rooms on the ground floor. Tolstoy taught the older boys in his study, while Sonya had a group of about ten pupils, mostly girls, whom she taught in another room. In the mornings they taught their own children, and after lunch they all pitched in to help teach at the school, including eight-year-old Sergey and seven-year-old Tanya, who were given the task of teaching the alphabet in the hall to the youngest pupils.[74] Five-year-old Ilya started out as a teacher too, but he proved to be far too strict with his pupils. His contract was terminated after he ended up fighting with his charges too often.[75] As an adult, Ilya could still remember the intense smell of sheepskin that the village children brought with them into the house, and the delightful anarchy that reigned in the schoolroom. Tolstoy allowed the children to sit where they wanted, get up when they wanted and answer questions all together – it was certainly a long way from regimented learning by rote.[76] The school broke up for the summer months, but teaching was not resumed in the autumn: Tolstoy had moved on to new pastures.

Tolstoy itched to see his *ABC* in print once he had handed over the manuscript, and eventually he lost patience with his publisher, who was proceeding at a snail's pace. The American primers Eugene Schuyler procured for him had given him the idea of using large typefaces and a particular design in the earlier pages of his *ABC* in order to make it easier for children to learn pronunciation, but this presented the typographers with a headache, as they were simply not used to printing anything other than with standard typefaces.[77] In May 1872 Tolstoy managed to transfer publication to Petersburg, having persuaded his friend Strakhov to oversee operations.[78] Strakhov, who had made his first visit to Yasnaya Polyana the previous summer, had already helped by producing modern translations of the old Slavonic texts, and now Tolstoy asked him also to grade the stories in the reading primer according to whether he liked them or not.[79] The 758 pages of the *ABC* finally appeared in November 1872, but its initial print run of 3,600 copies also proved to be its last. The next time the book appeared again in this format was in 1957, when a facsimile edition constituted volume twenty-two of the 'Jubilee' edition of Tolstoy's *Complete Collected Works*.

Despite the high price of fifty kopecks for each constituent part of the *ABC*, Tolstoy had high expectations for its success and began thinking about the second edition even before it had been published.[80] He was to be bitterly disappointed. First of all, the book did not receive official approval for use in schools, despite Tolstoy sending a letter explaining its virtues to his distant relative Count Dmitry Tolstoy, the Russian Minister of Education.[81] Secondly, Tolstoy's desire to make some money from the publication got the better of him. He offered booksellers a twenty per cent discount, but insisted

3. Page eight from the 1872 edition of Tolstoy's ABC book, showing the letters 'k' for kolokol
(bell), 'l' for lozhka *(spoon) and 'm' for* medved *(bear).*

they paid in cash up-front, and so lost both their goodwill and valuable mar-
keting potential. Sonya's younger brother Pyotr Bers, who lived in Petersburg,
had been put in charge of sales, and he took a dim view of Tolstoy's attempt
to break the power of booksellers in controlling distribution. His flat doubled
up as a warehouse, and so he ended up being left with hundreds of unsold
copies. The almost uniformly negative reviews which started appearing also
did nothing to help sales of the *ABC*. Some critics objected to the dull grey

paper it was printed on and the paucity of illustrations (twenty-eight), while others complained about the lack of any kind of introduction to explain for whom the book was intended.[82] They were all suspicious of Tolstoy's new-fangled methods.

A writer as thin-skinned as Tolstoy could not fail to be stung by the criticism, but his belief in the *ABC* never wavered. Once he had published an open letter to the *Moscow Gazette* in June 1873 setting out what he regarded as the shortcomings of the teaching methods then in use, he calmed down. First, he decided to unbind the 1,500 unsold copies of his *ABC* and repackage them as twelve individual small volumes – they went on sale for between ten and twenty-five kopecks each.[83] Then a dozen young teachers from rural schools in the area came to spend a week at Yasnaya Polyana in October to study his methods.[84] In January 1874 Tolstoy was given the opportunity to defend his approach to the Moscow Literacy Committee, which accepted his proposal to conduct an experiment comparing his teaching methods with those that had been officially adopted. When the results of this experiment were inconclusive, he published a fifty-page *profession de foi* about his teaching methods in the august and widely read journal *Notes of the Fatherland* which finally provoked wide public debate.[85] 'On Popular Education' is Tolstoy's heartfelt pedagogical manifesto.

Tolstoy goes into extraordinary detail in his discussion of pedagogical methods in 'On Popular Education', and shows deep knowledge of the educational provision in his own district. He summarised the flaws of Russian primary education as: '(1) lack of knowledge of the people, (2) the attraction of teaching what the pupils already know, (3) a tendency to borrow from the Germans, and (4) a criticism of the old without the establishment of new principles.'[86] Tolstoy had strong ideas about how Russian children should be taught letter and syllable formation, and was adamant that the phonetic method that had been adopted from Germany was not practicable in Russia, and certainly not suitable for disadvantaged peasant children. In some respects, he was ahead of his time, as what he was advocating later became axiomatic in twentieth-century remedial education.[87] Tolstoy's *ABC* was eventually approved by the Russian government in September 1874. Even repackaged, it had continued to sell poorly, and Tolstoy complained that he made a loss of 2,000 roubles,[88] but he was now keen to revise it.

To begin with, Tolstoy's plans for revision were minor, but typically for him, he ended up producing an almost completely new book. Something similar had happened with *War and Peace*, which he revised in 1873 for a new, third edition. His new frame of mind led him to turn six volumes into four, translate all the French text in the novel into Russian and place all his historical digressions into a separate epilogue. Strakhov was also instrumental in this project. For his *New ABC*, as it was now called, Tolstoy actually heeded his critics by providing an introduction and reducing the cost.[89] He wrote more than 100 new miniature stories, but by separating the 'ABC' section from the reading primer, he reduced the overall size of the book to ninety-two pages. It went on sale for a much more reasonable fourteen kopecks.[90] The *New ABC* proved to be as successful as the first edition had been a failure. It was published in February 1875, was swiftly recommended by the Ministry of Education, and became a best-seller, running into twenty-eight editions during Tolstoy's lifetime, with print runs of up to 100,000. Over a million copies had been sold by the time of his death. No other textbook was more widely read in pre-revolutionary Russia.[91] The poet Anna Akhmatova was just one of scores of Russians who benefited from Tolstoy's child-centred approach in learning their alphabet. The new primer, now entitled *Russian Books for Reading*, was based on the texts used in the first edition and was published later in October 1875. Since most of the first book from the 1872 edition had gone into the *New ABC*, Tolstoy produced twelve new stories and fables for the first of the four parts.[92] They proved equally popular with Russian children.

Tolstoy had conclusively proved that he wanted to improve the deplorable literacy levels in Russia, and that he cared deeply about Russian boys and girls of all classes discovering the joys of their native language when they learned to read. But what about his own children? What kind of a teacher was he to them? What was it like being used as a guinea-pig for his educational ideas? What was it like, indeed, growing up with a famous writer for a father? In October 1872 Tolstoy responded to Alexandrine's request that he for once tell her something about his children – for the most part, his letters to her, as to everyone else, concerned his current projects and intellectual preoccupations. It was indeed rare for Tolstoy to talk much about his family in his letters, and the thumbnail sketches he provides of his six children are thus often quoted.

Tolstoy described fair-haired Sergey, his eldest, as being bright, with a natural ability for mathematics and art. He was a good pupil, he told

Alexandrine, and proficient in gymnastics, but rather gauche and absent-minded. Tolstoy was flattered to think Sergey reminded some people of his brother Nikolay, who had been famous for his lack of ego. Unlike Sergey, sensitive, pink-cheeked Ilya was always healthy, Tolstoy wrote, but he did not like studying much. Also unlike Sergey, he was a great original, and rather pugnacious, but at the same time he had a great capacity for tenderness, and had an infectious laugh. Tolstoy was confident that Sergey would excel in any environment, but he felt that Ilya would always need the strong leadership of someone he respected. Eight-year-old Tanya was very like her mother, Tolstoy wrote, and was already very maternal, liking nothing better than to take care of her younger siblings. Lev junior, then three and a half, he described as lithe, graceful and very capable, but for sickly little Masha, whom he described as 'very clever and unattractive', he foresaw a life of seeking and not finding. 'Skin white as milk, blonde curly hair; strange, large blue eyes – strange because of their deep, serious expression' – Tolstoy felt she would be a mystery to everyone. He openly confessed to Alexandrine that he found children in general hard to deal with until they were about three years old, but described Pyotr, the youngest, as a wonderful, bouncing six-month-old baby.[93]

As Sonya later emphasised, her husband's work was always the most important thing in his life,[94] and she would later actually reprove him for his neglect of the younger children when he became a full-time campaigner on behalf of the oppressed. He was the one to make all the decisions about how the children would be educated, however, and was a charismatic figure when they were growing up, all the more so because they saw him less. It was in the 1870s that Tolstoy was most active and involved as a father, particularly in the first half of the decade, before he became swept up by the writing of *Anna Karenina* and the spiritual crisis which immediately followed it. The elder Tolstoy children consequently received considerably more attention from their father than their younger siblings who grew up in the 1880s, as would become apparent in the case of Andrey and Misha, who later showed no interest whatsoever in living according to their father's teachings. The younger Tolstoy children also grew up with no memory of their parents being happily married, unlike the three eldest, who as adults all wrote revealing memoirs of their idyllic early years at Yasnaya Polyana.[95]

Even though the Tolstoy children saw less of their father than their mother, his influence was certainly greater when they were young: his word was law. When they were very young, it was always an event whenever he appeared in the nursery, and throughout their childhood they cherished the times he spent with them. In the 1870s the Tolstoy children remembered their father still being full of joie de vivre, and somehow life became more interesting for them when he was present, as he seemed to possess a special energy. He hated to be disturbed while he was working, and insisted on complete peace and quiet, but at other times he was often in high spirits, with the exuberance of an overgrown child himself. As an aficionado of physical exercise and the benefits of being outdoors in the fresh air, he enjoyed taking his children riding, swimming and skating. Tolstoy was particularly keen that his sons take up gymnastics, but he was not at all keen on toys, which were banished from the nursery, forcing Sonya to produce horses and dogs out of cardboard, and sew rag-dolls herself so the children had something to play with. Tolstoy compensated for depriving his children of conventional playthings by granting them the greatest possible liberty. What he hated most of all in his children were lies and rudeness, and to see them eating from their knife; he punished their misdemeanours by simply ignoring them. The Tolstoy children found it impossible to lie to their father, and sometimes found it hard to face his steely gaze, as they were convinced he could read their thoughts. They never doubted his love for them, but since he regarded it as a weakness to exhibit tenderness towards his sons, he was not always demonstrative. Indeed, Ilya could not remember ever being caressed by his father. Tolstoy was always much more physically affectionate with his daughters.

With his own children, Tolstoy was a rigorous and exacting teacher, and it was sometimes hard keeping up with him (Tanya dreaded her maths lessons with her father as he could be very impatient). Not only did the word 'can't' not exist in his vocabulary, but he always went at a cracking pace, just like the fast trot he maintained on horseback. The Tolstoy children were taught by both their parents, with their father taking them for mathematics, Latin and Greek, while their mother was responsible for Russian and French lessons. Then there was a local priest who came twice a week to teach the Scriptures, a drawing teacher for Tanya later on, and a succession of resident tutors, several of whom were foreign. Since Tolstoy admired many aspects of British education, the first of the many tutors hired for the three eldest children was an English governess, Hannah Tarsey, who arrived in November 1866. Neither

Tolstoy nor Sonya knew English well, so before her arrival they read their way through Wilkie Collins's *A Woman in White*.

Hannah Tarsey was the daughter of the gardener at Windsor Castle, and she arrived in Russia with her sister Jenny, who was taken on by another family. At nineteen, Hannah was only three years younger than Sonya. The two could not communicate at all at first,[96] but she was hard-working and friendly, and was to become an adored member of the family. Soon she had the children on a regime of regular baths, and introduced the family to Christmas pudding and the custom of setting it alight (recipe no. 26 in Sonya's recipe book: 'Plump-puding'). Hannah obviously missed Sunday roasts at home in Berkshire, as she also tried out Yorkshire pudding on the Tolstoys (recipe no. 132: 'Pastry baked for Roast Beef'). Hannah threw herself into Russian life, and stayed with the Tolstoys for six years, but she suffered from poor health and at the end of the summer in 1872 left to become governess to the children of Sonya's sister Tanya in the Caucasus. Her health improved in the more temperate southern climate there and two years later she married into impoverished Georgian royalty by becoming the wife of Prince Dmitry Machutadze (and won over her in-laws by eventually making a success of the family's sheep-cheese business).[97] Fyodor (Theodor) Kaufmann was installed as the boys' tutor when Hannah left, and he gave all the children German lessons. He fell for the blonde and pretty Dora who replaced Hannah as the girls' governess, but she did not last long, as she proved incapable of exerting any authority. This was partly because Tolstoy had a golden-haired Irish setter of the same name (he liked to name his dogs after characters in novels by Dickens). That made it even harder for anyone to take Dora seriously. Then came Emily, who was quiet and serious and cried a lot.

The Tolstoy children saw far more of their tutors and governesses than they did their father, or even their mother, who was always busy sewing clothes for them or attending to domestic matters when she was not copying out manuscripts. Their upbringing was also influenced by other members of the populous household in which they lived, amongst whom were some eccentric characters. First of all there was the ageing Aunt Toinette in her cap and shawl, whose room was full of icons in silver frames that were polished by her maid Aksinya Maximovna, who by then was equally doddering. The children associated Aunt Toinette with the smell of cypress, and drawers in her commode full of gingerbread, which she would treat them to sometimes.

She was kind, but the children found both her and her companion very dull. Natalya Petrovna always chuntered on about landowners, army officers and monasteries, and to Sergey she always seemed to speak as if she had a mouthful of kasha. Then there were all the servants – the family's former serfs. The most venerable of them was Agafya Mikhailovna, the old maid of Tolstoy's grandmother, who had in later years tended the sheep and worked as the family's housekeeper, and was now living on a pension on the estate. She was a tall, thin and slightly scary figure for the children when they were small, but she was a beloved member of the household, who before Tolstoy was married used to sit quietly by the samovar reading the lives of saints on cold winter evenings. She was affectionately known by everyone as the 'dog governess', as she lived, in a state of some squalor, with all the family's borzois and other hunting dogs. The small, round Maria Afanasievna Arbuzova, who was nanny to the five eldest Tolstoy children, was also greatly loved. She became housekeeper after Hannah arrived, and always spoiled the children, furtively giving them Persian dried apricots and other treats from the pantry. Both she and her two sons Pavel and Sergey, also trusted family servants, were very close to the Tolstoy children. Pavel later taught Tolstoy the art of cobbling, while Sergey became Tolstoy's personal servant after the faithful Alexey Stepanov retired. The mild-mannered Alexey, for whom the children had a great respect, had originally been a Yasnaya Polyana house serf, and had accompanied Tolstoy to the Crimea. He was married to Dunyasha Bannikova, the daughter of Tolstoy's first tutor, and when Ilya was born in 1866, Tolstoy promoted him to become the estate manager. The Tolstoy children had deep connections to nearly everyone in the household. Evlampia Matveyevna, who had acted as Sergey's wet-nurse, for example, was the wife of the Yasnaya Polyana coachman Filipp Rodionov, who looked after the boys' ponies.

In order to accommodate their burgeoning family, as well as the foreign tutors, the Tolstoys were soon obliged to build a large new extension on to their house. They had built the first extension back in the summer of 1866, and at the end of 1871 they created a large new drawing room and dining room upstairs, and a study for Tolstoy downstairs, with a spacious wooden veranda outside for summer repasts.[98] The additions destroyed the symmetry of the two identical wings that had once flanked the manor house Tolstoy had sold to pay his gambling debts, but provided much-needed extra room. The second and final extension was completed in December 1871, and was ready for Christmas, which was always one of the most joyous times of year for the Tolstoy children. As well as supervising the scrubbing of floors and the hanging of pictures after all the painting and decorating was finished, Sonya retrieved from storage antique candelabras and old family tableware, as well as sewing masquerade costumes and gilding walnuts in preparation for the arrival of the family's guests just before midnight on Christmas Eve in three sleighs. More guests arrived the following day, and after the tree had been decorated there was ice-skating and tobogganing, with everyone collapsing of fits of laughter when they took a tumble or landed in a snowdrift. That year, as well as the seven Tolstoys plus Hannah, Aunt Toinette and Natalya Petrovna, there was Sonya's uncle Kostya, Tolstoy's aunt Polina and his nephew and nieces Kolya, Varya and Liza, plus the latter's husband Leonid Dmitrievich, Tolstoy's old friend Dmitry Alexeyevich Dyakov and his daughter Masha plus Sofya, her former governess and another visiting English governess, Katie – all in all, twenty sat down to dinner. Late into the evening, Uncle Kostya started playing a waltz, and soon everyone was dancing, followed by the hilarious spectacle of watching the rotund, red-bearded Dmitry Alexeyevich striking up a Cossack dance with Leonid Dmitrievich.

Christmas in Russia was about the only time the Tolstoy children were allowed toys. Tanya in particular cherished the dolls her godfather Dmitry Alexeyevich gave her – they were invariably called Masha, after his daughter, who turned sixteen in 1871, and whom she clearly idolised. Christmas was also the time for wearing masks, cross-dressing, and dressing up as animals, and the second day of festivities that year saw Tanya dressing up as a powdered Marquis in a long blue robe, accompanied by her brother Sergey as the Marquise. Ilya put on a red skirt, Katie transformed herself into a clown, Liza became a muzhik, and Sonya donned Russian national dress. Next came the appearance of Uncle Kostya and Kolya as the traditional dancing bears, led by Dmitry Alexeyevich in bast shoes, who was accompanied by a leaping goat whom the children gleefully recognised as their father.[99] This was one of the happiest times at Yasnaya Polyana, and also one of the last happy times.

When they were young, the elder children also used to look forward to the summer months when people came to visit. Their father's friends (such as Afanasy Fet and his wife, Sergey Urusov and Nikolay Strakhov) usually came to stay for a few days, but their aunt Tanya and their cousins Dasha, Masha and Vera, who were all under five in 1871, would take up residence in the other wing for over a month every summer. Sonya's younger brother Stepan ('Uncle Styopa') also spent every summer at Yasnaya Polyana from 1866 to 1878 while he was in his teens. Sometimes grandmother Lyubov came to stay (she was now living in Petersburg), and Aunt Polina would make regular visits from the convent in Tula which was now her permanent home. Summer had truly arrived after the buttercups appeared in the lawn in front of the house, and the children's summer clothes had been unpacked and no longer smelled of camphor. It was the time for picnics with the samovar by the stream under the shade of an oak tree, with the girls reading poems aloud. It was the time for mushroom gathering and evening bonfires, sometimes with the thrill of watching the express train speed by the nearby village of Kozlovka. Summer was also the time for jam-making, a ritual that took place every year in the garden under the lime trees, accompanied by clouds of bees and wasps buzzing overhead. Barefoot village girls would come up to the porch on hot afternoons bearing plates of mushrooms and strawberries to be exchanged for a few kopecks.

For the two elder Tolstoy boys, summer also meant taking a net into the fields to hunt for butterflies, or riding through oak woods and dewy glades full of forget-me-nots on their Kirghiz ponies, Sharik and Kolpik. If they were lucky, their father would accompany Sergey and Ilya on his English stallion, and more often than not they would tie them to the birch trees next to the bathing hut and go swimming in the pond. Used to having at least a shack to change in when she was growing up, Sonya had been shocked when she had first arrived at Yasnaya Polyana to discover there was nothing but the bare bank, but this was in keeping with Tolstoy's enthusiasm for living the natural life. When Sergey was a baby, Tolstoy also bought some unbleached linen in the village and ordered Sonya to make traditional peasant shirts with a skewed collar for him, like the ones he himself wore and became identified with (which later even came to be named the *tolstovka* after him). Sonya dutifully complied, but she also made little shirts out of her fine muslin blouses for Sergey to wear under the rough linen.[100]

Just twice, in 1873 and in 1875, the Tolstoy family went away for their summer holidays, to their new estate out in the steppe of Samara province, over 500 miles away to the east. It was a huge adventure for the children, and an enormous undertaking for their parents. Tolstoy had made the trip several times already for health reasons: he was a great advocate of koumiss, the fermented mare's milk produced by the nomadic Bashkirs. He made his first trip to the steppe in the summer of 1862, before his marriage, and then returned in 1871 and 1872, leaving Sonya and the children at home. In 1871 he took Stepan Bers (now sixteen) and his old servant Vanya Suvorov with him, and was away for six weeks.[101] At that time, there was no railway beyond Nizhny Novgorod, which was already two days away from Yasnaya Polyana, and just to get to the remote steppe village where Tolstoy undertook his koumiss cure required a two-day passage on a Volga steamer, and then a further two days of travel in a *tarantass* from Samara, which lay on the main highway to Central Asia. What awaited at the end of the journey was mile upon mile of scorched, treeless steppe, a round felt tent, an almost exclusive diet of mutton, and gallons of koumiss.

A primitive Bashkir village in the middle of nowhere was not every Russian's idea of the ideal health resort. Much more fashionable at that time was to go abroad, either to the German spas, or to the French Riviera. Those who wished to stay within the Russian Empire were also now spoiled for choice: they could enjoy the bracing sea air at a lido on the Baltic, take the waters at the resorts that had sprung up around the mineral springs in the Caucasus, such as Kislovodsk or Pyatigorsk, or patronise the increasingly popular seaside town of Yalta in the balmy Crimea, where the Romanovs vacationed. It had been a long time since Tolstoy cared for fashion, however, and he positively relished the lack of amenities, writing merrily to Sonya to tell her the complete absence of beds, crockery and white bread (food was consumed from wooden bowls without cutlery) would be more than her 'Kremlin heart' could stand.[102]

The Bashkirs were originally nomadic horsemen from the southern Urals who lived between the Kama and Ural rivers, east of Samara. A Turkic-speaking Moslem people, they were forced to acknowledge Russian supremacy after the conquest of Kazan in the mid-sixteenth century, but then gradually found themselves becoming a minority as Russians and other ethnic groups from the Volga region settled in the lands they had for centuries believed belonged to them.[103] This was frontier territory for the Russians, who in the eighteenth century proceeded to build a line of forts from Samara to the new town of Orenburg, in preparation for advancing into Kazakhstan and beyond (Samarkand was conquered for the great White Tsar's new province of Turkestan in 1868). While the Bashkirs had been brutally subjugated by the middle of the eighteenth century, and their lands fully absorbed into the Russian Empire, they were given a special tax status and they tried to maintain their traditional way of life amongst the more numerous Russians who steadily colonised their fertile pastures. One of these Russians was Tolstoy.

Tolstoy might have poured a lot of his own money into publishing the first edition of his *ABC*, but he had large reserves from sales of *War and Peace*, and at this stage of his life he was eager to increase them. Bashkir land was very cheap, and Tolstoy had an eye to making a profitable deal by buying some land, and pocketing the proceeds of its cultivation. Two weeks after his arrival he made a decision to buy nearly 7,000 acres for a total cost of 17,500 roubles. He explained to Sonya by letter that with two good harvests he would recoup his investment, but that they would need to spend the following summer living there to make that possible. He described the hilly landscape to his wife as picturesque, although he admitted there were no trees, and he also acknowledged there was no shade at all, but to compensate there was 'steppe air, bathing, koumiss, and riding'. Tolstoy assured Sonya that he wanted her approval first, but he went ahead anyway, even before he had received her reply. As it happened, she was not at all enthusiastic: 'If it's profitable, that's your business, and I don't have an opinion on the matter. But it would have to be extreme necessity that would want to force a person to live in the steppe without a single tree for hundreds of miles, as one would never go there willingly, particularly with five children.'[104]

In the summer of 1871 Tolstoy and his two companions lived in a huge Bashkirian *kibitka* (tent) belonging to the local mullah, with feather grass serving as flooring. It had formerly been a mosque, and featured a table and one chair, oats for the horses, a black dog and lots of hens who brought disorder, but also a regular supply of eggs. Tolstoy got up at dawn every day, he wrote to Sonya, and after three cups of tea, would go outside to watch the herds of horses coming back over the hills (about 1,000 of them, he reckoned). Then it was time to drink koumiss, produced in leather churns behind curtains by the Bashkir women, but served always by the men. Afterwards, he told Sonya, he would usually walk into the village to consort with other people who had come from Russia for the koumiss cure, including a Greek teacher who helped him read Herodotus. Sometimes there was some shooting (for bustard, ruff, and the occasional wolf), and there was always great deal of hospitality from the Bashkirs they visited due to Tolstoy's aristocratic title. At the end of June Tolstoy and Stepan travelled fifty miles east, in a cart pulled by the horse he had bought for sixty roubles when he arrived, to Buzuluk, a town with several churches, mostly wooden houses and a bustling trade in grain, tallow and hides.[105] After spending a rough night at the halfway point in their exhausting journey across the steppe, Tolstoy slept soundly when they finally arrived – indeed, he slept so deeply he did not notice the bedbugs crawling all over him – but soon his mind was taken up with the colourful fair they had come to see. About a dozen different nationalities had converged to trade Kirghiz, Cossack and Siberian horses.

Tolstoy returned home to Yasnaya Polyana that year in high spirits, and in much better health, having gloried in the dry heat of the steppe, the clear air and bright skies. In the end he went back to Samara the following summer without Sonya, since she had just given birth to Pyotr (Petya), their sixth child, and as his companion he took with him instead Timofey Fokanov, a Yasnaya Polyana peasant, who was going to became the first manager of his property. This trip was more difficult in many respects. The harvest in 1871 had been very poor, but the harvest in 1872 was the worst in decades, causing problems which would only worsen the following year. Tolstoy was staying in a house rather than a tent this time – the house on his new *khutor* (homestead), but it left something to be desired. The first impression was very pleasant, he wrote to Sonya, although there was no water in the pond. He also admitted that the house was old and drab, and had only two rooms, but it would be absolutely fine for all of them, he reassured her brightly.[106] That summer Tolstoy was very preoccupied with his first *ABC* book, which was now finally being printed, so in the end he came back early, after only three weeks.

Whatever qualms Sonya had about living out in the steppe, she managed to suppress them the following summer, when the entire family headed east. In June 1873 sixteen members of the Tolstoy household gathered in the drawing room, shut the doors and sat in silence for a few moments to prepare for the journey ahead, then completed the ritual by getting up and crossing themselves. A caravan of carriages and carts then transported them to Tula to catch a train, and in Nizhny Novgorod they boarded the steamer for Samara. When they stepped on board, they already felt they were in Asia when they saw the exotic robes and skullcaps of the various Tatars and Persians travelling in third class, and particularly when they heard them speak. During a refuelling stop in Kazan, Tolstoy got off with the eldest boys, Sergey and Ilya, to show them where he used to live, and it was not until the boat had travelled several miles further down the Volga that Sonya realised they had failed to re-embark. As she notes in her autobiography, the captain would not have turned back for a 'mere mortal', but since Tolstoy was a count, it was different.[107] From Samara the family travelled in an enormous old carriage pulled by six horses, donated by Tolstoy's friend Urusov, which had been brought from Yasnaya Polyana. It was a long, hot and dusty journey, punctuated by a night spent at a peasant coaching inn. For the elder children, who slept outside on hay under the stars, and had never seen such a strange landscape, everything was a great novelty.

When they finally arrived, the Tolstoys had difficulty cramming themselves into the small and extremely basic residence on their new estate. In the end, Tolstoy and Stepan took up residence in a kibitka, and the boys and their German tutor slept in the barn. Sonya's qualms, it turned out, were fully justified. The dried dung used as fuel did not burn well, and smelled disgusting; there were clouds of flies everywhere during the day, while large black beetles would drop from the ceiling and start running all over the tablecloth as soon as the candles were lit. The only neighbours for miles around were Bashkirs and peasants. Sonya put on a brave face, however, and did her best to make sure everyone enjoyed their stay. Tolstoy was conscious they were all there because of him, and also did his best to keep everyone amused. He invited an elderly Bashkir to provide the koumiss that summer, which he had almost on tap. Muhammed Shah brought along his wives and daughters-in-law plus ten mares, and pitched his kibitka near to the Tolstoys' house. Every morning various members of the family, plus Hannah, who had come up from the Caucasus to join them, went to sit cross-legged on the carpets in the kibitka and drink from the wooden bowls proffered by Muhammed. The Bashkirs had not adapted well to leading sedentary lives, like the Russian settlers, and Muhammed spoke wistfully about the lands they had lost to peasant farmers from Tambov or Ryazan, who were distinguishable by the colour and styling of their clothes.

Tolstoy certainly derived health benefits from downing up to eight bowls of koumiss at a sitting, and he loved going to Orenburg and Buzuluk to the horse fairs, on one occasion buying a whole herd of wild steppe horses. But that summer he was preoccupied with the drought, and the famine in the area that was beginning to follow the third consecutive failed harvest. There was absolutely no prospect that his optimistic forecast of being able to recoup his investment in two years was possible now. Sonya egged him on to do something, and the new governor's staggering lack of concern goaded him into action.[108] Indeed, the new governor's only action was to put pressure on those peasants who were in tax arrears with the administration. Tolstoy spent two weeks travelling round each of the districts in a fifty-mile radius of his homestead in order to assess the problem, and then he put together a detailed inventory of twenty-three households in Gavrilovka, the nearest village. It included information about the number of cattle each family owned, the size of their property, how much they had sown and harvested that year and the extent of their debts. Then he sat down and wrote a letter to the editors of the *Moscow Gazette* to ask for the government and the public to come forward with aid. He also wrote to Alexandrine, asking her to raise the issue at court.

There was no area of Russia so dependent on the outcome of the harvest each year as Samara province, he wrote in his letter. Everywhere he had gone, he wrote, he had encountered the same situation: signs of approaching famine which threatened to engulf ninety per cent of the population in the province: 'There are no men anywhere, they have all gone off to look for work, leaving at home thin women, with thin and ailing children, and old people. There is still grain, but it is running out; dogs, cats, calves, and chickens are thin and hungry, while beggars keep coming up to the window and they are given tiny crusts or refused.'[109] Aware that the authorities' preferred course of action was simply to ignore this disaster (they had already tried to pin the blame for the approaching famine on the peasants by arguing it was due to their drunkenness and laziness), Tolstoy included in his letter all the data he had collected, verified in writing by the local priest, and endorsed with a stamp by the village elder, who of course was illiterate. His research had been very thorough:

> 1. Savinkin [household]. Old man of 65 and old woman, 2 sons, one
> married, 2 girls. 7 mouths to feed, 2 workers. No animals: no horse, no cow,
> no sheep. The last horses were stolen, the cow died last year, the sheep have
> been sold. They sowed eleven acres [last year]. *Nothing* grew, so there was
> nothing to sow [this year]. No stores of grain. Poll tax of 30 roubles due for

the last two periods; for loans from last year 10 and a half roubles; private debt for borrowing train 13 roubles; total 53 and a half roubles ...

19. Khramov [household]. Six mouths to feed and one baby, one worker. Animals: 2 horses, 3 cows, 5 sheep. Sown: 9 and a half acres and nothing has grown. Debt: 28 roubles and 48 kopecks ...[110]

Tolstoy's letter was published on 17 August, while the family was travelling home to Yasnaya Polyana, and quickly reproduced in many other newspapers. It was the factual detail of Tolstoy's inventory which struck Russian readers, for he was not just warning of imminent tragedy on a large scale, but providing some of the very first statistical information about the peasantry ever collected. Liberal politicians in Europe had been championing the collection of empirical data from populations as a valuable tool of social progress since the early nineteenth century, but the spectre of politics had severely impeded the development of the new discipline of statistics in Russia. Nicholas I had been so cautious about Russian society being placed under the microscope (particularly where serfdom and state institutions were concerned) that he had simply censored a lot of statistical work. As a consequence, next to no statistical knowledge of the Russian peasantry was acquired prior to the Emancipation of Serfdom Act of 1861, despite peasants representing the vast majority of the population. Attitudes predictably changed in the 1860s, but it was not until the 1880s that poorly paid members of the intelligentsia began conducting censuses in villages on behalf of the *zemstvo* (local government), and it was not until 1897 that the first national census took place. Tolstoy's letter about the famine in 1873 caused a national outcry, and resulted in donations of nearly 2 million roubles and 344,000 kilograms of grain. Through these donations, which came both from central government and from the populace at large, much of the suffering was either prevented or alleviated. This was Tolstoy's first clarion call about the reality of many Russian peasants' lives, and it would not be his last.

· 9 ·

NOVELIST

At that time he read a lot of English family novels and sometimes joked about them, saying, 'These novels always end up with him putting his arm *round her waist*, then they get married, and he inherits an estate and a baronetcy. These novelists end their novels with him and her getting married. But a novel should not be about what happens before they get married, but what happens after they get married.'

Reminiscence of Tolstoy's son Sergey[1]

TOLSTOY HAD BEEN ITCHING to get back to fiction ever since he delivered the manuscript of the last part of his *ABC* to the printers in February 1872. This time there was none of the restless casting around for a subject as there had been at the end of *War and Peace*. Tolstoy now knew exactly where he was going, but his imagination was not yet captured by the unruly curls of a beguilingly beautiful society woman destined to become one of the greatest of literary heroines. His mind was instead occupied by the relentless energy and alcohol-fuelled sadism of a seven-foot-tall syphilitic buffoon who also happened to be Russia's first great revolutionary: Peter the Great. To be fair, Tolstoy only uncovered these traits during the course of his painstaking research, but they led him to the realisation that he no longer wanted to write a novel about the 'tsar-reformer'. It was this discovery which made him receptive to the chance flash of inspiration which then launched *Anna Karenina*, but it came at the end of a very serious engagement with the available sources on late-seventeenth- and early-eighteenth-century Russian history. Tolstoy tried to start his novel about Peter the Great thirty-three times.[2]

Tolstoy was not the only Russian artist interested in Peter the Great in 1872, for this was when the composer Musorgsky started to plan an ambitious new historical opera set at the time of Peter's accession. But there was a particular reason why Peter I was in the public eye that year: it was the bicentenary of his birth. Nicholas I had actively encouraged the cult of Peter's personality during his reign, and the anniversary was celebrated with due pomp and circumstance. A new battleship was named after Peter, a statue of him was put up in Petrozavodsk (St Petersburg was not the only city he founded bearing his name), and Tchaikovsky wrote a cantata in honour of the occasion, to name just some of ways in which the bicentenary was marked. There was also a flurry of new publications – 1,049 to be exact,[3] and a great deal of eulogy from Russian historians, some of whom were still inclined to see Alexander II, the country's next 'great reformer', as a latter-day Peter. Amongst those who idolised Peter the Great was the nation's leading historian, Professor Sergey Solovyov, newly appointed as Rector of Moscow University. 'Two hundred years have passed since the day that the great man was born,' he intoned in the first of his twelve 'Public Lectures about Peter the Great' in 1872. 'Everywhere one hears the words: we must celebrate the bicentenary of this great man; it is our duty, our holy, patriotic duty, because this great man is one of us, a Russian man.'[4]

Solovyov was a scholar of Tolstoyan industry who also published on a Tolstoyan scale. He had read the twelve volumes of Karamzin's pioneering *History of the Russian State* (1806–1826) at least a dozen times by the time he was thirteen, and then in 1851 he started publishing his own history of Russia – a project which would absorb him until his death in 1879. Karamzin had covered Russian history up until the accession of the first Romanov tsar in 1613, but the twenty-nine volumes of Solovyov's *History of Russia from the Earliest Times* extended the survey up to 1774, the year of the Pugachev Rebellion (which was brutally crushed by Catherine the Great). Tolstoy, of course, read Solovyov's magisterial history very carefully, and particularly those volumes concerning the reign of Peter the Great. Solovyov sought to present a unified view of Russia's evolution as a nation. As a pronounced Westerniser who believed in historical progress, he saw Peter's reforms as a natural and inevitable development which had placed Russia on the path to the rule of law, and brought her closer to European civilisation. For Tolstoy, however, Solovyov's history revealed pre-Petrine Russia as a country of 'cruelty, theft, beatings, coarseness, and an inability to do anything', and it signally failed in his opinion to acknowledge the contribution of the people in turning Russia into the great and united state that made such great strides in the eighteenth century. He was inevitably critical of yet another history which seemed to concentrate on the policies and actions of Russia's rulers.[5] Tolstoy shared Solovyov's admiration for Peter's down-to-earth tastes, but not much else.

In order to gain a sense of what it was like to live in Russia during Peter's reign, Tolstoy surrounded himself with an enormous number of books and articles. They ranged from the thirty volumes of Ivan Golikov's reverent *Deeds of Peter the Great, Wise Reformer of Russia*, published at the end of the eighteenth century, to the latest contemporary portraits by Slavophile historians, whose attitude to Peter's reign was far more ambivalent. And then there were studies by historians such as Mikhail Semevsky, who respected Peter's achievements but was repelled by his sacrilegious, Rabelaisian behaviour. General histories, monographs, memoirs, diaries, letters – Tolstoy devoured everything he could lay his hands on.[6] He also perused pictures and contemporary portraits.

Musorgsky also revelled in the profusion of new books and articles which were gradually filling in the blank spots of Russian history, but he was extremely sceptical as to whether Peter's reforms had really been beneficial. In the letter he sent to Stasov in June 1872, written in his typically opaque style, Musorgsky asserted that Russia had not progressed as a nation:

> The power of the black earth will reveal itself when you dig down to the very bottom. It is possible to dig the black earth with tools alien to it. And at the end of the seventeenth century they did dig Mother Russia with *just* such tools, so she did not immediately realise what they were digging her with, and, like the black earth, she opened up and began to breathe. And so she, our beloved, received actual and privy councillors, who never gave her,

the long-suffering one, the chance to collect herself and to think: '*Where are you pushing me?*' ... 'We've moved forward!' – you lie – 'We're still stuck back there!' ...[7]

Musorgsky was overwhelmed by the task of having to fashion a libretto himself from the many disparate primary sources he was working with, and he never managed to finish the score for his opera. Tolstoy was not at all perturbed by the dimensions of his task, but his project never even got off the ground, as the more he read about Peter the Great, the less he attractive he became as a potential character in a novel. He was disappointed by the personality of Russia's first emperor, later dismissing him as a 'drunken jester'.[8]

Musorgsky's alcoholism also played a part in diminishing any interest Tolstoy might have had in his music (it drove the composer to an early death in 1881, when he was just forty-two). Although he was later surprised how much he liked the Musorgsky songs performed for him in 1903, Tolstoy generally had little interest in contemporary Russian music, and remained oblivious to its achievements. Tolstoy and Musorgsky had a surprising amount in common, however, despite never coming into contact. They shared a passion for Russia and its history, a deep interest in the rich textures of the Russian language (while Tolstoy was composing his *ABC*, Musorgsky was reproducing children's speech in his exquisite song cycle *The Nursery*), and a studious concern for authenticity which embraced the tiniest detail. In trying to conceive a way of writing about Peter the Great's Azov campaigns against the Turks, in January 1873 Tolstoy wrote to a family acquaintance who lived in the south of Russia to ask very precise questions about the landscape by the River Don. What were the riverbanks like? What sort of grasses grew there? Were there bushes? Was it pebbly? Tolstoy certainly entertained high hopes for his Peter the Great novel,[9] but he found he could not breathe life into his many drafts, no matter how hard he tried. It is somewhat ironic that in February 1873, just as the public was informed of his latest work in progress in a newspaper column, he was on the verge of giving it up.[10] Within weeks he would be seized with a desire to write on contemporary themes, setting his new novel in the turbulent age in which he lived.

As historians fleshed out a more rounded picture of Peter the Great in the more permissive atmosphere under Alexander II, a growing number of people began to question the official view of his reign, including Tolstoy's American visitor Eugene Schuyler, whose own 'historical biography' was published in 1884.[11] It is likely he and Tolstoy discussed their shared fascination with Peter the Great at some point during his week-long stay at Yasnaya Polyana in 1868. In the course of his research, Schuyler came to believe Peter had forced Europeanisation on to Russia too early.[12] Since subsequent Russian rulers had then concentrated resources on increasing the nation's military prestige at the expense of domestic reform (a scenario which would, of course, be played out again in the twentieth century), the cost of Peter's reforms had in fact been paid by those who had least benefited from them – the millions of serfs who made up the majority of the population. The 'Great Reforms', when they eventually arrived in the 1860s, came too late, and certainly did not go far enough in the eyes of most educated Russians. But Tolstoy was typically neither on the side of the krepostniks – those members of the right-wing landed gentry who regretted the Emancipation of Serfdom Act – nor was he with those members of the intelligentsia on the left who sought more radical reform. He would take on both sides in *Anna Karenina*.

Tolstoy's knowledge of the huge discrepancy between his own unmerited position of privilege and the poverty and backwardness of the peasantry was becoming increasingly painful for him as time went on, and made it morally difficult for him to continue writing for the educated classes. This is why he devoted so much time to his *ABC*, which he regarded as the most important thing he had ever done. At that time in his career, it was the best way he could find of personally helping to remedy a situation in which all the landed gentry were complicit. The utopian approach to the country's social problems taken by many of Russia's idealistic young students was far less practical. Just as Tolstoy was abandoning his Peter the Great novel in the spring of 1873, at a time when it seemed that his *ABC* project was turning into a complete fiasco,[13] the more radical members of Russia's student intelligentsia were beginning to think of revolution as the only solution to the country's ills. Inspired by the populist ideas of thinkers like Alexander Herzen, who had advocated a Russian brand of socialism designed to enable the peasantry to bypass capitalism, they headed for the countryside to have direct contact with the people by distributing propaganda and setting up workshops and co-operatives.

The high-water mark of the 'Going to the People' movement was the summer of 1874 when the Russian countryside was invaded by literally thousands of earnest young 'nihilists' (the moniker they had been labelled with ever since the publication of Turgenev's *Fathers and Sons* in 1862, which denoted their scepticism towards accepted authorities). Many of them were women. But since most of these students came from the cities, and were essentially middle class, they had next to no direct knowledge of the peasantry, and they badly miscalculated. As it turned out, the peasants' innate conservatism made them indifferent if not downright hostile to the students' efforts to incite them to overthrow their tsar. Against all odds, they retained a deep loyalty and affection for the Romanovs. The peaceful 'Going to the People' movement failed, and the wave of arrests which followed led the more extreme Populists to turn to terrorism at the end of the 1870s. It was against this background of social upheaval that Tolstoy would set *Anna Karenina*. The casting of only a minor character as a nihilist belies the fact that in its defence of marriage and conservative family values, the whole novel is an assault on the kind of views espoused by the radical intelligentsia, for whom female emancipation was entirely consonant with their political goals.[14] The aristocratic Tolstoy would never have deigned to engage in a direct polemic with his opponents, whose uncompromising stance was partly driven by the fact that, coming from poor backgrounds, they had nothing to lose. In its searching analysis of marriage as an institution, however, *Anna Karenina* is certainly an indirect response to the kind of women's liberation championed in such classic nihilist texts as Chernyshevsky's 1862 novel *What Is to Be Done?*, which celebrates 'free love'.

The seeds had been sown back in February 1870, when Tolstoy had begun drafting his article about the 'woman question', joining Strakhov in a comprehensive rejection of John Stuart Mill's call for equality between the sexes. This was exactly when he first conceived the idea of writing a novel about a society woman who commits adultery. Then on a dark, cold evening in January 1872, a thirty-five-year-old woman called Anna Pirogova arrived at Yasenki station, just down the road from Yasnaya Polyana, with a bundle containing a change of underwear. After crossing herself, she threw herself under goods train No. 77. Anna Pirogova was a distant relation of Tolstoy's wife. She had become the housekeeper and lover of his friend and neighbour Alexander Bibikov, then in his early fifties, with whom he had set up his short-lived distillery some years earlier. Bibikov had informed Anna he was going to marry his son's governess, an attractive German girl.[15] In a rage of jealousy and anger, she had sent him a note accusing him of being her murderer before taking her own life.[16] Tolstoy went to the autopsy. He was badly distressed by seeing the mangled corpse of the grey-eyed, well-built woman he knew well. This was one of the first railway suicides on Russia's young but rapidly expanding network, which had increased from about 500 miles of track at the time of Nicholas I's death to over 10,000 by the 1870s. It was undoubtedly the first suicide at Tolstoy's local station. He used the 'iron road' himself, of course, but he loathed this intrusion of modernity into his rural sanctuary, and he would shore up the complex architectural structure of *Anna Karenina* by thematically aligning events connected with the railway in his novel with death and destruction.

Another immediate stimulus for *Anna Karenina* came from France. In March 1873 Tolstoy wrote to his sister-in-law Tanya to ask if she had read *L'Homme-femme*, an essay by Alexandre Dumas fils which had created a storm in Paris the previous year and had already been reprinted several dozen times.[17] Dumas wrote his essay as a reaction to coverage in the French press of the trial of a man who had murdered his 'unfaithful' wife, from whom he had separated. Specifically he was responding to an article which deplored the French laws which virtually condoned such crimes (the man was sentenced to a mere five years), and proposed divorce as the solution. This could never have been an option in this case. After a brief period following the French Revolution when France had the most liberal divorce laws in the world, divorce had been made illegal there in 1816 and would remain so until 1884.[18] For Dumas, marriage was a bitter, irreconcilable struggle between the sexes in which the woman prevails, but he argued that in this case the husband was ultimately the moral arbiter, and so had the right to kill an unfaithful wife who continued to be recalcitrant. Tolstoy was deeply impressed with Dumas's analysis of marriage. As well as introducing a discussion of his essay in one of the early drafts of *Anna Karenina*,[19] he would take issue with many of its fundamental points in his account of Levin and Kitty's marriage. He would also engage, of course, with the entire tradition of the French novel of adultery that had been created by authors such as Flaubert, Zola and Dumas.[20]

Dumas's own life, meanwhile, or rather that of his wife, provides interesting commentary on the themes of *Anna Karenina*, for he was married to Nadezhda Naryshkina, a Russian aristocrat who had committed adultery and borne an illegitimate child. Naryshkina had also been involved in an infamous murder case in Moscow in 1850 which shocked and thrilled Russian polite society, Tolstoy included. She was a captivating woman who had been married at a young age to Alexander Naryshkin, a scion of one of Russia's most distinguished aristocratic families. After bearing him a daughter, she resumed her career as one of the grandes dames of Moscow high society, and was renowned for arriving last at soirées, preferably no earlier than midnight. Tolstoy, who was her contemporary, was also living in Moscow at this time, and he described her as 'très à la mode' in a letter to Aunt Toi-nette. In 1850, when she was twenty-five, she began an affair with a Vronsky type – a handsome, wealthy aristocrat called Alexander Sukhovo-Kobylin, who was a talented dramatist and had the reputation of being a Don Juan. Naryshkina then became caught up and later implicated in the murder of his French mistress, a crime for which Sukhovo-Kobylin was (probably wrongly) arrested and imprisoned, along with two serfs who were convicted and sent to Siberia. Pregnant with her lover's child, the flame-haired femme fatale hastily decamped with her daughter to Paris, where she immediately made a name for herself in the city's top salons. It was in Paris that she met Dumas, the illegitimate son of Dumas *père*, who had come to fame after the publication of his 1848 novel *La Dame aux camélias*, inspired by his relationship with a cel-ebrated Parisian courtesan (and later turned into Verdi's opera *La Traviata*). Naryshkina's husband refused to give her a divorce, also threatening to take their daughter away from her, and she was able to marry Dumas only after Naryshkin's death in 1864.

Tolstoy wrote to tell Toinette about the scandalous murder case which was a subject of Moscow gossip for many years,[21] and he may well also have heard about Naryshkina's high-profile relationship with Dumas during his later visits to Paris. Dumas's reflections on marriage in *L'Homme-femme* were clearly the product of his experience as husband to Nadezhda Naryshkina, with whom he had two daughters, and they struck a chord with Tolstoy. It was Aunt Toinette, however, who had perhaps the greatest influence on Tolstoy's views about adultery. In his memoirs, in which he writes about her at length, Tolstoy records telling her late one night about an acquaintance of his, whose wife had been unfaithful and absconded. When he expressed the view that his friend was probably glad to be shot of his wife, he describes how Toinette at once assumed a serious expression and urged instead forgiveness and compassion.[22] This is the precisely the sentiment Tolstoy voices through his unsung heroine Dolly in *Anna Karenina*. When Karenin tells Dolly about his predicament at the end of Oblonsky's dinner party in Part Four of the novel, she pleads with him not to bring shame and disrepute on his wife by divorcing her, as it would destroy her. Toinette's general view, that one should hate the crime, but not the person, was essentially Tolstoy's, and holds the key to why Anna Karenina is one of the most compelling and complex literary characters ever created.

The story of how Tolstoy actually came to begin *Anna Karenina* has gone down in the annals of Russian literary history, and involves Sonya, Toinette and his eldest son. Sergey, then nine years old, had been badgering his mother to give him something to read aloud to Toinette, who was by then old and frail and in need of diversion. Sonya recorded in her diary on 19 March 1873 that she had given Sergey the fifth volume of the family's edition of Pushkin, which contained his *Tales of Belkin*. Aunt Toinette apparently soon nodded off, and Sergey also lost interest in Pushkin's immortal prose, but Sonya was too lazy that day to take the book back to the library, and so left it upstairs on the windowsill in the drawing room. Tolstoy naturally picked it up, and a few days later he wrote excitedly to Strakhov to tell him he had been unable to put it down, even though he was reading the *Tales of Belkin* for about the seventh time. The volume also contained some unfinished sketches for novels and stories, including one fragment beginning 'The guests arrived at the dacha' which particularly caught Tolstoy's eye. He was riveted by how Pushkin got straight down to the action, without even bothering to set the scene first or describe the characters. After the thirty-three false starts with Peter the Great, this was a revelation for Tolstoy, and it showed him how he himself should proceed in his own fiction. (Oddly, he seemed to have forgotten that he had more or less used precisely this technique with *War and Peace*, which also begins at a high-society soirée.) 'I automatically and unexpectedly thought up characters and events, not knowing myself why, or what would come next, and carried on ...,' Tolstoy wrote unguardedly in the letter he drafted to Strakhov, which he later thought better about sending.[23] The idea of writing about the consequences of a woman's infidelity was there from the start,[24] but it would be a long time before his novel was called *Anna Karenina*, and began with that famous opening line:

All happy families are alike, each unhappy family is unhappy in its own way.

Everything was confusion at the Oblonskys' house. The wife had found out about the husband's liaison with the French governess previously living in their house, and had told her husband she could not live under the same roof as him ...

The narrator of Pushkin's fragment, which dates from the end of the 1820s, goes on to describe a drawing room filling with guests who have just attended a performance of a new Italian opera. The ladies take up position on the sofas, surrounded by gentlemen, while games of whist are started at tables nearby. Tolstoy also started the first draft of his as yet unnamed new novel with a scene in an aristocratic drawing room:

> The hostess had just managed to take off her sable fur coat in the hall and give instructions to the butler about tea for the guests in the large drawing room, when there was the rattle of another carriage at the front door ...[25]

As in Pushkin's fragment, the guests in Tolstoy's new novel have all just been to the opera – a performance of *Don Giovanni*, a work all about seduction and adultery. Their conversation focuses on the senior civil servant Mikhail Mikhailovich Stavrovich (the future Karenin) and his wife Tatyana Sergeyevna (the future Anna): she has been unfaithful, and he seems ignorant of the fact. The couple then arrive in person, followed later on by Ivan Balashov (the future Vronsky), who proceeds to have an intimate and animated conversation with Tatyana, scandalising those present. Stavrovich now realises the misfortune that has befallen him, and his wife is henceforth no longer invited to society events. It is a scene slightly reminiscent of the soirée at Princess Betsy's in Part Two of *Anna Karenina*.

In his first draft Tolstoy sketched out eleven further chapters. Tatyana (Tanya) becomes pregnant and Balashov loses a horse race when his mare falls at the last fence. Stavrovich then leaves Tatyana and moves to Moscow; she gives birth and her husband agrees to a divorce. Tatyana's second marriage is no happier, however, and after Stavrovich informs her their marriage can never be broken off, and that everyone has suffered, she drowns herself in the Neva. Balashov goes off to join the Khiva campaign (Russian troops attacked the city and seized control of the Khanate of Khiva in 1873, just when Tolstoy was writing).

Tatyana has a brother in the first sketch (a prototype of Oblonsky), while her husband has a sister called Kitty, but there is no trace of Levin and his brothers yet, nor any member of the Shcherbatsky family. Stavrovich is portrayed sympathetically, while his wife is intriguingly both 'provocative' and 'meek'. Tolstoy had never before sketched a synopsis of a fictional work in advance, but in any case this raw material soon changed significantly. He developed and dramatically expanded every part of this storyline in future drafts except for his evocation of the state of mind of Balashov's horse during the race, which he subsequently decided to cut. Balashov's English groom is called Cord, as in the final version of the novel, but his mare is not Frou-Frou yet. To begin with she bears the English name of 'Tiny', and is referred to as 'Tani' (as the name becomes when transliterated) and also as 'Tanya', thus drawing an indelible link with his lover, which remains in the final version, although the association is not articulated.

Tolstoy was nowhere near ready to give any of this material to Sonya to copy out yet. Instead, he started a new draft of the beginning of his novel:

> After the opera, the guests drove over to young Princess Vrasskaya's house.
> Having arrived home from the theatre, Princess Mika, as she was called
> in society, had so far only managed to take off her fur coat in the brightly
> lit hall in front of the mirror, which was festooned with flowers; with her
> small gloved hand she was still unhooking the lace which had caught on a
> hook of her fur coat …[26]

This time he called his heroine Anastasia ('Nana') Arkadyevna Karenina, and replaced her yellow lace gown with the black velvet she will wear to the ball in the final version. Her husband is now firmly called Alexey Alexandrovich, but her lover's name has switched from Balashov to Gagin. Tolstoy ended up discarding this draft, but he would save up the detail of the caught lace for Anna to unhook in the final version of the novel, when she is leaving Princess Betsy's soirée after her fateful encounter with Vronsky.

Tolstoy wrote several more pages, but he was already beginning to chafe at the bit. He wanted to write a novel of adultery, but he did not want to be constrained by writing only about St Petersburg high society, even if his attitude towards it was sharply critical. With a few exceptions (Stavrovich, for example, has a conversation with a nihilist on a train), his social radius was thus far stiflingly small, and so he decided to introduce in his third draft

4. The fourth draft of the opening of Anna Karenina, *1873*

the character of Kostya Neradov, a prototype of Levin. Neradov is a rural landowner, and both a friend of Gagin (the future Vronsky) and his rival for the hand of Kitty Shcherbatskaya, who also now makes her first appearance. The action, moreover, now moves to Moscow.

Tolstoy was gradually finding his way into his new novel. His fourth stab at an opening now received the title 'Anna Karenina', followed by 'Vengeance is Mine' as an epigraph. This draft begins with the familiar scene of a husband waking up after a row the night before with his wife, who has discovered his infidelity. 'Stepan Arkadyich Alabin' is almost Oblonsky. Anna comes to Moscow as peacemaker, and she meets Gagin at the ball. But still Tolstoy was not satisfied: there was no tension in the relationship between the Levin and Vronsky prototypes, as they were friends. He decided to change their names to Ordyntsev and Udashev, and now made them rivals for Kitty's hand rather than friends. It was time to try another beginning. Tolstoy took out a fresh sheet of paper and started a fifth opening draft:

> There was a cattle exhibition in Moscow. The Zoological Garden was full
> of people. Beaming with his pleasant, open face and full red lips, wearing
> his hat slightly tilted to one side on his thinning, light brown curly hair,
> the grey of his beaver collar merging with his handsome greying sideburns,
> Stepan Arkadyich Alabin, well known to all of Moscow society, was
> walking along …[27]

Ordyntsev, who is about to run into his old friend Alabin, has come up to
Moscow to show his calves and his bull.

This time Tolstoy carried on writing for quite a long while, but he was
to change tack yet again. He had now constructed solid foundations for his
novel by creating the 'Levin' storyline to act as a counterpoint to the Karenin
plot, with the 'Oblonskys' as the arch joining them together. For reasons of
structural balance, he now decided against his central character of 'Levin'
appearing in the first chapter, so he reserved the Zoological Garden for a
skating scene later on and returned to his previous idea of opening the novel
with 'Oblonsky' waking up after the row with his wife. He reworked the
crucial opening scenes four times to get them exactly right, and these were
the first chapters he gave Sonya to make fair copies of. Everything else stayed
in draft form.[28] In all, Tolstoy produced ten versions of the first part of *Anna
Karenina*, writing a total of 2,500 pages of manuscript before the novel was
complete.[29] Almost a century would pass before the story of how *Anna Karenina* was written could be told with accuracy. The manuscripts were partially
unravelled for publication in volume twenty of Tolstoy's *Complete Collected
Works*, published in 1939, but the first complete scholarly edition of the novel
appeared only in 1970, and that now turns out to contain errors.

On 11 May 1873 Tolstoy took a deep breath and finally wrote to tell Strakhov that he had spent over a month working on a novel that had nothing
to do with Peter the Great. He emphasised that he was writing a proper
novel – the first in his life.[30] Indeed, he had been writing the word *roman*
('a novel') at the top of the page on each new draft of his opening chapter.
At this early stage, he was still very excited by his new project, which he
told Strakhov completely 'enthralled' him.[31] But before he set off with the
family at the beginning of June for their summer trip to Samara, where he
was not intending to do much writing, a couple of events slowed his progress and cast the first shadows over a novel whose completion would prove

increasingly difficult. First came the unexpected news of the death of Tolstoy's five-year-old niece Dasha Kuzminskaya, the eldest daughter of Sonya's sister Tanya, who brought her children to stay at Yasnaya Polyana each summer. Dasha was adored by everyone, and her death brought the chilling realisation to Tolstoy that it could have easily been one of his own children. Sonya was grief-stricken. Tolstoy wrote a long letter of consolation to Tanya, and instructed her to learn by heart and recite Psalm 130 every day ('Out of the depths I cry to you, O Lord').[32]

Tolstoy was further upset that May on hearing that a Yasnaya Polyana peasant had been gored and killed by a bull he was untying.[33] He found it particularly troubling because this was the second such death in twelve months. Despite being in Samara on the previous occasion in the summer of 1872, Tolstoy had been held accountable by the coroner, who had placed him under house arrest while he investigated the incident. Tolstoy was incensed, both by having to submit to the authority of the young whippersnapper of a coroner who was curtailing his liberties, and by all the new laws which had introduced these procedures. He remembered the case of the peasant who had sat in Tula's jail for a year and a half under suspicion of stealing a cow before it was finally established that he was innocent, and he feared the worst. Bizarrely, Tolstoy was also summoned as a juror for another case at the same time, and was promptly fined for not attending court.[34] In the heat of the moment he seriously considered taking Sonya and the children to England, where he believed civil liberties were respected. On 15 September 1872 he even wrote to Alexandrine to ask if she could put him in touch with some 'good aristocratic families', to enable the family to have a 'pleasant' life in England. Although he admitted that he found European life repellent, he told her he could raise about 200,000 roubles if he sold up everything he had in Russia, which he reckoned would be enough to buy a house with some land near the sea.[35] The new legal system which had been introduced in Russia in 1864 had created Western-style courts and the need for Western-style lawyers and other legal professionals, and Tolstoy's other impetuous action was to begin writing a high-minded critical article titled 'The New Laws and Their Application'.[36] In due course, Tolstoy would express his contempt for the new institutions through his alter ego Levin in *Anna Karenina*.

Fortunately, Tolstoy did not usually stay in a state of apoplexy very long. The case against him was dropped, the article was never finished and the squires of Sussex never got to have a hot-headed Russian count as their neighbour. Following the second bull-goring incident in May 1873, Tolstoy spent three days tending to the injured peasant and was devastated when he eventually died.[37] It was not surprising he had not been able to concentrate on *Anna Karenina* that month, so when he returned home from the steppe at the end of the summer he was all the more eager to resume work on it. His health had been invigorated by all the koumiss he had drunk on his homestead, his conscience was clear after successfully publicising the famine that threatened to engulf Samara's peasant farmers, and he was still waiting for the Moscow Literacy Committee to respond to his invitation to organise a trial of the teaching methods he had championed in his *ABC* books. There was nothing to stop him going back to fiction, and he worked productively for about a month. Even having to sit for his first portrait did not distract him too much from his purpose at this stage. Indeed, it provided him with another source of raw material for *Anna Karenina*.

Pavel Tretyakov had been keen to acquire to a portrait of Tolstoy for his art collection since 1869, but his tentative attempts to broach the topic had so far been rebuffed. Tolstoy no doubt wondered, perhaps not without aristocratic snobbery, why he should give up valuable hours of his time so that an obscure Moscow merchant could put up a picture of him in his house. As the son of a merchant of the second guild who had grown up in the Zamoskvorechie, Tretyakov's beginnings were indeed humble, and he remained a personally abstemious and self-effacing man, but the immensely profitable textile business he built up with his brother, combined with his passion for art, ensured he did not remain obscure for long. He may have had a total of six paintings in 1860, but by the time Kramskoy painted Tolstoy's portrait in 1873, Tretyakov was already planning a separate building to house his expanding collection. In 1881 it was opened to the public, thus fulfilling Tretyakov's great dream of establishing a national gallery of Russian art. In 1892, when he donated his collection to the city of Moscow (six years before the opening of the Russian Museum in St Petersburg, which was founded on the initiative of Alexander III), the Tretyakov Gallery contained nearly 3,000 works of art.[38]

As a passionate Slavophile, Tretyakov had decided to concentrate exclusively on Russian painting, and in particular on contemporary works which expressed the national spirit. In the 1860s painting had become as vibrant as literature and music in Russia, and at the end of the decade Tretyakov decided his gallery should also include portraits of the greatest new figures in the Russian arts. For the first time in Russia's history there was a whole phalanx of professional writers, composers and painters proud of their nationality, and producing work of international quality that was becoming known abroad. As well as buying portraits of artists who were already deceased (such as Fyodor Moller's 1841 portrait of Gogol, who died in 1852), Tretyakov set about commissioning new works, and in 1872 Perov painted Turgenev and Dostoyevsky. As luck would have it, Ivan Kramskoy, Russia's leading portrait painter, happened to spend the following summer in Tula province, and when he realised his dacha was just down the road from Yasnaya Polyana, he decided to wait for the count's return from Samara. On 5 September he persuaded Tolstoy to agree to pose for him, and started work the next day.

Kramskoy was in many ways a painter after Tolstoy's own heart: he came from a lowly background and was deeply committed to national subjects and contemporary issues, but more importantly in 1863, while still a student, he had led a famous rebellion against the Imperial Academy's classical strictures in the name of artistic freedom.[39] This did not stop him becoming an academician in 1869, however. (Tolstoy himself was elected as a corresponding member of the literary section of the Academy of Sciences in 1873.) Kramskoy spent about a month working on two paintings: one for Tretyakov and another portrait for Yasnaya Polyana, stuffing one of Tolstoy's trademark blouses with bed linen and tying it with a belt so he could concentrate on the writer's face during their sessions, and minimise the time he had to pose for him. His portrait of the author sitting in a relaxed pose, hands folded in his lap but staring intensely straight ahead, with his mind probably on his latest draft of the opening of *Anna Karenina*, was immediately and universally acclaimed as an astounding likeness. It is this portrait, which seems to have captured Tolstoy's difficult and complex character as well as his greatness, and simultaneously portrays him both as a quintessential Russian peasant and as an aristocrat, that began to give rise to the popular perception of him being of towering physical stature. Kramskoy was electrified by Tolstoy's personality, and later claimed that he had never seen a more handsome man than Tolstoy when he was astride his horse dressed to go out hunting.[40] Tolstoy may have regretted the time he gave up to sit for Kramskoy, but he squirrelled away all sorts of details that later came in very useful when writing the chapters in *Anna Karenina* about the artist who paints Anna's portrait.

The singleness of purpose emanating from the expression fixed in Kramskoy's portrait was what enabled Tolstoy to write to his friend Fet in between sessions on 23 September 1873 and tell him that he was already finishing *Anna Karenina*. In a letter sent to Strakhov on the same day he was more candid, but still optimistic about finishing his novel by the end of the year. Before signing off, he mentioned his interest in the murder of Anna Suvorina, which Kramskoy had just told him about. Just days earlier the thirty-three-year-old mother of five had been shot in the face with a revolver in a fashionable hotel on the Nevsky Prospekt in St Petersburg. She had been murdered by her lover, a young former officer and family friend called Timofey Komarov, who then proceeded to shoot himself.[41] Even at a time when there seemed to be a rash of suicides in Russia, it was a sensational case, covered in all the newspapers.[42] Tolstoy was interested because he knew the victim's husband. Back in 1861 he had paid Alexey Suvorin, then a penniless writer, fifty roubles for a story he had commissioned for his *Yasnaya Polyana* journal, and he was shortly to resume contact with him. Originally from a peasant background, Suvorin was now a successful journalist and publishing supremo, and was fast becoming a power in the land. (Kramskoy would paint his portrait in 1881, by which time he was editor of Russia's most popular newspaper.)

Tolstoy was, of course, also interested in the Komarov case because he was writing a novel in which his hero Levin thinks about suicide, his heroine's lover Vronsky attempts suicide, and his heroine Anna actually does commit suicide. The fact that in his letter to Strakhov Tolstoy also mentions Goethe's *Werther* and a schoolboy who took his own life because he had trouble learning Latin confirms that suicide was in his mind at this time. Nor was his interest purely academic, as he would shortly be contemplating his own voluntary exit. In his writing, Tolstoy was in some ways following a trend as it was just at this time that the incidence of suicide in Russia reached what has been described as epidemic proportions. This may have been partly a mass-hysterical reaction to the widespread and often daily coverage during the early 1870s of suicide in the Russian press, which had finally been unmuzzled in the 1860s and now also covered the new public trials.[43]

Tolstoy ploughed on with *Anna Karenina* in October and November 1873, but there were further disruptions. As soon as Kramskoy packed up his easel and returned to St Petersburg, he was host to the group of village schoolteachers whom he had invited to discuss his teaching methods. They stayed at Yasnaya Polyana for a week.[44] Then on 9 November the Tolstoys suffered their first bereavement with the sudden death of their youngest son, the previously healthy eighteen-month-old Pyotr (Petya). Shortly after that, Sonya's sister Tanya Kuzminskaya's pregnancy ended in a stillbirth.[45] The family was devastated, particularly Sonya (who a few months later was also to lose her nineteen-year-old brother Vladimir, who died just after joining the hussars[46]). On the clear frosty day when they were burying Petya next to his grandparents, Tolstoy started to think for the first time about where he would be buried. At this point he was still fairly sanguine, and in letters he wrote at the time he explained that the death of his brother Nikolay had in some way inured him to the pain of loss. He reasoned that the death of any other of the five elder children in the family would have been harder,[47] as this was like losing one's little finger.[48] He was also frank that this 'screaming' baby had not yet been a source of any delight for him.[49]

Sonya, who was four months pregnant when Petya died, felt differently. No other of her children had been so attached to her, and radiated such cheerful spirits and goodness, she wrote to her sister Tanya. She still kept expecting her jolly, chubby little boy to call out to her. Because of the weight of the grief she was carrying in her heart, she also feared for the new baby she had felt move inside for the first time just as Petya was dying. Her last memory of him was of the sun pouring in through the church window on to his body in its little coffin, and turning his hair gold. Christmas was a quiet affair at Yasnaya Polyana that year. While the children were outside tobogganing, Sonya sat inside getting on with copying and household chores, and looking forward to the evening troika rides that they organised as their entertainment. But the recent deaths had almost totally taken away her capacity to find happiness and tranquillity, she told Tanya.[50]

Tolstoy had now been working on and off on his novel for nine months. At the end of 1873 he confided to Nikolay Strakhov that his work on *Anna Karenina* had gone well up until that point, even very well. He calculated that he had seven printer's sheets all ready to be typeset, and he decided he would go ahead and print them as the first part of his novel in book form, without prior publication in a journal.[51] Accordingly, in January 1874 Tolstoy went to Moscow to draw up an agreement for publishing *Anna Karenina* with Mikhail Katkov's printing house. He turned to Katkov's press as it had just produced a print run of 3,600 copies of his collected works in eight volumes (about 1,000 of them sold in the first year, at a price of twelve roubles).[52] Technically this constituted the third edition of Tolstoy's writings, since he counted the appearance of his work in journals as the first. The two-volume 'second' edition which had been published in 1864 was now swelled by *War and Peace*, but in the new format: four rather than six parts, with all the French translated into Russian and the authorial ruminations about history placed together in a new epilogue. The revisions to *War and Peace* had been partly dictated by the momentous changes wrought in Tolstoy's thinking by his work on the *ABC* books, and his new ideas about reforming the way he wrote would also have an impact on *Anna Karenina*. Tolstoy was, of course, still very preoccupied with his educational work. It was during this brief visit to Moscow in January 1874 that Tolstoy appeared before the Moscow Literacy Committee, which accepted his proposal that his teaching method be tried out alongside the official method then in use.

Tolstoy worked furiously to finish the first part of *Anna Karenina* at Yasnaya Polyana while the six-week teaching trial was conducted in Moscow. He was still making up his mind about how his new novel should begin. At some point during this time he crossed out *Anna Karenina* as a title and wrote in *Two Marriages*, and inserted titles for each chapter, such as 'Family Quarrel', 'Meeting at the Railway Station', 'The Ball'. He also replaced the modern Russian words of his earlier epigraph ('Mine is the Vengeance') with the Church Slavonic equivalent taken from the Bible, and gave Stepan Arkadych the surname of Oblonsky (now relegating Alabin to his dream). Before he took the manuscript to the printers during his next visit to Moscow in early March, he had changed his mind again, however: now the novel once again bore the title *Anna Karenina*, and Levin was Tolstoy's new and final name for Ordyntsev, which he and many of his friends pronounced 'Lyovin', like his first name, Lyov (*Лёв*), in accordance with Russian practice.[53] To Sonya, her husband was always Lyovochka. Tolstoy estimated that the manuscript of Part One which he handed over for typesetting in March constituted about a sixth of the total word-count for the novel, and he was still confident *Anna Karenina* would soon be finished. He did not manage to complete the novel in 1874, in 1875, or even in 1876, however. The concluding sentence was not written until 1877.

Sonya had started making a fair copy of Part Two while Tolstoy was in Moscow in January,[54] but in April she had to stop to give birth to Nikolay, their seventh child, whom they could not help calling Petya.[55] The joy was not unalloyed, as a few weeks earlier there had been another stillbirth in the family, suffered by her sister-in-law Maria Mikhailovna, Sergey's wife.[56] Tolstoy also stopped work on *Anna Karenina* at this point. The trial comparing his teaching method with the one officially approved by the Russian government had now come to an end, and the results were inconclusive. Far from being deterred, however, Tolstoy was even more determined to fight for his educational ideas to be recognised. He could not let matters stand, as this meant far more to him than his fiction. First he sent a letter to the Minister of Education, in which he argued that the 'pedantic' German teaching system approved by the ministry would not help the cause of popular education because it was based on 'pointlessly complex and false principles' and was 'completely alien and even contrary to the spirit of the Russian language and people'.[57] His offer to put together a comprehensive teaching and learning programme for popular education was not taken up. At this point he decided to move into the public arena, and he now threw his energies into writing the long article on popular education mentioned earlier that he regarded as his personal credo. *Anna Karenina* was set aside.

The more deeply Tolstoy immersed himself in his educational crusade, the more rapidly his enthusiasm for his novel diminished. Indeed, on 10 May 1874 he informed Strakhov that he frankly no longer liked it,[58] and later in the month he decided to bring the printing process to a halt.[59] But there was another reason Tolstoy's heart was no longer in continuing *Anna Karenina*. His *tyotushka* (auntie) Tatyana Alexandrovna – Toinette, his surrogate mother – died on 20 June. She was eighty-two. Tolstoy frankly admitted to Alexandrine in a letter that for the last few years, as her life had ebbed away, she had not been part of their family life, particularly after she had moved at her request to a downstairs room, so as not to leave bad memories, but her death made a deep impression on him. In her last years she had confused Tolstoy with his father, whom she had worshipped, and called him Nicolas. He would drop in on her room late at night, when she and Natalya Petrovna were already sitting in their dressing gowns and nightcaps, with shawls round their shoulders, and would help lay out the cards for patience with her at the small table in front of her bed.[60] 'I've lived with her my whole life. And I feel awful without her,' he wrote to Alexandrine. Toinette had been loved and respected by everyone. Tolstoy described to Alexandrine how peasants from every house in the village had stopped the funeral procession so they could give money to the priest for him to say prayers to her memory.[61]

The summer was never a time when Tolstoy sat inside at his desk very much and Yasnaya Polyana soon filled with relatives and friends. Strakhov tried to rekindle his interest in *Anna Karenina* in July 1874 when he came to stay, but Tolstoy had lost momentum by that time, and referred to his novel now as 'vile' and 'disgusting'.[62] The only positive result of his picking up the proofs of the thirty chapters that had already been typeset was the decision he took to write the whole beginning again.[63] In August Tolstoy took his eldest son Sergey for a short trip to their Samara estate, so there was a further hiatus. One of the main reasons Tolstoy did go back to *Anna Karenina* that autumn was that he needed money. He had invested heavily in his Samara estate, and that summer estimated that he made a loss of about 20,000 roubles. After three years of drought there was a bountiful harvest generally in the Samara region in 1874 – except on the land that he had sown, he noted sardonically.[64] The family's German tutor had left, the children were growing up, and Tolstoy was also on the hunt for new teachers for them. That meant paying a wage of between 300 and 600 roubles a year for a governess for Tanya and Masha, and between 500 and 1,000 roubles for a tutor to teach Sergey, Ilya and Lev. Meanwhile, he suddenly needed 10,000 roubles as the deposit on some extra land he was purchasing next to his Nikolskoye estate, and his friend Afanasy Fet refused to give him a loan.[65] One tactic was to chop down some of the forest on the estate, and sell the wood (which is something that Oblovsky does in *Anna Karenina*),[66] but the surest source of revenue was royalties. There was no money in education, as Tolstoy had learned to his cost (he had not yet published his *New ABC*), which meant he had to get on with his novel, and he now changed his mind in favour of printing *Anna Karenina* in instalments in a monthly journal.

Tolstoy could only reasonably ask for 150 roubles per printer's sheet for his article on popular education, but there was more than one journal interested in *Anna Karenina*, and he reckoned he could drive a hard bargain for it. He had sold *War and Peace* for 300 roubles per printer's sheet, but for *Anna Karenina* he held out for 500 roubles, with an advance of 10,000 (the exact sum he needed). No other writer in Russia could hope to earn what would be a total of 20,000 roubles for a novel, and after protracted negotiations, in November Tolstoy finally opted to publish in Katkov's *Russian Messenger*. This was galling for the editors of *Notes of the Fatherland* in St Petersburg.

They had agreed to publish Tolstoy's outspoken article on popular education more or less on the assumption that they would have first refusal on his next novel, and now they were left with the awkward task of accommodating the count's mixture of highly idiosyncratic nihilism and conservatism in a journal known for its openly Populist, left-wing orientation.

Now all Tolstoy had to do was finish *Anna Karenina*, which was easier said than done. He had extensively written and rewritten the opening chapters, so he could buy time to begin with, but the bulk of the novel, now that he no longer wanted it to be just the story of high-society marital infidelity, was as yet unwritten. The problem was that in 1874, and for most of 1875, his heart was still in pedagogy. He was in charge of seventy schools in his district, working on the proofs of his *New ABC* and developing proposals for teacher training.[67] Fiction seemed trivial by comparison, not least the tawdry story of an adulterous love affair. Having found it impossible to sustain his interest in writing a novel of adultery on the French model, he had found a way out by broadening its scope and introducing an autobiographical character through whom he could explore topics that interested him, such as ploughing techniques, but writing *Anna Karenina* was still profoundly irksome. Tolstoy wrote to tell Alexandrine in December 1874 that he had once again become entranced by the thousands of little children whose education he was involved with, as he had been fifteen years earlier when he had first started his school. When he went into a school, he told her, and saw a 'crowd of ragged, dirty, thin children, with their bright eyes and often angelic expressions', he felt like someone trying to save people from drowning. He wanted to save all the little Pushkins and Lomonosovs who would otherwise perish.[68] To his publisher Katkov he even declared openly that every single page of his *ABC* had cost him more effort and had more significance than all the fictional writings for which he received 'undeserved praise'.[69]

Sonya felt differently: she wondered whether it was worth her husband investing all his energy in a tiny corner of Russia – the district in Tula province where they lived. Writing to her sister Tanya, she did not conceal the fact that she heartily despised all her husband's works with arithmetic and grammar. She was longing for her husband to get back to writing novels, which was an activity she both respected and loved:

> I teach, breast-feed like a machine, from morning to night and from night to morning. I was copying out the *ABC*, but when I saw that it was not

going to come to an end soon, I got so fed up with all those short words, and phrases such as 'Masha ate kasha' and so on that I gave up – let some clerk write it out. My work was copying out the immortal *War and Peace* or *Anna*, but that was boring.[70]

Sonya and Lyovochka were beginning to grow apart. Sonya was tiring of the monotony and grind of her daily life, and was frequently ill. Her husband was beginning to be assailed by existential despair.

Subscribers to the *Russian Messenger* finally started reading *Anna Karenina* at the beginning of 1875, when the first chapters of the novel appeared in the January issue, nestled amongst materials as diverse as an article about the reform of Russian universities, an instalment of Wilkie Collins's detective novel *The Law and the Lady* (only just published in England), notes on the defence of Sebastopol by a 'Black Sea Officer', a sketch of China and an article about education.[71] It is unlikely readers dwelled long on the dry disquisition about the teaching of logic in high schools when there was a new novel by Count Tolstoy to read. The first chapters of *Anna Karenina* caused a sensation, and Strakhov wrote to tell Tolstoy that he had seen even the most highbrow people in St Petersburg jumping up and down in excitement.[72] The first instalment ended with Anna leaving the ball early, having danced the mazurka with Vronsky, and thus brought Kitty's dreams crashing to the ground. Russian readers could not wait to read more. Sonya, the faithful copyist, had a right to feel hard done by when there were people blackening her reputation after Tolstoy's death, for she had contributed several details to the crucial scene at the ball by acting as her husband's fashion consultant and advising on Anna's toilette:

> She was not in lilac, which Kitty had so set her heart on, but in a low-cut black velvet dress, revealing her ample shoulders and a bosom like old chiselled ivory, rounded arms and tiny slender hands. The entire dress was trimmed with Venetian lace. On her head, in her black hair, unaugmented by any extension, was a small garland of pansies, and there was another on the black sash ribbon around her waist, between pieces of white lace.[73]

Tolstoy dressed Anna in a black dress, but it was Sonya who suggested the fabric should be velvet, and accentuated the overall sensual impression by making the lace around her waist white.[74]

In the second instalment of *Anna Karenina*, which appeared in the February issue of the *Russian Messenger*, readers sympathised with the grieving Kitty and Levin, both now spurned. They thrilled to Anna's romantic night-time encounter with Vronsky at a remote railway station in the middle of a snowstorm, but they were probably slightly disconcerted by the way this instalment ended. In the middle of chapter 10 of Part Two came two coy lines of dots representing the moment when Anna and Vronsky become intimate with each other.[75] They were followed by a passage in which the sexual act was clearly associated with murder:

> As she looked at him, she felt physically humiliated, and she could say nothing more. He meanwhile was feeling what a murderer must feel when he looks at the body he has robbed of life. That body he had robbed of life was their love, the first period of their love. There was something terrible and loathsome in the memories of what this terrible price of shame had bought. Shame at her spiritual nakedness oppressed her and communicated itself to him. But in spite of the murderer's deep horror before the body of his victim, the body must be hacked to pieces and hidden – the murderer must take advantage of what he has gained by murder.

Tolstoy experienced the first of several bruising encounters with his editor over this chapter. Katkov objected to his 'vivid realism', and asked him to tone it down. Tolstoy refused to change a single word, however, arguing that this was one of those parts on which the 'whole novel' depended.[76]

All in all, February 1875 was not a good month for Tolstoy. If he felt completely indifferent to all the accolades he was receiving for *Anna Karenina*, it was because there had been another death in the family.[77] This time it was Nikolay, their ten-month-old baby, who passed away after three weeks of harrowing illness. It was particularly agonising for Sonya, who was still breast-feeding. Instead of the sunshine which had accompanied Petya's funeral, the day of Nikolay's burial was one of the coldest that winter – minus twenty degrees, with fierce, biting winds which tore at the muslin he was wrapped in and the crown on his head, traditionally a part of Orthodox funerals. Sonya told Tanya that she felt as if she had turned to stone.[78] Three months later, she was pregnant again.

There were further instalments of *Anna Karenina* in March and April

1875, but Russian readers then had to wait eight months for the next chapters to be published. The reason for the delay was simple: Tolstoy had not finished them. It was unprecedented for the serial publication of a novel to be interrupted in this way, and only a writer of Tolstoy's stature could have got away with it. He could not back out of his deal with Katkov, but he found it hard to muster the necessary enthusiasm to carry on. He was still wrapped up in his educational ideas, and preoccupied with the publication of his *New ABC*, which won immediate acclaim as soon as it appeared in June 1875. He was also becoming very depressed and needed distraction.

That summer the whole family returned to Samara, accompanied by Sonya's brother 'Uncle Styopa', their English governess Emily Tabor and Jules Rey, the bespectacled but athletic Swiss tutor who had arrived at Yasnaya Polyana that January.[79] He was a spruce, neatly turned out young man of twenty-three with a secret drink problem, and he made a bee-line for Emily.[80] At the beginning of August Tolstoy organised a traditional Bashkir horse race – five laps of a three-mile circular course marked out on his land – for which he offered prizes.[81] Tents sprang up all around it in the days leading up to the race as Bashkirs arrived with their horses, and Tolstoy offered a lame foal and a few sheep for the feasting that went on beforehand. It was thrilling for the Tolstoy children, who had never encountered throat singing or the traditional dancing that accompanied the songs performed on the *quray*, the long Bashkir flute. Thirty-two riders took part in the race, which drew hundreds of spectators. A handful were local Russians, including Tolstoy on a mount he had bought specially for the occasion, but the rest were Bashkir and Kirghiz horsemen, one of whom claimed the top prize of a rifle. It was a far cry from the horse races in *Anna Karenina*, attended by the court. Tolstoy was hatching a plan to start breeding horses, and he brought home some Kirghiz horses, prized for their speed and stamina, as well as two donkeys christened Bismarck and MacMahon after two opponents in the Franco-Prussian War.[82]

Back in Yasnaya Polyana at the end of August, rested and sunburnt, Tolstoy declared that the experience of witnessing first-hand the clash of sedentary Russian and nomadic Bashkir lifestyles, and putting up with flies and dirt out on the steppe, was infinitely superior to listening to speeches in the English Houses of Parliament, which he regarded as a dubious privilege. He had not picked up a pen for two months.[83] He forced himself to return to 'boring, banal' *Anna Karenina* in the autumn of 1875, but both he and

Sonya were soon in low spirits again. On 12 October Sonya wrote in her diary that their excessively isolated country life was now unbearable, and that the monotony of her routine over months and years had led to an overwhelming apathy and indifference to everything which she could no longer fight. Her husband's gloom was infectious: 'He sits miserably and despondently for days and weeks on end without doing anything, without work, without energy, without joy and seems to have reconciled himself to this state of affairs. It is a kind of moral death, but I don't want to see it in him, and he himself can't go on living like *this*.'[84]

At the end October Sonya fell gravely ill with peritonitis, and then went into labour. Varvara, born three months premature, died a few hours after she was born.[85] 'Fear, horror, death, children cavorting, eating, fuss, doctors, falsity, death, horror' was how Tolstoy defined the situation at Yasnaya Polyana in a letter to his correspondent Fet.[86] A further source of stress was that the house was full of people just at that time. After Toinette's death the previous summer, Tolstoy's other aunt, seventy-eight-year-old Polina, had moved to Yasnaya Polyana from her Tula convent, and she took over running the household while Sonya was ill, but there were also lots of guests: Sonya's brother Sasha and his wife, her uncle Kostya Islavin, Pyotr Samarin and his wife and another family friend. On the most critical day of Sonya's illness, Jules Rey's sister arrived from Geneva to become the children's new governess.[87]

Tolstoy found some solace in writing a very long letter to Strakhov about philosophy, but ended up confronting the meaning of life and the inescapable truth that his own life was just an 'empty and stupid joke'. He had just turned forty-seven, and he felt he was entering old age – a time when there was no longer anything in the 'outside world' that interested him, and all he could see ahead was death. He had now started the long descent back to where he had originated, he wrote, aware that whatever his desire – breeding a particular kind of horse, shooting ten hares in one field, learning Arabic – it could not bring him any true satisfaction. His only hope was that he had understood the meaning of life wrongly.[88] Meanwhile, to be on the safe side, he went hunting without a gun, so that he could not turn it on himself, and boasted to his brother Sergey that he had managed to bag six hares with his dogs without firing a shot.[89]

Sonya did not have the luxury of contemplating the meaning of life. Usually she was too busy with household chores, and now, not the first time, she was actually close to death. Her long convalescence was immediately beset by new problems. Jules Rey's sister was not a success as a governess, and there was friction: soon Sonya could no longer bear her.[90] And then, in December 1875, came the slow, painful demise of *tyotushka* Polina.[91] It was Sonya who had to look after her during her last illness when she was confined to bed. It was Sonya who had to change her soiled bed linen and suffer her shouting and cursing from the pain that the slightest movement caused her. Polina, who conversed in French with her nephew to the last, was terrified of dying, and finally passed away after great suffering on 22 December. She was buried two days later. It was another quiet Christmas.[92]

Tolstoy was greatly saddened, as the last living link with his parents had now been irrevocably sundered. As he wrote to Alexandrine in March, the death of this old woman had affected him profoundly – more than any other. Despite feeling as fed up with *Anna Karenina* as with a 'bitter radish',[93] he had to soldier on, however. Another third of the novel was printed in the first four issues of the *Russian Messenger* in 1876. The April issue contained a substantial section of Part Five, ending with a chapter recounting the last days of Levin's brother Nikolay.[94] As with many other parts of *Anna Karenina*, Tolstoy drew on his own personal experience to write it. For the character of Nikolay, he recalled aspects of his eccentric late brother Dmitry, and also resurrected in his memory the last days of his dearly loved brother of the same name who had died in his arms. Death seemed to be everywhere. Tolstoy told his one surviving brother Sergey in February that, like his character Levin, he was finding it impossible to get away from thoughts of death, and the notion that nothing else remained for him in life.[95] Sergey was familiar with the feeling as he himself was a depressive, but so was their sister Maria, who wrote to Tolstoy from Heidelberg in March 1876 to tell him she had been feeling suicidal too:

> I'm in such an appalling moral state, loneliness is affecting me so *dreadfully*, with the constant worry which hangs over on me like the sword of Damocles, and which I think about day and night, that I sometimes get frightened. Thoughts of suicide have begun to hound me, I mean really hound me and so relentlessly that it's become a kind of illness or madness.[96]

Maria's 'constant worry' was Elena, the illegitimate daughter she had given

1. *Tolstoy in his army uniform as a newly promoted ensign in Moscow in 1854, shortly before transferring to active duty in Bucharest. He decided to make the journey from the Caucasus, where he had been stationed, via Yasnaya Polyana, which involved a detour of about six hundred miles.*

2. Tolstoy with his brother Nikolay in Moscow shortly before travelling to the Caucasus, where he would enlist in the army, 1851.

3. *Sergey, Nikolay, Dmitry and Lev Tolstoy in Moscow, February 1854. This was the last time the four brothers were all together. They met during Tolstoy's month of leave, before he travelled south to fight in the war against Turkey.*

4. *The writers associated with the journal* The Contemporary, *St Petersburg, 1856. From left to right: Goncharov, Turgenev, Tolstoy, Grigorovich, Druzhinin and Ostrovsky. This picture was taken by the celebrated 'patriarch of Russian photography' Sergey Levitsky, and Tolstoy later hung it on the wall of his study at Yasnaya Polyana.*

5. Tolstoy in Brussels, March 1861. Tolstoy was at this point nearing the end of his second and final trip abroad. He had been away for nine months, during which time his brother Nikolay died in the south of France, and he had studied foreign educational methods in preparation for developing his own pedagogical activities.

6. Alexandra Andreyevna Tolstaya (Alexandrine), 1860s. Tolstoy enjoyed a close friendship with his father's cousin, who was an attractive woman of formidable intellect. As a lady-in-waiting at court, she later became very useful as a conduit for letters of appeal when Tolstoy took up the cause of social and religious injustice, but there was friction when he abandoned his Orthodox beliefs.

7. The future Sofya (Sonya) Tolstaya and her younger sister Tatyana (Tanya) Bers, Moscow
1861 . This photograph was taken the year before Tolstoy married Sonya. The sisters remained
close, and it was in letters to Tanya that Sonya gave the most honest account of her life at
Yasnaya Polyana.

8. Sonya in the drawing room at Yasnaya Polyana, 1902. This corner of the spacious drawing
room was where the family and their guests would traditionally gather for evening tea.
Above Sonya's head is a portrait of Tolstoy's profligate grandfather, Ilya Andreyevich.

9. *The old Yasnaya Polyana mansion built by Sergey Volkonsky, where Tolstoy was born in 1828, and which he sold to a neighbouring landowner after heavy gambling losses in 1854. It was dismantled and moved, brick by brick, to the new owner's estate twenty miles away, where this photograph was taken in 1892.*

10. *Tolstoy's house at Yasnaya Polyana before the addition of a final extension in the 1890s. Originally, this building was intended as one of two identical guest wings which flanked the old mansion. Tolstoy made it his main residence when he retired from the army after the Crimean War. Extensions were added in the 1860s, 1870s and 1890s to accommodate his burgeoning family and the retinue of tutors and governesses.*

11. Ivan Kramskoy, portrait of Tolstoy, Yasnaya Polyana, 1873. This portrait was acquired by the merchant Pavel Tretyakov for his growing collection of Russian art. Tolstoy had initially turned down requests to sit for a portrait, but was persuaded to change his mind by the personal charm of the celebrated painter Ivan Kramskoy, who had been staying at a dacha near to Yasnaya Polyana.

12. Repin, Tolstoy ploughing, Yasnaya Polyana, 1887. Tolstoy started working in the fields as a young man in the late 1840s, and increased his time working alongside the peasants as his feelings of guilt over their exploitation grew. After he turned his back on writing fiction for the upper classes, he preached that each person should live by the sweat of their brow, working the land. He was about to turn sixty when this portrait was painted.

13. Repin, Tolstoy in his study at Yasnaya Polyana, 1891. Tolstoy moved his study at Yasnaya Polyana several times, but this famous arched room on the ground floor, where old Prince Volkonsky had used to hang cured meats, was where he worked in the early 1860s and from 1887 to 1902. It was where he began War and Peace, *and where he later worked on* The Kreutzer Sonata *and* Resurrection.

14. Repin's first portrait of Tolstoy, 1887. Repin had met Tolstoy back in 1880, but he wanted to get to know him well before attempting his first portrait. By this point, Tolstoy had gone through his spiritual 'crisis' and achieved international celebrity for works such as Confession *and* What I Believe, *both of which were banned in Russia.*

15. Sonya standing by a portrait of her deceased son Ivan (Vanechka), Yasnaya Polyana, 1897. Sonya was devastated by the death of her youngest son Ivan, who is seen here in the portrait hung above an informal shrine to his memory. Sonya took up photography after Vanechka's death, and enjoyed setting up shots such as this one, arranged on the balcony at Yasnaya Polyana.

16. *Tolstoy and his Starley Rover bicycle, 1895. Tolstoy had an irrepressible appetite for trying out new enthusiasms, and when he was sixty-five, just after Vanechka Tolstoy died, he took up cycling. After buying a British-made bicycle, he went to have lessons, and then successfully acquired the licence which permitted him to cycle around Moscow.*

17. Tolstoy and Sonya, August 1895. Their youngest son Vanechka had died six months earlier, so they are still in mourning.

18. *The Tolstoy children with their mother in Gaspra, Crimea, 1902. From left to right: Ilya, Andrey, Tanya, Lev, Sonya, Misha, Masha, Sergey, Alexandra. Tolstoy came close to dying during a long period of illness which started in 1901, after he was excommunicated. Despite his hatred of luxury, he accepted an invitation to spend the winter at a palatial villa in the more temperate climate of the Crimea. Members of his close family all came to visit, thinking they would be paying their last respects. In 1902, the Tolstoys' eldest child Sergey was nearly forty, while their youngest, Alexandra, was eighteen.*

19. Tolstoy and his sister Maria (Masha), 1908. Despite the fact that his sister became a nun, Tolstoy remained always very close to Masha, who had earlier led an unhappy life, with marriage to an abusive husband and the stigma of an illegitimate child.

20. *Tolstoy on horseback in the environs of Yasnaya Polyana, 1908. Tolstoy was a passionate horseman from early childhood. There was a point at the end of his life when he came to see even riding as a self-indulgent activity when there were peasants starving around him, and he pondered giving it up. He reasoned that his horse was old, however, and so continued riding.*

21. *Tolstoy at the opening of the People's Library in Yasnaya Polyana village, 31 January 1910. As a young man, Tolstoy had been passionate about setting up schools, since there was no provision for the peasants to receive any education. This village library, set up by the Moscow Literary Society, consisted of one small room with two bookcases. Pictured with Tolstoy are four pupils of his first Yasnaya Polyana school.*

22. Repin, Lev Tolstoy Barefoot, *1901. This famous portrait of Tolstoy 'at prayer' in the grounds of Yasnaya Polyana was first exhibited in St Petersburg just after Tolstoy was excommunicated, and drew hundreds of admirers who adorned it with flowers as if it was a popular icon. Seeking to avoid public disturbances, the authorities ordered it to be withdrawn when the exhibition travelled on to other cities.*

birth to in September 1863, months after the Tolstoys' first child Sergey was born.[97] In 1876 Elena turned thirteen, and Masha, as a widowed single woman, was still too ashamed to bring her to Russia.

Russian society had begun to change rapidly in the 1860s, but the patriarchal structures enshrined in law by the state remained in place. Tolstoy struck a chord with thousands of female readers suffering unhappy marriages when he wrote *Anna Karenina*. Even though few had the bravery of Anna Arkadyevna, they identified with her. The paradox of Tolstoy writing with such sympathy about Anna while at the same time writing a novel which clearly condemns adultery is partly explained by the fate of his sister Masha, whose unhappy experience of marriage was one of the many life stories which served as the raw material for his 'family' novel. It is as almost as if Masha read her brother's mind, as in the letter she sent him in March 1876, she also spoke of the bitter life lessons she had learned, and directly identified herself with his heroine. 'If all those Anna Kareninas knew what awaited them,' she wrote, 'how they would run from ephemeral pleasures, which are never, and cannot be pleasures, because nothing that is *unlawful* can ever constitute happiness.' This, of course, was Tolstoy's own view.

Until the publication of Tolstoy's correspondence with his siblings in 1990, Masha was a somewhat shadowy figure in Tolstoy's biography,[98] but she was an important person in his life, and they remained close (his letters to her are some of the most touching he ever wrote). Masha had lived to regret her marriage to Valerian Petrovich Tolstoy and buried her sorrows in foreign travel, travelling with her children to spas where she could treat the various illnesses she believed she was suffering from. It was in Aix-les-Bains in 1861 that she met the handsome Swedish Viscount Hector Victor de Kleen, with whom she spent the next two winters in Algiers. Her brothers learned they were living together when she made a trip back to Russia in the summer of 1862, just when Tolstoy was about to get married. The following autumn, fearing their censure, she wrote from Geneva to tell them she had given birth to a little girl. Both Tolstoy and his brother Sergey had fathered illegitimate children themselves, and were sympathetic. Tolstoy hastened to reassure Masha of their support, and resolved to try to help her.[99] In January 1864 he and Sergey met with Valerian Petrovich, who acknowledged his responsibility in the breakdown of the marriage and agreed to a divorce. Tolstoy obtained the necessary permission from the bishop, and then sent the documents for

Masha to sign and return. She was scared to set things in motion, however, as Valerian Petrovich sent her a threatening letter, telling her a divorce would 'harm his position and bring him a great deal of unpleasantness'. In a letter to Toinette she asked pitifully if she had the right to go through with it, even though he had made her suffer so much.[100]

Masha was understandably hesitant about going through with divorce. It was extremely rare in Russia, and the risk of social disgrace was very real. In 1857, the year in which divorce first become possible in an English court of civil law, the sanctity of marriage as a religious institution in Russia was upheld by the publication of the third edition of the Imperial Law Code. A divorce in Russia could only be obtained through the Church, which viewed marriage as a holy sacrament which could not be dissolved,[101] and accorded illegitimate children no legal rights. Article 103 of Chapter 1 in Volume One of the Law Code specifically forbade married couples from living apart, except in cases of exile to Siberia, while articles 106 and 108 upheld male authority within wedlock:

> A husband shall love his wife as his own body and live with her in harmony; he shall respect and protect her, forgive her shortcomings, and ease her infirmities. He shall provide his wife nourishment and support to the best of his ability … A wife shall obey her husband as the head of the family, abide with him in love, respect and unlimited obedience and render him every satisfaction and affection as the mistress of the house …[102]

Female subjugation was not exclusive to Russia, of course, but the state had a vested interest in supporting patriarchal structures, as it equated domestic stability with political stability. Tolstoy could have picked no better way of portraying the disintegration of late imperial Russian society than to decide to write a novel with the theme of the 'family'.

Over the course of the nineteenth century the Orthodox Church had made marital separation more rather than less difficult. Petitions for divorce had to be made to the diocesan authorities, and entailed an expensive, bureaucratic and lengthy process, with nine separate stages. Adultery, furthermore, could only be proved with the testimony of witnesses, as Alexey Alexandrovich discovers to his horror when he goes to consult the 'famous St Petersburg lawyer' in Part Four of *Anna Karenina*. It is thus hardly surprising so few petitions were made – seventy-one in the whole of Russia in 1860, and only seven made on the grounds of adultery.[103] But with the Great Reforms, urban growth and the expansion of education came new attitudes towards marriage, and pressure to simplify and update divorce, so it was a constant topic of discussion in the ecclesiastical press in the second half of the nineteenth century.[104] A committee set up by reformers in 1870 proposed transferring divorce proceedings to the civil courts, thus saving the ecclesiastical authorities from having to investigate such matters, 'which are full of descriptions of suggestive and disgusting scenes, in which the whole stench of depravity is often collected'.[105] In May 1873, just when Tolstoy was starting *Anna Karenina*, the Holy Synod overwhelmingly rejected this proposal, as it did a proposal to introduce civil marriage (which had already been introduced elsewhere in Europe) on the grounds that it was 'legalised fornication'. Nevertheless, the number of divorces rose steadily, from 795 in 1866 to 947 in 1875.[106] Both Sonya's elder sister Liza (the clever one Tolstoy had shrunk from marrying) and their brother Alexander obtained divorces during this period.[107]

Tolstoy's research on behalf of his sister served him well when dealing with the topic of divorce in *Anna Karenina*, as did the experience of witnessing divorce proceedings close at hand. In 1868 his old friend Dmitry Dyakov's sister Maria Alexeyevna divorced the stuffy, Karenin-like Sergey Sukhotin, having created a scandal by abandoning him and their young children for another man, with whom she had an illegitimate child.[108] In the event, his sister Masha did not need to go through with the divorce from her husband, as the weak-willed and impoverished viscount returned to Sweden to marry someone with better financial prospects, leaving Masha mired in debt. His family had been reluctant to see him marry a woman with four children who would also soon bear the stigma of divorce, and had persuaded him to leave her. Masha returned to Russia and Valerian Petrovich died the following year, but she remained deeply unhappy in her personal life, having left her daughter Elena behind in Switzerland. As she wrote in the desperate letter to her brother in 1876 in which she likened herself to Anna Karenina, she knew of no single woman from their background with the 'courage' to admit to the existence of an illegitimate child.[109]

Tolstoy himself certainly contemplated divorce too on occasion, but his increasingly troubled marriage was stable and conventional when compared to the marriages of his relatives and friends. His brother Dmitry spent his last years living with a former prostitute (as Nikolay does in *Anna Karenina*), and his brother Sergey was married to a gypsy. While Tolstoy was trying to rescue Masha in 1864, and write *War and Peace*, he suddenly found himself also having to deal with the romantic crisis Sergey had become embroiled in. The previous summer, after his fourteen-year relationship with Maria Shishkina, the gypsy singer from Tula whom he had 'bought out' from her choir, Sergey had suddenly fallen madly in love with Sonya's vivacious sister Tanya (with whom Tolstoy himself was also slightly enamoured, if the truth be told). Sergey proposed to Tanya, but quite apart from the fact that he was twenty years older (Tanya was a very young seventeen), he already had three children with Maria Shishkina and was expecting a fourth. In the end, his conscience got the better of him. It broke his heart to see Maria praying on her knees in front of an icon in floods of tears, and meekly submitting to fate.[110] In June 1865, a month after his daughter Vera was born, he broke off the engagement.[111]

Both Tanya and Sergey married in 1867. Tolstoy was opposed to Tanya marrying her cousin Alexander Kuzminsky, as he thought she would be a good wife for his old friend Dmitry Dyakov, who had just been widowed. There was something distinctly curmudgeonly about the distaste he expressed ten years later when Dyakov (then fifty-five) married his daughter Masha's former governess Sofya Robertovna, who was thirty-two.[112] After all, 'Sofesh', as she was affectionately known, was the same age as his own wife, and two years older than Tanya.[113] After Sergey finally married Maria they moved to his Pirogovo estate. They were to have a total of eleven children, of whom four survived, but their marriage was not happy. Maria felt painfully aware of their different social backgrounds, and was shy and retiring in the company of her brother's family. Tolstoy always showed Maria Mikhailovna the greatest of respect, and repeatedly invited her to accompany Sergey to Yasnaya Polyana, but she was reluctant to come, even when Sonya had the idea of asking her to become godmother to their son Andrey, born in December 1877.

If Tolstoy had essentially stopped keeping a diary while he was writing *Anna Karenina*, it was partly because he was able to give voice to matters that concerned him on the pages of his novel. Through the relationship of Levin and Kitty he had wanted to chart a 'third way' between the European-style marriage favoured by Anna, notable for the small number of children, and the 'traditional' peasant-style marriage of Dolly, who raises a large number of children despite being from the same noble background as Anna. Over the course of the novel Tolstoy had woven many thinly disguised autobiographical details into the story of Levin's courtship and marriage of Kitty (the communication via letters written in chalk, the oversight of leaving out a clean shirt for Levin to wear to the wedding and so forth), but in the second half of Part Six, he began to voice through Dolly one particular immediate concern: his horror of contraception.

After the death of Varvara in November 1875, Sonya's health had remained precarious, and in January 1877 she made her first visit to St Petersburg to spend a week with her mother (whom she had not seen for three years) and consult the famous Dr Botkin, court physician to the Tsar. She also met Alexandrine for the first time, who immediately wrote to tell Tolstoy how much she liked his wife. She told him that she had found 'Sophie' sincere, intelligent, warm and straightforward, and had taken to her at once. It was Alexandrine who also conveyed a euphemistic message from Dr Botkin about Sonya's 'health' which resulted in her becoming pregnant again in a matter of weeks.[114] Since the death of Varvara, Sonya had so dreaded having another child that she had done everything in her powers to avoid becoming pregnant, including considering contraception, and it had clearly had an impact on the marriage. It was just at this time that Tolstoy wrote the chapter in *Anna Karenina* in which Dolly reacts with extreme shock to Anna's revelation that she has been using contraception. For Dolly, and for Tolstoy, contraception was immoral.

While Sonya was in Petersburg, Tolstoy got on with finishing *Anna Karenina*, turning to Trollope for light relief. He was reading *The Prime Minister*, the penultimate of the six Palliser novels, and recommended it highly to his brother Sergey.[115] *Anna Karenina* reflects Tolstoy's engagement with the French novel of adultery, but also his enthusiasm for English fiction, which he highly revered – he once stated quite baldly that English books were the best, and that he always found something fresh and new in them.[116] The English novel Anna reads on the train at the beginning of *Anna Karenina* may well have been by Trollope, since it mentions Members of Parliament, fox-hunting and peers.[117] Trollope had decided early on that his spirited heroine Lady Glencora would grow to love her upright, dry, statesman husband Plantagenet, who is altogether more benign than his Russian counterpart Karenin. And without the burden of a didactic tradition to weigh him down, opting for a happy ending was unproblematic for a writer devoted to his full-time job at the Post Office. Trollope was mercifully immune to the kind of self-doubt which increasingly bedevilled Tolstoy as he struggled to finish *Anna Karenina*.

Tolstoy finally finished *Anna Karenina* in 1877. Russian readers had certainly been patient. They had, after all, begun reading it two years earlier, and they were probably as disconcerted as Tolstoy's editor was when the instalments had suddenly stopped in April 1875, a third of the way into the novel, and again in 1876. Katkov had even felt obliged to publish a notice explaining that the hiatus was not due to the journal's editors but to 'circumstances preventing the author from completing his novel', whose publication, they hoped, would now continue 'without interruption'. Tolstoy's readers remained enthusiastic, however. One young acquaintance of Tolstoy later recalled that he and his fellow students waited with bated breath for each new issue of the *Russian Messenger*, and then immediately 'devoured' every page whenever there was an instalment of *Anna Karenina*.[118] But Tolstoy was fairly nonplussed when Strakhov wrote from Petersburg in May 1877 to tell him that the most recent reviews were hailing him to be a writer as great as Shakespeare, and that even Dostoyevsky was waving his arms about and calling Tolstoy a 'god of art'.[119] Dostoyevsky, however, would shortly change his tune when he came to read the novel's final chapters, in which Tolstoy threw down the gauntlet to Pan-Slavists like himself.

Anna Karenina was nothing if not topical, and Tolstoy's slow progress enabled him to reflect in its pages not just the most recent debates about agriculture, but also the latest political developments as they unfolded in Russia. Here Tolstoy was in new territory, but his increasing indifference to purely artistic questions made him fearless about voicing unpopular opinions and set him on a collision course with the Russian establishment. The April 1877 issue of the *Russian Messenger* contained the last chapters of Part Seven, which end with Anna's death, and they were greeted with wide acclaim. This issue should have also contained the novel's epilogue (as Part Eight was originally called), but Tolstoy had once again fallen out with his editor, and he was still awaiting a third set of revised proofs in mid-May.[120] The sticking point was politics, and specifically the 'unpatriotic' opinions expressed in the novel about the Russian volunteer movement in aid of the Serbs, who since the end of June 1876 had been at war with the Ottoman Empire. This is the movement which Vronsky joins at the end of *Anna Karenina*: we see him getting on a train at the Smolensky station in Moscow as he sets off on a journey from which we know he will never return.

The Serbo-Turkish War was just one aspect of the 'Eastern Question' which reared its head once again in the 1870s, this time driven by the Balkan nations' desire for liberation from centuries of Ottoman rule. Pan-Slavists saw the conflict as a golden opportunity to further their goal of uniting all the Slavic nations, ideally under Russia's sovereignty. The fact that Pan-Slavism had its roots in Russia's diplomatic isolation and humiliating defeat in the Crimean War was not lost on Tolstoy, whose experience fighting in that campaign had turned him into a committed pacifist. He found this new war greatly troubling. He had no wish to be caught up in contemporary politics, but his concern over the events unfolding in the Balkans caused him to put aside his disdain for the press temporarily and follow the war's progress. Foreseeing Russia's ineluctable involvement in the Serbo-Turkish War, he had actually gone to Moscow to find out more about it in November 1876. He was there when Alexander II gave a speech from the Kremlin in which he gave the Turks an ultimatum, and could not have avoided the patriotic crowds lining the streets and shouting, 'War! War!' along with the customary 'Hurrah!'[121] What really made Tolstoy's blood boil was the part he believed was played by the press and the 'Slavic Committee' in whipping up enthusiasm for war, and in the last pages of *Anna Karenina* he began to speak out.

Moscow had always been the epicentre of Russian Pan-Slavism. The first charitable Slavic Committee had been founded there in 1858 to provide support to Slavic peoples under Ottoman or Habsburg rule, and the city hosted the second Slavic Congress in 1867. In 1877, the Slavic Committee was run by the Slavophile journalist Ivan Aksakov, with active support from his wife Anna, and Tolstoy wrote in particularly withering tones to Fet about her self-appointed role in artificially drumming up support for war when he returned home from his Moscow visit.[122] Anna Aksakova, daughter of the poet Tyutchev, was Tolstoy's old acquaintance, and formerly the governess to Alexander II's youngest children (when she married in 1866 she had been succeeded by Alexandra Andreyevna Tolstaya – Alexandrine). Another key figure in Moscow's Slavophile circles was the former guards officer Alexander Porokhovshchikov. In 1872 he built the Slavic Bazaar Hotel close to Red Square to be an embodiment of his vision of Slavonic brotherhood; the deliberately pre-Petrine style of its design was complemented by its interiors while the main dining room featured an enormous canvas depicting Russian, Polish and Czech composers commissioned from the young artist Ilya Repin. It was from here that Porokhovshchikov organised the recruitment of Russian volunteers for the Serbo-Turkish War,[123] and as an eligible retired officer, this is where Vronsky would have come to enlist in *Anna Karenina*.

Russia went on to declare war on the Ottoman Empire in April 1877, just as Tolstoy was writing his epilogue to *Anna Karenina*. As a prominent Pan-Slavist, and also the editor of an influential conservative newspaper, Katkov was incensed to see the volunteer movement dismissed in Tolstoy's manuscript as a 'fashionable enthusiasm' for the idle rich. He also did not like to see the press criticised for claiming to represent the 'voice of the people', and publishing 'much that was unnecessary'. For his part, Tolstoy was infuriated that a 'mere journalist' should dare to try to correct his manuscript. He had never made any attempt to hide the fact that the sentiments voiced by Levin and old Prince Shcherbatsky were his own. To his friends he openly declared that newspapers were 'a most evil thing, and it would be better if they did not even exist'. He reiterated that the Russian people neither knew anything about the Slavs, nor wanted to fight.[124] Tolstoy refused point-blank to make the changes Katkov demanded, and in the end withdrew his manuscript in order to publish it separately. Katkov retaliated by publishing a statement in the *Russian Messenger*:

> In the previous issue the words 'to be concluded' followed the novel *Anna Karenina*. But the novel really ends with the death of the heroine. According to the author's plan, a short epilogue was to have followed, in which readers could have found out that Vronsky, grief-stricken and confused after Anna's death, sets off for Serbia as a volunteer, and that all the other characters are alive and well, with Levin staying in his village and getting angry at the Slavic Committees and the volunteers. The author may perhaps develop these chapters for a separate edition of his novel.[125]

Tolstoy was naturally even more furious when he read this, and immediately sat down to draft a letter to Alexey Suvorin, now the editor of the St Petersburg *New Times*, in which he objected to the way in which his epilogue was dismissed as being of little value, but then summarised anyway. 'How about summarising the rest of the novel in ten lines?' he thundered: 'There was a lady who left her husband. After falling in love with Mr Vronsky, she grew angry with various things in Moscow and threw herself under a train ...'[126] Tolstoy also objected to Katkov's instruction to the reader as to how to interpret *Anna Karenina*, that is, as a 'novel about high society', and greatly resented being effectively told how to end it. But it was Sonya, signing as 'C[ountess] S[ofya] ***' and quoting from her husband's draft, who finally announced to the readers of *New Times* why the epilogue to *Anna Karenina* was not published in the *Russian Messenger*.[127]

No doubt the Russian public was gratified with the explanation, but not all readers relished the epilogue. Levin's disparaging remarks about the Balkan Question and the Russian Volunteer Movement were highly contentious, and ran exactly counter to those of Tolstoy's great rival Dostoyevsky, whose messianic nationalism (or jingoistic Orthodox megalomania, depending on your viewpoint) was centred on Russia's role as crusading saviour in the Balkans. Although Dostoyevsky and Tolstoy never met, they were, of course, aware of each other, but were natural antipodes who found many shortcomings in each other's work. As a journalist, it was more or less incumbent upon Dostoyevsky to deliver a verdict on Tolstoy's novel, and after much prevarication he finally came out in print with an opinion of *Anna Karenina* in early 1877. Tolstoy, however, never returned the compliment of publicly commenting on any of Dostoyevsky's fiction, remaining, as always, aloof.

To begin with, Dostoyevsky was generous with his praise of *Anna Karenina*. He was particularly enthusiastic about Levin as a literary character, and he devoted several pages to the novel in the February issue of his *Diary of a Writer*, the independent monthly journal he had started up in 1876 to explore the character and destiny of the Russian people. But when he read the epilogue later in the year, Dostoyevsky was beside himself. In the July–August issue he lambasted Levin for being egocentric, unpatriotic and out of touch with the Russian people.[128] He took a dim view of Levin's claim that the Russian people shared his lack of concern for the predicament of the Balkan Slavs, and took strong exception to his declared unwillingness to kill, even if it resulted in the prevention of atrocities. It is here, of course, that we meet in embryonic form the idea of non-resistance to violence which would lie at the heart of the new religious outlook which Tolstoy would develop over the next decade. People like Tolstoy were supposed to be our teachers, Dostoyevsky concluded at the end of his lengthy tirade, but what exactly were they teaching us? Needless to say, Dostoyevsky did not receive a response either in 1877 or in the years leading up to his death in January 1881. But Tolstoy made up for that by then spending the next thirty years of his long life doing little else but answering that very question.

PILGRIM, NIHILIST, MUZHIK

If I was on my own, I wouldn't be a monk, I would be a holy fool – that is, I wouldn't cherish anything in life, and would do no one any harm.
                    Letter to Nikolay Strakhov, 6 November 1877[1]

AS SOMEONE WHO CAME TO BELIEVE fervently in the idea that our lives are made up of seven-year cycles, and who was also extremely superstitious, Tolstoy was bound to look upon his forty-ninth year as being of special significance – particularly since this birthday fell in the seventh year of the seventh decade of the century. And so it was, for looking back in October 1884, when seven more years had passed, he realised that the most radical change in his life had indeed been, as he put it numerically in a letter to his wife, '7 × 7 = 49'.[2] It was in 1877 that Tolstoy began to tread more firmly on the path he had first tentatively started out on when he set up his Yasnaya Polyana school – the path of living in accordance with Christian ethics. Twice he had been diverted – when he married and again when he committed himself to writing *Anna Karenina*. But this time there was to be no straying, and the further he progressed along the path that was taking him away from his artistic calling as a novelist, and also away from his wife, the lighter his step became. He did not stop writing fiction entirely, but it became secondary to the more pressing task of exposing the hypocrisy and immorality he saw around him.

It was perhaps inevitable that a man who did nothing by half-measures would experience something beyond the typical mid-life crisis. The decade following Tolstoy's forty-ninth birthday would indeed turn out to be the most tumultuous in his life thus far. Moving to Moscow was the event which loomed largest for the rest of his family during this period (it was a life-changing experience for all the children and certainly for Sonya, after the long years of being sequestered at Yasnaya Polyana). But that was not what Tolstoy was referring to when he defined these years as a time of tempestuous inner struggle and change. He became a devout Orthodox communicant, then a trenchant critic of the Church. He undertook a root-and-branch study of all the major world religions and wrote a searing work of spiritual autobiography about his quest for the meaning of life. He produced a new translation of the Gospels, and set out to follow Christ's teaching. And then he began protesting loudly in the name of that teaching against the Orthodox Church. At the end of the 1880s Alexander III would brand Tolstoy as a godless nihilist, and a dangerous figure who needed to be stopped.[3]

There was a journey to be undertaken before Tolstoy reached the point of formulating and articulating his new ideas, however, and it began with a period of intense religious searching, as reflected in the chapters at the end of *Anna Karenina* where Levin questions the meaning of life. The spiritual crisis that Dostoyevsky underwent during his years of Siberian exile in the early 1850s resulted in him jettisoning atheism and socialism and embracing Christianity, specifically Russian Orthodox Christianity, with ever greater fervour. Tolstoy did more or less the opposite, the spiritual crisis he underwent at the end of the 1870s resulting in him jettisoning not just Russian Orthodoxy but a large part of Christianity too. But he began his spiritual crisis by first becoming devout – the most devout he had ever been in his life.

Up until this point, Tolstoy had only notionally been a member of the Orthodox faith he was baptised into, like most members of his class. He had given up praying at sixteen and lost his belief at eighteen, but in his late forties he began to yearn for the guidance provided by strong religious beliefs. Writing to Alexandrine at the beginning of February 1877, Tolstoy confessed that for the past two years he had been like a drowning man, desperate to find something to hold on to. He told her he had been pinning his hopes on finding salvation in religion, that he and his friend Strakhov were both agreed that philosophy could not provide the answers, and that they could not live without religion. At the same time, he wrote, they just could not believe in God.[4] A month later, however, Tolstoy had changed course totally, and almost on a whim, after conversations with his 'materialist' doctor Grigory Zakharin and Sergey Levitsky, the celebrated 'patriarch' of Russian photography who had taken the group portrait of *The Contemporary*'s writers in Paris back in 1856.[5] He started reading the theological writings of the Slavophile thinker Alexey Khomyakov, just like his character Levin at the end of *Anna Karenina*.[6] Like Levin, he found them wanting. Even so, he was soon saying his prayers every day as he had in childhood, going to church on Sundays and fasting on Wednesdays and Fridays.

Tolstoy's newfound religious fervour did not stop him from going off hunting with his friends for wolves and elk, or seeking to publish his fiction profitably – yet. He had come back to his old publisher Theodor Ries to arrange for the separate publication of 'The Eighth and Last Part' of *Anna Karenina* after the *Russian Messenger* debacle, and soon after it appeared in print in July 1877 he handed over a slightly revised version of the complete novel for its first publication in book form the following year. The 1878 edition was never reprinted. By subsequently including the novel as part of his collected works, Tolstoy cunningly obliged all those who wanted their own copy to splash out on the complete set. In May 1878 he ascertained from his Moscow distributor that there were 2,700 copies left of the original print run of 4,800, and 800 unsold copies of his nine-volume collected works. The new, fourth edition of his collected works, planned for 1880, would be swelled by the addition of two final volumes incorporating *Anna Karenina*, and would go on sale for sixteen and a half roubles. If 5,000 copies were printed, Tolstoy wrote to Strakhov, that meant a total revenue of 82,500 roubles, of which 20,000 would go on printing costs, but he would sell the distribution rights for 30,000 roubles, so he stood to do extremely well out of the deal.[7]

Tolstoy remained, as ever, a shrewd businessman when it came to financial negotiations. Nevertheless, there were also clear signs of his new piety. In the summer of 1877, accompanied by Strakhov, Tolstoy made the first of several visits to the famed Optina Pustyn Monastery in Kaluga province, some 135 miles west of Yasnaya Polyana. Tolstoy hoped to be granted an audience with Elder Ambrosy. He had heard about Ambrosy from his aunts, who had instilled in him and his siblings a reverence for Optina Pustyn from an early age.[8] His devout aunt Aline was even buried there, having made annual pilgrimages from Yasnaya Polyana. Tolstoy also knew about Ambrosy from his peasants. After a full day's travel, he and Strakhov arrived at three in the morning in their *tarantass*. Tolstoy did not want to be accorded special treatment because of who he was, and so they put up in the monastery's spartan and crowded hostel. It turned out that Father Feoktist, the monk running the monastery hostel, was one of his family's former serfs, however, and as soon as Count Tolstoy's identity was known, there was pressure on him to move to the more luxurious quarters available, which he resisted.

There were reasons why Tolstoy chose to come to Optina Pustyn rather than any other monastery. Despite its sixteenth-century foundations, the anti-clerical reforms launched by Peter the Great and continued by Catherine the Great had almost forced it to close at the end of the eighteenth century, by which time there were only three monks left, and one of them was blind.[9] From this moribund state, however, Optina Pustyn recovered to become the centre of an extraordinary religious revival in the nineteenth century. This was due to its charismatic 'elders'. An elder (*starets*) was a monk who through long ascetic practice, constant prayer and solitude had become an unofficial leader of the spiritual life of his monastery.[10] Believing they possessed powers of healing and clairvoyance in addition to unusual wisdom, thousands of lay visitors would come annually from all over Russia to seek guidance from Elders on a wide array of problems in their lives. Many petitioners were peasants, but Optina Pustyn also attracted large numbers of the Russian intelligentsia, including many noted writers.[11]

The ancient tradition of eldership was brought to Russia by disciples of the eighteenth-century spiritual leader Paisy Velichkovsky. At the age of seventeen, after taking his monastic vows, Paisy moved from his native Poltava to Mount Athos, where he established a hermitage and immersed himself in the Eastern Christian practice of Hesychasm ('inner stillness'). In 1764, after two and a half decades of attempting to reach a state of perpetual prayer and reconnect with the traditions of the early Church Fathers, he was invited to revive spiritual life in Moldavia. By the time of his death in 1794, the monastery he founded at Neamt had around 700 monks. As well as introducing eldership to the Slavonic world, Paisy Velichkovsky left an important legacy of published writings on prayer which were very influential on the monks who revived Optina Pustyn in the dark days of the early nineteenth century. The mystical texts he compiled for his Slavonic *Philokalia* ('love of the beautiful'), in particular, cemented the vital link he had forged with the Hesychast traditions of Mount Athos and the early Christians who had lived in the desert. The nineteenth-century Russian elders who followed Velichkovsky's example were monks who emulated the Church Fathers by living in a remote hermitage, which was the nearest equivalent in Russia to retreating to the desert, and it is no coincidence that the word *pustyn'* (hermitage) is related to the word *pustynya*, which means desert as well as wilderness. To ensure a stricter and more solitary existence than that of regular monks, however, the elders also lived in a *skete* – a kind of monastery within a monastery. At the time of Tolstoy's visit, the elder in charge of Optina Pustyn was Ambrosy, who was by then sixty-five, and one of the most famous men in Russia. It was Ambrosy upon whom Dostoyevsky would model his character of Zosima in *The Brothers Karamazov* following three meetings with him during his pilgrimage to Optina Pustyn in 1878.

Tolstoy was not best pleased that his cover was blown when he arrived at the monastery in May 1877, but it did mean that he was granted an audience with Ambrosy straight away. So many people came to see the elder that the vast majority would have to wait days or even weeks before being granted access (women were not allowed into the hermitage itself, but thronged round a specially built extension to Ambrosy's cell).[12] The spiritual assistance people requested was extremely varied. Mothers sought his advice on how to bring up their children, merchants wanted to know whether to make a particular purchase or not, uncles consulted him about whom their nieces should marry, while innumerable others sought prayers which might effect a cure for a grave illness, or merely some comfort in their afflictions.[13] Tolstoy came to Elder Ambrosy with no particular agenda, other than a hope that he might find answers to the spiritual questions which tormented him. After heeding Ambrosy's suggestion that he go to confession and take communion, Tolstoy stood through the four hours of the monastery's vespers service. He also spent time during his pilgrimage talking to the monastery's archimandrite (a Guards officer in his previous life), but his heart was most deeply touched most by the ingenuous humility of Father Pimen, a former decorator whose

5. Father Ambrosy, the Elder at Optina Pustyn Monastery, whom Tolstoy visited for the first time in 1877

kind and down-to-earth ways had made him very popular with female supplicants. At one point in Tolstoy's conversation with the archimandrite, Pimen quietly nodded off on his chair,[14] but he was not as sleepy as he seemed. He later commented that Tolstoy had said a lot of eloquent but empty things, and should think about his soul. Ambrosy, meanwhile, later recounted to a friend of Strakhov, after a long sigh, that he had found Tolstoy challenging. In 1907 this friend published what the Elder had told him about Tolstoy:

> His heart seeks God, but there is muddle and a lack of belief in his thoughts. He suffers from a great deal of pride, spiritual pride. He will cause a lot of harm with his arbitrary and empty interpretation of the Gospels, which in his opinion no one has understood before him, but everything is God's will.[15]

This same acquaintance told Strakhov privately at the time, however, that the Holy Fathers had thought Tolstoy had a 'wonderful soul', and were particularly pleased that he did not suffer from intellectual pride, unlike Gogol, who had visited the monastery in 1850. Wherever the truth lies, Tolstoy was buoyed by his first pilgrimage to Optina Pustyn – he was genuinely impressed by the wisdom of the monastery's elders, and by Father Ambrosy's spiritual powers in particular.[16] Meanwhile, his own faith was strengthened. When he returned to Yasnaya Polyana at the end of July, he started having long conversations with the local priest and getting up at dawn to go to early matins, saddling his horse himself so as not to wake his servant.[17]

Russia had finally declared war on Turkey in April 1877, just as Tolstoy was finishing *Anna Karenina*. In the middle of August, accompanied by Sonya and various other members of their family, Tolstoy went to visit the Turkish prisoners of war who were being held at an old sugar factory on the road to Tula. He had hoped to start a new historical novel that summer, but news from the front kept preventing him from being able to concentrate, regardless of whether he was in a good or a bad mood, he wrote to Strakhov.[18] Tolstoy naturally could not help remembering being stationed himself on the Danube, before being transferred to the disastrous Sebastopol campaign during the Crimean War, and for a while he pondered writing Alexander II a letter about the state of Russia, and the reasons for the army's failures in the most recent hostilities with Turkey. But it was religion that was uppermost in his mind, and so it was faith that he wanted to talk about to the Turkish prisoners of war, not politics. He wanted to know whether they each had their own copy of the Koran, and who their mullah was.[19] Tolstoy's religious quest took him well beyond Russia's borders. The books which he asked Strakhov to send him later in the year included the Protestant theologian David Friedrich Strauss's *Old and New Faith*, a work which had caused almost as much scandal in Germany in 1872 as his 'historical' *Life of Jesus*, in which he had denied Christ's divinity some thirty years earlier. Tolstoy also asked Strakhov to procure for him Ernest Renan's *Life of Jesus*, an equally notorious volume with the same title which had provoked a storm of controversy in the Catholic world, and which had been banned in Russia ever since its first publication in France in 1863. Other authors who interested Tolstoy at this time were the orientalists Eugène Burnouf, who had published a history of Indian Buddhism in 1844, and his student Max Müller, later regarded as the father of *Religionswissenschaft*. Müller had become Oxford's first Professor of Comparative Theology in 1868, and wrote extensively on Indian philosophy and Vedic religion.[20]

Strakhov continued to be a sounding-board for Tolstoy's ideas, but he was not thirsting for faith in the same way, and so did not accompany his friend on the next leg of his spiritual journey. As Elder Ambrosy had noted during their visit to Optina Pustyn, Strakhov's lack of belief was deeply entrenched; faith for him was 'merely poetry', despite an attraction to the monastic way of life which inspired him to travel to Mount Athos in 1881.[21] At Yasnaya Polyana, Tolstoy's newfound religious fervour was greeted with slight bemusement, particularly by Sonya, for whom Orthodox belief had always been an unobtrusive but integral part of her life. She was glad her husband had 'calmed down' after the violent mood swings of the previous years (particularly the periods of deep depression), and she could only rejoice that his character seemed to be changing for the better. In her diary, she was optimistic that Tolstoy had somehow reached the end of his spiritual journey:

> Although he has always been modest and undemanding in all his habits, he is now becoming even more modest, meek and patient. And this eternal struggle that he began in his youth, aimed at achieving moral perfection, is being crowned with complete success.[22]

She must have winced later at her naïvety. Tolstoy's religious strivings certainly brought some peace and harmony to Yasnaya Polyana, but he had begun to walk alone, for none of his family felt inclined to take Christianity as seriously as he did.

Tolstoy's greatest inspiration at this time came from an unlikely source. Vasily Alexeyev, a thin, rather frail young man with a wispy ginger beard and candid blue eyes, was the latest tutor engaged to teach his eldest children, and he would have a surprisingly powerful influence on Tolstoy's evolving religious philosophy during the next few years.[23] In many ways, he was a Tolstoyan *avant le lettre*. He arrived at Yasnaya Polyana in October 1877 after being recommended by the Tolstoys' midwife Maria Abramovich (Sonya was at this point two months off giving birth to Andrey, her ninth child), and he was to stay with the Tolstoys for four years.[24] Given his background in radical politics, the surprising thing is not that Sonya eventually asked him to leave, but that he stayed as long as he did.[25] Alexeyev was openly socialist and atheist, and yet he was a model of Christian ethics in his personal conduct. He provided Tolstoy with much-needed moral support at this critical time in his life, and Tolstoy defended him to the hilt whenever his pious friend Sergey Urusov tried to attack Alexeyev as a 'nihilist' and 'the son of the devil'. 'I know few people other than him who are not only good, but kind and religious in feeling,' Tolstoy assured Urusov, another time stressing his meekness, and devotion to serving others.[26]

Vasily Alexeyev was the son of a retired officer and minor landowner who had married one of his serfs, whom he was known to beat. He grew up in the far western province of Pskov, hundreds of miles from Moscow.[27] One of eight brothers and sisters, Alexeyev had excelled academically at an early age and won a place to study mathematics at St Petersburg University, where he became increasingly involved in left-wing politics. This was at the height of the Populist movement in the early 1870s and Alexeyev had got to know the revolutionary Nikolay Chaikovsky, leader of a circle involved in spreading socialist propaganda amongst the peasantry. It was Chaikovsky who introduced Alexeyev to Alexander Malikov, who was more of a religious idealist than a revolutionary and who came from a peasant background. Malikov had already spent time in prison and in exile because of his political beliefs, and now set his hopes on a mystical doctrine he had founded called Godmanhood, which combined socialist theory with Christian ethics. Seduced by his passionate oratory, Alexeyev became one of Malikov's followers, but the Russian government inevitably viewed attempts to disseminate the teaching of Godmanhood as revolutionary propaganda and promptly arrested him. Although Alexeyev was soon released due to the lack of incriminating evidence, his father disowned him.

Malikov and Alexeyev realised it was going to be impossible to put their ideas into practice in Russia, where they were seen as subversive. Along with about a dozen others, they decided to emigrate to America in 1875, hoping to fulfil their dreams of living a morally pure life in the Land of the Free. Chaikovsky was already there, having fled Russia to avoid arrest, and so was the positivist Vladimir Geins, another disillusioned revolutionary who had rechristened himself William Frey (the closest possible transliteration in Cyrillic of the English word 'free'). The group decided to settle in the Midwest. The southern part of Kansas had been acquired from the Native Americans only five years earlier, and land was extremely cheap. By pooling their resources, the group were able to buy 160 acres of land in Cedarville, near Wichita, for the total sum of twenty-five dollars. Crowding into the two rooms of the small farmhouse on their holding, the young Russian pioneers attempted to set up a utopian agricultural commune.[28] Although they augmented the two horses and a cow already on the land with more livestock, and sowed corn and wheat, there were immediate problems. No one knew how to milk a cow, for example. The community started out with noble ascetic ideals, and was happy to give up alcohol, meat, coffee, tea and sugar, but the fanatical and dogmatic Frey also banned bread, arguing that only food in its 'natural' state was acceptable. Medicines were also banned by him. But what finally undid the commune were the weekly meetings of 'mutual criticism' and 'public confession' which only exacerbated the numerous personal tensions that arose. The experiment was a disaster and the commune barely survived two years.

In late May 1877 Alexeyev returned to Russia, now with Malikov's peasant wife Elizaveta and her two children in tow, one of whom was his. They had been dreadfully homesick in the American plains, and crossed the border on Trinity Sunday (Troitsa) to see young people dancing in the fields through the train window. In pre-revolutionary times, Russians traditionally celebrated Troitsa as the day on which the Holy Spirit descended on all of nature, not just the apostles. 'Green Yuletide', as it was also called in reference to the pagan traditions which accompanied all the major Christian holy days, was a particularly fertile and joyous time, when everything was in full bloom. It was also a date in the calendar particularly associated with youth, so it was a poignant day for Alexeyev to return to Russia – at twenty-nine he was four years younger than his future employer Countess Tolstoy. Trinity Sunday was celebrated at Yasnaya Polyana like everywhere else[29] – the Tolstoy children would go to church in their Sunday best bearing armfuls of flowers, then take part in the dancing. Sonya would plant flowers and the local village girls would ask the cuckoos how many years awaited them before they married, calculating their answer from the number of calls they heard.[30] Homes and village streets would be decorated with greenery, with bunches of carnations placed behind icons, and a profusion of periwinkles, peonies, cornflowers, violets and lilies placed on window-ledges. When Tolstoy went to worship that morning in May 1877 he would have encountered birch saplings and freshly cut grass and fragrant thyme strewn on the floor of the church. Along with other parishioners he would also have held a birch twig or flowers during the service as symbols of the Holy Spirit coming down to bring renewal.[31] As well as the ritual songs and dances that came after church on Trinity Sunday in Russia, village girls at Yasnaya Polyana would weave garlands which they would throw on to ponds and lakes, in the hope they would float – a sign of long life.

Given his moral convictions and his past experiences, Alexeyev was understandably reluctant at first to become tutor to the Tolstoy children. Despite being desperately poor and in need of a job, he recoiled at the idea of coming to live in the house of a count, where meals were served by white-gloved servants. When Tolstoy heard this, however, he took an immediate interest in Alexeyev, and persuaded him to come just for a visit. Alexeyev's doubts vanished as soon as they set off for a walk, during which he was closely questioned about his outlook on life. Tolstoy was a good listener, and Alexeyev was soon unbuttoning himself completely. He felt so uninhibited he even went into propaganda mode and showed Tolstoy the calloused hands he had acquired from all the manual labour he had done in America, imagining he was talking to an upper-class writer who had never picked up a tool. To his surprise, Tolstoy declared they were worth far more than the huge salaries earned by civil servants, and opened up to Alexeyev about his own ideals, sharing with him his despair at not being able to find answers to the questions that tormented him. He even showed Alexeyev the bough in the garden he had considered hanging himself from to escape from his afflictions. Tolstoy carried on talking to Alexeyev in his study for the rest of that day, and by evening Alexeyev had agreed to take the job, accepting Tolstoy's suggestion that he rent the cottage just outside the Yasnaya Polyana gates for his family. Soon he was coming to the house every morning at eight to have coffee with the children before starting lessons in Russian and mathematics with Sergey, Tanya and Ilya. Within a year he felt so at home in the Tolstoy household that he moved with his family into the guest wing which Sonya's sister stayed in during the summer months. The fact that he and Elizaveta were not actually married (which Sonya would not have approved of) was somehow glossed over.

Alexeyev was a gifted teacher and popular, particularly with fourteen-year-old Sergey, who became very attached to him. Sergey was the most musical of the Tolstoy children, and Alexeyev records in his memoirs his pupil playing Chopin's D Flat Major Prelude especially for him. Eleven-year-old Ilya, by contrast, only seemed interested in dogs and hunting, and took great delight in taking his violin outside and playing mournful sounds on it, attracting all the dogs in the vicinity to gather round and start howling in unison.[32]

There was, however, one time that Ilya also gave a bravura performance of some Chopin during Alexeyev's time as tutor. Tolstoy loved Chopin, and hearing one of his opuses played at an insane tempo with a torrent of mistakes prompted him to come out of his study and put his head round the door to see what was going on. Tolstoy realised that Ilya was playing to an audience. Ilya's *fortissimo* dynamics, with his foot hard down on the pedal, were for the benefit of Prokhor, the family carpenter, who was in the drawing room putting in secondary-glazing panes for the winter. The phrase 'for Prokhor' entered Tolstoy family lore, and was ever afterwards affectionately trotted out whenever any member of the family seemed to be showing off.[33]

Tolstoy's fondness for Vasily Alexeyev stemmed from the fact that he shared with him the same basic philanthropic impulse to improve the life of the peasantry. This very Russian priority was well summarised by the English positivist Edward Spencer Beesly when characterising Alexeyev's former partner William Frey after his death in 1888:

> He was filled with that extraordinary enthusiasm which prompts so many Russians of the well-born and wealthy class to strip themselves of all advantages and cast in their lot with the poorest, humblest and most miserable. I do not know where we are to find anything like it, except in the spirit which so often led persons of rank in the Middle Ages to fly from the world and embrace the privations and humility of monastic life. But among them the motive was unsocial – a selfish desire to save their own souls. These Russians are animated by a burning desire for social improvement. To some of them inequality is in itself shocking – the root and sum of all social evil. They plunge into the humblest life to escape in their own persons from this taint. They cannot be happy till they have freed themselves from it. Others perhaps embrace a life of poverty and manual labour for a somewhat different reason. They desire to spread their political and social aspirations among the mass of their poorer countrymen. They find that they are impeded in doing this by the barriers of rank and wealth. Such is their propagandist ardour, such their faith in their principles, that wealth, comfort, and material advantages of every kind seem to them cheap, if by sacrificing them they can gain the opportunity they desire of approaching and getting the ear of the people. Whatever we may think of the principles and reasoning which lead to this conduct, it is impossible not to admire the sincerity and enthusiasm of those who practise it. They

have subdued some of the strongest and most selfish of human impulses, whether they are turning the victory to the best account or not.[34]

Frey settled in England after the American escapade, but he would find his way to Yasnaya Polyana during the one brief trip he made to Russia before his untimely death, and make a deep impression on Tolstoy.

Alexeyev was convinced Tolstoy would dismiss him once he knew he was a socialist, but his employer was unperturbed.[35] Christianity was really the only sticking point in their long and frank conversations. Tolstoy was still a fully paid-up member of the Orthodox Church in 1878, and Alexeyev could not understand this. In an oft-quoted passage in his memoirs, he describes Tolstoy pointing one winter morning to the frosty patterns made on the window pane by the sun, which he compared to popular religious belief. The people see the patterns, he explained, whereas he wanted to look beyond them towards the source of the light. But Tolstoy's faith was intimately linked to popular religious belief, and Alexeyev observed that he went to church not simply to perform the rites alongside peasants, but to study exactly what it was the peasants believed in, because their faith was so strong. Tolstoy also wanted to learn how to make himself more comprehensible in the exposition of his religious beliefs, and over time he grew impatient with the impenetrable and high-flown Church Slavonic of the liturgy. If he himself could barely understand it, what hope was there that the peasants could glean its message? Tolstoy relayed to Alexeyev how in church he would hear the men discussing farming matters, and the women whispering the latest gossip to each other at the most solemn moments of the service, as if it had nothing to do with them. He would stand there hearing the constant thud of fingers on sheepskin as peasants crossed themselves unthinkingly beside him while the lofty language of the liturgy went far above the heads. It began to bother Tolstoy that the Church made so little effort to meet the spiritual needs of the peasants and he started to understand why so many of them were drawn to sectarian religions, which did at least attempt to explain Christ's teaching in plain Russian.

Tolstoy would get up most days around eight in the morning, and his children would usually run out to greet him as he headed downstairs to get dressed. Sometimes he would do a few turns on the parallel bars in the hall before returning upstairs for coffee in the small drawing room, next to the main family dining room. This is when Tolstoy and Alexeyev usually got into conversation, and Sonya was now sometimes alarmed by what she overheard her husband talking about while she was dressing. Having acquired the habit of staying up until the small hours to copy out manuscripts, Sonya tended to get up later, and since their bedroom was next to the drawing room, she could not help overhearing the constant conversations about religion and ethics. She was longing to hear Tolstoy talk about literature again. Writing on religion was never going to be a good earner, even for a writer of Tolstoy's fame. Sonya was unstinting in her praise of Alexeyev as a teacher in her auto-biography, and she was happy to declare that Tanya never learned as much from anyone else as she had from him. She recollected Alexeyev's love of hard work, and his warm-hearted, simple nature,[36] but in time she would see him as a threat to the family's emotional and financial stability.

At around eleven o'clock every morning Tolstoy would head back down-stairs with a cup of tea to go and work in his study, sometimes picking up the first bit of paper which came to hand even if it was an old envelope, in his desire to set down as quickly as possible whatever thought he had in his mind. He would not emerge again until four, which was his time to go riding or for a walk, sometimes breaking off a stalk of sweet-pea by the house to sniff at as he strode along in the summer months, as he loved the scent. At some point he began to take his daily constitutionals with Alexeyev, who often had diffi-culty keeping up with him. But Tolstoy needed Alexeyev by his side, as he one day confessed to his young friend that he was wildly attracted to a tall young woman called Domna who worked in the servants' kitchen. Her husband had been recruited into the army, and Tolstoy had been following her around and softly whistling to her to catch her attention. Finally he had struck up a conversation with her, and had arranged a rendezvous on a shady path under some nut trees in a distant part of the garden. Tolstoy confessed to Alexeyev that he had set off from the house only to be called back by Ilya, shouting from the window to remind him about his Greek lesson. After that bracing reality check, Tolstoy ensured that Alexeyev always accompanied him on his walks, and took steps for Domna to be 'removed' from view.[37] He found that praying was not much help when it came to battling his feelings of lust, but he certainly repented. The incident was to find reflection in a story he wrote in 1889 called 'The Devil', which also drew on his experiences with his peasant 'wife' Aksinya. For obvious reasons, Tolstoy stuffed the manuscript down the back of an armchair to keep it hidden from Sonya, and it was not published until the year after he died.

A new French tutor arrived at Yasnaya Polyana a few months after Alexeyev in January 1878. Hiding behind the false identity of 'Monsieur Nief' was the militant young anarchist Vicomte Jules Montels, who had served as colonel of the 12th Federated Legion in the Paris Commune in 1871. After its two-month reign of power came to an end, Montels had fled to Geneva, where he became an active member of the French exile group of the International Workingmen's Association (the First International), its 'propaganda and socialist-revolutionary action section' to be precise. In 1877, after six years of living with a death-sentence on his head, he found himself in Moscow getting on a train to Tula, disguised as 'Monsieur Nief'. He had been recommended to the Tolstoys by the wife of the Russian priest in Geneva. Sonya had some justification for later exclaiming to her husband, 'You found me two nihilists!' Yasnaya Polyana was beginning to turn into a hotbed of radical left-wing politics.

The Tolstoys learned the full story about their enigmatic French tutor only after he had left their employ in late 1879. In 1880 the Communards were amnestied and the dapper, mustachioed Vicomte Montels returned to France, taking with him the Tolstoys' French-Swiss governess Lucie Gachet. They later married and then moved to Tunisia, where Montels became editor of the *Tunis Journal*. Mademoiselle Gachet had arrived as a French teacher for Tanya and Masha in September 1876,[38] at around the same time as the latest English governess Annie Phillips, and had first been hotly pursued by the family's Russian tutor Vladimir Rozhdestvensky. The Tolstoys had been amongst the first Russians to acquire an English croquet set when they became available in Moscow in the 1870s, and they became avid players on warm summer evenings when the air was cooler. Rozhdestvensky took a particular delight in hitting Lucie Gachet's ball in the direction of the pond, telling her he was sending it to the frogs. Like Jules Rey, he had a drink problem, and was soon dismissed, no doubt to Mlle Gachet's relief. Sergey Tolstoy extended sympathy towards the family's young male tutors when he was writing his memoirs much later. They were always on display, as he put it, occupying a difficult position somewhere between servants and employers, and they were usually rather bored. As a consequence, when they were not at loggerheads with each other they tended to develop infatuations with the family's pretty young governesses.

Having sorted out the family's teachers at the beginning of 1878, Tolstoy was keen to get back to fiction, and his religious views did not yet interfere with those plans. Some twenty years after writing *War and Peace*, he was keen to write another historical novel, and he was still fixated on the Decembrist Uprising. Back in the early 1860s Tolstoy had found himself going back in time from the 1825 uprising to the 1812 war with Napoleon, and finally to the events of 1805 before feeling he was at the right place to begin. But he had got no further than the immediate aftermath of 1812 in *War and Peace*, so he had never followed Pierre Bezukhov's transformation into a Decembrist, or written about the uprising. Now, in the late 1870s, he began to be drawn to the events surrounding Nicholas I's accession, and to the Russo-Turkish War of 1829. At the same time he was also interested in writing a novel about Russian peasant settlers colonising new lands, such as the territories east of the Volga near Samara and Orenburg with which he was personally familiar. He was excited by the prospect of somehow combining both these topics, and 1878 was a year of frenetic activity in which he gathered a mass of historical material and oral testimony in order first to bring the period alive for himself. In February 1878 Tolstoy went to Moscow on a foraging expedition, and held the first of many meetings with various Decembrists and their descendants. He also started marshalling his friends in libraries and archives to send him materials, which meant renewing his contact with Pyotr Bartenev, the editor of the journal *Russian Archive*, and depending, as usual, on Strakhov. He also began bombarding relatives with contacts in high places (such as Alexandrine and Sonya's uncle Alexander Bers) with requests for help with primary sources. Tolstoy had further meetings with Decembrists in Moscow in March before travelling on St Petersburg to continue his research, and also tie up a new property deal which enabled him to enlarge his Samara estate by over 10,000 acres.

Tolstoy had not been in the capital for seventeen years, and he did not like it any more in 1878 than in 1861. Alexandrine had offered Tolstoy accommodation with her brother on Mokhovaya Street, but he decided to stay with his old friend and mother-in-law Lyubov Bers in her apartment on Ertelev Lane, which was also right in the heart of the city. He arrived on 6 March and was back home within the week, disappointing many acquaintances who had hoped to see him (such as the painter Kramskoy), but he packed a lot into his four days in St Petersburg. He made a chilling visit to the St Peter and Paul Fortress, where the governor showed him the irons the Decembrists had been clamped in, but the cells where they had actually been held in 1825 were off-limits to all visitors except the Tsar and the chief of police. When he later drove past the equestrian statue of Nicholas I which had been erected in St Isaac's Square, Tolstoy realised that his revulsion for the man who in his opinion had destroyed the best part of the Russian aristocracy had increased.[39] A much more enjoyable visit was to the Imperial Public Library, where Tolstoy went to see Nikolay Strakhov and to meet the indomitable critic Vladimir Stasov, who had himself been imprisoned in the St Peter and Paul Fortress in 1849 for his involvement with the Petrashevsky Circle. Tolstoy was not so interested in Stasov the tireless and sometimes also tiresome propagandist of Russian national art as in Stasov the librarian, who had first been appointed specifically to research the reign of Nicholas I. For Tolstoy he was one more useful contact who could help him track down valuable historical sources.

Another notable event during Tolstoy's visit to St Petersburg was his attendance at one of the public lectures on the topic of 'divine humanity' given by a young religious philosopher with flowing locks called Vladimir Solovyov (son of the famous historian Sergey Mikhailovich). It was a notable event, not because Tolstoy found the lecture interesting (he dismissed it as 'childish nonsense'[40]), but because it was the only occasion on which he and Dostoyevsky were in spitting distance of each other. Strakhov was a friend of both the great writers, but he honoured Tolstoy's request not to introduce him to anyone, and so the two passed like ships in the night, to their subsequent mutual regret. Much later, Tolstoy described in letters the horrible experience of having to sit in a stuffy hall which was packed so full that there were even high-society ladies in evening dress perched on window ledges. As someone who went out of his way to avoid being part of the crowd, and who disdained having anything to do with polite society or fashion, his blood must have boiled at having to wait until the emaciated figure of the twenty-four-year-old philosopher decided to make a grand theatrical entrance in his billowing white silk cravat. Tolstoy certainly did not have the patience to sit and listen to some boy 'with a huge head consisting of hair and eyes' spout pretentious pseudo-profundities. After the first string of German quotations and references to cherubim and seraphim, he got up and walked out, leaving Strakhov to carry on listening to the 'ravings of a lunatic'.[41] The rest of Tolstoy's time in St Petersburg was taken up with concluding his property deal and meeting historians, including Mikhail Semevsky, editor of the important journal *Russian Antiquity*, who promised to send him unpublished Decembrist memoirs from its extensive archives.[42] Otherwise Tolstoy spent time with family. Apart from Sonya's younger brothers Pyotr, Stepan and Vyacheslav, the one person Tolstoy wanted to see during his stay in Petersburg was Alexandrine, whom he had not seen since 1860. They had several long and (for her) reassuring conversations about religion, and Alexandrine noted in her diary how happy she was to see him after so many years. Indeed, she had initially feared she might expire under the weight of all the things she wanted to share with him. Tolstoy seemed nicer to her than ever before, and on the day he left Petersburg, she registered in her diary their discussions about religion:

> After many years of seeking the truth, he has finally reached the jetty. He has constructed this jetty of course in his own way, but the One leading him is nevertheless the same One and Only Comforter. Lev is now at the beginning of a new work, and I am sure this confession of his faith, or rather the confession of his new faith will now be reflected in it.[43]

One positive outcome of Tolstoy's new Christian outlook was his desire to save his soul, as he put it, which meant being at peace with the world. There was, of course, one conspicuous person he needed to make his peace with, and that was Turgenev.

Tolstoy had gone to Petersburg during Great Lent, the traditional time for penitence, and he wrote to Turgenev on the penultimate day of the forty-day fast. Filling two pages with his imperious, aristocratic handwriting, he apologised to his old friend and proposed that they bury their differences. It is tempting to think that Tolstoy's recent trip to St Petersburg had played a part in prompting this peace-offering. The last time he had been in the capital was 1861, and his return to the city must have brought back a flood of memories – of first meeting and becoming friends with Turgenev there in 1855, of arguing with him over the way he had treated his sister during his visit to Petersburg in 1859,[44] and of no doubt feeling still angry with him when he returned the following year with Masha and her children Varya, Liza and Nikolay, when they had walked together through the city to visit St Isaac's Cathedral and the Bronze Horseman. It is likely Turgenev came into

Tolstoy's mind again on this visit seventeen years later when he walked across St Isaac's Square to visit Alexandrine in her apartment in the Mariinsky Palace. Now that he was nearly fifty years old, and his outlook and ambitions quite different, perhaps he suddenly realised the absurdity of his feud with Turgenev. It was with surprise and delight that Turgenev received Tolstoy's letter at home in France. Responding at once with a page and a half of his own neat, diffident handwriting, he enthusiastically agreed that they should renew their friendship, and promised to visit during his trip to Russia later that summer.[45]

During Holy Week in 1878, shortly after writing his letter to Turgenev, Tolstoy prepared to take communion. He had been reading the Gospels and Renan's *Life of Jesus*, and he decided to start keeping a regular diary again for the first time in thirteen years. After Easter he made another trip to Moscow for further meetings with Decembrists, and to talk to publishers about the next edition of his writings, but he also wanted to attend the annual Easter debates about faith between the Orthodox faithful and Old Believers which had been taking place in the square in front of the Kremlin Cathedrals since the seventeenth century. Tolstoy had never taken any noticeable interest in sectarians before, but now he became increasingly drawn to them. In March he had asked Stasov to send him the autobiography of the Archpriest Avvakum and other Old Believer 'raw materials',[46] and began educating himself about this powerful underground current of Russian society. During his six-week koumiss cure in Samara later that summer, Tolstoy pursued his new interest further: he went to talk to the 'Molokans' – sectarians who lived amongst the Bashkirs and Russian peasant colonists. They were on the fringes of society and on the fringes of the empire for a good reason.

Religious dissent had a long and eventful history in Russia which the government had done its best to suppress over the centuries. Orthodoxy was the official religion, and the state made vigorous efforts to try to ensure the population conformed to it, seeing the Church as a useful tool in promoting and maintaining civil obedience in the face of the potentially dangerous political threat of dissent. The ecclesiastical authorities had little choice but to acquiesce with state policy, since they was actually subordinate to it. In 1721 Peter the Great had abolished the once-powerful Moscow Patriarchate and replaced it with the Holy Synod, a secular institution headed by a lay person, the better to consolidate the power of the autocracy. Yet this fatal undermining of the Church's moral authority, combined with an influx of Protestantism from German settlers, had only led to sectarian religions becoming more popular. The government systematically understated their numbers, but by the nineteenth century there were millions of Russians who had turned away from Orthodoxy, and who were at best discriminated against, or actively persecuted. It has been estimated that as many as a quarter of the Russian Empire's population were sectarians by the time of the 1917 Revolution.[47]

The largest group of religious dissenters in Russia were the Old Believers, a group who had refused to go along with Patriarch Nikon's reforms to the rite in the 1660s and so caused a schism in the Church which had far-reaching repercussions. In part because Constantinople (and with it the entire Byzantine Empire) had fallen into the 'heresy' of Islam after being conquered by the Ottomans in the fifteenth century, thousands of zealous Orthodox believers in old Rus insisted on clinging to the rituals and wordings to which they had become accustomed, regardless of the fact that they had gradually diverged from Greek practice over the centuries. Far from this being a Reformation in the Russian Orthodox Church, it amounted to the opposite, as large numbers actively resisted change – perhaps as many as half the total population at that time.[48] Becoming known as *staroobryadtsy* ('adherents of the old rite') or *raskolniki* ('schismatics'), the Old Believers caused the first serious weakening of the Russian Orthodox Church, and they were dealt with ruthlessly, with many choosing the path of mass self-immolation rather than suffer exile to Siberia or capitulation. One of their leaders was the Archpriest Avvakum, who was eventually burned at the stake in 1682, leaving behind the remarkable autobiography which Tolstoy asked Strakhov to send him in 1878. The fact that this document (the first masterpiece of Russian literature written in the living vernacular) was officially suppressed until 1861 speaks volumes about the authorities' identification of religious dissent with popular rebellion. The repressive measures were particularly harsh during the reign of Nicholas I, and it was only after his death, as part of the liberalisation introduced by Alexander II, that it first became possible to write about the Schism (a change in policy which Musorgsky took full advantage of with the composition of his second opera *Khovanshchina*, which ends with old Believers committing suicide).

As the religious and political thinker Nikolay Berdyaev remarked in 1916, sectarianism was in fact an 'integral part of the spiritual life of the Russian people'.[49] Alongside the vast numbers of Old Believers were many other groups whose sectarian origins in some cases actually pre-dated the Schism. Many were offshoots of the mystical *Khristovery* ('Believers in Christ') or *Khlysty*, as they became known, whose peasant founder was believed to be the Lord of Sabaoth himself.[50] These included the *Skoptsy* ('self-castrators'), who appeared in the eighteenth century, and the *Skakuny* ('jumpers') who appeared in the nineteenth century. There were also radical schismatics who sought to break all ties with society: the *Stranniki* ('wanderers'), *Pustynniki* ('hermits') and *Beguny* ('runners'). And then there were a number of 'rationalist' and quasi-Protestant sects who were to hold a particular interest for Tolstoy. One group he was later to become deeply involved with were the *Dukhobory*, a pejorative label which the 'spirit-wrestlers' turned to their own advantage by styling themselves as *Dukhobortsy* ('wrestlers in the name of the Holy Spirit'). Tolstoy also had deep respect for the *Molokany* ('milk-drinkers'), or 'spiritual Christians' as they called themselves, a large number of whom lived out in the steppe beyond Samara.

Old Believers and sectarians were granted limited privileges in a decree of 1863, but these were not turned into full civil rights until 1905, when all religious dissenters were finally allowed to practise their faith without fear of persecution. By and large, the adherents of Russian sects came from peasant backgrounds and lived in thinly populated areas on the edges of the empire, either because they had been deported by the government to keep them from contaminating the Orthodox population, or because they had fled to avoid persecution. There was one important exception, and that was the upper-class Protestant evangelists in St Petersburg and Moscow whom Tolstoy satirises towards the end of *Anna Karenina*. Tolstoy was not the only Russian to want a Church which communicated its message in an intelligible language. A century and a half of the Orthodox Church being part of Russian official-dom had led to apathy and disillusionment amongst the educated classes and when Granville Waldegrave, 3rd Baron Radstock, first travelled as a missionary from London to St Petersburg in 1874, he was greeted with open arms by Russian aristocrats, who welcomed his message of personal salvation through independent Bible study. The New Testament had first been translated from Church Slavonic into modern Russian in 1823, but then suppressed by the Orthodox Church for political reasons. It first became widely available in

1876, and then thousands of copies started to be disseminated as a result of the missionary activities of Baptists and figures such as Lord Radstock. The first complete Bible in Russian followed in 1882.

When Radstock was inevitably banned from Russia in 1878, the 'Radsto-kisty' became 'Pashkovtsy'. Colonel Vasily Pashkov took over Radstock's missionary activities until he too was sent into exile abroad in 1884. By that time his Society for the Encouragement of Spiritual and Ethical Reading had already distributed millions of pamphlets amongst the peasants, and caused a mass exodus from the Orthodox Church.[51] The religious revival sparked by the conservative and upper-class 'Pashkovites' arose partly to counter the rising tide of atheism embraced by the young generation of Russian nihilists who preached the religion of socialism. One tangible result was the capacity attendance at lectures like the one given by Vladimir Solovyov which Tolstoy had gone to.[52] Tolstoy was keenly interested in knowing more about Radstock. Indeed, he had met one of his followers and found him very persuasive, but had never met the baron himself. Alexandrine, however, knew him well, and at Tolstoy's request provided him with full details about Radstock's activities by letter in March 1876. It all went into *Anna Karenina*. In May 1877 Alexandrine wrote from Tsarskoye Selo to tell Tolstoy that she had spent the previous evening with the Empress, and that the closing chapters of Part Seven of *Anna Karenina* had been read aloud to the assembled company. She reported that everyone had laughed heartily at his merciless caricature of Radstock's followers.[53]

Tolstoy had little time for aristocratic religious dissenters who became Christian evangelists without changing their privileged (and to his mind corrupt) lifestyles, but peasant sectarians were something else entirely. He must have been aware of the Molokans out in Samara ever since he had first spent time in the steppe, but it was only now that he wanted to meet them and talk to them about their beliefs. Conversations about religion with the Molokans were the highlight of Tolstoy's stay in Samara in the summer of 1878. The Molokans were apparently so-called because of their refusal to cease the consumption of milk products during the 200 fasting days in the Orthodox calendar, but others argued that they took their name from a river in southern Russia. Like many of the 'rational' sects in Russia, the Molokans distinguished themselves from the general peasant population by eschewing alcohol and leading modest, industrious lives.[54] They dispensed not only with all rituals (from holding services to crossing themselves), but also with clergy, sacred buildings and artefacts such as icons, engaging instead in independent Bible study.

The Times' correspondent Donald Mackenzie Wallace, who visited the same area of the steppe beyond Samara where Tolstoy had his estate in the early 1870s, was greatly intrigued by the Molokans, but ascertaining the exact nature of their beliefs through direct questioning proved to be frustratingly difficult. It was only through a lengthy process of innocently comparing the weather and crops in Russia with the weather and crops in Scotland, and then gradually moving on to religion, that he was finally able to make headway during a conversation with one local Molokan peasant. Mackenzie Wallace came to the conclusion that there were strong similarities with the Presbyterian Church:

> When the peasant heard that there is a country where the people interpret the Scriptures for themselves, have no bishops, and consider the veneration of Icons as idolatry, he invariably listened with profound attention and when he learned further that in that wonderful country the parishes annually send deputies to an assembly in which all matters pertaining to the Church are freely and publicly discussed, he almost always gave free expression to his astonishment, and I had to answer a whole volley of questions. 'Where is that country?' 'Is is to the east, or the west?' 'Is it very far away?' 'If our Presbyter could only hear all that!' [55]

When he was out in the steppe, Mackenzie Wallace also enjoyed the hospitality of the Bashkirs in a kibitka, and his description of the way dinner was prepared and consumed may partly explain why the fastidious Frenchman Jules Montels, who had accompanied Tolstoy's sons Ilya and Lev on their trip in 1878, did not terribly enjoy his time on the steppe. It was a long way from the bistros of Paris:

> A sheep was brought near the door of our tent, and there killed, skinned, cut up into pieces, and put into an immense pot, under which a fire had been kindled. The dinner was not less primitive than the method of preparing it ... There were no plates, knives, forks, spoons, or chop-sticks. Guests were expected all to eat out of a common wooden bowl, and to use the instruments with which Nature had provided them ... The fare was copious, but not varied – consisting of boiled mutton, without bread or other substitute, and a little salted horse-flesh thrown in as an *entrée*. [56]

Sonya had planned to stay behind that summer while Sergey took the annual end-of-year school exams (to ensure he was on target for university entrance), but the telegraphist missed out the crucial words 'do not' from Tolstoy's telegram: 'House, water, horses, carriages good; but dung, flies, drought; [do not] advise you come.' She duly arrived with the rest of the family. Strakhov also came out to the steppe for the first time that summer, and he greatly enjoyed the 'oceans of wheat and endless herds of horses and flocks of sheep', but could not help noticing Tolstoy was restless and out of sorts.[57]

On 8 August, two days after everyone arrived back at Yasnaya Polyana, Turgenev arrived for his first visit in nearly twenty years. He had never met Sonya, let alone any of the six children, who now ranged in age from fifteen down to nine months, and it was a joyous reunion. Meeting the tall, white-haired writer with the sad, kind eyes was very exciting for the children, and Sonya made him play chess with Sergey, so her son would have a story to dine out on later (he was soundly beaten).[58] Turgenev's second visit a month later, when he was on his way back to Paris from his estate in Oryol province, was less euphoric. Despite his new Christian-inspired humility, Tolstoy could only deal with Turgenev in small doses. He still felt riled that Turgenev only 'played at life', and realised that they would never be fully reconciled. That summer Tolstoy had built himself a hut in the woods so he could work in peace and quiet; one day Sonya found them both there arguing heatedly with each other. The usually mild-mannered, urbane Turgenev was gesticulating wildly, red in the face. After so much time apart, Turgenev had no real inkling of the changes taking place in his friend's spiritual life, and the biggest shock for him was encountering Tolstoy's new, dismissive attitude to his own published fiction. The Tolstoy he knew, after all, was the peerless writer who effortlessly outclassed his entire generation, and he was bewildered by this uncompromising new stance.[59]

Tolstoy's decision to move his study to another room in the house that autumn was perhaps a symptom of his changing outlook during this time. He was still trying to get his novel about the Decembrists off the ground, but he derived more enjoyment from reading Dickens (*Martin Chuzzlewit* and *Dombey and Son*). In February 1879 he eventually gave up with the Decembrists, just as he had with his Peter the Great novel. He had produced seventeen different versions of an opening chapter, and twelve of them were set in a peasant environment, but his heart was not in it. The problem, he found, was

not so much that the Decembrist movement owed its origins to Russian officers coming into contact with French ideas during their occupation of Paris
after the defeat of Napoleon, but that so many of the Decembrists were in
fact French Catholics who had escaped to Russia after the 1789 Revolution.[60]

One person disappointed never to see the publication of the Decembrist
novel was Monsieur Nief, or rather Jules Montels, himself a revolutionary
who had been forced to flee from France. Although he describes Tolstoy
as a 'model husband, excellent father, relatively rich', it was his memories
of Tolstoy's research for 'The Decembrists' which stood out for him during
the two years he lived at Yasnaya Polyana. This is the subject of the short
memoir he published in an anarchist journal in Paris immediately after Tolstoy's death. Montels must have found it hard not to blow his cover while
he talked to Tolstoy about the Decembrists. He was clearly electrified when
Tolstoy showed him the original letter written by the Decembrist leader
Sergey Muravyov-Apostol to his parents on the eve of his execution in 1826.
The letter, written in French, 'in that fine and expansive handwriting of our
grandfathers' ('de cette bonne et grosse écriture de nos grands pères'), had been
entrusted to Tolstoy by Muravyov-Apostol's elder brother Matvey, whom
Tolstoy met in February 1878 in Moscow. Matvey Muravyov-Apostol spent
thirty years in exile in Siberia before returning to settle in Moscow after the
1856 amnesty.[61] In 1910 Montels felt there must have been a sensational reason
for the disappearance of what would have been an explosive novel showing
how a generation of young Russians acquired ideas of 'Liberté et Justice'. He
wondered whether the *comtesse* (i.e. Sonya) had burned the manuscript, or
whether a jittery government, reeling from three assassination attempts on
Alexander II between 1879 and 1880, had ordered its destruction.[62] The truth
was rather more prosaic.

Tolstoy's interest in the Decembrists palled, but he could not sit still for
long. Poring over Prince Pyotr Dolgorukov's volumes on Russian heraldry
stimulated a creative interest in his own ancestors, so he now turned back to
the eighteenth century, and pondered writing a novel about the fate of one of
his ancestors. There was a story in his family that one of his maternal great-
uncles had been exiled to Siberia for some murky deed, and he was curious
to know more, so he fired off a barrage of letters to friends and relatives.[63]
A distant relative wrote back to tell him that, according to family lore, his
great-uncle Vasily Gorchakov had been sent to Siberia for bringing back to

Russia a grand piano stuffed with banknotes. That was enough to fire Tolstoy's imagination: he drafted four beginnings of a new novel, and one of
them was written in the 'uneducated', simple language he had pledged to use
when he was writing stories for his *ABC*. He reiterated this vow to Sonya in
1878, by saying that anything he wrote in future would be in a language simple
enough for children to understand every word.[64] As it turned out, none of
Tolstoy's contacts could produce any more information about Gorchakov's
case, so that project was stopped in its tracks.

Tolstoy now switched his attention back to the time of Peter the Great
and his successor Anna Ioannovna (who reigned from 1730 to 1740), this time
sketching out a novel which would explore its 'unofficial' history – including that of the Old Believers.[65] Alexandrine had difficulty keeping up with
Tolstoy's plans for his new novel. One moment he was asking for help with
materials about the Decembrists, then he was interested in his ancestor Vasily
Gorchakov, and now in March 1879 he asked her to help him gain access to
secret archives relating to early-eighteenth-century Russian history. At the
same time he asked for her help in securing the release of three Old Believer
bishops who had been sitting in a prison in Suzdal for twenty-two years as
'religious criminals'. One of them was ninety. Tolstoy had found about their
plight from another Old Believer bishop he had been meeting with in Tula.[66]
All that month, in fact, he had been spending time on the highway linking
Moscow and Kiev which ran close to Yasnaya Polyana, and talking to the
crowds of pilgrims making their way to the 'holy places' on foot.

Tolstoy had given up thinking he could ever gain any religious insight
from people who came from his own class, and whose lives seemed to be a
contradiction of their faith. But for the poor and illiterate, be they monks,
peasants or sectarians, religion seemed to be an indispensable part of their
lives, and it was from them that Tolstoy finally discovered the truth about
faith and salvation which he had been seeking. Some of them were Stranniki – wanderers who spent their lives going from monastery to monastery,
carrying all their worldly goods in a bundle on their back. Tolstoy walked a
part of the way with some of the pilgrims he met. One was an old man of
ninety-four, heading to Kiev for the fourth time. Others walked barefoot
or carried heavy chains as penance. They had already walked well over 100
miles from the Trinity St Sergius Monastery outside Moscow, and they had
another 400 to go.

Tolstoy began to feel it was time he too went on another pilgrimage. While researching his latest project he had become very interested in the fate of his ancestors Pyotr Andreyevich Tolstoy and his son Ivan Petrovich who had both died in exile at the prison-monastery on the remote Solovetsky islands in the 1720s. Naturally, Alexandrine received another letter asking if she could help him provide any information about the first Count Tolstoy, who had been one of Peter the Great's most trusted statesmen.[67] Meanwhile, Pyotr Andreyevich's descendant conceived the idea of travelling up to the Arctic waters of the White Sea himself that summer, and in May he wrote to Strakhov to ask if would like to accompany him.[68] Thousands of pilgrims undertook the long journey north during the brief summer months to the fifteenth-century monastery, which was one of the holiest places in Russia, but it turned out that Strakhov did not want to be one of their number.

In the end, Tolstoy went to Kiev, the cradle of Russian civilisation, to visit the famed Caves Monastery which dated back to the early eleventh century. He had high expectations, having been inspired by his conversations with all the wanderers he had talked to, who had told him that the monks in Kiev lived as ascetically as the early Church Fathers.[69] He was to be bitterly disappointed: as far as he could see, the holy relics on show were fakes, and the monk he went to talk to about faith turned him away, saying he was too busy. Tolstoy presumed it was because he had dressed as an ordinary pilgrim, and did not reveal his true identity, which would have commanded greater respect.[70] What he did not take into account, however, was that he was one of the hundreds of thousands of pilgrims who arrived in Kiev every year, and the monastery had difficulty coping. There were some who arrived on foot, but large numbers, including Tolstoy, were able to use the new railway network to travel comfortably by train, and the huge increase in visitors posed a very real threat to the spiritual integrity of sacred institutions which were traditionally used to silence and contemplation.[71] Be that as it may, Tolstoy's pilgrimage to the Caves Monastery in Kiev was a turning point on his religious journey.

In the autumn of 1879 Tolstoy's thoughts returned yet again to his historical novel. He went to Moscow in September to do some more foraging in the archives. All year, the archivist of the Ministry of Justice had been sending him materials relating to Russian criminal cases in early-eighteenth-century Russia. In October he would send further documents which shed light on how the people had related to Peter the Great's reforms, but by this time

Tolstoy had lost interest. It was religious questions which were at the forefront of his mind during that visit to Moscow, and he now urgently wanted some answers. Tolstoy wanted to know, for example, why the Church had prayed for the imperial army to prevail in the recent Russo-Turkish War, when killing people went against one of the most basic tenets of the Christian faith. He wanted to know why the Orthodox Church was intolerant of people who practised other faiths, whether they were Catholics or Protestants, Old Believers or sectarians. And at a time when increasing numbers of revolutionaries were being executed, he wanted to know why the Church in Russia supported capital punishment.[72] In order to try to find some answers to these pressing questions, Tolstoy went straight to the top of the ecclesiastical hierarchy. He had meetings with Moscow's august Metropolitan Makary, and with the Bishop of Mozhaysk, and then travelled out to Sergiev Posad, to visit the most important monastery in Russia. Named after St Sergius of Radonezh, who founded it in the fourteenth century, the Trinity St Sergius Monastery was by the time of Tolstoy's visit a vast and wealthy institution with some 400 monks and roughly half a million annual pilgrims. That year, Tolstoy was one of them.[73]

Father Nikon was deputed to show Tolstoy round the monastery's cathedrals, and also the sacristy, where some of the chains worn by ascetic monks in the past were on display. Tolstoy was not impressed to learn that the tradition had not been maintained by the monastery's monks. After attending a meeting of the Moscow Spiritual Academy, which was based there, one of its eminent faculty innocently asked him when his next novel was coming out. Quoting a verse from the second book of Peter, Tolstoy spat back that he did not want to be like a dog returning to his own vomit. Those present were probably too shocked to be impressed by his close familiarity with the Gospels, but they were certainly left in no doubt as to how he now related to his artistic works. Tolstoy submitted the monastery's archimandrite to the same volley of questions he had posed to the representatives of the Church in Moscow. He was not satisfied by any of the answers he received. The archimandrite was rather shocked to encounter such pride, and produced the verdict: 'I fear it will end badly.'[74]

After returning home to Yasnaya Polyana in early October, Tolstoy made a note in his diary: 'The Church, from the present day all the way back to the third century, is one long series of lies, cruelty and deception.' By its very nature, he went on to observe, religious faith cannot submit to political power.[75] The tide had turned. In December Tolstoy went to talk to the Bishop of Tula about the faith of the common people, about pilgrimage and asceticism, and evidently scared the living daylights out of him by pinning him to the wall with his 'burning questions' and allowing no compromises.[76] The bishop advised the count to talk to Father Alexander, another priest in Tula, and Tolstoy typically acted on his suggestion immediately. It was Father Alexander who recommended that he study Metropolitan Makary's *Dogmatic Theology*. Metropolitan Makary was a high-ranking church figure, but also a prolific scholar renowned for his thirty-volume *History of the Russian Church*. His authoritative *Orthodox Dogmatic Theology* was an award-winning five-volume work which went into many editions. Tolstoy wasted no time in obtaining a copy, and then sat down to study it very carefully.[77] He now had a project: he would put Orthodox theology to the test. He also began to write down the story of his spiritual journey, and embark on his own translation of the Gospels.

While Tolstoy's soul was in ferment, family life went on around him at Yasnaya Polyana. Lessons, birthday parties, weddings, musical evenings, picnics, housework, and visits from family and friends all continued as usual. Sonya was always busy. When she was not teaching the children she was running the household, and she had very little time to herself. She had also been pregnant for most of 1879, and on 18 December, just after Tolstoy started getting to grips with Orthodox dogma, she gave birth to their seventh son, Mikhail (Misha). Another small baby meant postponing again any time for herself. That spring she had enjoyed doing some gardening, with the help of Jules Montels (who was also very deft at producing omelettes and cups of hot chocolate for their summer picnics). The window boxes and flower-beds she had sown with stocks, asters, verbena and phlox brought wonderful colour and heavenly scent. Sewing clothes, which also occupied her that spring, was not nearly as enjoyable as sowing seeds. She had to sew summer clothes for all her six children and it became very arduous. 'I've been sewing away and I'm now sick to death of it and totally desperate,' she wrote to her sister Tanya in March 1879. 'I've got throat spasms, my head hurts ... but I've still got to keep sewing. Sometimes I want to break down these walls and escape to freedom.'[78] Tolstoy had been to Moscow twice that autumn, but Sonya had not even gone beyond the gates of Yasnaya Polyana. In January 1880 she wrote a particularly plaintive letter to her sister Tanya:

My captive life is sometimes so hard! Just think, Tanya, I haven't been out of the house since September. The same prison, even if it's quite bright in the moral and material sense. But sometimes there is still the feeling that someone has locked me up, keeping me here, and I want to push everything away, break everything around me and break out no matter where – as soon as I can![79]

More than ever before, Sonya now lived for the summer months, when Tanya brought her family to stay. She often felt very lonely, and longed to enjoy herself amongst the bright lights of the big city. She had initially welcomed her husband's embrace of Russian Orthodoxy, but now he seemed to be losing his exuberant joie de vivre. He seemed to be less and less interested in the family, and also in running the estate. She was not mistaken. Tolstoy wrote to Strakhov in October 1880 that he had been misguided all his adult life by equating goodness first with his aspirations to be awarded the St George Cross, then with the writing of novels and owning land, and finally with having a family, as he now knew that true goodness could only be found in the Gospels.[80]

In 1880 Tolstoy began to break with old friends and relatives, who were left feeling hurt and confused. In January he went to St Petersburg to hand over the final payment for the land that he had bought, and he went to see Alexandrine the day after he arrived. After telling her he now rejected the divinity of Christ, he had a violent argument with her which lasted all morning, and he returned to continue it that evening, leaving her so agitated she could feel her heart thumping in her chest. After being unable to sleep that night, Tolstoy then left Petersburg first thing the next morning, and Alexandrine felt deeply wounded that he did not come to say goodbye.[81] Tolstoy's sister Masha also became intensely religious at this time, but her spiritual journey took her in the opposite direction, deep into the bosom of the Orthodox Church. Her only son Nikolay had married in October 1878, with Tolstoy as best man, but the following summer, just as her illegitimate daughter Elena was finishing her education in Switzerland and Masha was preparing to bring her to settle in Russia, he died of typhoid.[82] It was a terrible blow for Masha, from which she never really recovered. Instead, under the spiritual guidance of Elder Ambrosy at Optina Pustyn, she became more and more devout, and eventually in 1888 she decided to become a nun. After a stint in a convent in Tula, she settled in a convent near to Optina Pustyn, where she would remain for the rest of her life. Masha remained close to her brother, but they had no common ground when it came to religion.

It took a while for Tolstoy's friends to acclimatise to his new state of mind. Nothing seemed to be able to faze Strakhov, but the deeply religious Sergey Urusov could not accept Tolstoy's new views, which he regarded as heretical, and their friendship foundered. Tolstoy's friendship with Afanasy Fet also disintegrated. Ironically, it was just when Tolstoy decided he wanted to abandon belles-lettres under the influence of his new religious views that his fiction began to become available to the French and English-speaking worlds. The combined *Childhood and Youth* appeared in English in 1862,[83] but it was not until Eugene Schuyler published his translation of *The Cossacks* in 1878 that there was anything else available by Tolstoy. Turgenev's friend, the Russian specialist and translator William Ralston, was rebuffed by Tolstoy when he wrote to him asking for biographical information in preparation for an article he was writing about him in October 1878.[84] 'I cannot partake the temporary illusion of some friends of mine, which seem to be sure, that my works must occupy some place in the Russian literature,' Tolstoy wrote back in decorous but distinctly Russian English to Mr Ralston's address in Bedford Square, London. 'Quite sincerely not knowing, if my works shall be read after 100 years, or will be forgotten in 100 days,' he continued, 'I do not wish to take a ridiculous part in the very probable mistake of my friends.'[85] Ralston filled in the blanks with the help of Turgenev, and published his pioneering article on 'Count Leo Tolstoy's Novels' in 1879. For the subject of *Anna Karenina*, Ralston wrote, Tolstoy had chosen 'society as it exists at the present day in Russian aristocratic circles, combining with his graphic descriptions of the life now led by the upper classes, a series of subtle studies of an erring woman's heart.'

Ralston was right on the mark in claiming *Anna Karenina* had made more money for its author than any other previous work of Russian literature, but some way off it when he speculated that *Anna Karenina* and *War and Peace* were unlikely to be translated into English.[86] In fact, the first French translation of *War and Peace* had already appeared in the same year as his article, and it had been this momentous event which prompted Turgenev to promote Tolstoy as a great novelist in his letter to Edmond About in January 1880. English translations soon followed. In May 1880, Turgenev came to spend a couple of days at Yasnaya Polyana. It was now three years since Tolstoy had finished *Anna Karenina*, and he had published nothing new since. Turgenev was hopeful that his friend would come back to fiction. He was also hoping he could persuade Tolstoy to take part in the Pushkin celebrations in Moscow the following month, but he was to be disappointed on both counts. Probably about the only thing they agreed on now was hunting, for which they still shared a passion.

While it is hard to imagine Tolstoy standing beside Dostoyevsky and Turgenev to honour Russia's first truly great writer at this stage in his career, his refusal does in retrospect look a little churlish. The occasion for the celebrations was the unveiling of the first statue of Pushkin in Russia. It was scandalous that it had not happened sooner (Pushkin died in 1837), but none of the nineteenth-century tsars was prepared to sanction the official veneration of a rebellious and subversive poet fatally wounded in a duel. What was therefore important about this statue is that it was paid for entirely by public subscription, and its unveiling was a cause for celebration precisely because it had nothing to do with the government. The fact that Turgenev came especially from Paris for the occasion, and that Dostoyevsky, who was gravely ill, broke off writing *The Brothers Karamazov* at his country house south of Novgorod to come and take part, speaks eloquently about the importance of this occasion as a public event, which lasted for four days and was widely seen as a triumph for the Russian intelligentsia, and for Russian culture generally. As Turgenev said in his speech, the whole of educated Russia had in some way contributed to the erection of the statue, and this was a sign of its love for one of its greatest fellow countrymen. It was Pushkin, he proclaimed, who had completed the final refinement of 'our language, which in its richness, force, logic and beauty of form is acknowledged by even foreign philologists to be the best after ancient Greek'. Pushkin, he said, 'spoke with typical images, and immortal sounds embracing all aspects of Russian life'. Tolstoy did not care much for 'educated Russia', and now scorned the intelligentsia, and yet he was in some ways biting the hand which had fed him, for as a writer he too owed an enormous debt to Pushkin.

Turgenev's rhetoric was nothing compared to Dostoyevsky's messianic identification of Pushkin with Russia and Christ, which was greeted by an ecstatic thirty-minute ovation. Writing to his wife afterwards, Dostoyevsky told her 'strangers in the audience were weeping, sobbing, embracing one another, and *swearing to one another to be better, not to hate each other in the future, but to love*. Even Turgenev was moved to embrace his old opponent.[87] Tolstoy was at this very moment immersed in Christ's teaching of brotherly love, as he had begun to coordinate and translate the Gospels, but his ego would never have permitted him to join in the communal rejoicing at this extraordinary, unparalleled event. Many years later he explained that, much as he valued Pushkin's genius, he had not gone to Moscow because he felt there was something unnatural about such celebrations, something, which, while not exactly false, did not meet his 'emotional requirements'.[88]

Tolstoy's conspicuous absence from the celebrations in Moscow was certainly much commented on. Rumour had it that he was ill, going mad, or already mad. Dostoyevsky was tempted to travel to Yasnaya Polyana to meet Tolstoy finally, but decided against it. In little over half a year he would be dead, and only then, sitting alone at dinner one cold, dark February evening, having arrived home late, and crying into his plate, did Tolstoy realise quite how dear Dostoyevsky was to him.[89] When he had been ill the previous September, Tolstoy had re-read *Notes from the House of the Dead*, the book which allegorises Dostoyevsky's spiritual rebirth during his years of hard labour in a Siberian prison, and he had marvelled at its 'sincere, natural and Christian point of view'. He had asked Strakhov to pass on affectionate greetings to Dostoyevsky,[90] who was terribly pleased by this, but less so by Tolstoy's lack of reverence for Pushkin. Strakhov tried to mollify Dostoyevsky by saying that Tolstoy had become even more of a 'free-thinker' than he had been before.[91] Tolstoy's belated appreciation of Dostoyevsky is revealing of his sentimentality, for the truth is that he was utterly repelled by the mixture of piety and patriotism in Dostoyevsky's later worldview. The feeling was mutual. Alexandrine had become close to Dostoyevsky shortly before he died, and the writer had bristled with indignation when she showed him some of Tolstoy's recent letters about religion.[92]

Sonya reported to Strakhov in March 1880 that her husband was working to exhaustion and getting terrible headaches, but could not be torn from his desk.[93] Tolstoy was, in fact, so excited by the challenge of confronting the Orthodox Church that he carried on working through the spring and into the summer, contrary to his usual routine.[94] There was no rest cure in Samara in 1880, but just three short trips to Moscow in late autumn to find new teachers for the children. One by one, the eleven volumes of the latest edition of his writings went on sale, but another year passed without Tolstoy venturing into print with anything new. He was aware that he would face difficulties with publishing all three of the projects he was working on now, but bringing them to completion was a matter of life importance to him. Their eventual publication abroad would set the seal on the antagonistic position he had taken up in relation to the Orthodox Church, and from that point on there would be no going back.

Once Tolstoy had worked through the 1,000-plus pages of Makary's *Orthodox Dogmatic Theology*, as well as other key expositions of the Eastern Christian doctrine by authors ranging from St John of Damascus to other recent Moscow metropolitans, he began his critical exegesis, setting out in painstaking detail its major flaws, as he saw them. The Tula priest who had originally recommended that Tolstoy read Makary was startled to receive a second visit from the count a year later. Tolstoy declared that he had read *Orthodox Dogmatic Theology* from cover to cover, and furthermore, he informed Father Alexander with evident satisfaction, his year of study had not only *not* convinced him of the truth of Orthodox dogma, but in fact the opposite. He now realised that the apostles had actually distorted Christ's teaching. Indeed, when he had come to see that Orthodox doctrine was just an artificial confection of often opaque and contradictory expressions of faith, he said, he began to understand why Russian seminaries produced so many atheists. Here Tolstoy was alluding to the many graduates of seminaries who had become revolutionaries. Chernyshevsky, who was still languishing in Siberian exile, was one, and in the 1890s Iosif Dzhugashvili (Stalin) would become another.[95]

The first draft of Tolstoy's own weighty *Investigation of Dogmatic Theology* was finally finished in 1882.[96] He does not pull any punches in it, at one point calling Makary an outright liar, dismissing the doctrine of the Trinity as a 'vile, criminal, blasphemous lie' and subjecting it to ridicule by describing biblical mysteries in his own words (as in 'God had a three-way conversation with his son and the Holy Spirit').[97] As Tolstoy goes on, his tone becomes more aggressive. He does not just refute the notion that Christ redeemed all of mankind by dying on the cross, since people afterwards were 'just the same', but goes on to accuse the Church of inventing the sacraments and the idea that Christ was divine sometime back in the third century. Pointing out that he is probably the only person to have read Makary from cover to cover apart from seminarists studying for exams, Tolstoy ends his obloquy with the allegation that the Orthodox Church no longer enjoyed any moral authority amongst either the educated classes or the common people in Russia. Tolstoy toned down his criticisms for publication in 1891, but only a little.[98]

Aware that readers of his novels might be a little taken aback to be confronted suddenly by a tendentious theological monograph in which the minutiae of Orthodox doctrine were submitted to rational scrutiny, Tolstoy felt he should preface it with a personal account of how he had come to embark on his critique of the Church.[99] The much briefer, and frankly far more readable, *Confession* was thus initially entitled 'Introduction to an Unpublished Work', and was completed in 1880. Bearing obvious comparison with the Confessions of Augustine and Rousseau, Tolstoy's interrogation of the meaning of life begins in his childhood, and charts his spiritual evolution with a painful and engaging honesty which Sonya summarised in notes made in her 1881 diary. She writes that her husband saw the 'light', as he put it, when he realised the source of 'goodness, forbearance and love' amongst the people was the Gospels, not the Church. It was the Church which had, in fact, obscured this message by insisting that salvation was only possible through the sacraments of christening, communion, fasting and so on. Tolstoy's 'whole outlook was illuminated by this light', she wrote, leading him to see millions of people as his brothers, his conscience greatly troubled by the poverty and injustice he saw around him.[100]

Fundamental to Tolstoy's repudiation of Orthodox doctrine was his own new 'unified' translation of the Gospels, which he worked on intensely in the second half of 1880 and 'finished' in July 1881. He was aware that he needed to work further on it, but at that point wanted to move on to other things. Tolstoy now considered his *Union and Translation of the Four Gospels* to be the most important thing he had done in his life.[101] With the assistance of Ivan Ivakin, the new family tutor who arrived in September 1880, he methodically worked his way through the New Testament in the original Greek, using academic editions supplied by the ever-helpful Strakhov. These included the authoritative edition produced in the 1770s by Johann Griesbach, Professor of Theology at the University of Jena, whose philological rigour had launched a new era in biblical scholarship, and the heavily annotated new French translation produced by another Protestant theologian, Professor Edouard Reuss, based at the University of Strasbourg.[102] Tolstoy's aim was to make sense of the morass of contradictions and obscurities he found in the Scriptures, clarify their central message, and extract some practical moral guidance which could be applied to daily living.

The experience of going back to the original texts was a revelation to Tolstoy. Drawing from each of the four Gospels to produce one unified text ('since they set out the same events and the same teaching, although in conflicting ways'), and accompanying it with his commentary, Tolstoy produced twelve titled chapters which follow Christ's life from birth to death. Each biblical excerpt in his version is given firstly in the original Greek, secondly in a modern Russian translation of the Church Slavonic biblical text (which would have been as archaic to a nineteenth-century Russian ear as the English of the Wycliffe Bible would have seemed to a nineteenth-century British ear), and thirdly in his own more accessible version. For the latter, he deliberately used colloquial words wherever possible, with a peasant readership in mind.

This is no ordinary summary of the New Testament, for the Jesus Christ in the Gospel according to Lev is a Christian after Tolstoy's own heart: an ordinary man who is critical of organised religion, and unafraid to speak out against attempts to obstruct his ethical message. The Jesus projected by Tolstoy is a lone crusader swimming against the current of public opinion, a 'humble sectarian' with whom he could identify, as well as look up to morally.[103] This was paramount, and one is reminded of his practice as a novelist. It is striking that what he had most admired about Peter the Great when he had sought to write a novel about him, for example, was his huge energy and productivity – qualities he himself possessed in abundance. Tolstoy essentially stripped the Gospels down to their moral message. By discarding accounts of Christ's baptism and early childhood, all miracles, the story of the Resurrection, anything referring to Jesus as a divine or historical figure, and passages highlighting the special mission of anointed apostles, Tolstoy ended up with about half of the original texts from the New Testament. He did, however, retain all direct quotations of Jesus' speech, which means the Gospel according to St John features far more than the Gospel according to St Mark, which includes many miracles. The key importance of St Matthew's Gospel for Tolstoy was due to the Sermon on the Mount, which was to become the cornerstone of his teaching.[104]

Ivan Ivakin, the new tutor at Yasnaya Polyana, was a Moscow University graduate, and at first he could not understand why Tolstoy wanted to talk about the finer details of New Testament wording, since the gossip columns in Russian newspapers at the time were still talking about him writing a novel about the Decembrists. Ivakin was soon initiated into Tolstoy's work in progress, and when it became clear that his knowledge of Greek was far superior to that of his employer, he was immediately inveigled into helping out. The pale-faced young man with exceptionally slender fingers left some vivid memoirs of his time at Yasnaya Polyana. It has to be said, he was not very impressed with Tolstoy's command of Greek, and took a rather wry view of his selective and distinctly unacademic approach, which jettisoned concrete details: "'Why should we be interested to know that Christ went out into the courtyard?" he would say. "Why do I need to know that he was resurrected? Good for him if he was! For me what is important is knowing what to do, and how I should live.'"[105]

Ivakin clearly found it sometimes a little challenging to work with Tolstoy, since the 'inimitable' author was even *parti pris* when it came to translating the New Testament passages dealing with ethics which survived his ruthless editing. In *War and Peace*, Tolstoy had manipulated events and people to suit the particular view of history he was proposing. Now he wanted Christ's apostles to confirm views he had already formed:

> Sometimes he would come running to me from his study with the Greek Gospel and ask me to translate some extract or other. I would do the translation, and usually it came out the same as the accepted Church translation. 'But couldn't you give this such and such a meaning?' he would ask, and he would say how much he hoped that would be possible.[106]

Tolstoy spent a particularly long time mulling over the opening paragraph in the Gospel of St John ('In the beginning was the Word, and the Word was with God ...'). He fairly swiftly decided to interpret the Greek *logos* as 'reasoning' rather than 'the word' (the Russian word *razumenie* implying both rational enquiry and understanding), but he then came up against the problem of translating *pros ton theon* ('with God'), which the first Church Slavonic Bible renders as 'from God'. Dismissing the literal meaning of 'towards God' as meaningless, and condemning the Vulgate 'apud Deum' and Luther's 'bei Gott' as meaningless and also inaccurate, Tolstoy's far more radical version, on the basis of a lengthy discussion of the preposition *pros* was 'and reasoning replaced God'.[107]

6. Konstantin Pobedonostsev, Chief Procurator of the Holy Synod from 1880 to 1905

By the time Alexander II was finally assassinated by revolutionaries on 1 March 1881, Tolstoy was ready to become, if not quite a Protestant, certainly a protestant in terms of the Orthodox Church, and his boldness was compared on more than one occasion with that of Luther, Jan Hus and Calvin.[108] Horrified by the thought of the conspirators being executed, Tolstoy sat down and wrote a letter to the new tsar, Alexander III, pleading for clemency in the name of Christian forgiveness. He then wrote a letter to the Chief Procurator of the Holy Synod, Konstantin Pobedonostsev, asking him to pass his letter on to the Tsar, and another to Strakhov, asking him to hand both letters over to Pobedonostsev. Sonya reacted with equanimity to having to go into national mourning by dressing in black crêpe from head to foot,[109] but she was aghast at her husband's latest action. It had been bad enough while he had been devout, and had insisted on observing the fasts on Wednesdays and Fridays. To retaliate, she had insisted on providing non-Lenten food for Vasily Alexeyev and Jules Montels, neither of whom were Orthodox, despite their readiness to eat what was offered, and she had then enforced the family's Lenten diet even more strictly when she noticed Tolstoy's faith wavering. On Good Friday, the strictest day of fasting, temptation had got the better of Tolstoy and he gave up eating Lenten food for ever after tucking into some of the meat that had been prepared for the two tutors. Sonya also stopped copying her husband's new manuscripts. She had found the pedagogical materials turgid, but the theological writing was far worse, and she confided in a letter to her sister Tanya that she had thought of leaving Tolstoy that spring. She reckoned that life at Yasnaya Polyana had been a lot better without Christianity.[110] She was also pregnant again.

The friction between the Tolstoys was now coming out into the open more and more frequently. When Sonya overheard Vasily Alexeyev supporting her husband's plea for clemency for the Tsar's assassins one morning over coffee, she exploded, terrified at the repercussions that Tolstoy's letter might cause. Alexeyev realised it was time for him to leave Yasnaya Polyana, and he asked Tolstoy for permission to make a personal copy of his Gospel translations to take away with him, knowing they could never be published in Russia. Since time was not on his side, he restricted himself to copying Tolstoy's Gospel excerpts and the general summaries in each chapter. This text was later prefaced by Tolstoy's introduction and entitled *Gospel in Brief*. It would be the first of his religious works to be published abroad. During World War I, Tolstoy's *Gospel in Brief* made a profound impression on Ludwig Wittgenstein, who chanced to find it in a bookshop in Galicia. He later claimed it had virtually kept him alive.[111]

Friends and relatives who came to visit Yasnaya Polyana in the spring of 1881 were drawn into vituperative arguments about capital punishment and the Church, and Sonya started to worry that her husband's Christian charity was going to result in him giving away all they had to the poverty-stricken peasants who were coming to Yasnaya Polyana in ever increasing numbers, knowing they would not leave empty-handed. To begin with, Tolstoy wrote a thumbnail sketch of each petitioner down in his diary, noting, for example, one old woman's tears dropping on to the dust and another peasant's toothless smile (Tolstoy himself was toothless by this time).[112] Needless to say, Pobedonostsev refused to pass on Tolstoy's letter to the Tsar, and the conspirators were hanged in early April. 'Our Christ is not your Christ,' wrote Pobedonostsev crisply in the letter he finally sent Tolstoy in June.[113] Tolstoy brought his work on the Gospels to a halt that month, because he wanted to make another pilgrimage to Optina Pustyn. This time, instead of Strakhov, he took along as companion his servant Sergey Arbuzov, and instead of travelling by train he went on foot, dressed like a muzhik, complete with bast shoes specially commissioned from a peasant in the village.

They spent the first night sleeping on straw in an old woman's peasant hut, where they were woken at dawn the next morning by the swallows nesting in the roof. Four days later they arrived at the monastery, where they were put up without ceremony together with other peasant pilgrims in a dormitory infested with bedbugs. When word got out that the scruffy looking old peasant was actually Count Tolstoy in disguise, he was obliged to move to more salubrious accommodation, but it did mean that he was again granted an immediate audience with Elder Ambrosy, rather than having to wait almost a week. Tolstoy had not come to Optina Pustyn this time to find religious solace, but to challenge Ambrosy and the other monks about the Orthodox Church's distortion of Christ's teaching. He went away dissatisfied, having at one point demonstrated his superior knowledge of the Gospels.[114] On the way home, Tolstoy and his servant walked as far as Kaluga, which had quite a large population of sectarians, including Molokans and two offshoots of that sect, Subbotniks ('Sabbatarians') and Vozdykhantsy ('Sighers'), a tiny new faction whose believers, instead of crossing themselves, sighed while lifting their gaze upwards. Tolstoy set off to find them as soon as he learned this, to talk to them about their faith. He had been sickened to see the Optina Pustyn monks treat the destitute pilgrims with contempt while deferring to wealthy visitors, but he found the rest of the trip very invigorating.

In July 1881, a month after returning home, Tolstoy set off for his Samara estate with his son Sergey, who had just passed the end-of-school exams which were a requirement for university entrance. He felt listless there this time. He no longer had the stomach for working to make his land profitable, and the poverty in the region seemed to be even more starkly evident than in previous years. During this trip he had further contact with the Molokans, and attended one of their prayer meetings, after which two of their leaders came to visit him so they could continue the conversation. Naturally, Tolstoy was preaching to the converted when he read them extracts from his *Gospel in Brief*, for they also thought the Orthodox Church had mutilated Christ's teachings. On 19 July Tolstoy made an interesting new acquaintance when he met Alexander Prugavin, a young ethnographer who had become interested in the Russian sectarians after meeting many of them while exiled in the far north. Since 1879 Prugavin had been publishing articles in progressive journals about Russian schismatics and sectarians, ranging from the three

Old Believer bishops Tolstoy had tried to help to the Pashkovites. Tolstoy was particularly interested to hear from Prugavin about a Tver peasant called Vasily Syutayev who had started preaching brotherly love and the abolition of private property. As soon as he learned from Prugavin that one of Syutayev's sons had refused to do military service, Tolstoy immediately declared that he wanted to meet him. The opportunity would soon present itself.

During his month out on the steppe, Tolstoy was affectionate in his letters to Sonya. He felt guilty. Many years earlier they had decided they would move to Moscow when the time came for Sergey to go to university, and that day had now dawned. With so much political unrest amongst the student body following the assassination of Alexander II, Sonya felt it was even more important to protect her son from being caught up in the revolutionary movement by going to live in Moscow herself. But this was also the liberation she had been longing for, particularly during the last few years when her husband had shunned any kind of social life, turning his back on his career as a successful novelist and condemning the depravity of their lifestyle. For Tolstoy, moving to Moscow was a nightmare prospect, and he had so far refused to help Sonya find somewhere for them to live. She was six months pregnant when she went flat-hunting in Moscow before he left for Samara, and she had to face the hot and dusty city the following month again in order to prepare everything for the family's arrival. Tolstoy suddenly felt remorse at having neglected her and left her to do everything on her own. He promised to help her on his return, and show willing, yet when he returned home and found the house full of summer guests, he once again felt the painful contrast between his beliefs and his surroundings.[115]

The nine Tolstoys left Yasnaya Polyana on 15 September, and took up residence in a rented apartment in a house in the best residential area of Moscow. Sergey became a student in natural sciences at Moscow University and Ilya and Lev became pupils at the very popular private boys' school founded in 1868 by Lev Polivanov, who had masterminded the Pushkin celebrations the year before. Later that autumn, Tanya became a student at the main art school in Moscow. Despite Tolstoy's pledge to help Sonya in Moscow, he soon forgot it. It was sheer misery for him to move to the city, and Sonya told her sister by letter that he was neither sleeping nor eating and had sunk into apathy, while she had spent the first two weeks constantly in tears. After he had arrived in Moscow, Tolstoy had gone to visit the city's slums, and had then returned home, walked up carpeted stairs to their new home and sat down to dinner, waited upon by two servants in white tie and tails.[116] The close proximity of luxury and poverty sickened him.

Relief came when Tolstoy escaped Moscow at the end of the month to go north to Tver province and meet Vasily Syutayev, the peasant sectarian Prugavin had told him about. Apart from their difference in social backgrounds, Syutayev was almost Tolstoy's mirror image in terms of their religious beliefs, which astonished him. Syutayev's doctrine of brotherly love was derived exclusively from the modern Russian translation of the New Testament, which he knew by heart, and like Tolstoy, he had dedicated his life to pursuing the ideal of self-perfection. Syutayev, who later came to visit Tolstoy in Moscow, was to become a source of deep inspiration for him.[117] Another source of spiritual support for Tolstoy at this time would come from his correspondence with his family's former tutor Vasily Alexeyev, and from his friendship with the librarian of the Rumyantsev Public Library, Nikolay Fyodorov, whose asceticism made Tolstoy's simple tastes seem positively sybaritic.

By the beginning of October Tolstoy was back in Moscow and trying to work. The walls in the flat proved to be paper-thin, however, so there was constant noise and he could not concentrate, for which he squarely blamed Sonya. He was also unhappy about her spending money needlessly. How could she have wasted twenty-two roubles on an armchair when that money could have bought a peasant a horse or a cow? Things improved a little after he rented two small rooms in another wing of the house for six roubles a month. Finally, he had some peace of mind, and to salve his conscience he crossed the Moscow river to go and chop wood every afternoon with the peasants on the Sparrow Hills. But relations with Sonya were no better. Two weeks before she gave birth, Sonya wrote again to Tanya to tell her that her husband had reduced her to complete despair. Tolstoy told his diary it had been the most painful month in all his life.[118] Alexey was born on 31 October. A few weeks later Tolstoy published a story about an angel in the new children's journal edited by Sonya's brother Petya. It was his first publication in four years.

Tolstoy had been working sporadically on the short story 'What Men Live By' throughout 1881. Utterly different from *Anna Karenina*, his last published work, which was a sophisticated novel aimed at an educated audience, this new work was a story from peasant life, and a parable which put forward his new Christian views about love. A reworking of a well-known legend about an angel sent to earth by God to learn 'what men live by', the story had been told to him by Vasily Shchegolenok, one of the last living peasant 'reciters' of oral folk epics from the Russian north. He had come to stay at Yasnaya Polyana in 1879 when he was already an old man (and still illiterate), and Tolstoy had listened to him with rapt attention. He took particular care to write 'What Men Live By' in a simple and lucid language, and incorporated several of the folk expressions he had heard during his conversations with Shchegolenok, and also with the pilgrims and wanderers on the road to Kiev near Yasnaya Polyana. Despite its simplicity, Tolstoy's work on the story was characteristically meticulous. He produced thirty-two manuscripts and nine different beginnings before being satisfied with the draft he submitted for publication. The eight epigraphs about love which preface the story are taken from his own version of St John's Gospel. Writing morally engaged fiction in a clear and simple style was one way Tolstoy planned to propagate his Christian ideals. He also now felt a need to protest in public about the evil he saw around him, and this was something he would do in an increasingly loud voice for the remaining three decades of his life.

· II ·

SECTARIAN, ANARCHIST, HOLY FOOL

There is one way to live joyously and that is to be an apostle. Not just in the sense of going around and talking, but in the sense that your arms, and your legs, and your stomach, and your sides as well as your tongue all serve the truth ...

Letter to Vasily Alexeyev, December 1884[1]

TOLSTOY'S CRUSADE to bring Christian principles into the lives of educated Russians began with a newspaper article he published on 20 January 1882. He had been shocked by the degradation and poverty he encountered when he went to visit a doss-house in one of Moscow's worst slum areas a few weeks earlier, and when he learned that a census was to be held in the city, he seized the opportunity to speak out. It was not the first time he had appealed to the consciences of his fellow countrymen, as he had publicised the plight of starving peasants during the Samara famine in 1873, and been successful in raising millions of roubles in aid. Now, however, his mission was not merely humanitarian but religious – he did not want cash but Christian brotherly love. Tolstoy was also determined to lead by example, having applied to be one of the eighty people appointed to supervise the census. He specifically requested to work in one of the poorest districts, moreover, near to where he himself lived in the western part of the city. The night before Tolstoy's article 'About the Census in Moscow' appeared on the front page of one of the city's most popular daily newspapers, he went to the city Duma to read it out to the organisation committee, and then distributed hundreds of copies to everyone involved in conducting the census when it began three days later.

Tolstoy was profoundly disturbed by the prospect of the 2,000 (mostly student) census-takers entering crowded, infested tenements to ask routine statistical questions of people dying of starvation, and he wasted no time in his article in confronting the issue:

> What does this census mean for us Muscovites conducting the census who are not academics? Two things. Firstly, we will probably discover among the tens of thousands of us who live on an income running into the tens of thousands that there are tens of thousands of people without food, clothes and shelter; and secondly, that our brothers and sons will be going to look at all this, and calmly noting down on the forms how many are dying of hunger and cold.
>
> Both of these things are very bad.[2]

True to the anarchic spirit which would become more and more apparent in Tolstoy's thought during the following decade, he rejected the idea of institutional involvement, either at the government or the philanthropic level, likewise conventional charitable enterprises such as fundraising balls, bazaars and theatre performances. Money, he insisted, was in itself an evil, so there should be no public proclamations of the sums donated by wealthy individuals. Throwing money at the problem was no substitute for practical assistance as far as he was concerned, and merely let people off the hook. Tolstoy took his inspiration straight from the New Testament, by paraphrasing Jesus's parable of 'The Sheep and the Goats' in St Matthew's Gospel: 'For I was hungry and you gave me something to eat, I was thirsty and you gave me something to drink, I was a stranger and you invited me in, I needed clothes and you clothed me, I was sick and you looked after me, I was in prison and you came to visit me.'[3] Tolstoy urged Muscovites to overcome their fears of coming into contact with the bedbugs, fleas, typhoid, diphtheria and smallpox which were rife in the filthy conditions the poor were forced to live in. He called on the young census-takers to sit down with those in need, and show them love and respect by talking to them about their lives.

Unfortunately for Tolstoy, some census-takers were so impoverished themselves that they undoubtedly greeted this exhortation to practise Christian charity with bemusement. One of them was a twenty-two-year-old medical student called Anton Chekhov, then living in Moscow's red-light district in the north of the city. His father was a former small-time merchant who had fled their provincial hometown after going bankrupt, and Chekhov had started contributing to low-grade comic journals in order to keep his family afloat. Working as a census-taker provided him with a few extra kopecks, and also good material for his next humorous piece, which as usual he signed with a nom de plume, thinking ahead to the future scholarly publications he dreamed of writing. The official census consisted of fifteen standard questions relating to name, gender, age, marital status, place of birth, faith, occupation and so on. In the 'Supplementary Questions to the Personal Forms of the Statistical Census Suggested by Antosha Chekhonte', a further ten questions were added, including:

> 16. Are you a *clever* person or a *fool*?
> 17. Are you an honest person? a swindler? a robber? a scoundrel? a lawyer? or?
> 20. Is your wife blonde? brunette? chestnut? a redhead?
> 21. Does your wife *beat* you or *not*? Do you *beat* her or *not*?
> 22. How much did you weigh when you were ten years old?
> 23. Do you consume hot drinks? *yes* or *no*?[4]

It is unlikely that Tolstoy ever read *The Alarm Clock*, where this irreverent skit appeared, but he would develop a great admiration for the short stories Chekhov wrote for literary journals later on in his career. If Chekhov paid scant attention to 'About the Census in Moscow' for his part, he nevertheless regarded Tolstoy as Russia's greatest living artist, and would also succumb for a while to his hypnotic powers of rational argument.

Tolstoy failed in his mission to induce Muscovites to show brotherly love to the poor, as his appeal only resulted in him receiving requests for financial help, and misunderstanding on the part of the press, but his article nevertheless won him an early follower. Indeed, the article's impact on the painter Nikolay Ge was so tumultuous that he left his remote farmhouse in the Ukraine and got on a train to Moscow so that he could come and embrace the 'great man' who had written it. Like Tolstoy, Ge (a descendant of a French émigré called Gay) had become preoccupied with religious and moral questions in the 1870s and had come to the same conclusions: art should not be practised for commercial gain, while engaging in physical labour was the path to saving one's soul. In early March 1882 Ge turned up at Tolstoy's front door in Moscow, and the discovery of their shared beliefs led to the blossoming of a close friendship.[5]

Ge was lucky to find Tolstoy at home. Several times that spring Sonya was left to fend on her own while her husband retreated to Yasnaya Polyana to recuperate from the trauma of living in Moscow, which he condemned as a 'foul sewer'.[6] For the first time, however, Sonya found herself almost wishing Tolstoy would stay at Yasnaya Polyana.[7] She had her hands full with the family (two of their eight children were under five in 1882), but she was also beginning to take her first steps into Moscow society. As Countess Tolstoy she had an entrée into all the best drawing rooms, and as the wife of the famous novelist she was now also a celebrity in her own right, and she found it rather intoxicating being the centre of attention for once. She had missed out on going to balls and soirées in her youth, but now she prepared to live vicariously through their daughter Tanya, who was about to turn eighteen, and as keen to dress up and go out as she was. Sonya was only thirty-eight in 1882, and still very attractive. Tolstoy, by contrast, desired only to simplify his life now, and wanted nothing to do with the conventions of polite society. Instead he gravitated towards peasant sectarians like Vasily Syutayev and ascetics like the 'Moscow Socrates' Nikolay Fyodorov, the eccentric philosopher-librarian of the Rumyantsev Library who deplored all material possessions (even refusing a salary), and slept on bare planks covered only by his threadbare overcoat.

Vasily Syutayev came to visit Tolstoy after the census, and his arrival caused a great stir in Moscow. The tiny sect that he had established in Tver was the subject of a recently published article in the new journal *Russian Thought*, and such was Syutayev's popularity that one art shop in Moscow even stocked copies of his photograph for purchase.[8] Tolstoy also encouraged his new friend Ilya Repin to come and paint Syutayev's portrait in his study.

Family friends who came to visit Sonya were so curious about the peasant prophet that they abandoned the drawing room in order to go to Tolstoy's study and hear what he had to say. His sister Masha was particularly piqued to have her conversation with Syutayev interrupted, and hoped he would be able to go and have a cup of tea with her one evening so they could continue their discussion.[9] Syutayev's visit to Moscow was cut short, however, when word of his presence in the city reached Prince Dolgorukov, the city's governor general, who swiftly despatched one of his gendarmes to arrest him and send him back to Tver (where the local clergy had already taken him to court for refusing to christen his son). Tolstoy refused to speak to the young gendarme, and slammed the door in his face, prompting Dolgorukov to send round one of his officials, Vladimir Istomin, who was a family friend. Tolstoy's brusque response to Istomin's invitation to come and explain himself to Prince Dolgorukov was that the governor general could perfectly well come and see him himself if he wanted to talk to him. Syutayev and Tolstoy were henceforth prohibited from seeing each other.[10]

Sectarian, Repin's portrait of Syutayev, was acquired for Tretyakov's gallery on Tolstoy's recommendation. In due course Repin would paint a series of celebrated portraits of Tolstoy, with whom he now embarked on a thirty-year friendship. He had first acquired fame in 1873 with an epic canvas depicting a group of destitute peasants forced into earning a demeaning living by hauling barges up the Volga, and henceforth had come to be seen as the 'Tolstoy of painting'. There was thus an inevitability to him meeting the Tolstoy of literature, just as there was an inevitability to the author of *An Investigation of Dogmatic Theology* challenging Repin on the subject of his painting *Religious Procession*, which is what he had been working on when he received a surprise visitor at his Moscow studio one evening in the autumn of 1880. The subject of Repin's painting – the annual procession accompanying the twenty-mile journey of one of Russia's most precious icons from the Znamensky Cathedral in Kursk to the Korennaya Hermitage where it first appeared – represented for Tolstoy the epitome of Russian Orthodox ritual and superstition, and he could not see the point of making it the subject of a painting.

Since the time it had first taken place in the early seventeenth century, the Kursk procession had been drawing Russians from all sections of society in ever greater numbers. There were a few dozen members of Syutayev's sect, but well over 60,000 people took part in the three-mile-long Kursk procession by the 1880s, including mounted police, pilgrims carrying the wonder-working icon, deacons carrying banners, choristers, clergy, the provincial governor and his staff in full dress uniforms, the Bishop of Kursk in ceremonial regalia, officials and their families, merchants and peasants, all in strict hierarchical sequence.[11] Whether or not Tolstoy's reproof had anything to do with it, by the time *Religious Procession in Kursk Province* was finished three years later, Repin's painting had been transformed into a thinly disguised attack on Russia's entrenched caste system, with strong hints that it was maintained by means of brutality and violence. The canvas attracted 4,000 visitors in one week when it was first exhibited in 1883 due to its provocative content, and was acquired for the Tretyakov Gallery at the record price of 10,000 roubles, despite Repin's refusal to tone down its trenchant social criticism.[12]

Two very different worlds had merged during Syutayev's visit to the Tolstoy household in 1882, but this was an exception. As Tolstoy and his wife were very well aware, their paths were now diverging. 'The difference between my husband and myself came about, not because *I* in my heart went away from him,' Sonya wrote later; 'I and my life remained the same as before. It was *he* who went away.'[13] Perhaps if she had not endured twelve pregnancies, three miscarriages and ensuing bouts of serious illness, and had not borne the responsibilities of running a large household on her shoulders, she could have followed her husband on his spiritual journey and spent her time reading books. She had grown into adulthood under his tutelage, and now she was expected to renounce all the values he had inculcated in her and meekly follow him. But she wondered how it would be possible to eke out an existence on next to no income with eight children to clothe and feed.

Undeterred by his setback with the Moscow census, Tolstoy now channelled his missionary zeal into the written word. Apart from his article about the census and his story 'What Men Live By', he had not published anything new since the last instalment of *Anna Karenina* appeared in 1877. Five years on, he was ready to disseminate his newfound religious ideas to the wider public, and he began that process by reading the manuscript of his *Confession* to Sergey Yuriev, one of the editors of the journal *Russian Thought*. Not least because Tolstoy had burned his bridges with Katkov and the *Russian Messenger* over his views regarding the Serbo-Turkish War, *Russian Thought* was the obvious journal to turn to. Based in Moscow, it had immediately acquired a distinguished reputation for its liberal views when it was founded in 1880 – Tolstoy's friend Prugavin, for example, had already published several articles about schismatics and peasant sectarians in it.[14] Yuriev agreed to publish *Confession* as soon as he heard it, and within a few weeks Tolstoy was holding the proofs in his hands. The projected May issue of *Russian Thought* was duly submitted to the office of the religious censor, and after Tolstoy complied with requests for revisions, both he and Yuriev were hopeful of the issue being approved for publication.

At this point, *Confession* was still entitled 'Introduction to an Unpublished Work' – the work in question being *An Investigation of Dogmatic Theology*, his response to Metropolitan Makary's *Orthodox Dogmatic Theology*. All secular writing which touched on questions of faith, or was related to the Church in some way, had to be submitted for approval by the religious censor committee. Its members were based at the Trinity St Sergius Monastery outside Moscow, but were beholden to the Holy Synod, the secular governing body of the Russian Orthodox Church, which had its headquarters in St Petersburg. On 21 June the committee finally gave its verdict. On the basis of a close examination of Tolstoy's text, Archpriest Filaret, Rector of the Moscow Theological Seminary, came to the conclusion that Tolstoy's attitude to Orthodoxy was disrespectful and so his article was therefore inadmissible. The committee demanded that it be cut from each printed copy of the journal and destroyed by the police. Despite this edict, which made headline news in the press, *Confession* was soon widely read. Such was the interest aroused by any new work by Tolstoy that several senior figures in the government demanded to be sent copies before they were destroyed, and these soon circulated. Multiple copies were also made from the few offprints of the final proofs which had remained in the *Russian Thought* editorial office. These were then hectographed or lithographed and distributed throughout Russia with the help of a student organisation in Petersburg which specialised in this kind of samizdat (and whose main warehouse was ironically a Petersburg apartment whose owner had an indirect connection to the Minister for Internal Affairs – head of the Russian police). *Confession* became available for purchase at three roubles a copy, and thus reached a far wider readership than it would have done through the legitimate means of the 3,000-circulation *Russian Thought*.[15] Turgenev even heard about it in Paris, and wrote to ask Tolstoy for a copy. Despite finding it rather depressing to read (its argument was based on false principles in his opinion, which led to a kind of nihilistic negation of all forms of human life), he nevertheless still regarded Tolstoy as the most remarkable individual in Russia.[16]

Tolstoy viewed *Confession* as the first part of a tetralogy, of which the second and third parts, his *Investigation of Dogmatic Theology* and *Union and Translation of the Four Gospels* remained unpublished. Completing a first draft of the fourth part, *What I Believe*, became his task for the summer of 1882. If the first three parts of this major new project were designed to expose the falsity of the Church's doctrine, the goal of *What I Believe* was to reveal the true meaning of Christianity, as set out in the Gospels. For Tolstoy, that meaning was essentially contained in Jesus's Sermon on the Mount (Matthew, 5–7), which alone offered the possibility of creating heaven on earth in his opinion. He was also convinced that it was the Church's teachings which actually made it impossible to follow the prescriptions of the Sermon on the Mount to the letter.[17]

Completing the first draft of *What I Believe* produced a state of spiritual euphoria in Tolstoy, and reawakened a desire which had lain dormant ever since he had set out on his quest to live a life consonant with the religious and moral principles he had painfully been hammering out for himself. He wanted to leave his family and make a complete break with his former life, but voicing this desire aloud to his wife resulted in the first serious rift between them. The violent row on a hot August night which led to them sleeping apart was not easily forgotten. Sonya had devoted her life to her husband and his writings, and to bringing up their children. She was already angry that he had been neglecting them ever since they had moved to Moscow, and the thought of him leaving altogether was devastating. Tolstoy was, in fact, deeply conflicted. He was repelled by his family's patrician lifestyle, but he still loved Sonya deeply – they would have two more children during the next few difficult years – and he had a keen sense of his obligations. In the spring of 1882, after resigning himself to the fact that his family was going to live in Moscow whether he liked it or not, Tolstoy went house-hunting. Days after delivering the proofs of *Confession* to the editorial office of *Russian Thought*, he finally decided to buy an old wooden house for them in a quiet back street on the outskirts of the city centre. He had been to visit it several times and negotiated a price of 36,000 roubles. He then spent part of the summer carrying out improvements and repairs so the family could move in at the beginning of autumn.

The house, which dated back to 1808, had belonged to a merchant couple who had bred large numbers of dogs, and was not in a fashionable residential area.[18] Sonya was crestfallen when she first came to Dolgo-Khamovnichesky Lane and set eyes on the rather shabby and nondescript house, which had a lunatic asylum and a brewery for neighbours and stood opposite a textile factory. But it had a lush, tranquil garden which made it seem more like a country estate than an inner-city house, and Tolstoy's mind was made up by the profusion of roses, gooseberry bushes and fruit trees it contained.[19] Tolstoy worked conscientiously that summer: as well as whitewashing, wall-papering and plastering, there were stoves to repair, parquet floors to lay and pieces of furniture to buy. The family moved in on 8 October, happy to be settled at last in what would be their home for the winter months. While Sonya became caught up in a hectic whirl of activities, as she sought to keep all the children under control as well as entertain them, Tolstoy consoled himself that autumn by studying Hebrew with a Moscow rabbi, who was rather taken aback to find his pupil arguing with him about the meaning of certain passages of the Old Testament after only a few lessons.[20]

As time went on, Tolstoy sought to bring more aspects of his life into line with his religious ideals, and 1883 was a pivotal year in this regard. He now wore peasant clothes in the city as well as at home in the country, dispensed with his title wherever possible and tried to avoid having to be waited upon, but he was conscious that there was a lot more he could do. While visiting Yasnaya Polyana that May, after doing what he could to help put out a fire in the village which destroyed twenty-two peasant homes, he took the first steps in divesting himself of his property, including his literary works, by handing to Sonya power of attorney. Immediately afterwards he travelled for the last time to Samara, where he sold his horses and cattle. He also divided up his land there into five plots to let to peasants.[21] During his month on the steppe, Tolstoy engaged in heated discussions with a peasant revolutionary living under police surveillance, and endeavoured to show him and his comrades that the use of violence was both immoral and futile.[22] He also wrote to Sonya to tell her he had renewed his contact with the local Molokans, with whom he had further long conversations about Christianity. He knew full well that this contact would come to the attention of the police, but despite Sonya's qualms, his response was 'Let them report it'.[23]

Fearless as Tolstoy was, he was probably unaware of the extent of the police operation which had been mounted to follow his every move. At the same time, the police probably had no idea quite how much trouble Tolstoy was going to cause them in the coming years. His meetings with Prugavin and the Molokans out on the steppe had been immediately reported to the Bishop of Samara by a local priest back in the summer of 1881, and since then, the matter had then been transferred to the Ministry of Internal Affairs in St Petersburg, which now began to monitor his 'harmful activities'. In September, for the first time since 1862 (when his peasant school activities had resulted in Yasnaya Polyana being searched for seditious material), Tolstoy was placed under permanent covert surveillance.[24] In December that year Tolstoy was improbably nominated to be the next Marshal of the Nobility in his district by the Tula local government, which had not yet been informed about the surveillance activities. Unaware that Tolstoy had immediately turned down the appointment, Konstantin Pobedonostsev, Chief Procurator of the Holy Synod, wrote to warn the new Minister of Internal Affairs, Count Dmitry Tolstoy (the distant relative who in the 1870s had been Minister of Education):

> In recent years Count Tolstoy's fantasies have suddenly changed once
> again, and he has succumbed to religious mania. This has resulted in
> his complete estrangement from Christianity – in the sense of belief.
> He has put together a retelling of the Gospels in his own words with a
> commentary, full of cynicism, in which he preaches Christian morality in
> the rational sense, rejecting the teaching of a personal God and the divinity
> of Christ the saviour. He had intended to publish this work abroad,
> but refrained after earnest pleading from his wife (his last child has not
> been christened, despite his wife's entreaties), and it is now circulating in
> manuscript. He is in contact with all the rational sects, the Molokans, the
> [Syutayevites] and so on …[25]

Tolstoy's movements during his trip to Samara in the summer of 1883 were indeed watched closely. A local police agent reported that Tolstoy had tried to preach the principle of equality to a group of peasants, whom he had exhorted to renounce private property, and reject the government. A few days later it was reported that he had been persuading peasants that they were wasting their time decorating churches and going to services.[26] From now on, the police would sedulously follow Tolstoy's every move, noting in its regular bulletins his arrivals and departures from Moscow.[27]

Tolstoy returned to Yasnaya Polyana that July to find a brief letter from Turgenev, with whom he had been in affectionate correspondence. Turgenev informed him he was now on his deathbed, but that was not the main reason for writing:

> I'm actually writing to you in order to tell you how glad I was to be your contemporary, and to put to you my last, sincere request. My friend, return to literary activity! This gift has come to you from where everything else comes from. Oh, how happy I would be if I could think that my request makes an impact on you!! I am a finished man – the doctors do not even know what to call my malady, Névralgie stomacale goutteuse. I can't walk, I can't eat, I can't sleep, but so what! It's even boring to repeat all this! My friend, great writer of the Russian land – heed my request! Let me know that you have received this note, and let me once again embrace you, and your family very, very warmly, can't write more, too tired.[28]

Tolstoy was deeply touched by this letter (although he was later probably rather annoyed when Turgenev's phrase 'great writer of the Russian land' became a cliché regularly fixed to his name). Turgenev died the following month, unaware that his friend had in fact partially returned to literature. In 1881 Tolstoy had started work on a new novella which would in time receive the title *The Death of Ivan Ilych*. He had put it aside in 1883, but would return to work on it the following year, placating Sonya, who also longed for her husband to return to fiction so that she could once again be part of his creative life as his copyist.

Although Tolstoy did not return to literature in the way Turgenev would have liked (fiction would never claim his attention again in the way it had earlier), he was nevertheless keen to honour his friend. He therefore readily agreed to speak at the commemorative meeting of Moscow's venerable Russian Literature Society that was planned for late October 1883, perhaps prompted by his conscience, having rather arrogantly refused to take part in the Pushkin celebrations in 1880. When it became known that Tolstoy was going to give a public lecture, the news spread rapidly throughout the city and was considered sufficiently important to be reported in the press. The head of press censorship wrote at once to inform the Minister of Internal Affairs: 'Tolstoy is a lunatic, you can expect anything from him; he may say incredible things and there will be a huge scandal'. Dmitry Tolstoy took action by informing the Moscow governor, Prince Dolgorukov, who promptly banned the commemorative meeting from taking place. There was bitter disappointment amongst the Moscow intelligentsia.[29]

Count Dmitry Tolstoy was forced to deal with his anarchic relative about another matter that autumn. Tolstoy was appointed to be a juror for the Tula regional court, and his refusal to serve on religious grounds was again reported in Russia's main newspapers. Fearing that the authority of the courts might be undermined if others followed his example, this time Dmitry Tolstoy expressed his concerns to the Tsar.[30] But Tolstoy was now unstoppable. In 1883, instalments of *Confession* began to appear in the revolutionary émigré journal *The Common Cause*, which was based in Geneva.[31] The first separate edition of *Confession*, as it was now called, was produced by the journal's publisher Mikhail Elpidin the following year. Elpidin was another former seminary student turned revolutionary who had escaped from prison and fled abroad, where he also published the first edition of Chernyshevsky's *What Is to Be Done?* in 1867. The émigré edition of *Confession* was reprinted many times. In June 1883 a French translation of Tolstoy's *Gospel in Brief* was also published in a Paris journal. Its translator, Leonid Urusov, the vice-governor of Tula, and a friend sympathetic to Tolstoy's views, had already started working on a French translation of *What I Believe*.[32] Tolstoy had planned to 'publish' *What I Believe* in *Russian Thought*, anticipating that hectographed copies of the proofs would circulate, following certain prohibition by the censor, as had been the case with *Confession*. It was now too voluminous to be submitted as an article, however, and Tolstoy resolved to publish it as a book instead.[33] The work on *What I Believe* had been intense, but in early October, exhausted but jubilant, he was ready to hand the manuscript over for typesetting. He made an interesting new acquaintance when he stopped off in Tula on his way to Moscow. The Sanskrit scholar Ivan Minaev, Professor of Comparative Philology at St Petersburg University, was Russia's greatest expert on Buddhism, and had travelled extensively in India. Tolstoy's interest in the Eastern religions was to grow exponentially in the last decades of his life, and he grilled Minaev for over five hours on the precise aspects of Buddhism on which he wanted clarification.[34]

Although Tolstoy felt extremely lonely in the midst of his uncomprehending family, he was beginning to find more people from an educated background with whom he could have meaningful conversations, either in person or by letter. The first had been his children's teacher Vasily Alexeyev, who had moved out to work on his Samara estate in 1881, and with whom he was still in regular contact. People were also beginning to make their way to him. At the end of 1882 Tolstoy had embarked on an intense, brief correspondence with a former university student exiled on his father's estate in Smolensk province.[35] But it was in Vladimir Chertkov, who came to visit Tolstoy in Moscow in October 1883, that he found his greatest kindred spirit and most devoted disciple. From this point until Tolstoy's death Chertkov would occupy an ever more important role in his life as his closest friend and partner in their shared mission to disseminate what they saw as true Christianity.

Chertkov was twenty-nine when they met, Tolstoy fifty-five. He did not have a title, but his background was even more distinguished than Tolstoy's. Both his parents were descended from old aristocratic families (one paternal relative had founded the Chertkov Library which Tolstoy had worked in when he was writing *War and Peace*), and they were very close to the court. The future Alexander III was Chertkov's playmate when he was a child, while Alexander II was a regular visitor to the family's opulent mansion in St Petersburg while he grew up, and showed him particular favour from a young age. As well as inviting Chertkov and his parents to holiday at the Romanov palace in Livadia in the Crimea, the Tsar singled him out during cavalry parades. At the age of nineteen, after an elite education, Chertkov had followed his father into the army, where a brilliant career awaited him.[36] 'Le beau Dima', as he was known, was enormously wealthy, as well as being tall, handsome, and on the guest list of all the most exclusive balls and social gatherings. He was also famous for a certain eccentricity: his refusal to dance with Empress Maria Fyodorovna on one occasion had caused a sensation in a world which took protocol very seriously. In 1879 Chertkov had taken an eleven-month leave, which he spent in England, and shocked his parents soon after his return by informing them of his decision to resign from the army. Since 1881 he had been living at Lizinovka, his parents' enormous estate in Voronezh province, where he had thrown himself into philanthropic works for the benefit of the peasants by setting up schools, libraries and training facilities.[37]

Chertkov's desire to devote his life to the peasantry was not the only

7. Vladimir Chertkov as a young man, 1880s

reason he was drawn to Tolstoy. He was also inspired by unorthodox Christian ideals which he initially inherited from his mother, who had become a Protestant evangelist after the untimely deaths of her eldest and youngest sons. It was his dynamic mother, Elizaveta Ivanovna, who had been instrumental in bringing Lord Radstock to Russia in 1874. It was she who had effected his introduction to all the best salons in St Petersburg, and introduced him to her brother-in-law, Colonel Vasily Pashkov, who carried on Radstock's work after he was expelled from Russia in 1878. One of the richest men in Russia, Pashkov also came from the aristocracy, but after becoming an evangelical Christian he had eschewed high society salons for prayer meetings held at his house, which sometimes attracted over 1,000 followers. He had also founded the Society for the Encouragement of Spiritual and Ethical Reading which disseminated copies of the Gospels translated into Russian, and other edifying literature. When Chertkov had gone to England, he naturally met with Lord Radstock,[38] who gave him introductions to the British aristocratic and political elite, including the future Edward VII.[39]

Chertkov had practised a Christian way of life since returning from England, but he was not an evangelist like his mother. His religious views were much more in tune with Tolstoy's beliefs, which explains why, when they met, it felt to them almost as if they were already old friends. Tolstoy was the first person Chertkov had ever known who shared his views on the incompatibility of Christianity with military service.[40] As for Tolstoy, he was dazzled by his young visitor, and the bond that was immediately formed between them was strengthened by not only their shared religious convictions, but also their common aristocratic background.[41] Chertkov had found his messiah and Tolstoy had found the confidant he had longed for. Throughout their friendship, much of their communication was by letter: their correspondence fills five separate volumes of Tolstoy's collected works in the edition which Chertkov launched in the 1920s. Tolstoy had also found in Chertkov an unexpected source of protection, for his friend's formidable connections to the court meant they could embark on their programme of planned activities with a degree of impunity.[42] As well as proposing a publishing venture, Chertkov wanted to help disseminate Tolstoy's writings abroad, and soon after their first meeting he began translating *What I Believe* into English, a language of which he had a flawless command.[43]

Another new friend who provided crucial moral support in the later stages of finishing *What I Believe*, when Tolstoy felt like a 'writing machine', was Nikolay Ge, who came to Moscow to paint his portrait in 1884. In contrast to Kramskoy's portrait, in which the writer's gaze is firmly fixed on the viewer, Ge depicted Tolstoy sitting pen in hand at his desk, his head bowed over his manuscript in deep concentration.[44] By deliberately not showing Tolstoy's eyes, Ge broke with the conventional rules of portraiture, and many were shocked when his painting was first exhibited. Like Tolstoy, Ge was a firm believer in manual work (his speciality was building stoves), and he was one of the first 'Tolstoyans'. He tried to follow Tolstoy's precepts to the letter, and became a fanatical vegetarian, sometimes eating almost nothing at all. He also tried valiantly to make himself eat things he did not like, so refused buckwheat and chewed his way penitently through dishes of wheat grain with either hemp oil, or no oil at all, rather than butter. In 1886 he gave away all his property to his family. Like Tolstoy, he had a wife who did not share his views.[45]

Tolstoy's strategy for getting *What I Believe* past the censor was to write from a deliberately subjective point of view, print only fifty copies and set the price at an eye-watering twenty-five roubles, but he was deluding himself if thought his unequivocal rejection of both secular and ecclesiastical power would be condoned.[46] On 18 February 1884 the thirty-nine copies remaining at the printer were confiscated, but to Tolstoy's delight they were not destroyed. Instead they were sent to Petersburg, where, along with the eight copies which Tolstoy had been required to submit for inspection, they were delivered to the many high-ranking figures in the government and the imperial court who were anxious to read Tolstoy's latest work. They then passed the book on to others. In no time, *What I Believe* was also being lithographed and sold for four roubles a copy.[47] Tolstoy himself was a willing accomplice in the illegal samizdat operation, and paid scribes fifteen roubles to make copies of his manuscript for distribution.[48] French, German and English translations were soon underway.

What I Believe was an important work for Tolstoy, and one he had been building up to in his previous religious writings. He took particular care with its exposition as it was the first systematic explanation of his religious and ethical views, his 'creed'. Tolstoy wanted a religion which would stand up to rational scrutiny. He wanted a clear, straightforward set of rules to follow in his daily life, and he found them in Christ's five commandments in his Sermon on the Mount, which can be briefly summarised as follows:

1. Live in peace with all men ('anyone who is angry with his brother will be subject to judgement').
2. Do not lust ('anyone who looks at a woman lustfully has already committed adultery with her in his heart') and do not divorce ('anyone who divorces his wife, except for marital unfaithfulness, causes her to become an adulteress, and anyone who marries the divorced woman commits adultery').
3. Do not swear ('Do not swear at all: either by heaven, for it is God's throne; or by the earth, for it is his footstool; or by Jerusalem, for it is the city of the Great King').
4. Do not resist evil ('If someone strikes you on the right cheek, turn to him the other also').
5. Do not hate ('Love your enemies and pray for those who persecute you').

If everyone followed these commandments, there would be no more wars and no need for armies. Indeed, living a Tolstoyan Christian life would eradicate the need for courts, police officers, personal property and any form of government. Morality was the cornerstone of Christianity for Tolstoy, and he now saw life in simple black-and-white terms. As he writes in *What I Believe*:

> Everything which used to seem good and noble to me – ambition, fame, education, wealth, a complex and sophisticated lifestyle, environment, food, clothes, and formal manners – has become bad and sordid. Everything which seemed bad and sordid – the peasant lifestyle, obscurity, poverty, crudity, simple surroundings, food, clothes, manners – has become good and noble.[49]

It was not surprising that Nikolay Berdyaev later defined as one of Tolstoy's many paradoxes the fact that this man who was Russian to the core of his being started preaching 'Anglo-Saxon religiosity',[50] for there were striking parallels with the reformist views that Matthew Arnold had been promoting in Victorian England in the 1870s.

Like Tolstoy, Arnold had increasingly turned to religious questions later in his career, although in his case he was impelled by a desire to navigate the crisis caused by the resistance of the Church of England's conservative theologians to the onslaught of scientific, rational thought (Darwin's *Origin of Species* had been published in 1859). Tolstoy, of course, had met Arnold briefly in London in 1861, and when in 1885 he read *Literature and Dogma: An Essay towards a Better Apprehension of the Bible*, the controversial book Arnold published in 1873, he exclaimed excitedly in a letter to a friend that he had found half of his own ideas in it.[51] Tolstoy ensured that Arnold was sent a copy of *What I Believe* as soon as it appeared in translation. It was, incidentally, Matthew Arnold who first awakened a serious interest in Tolstoy in England, where he was largely unknown until the middle of the 1880s. In the essay he published in 1887, a few months before he died, Arnold introduced British readers to Tolstoy's fiction. As well as presenting a strong case for the superiority of *Anna Karenina* to *Madame Bovary*, it is interesting to note that he also presented a summary of Tolstoy's religious philosophy to date. While sympathetic to its general thrust, Arnold had some judicious comments to make. Even without having the opportunity to read any of Tolstoy's later religious writings, Arnold's main exposure of the basic flaw in Tolstoy's thinking, based on a reading of *What I Believe*, is in many ways unsurpassed in its lucidity and concision:

Christianity cannot be packed into any set of commandments. As I have somewhere or other said, 'Christianity is a source; no one supply of water and refreshment that comes from it can be called the sum of Christianity. It is a mistake, and may lead to much error, to exhibit any series of maxims, even those of the Sermon of the Mount, as the ultimate sum and formula into which Christianity may be run up.'[52]

Tolstoy was not a man to make concessions, however. In the spring of 1884, as he recovered from the exhaustion of completing the initial writing of *What I Believe* and then the various stages of proofreading (the number of changes he introduced at the first stage cost him about the same as the sum he was charged for the typesetting), he learned how to cobble shoes, and read Confucius and Lao Tzu.[53]

Family life in the Tolstoy home in Moscow was rather surreal in the early part of 1884. In one part of the house, Tolstoy was paring his footprint on the earth down to a minimum and castigating such depraved activities as physical adornment and dancing at balls, closely watched by the governor general.[54] In another part of the house, Sonya and Tanya were dressing up in tulle and velvet to go to society balls where they fraternised with the governor general, who went out of his way to be friendly and curry favour with them.[55] Sonya was still breast-feeding their two-year old son Alyosha, and she was pregnant again, but she was determined to enjoy herself. Tolstoy deplored the money his wife was spending on Tanya's coming-out that season. Each dress alone cost up to 250 roubles, and he was well aware that twenty-five horses could have been bought with that money. He was also pained to think of the old coachmen shivering in the cold outside grand mansions while their employers partied, and so he absconded back to Yasnaya Polyana for a while to rest his frayed nerves. Sonya was also pained to think of her husband sitting in his dirty woollen socks at home, sewing misshapen boots for their old servant Agafya Mikhailovna, while their teenage sons Ilya and Lev were being delinquent and neglecting their schoolwork. She was fed up with him being a 'holy fool', she complained to her sister, reneging on his duties as a father, and no longer even interested in being part of family life.[56] While Sonya wrote complaining letters to her sister Tanya, Tolstoy recorded in his diary, and in letters to Chertkov, the discord with his wife which prevented him from aligning their family's life with his convictions. He felt he was the only sane person living in a madhouse run by madmen. But it was Tolstoy who was the madman according to his brother Sergey, who had as little sympathy for his suffering as Sonya.[57]

Relations continued to be strained that summer when the family moved back to Yasnaya Polyana, and Tanya arrived as usual to take up her summer residence in the other house, along with her children (as a rule, her husband, Alexander Kuzminsky, did not join them). The summer days which Sonya spent with her sister were still the happiest time of year for her, but she was increasingly living apart from her husband. He had now started getting up even earlier, so he could do more physical work, and spent long days mowing with the peasants. He now also gave up eating meat, stopped drinking wine and tried to give up smoking.[58] His personal self-discipline was not sufficient to maintain a cool head in his altercations with Sonya, however, and by early June he was longing to leave Yasnaya Polyana and move away from his family. There was a particularly bitter argument with Sonya about money on 17 June, just before she gave birth. Late that afternoon Tolstoy decided to leave, and he got halfway to Tula before feelings of guilt made him turn back. When the two bearded young men playing cards in the house (two of his sons) told him the rest of the family were outside playing croquet he retreated to his study, to be woken at three in the morning by Sonya, who had gone into labour.

The birth of Alexandra (Sasha) was not a happy occasion – Sonya had not wanted another child, she had dreaded giving birth, and she hired a wet-nurse this time in a fit of pique. Later she explained in her autobiography that Tolstoy was perennially so cold and unpleasant with her during this time, and so unhelpful around the house, that she felt no compunction about defying him in this matter.[59] That July she was so unhappy that she could not refrain from unburdening herself in a letter to her husband's former confidante Alexandrine. 'Lyovochka has never been before in *such* an extreme frame of mind,' she wrote, describing how difficult it was to find any common ground between them where they could both make compromises. She also found it hard that Tolstoy was complaining about her in letters, and telling his correspondents how lonely he was.[60] Alexandrine was no doubt sympathetic. Her irascible relative had barely been in touch since they had fallen out over their divergent views on Christianity, and then suddenly that spring she had been bombarded with four letters from him in quick succession. Tolstoy wanted her to intercede on behalf of Anna Armfeldt, the widow of a Moscow University professor. Her daughter Natalya was a revolutionary who had been sentenced to fourteen years' hard labour in Kara, a particularly harsh prison in eastern Siberia, just north of the border with China (where convicts worked the gold mines). Natalya had fallen ill with tuberculosis, and her mother wanted to be able to settle near her.[61]

Tolstoy's relations with Sonya improved somewhat when post-natal complications made her ill.[62] Tanya reported to her absent husband in July that her sister was still weak, and that her brother-in-law was still preaching about the need to sell everything up and dismiss the servants, but he became more solicitous.[63] One rare source of merriment during these tense years was the Yasnaya Polyana post box. Every member of the household was invited to drop unsigned stories, news items, poems and anecdotes into a locked box placed on the landing by the grandfather clock for Sunday evening readings around the samovar. On 22 August 1884, which was Sonya's birthday, Tolstoy compiled twenty-three medical histories for the mentally ill inmates at the Yasnaya Polyana hospital, who all suffered from a particular mania. He began with himself, describing his own mania as *Weltverbesserungswahn* (a desire to improve the world), and its symptoms as a dissatisfaction with the status quo, condemnation of everyone but himself, an annoying loquacity with no thought for his listeners, and frequent descents from anger and irritability to an unnatural lachrymose sensitivity. He prescribed complete indifference from everyone around him to anything he might say as his cure.

Tolstoy diagnosed his wife as suffering from *petulantia toropigis maxima* (unruly haste), a condition causing the patient to believe that everything depends on her, and a concomitant fear that she cannot manage to do everything.[64] In her autobiography, Sonya records some of the 'Ideals of Yasnaya Polyana' that were posted:

- Lev Nikolayevich: Poverty, peace and harmony. To burn everything he used to have reverence for, and to have reverence for everything he has burned.
- Sofya Andreyevna: Seneca. To have 150 babies who will never grow up.
- Tatyana Andreyevna: Eternal youth, female emancipation.
- Ilya Lvovich: To carefully conceal from everyone that he has a heart, and to give the impression that he has killed 100 wolves.[65]

Sonya did not have much time to read, but she enjoyed leafing through a French edition of the Roman Stoic philosopher's complete works, which their friend Leonid Urusov had lent her, along with Marcus Aurelius, Plato and Epictetus.[66] Tolstoy was on to the transcendentalist philosophy of Ralph Waldo Emerson by this time.

By the autumn of 1884 family relations were much improved, partly because Tolstoy had been able to stay behind for a few weeks after everyone left for Moscow, and live according to his ideals. He dismissed the cook and the caretaker, cooked his own simple dishes like baked turnip, lit the samovar himself, stopped using horses and walked every evening down to the railway station to post his letters to Sonya and pick up the post.[67] He also took walks during the daytime to the highway to resume his conversations with pilgrims. He wrote to Sonya about meeting two old Stranniks from Siberia who had dedicated themselves to a life of permanent pilgrimage and were returning from Jerusalem and Mount Athos, a journey which they had undertaken without a single kopeck to their name. On another day he met two old gentlemen from the far north of Russia, whom he invited back to Yasnaya Polyana for tea – they completely drained the samovar. Tolstoy finally gave up hunting that autumn, having discovered, apart from a feeling of shame, that when he went out on horseback with his dogs he now hoped his quarry would get away. This meant a major change in his routine (his daughter Tanya had noted in her diary that he had killed fifty-five rabbits and ten foxes during the course of one autumn a few years earlier).[68] Tolstoy also now decided to take over the running of all the farming at Yasnaya Polyana from his steward,[69] and his spirits rose when Sonya decided she would not take their daughter Tanya into society for a second season, or attend any high-profile social events herself. But the dynamics within the family were also beginning to change, which raised Tolstoy's spirits. Although Tolstoy's relationship with his sons remained largely cool, his elder daughters, particularly Masha, were slowly coming round to his point of view.

In November 1884 Tolstoy published two of the draft openings to his abandoned novel about the Decembrists. It was the first fiction he had published for an educated audience since *Anna Karenina*, but his heart was now in a new project conceived by Vladimir Chertkov. Tolstoy had been engaged in a lively correspondence with Chertkov (whom he had already sent thirty-six letters since their meeting the previous year), and amongst their topics for discussion was a plan to produce quality literature for the masses. Chertkov wanted to emulate the pamphlets which had been put out under the auspices of the (now banned) Society for the Encouragement of Spiritual and Ethical Reading by Vasily Pashkov, who had just been sent into permanent exile by the government. He had met Pashkov in England that summer, and realised that inexpensive publications for the masses offered an excellent means to promote Tolstoy's new creed.[70] Tolstoy was only too keen to collaborate, and they discussed these plans further when Chertkov came to Moscow in November. After a productive meeting with Ivan Sytin, an enterprising young publisher of popular woodcuts and pictures who had worked his way up from lowly beginnings as an apprentice in a bookshop, Chertkov was ready to sign a contract. The new publishing house they set up was given the name 'Posrednik' (The Intermediary), and they agreed they would publish superior but accessible Russian and foreign literature in translation with illustrations for a few kopecks a copy. That they were able to do so may well have been due to Chertkov's mother, who gave her son a 20,000-rouble annual allowance – more than the Tolstoy family's entire expenditure in a year.[71] Chertkov's wealth proved to be a rare but lingering bone of contention between him and Tolstoy.[72]

In April 1885 Chertkov opened a bookshop in Moscow, set up a warehouse in St Petersburg and hired a young female assistant, whom he would later marry, and a co-editor, Pavel Biryukov, who was to become another of Tolstoy's devoted friends and disciples (in time he would write a voluminous and reverential biography). Biryukov was a graduate of the Naval Academy, and had been working as a physicist in the main observatory in St Petersburg. He came from the nobility, but occupied a far lower place in the pecking order than either Chertkov or Tolstoy, which became a stumbling block when he tried to marry Tolstoy's daughter Masha a few years later.[73]

The Intermediary was a huge success – 12 million of the little books it produced were sold in the first four years of its existence. They filled a real gap in the market, where previously there was little available to the burgeoning numbers of literate peasants and urban workers beyond saints' lives and crudely written stories of a very low literary quality. Tolstoy advised Chertkov on which foreign authors to publish (including Dickens and Eliot), but he also made a very valuable original contribution himself. The Intermediary presented him with an opportunity to pick up the work of his *ABC* where he had left off, and, in fact, one of The Intermediary's publications was his story 'Captive in the Caucasus', which he had written back in the 1870s for his *ABC*.[74] He also wrote twenty finely executed new stories over the next few years for The Intermediary, and a select few journals.[75] These brief tales were considerably better crafted than the boots he made, which he proudly described to Sonya as 'un bijou'. Tolstoy was an expert at retelling fables and folk stories in a vivid and simple way, deploying humour and an admirably light touch with the moral each contained.

While Tolstoy was busy writing stories for the masses, his wife was learning the ropes in a different area of the publishing sector. Her very real anxieties about the family's loss of income had led Tolstoy to suggest that she produce the next editions of his collected works and his *ABC* books. Previously the sales of Tolstoy's collected works had been handled by the husband of his niece Varya (Masha's daughter). Sonya now decided to retain the rights to the publication of her husband's works, and to convert the outbuilding at their Moscow house into a warehouse. In January 1885 Sonya got down to business, and the proofs for the new, fifth edition started arriving the following month. New works by Tolstoy completed since 1881 which were earmarked for the new twelfth volume of this edition included his novella *The Death of Ivan Ilyich*, 'Strider', and a couple of the stories Tolstoy had just written for The Intermediary, including 'The Tale of Ivan the Fool'.[76] In February Sonya set off to St Petersburg to obtain permission for this volume to be published, and also to consult Dostoyevsky's widow about the most profitable way to go about her new publishing venture. One of the most valuable pieces of advice from Anna Grigorievna was to give booksellers only five per cent discount.[77] She also recommended that Sonya should not insist on each volume being published in chronological order. Sonya proved to be an accomplished businesswoman. The twelfth volume was banned, but in November 1885 she was already making her second visit to St Petersburg to lobby for the ban to be lifted (it was eventually published in 1886), and to initiate the process of publishing the sixth edition of Tolstoy's works.[78] By 1889 she was already releasing the eighth edition.[79]

Letting Sonya publish everything he had written before his spiritual crisis (plus the occasional new work of fiction) was Tolstoy's concession to her, and he helped her with the proofs, but he was much more interested in proselytising. Since 1882 he had been working on and off on a major new treatise, *What*

Then Must We Do?, which drew on his experiences in the Moscow slums while working for the census. Its topics were poverty, exploitation and the evils of money and private property, but the solution to these perennial problems was not technology or modernisation, but physical labour, humility and personal endeavour:

> So these are the replies I found to my question: What must we do?
>
> First: not to lie to myself; and – however far my path of life may be from the true path disclosed by my reason – not to fear the truth.
>
> Secondly: to reject the belief in my own righteousness and in privileges and peculiarities distinguishing me from others, and to acknowledge myself as being to blame.
>
> Thirdly: to fulfil the eternal, indubitable law of man, and with the labour of my whole being to struggle with nature for the maintenance of my own and other people's lives.[80]

At the end of 1884 Tolstoy handed over the first chapters for publication in *Russian Thought*. Despite the eternal optimism of his editors, the censor vetoed their publication, but copies were naturally made from the proofs for informal distribution.

Tolstoy's religious works were now also beginning to reach a wide audience abroad: in 1884 Mikhail Elpidin had published *Confession* as a separate book for the first time in Geneva, and in 1885 French, German and English translations of *What I Believe* were published. In the volume *Christ's Christianity*, published in London, Chertkov included his translations of *Confession* and *The Gospel in Brief* along with *What I Believe*. Readers outside Russia thus became acquainted with Tolstoy's religious writings and his major fiction simultaneously, as if his entire career to date had been telescoped: while the first French translation of *War and Peace* appeared in 1879, it was not until 1885 that *Anna Karenina* was also published in French translation. The first English translations (completed by the American Nathan Haskell Dole) of both novels appeared in 1886.[81]

While Tolstoy was keen to disseminate his ideas abroad, it was in Russia that he wanted to make an impact, and the first concrete sign that he was succeeding came in the spring of 1885, when it became known that a young man had refused to serve in the army on the grounds of his Tolstoy-inspired religious convictions.[82] A number of writers and thinkers now started to make an impact on Tolstoy's thought, as it continued to evolve. Although he had by now articulated the major tenets of his new worldview, he remained very receptive to currents of thought which seemed to echo or amplify his own ideas, and there were three important people who shaped his thinking in 1885: an American political economist in New York, a self-educated peasant in Siberia, and an émigré religious positivist based in London.

Henry George, who rose from humble origins in Philadelphia to stand against Theodore Roosevelt for Mayor of New York in 1886, was an evangelical Protestant who wrote a best-selling book in 1879 about social inequality called *Progress and Poverty*.[83] Articles about this book began appearing in the Russian press in 1883, and in February 1885 Tolstoy started reading the book itself. He was riveted by George's central idea that all land should become common property. Regarding it as a major turning point, he predicted that the emancipation from private ownership would be as momentous as the emancipation of the serfs.[84] George's philosophy was inspired by the observations he had made during his extensive international travels. He had noticed that poverty was greater in populated areas than in those which were less developed. In his book he argued for a single tax, so that private property, and ultimately poverty, could be eliminated. Tolstoy was all for the abolition of private property, but at this point he was quite hostile to the idea of a tax applied by a government, due to the element of coercion inherent in such an action. Nevertheless, he would come to change his mind a decade later, and wholeheartedly embrace George's proposals.

In July 1885 Tolstoy found himself being stimulated by another thinker in whom he recognised a kindred spirit when a political exile in Siberia sent him a manuscript by Timofey Bondarev. He had first read about *The Triumph of the Farmer or Industry and Parasitism* a few months earlier in a journal article, and was curious to read it. Taking his inspiration from Genesis 3: 19 ('By the sweat of your brow you will eat your food ...'), Bondarev argued that it was each person's moral and religious duty to earn their bread through physical labour, regardless of their social station. Tolstoy was electrified by the ideas contained in this manuscript, and by the author's passionate diatribe against the wealthy ruling classes. He was also struck by the rich mixture of biblical and colloquial language the treatise was written in, and he read it aloud to everyone at Yasnaya Polyana on the day he received it. He then set about

8. Pencil drawing by Repin of Tolstoy reading in his grandfather's chair at Yasnaya Polyana, 1887

writing to the author, and finding out more about him. Timofey Bondarev, it turned out, was a former serf from southern Russia. In the 1850s, at the age of thirty-seven, he had been forced to abandon his wife and four children when his owner recruited him into the army, where he faced the standard period of conscription of twenty-five years. In 1867, after serving for ten years, Bondarev was arrested for renouncing his Orthodox beliefs and becoming a Subbotnik ('Sabbatarian' – a splinter group of the Molokans). He was exiled for life to a remote village on the Yenisey river, not far from Mongolia, along with other sectarian 'apostates'. As he was the only person who could read and write in the village, he set up a school, in which he taught for thirty years. He devoted the rest of his time to tilling the land and writing his treatise.

Tolstoy agreed with 'everything' in the treatise, and entered into an enthusiastic correspondence with Bondarev, telling him that he frequently read out his manuscript to his acquaintances, though adding rather tactlessly that most of them usually got up and walked out. He also confided to Bondarev that this had given him the idea of narrating his manuscript whenever he had boring visitors: it was a successful ploy in getting rid of them.[85] Tolstoy went out of his way to get Bondarev's manuscript published. After its inclusion in the journal *Russian Wealth* was censored at the last moment in 1886, he persevered, only to see it being physically cut from *Russian Antiquity* in 1888. Eventually an edited version of Bondarev's manuscript, accompanied by an article by Tolstoy, appeared later in the year in *The Russian Cause*, its editor receiving a caution from the Ministry of Internal Affairs as a result.[86] Much later it was published by The Intermediary, prefaced by Tolstoy's introduction.[87] Both Bondarev and Syutayev were pivotal figures for Tolstoy in his quest to persuade people to live in harmony with the land, as he made clear in a footnote to *What Then Must We Do?*, which he finally finished revising in 1886:

> In the course of my lifetime, there have been two Russian thinking people who have had a deep moral influence on me, enriched my thinking, and clarified my worldview. These people were not Russian poets, scholars or preachers, but are two remarkable men who are alive today, and have both spent their whole lives working on the land – the peasants Syutayev and Bondarev.[88]

Another crucial person in Tolstoy's campaign to promote a life of non-violence in harmony with the land was William Frey, the gifted son of an army general from the Baltic nobility who had abruptly turned his back on a brilliant military career in St Petersburg in the 1860s in order to seek the truth. In 1868, at the age of twenty-nine, after dabbling with radical left-wing politics, Frey emigrated with his bride to America and changed his name from Vladimir Geins to the symbolic Frey ('free'). In the mid-1870s he had been part of the disastrous Kansas commune along with Vasily Alexeyev and Alexander Malikov, but in 1884 he moved with his family to London, by this time a fervent positivist, and a devotee of Comte and Spencer. The following summer he set off to preach the 'religion of mankind' in Russia, where he very quickly came across samizdat copies of *Confession* and *What I Believe*, which made a deep impression on him. After sending Tolstoy a sixty-page letter outlining the superiority of the 'religion of mankind', he received an invitation to visit Yasnaya Polyana, and he arrived in October 1885.[89] Tolstoy was enchanted by Frey, whom he described as a serious, clever and sincere person with a pure heart. He was not persuaded by Frey's arguments about religion, but he was encouraged by his example to persevere with his efforts to give up meat, alcohol and tobacco. And he was captivated by Frey's stories of life in the Wild West, and his experiences of living in communes where there was no private property, and where everyone worked with their hands rather than with their heads.

Frey was interesting, Tolstoy wrote teasingly to his sister-in-law Tanya, because of his absolute refusal to recognise 'Anke Cake', which was his ultimate symbol of bourgeois self-satisfaction and unearned privilege. Anke Cake was served on special occasions at Yasnaya Polyana, and was named after a friend and medical colleague of Sonya's father, also of German descent. In her recipe book, Sonya does not provide instructions, merely a list of ingredients:

Anke Cake
1 pound of flour
½ pound of butter
¼ pound of caster sugar
3 egg yolks
1 glass of water
The butter should come straight from the cellar, it needs to be on the cold side.

Filling
Melt a quarter of a pound of butter, then mix in two eggs, half a pound of caster sugar, the grated rind of two lemons and the juice of three lemons. Heat until it is as thick as honey.[90]

There was also a sour cream version, which involved mixing ten eggs with twenty dessert spoons of sour cream, a cup of sugar, and two dessert spoons of flour, lining a tin with jam, pouring the mixture onto it and baking it in the oven.[91] The puritanical Frey would have considered it immoral to partake of something so rich and indulgent, and Tolstoy was now of the same opinion. Frey had a further meeting with Tolstoy in Moscow that December, but he was forced to leave Russia in March 1886 after failing to win over Tolstoy, or indeed anyone else, to his religion of mankind. He returned to London, where he died in extreme poverty of tuberculosis two years later at the age of forty-nine. Tolstoy recollected that he was one of the 'best' people he had ever known.[92]

Tolstoy had focused his energies in the first half of the 1880s on articulating and disseminating his new worldview. In 1886, after he finished setting out the practical proposals contained in *What Then Must We Do?*, he turned to the abstract realm of ideas. His new project was initially conceived as a treatise 'about life and death', in which he wanted to set out the philosophy underpinning his ideas. Even though he may have stopped feeling suicidal, thoughts of death had never left Tolstoy, as can be seen from all three of his major artistic works written in the 1880s (*The Death of Ivan Ilych*, *The Power of Darkness* and *The Kreutzer Sonata*), the last two of which deal with violent death by murder. Death was also never far away in Tolstoy's personal life, but he now had a new attitude to it. In the late summer of 1885 he had been saddened to hear of the death of his faithful friend and supporter Leonid Urusov, whom he had accompanied him on a trip to the Crimea that spring (it was the first time he had been back to Sebastopol since the war).[93] More testing, however, was the experience of death in the family: in January 1886 four-year-old Alyosha died. Tolstoy discovered that he was now able to approach the death of his youngest son with equanimity. He wrote to tell Chertkov that he had previously regarded the death of a child as cruel and incomprehensible, but now saw it in a positive light.[94]

Sonya's only response to Alyosha's death was grief, but despite feeling distraught, she shrank from paying the 250 roubles required for burial at the prestigious cemetery next to the Novodevichy Convent, which was close to their house. Instead, she and the family's nanny placed the small coffin in the sleigh they had only recently used to take Alyosha to the zoo, and travelled north of Moscow to bury him at Pokrovskoye, where the Bers family had rented a dacha when she was a young girl.[95] In November 1886 Sonya had to cope with another death when her sixty-year-old mother fell gravely ill, and she too travelled to the Crimea. She was with her mother in Yalta during her last days.[96] If Tolstoy barely seemed to register the demise of Lyubov Alexandrovna, his old friend from childhood,[97] it was perhaps because he himself was seriously unwell that autumn. Death was an ever-present subject in his conversations, and in his correspondence.[98]

The thirty-five chapters of Tolstoy's voluminous treatise about life and death, which was later given the final title *On Life*, present the philosophical foundations underpinning his new worldview. He invested a great deal of mental energy in the exposition of his ideas, writing over 2,000 pages before the manuscript was complete in August 1887.[99] Sonya agreed to copy it out, which helped to create a peaceful atmosphere between them during its composition. Although she still could not accept the fundamental proposition that one should reject the 'material, personal life' in favour of the life of the spirit and 'universal love', as she noted in her diary,[100] she liked the fact that it was not tendentious like his earlier religious writings. Nevertheless, a work which replaced religious doctrine with reason and personal conscience never stood a chance of being approved by the censor. It had been planned that the 600 copies printed in 1888 would constitute a new thirteenth volume of Tolstoy's collected works, but the Holy Synod ordered their confiscation. All but three copies were burned, and the first publication of *On Life* was the French translation which appeared in 1889. The Archbishop of Kherson, who had examined the treatise, confided in a letter to one of Tolstoy's acquaintances that the Holy Synod was now seriously considering anathematising him.[101]

After *The Death of Ivan Ilych*, which had won many accolades from critics, Tolstoy wrote only two major artistic works in the late 1880s: the play *The Powers of Darkness*, and the novella *The Kreutzer Sonata*. He had first tackled the dramatic genre back in the 1860s, but had taken neither of his efforts back then very seriously. Now he was drawn towards popular drama. The books published by The Intermediary had already immeasurably improved the calibre of literature available to the peasantry, and Tolstoy wanted to transform the crude repertoire of drama on offer to the masses. He began in the spring of 1886 with a comedy on the evils of alcoholism called *The First Distiller*. It was published by The Intermediary and then staged in June at the open-air theatre attached to a porcelain factory outside St Petersburg. Despite the rain, 3,000 workers made up an enthusiastic audience. Two years later it was banned by the theatrical censor for featuring imps and devils, and an act set in hell.[102]

The Powers of Darkness, which is also drawn from peasant life, is a much more serious work. Based on a recent criminal case involving murder and adultery heard in the Tula court, it was completed in the autumn of 1886. The theatrical censor immediately banned it. This was a setback, as the script had already been typeset at three different printers, and Tolstoy had agreed that the play could be performed for the actress Maria Savina's benefit night – he himself was very keen to see it staged. Sonya fired off a letter to the government's head of censorship, Evgeny Feoktistkov, who expressly forbade its performance, but did now consent to its publication. Over 100,000 copies were printed in the first months of 1887, including an edition with The Intermediary which sold for three kopecks.[103] Meanwhile, Chertkov started a sophisticated public relations operation. As anticipated, the reading he organised at the home of Countess Shuvalov, using his formidable society connections, soon set people talking. Not only was it reported positively in the press, but soon the Tsar's curiosity was aroused. A special reading was arranged for him in the Winter Palace on 27 January, which was attended by the Empress, grand dukes and duchesses, and other members of the court. Alexander III declared that he liked the play very much, and ordered it to be staged by the Imperial Theatres. He was soon forced to back down, however, after being reprimanded by Pobedonostsev. The Chief Procurator had been horrified to learn of the Tsar's irresponsible attitude to the 'crude realism' and 'denigration of moral feeling' in this appalling play – he told the Tsar he had never seen anything like it.[104]

There was much worse to come. *The Kreutzer Sonata*, a worthy successor to *Anna Karenina* in terms of its association of carnal love with extreme violence, would be his most scandalous work yet. It owed its inspiration to several sources. First of all there was an anonymous female correspondent who wrote to complain to Tolstoy in February 1886 about the distressing situation of women in contemporary society, and their debasement by men.[105] Then there was the acquaintance who told a story about once sitting in a train carriage opposite a man who confessed that he had been unfaithful to his wife. And there was a direct musical stimulus: on several occasions in 1887 Tolstoy's son Sergey, a fine pianist, accompanied Lev and Misha's violin teacher Yuly Lyasotta in performances of Beethoven's Violin Sonata No. 9, the Kreutzer Sonata, both in Moscow and at Yasnaya Polyana. Tolstoy certainly knew Beethoven's Kreutzer Sonata very well, and it was one of relatively few opuses to feature on the list of his favourite musical works later compiled by Sergey.[106] It is the first of the sonata's three movements which has the greatest parallel with the story. The frenzied dialogue between violin and piano in its central *presto* section performed by Pozdnyshev's wife and her male violinist partner suggests to Pozdnyshev a dialogue of a different kind, which provokes him to fits of jealousy he can eventually no longer control.

On one of the occasions when the sonata was performed at the Tolstoys' home, the painter Repin was present, and Tolstoy even toyed with the idea of his friend accompanying his story with a painting.[107] Tolstoy would have certainly discussed his ideas for the story with Repin, for he found himself posing for another portrait in the summer of 1887 during the painter's stay at Yasnaya Polyana. They had been acquainted for seven years by this point, but Repin had bided his time, clearly wanting to get to know Tolstoy better before fixing him on canvas. The portrait, which depicts him sitting calmly in a chair with a book in his hand, dressed in black, seemed to many to be reminiscent of an Old Testament prophet.

Another oblique source for *The Kreutzer Sonata* were certain events in Tolstoy's own family life which touched a raw nerve. In the autumn of 1887 his second eldest son Ilya proposed to his sweetheart Sofya Filosofova. Tolstoy was a concerned father, as the couple did not have very good prospects and were both very young: Ilya was twenty-one, Sofya was twenty. Ilya had failed to graduate from his lycée, so was ineligible for university, and he had returned from spending two years in the army without any plans for earning his living. The Tolstoys were friends with his fiancée's family, but they were well aware she was no better off: her father worked at the Moscow art school where Tanya had trained. Tolstoy wrote Ilya several letters entreating him to consider carefully the step he was about to take, but his son's heart was set. There were further reasons why Tolstoy should have marital relations at the forefront of his mind at this time. In September 1887 he and Sonya celebrated their twenty-fifth wedding anniversary, and his wife was pregnant again. Their son Ivan (Vanechka) was born on 31 March 1888, a month after Ilya's marriage. On Christmas Eve of that year their first grandchild Anna was born.

Apart from the Tolstoys' eldest child Sergey (who had left Moscow University and was now working for the Tula peasant bank), only Ilya lived away from home at this time.[108] In the spring of 1889 Tolstoy went to visit him and his family, and was appalled to find coachmen, carriages, horses and other trappings of a comfortable lifestyle which he felt they should abjure. Ilya was not the only one of his sons with whom Tolstoy seriously fell out during these years.[109] His third eldest son Lev, then in his last year of school, constantly argued with him. Tolstoy also seriously risked falling out with his daughter Masha, whom his follower Pavel Biryukov proposed to at the end of 1888. Sonya was not prepared for her daughter to marry a 'Tolstoyan', even if he was of noble background, and she blocked it. Biryukov went away to lick his wounds but reappeared in Tolstoy's life in 1891 after sailing to Japan with the future Nicholas II on his nine-month 'grand tour'.[110] Masha accepted her lot meekly. Since she was Tolstoy's favourite daughter, whom he relied upon for assistance and moral support, he was secretly glad, and he himself would later thwart Masha's romantic dreams on more than one occasion in a selfish attempt to keep her near him. Tolstoy had little to do with his youngest children Andrey, Misha and Alexandra, eleven, nine and four respectively, who barely saw their father, let alone baby Vanechka. Unlike the elder children, whom he had personally taught, the youngest came under the care of tutors and governesses, and were essentially brought up by Sonya.

Ilya's marriage, and the births of his son and granddaughter in quick succession, had a profound effect on Tolstoy, particularly the birth of Vanechka, which had been very difficult for Sonya. She was forty-three, he was fifty-nine, and he felt ashamed that while he had successfully been able to fight the temptation to drink wine and eat meat, he had been unable to master his physical desire for his wife, particularly knowing how reluctant she was to become pregnant again. He despised himself for his weakness, and ended up venting his self-loathing in his fiction, which Sonya perceived as barbs personally directed at her. Having exalted the sanctity of marriage in *What I Believe* a few years earlier, Tolstoy now regarded it as an institution to be roundly condemned. He had always taken violent exception to the idea of marriage without children, but now even procreation could not redeem its sinfulness. Not for the first time in his life the mercurial writer had changed his tune. Well might Sonya find her husband's sudden advocacy of chastity, even within marriage, hypocritical and hard to take. According to her first Russian biographer, she became pregnant yet again in 1890, and was relieved to miscarry.[111]

Tolstoy had started *The Kreutzer Sonata* in 1887, but most of the work on it took place in the spring and summer of 1889. One book which made an impact on him during this time was a practical guide to gynaecology and midwifery called *Tokology: A Book for Every Woman*, which was issued by the Sanitary Publishing Company in Chicago in 1883 ('tokology' comes from the Greek word for obstetrics). It had been sent to him by its author Dr Alice Bunker Stockham, who had been brought up as a Quaker, and was one of the very first women to qualify as a doctor in the United States. Having specialised in gynaecology, she came to believe that women should not have continual pregnancies, and that men should control their sexual urges.[112] She also advocated abstinence from alcohol and tobacco and campaigned against prostitution. The book was of interest to Tolstoy for religious rather than medical reasons, he later told his daughter Tanya, and he wrote in November 1888 to tell Alice Stockham in his slightly creaky but elegant English that it was 'truly a book, not only for woman but for mankind':

> Without labour in this direction mankind cannot go forward; and it seems to me especially in the matter treated in your book in chapter XI ['Chastity in Marital Relations' – Stockham discouraged sexual relations during pregnancy], we are very much behindhand. It is strange, that last week I have written a long letter to one of my friends [Chertkov] on the same subject. That sexual relation without the wish and possibility of having children is worse than prostitution and onanism, and in fact is both. I say it is worse, because a person who commits these crimes, not being married, is always conscious of doing wrong, but a husband and a wife, which commit the same sin, think that they are quite righteous.[113]

Tolstoy had indeed just written to Chertkov to castigate himself for the fact that it was too late to atone for having lived 'like an animal'.[114] In October

1889, the month in which his sister Masha decided to take the veil (she spent a year living with 400 nuns at a convent in Tula before moving to the convent next to Optina Pustyn), Alice Stockham came to visit Tolstoy at Yasnaya Polyana.[115] She probably quickly discovered that they were not in complete agreement about everything – she was not as uncompromising as Tolstoy, for example, when it came to condemning all sex that was not for procreative purposes,[116] but they enjoyed rewarding conversations about the American sects which practised chastity. In 1892 a translation of her book with an introduction by Tolstoy was published in Russia. It was because Stockham viewed childbirth in such sacred terms that she promoted the idea of sexual continence. Nevertheless, her novel ideas about a spiritualised form of human intimacy were not always well received. In her later book on the 'ethics of marriage', her 'method of promoting marital happiness [whereby] sexual intimacy may take place without completing the act' received withering scorn from a critic writing for a scholarly journal.[117]

Completion of the ninth and final draft of *The Kreutzer Sonata* provoked the question of where it could be published. Chertkov wanted the story for The Intermediary, Sonya wanted it for the new edition of the collected works, while Tolstoy now only cared about renouncing his copyright and avoiding arguments. On this occasion Tolstoy's story started circulating in samizdat even before it was submitted to the censor. The manuscript was taken to St Petersburg by Tolstoy's niece Masha Kuzminskaya, who arranged a reading attended by thirty friends, including Alexandrine and Nikolay Strakhov. After another late-night reading at the offices of The Intermediary, the editorial staff portioned the manuscript amongst themselves and then sat up all night to copy it before returning it to the Kuzminskys the next morning. Within a few days, much to Tolstoy's chagrin (he was only ever content to disseminate his work after the proofreading stage, which always involved him making myriad corrections), 300 lithographed copies appeared, which themselves were soon copied and distributed further. The story soon became the hottest property in St Petersburg, and sold for the exorbitant sum of ten, and sometimes even fifteen roubles (Sonya sold Tolstoy's entire collected works for eight roubles).[118]

It was agreed that *The Kreutzer Sonata* would be published first in an ephemeral weekly newspaper which did not have such strict censorship, and then handed over to Sonya,[119] but rumours that it would be banned even from this publication started spreading at the beginning of December 1889. They were confirmed later that month.[120] In the detailed review of the story Pobedonostsev sent his colleague Evgeny Feoktistov in February 1890, he conceded it was a 'powerful' work, and that he could not in good conscience ban a story which promoted chastity in the name of morality, but the overwhelmingly bleak message this sent out about the future of the human race made it unacceptable for publication. Alexander III enjoyed the story as much as *The Power of Darkness* when it was read to him at the Winter Palace, but his wife was shocked – as Theodore Roosevelt would be when translations reached the United States later that year. As US Attorney General, he forbade the distribution of the newspapers which printed it. By February 1890 illegal copies of *The Kreutzer Sonata* were being read all over Moscow, as we know from statements by Anton Chekhov, who had largely left his medical career behind and was by now a celebrated writer. He had been publishing under his own name in Russia's most prestigious literary journals for twelve years at this point, and was just beginning to appear on Tolstoy's radar. In the letter that Chekhov wrote to his friend Alexey Pleshcheyev about *The Kreutzer Sonata*, his typically incisive, clear-sighted observations bring a breath of fresh air into a debate that was highly charged:

> Did you really not like *The Kreutzer Sonata*? I don't say that it is a work
> of immortal genius – I'm not able to judge that – but I do consider that,
> compared to most of what is being written today both here and abroad,
> it would be hard to find anything to compare with the importance of its
> theme and the beauty of its execution. Aside from its artistic merits, which
> are in places stupendous, we must above all be grateful to the story for
> its power to excite our minds to their limits. Reading it, you can scarcely
> forbear to exclaim: 'That's so true!' or alternatively 'That's stupid!' There
> is no doubt that it has some irritating defects. As well as those you have
> listed, there is one for which it is hard to forgive the author, and that is his
> arrogance in discussing matters about which he understands nothing and
> is prevented by obstinacy from even wanting to understand anything. Thus
> his opinions on syphilis, foundling hospitals, women's distaste for sexual
> intercourse and so on, are not only contentious but show what an ignorant
> man in some respects he is, a man who has never in his long life taken the
> trouble to read one or two books written by specialists on the subject. But
> at the same time the story's virtues render these faults so insignificant that

they waft away practically unnoticed, like feathers on the wind, and if we do notice them they serve merely to remind us of the fate of all human endeavour without exception, which is to be incomplete and never entirely free of blemishes.[121]

Chekhov undertook his momentous journey to study the notorious penal colony on the island of Sakhalin in the summer of 1890, and when he came back that autumn he was able to read the afterword that Tolstoy had now written – also in samizdat. In response to the furore caused by his story, Tolstoy clarified that chastity was merely an ideal, and that he was not advocating the end of the human race. The time Chekhov spent in Siberia changed him, and also his view of Tolstoy's story, as in the letter he wrote in December 1890 to his great friend Alexey Suvorin (editor of *New Times*), his outlook was quite different:

> Before my trip, *The Kreutzer Sonata* was a great event for me, but now I find it ridiculous and it seems quite absurd … To hell with the philosophy of the great men of this world! All great wise men are as despotic as generals and as rude and insensitive as generals, because they are confident of their impunity. Diogenes spat in people's beards knowing nothing would come of it; Tolstoy lambasts doctors as scoundrels and exposes his ignorance of the important issues because he is another Diogenes whom no one will arrest or criticise in the newspapers …[122]

By the spring of 1891 *The Kreutzer Sonata* had still not been published, and Sonya decided to take matters into her own hands. Despite the personal affront she felt with regard to the content of *The Kreutzer Sonata*, she was keen to see it in print – in her edition. Accordingly, she had gone ahead and had the story typeset in Moscow, but a decision was made on 25 February that neither the story nor the afterword Tolstoy had written could be included in the thirteenth volume of his collected works. On 1 March, the day after the tenth anniversary of the assassination of Alexander II, Tolstoy was even formally anathematised for the first time in a sermon read in Kharkov, which was then published. *The Kreutzer Sonata* was condemned as an 'incoherent, filthy and amoral story'. Ten days later Sonya received word about the ban, and on 28 March she set off for St Petersburg with the intention of petitioning for an audience with the Tsar, so she could ask him personally for permission to publish *The Kreutzer Sonata*. It was granted on the proviso that the story was only published as part of the multi-volume collected works that were less readily available to vulnerable younger readers. Alexander III was, in fact, very gracious, and in an apparent nod to rumours that Vladimir Chertkov was the illegitimate son of Alexander II, Sonya noted in her diary that their tone of voice and manner of speaking were somewhat similar.[123] Empress Maria Fyodorovna, who also received Sonya, was just as solicitous as her husband.[124] The thirteenth volume of Tolstoy's collected works appeared in June 1891.[125] Naturally Pobedonostsev was furious when he learned of the Tsar's leniency.[126] That Alexander III was consistently indulgent towards Tolstoy's subversive activities makes one wonder whether he was protected by his friendship with the influential Chertkov. There is certainly an eerie resemblance between photographs of the young Alexander III and Vladimir Chertkov – perhaps they really were half-brothers.

Sonya's trip to St Petersburg was another nail in the coffin of the Tolstoys' marriage. Tolstoy regarded the very idea of petitioning the Tsar as demeaning, and he wished for no profits to be made from his writing. Sonya, on the other hand, felt bound to earn money even if just to pay for the upkeep of their nine children. Unceasing arguments now led Tolstoy to make a decision to renounce all his property. In April 1891 the entire family gathered at Yasnaya Polyana to sort out the allocations on an equal basis. Sergey, for example, received Nikolskoye, which had once belonged to Tolstoy's brother Nikolay, but was obliged to pay his sister Tanya and his mother a certain sum of money over the next fifteen years. Lev received the Samara estate and, as the youngest, three-year-old Vanechka by tradition received the bulk of Yasnaya Polyana, along with Sonya. Masha, as her father's devoted daughter and follower, renounced her share (although she would change her mind when she eventually married in 1897).[127] The arguments with Sonya continued when Tolstoy insisted she send to the press a letter announcing his renunciation of the copyright on his writings. It finally appeared in all of Russia's major newspapers on 19 September 1891.[128]

The whole experience of dividing up his estate reminded Tolstoy of a famous literary antecedent, and he told his children to go away and read *King Lear*.[129] It was probably the only time in his life that he actually recommended Shakespeare, but he had clearly been ruminating on *King Lear* for a while.

In 1888 he had talked about the play to the campaigning journalist William Stead, who arrived in Yasnaya Polyana that May fresh from his audience with Alexander III in St Petersburg (he seems to have been the only man ever to have interviewed a Russian tsar). Stead was anxious to quiz Tolstoy about English authors: 'Shakespeare, of course, came first,' he later recalled. 'He said that most of his plays were translated into Russian, and some of them were very popular. "Which most?" I asked. "*King Lear*," said he, instantly; "it embodies the experience of every Russian *izba*."'[130] The nearest British equivalent to Tolstoy in terms of his zeal to expose the hypocrisy of Victorian society, and focus attention on poverty and vice, Stead was a controversial figure, but also a committed pacifist (he was on his way to take part in a peace congress in New York in 1912 when he went down with the *Titanic*).[131] The character of King Lear at the end of Shakespeare's play, meanwhile, is English literature's nearest equivalent to the holy fool (*yurodivy*) – that peculiarly Russian form of sainthood to which Tolstoy aspired, and which is not encountered in any other religious culture.

Russia's holy fools deliberately challenged social conventions to mock the falsehood of the temporal world, unafraid of speaking the truth to all classes, including rulers. Relinquishing all material comforts, they dressed in rags and led ascetic lives like the vagabond Stranniks, voluntarily accepting humiliation and insults in order to conquer their pride and thus achieve greater humility and meekness. Since they lived amongst people, unlike hermits in monasteries, and so were in the public eye, they went out of their way to avoid being accorded any respect for their piety, and welcomed censure. Tolstoy had known and revered holy fools from the days of his childhood, thanks to his pious aunts who welcomed them to Yasnaya Polyana. *Childhood*, his first work of fiction, notably features a holy fool, as does *War and Peace*, and it can been argued that three other characters in that novel, Pierre, Natasha and Kutuzov, are 'stylised' holy fools.[132] Pashenka, the heroine in 'Father Sergius', the story Tolstoy worked on between 1890 and 1898, is another version of the holy fool. Back in 1877 Tolstoy had told his friend Strakhov that he most wanted to be a holy fool rather than a monk, and after his religious crisis he expressed the view that the best path to goodness was to be an involuntary holy fool. But projecting oneself as worse than in reality was a conscious act for a holy fool, and was a strategy adopted by Tolstoy from the time he wrote his historic letter to Alexander III in 1881. His merciless self-criticism allowed him to express himself more freely with the Tsar. Tolstoy's self-flagellation continued until his last days. In August 1910, just a few months before his death, he noted in his diary that he had never encountered anyone else who had the full complement of vices – sensuality, self-interest, spite, vanity and, above all, narcissism.[133]

As pointed out earlier, Sonya took a dim view of her husband donning the mask of the holy fool. For him, however, it was a fundamental medium for the communication of his message. In this regard, a comment Tolstoy made in his diary when he was writing *The Kreutzer Sonata* in August 1889 is revealing. 'I need to be a holy fool in my writing too,' he noted, realising that perfect execution alone would not make his arguments more convincing.[134] Sadly, Chekhov for one was unimpressed, to judge from further disparaging comments in his letter to Suvorin of December 1890. Dismissing in withering terms Tolstoy's afterword to *The Kreutzer Sonata* as the product of a holy fool, he asserts that his philosophy is 'not worth even one of the little mares in "Strider"'. (Tolstoy's superlative story about a horse, which he had begun many years earlier, when he still had ambition as an artist, was finally completed and published for the first time in 1886.[135])

As much as the holy fool is integral to the Russian Church, the character of 'Ivan the Fool', is integral to Russian folklore.[136] 'The Tale of Ivan the Fool', a popular story for The Intermediary which Tolstoy dashed off in an evening in 1885, was one he particularly cherished.[137] The story was published the following year in Sonya's first edition of the collected works, and also by The Intermediary, but was eventually banned by the religious censor as a work unsuitable for mass readership. The authorities took exception to the way in which the story promoted the idea of a kingdom which had no need for an army, money or intellectuals, while its tsar should at least be 'no different from a muzhik'.[138] In fact, even some of Tolstoy's closest friends took exception to its bald moralising and its denigration of intellectual endeavour in favour of physical labour.

By the summer of 1891, after the controversy surrounding *The Kreutzer Sonata* had died down, Tolstoy found himself struggling to concentrate on the new treatise he had begun the previous summer about non-violence. He had ideas for new fictional works which he wanted to develop (the future novel *Resurrection* and the story 'Father Sergius'), and he also wanted to complete an article about gluttony. He had been greatly impressed with Howard

Williams's history of vegetarianism, *The Ethics of Diet: A Catena of Authorities Deprecatory of the Practice of Flesh-Eating*, which had been published in London in 1883, after serial publication in *The Dietetic Reformer and Vegetarian Messenger* (the monthly journal of the Vegetarian Society), and he wanted to write a preface for its Russian translation. His article, 'The First Step', was completed in July, after a sobering visit to the abattoir in Tula, and published the following year in the journal *Issues in Philosophy and Psychology*, which was edited by his friend Nikolay Grot, a professor at Moscow University.[139] If the article came hard on the heels of *The Kreutzer Sonata*, it was because Tolstoy drew a direct link between gastronomic and sexual indulgence, arguing that carnal consumption stimulated carnal desire. Like chastity, vegetarianism was a precondition of the Christian ascetic life to which he aspired.[140] Tolstoy was bound to become a hero of the animal rights movement, for he did not, as it were, mince his words when graphically describing the cruelties involved in the slaughter of animals:

> Through the door opposite the one at which I was standing, a big, red, well-fed ox was led in. Two men were dragging it, and hardly had it entered when I saw a butcher raise a knife above its neck and stab it. The ox, as if all four legs had suddenly given way, fell heavily upon its belly, immediately turned over on one side, and began to work its legs and all its hind-quarters. Another butcher at once threw himself upon the ox from the side opposite to the twitching legs, caught its horns and twisted its head down to the ground, while another butcher cut its throat with a knife. From beneath the head there flowed a stream of blackish-red blood, which a besmeared boy caught in a tin basin. All the time this was going on the ox kept incessantly twitching its head as if trying to get up, and waved its four legs in the air. The basin was quickly filling, but the ox still lived, and, its stomach heaving heavily, both hind and fore legs worked so violently that the butchers held aloof. When one basin was full, the boy carried it away on his head to the albumen factory, while another boy placed a fresh basin, which also soon began to fill up. But still the ox heaved its body and worked its hind legs …
>
> … [W]e cannot pretend that we do not know this. We are not ostriches, and cannot believe that if we refuse to look at what we do not wish to see, it will not exist. This is especially the case when what we do not wish to see is what we wish to eat. If it were really indispensable, or, if

not indispensable, at least in some way useful! But it is quite unnecessary, and only serves to develop animal feelings, to excite desire, and to promote fornication and drunkenness. And this is continually being confirmed by the fact that young, kind, undepraved people – especially women and girls – without knowing how it logically follows, feel that virtue is incompatible with beefsteaks, and, as soon as they wish to be good, give up eating flesh.[141]

Contemporary writers may not be following the same spiritual path as Tolstoy, but the fact that revelations of animal cruelty in the twenty-first century still have the capacity to shock shows that we still behave like ostriches. Over a century after Tolstoy's 'First Step' was published, many abattoirs are only a little more humane.[142]

There is a grim irony about the fact that Tolstoy's broadside against needlessly excessive consumption was written just as reports of a major famine started reaching him. The Volga and central 'black earth' regions had already suffered two poor harvests in consecutive years, and in 1891 there was a drought which affected about 14 million people in an area stretching across thirteen regions in the European part of Russia, all the way from Tolstoy's own Tula region in the west to Samara, hundreds of miles to the east. The combination of adverse weather conditions, outdated farming implements, poor transportation and the Russian government's failure to act in time, compounded by its further failure to provide adequate help for peasants who were already desperately poor and malnourished, was fatal. Half a million people died of cholera alone. The crisis was certainly not helped by Russia's centralised government with its bloated and inefficient bureaucracy, since officials had little conception of what was actually really going in the provinces, and little autonomous power.

Tolstoy's ideas had begun to win him increasing numbers of followers by the end of the 1880s, but he also had his share of critics. In 1891, however, when he seized the initiative to help victims of the famine which had begun to rage in Russia, Tolstoy assumed an unassailable position of national moral leadership to the extent that his strident religious views were subsequently indulged more as eccentricities, at least by the people. Despite Chekhov's impatience with Tolstoy's retrogressive ideas, he was serious about placing him as the No. 1 most important person in Russia in December 1890 (he categorised himself as No. 877),[143] and he had nothing but admiration for his famine relief work. As he wrote in another letter exactly a year later, 'You need the courage and authority of a Tolstoy to swim against the current, defy the prohibitions and the general climate of opinion, and do what your duty calls you to do.'[144] Chekhov did sterling work himself during the famine, but Tolstoy got there first, and he put the Russian government to shame.

Tolstoy soon became intensely irritated that the Russian affluent classes were up in arms about the approaching crisis in the summer of 1891. Dire poverty was an everyday reality for most peasants, so why was it they only wanted to help the peasantry during the extreme conditions of a famine?[145] In September he went off on horseback round Tula province to see for himself what was happening, having already resolved not to spend that winter in Moscow. At the end of the month he returned home and started writing an article, 'About the Famine', in which he excoriated the educated classes for their indifference to the plight of all those millions of peasants who barely managed to subsist even in normal circumstances. On 15 October he sent his devastating report to *Issues in Philosophy and Psychology*, and ten days later Nikolay Grot wrote to give Tolstoy the unsurprising news that the issue in which it was slated to appear had been confiscated by the censor. The next day Tolstoy set off for Ryazan province with his eldest daughters, Tanya and Masha, ready to do what he could to help: the plan was to live at his friend Ivan Rayevsky's estate and set up soup kitchens and provide practical help to the peasants in the area. Rayevsky had come to visit Tolstoy that summer to tell him about what was going on, and it was his selfless devotion to the cause which inspired Tolstoy himself to act (he tragically died of influenza a month after Tolstoy's arrival).[146]

Tolstoy's twenty-two-year-old son Lev went off to his newly inherited estate in Samara to help out with the famine there, electing to take a period of leave from his university studies, but the experience was traumatic, and took a great toll on his frail health – the conditions were so extreme in Samara that it was hard just to produce any foodstuffs at all, let alone set up soup kitchens.[147] Sonya still had four children between the ages of three and fourteen to look after at home in Moscow, so was housebound, but she was keen to help as well. On 3 November 1891 she published an appeal for help in the *Russian Gazette* (it was also printed in many newspapers in Europe and the United States), and she received 9,000 roubles in the first week alone.[148] It was not just the wives of wealthy tea-merchants in Kyakhta, on the border with China, who sent Sonya money – donors included Old Believer fishermen in Bessarabia who gave up most of their earnings, a retired lieutenant-colonel in Nizhny Novgorod who donated his pension, as well as postmen, village schoolteachers and even peasants.[149] Sonya was glad to be able to contribute, as she recalls in her autobiography:

> I bought trucks of corn, beans, onions, cabbage, everything needed for the feeding centres where the famine-stricken poor from the villages were fed. To pay for this, I received money which was sent to me in considerable sums. From the material sent to me by textile manufacturers I had [bed linen] made by poor women for small wages, and I sent it to the places where it was needed most, chiefly for those suffering from typhoid.[150]

From her Moscow base, Sonya coordinated donations, and published regular bulletins over the next few months detailing the contributions received. She also spent days sewing shirts from the fabric supplied by the great textile magnate Savva Morozov, together with Dunyasha Popova, the family housekeeper, the nanny and the English governess.[151]

Tolstoy's mind was naturally taken back to the events of 1873 in Samara, when he first had seen the effects of famine in Russia. Ever since writing his article about the Moscow census back in 1882, Tolstoy was adamant that just throwing money at such a deep-rooted problem was no remedy: what was needed above all was practical action. After settling in at Rayevsky's estate in the village of Begichevka, Tolstoy wrote another article on the famine. 'A Terrible Question' (the question being whether could Russia feed itself) was duly published in the *Russian Gazette* on 6 November. Thus began months of getting up early every day, setting up and operating free soup kitchens, supervising volunteers and buying provisions with the donations received (Tolstoy himself took 600 roubles of his own money with him). By the end of November there were thirty soup kitchens up and running, and by the end of December there were seventy. They were vitally needed. Tolstoy wrote to tell Sonya that he had been to a village where there was only one cow for every nine households, and to another where nearly all the inhabitants were destitute. By January 4,000 peasants were receiving free food every day.[152]

The government had initially discouraged ordinary Russians from becoming involved in famine relief, but they were obliged to change policy in the face of their own helplessness. Nevertheless they were alarmed by Tolstoy's activities, and sent out a circular to all Russian newspapers forbidding them to publish any articles by him. The editor of the *Russian Gazette* had received a reprimand for publishing 'A Terrible Question', but on 10 December he went ahead and published its sequel: 'About Ways to Help the Population Suffering from the Failed Harvest'. Chekhov exclaimed the next day in a letter to Suvorin that Tolstoy was no longer just a man, but a 'giant, a Jupiter', and immediately contributed an article of his own to the collection of essays put together by the newspaper. Tolstoy's friend Nikolay Grot, meanwhile, called him a 'spiritual tsar' on whom all of Russia's hopes were pinned at this difficult time.[153] But an enormous scandal was brewing. 'About the Famine' had now finally been approved for publication after drastic editing, and it was published in *The Week* in early January 1892. Tolstoy also wanted his uncensored text to be known abroad, and he now got in touch with various foreign acquaintances to ask them to translate it. Isabel Hapgood produced a translation for publication in America, and she printed an announcement in the New York *Evening Post* that she was setting up a campaign to raise funds to help those starving in Russia (contributions had already started arriving from England, France and Germany).[154] Emile Dillon, an English academic who had been teaching at the University of Kharkov, placed his translation of Tolstoy's article in the *Daily Telegraph* on 14 (26) January. It was given the inflammatory title 'Why Are Russian Peasants Starving?'. As Tolstoy had hoped, extracts were then translated back into Russian for the press at home, but his words were twisted by right-wing publications, and immediately denounced by the more reactionary journalists as the most dangerous revolutionary propaganda. Tolstoy found himself being branded as the Antichrist, and as someone inciting the peasants to revolt.[155]

There was no way the liberal-minded Nikolay Grot could publish Tolstoy's article in his journal now. Conversations at court revolved around whether Tolstoy should be locked up in the Suzdal Monastery prison (the traditional place of incarceration for heretics in Russia), sent into exile abroad, or committed to a lunatic asylum (the link between holy fools and madness was well established in Russia).[156] In faraway Smolensk there was even a rumour that Tolstoy had already been exiled to the Solovetsky Monastery prison (the place of his ancestor Pyotr Andreyevich's incarceration), and before the writer and journalist Jonas Stadling left his native Sweden to volunteer, he heard reports that Tolstoy was a 'prisoner on his estate, and that he was to be banished from the country'.[157] But once again Alexander III opted for clemency – not for the first time was Alexandrine forced to answer for her wayward relative at court, but her very proximity to the Tsar was a guarantee of his safety.[158] Tolstoy was longing for martyrdom, so was infuriated that he could continue unhindered. But as Suvorin pointed out in a letter he wrote at the time, Tolstoy was the only person who managed to do anything, while everybody else had to clothe their ideas 'in velvet' in order for any action to be taken: 'they are persecuting him, but to no avail; he can't be touched, and even if he is, he will just be pleased, for how many times has he said to me: "Why aren't they arresting me, why aren't they putting me in jail?" It's an enviable lot.'[159]

Sonya was concerned that their whole family was on the brink of ruin, and she wondered what had happened to Tolstoy's doctrine of love and pacifism.[160] Her commitment to the cause had brought them together, however, which made him very happy, and she also came out to Begichevka for a ten-day visit at the end of January 1892.[161] She had been collecting donations and publishing reports, and now she saw for herself emaciated, shivering peasants dressed in rags, their sad expressions speaking of the humiliation they felt to receive charity.[162] She also saw what difficult and exhausting work it was for her husband and daughters (Tolstoy sometimes sat up until three in the morning in an attempt to continue with his writing). Apart from the physical challenges of working during the freezing winter months in villages where people had no means of feeding themselves or heating their homes, the sheer scale of the disaster was sometimes demoralising – it was impossible to help everyone. When she returned to Moscow in February, Sonya found herself having to nurse Vanechka (just about to turn four), who was seriously unwell again, and conduct a damage-control operation. The repercussions of Dillon's translation of Tolstoy's article in the *Daily Telegraph* amongst ministers and court officials were such that she was obliged to send mollifying letters, and make repeated visits to Governor General Grand Duke Sergey Alexandrovich and his wife Elizaveta Fyodorovna.[163]

The Tolstoys' famine-relief work proved to be infectious; soon they were joined by friends and relatives who wanted to help, and then by foreign volunteers like Jonas Stadling, who arrived in February 1892. In the book he later published about his experiences, Stadling described accompanying Tolstoy's daughter Masha on her visits on his first day, including one to a school:

> We stopped at one of the *izbas*, in which the Count had opened a school and eating-room. For some time after our entrance we could see nothing distinctly, but our feet told us that the naked soil served as floor. When our eyes grew accustomed to the gloom we saw a number of benches, and standing between them about thirty children, silently looking at us … In one corner were a couple of elderly people. From the neighbourhood of the [stove] came heavy breathing, and lying on top of it, we saw three children, covered with black small-pox. I suggested that these ought to be removed at once, and the Countess replied that it would be done as soon as possible, but as there were no hospitals, and almost every house was infected, it was not easy to isolate the sick. These poor children had been brought to the school 'because it was warm there'.[164]

When there was no longer any money to pay the teachers, the local schools had been forced to close, but Tolstoy had done what he could to reopen some of them. Stadling was full of admiration for all the Tolstoys – for the indefatigable Sonya, dealing on her own with an enormous correspondence in Moscow, for Lev Lvovich, heading the relief effort in Samara (where Stadling also volunteered), and the two dedicated daughters Tanya and Masha, who assisted their father not only with the operation of the soup kitchens and the establishment of separate premises for feeding children, but also with the procurement of feed for the horses and the distribution amongst the peasants of fuel, seed for planting, and flax and bast, to give them some work.

By the autumn of 1892, when Tolstoy eventually returned to Yasnaya Polyana, donations of over 100,000 roubles, plus two ships from America with a cargo of flour, grain and potatoes, had helped with the setting up of 212 emergency soup kitchens in four districts, which had functioned until July. Along with teaching at the Yasnaya Polyana school, and his work on the *ABC* books, Tolstoy later declared that this had been one of the happiest times of his life. In September he returned to Begichevka for another visit, and carefully toned down his language when he wrote a moving account of how the donations received between April and July had been used. It was published on 31 October in the *Russian Gazette*, and at least 5,000 extra copies had to be printed to meet the demand.[165] Tolstoy would continue to make further visits to Begichevka in the winter of 1893, but he was now free to spend more time working on the treatise about non-violence which he had begun two years earlier. He had worked further on it during the three weeks he had spent resting in Moscow back in January, and in April Chertkov had sent out to him in Begichevka not only his latest manuscript, but also a young peasant with good handwriting keen to work as a copyist. Tolstoy had thus been able to continue writing, and now that he was back in the peace and quiet of Yasnaya Polyana he was able to give his treatise his full attention.

After Tolstoy's religious writings began to be published abroad, he had started to receive letters, books and pamphlets from enthusiastic readers from all over the world who were sympathetic to his cause. When Alice Stockham had come to visit Yasnaya Polyana, Tolstoy had been greatly interested in what she had to tell him about all the various branches of Christianity in America which were 'moving towards practical Christianity, towards a universal brotherhood and the sign of this is non-resistance'.[166] He began to learn for the first time about Universalists, Unitarians, Quakers, spiritualists, Swedenborgians and also Shakers. On 30 March 1889 the Shaker Asenath Stickney had sent Tolstoy photographs of the leaders of their community, and two books: *The Shaker Answer* and George Lomas's *Plain Talks upon Practical Religion: Being Candid Answers to Earnest Inquirers*. In the autumn of 1889 Tolstoy entered into correspondence with another Shaker, Alonzo Hollister, explaining where he agreed and disagreed with their beliefs.[167] Tolstoy also now came into contact with the Quakers, who had preached non-resistance for over 200 years, and refused to take arms even in self-defence. Wendell Garrison, who edited a journal called *Non-resistance*, sent Tolstoy works by his father, the famous abolitionist and social reformer William Lloyd Garrison (who had died in 1879). And in 1889 Tolstoy was also sent Adin Ballou's *Catechism of Non-violence*, which he was very impressed by. Ballou was an abolitionist pastor who had formed a utopian community to live a rigorous life of Christian non-violence in Massachusetts back in 1841. Tolstoy exchanged warm letters with the eighty-seven-year-old pastor in the last year of his life.[168]

As Tolstoy's ideas matured, partly under the impact of all the new kindred spirits with whom he had come into contact, he had come to realise that there was one more important book he needed to write after *What I Believe*. The idea of non-resistance to violence was a central plank in his religious and ethical system, but he did not feel his exegesis had been sufficiently wide-ranging in works he had published thus far. As Jonas Stadling described it after conversations with Tolstoy at Begichevka, the new book was going to be 'a kind of counterblast to the increasingly martial spirit of the time, that seemed almost personified in the young German Emperor'.[169] Tolstoy had thought initially that he would be able to write this new book quickly, and he already had a full draft two days after his return to Yasnaya Polyana, but he would not be satisfied with his manuscript for another year. *The Kingdom of God Is Within You* became his magnum opus amongst his religious writings, and its importance can be gauged by the fact that when Tolstoy finally finished it in May 1893, he had written over 13,000 manuscript pages – almost as many as he wrote for *War and Peace, Anna Karenina* and his later novel *Resurrection* put together.[170] It was also his most strident work yet.

Tolstoy begins by discussing some of the people who had felt moved to express their support after reading *What I Believe* by sending him letters, brochures and books. He also answers his critics, before going on to assert that neither believers nor non-believers understand Christianity, and that it is impossible to live as a true Christian in conventional society. Finally, he analyses contemporary attitudes to war and the meaning of conscription, and is categoric about the fundamental incompatibility of Christianity with any form of government. By the end of the book Tolstoy is no longer able to maintain the calm tone with which he begins his treatise. In his twelfth and incandescent last chapter he recounts meeting a battalion of 400 soldiers when he was on his way to Begichevka for the last time. Armed with rifles, they were travelling by special train to quell disturbances amongst the starving peasants whom he had been trying to help. For Tolstoy, this served only to confirm the validity of his ideas.[171] In July 1892 Tolstoy set out a useful summary of the main ideas in his treatise in a letter to Charles Turner, an English teacher who had settled in Russia, and translated some of his works:

> In this book there are three main ideas: 1) Christianity is not only worship of God and a doctrine on salvation, as it is understood by the majority of false Christians, but is first of all a different understanding of life, which changes the whole structure of human society; 2) from the time of the arrival of Christianity there have been two opposing tendencies: one

that has been clarifying over time the new and genuine understanding of life which it has given people, and another which has been distorting Christianity and turning it into a pagan doctrine; in our time that contradiction has become particularly acute and is fully expressed in universal armament and general military conscription; 3) the necessary solution of this critical contradiction, which has been concealed by an absurd degree of hypocrisy in our time, can only happen through the sincere effort made by each individual person to coordinate one's life and actions with those moral foundations one considers to be true, regardless of the demands of family, society and government.[172]

In March 1893, as soon as *The Kingdom of God Is Within You* was finished, Tolstoy started despatching his manuscript abroad for translation and publication. French and Italian translations appeared at the end of 1893, and in a letter to Tolstoy of 29 October Nikolay Strakhov reported from St Petersburg that the religious censor had deemed the French translation of *The Kingdom of God Is Within You* to be the most harmful foreign book it had ever had occasion to ban from distribution in Russia. The French and Italian translations were followed in early 1894 by a German translation and three in English, two of which were published in London and one in America. One of these editions reached a twenty-five-year-old Indian lawyer working in South Africa called Mohandas Gandhi. He was already practising non-violence, but had succumbed to doubts which were completely and immediately erased when he read Tolstoy's text. Gandhi was particularly struck by the fact that Tolstoy practised what he preached, and was not willing to compromise when it came to searching for the truth.[173]

The first Russian edition of *The Kingdom of God Is Within You* appeared in early 1894, although even this émigré publication was abridged – the two pages about Kaiser Wilhelm had to be removed, as well as derogatory references to Catherine II, who was born a German. By this time Tolstoy's text had circulated widely in Russia via samizdat, but copies of the Russian edition published in Germany were also smuggled in. A secret government memo in May 1894 expressed alarm at the number of copies that had already been imported into Russia illegally, and advised that all typographers, lithographers and even individuals in possession of typewriters were to be put under close covert surveillance. For some reason, typewritten copies particularly proliferated in the 'southern provinces'. The first unexpurgated Russian edition of *The Kingdom of God Is Within You* was published in 1896 in Geneva by Mikhail Elpidin.[174] Alexander III had earlier declared that he did not want to add a martyr's crown to Tolstoy's fame by exiling him, but he was horrified by this new book, which he read a few months before his untimely death in the autumn of 1894. Even he now itched to be able to bring his rebellious subject to task.[175]

ELDER, APOSTATE AND TSAR

Someone said that each person has their own specific smell. However strange it may seem, I think Tolstoy has a very devout, church-like smell: cypress, vestments, communion wafers …

Valentin Bulgakov, diary entry, 12 February 1910[1]

WITH THE PUBLICATION of *The Kingdom of God Is Within You* in 1893, Tolstoy's 'gospel' was complete. It was not a coincidence that the illegal printing presses which produced copies for distribution in Russia also handled revolutionary propaganda. Except for his complete and utter commitment to non-violence, Tolstoy also sought to bring down the Russian government. As the Polish Marxist theorist Rosa Luxemburg was later to comment:

> The criticism to which Tolstoy has submitted the existing order is radical; it knows no limits, no retrospective glances, no compromises … The ultimate destruction of private property and the state, universal obligation to work, full economic and social equality, a complete abolition of militarism, brotherhood of nations, universal peace and equality of everything that

bears the human image – this is the ideal which Tolstoy has been tirelessly preaching with the stubbornness of a great and vehement prophet.[2]

In the years to come Tolstoy would write dozens more articles in which he set out his religious and ethical views. Some of them, such as 'Thou Shalt Not Kill' (written in response to the assassination of King Umberto I in 1900), and 'I Cannot Be Silent' (prompted by the news that twenty peasants had been hanged in 1908 for attempted robbery), were occasioned by specific events. Others, such as 'Religion and Morality', 'The Law of Violence and the Law of Love' and 'The Essence of Christian Teaching' expressed his thinking as it continued to evolve in the last decade and a half of his life. They were all essentially variations on a theme, and mostly quite a lot shorter, but also quite a lot more abrasive.

Tolstoy had already proved to be a remarkably effective apostle. Capitalising on the fame he had already acquired as a writer, he began winning converts to his version of Christianity almost immediately he started disseminating his new beliefs in the 1880s. When he had first set out on his crusade, he had complained of loneliness, and had actively sought out kindred spirits. A decade later it was the kindred spirits who came to him – in droves, from all over the world, more often than not conceiving their journey as a 'pilgrimage'. Where Tolstoy previously used to have two or three visitors a week at most in the early 1880s, there were sometimes as many as thirty-five people a day wanting to see him during the last years of his life.[3] There were those who approached him with reverence as an elder (*starets*), hoping he would provide spiritual guidance and give them answers to diverse problems, and then there were others who wanted to see him in the flesh simply because he was such a celebrity.

Just how famous Tolstoy became can be ascertained from the way in which the British journalist William Stead prefaced his account of the week he spent at Yasnaya Polyana in 1888:

In Russia and out of Russia, I have found people more interested in the personality of Count Leo Tolstoi, the novelist, than in that of any other living Russian. He is the first man of letters in contemporary Russia, but that alone would not account for the widespread interest in his character. He is a great original, an independent thinker, a religious teacher, and the founder of a something that is midway between a Church, a school, and a socio-political organisation. He not only thinks strange things, and says them with rugged force and vivid utterance – he does strange things; and what is more, he induces others to do the same. A man of genius who spends his time in planting potatoes and cobbling shoes, a great literary artist who has founded a propaganda of Christian anarchy, an aristocrat who spends his life as a peasant – such a man in any country would command attention. In Russia he monopolises it, and the fame of his originalities has spread abroad so far until it is probable that there are more people anxious to 'hear about Tolstoi' in Boston and San Francisco than there are even in Petersburg and Moscow.[4]

Tolstoy's major artistic and religious writings had only appeared in translation a couple of years earlier yet he was already a household name throughout the world. The Swedish playwright August Strindberg was profoundly affected by Tolstoy's ideas when he came across them in Paris in 1885:

> Tolstoy, whose recently translated novel *War and Peace* has aroused the admiration of the Parisians, Tolstoy, a Count, a wealthy man, a decorated soldier from the battles at Sebastopol, a brilliant writer, has broken with society, turned his back on literary writing and in the polemical works *Confession* and *What I Believe* has taken Rousseau's side, declared war on culture, and has put his teaching into practice himself by turning himself into a peasant.[5]

Strindberg wrote his book *Among French Peasants* (which was published in 1889) under the immediate influence of Tolstoy's ideas. Matthew Arnold had fired the imagination of British readers, while a pioneering study of the Russian novel published in 1886 by the Vicomte Eugène-Melchior de Vogüé (who had served at the French Embassy in St Petersburg in the late 1870s and early 1880s, and married a Russian noblewoman) served to fuel the European reading public's intense interest in Tolstoy on the Continent.[6] In 1887 an American critic published an article in *Harper's Bazaar* about the tumultuous reaction to the sudden arrival of Russian literature in the English-speaking world, describing Tolstoy as the greatest ever writer of fiction, 'living or dead'.[7] At the end of the decade a German writer set off to Yasnaya Polyana to do research: the first biography of Tolstoy was published in Berlin in 1892, two years before one even appeared in Russia.[8] Tolstoy was sixty-four.

9. Cartoon showing 'Tolstoy at work', published in 1908

The dynamics of Tolstoy's life had changed radically while he had been formulating his doctrine of brotherly love and non-resistance to violence in the 1880s. He had become teetotal, a vegetarian, he had given up smoking and hunting animals, and he had also stopped handling money insofar as it was possible. In the 1890s the dynamics of his life were to change again, and not just because he took up bicycling at the age of sixty-five, and soon needed a secretary to help him deal with the voluminous correspondence he found himself conducting with readers from all around the world. When he now went head to head with the Russian government by taking up the cause of persecuted sectarians scattered across the country, its ministers responded by sending his closest followers into exile, and excommunicating him from the Orthodox Church – which only increased his fame. The dynamics of Russian life also changed in the 1890s. Nicholas II, the last Romanov, ascended to the throne in 1894 amidst growing social and political unrest, and the rapid development of new technologies which began to revolutionise daily life. Before he died in 1910, Tolstoy lived to see the movie camera, the motor car, the phonograph and the typewriter, and even talked to Chekhov on the telephone.

Remarkably, Tolstoy found time to write fiction during the hectic last period of his life, when he was also sometimes extremely unwell. Apart from his novel *Resurrection*, completed in 1899, he worked on a handful of superlative stories, and also composed a substantial treatise on the meaning of art. These works were written alongside all the religious articles and diatribes against the immoral practices of the tsarist regime, which remained as reactionary as it had been under Alexander III. But Tolstoy's main writing project at the end of his life was the compilation of several exhaustive volumes of daily sayings and maxims from his favourite writers and philosophers. He was in need of their solace, as he was unhappy for much of the last fifteen years of his life. He still felt obligations to his family, but found it endlessly painful having to put up with the trappings of his once seigneurial lifestyle when he was longing to take to the road as a penniless and penitent Strannik. And as his friend Vladimir Chertkov assumed ever more influence over his affairs, Tolstoy's relationship with his wife steadily deteriorated.

Sonya had grown up in fairly humble surroundings despite her parents' flat being located in the Kremlin, so when she married Tolstoy she had adapted quickly to Yasnaya Polyana, but its spartan furnishings invariably took foreign visitors by surprise. The intrepid American traveller George Kennan, for example, who came to Yasnaya Polyana in June 1886 after travelling across Siberia, was clearly expecting Tolstoy's study to be a bit grander:

> The floor was bare; the furniture was old-fashioned in form, with two
> or three plain chairs, a deep sofa, or settle, upholstered with worn green
> morocco, and a small cheap table without a cover. There was a marble bust [of
> Tolstoy's brother Nikolay] in a niche behind the settle, and the only pictures
> which the room contained were a small engraved portrait of Dickens and
> another of Schopenhauer. It would be impossible to imagine anything

plainer or simpler than the room and its contents. More evidences of wealth and luxury might be found in many a peasant's cabin in Eastern Siberia.[9]

Anna Armfeldt had asked Kennan to smuggle out a manuscript copy of *Confession* to her daughter Natalya in the convict mine at Kara, and he had been so shocked by what he had seen of the Russian penal system in Siberia that it turned him into a vociferous opponent of the tsarist regime. Tolstoy was consequently extremely interested to hear what he had to say. Kennan's book *Siberia and the Exile System* was banned from Russia along with its author as soon as it was published in 1891.

Sonya did not need to live in luxury, and she even did not mind the additional burden of having to prepare special dishes at mealtimes for her husband and the growing number of vegetarians at Yasnaya Polyana. Tanya and Masha became vegetarians like their father, and all the Tolstoyans, beginning with Chertkov, refused to eat meat. Then there were other loyal friends of Tolstoy who were vegetarians, like the painter Repin, whose colourful companion Natalya Nordman at one point promoted a diet of grass and hay.[10] All of that the conventional Sonya could just about tolerate, but she did not warm to her husband's followers. 'These people who are adherents of Lev Nikolayevich's teaching are all so unlikeable! Not one normal person,' she exclaimed in her diary in August 1890.[11] In general, she viewed the Tolstoyans as the opposite of the *svetskie* (polite society) people from her own milieu, and by playing on the word *svet*, which means 'light' as well as 'society' and 'world', Sonya took to calling them *tyomnye* (dark). She noticed *tyomnye* Tolstoyans coming out of the woodwork as soon as illegal copies of *The Gospel in Brief* and *Confession* started circulating. Sonya made an exception initially for the highborn Chertkov, who had exquisite manners, and also the artist Nikolay Ge, who became a friend of the whole family (he died in 1894). She also tolerated Pavel Biryukov ('Posha'), who was meek and intelligent, but she found the sectarians and peasants hard to deal with, and positively recoiled from the social misfits who seemed to be drawn to her husband like magnets, and became fanatical followers, having failed to carve conventionally successful careers for themselves. Sonya recorded in her diary the knock on the door that woke them all up at four in the morning one icy January day in 1895, for example: the visitor turned out to be a 'bedraggled, flea-bitten, *tyomny*' who was desperate to marry their daughter Tanya.[12]

Despite her feelings of distaste, Sonya had to learn to live with *tyomnye* Tolstoyans in their midst. One devoted early follower of her husband was a woman of her own age, Maria Alexandrovna Schmidt, an unmarried teacher at a prim Moscow girls' school. In March 1884 Maria Alexandrovna had turned up on Tolstoy's doorstep with her friend Olga Barsheva and asked him for a copy of his *Gospel*. When Tolstoy informed her he only had it in manuscript, she responded brightly that they would be happy to copy it. And so the two friends divided the manuscript up, and spent several evenings in Tolstoy's study becoming acquainted with his ideas. Soon Maria Alexandrovna was taken on as an assistant to Tolstoy's main copyist at that time, Alexander Ivanov. Her services were soon required, as Alexander Ivanov was an alcoholic former officer who often absconded on drinking bouts. He did very good work on the days that he was sober, but Tolstoy had to rescue him from various slums on a regular basis.[13] Maria Alexandrovna's life changed utterly when she was won over to Tolstoy's *Gospel*. She had been an ardent Orthodox Christian, but she now took down her icons and replaced them with Tolstoy's portrait.[14] She also resigned her teaching position, went with her friend Olga to join one of the first Tolstoyan communes down in the Caucasus, then in 1893 came back north when Olga died. By this time she wanted to be near Tolstoy, with whom she had become close friends. After settling into a tiny thatch-covered *izba* on Tanya Lvovna's newly inherited land, three miles away from Yasnaya Polyana, she led a model Tolstoyan life until the end of her days. Sometimes she would come up to Yasnaya Polyana when Tolstoy's sister was making her annual summer visit from her convent, and her skeletal frame stood in stark contrast to the rotund figure of Maria Nikolayevna, who was famously fond of eating. It was Maria Alexandrovna, with her abstemious diet of cabbage soup and grain, who somehow seemed far more like a nun.[15]

Maria Alexandrovna relished living like an anchorite by the sweat of her brow with the help of her vegetable patch and her cow Manechka, but there were other Tolstoyans who wanted the security of feeling they were part of an organisation. In 1893, before *The Kingdom of God Is Within You* was even finished, let alone copied and distributed, unfounded rumours started flying of an imminent Tolstoyan congress. Tolstoy was both amused and horrified at the idea. 'That's wonderful!' he exclaimed. 'We'll turn up to this congress and set up some kind of Salvation Army. We'll get a uniform – some hats with a cockade. Maybe they will make me a general. Masha can sew me some blue trousers.'[16] Tolstoy was happy to show leadership by setting out and imparting to the world what he believed to be the truth, but he did not want actually to lead anything – the whole point was to get away from organisations. In his ideal world, in fact, there would be no organisations, yet he could not avoid a movement forming amongst those attracted to his ideas, and many of his followers were fanatics. The other unsavoury side of Tolstoyanism for Sonya was the 'militancy' with which her husband's followers clung to the doctrine of non-violence, thereby placing themselves in an openly antagonistic position with regard to the Russian government. There were inevitable unpleasant repercussions, but these only seemed to goad Tolstoy to campaign more vigorously for human rights, at both ends of the social spectrum.

One person who received Tolstoy's direct support was Prince Dmitry Khilkov, who became a key figure amongst the Tolstoyans (before he went over to the other side and became a revolutionary).[17] Khilkov was a graduate of the prestigious Corps des Pages in St Petersburg, and the youngest officer to be appointed a colonel in the Russian army.[18] Like Chertkov, who was four years older than him, Khilkov turned his back on a brilliant military career. By the time he resigned from the army in 1884, the experience of killing a Turkish soldier in the Russo-Turkish War while serving in a Cossack regiment, and contacts with sectarians while stationed in the Caucasus, had turned him into a pronounced pacifist, and a Christian after Tolstoy's heart. Inspired by reading Tolstoy's *What I Believe*, he, went back to his estate in Kharkov province, sold the land to his peasants for a fraction of its real value, built himself a simple farmhouse to live in, threw away his Western-style clothing and started leading a simplified, agricultural life. In 1887, when he was twenty-nine, Khilkov came to Moscow to meet Tolstoy, with whom he established an instant rapport.[19] The concern Khilkov had shown for sectarians, ethnic minorities and rank and file soldiers (whose conditions had barely improved since the Crimean War) had already attracted the attention of the secret police, and their surveillance activities only intensified after he became friends with Tolstoy.

Khilkov turned his small thatched farmhouse into a local centre of Tolstoyan Christianity, and opened a library so that peasants could read the central texts in the Tolstoyan canon, which aroused hostility among landowners and clergy. Things came to a head in 1891. In March, following Khilkov's successful missionary activity in the area, Tolstoy was anathematised in Kharkov cathedral, and then in August Khilkov wrote to tell Tolstoy about his frosty encounter with Father Ioann (John) of Kronstadt, with whom he had argued about baptism.[20] He had been curious to set eyes on this charismatic priest when he came on a visit to Kharkov as he had attracted a large following amongst the populace, and so had acceded to his mother's request that he go and meet him, but it had not gone well. Khilkov's mother was outraged that her son had not consecrated his recent marriage in a church, or baptised his one-year-old child, thus depriving him by law of his title. In November Chief Procurator Pobedonostsev wrote to Alexander III to warn him of the dangers of the impact of Tolstoyanism on the peasantry in an area where there was already unrest. Out of the 6,000 parishioners in Khilkov's district, he wrote, only five old women were now going to church, and large numbers were refusing to enlist in the army.[21] The authorities now moved quickly. In January 1892 Khilkov was exiled to the Caucasus, causing Tolstoy to express envy, but those feelings were tempered in October the following year. With the blessing of Father Ioann of Kronstadt, his mother arrived in the Caucasus accompanied by police officers. Princess Khilkova proceeded to remove her three-and-a-half-year-old grandson and two-year-old granddaughter from their horrified parents and take them back to St Petersburg, where she christened them without their parents' consent.[22] Tolstoy wrote a letter to Alexander III to protest, and Khilkov's wife travelled to St Petersburg to petition the Tsar personally, but to no avail, despite the public outcry.

Khilkov's Tolstoyan ministry had certainly produced results. The peasant schoolteacher Evdokim Drozhzhin was rapidly converted to Tolstoyanism after meeting Khilkov in 1889, and two years later he was jailed after he refused to enlist when called up for military service. There were to be many other conscientious objectors who refused to be conscripted on religious grounds, but Tolstoy took a particular interest in Drozhzhin, and was deeply concerned when he was first kept for twelve months in solitary confinement, and then sent to serve in a disciplinary battalion in Voronezh. The conditions were truly brutal, as Chertkov discovered when he visited Drozhzhin, and he successfully campaigned to have him transferred to a regular prison, but it was too late. In January 1894, at the age of twenty-eight, Drozhzhin died of consumption at the start of his nine-year sentence. Tolstoyanism had claimed its first martyr, but there were chroniclers and hagiographers ready to spring into action, as well as secret police agents watching like hawks. In June, soon after Tolstoy's follower Evgeny Popov finished a book about Drozhzhin, his home in Moscow was searched by the police and the manuscript confiscated. A few months later the Russian press was placed under orders not to publish anything at all about Drozhzhin.[23] Popov nevertheless managed to resurrect his book from drafts that had carefully been stored elsewhere, and Tolstoy completed it by writing a foreword. There was, of course, no chance it would pass the censor in Russia, and it was published in Berlin in 1895.[24]

The son of an impoverished noble from Perm province, Popov had joined Tolstoy's growing number of followers in 1886 when he was twenty-two. Convinced that Tolstoy could tell him about the meaning of life, he one day got on a train to Yasnaya Polyana to go and talk to him. Before long he had become a vegetarian and was tilling the land. After separating from his wealthy young wife, who did not share his new beliefs, Popov led a rather peripatetic existence, moving from one Tolstoyan colony to another, but then went to work for The Intermediary in Moscow. In 1889 Popov got to know Tolstoy better when he accompanied him on his annual three-day journey by foot from Moscow to Yasnaya Polyana at the beginning of the summer. This was the third time Tolstoy had undertaken to walk the full 120 miles home. He would take with him only a small bundle, plus a notebook and pencil, so he could jot down ideas and stories he heard along the way, and would find overnight accommodation with hospitable peasants. It was his way of protesting against the intrusion of the railways into rural Russia, which had brought about mass peasant migration into the cities.

As well as working for The Intermediary, Popov also spent some time at the main headquarters of the Tolstoyan movement at Chertkov's estate in Voronezh province. In 1892 he was employed for a time as Tolstoy's copyist at Yasnaya Polyana, and assisted him in the famine relief effort at Begichevka. After next writing the book about Drozhzhin, he collaborated with Tolstoy on a Russian version of Lao Tzu's *Tao Te Ching* for The Intermediary. This was a project which Tolstoy cared deeply about. Victor von Strauss had produced the first German translation of the *Tao Te Ching* in 1870, and this was the text which Popov translated into Russian.[25] Tolstoy checked over Popov's translation and wrote an introduction to them, explaining that the basic teaching in the *Tao Te Ching* was the same as in all great religions. Back in the 1870s he had chiselled away at his translations of Aesop's already pithy fables in order to distil their essence, and it is not hard to see why Tolstoy was drawn to Lao Tzu's lapidary insights, which accorded so much with his own hard-won beliefs:

> People wearing ornaments and fancy clothes,
> carrying weapons,
> drinking a lot and eating a lot,
> having a lot of things, a lot of money:
> shameless thieves.
> Surely their way
> isn't the way.[26]

Tolstoy's attraction to the religions of the Orient only increased towards the end of his life. Some people even argued that his pared-down belief system had more in common with Buddhism than with Christianity.[27]

After translating Lao Tzu, Popov took up the cause of another Tolstoyan conscientious objector, who was about to be exiled to Siberia after serving his term in a disciplinary battalion. While visiting him at the central transit prison in Moscow in December 1894, Popov was intrigued by three men dressed half like peasants, half like Cossacks.[28] They were Dukhobors – 'wrestlers in the name of the Holy Spirit' – and they had come up from their home in the Caucasus to meet with Pyotr Verigin, who was their leader. Verigin had already spent seven years in exile in the northern province of Arkhangelsk, following disputes with other Dukhobors over his leadership, and he was now about to be sent to Berezov, in the Siberian province of Tobolsk, where he faced another seven years of exile. Popov introduced himself to the three Dukhobors, swiftly arranged another meeting to which he could bring Tolstoy when he heard their story. It was to be a fateful encounter.

The lack of historical records makes tracing their origins difficult, but the Dukhobors seem to have emerged from disparate groups of like-minded religious dissenters in the Ukraine who were forced to settle along Russia's southern borders at some point in the eighteenth century. It was only under Nicholas I that they formed a distinct community, however, when in the 1830s they were again forcibly resettled by imperial decree in the more remote reaches of the Russian Empire's new Caucasian territories, close to the border with the Ottoman Empire. Like many peasant sectarians, the Dukhobors acquired a reputation for their abstemious, hard-working and humble way of life. Believing, like Tolstoy, that 'The Kingdom of God is Within You', they revered the sanctity of all human life, thus were opposed not only to taking up arms, but to almost every aspect of the Russian Orthodox Church, since it supported the state during warfare. This meant rejecting all rituals, sacraments, icons, clergy, sacred buildings, and also the Scriptures themselves, in favour of seeking guidance from the voice of individual conscience. The Dukhobors first came into serious conflict with the Russian government in 1887, when military conscription was introduced in the Caucasus, and the situation worsened in 1894, when all Russian citizens were required to swear allegiance to the Tsar.[29]

Before his first meetings with the Dukhobors, Tolstoy knew very little about their beliefs, since their existence was officially frowned upon and barely documented. Tolstoy could not meet Verigin himself, who was imprisoned like a convicted criminal while awaiting his departure for Siberia, but on 9 December 1894 Popov and Biryukov accompanied him to a meeting with the three Dukhobors who had come to see Verigin off, one of whom was his brother Vasily. To his delight, Tolstoy discovered that the Dukhobor views on private property, organised religion, secular authority and non-resistance to violence were remarkably similar to his own. Verigin had already made this discovery. Even before he had started reading Tolstoy's banned religious writings (procured via contacts with political exiles in the far north) he had begun inciting Dukhobors to renounce tobacco, alchohol and the eating of meat. Now he realised that a concerted application of the principles contained in Tolstoy's writings offered an effective means for the Dukhobors to stand up against the government. He started plotting various strategies for mass resistance.[30]

Chertkov passed through Moscow that December. He was on his way to St Petersburg where he planned to campaign for Dmitry Khilkov's children to be returned to their parents, and he persuaded Tolstoy to have his photograph taken with him and the other Tolstoyans involved with The Intermediary. As well as Popov and Biryukov, there were two other young recruits: Ivan Tregubov, yet another priest's son who had graduated as an atheist from a seminary, and Ivan Gorbunov-Posadov, the son of an engineer.[31] Tolstoy's loyal daughters Tanya and Masha were put out by the covert way in which Chertkov had arranged this group portrait of five male Tolstoyans with their 'teacher', as they were used to being privy to their father's activities and were deeply involved in his work themselves. As for Sonya, it was one step too far, and as soon as she found out she marched off to the photographer's studio to collect the negatives and deface them. She then sat up until three in the morning trying to erase Tolstoy's face from the picture with one of her diamond earrings. It was fine for pupils at a school to have group photographs, she thought, but the idea of institutionalising Tolstoyanism was abhorrent to her. She felt it did not become her husband's status as a great writer to be pictured alongside such dubious people, and feared that thousands of people would want to buy copies of the photograph.[32] Tolstoy acquiesced, but Chertkov later more than made up for the loss of this early group portrait by bringing an English professional photographer called Thomas Tapsell to Russia to help him take hundreds of images of the great man for posterity. Tolstoy was a vain man, and he acquiesced to that too.[33]

Tolstoy had been putting the finishing touches to a new story in the month that he met the Dukhobors. 'Master and Man' (the Russian title 'Khozyain i rabotnik' literally means 'The Master and the Worker') is about a rich landowner who redeems his selfish, avaricious ways in the middle of a snowstorm by sacrificing his life for that of his downtrodden peasant. The news that Tolstoy was going to publish this story, for nothing, in the expensive Petersburg journal *Northern Messenger* (its annual subscription was thirteen roubles) provoked another outburst from Sonya, who felt betrayed and jealous, not least because the editor was a young woman. She wanted the rights to new fiction by her husband, and in the first of many over-dramatic 'suicide attempts' she ran out into the snowy street late one January night in just her dressing gown and slippers.[34] Peace was temporarily restored after Tolstoy brought her back into the house and agreed to her demands. Along with its appearance in *Northern Messenger*, his new story was published simultaneously as a supplement to the thirteenth volume of Sonya's edition of the collected works (10,000 copies sold for fifty kopecks in a matter of days), and also by The Intermediary (15,000 copies sold for less half that price in four days flat). A 'popular' edition which went on sale for three kopecks was then published and reprinted several times.[35]

Sonya's suicide attempts were really just desperate ploys to seek attention: she was exhausted by the stress of caring for six-year-old Vanechka, who was frequently sick, and by the struggle to keep her marriage going and raise their four youngest children on her own. In the event, petty concerns about money and personal loyalties were soon pushed to one side as the Tolstoys suffered a terrible bereavement just before the story appeared in print. Days before his seventh birthday their youngest son Vanechka died of scarlet fever. This time both parents were equally devastated, as the angelic, frail Vanechka had been universally adored by everyone in the family for his preternatural goodness and his supposed likeness to his father. Tolstoy, indeed, had already begun to nurture dreams of Vanechka carrying on his work after his death. His sister Masha, who had been visiting Moscow from her convent, prayed constantly over Vanechka in his last few hours, then helped comb his long, blond hair and dress him in a white shirt after he passed away. Numb with grief, Sonya wrote to tell her sister Tanya how she had placed a small icon on Vanechka's chest, and lit the traditional candle by his head. For the next three days the nursery filled with flowers, and then came another sleigh-ride north of the city to the graveyard of the Church of St Nicholas at Pokrovskoye, to bury Vanechka next to his brother Alyosha.[36] 'Mama is grief-stricken,' wrote Masha to a friend. 'Her whole life was in him, she gave him all her love. Papa is the only one who can help her, he's the only one who can do that. But he is suffering terribly himself, and keeps crying all the time.' For Tolstoy, indeed, this death was on a level with that of his brother Nikolay.[37]

The death of Vanechka was a major turning point for both his parents. Grieving for Vanechka brought them together, and Tolstoy thought about taking Sonya that summer to Germany for a rest (she had never been abroad, and had a longing to hear Wagner's *Ring* cycle at Bayreuth), but that plan had to be shelved when it became clear that they would probably not be allowed to return to Russia.[38] Sonya stopped writing in her diary for over a year, and never really recovered. Tolstoy started making notes in his diary about how he wanted his own death to be handled, which would ideally lead to him being buried in the most humble cemetery possible, with no flowers, preferably no priest, and definitely no obituaries.[39] He also employed a classic displacement technique to deal with his grief: he learned to ride a bicycle.

The British-made 'safety' bicycle, which was the first to replace the penny-farthing and become commercially successful, was a newfangled form of transport just coming into vogue in Russia. Tolstoy equipped himself with a 'Rover' (a popular model first developed in Coventry in 1885 by the inventor of the modern bicycle John Starley) and went off to have lessons. These

10. Tolstoy skating in the back garden of his Moscow house in 1898, photograph taken by Sonya Tolstaya

were held in the Moscow Manège, the long classical building in front of the Kremlin used for parades, where he had once learned to fence. Tolstoy acquired a reputation for riding alone, apart from the other trainee cyclists, with an intense look of concentration on his face. Once he had demonstrated his proficiency to the police and acquired a licence, he was free to pedal round the city. The high-minded Evgeny Popov disapproved of his mentor indulging in such a frivolous activity, but Tolstoy saw cycling as a kind of 'innocent holy foolishness', and did not care what people thought of a sixty-six-year-old man on wheels.⁴⁰ That summer Tolstoy took his bicycle to Yasnaya Polyana and exhausted himself by going on rides all the way to Tula and back.⁴¹ As with all his enthusiasms, cycling became an obsessive passion for a while, and Tolstoy even managed to persuade the pianist and composer Sergey Taneyev to take it up. Taneyev, then thirty-nine, was a family acquaintance who some-times went ice-skating with Tolstoy.⁴² Apart from being rather portly, he was extremely short-sighted and slightly cross-eyed, and did not like going out at night without a chaperone for fear of stumbling, but he was very game. Taneyev was also very game about playing the piano for Sonya. It was in music rather than sport that Sonya sought consolation from her grief.

Since her sister was not coming to Yasnaya Polyana in the summer of 1895, Sonya offered the wing to Taneyev for a peppercorn rent, and in June he arrived to spend a month, accompanied by his wrinkled old nanny Pelageya Vasilievna and his seventeen-year-old composition pupil Yury Pomerant-sev.⁴³ Taneyev filled the house with exquisite piano music during his stay, and unwittingly became an emotional crutch for Sonya while she mourned the loss of Vanechka. Music acted as a kind of tranquilliser for her. Tolstoy had been affectionate and caring that spring, but he soon became preoccupied again with his missionary activities. It was Chertkov he wanted to spend time with. They had been exchanging frequent and sometimes very long letters, but had been able to meet only rarely during the first decade of their friend-ship, and usually only when Chertkov was passing through Moscow on the way from his estate to St Petersburg or vice versa. In 1894 all that had changed when Tolstoy found a dacha near Yasnaya Polyana for Chertkov, his frail wife and five-year-old son Vladimir (also known as Dima, like his father). It meant Tolstoy and Chertkov could spend finally long summer days in uninterrupted conversation. The Chertkovs returned to spend their summers in the house in 1895 and in 1896, so it is not surprising that Sonya found Tol-stoy's emotional absence hard to bear. Taneyev was a placid, unobtrusive sort of person, completely wrapped up in his music, but he provided a sympathetic ear to Sonya, who was clearly very lonely.

To begin with, Tolstoy did not mind – he and Taneyev played a lot of chess together, and he certainly enjoyed the composer's peerless performances of the classical repertoire of which he was so fond. Taneyev had been a pupil of Tchaikovsky and Nikolay Rubinstein, and in 1875, at the age of just nineteen, had been the first Moscow Conservatoire student to graduate with the Gold Medal in composition and performance. That year he had been the soloist in the premiere of Tchaikovsky's Piano Concerto No. 1, and in 1878 replaced him as teacher at the Moscow Conservatoire (his many pupils would include Scriabin and Rachmaninov). Tolstoy even shared an enthusiasm for Esperanto with Taneyev, who was unusual in being one of Russia's first speakers of the language – he wrote songs with lyrics in Esperanto, as well his frankly rather unexciting diary entries. Tolstoy had nothing but praise for Esperanto's inventor Lazar Zamenhof and the book he published in 1887: *Lingvo internacia. Antaŭparolo kaj plena lernolibro* (International Language. Foreword and Complete Textbook).

A native Russian speaker from Białystok in the Jewish Pale of Settlement, Zamenhof published under the pseudonym Doktoro Esperanto (Doctor Hopeful), a name which expressed his dream that Esperanto would bring peace and understanding between peoples all over the world. Tolstoy expressed his support for the language in a letter he wrote to some Esperanto enthusiasts in early 1894. He told them he had received Zamenhof's book soon after it was published, and claimed to have learned to read the language fluently in two hours. This gave the resourceful Tolstoyans the idea of using the journal *Esperantisto* as an ideological platform. In May 1895 *Esperantisto* published translations of both Tolstoy's 1894 letter and his article 'On Reason in Religion'. The Russian government reacted by promptly banning any further imports of the journal from its editorial base in Nuremberg. By August *Esperantisto* was forced to close, since three-quarters of its 600 subscribers lived in Russia. Amongst them must have been Taneyev.[44]

A shared love of Esperanto was unfortunately not sufficient to prevent Tolstoy developing absurd feelings of jealousy towards the hapless Taneyev, despite the fact that the composer was a confirmed bachelor. Taneyev was clearly extremely fond of his young pupil 'Yusha' Pomerantsev, who studied harmony and counterpoint with him for several years, and was frequently by his side, but the composer's lifelong companion was his old nanny. As one former student later commented, Taneyev simultaneously experienced fear, respect and contempt towards 'ladies', their appearance at his home invariably throwing him off kilter and making him less 'straightforward and natural'.[45] Taneyev's ecstatic comments about bicycling, moreover ('I think that even the experiences of newly-weds on their wedding night cannot compare with the sensations experienced by a bicyclist'), ought to have been enough to put Tolstoy's mind at rest.[46] Some might even argue that Tolstoy should have been indulgent of his wife simply for sitting through the premiere of Taneyev's interminably long opera *The Oresteia* at the Mariinsky Theatre in October 1895 (which rapidly disappeared from the repertoire after he refused to cut it).

Taneyev was hardly a surrogate husband, more someone for Sonya to talk to, particularly about the day-to-day matters concerning life at Yasnaya Polyana which Tolstoy had washed his hands of years before. Tolstoy might have been magnanimous, even if he did think his wife was making a fool of herself by fawning on a man much younger than herself. After all, he was doing the same now that Chertkov had replaced her as the chief object of his affections and confidences. Later on, Sonya would actually accuse her husband of having a homosexual relationship with Chertkov.[47] It is a charge that cannot be substantiated, although the tone of many of Tolstoy's letters to his younger friend just after he was deported to England is sometimes that of an infatuated adolescent, and his affection was at least reciprocated with an obsessive devotion on Chertkov's part.[48]

Sonya's dependency on music after Vanechka's death stimulated Tolstoy to reflect further on questions of aesthetics which would be fully articulated a few years later in his treatise *What is Art?*, but his central mission in the 1890s was as a non-violent Christian soldier fighting for truth and justice. It was extremely gratifying to him that his ideas were now beginning to bear fruit abroad. When a British businessman called John Kenworthy had stumbled across Tolstoy's writings in America in 1890, for example, they had completely changed his life. He abandoned all desire to settle in America and make money, and returned home to England to live and work amongst the poor in the East End of London. In 1893 he published a book entitled *Anatomy of Misery: Plain Lectures on Economics*. To the vegetarian pacifist Ernest Crosby, a reforming American lawyer and Tolstoyan, Kenworthy described the day in March 1894 when he received his first letter from Tolstoy as the happiest in his life.[49] For his part, Tolstoy told Kenworthy that it was a 'joy' to be in communication with him, and that he had not only read his book, but had commissioned a Russian translation.[50]

In May 1894 Kenworthy became honorary pastor of the newly established 'Croydon Brotherhood Church', a Tolstoy-inspired organisation whose congregation, according to one member of its committee of management, included every possible kind of crank, including 'Atheists, Spiritualists, Individualists, Communists, Anarchists, ordinary politicians, Vegetarians, Anti-vivisectionists and Anti-vaccinationists'.[51] In October that year Tolstoy acquired another British follower when he received a letter from Arthur St John, a former officer in the Inniskilling Fusiliers in his early thirties. St John wrote to tell Tolstoy that after reading *The Kingdom of God Is Within You* while returning from Burma on sick leave, he had left the army and joined an agricultural community. He commented later about the power of Tolstoy's inspiration:

> It had so tremendous an effect upon me that within two or three months I had given up my commission and found myself launched out in the world with no job and no capabilities for any work other than soldiering. I was clear about very little but among the little was Tolstoy's dictum that if you want to work for peace there was no use in preparing for war.[52]

All across Europe, Tolstoy's ideas were falling on fertile ground. In February 1895 Tolstoy heard about a twenty-six-year-old Slovak doctor called Albert Škarvan who had been so influenced by his religious writings that he had become a conscientious objector. When Škarvan refused to complete his military service, the Habsburg authorities first had him examined in a Viennese psychiatric ward, and then imprisoned him in a military jail.[53] Kenworthy, St John and Škarvan would all soon become actively involved in supporting Tolstoy's endeavours.

Tolstoy also had an ardent supporter in Russian-occupied Finland, where the nationalist movement was steadily gaining momentum in the face of recent militant Russification. Like his composer brother-in-law Jean Sibelius, Arvid Järnefelt was committed to Finnish independence, but his devotion to Tolstoy was greater. A lawyer who had spent two years studying Russian in Moscow in the late 1880s, Järnefelt first encountered Tolstoy's writings in 1891 while working in the civil service in Helsinki. Against his family's wishes, he abandoned his profession to become a full-time farmer, writer and cobbler, and even ceased sexual relations with his wife. Järnefelt translated some of Tolstoy's works into Finnish, and preached his ideas of land reform through his own writings.[54] In February 1895 Tolstoy wrote to thank him for sending him his recently completed autobiographical novella *My Awakening*

(*Heräämiseni*), and in particular the chapter he had helpfully translated into Russian which discusses why he could not become a judge.[55]

It gladdened Tolstoy's heart to develop contacts with like-minded Christian thinkers abroad, but his main concern was the plight of fellow-brethren in Russia who were persecuted for their beliefs. In May 1895, a few months after Tolstoy had first met with the Dukhobors in Moscow, Chertkov received a letter from the exiled Dmitry Khilkov in the Caucasus, who wrote to tell him that eleven Dukhobor soldiers had refused to go on Easter parade, and no longer wanted to continue their military service.[56] In June there was a mass burning of arms by Verigin's followers in protest against conscription. A ferocious wave of repressions followed. About 200 Dukhobors were jailed, while aggressive Cossacks were billeted to their villages and their families dispersed amongst Tatar, Armenian and Georgian communities. Tolstoy decided to take action. On 23 October his letter to John Kenworthy about the Dukhobors was published in *The Times* in London, along with an edited version of an account of what had been going on written by Biryukov, who had travelled down to the Caucasus to investigate.[57] That autumn Tolstoy wrote his first letter to Pyotr Verigin, and Chertkov began collecting materials documenting government persecution of the Dukhobors.

After deciding to relinquish the management of The Intermediary in 1893, Chertkov threw his energies into collecting materials on the persecution of sectarians in Russia. By 1902 he had a file consisting of 4,000 documents.[58] He also wanted to devote himself to the dissemination and preservation of Tolstoy's literary legacy; this, in fact, became his life's work. Since 1889 he had been systematically copying everything Tolstoy wrote and maintaining an archive of Tolstoy's new manuscripts, which were dutifully sent on from Yasnaya Polyana. Now he wanted to publish all of Tolstoy's banned works in England. He had been deliberating about whether to move there with his family, but shelved that idea, to Tolstoy's relief, when he heard that John Kenworthy had decided to relinquish the pastorship of the Brotherhood Church in order to found the Brotherhood Publishing Company. Chertkov invited him to Moscow. At their meeting in December Kenworthy was given the rights to publish Tolstoy's new work in English, and in February 1896 the members of his community sent Tolstoy a letter of support to the Dukhobors in the Caucasus which they asked him to pass on. It was in 1896 that Tolstoy began writing his magnificent short novel *Hadji Murat*, which he continued to work on until 1904 and which remained unpublished at his death. It is set in the Caucasus, during Russia's war with the Chechen and Daghestani highlanders. Although the story fictionalises an historical event – the capture by the Russians in 1851 of Hadji Murat, one of Imam Shamil's former henchmen – and draws on Tolstoy's own experiences fighting in the Caucasus, the story is also coloured philosophically by his new Christian beliefs, and inspired by the Dukhobors' heroic resistance.

The Dukhobors continued to prey on Tolstoy's mind throughout 1896 – a year in which Nicholas II was finally crowned in Moscow, and thousands were crushed to death or injured during the celebrations which followed. The combination of this horrifying spectacle with the magnificent splendour of state pageantry seemed eloquently to sum up the extremes of Russia's autocratic regime. In December that year Chertkov completed a direct appeal for help for the Dukhobors with the assistance of Biryukov and Tregubov. They published it in England in early 1897 together with an afterword by Tolstoy. Chertkov then went on to Petersburg to start active campaigning, but the Russian government intervened. Before Nicholas II's coronation, Pobedonostsev had despaired of Tolstoy in a letter:

> It's terrible to think of Lev Tolstoy, as he's spreading a terrible infection of anarchy and atheism throughout the whole of Russia! It's as if he was possessed by the devil – but what should be done with him? Obviously he is an enemy of the church, an enemy of any government and any civil order. There is a suggestion in the Synod that he be excommunicated from the church to avoid any doubts and confusion amongst the people, who see and hear that the entire intelligentsia worships Tolstoy. Probably, after the coronation the question will arise: what should be done with Tolstoy?[59]

The moment had arrived to answer that question. From this point until Tolstoy's death thirteen years later, the Russian government deployed an effective strategy of leaving him alone, while taking punitive action against his followers. On 5 February Chertkov's Petersburg apartment was searched, and he was informed he was to be sent into exile for illicit involvement in the affairs of sectarians, and for spreading subversive propaganda. His powerful connections had not given him complete immunity, but they did ensure he was not sent to Siberia. Vladimir Ulyanov, a lawyer turned revolutionary from Simbirsk, was not so lucky. He had been languishing in a Petersburg jail for conspiring against Alexander III, and that same month was exiled to a village on the River Yenisey, south of Krasnoyarsk (he later renamed himself Lenin, after the Lena, another mighty Siberian river). Chertkov had the much gentler option of going to England, a country he loved. Biryukov and Tregubov were also dealt with leniently: they were exiled to villages in the empire's Baltic territories.

Accompanied by Sonya, Tolstoy came to St Petersburg to see his friends off – he had not been in the city since 1880, and it would be his last ever visit to the capital. The secret police had a field day, filing detailed reports on his every movement, including to the barber on Panteleimon Street where he had his beard trimmed. They even embellished their despatches with loving details about Tolstoy's couture (a short coat tied with a grey belt, dark trousers and a dark grey knitted hat one day, and a heavy coat with a lambswool collar, dark grey trousers and a grey felt hat the next).[60] Tolstoy was mobbed everywhere he went, and given a huge ovation at the railway station when he left to go back to Moscow. There were only two people he did not enjoy seeing. One was Chertkov's indomitable mother, Elizaveta Ivanovna, who loathed him for leading her only son astray (she also thought he was imbued with the spirit of the Antichrist for not acknowledging Christ's resurrection).[61] The other was his implacably devout old relative Alexandra Andreyevna, no longer his dear friend and confidante Alexandrine.[62]

Tolstoy was abandoned by another of his devoted followers in 1897: six months after Chertkov's departure, his daughter Masha suddenly announced that she was to be married. She was twenty-six, and had finally decided to insist on some independence after several potential engagements had been thwarted by her father.[63] Tolstoy was no happier about Masha marrying Nikolay Obolensky, the son of his niece Liza, who was a feckless youth without an income. He noted in his diary that seeing Masha get married to someone like Obolensky was like watching a thoroughbred horse being ruined by being made to carry water. He was also not happy about the fact that Masha now reneged on her earlier principles and demanded her share of the family property. But most importantly, Masha had been his faithful helpmeet – meek, quiet and always willing to help, so her departure from Yasnaya Polyana, even though she did not go far, left a huge hole in her father's life. It was Masha he loved best of all amongst his children.

Soon after Chertkov's departure, Masha's elder sister Tanya also began to loosen her ties to her father by beginning an affair with a man fourteen years older than her who had six children. She felt very guilty, feeling she had sullied herself. Mikhail Sukhotin was unhappily married to a woman who was gravely ill, and who in fact died later that year, but that did not make it easier. Tanya's previous romantic life had also been quite unhappy. It was difficult living in a house where all the attention was directed at her father. Everything revolved around him, and Tanya felt aggrieved that he gave his time to just about anyone who turned up to see him, but not to his own daughter.[64] She had been devastated in October 1886 when Chertkov, at the age of thirty-two, had married Anna Diterikhs, a general's daughter from St Petersburg. Anna Konstantinovna, or Galya, as she was universally known, was twenty-seven (Tanya was then twenty-two), and not only was she educated, having been one of the first graduates of the university courses that had finally been opened to women in 1878, but also beautiful – Yaroshenko had painted her portrait in his famous 1883 painting *The Student*. Galya was also earnest and principled, and completely committed to Tolstoyan ideals. It was not that Tanya was in love with Chertkov, but she admired him, and she felt dejected to be always on the sidelines, never quite beautiful, clever or noble enough to take centre stage.[65] Tanya had also been very drawn to the handsome Evgeny Popov while he was living at Yasnaya Polyana in 1894. He was exactly her age, but he was still technically married, and even less eligible in her parents' eyes than Pavel Biryukov, the Tolstoyan who had courted Masha.[66] Following the lead of her parents, who still read each other's diaries manically, Tanya showed Popov her diaries, and received his to read. Tolstoy also got to see his daughter's diary, and then he put a stop to the relationship.[67] He and Sonya were no happier about Tanya's liaison with Misha Sukhotin, but it led to a happy marriage.

Tanya had been a peacemaker for her parents, and she was keenly missed. In the summer of 1897 Masha lamented in a letter to Galya Chertkova that there was a sadness at Yasnaya Polyana, with each person dealing with their own issues, and feeling very lonely.[68] There certainly seemed to be many problems in both generations of the Tolstoy family that year. Sergey's marriage had gone wrong soon after he married in 1895, and in 1897 his wife divorced him after their son was born.[69] Ilya now had three children (a fourth had died before his second birthday), his wife Sonya was expecting another, and he was always short of money. Lev junior had recovered from the nervous break-down he had suffered after the famine-relief work out in Samara, and had married the daughter of the Swedish doctor who had cured him in Stock-holm, but, like most of his brothers, he was fanatically opposed to his father's views. After he and his wife moved into the wing at Yasnaya Polyana, there had been many bitter rows with Lev senior. The situation with the three youngest children was not much better. Andrey, who turned twenty in 1897, had been expelled from school for tearing up a picture of Nicholas II, and was leading a dissipated life. He was already a notorious womaniser, first angering his father by wanting to marry a peasant girl from Yasnaya Polyana whom he had become involved with at the age of fifteen, then absconding to the Caucasus where he fell in love with a Georgian princess, who in due course was also unceremoniously dropped.[70] Andrey constantly ran up large debts, and expected his mother to bail him out. Eighteen-year-old Misha, still at school in Moscow, was suffering teenage angst, and Alexandra (Sasha), who turned thirteen in 1897, had turned into a tomboy with an unwavering hostility towards her mother. This was hardly surprising as Sonya had neglected her youngest daughter from the moment she was born.

There were also problems over at Pirogovo. To the horror of Tolstoy's brother Sergey, whose way of life was very ancien régime, despite his uncon-ventional marriage, both his daughters had become fervent Tolstoyans. In 1897 Varya became the common-law wife of Vladimir Vasiliev, who was one of Sergey's peasants, and she left home. Her elder sister Vera was also a free spirit who shocked her father by having a child out of wedlock a couple of years later with Abdurashid Sarafov, a Bashkir who had come to Pirogovo to provide them with koumiss.[71] Tolstoy felt very guilty. In 1897 Sonya's strange obsession with Taneyev and his playing showed no sign of abating, and Tolstoy yearned again to leave home. At one point he got as far as writing a farewell letter to Sonya, but ended up stuffing it down the back of a chair after they made up.[72] Sonya agreed not to invite Taneyev to Yasnaya Polyana again, and Tolstoy channelled his feelings about music, and what he regarded as its dangerous powers, on to the page. The product was his iconoclastic treatise *What is Art?*, which he had been thinking about writing ever since his daughter Tanya had become a student at the Academy of Painting, Sculpture and Architecture in 1881.

What is Art? is of a piece with Tolstoy's religious writings, in that it promotes the sort of Christian art to which he himself aspired. Art for Tolstoy was to the ability to communicate universal feelings of brotherly love to the widest possible audience. Everything else is made the subject of condemnation as 'counterfeit art', namely:

> all novels and poems which transmit ecclesiastical or patriotic feelings, and also exclusive feelings pertaining only to the class of the idle rich, such as aristocratic honour, satiety, spleen, pessimism, and refined and vicious feelings flowing from sex-love – quite incomprehensible to the great majority of mankind.
>
> In painting we must similarly place in the class of bad art all the Church, patriotic, and exclusive pictures; all the pictures representing the amusements and allurements of a rich and idle life; all the so-called symbolic pictures, in which the very meaning of the symbol is comprehensible only to the people of a certain circle; and, above all, pictures with voluptuous subjects – all that odious female nudity which fills all the exhibitions and galleries. And to this class belongs almost all the chamber and opera music of our times, beginning especially with Beethoven (Schumann, Berlioz, Liszt, Wagner) – by its subject-matter devoted to the expression of feelings accessible only to people who have developed in themselves an unhealthy, nervous irritation evoked by this exclusive, artificial, and complex music ...[73]

Into the category of 'counterfeit art' falls most of modern Western culture, deplored by Tolstoy as degenerate and elitist, not to mention all the fiction he himself wrote before he became an overtly Christian artist (such as the novels *War and Peace* and *Anna Karenina*).

Looking back over the trajectory of Tolstoy's career, it is possible to see that he took pains to transform himself into a different kind of artist long before his religious 'conversion' at the end of the 1870s. The love and care he invested in his *ABC* books is testament to his desire to simplify his artistic expression, just as the distress and discomfort he experienced writing *Anna Karenina* is witness to the pangs of conscience provoked by his return to writing for an educated audience. Tolstoy was never less than a consummate artist, however. The simplicity of the message conveyed by his late masterpiece *The Death of Ivan Ilyich* belies the sophisticated means with which the story is constructed on both the narrative and thematic levels, and his hard-won clarity exerted a huge impact on younger writers like Chekhov, whose linguistic register is deliberately unpretentious and straightforward. Tolstoy certainly recognised Chekhov as a major artist – they had warmed to each other at their first meeting, when Chekhov visited Yasnaya Polyana in the summer of 1895 (stealing Tanya's heart, before Sonya nipped the development of any romantic feelings in the bud).[74] All the same, Tolstoy's impossibly narrow criteria meant that most of Chekhov's greatest stories (and all his plays) failed to make the grade as true art.

Of all the arts, Tolstoy regarded music as the most powerful, and also the most dangerous. He was a sentimental man, often reduced to tears by his favourite pieces, and it was probably his inability to control his emotional reactions to music as much as his moral scruples which made him condemn much of it. There is here a link here, of course, to Tolstoy's punitive attitude to female sensuality, which also exerted a hypnotic hold over him, and which he also censured on moral grounds in works like *The Kreutzer Sonata*. The writer D. H. Lawrence, for one, was incensed that the vibrant, warm-hearted Anna Karenina had to fall victim to Tolstoy's didactic urge and be essentially punished for her sexuality. As someone who in 1912 himself eloped with a married woman who had three children, Lawrence took strong exception to the idea that Tolstoy's admirably brave and passionate heroine should have to pay for committing adultery by committing suicide.[75] Similarly, Tolstoy seemed to find it easier to deal with the 'terrible power' of music by dismissing it.[76]

There was always a lot of music at Yasnaya Polyana, and the Becker concert grand in the main drawing room was at some point joined by a second, smaller model made by the same firm, which was reputed to be the best in Russia. (Jakob Becker, a German immigrant, had set up his piano manufacturing business in St Petersburg in 1841.) Both Tolstoy and his sister Masha were keen pianists who sometimes played for hours at a stretch (Sergey Tolstoy remembered his father sometimes playing until one in the morning in the 1870s while he was growing up), while Sonya also played, and her sister Tanya had a fine soprano voice. Of the Tolstoy children, Sergey and Misha were musically the most talented. Sergey went on to become a respected composer and ethnomusicologist who collaborated with the Indian Sufi musician and philosopher Inayat Khan, and he taught at the Moscow Conservatoire in the late 1930s. Misha was an accomplished pianist and violinist.

Apart from the family's amateur music-making (which involved lots of duets), there were also impromptu concerts given by the professional musicians who came to visit Yasnaya Polyana and the house in Moscow. These increased as Tolstoy grew more famous. Visitors ranged from the legendary Polish harpsichordist Wanda Landowska, who performed Rameau, to Boris Troyanovsky, the first great virtuoso balalaika player, whose repertoire consisted mostly of Russian folk tunes. Tolstoy personally invited this 'Russian Paganini' to Yasnaya Polyana in the summer of 1909, shortly before he played for Queen Alexandra at Windsor Castle. The opera singers Nikolay and Medea Figner came up to Yasnaya Polyana from their nearby dacha on a number of occasions and bewitched the local peasants with their powerful voices, while one winter's evening Shaliapin and Rachmaninov turned up to perform at the Moscow house. The musician to whom Tolstoy became closest, despite the almost fifty years difference between their ages, was the pianist Alexander Goldenweiser, whom he got to know in 1897. Goldenweiser often played Tolstoy's favourite Chopin pieces, and later became a trusted friend of Chertkov – the memoirs he began publishing in 1922 are heavily biased against Sonya.

Even Goldenweiser had to admit that Tolstoy was a dilettante when it came to music.[77] Tolstoy liked folk music and gypsy music, and most of Haydn, but otherwise was very selective about approving works by the other major western European composers. According to his son Sergey, Tolstoy liked Mozart's symphonies, some of his sonatas and a few of his arias, and he liked certain early Beethoven sonatas (definitely none of the late works). He liked some of Schumann's piano pieces and the *Dichterliebe*, one of Schubert's impromptus, and a handful of his Lieder. Otherwise his favourite composer, despite his general animus towards elite Western culture, was by far and away Chopin, which is somewhat ironic given that he was the salon musician par excellence.[78] Tolstoy certainly did not like Taneyev's own music, but then there was barely any contemporary music he had time for, Russian or otherwise. He professed to being choked by the news of Tchaikovsky's untimely death in October 1893, but he had not always been very complimentary about his music.

They had met in 1876 at the Moscow Conservatoire at Tolstoy's express insistence. Tchaikovsky was very flattered that Tolstoy wanted to meet him (he was still at a relatively early stage of his career) but he was a very retiring man, and found the one serious conversation they had very onerous. It was not just that he was constantly terrified the novelist's penetrating gaze would bore straight into the 'innermost recesses' of his soul, but that he also did not enjoy being lectured at about music. He recounted the gruesome experience afterwards in a letter:

> [N]o sooner had we met than he straightaway started expounding his views on music. According to him *Beethoven lacked talent*. And that was his starting point. So, this great writer, this brilliant student of human nature began, in a tone of the utmost conviction, by delivering himself of an observation which was both fatuous and offensive to every musician. What is one to do in circumstances such as this? Argue? … Although my acquaintance with Tolstoy has convinced me that he is a somewhat paradoxical, but good and straightforward man, even, in his own way, sensitive to music, all the same, my acquaintance with him, as with anyone, has brought me nothing but weariness and torment.

The meeting was followed by an evening of chamber music put on in Tolstoy's honour, which included a performance of Tchaikovsky's First Quartet, op. 11, written in 1871. The fabled *andante cantabile* of its second movement is based on a Russian folk tune which Tchaikovsky had heard a carpenter sing while he was composing at his sister's house in Ukraine, and it brought tears to Tolstoy's eyes. That, at least, Tchaikovsky found touching.[79]

Tolstoy went to very few public musical performances, so his knowledge of, say, Mozart's symphonies mostly came from four-hand piano arrangements. His antipathy to the artificial conventions of opera, meanwhile, was developed at an early age (and expressed through his faux-naive account of Natasha's night at the opera in *War and Peace*, which is seen as if through her eyes). Tolstoy even exhorted Tchaikovsky to abandon writing operas,[80] so his response to the performance of Wagner's *Siegfried* that he went to at the Bolshoi Theatre in 1896 was perhaps entirely predictable. Tolstoy writes more about Wagner than any other artist in *What is Art?* Criticism of the performance of *Siegfried*, and of Wagnerian opera, takes up an entire chapter. Taneyev shared a box with the Tolstoys at the performance they attended on 18 April 1896, and although he liked Wagner no more than Tolstoy, he was heartily ridiculed for following with a score and listening seriously.[81] Tolstoy arrived late, and walked out before the end.

As with his analysis of Metropolitan Makary's *Orthodox Dogmatic*

Theology back in 1880, Tolstoy was very *parti pris* when it came to analysing Wagner's *Siegfried* – in both cases he took two isolated works out of context as exemplary of the whole, the easier to demolish them. *Siegfried* is the third part of a tetralogy, and by common consent the least engaging part of *The Ring*, so was a surprising repertoire choice for the sleepy Bolshoi Theatre in 1894, several years before even the Mariinsky, Imperial Russia's premier opera house, had staged any of Wagner's music dramas – works which place special demands both on singers and orchestra. The Mariinsky would finally complete a distinguished *Ring* cycle in 1907, but this Bolshoi *Siegfried*, sung in Russian, while a valiant effort, left a lot to be desired. Attendance at one of the two isolated revival performances in April 1896 was hardly the appropriate basis for a general assessment of Wagnerian art.[82]

Tolstoy had more or less built an entire artistic and religious edifice on the foundation of one aspect of Christianity (the Sermon on the Mount), and although he can be forgiven for not reading Wagner's ponderous aesthetic writings, here was a classic case of him wilfully refusing to consider all the dimensions of a structure in his path that did not conform to his specifications in the rush to tear it down. Although Wagner and Tolstoy were in certain important respects poles apart (the composer's bombast and love of luxury spring to mind), there are also some intriguing parallels between them. Under the influence of Schopenhauer both formulated a religious vision based on a highly idiosyncratic theology of redemptive love which had little in common with traditional Christianity.[83] Redemption can be attained only by renouncing *eros* and practising compassion or *agape,* the word for love used in the New Testament: such are the lessons of Wagner's last work *Parsifal* and all of Tolstoy's late works from *The Death of Ivan Ilyich* onwards. Only love can redeem mankind and bring about a state where human beings can be at peace with themselves and with each other. Thomas Mann was quite correct when he wrote in 1933 that the pattern of Tolstoy's artistic career was identical to that of Wagner, for in both cases, everything in their later oeuvre was prefigured in their earlier works.[84] For all its enthralling narrative, for example, *War and Peace* is ultimately about sin (separation from God, and the absence of human relatedness) and redemption (the restoration of love), as can be seen by following Natasha Rostova's spiritual journey.

Mann's comparison of the consistency of Wagner's artistic evolution with that of Tolstoy is instructive, for both Wagner and Tolstoy came to distinguish the simple religion of love and compassion for the poor and oppressed that Jesus Christ had founded from the deforming edifice of the Christian church (it is striking that they both made a serious study of Renan's *Life of Jesus* in 1878). They both wished to revive the spiritual essence of Christianity by removing its superstitious elements and the Old Testament notion of a vengeful God in order to create a purer and more practical religion. And the pacifism and vegetarianism both espoused in their final years went hand in hand with their views on the regeneration of society and a corresponding desire to simplify their aesthetic style. Before he died in 1883, Wagner came to see vegetarians and anti-vivisectionists as the harbingers of cultural renewal, and, ever the Romantic idealist, he hoped that through the medium of religious art (specifically music, his kind of music) a culture of compassion would replace the contemporary 'civilisation' of power and aggression. Tolstoy came to the same conclusions, but naturally the religious art he had in mind was primarily of the verbal kind. Both Wagner and Tolstoy were anxious for the rest of the world to gain insight into Jesus' radical idea that responding to violence with more violence can only lead to the further desecration of nature.

Tolstoy's deliberations in *What is Art?* were the fruit of long reflection and characteristically intense study, but were not at all objective, and out of step with the age in which he lived. As the age of modernism dawned, Tolstoy himself was now an anomaly as an artist. It was in 1896, after all, that Chekhov's *Seagull* was first performed, a play which Tolstoy thought was complete rubbish. In his pointed comparison of 'new' and 'old' art in the play, Chekhov offers subtle comments of his own on the question of 'What is art?', but typically refuses to be partisan. Like his stories, his great plays stand on the cusp of a new aesthetic sensibility, indebted on the one hand to the legacy of Tolstoy's generation, but also heralding things to come. Tolstoy was still alive as Russian artists began to become leaders of the European avant-garde, and he died only three years before the Futurists declared in their manifesto *A Slap in the Face of Public Taste* that they wished to throw 'Pushkin, Dostoyevsky, Tolstoy etc. etc.' overboard from the ship of modernity.

Tolstoy's chaotic publishing habits had not improved over the course of his career; indeed, they became more chaotic in his last years when different versions of his works appeared in Russia and England. Apart from the problems with negotiating censors, Tolstoy continually revised his manuscripts, and then his proofs, and he also continually changed his mind about where and how he wanted his works to appear in print. This did not make it easy for his editors and translators, and that was certainly the case with *What is Art?*, the first English edition of which was prepared by Aylmer Maude, an important figure in anglophone Tolstoy studies. Maude was the son of an Ipswich vicar and a Quaker mother, and had moved to Moscow in the early 1870s when he was sixteen years old. While he was working as a manager of the Russian Carpet Company, he married Louise Shanks, who was also English but born in Russia, and later they pooled their considerable linguistic resources to become distinguished translators of Tolstoy's writings. Maude had fallen under Tolstoy's spell after first meeting him in 1888, and their conversations in the 1890s led him to the conclusion that he could not spend his life selling carpets. In 1897, when the Maudes moved back to London, they stayed first at the Brotherhood Church in Croydon, as Chertkov's family had done earlier that year, and then followed them to Purleigh, near Maldon in Essex, where the first English Tolstoyan colony had been set up the year before.

In 1896 the colony consisted of just three men, all anxious to chase the utopian dream of living off the plot of land that had been bought by the more affluent members of the Brotherhood Church, but their number had already risen to fifteen by the end of 1897, and there were a further thirty-five or so like-minded people living nearby. The Maudes contributed generously by donating two cows, providing meals and holding concerts at their farmhouse. It was in Essex that Aylmer Maude completed his translation of *What is Art?*, which was no small feat, as he himself has described in the biography of Tolstoy he started publishing in 1908:

> As proof followed proof, each covered with fresh alterations, excisions, and additions, often very illegibly written, it required the closest attention to keep the text correct and to discriminate between changes made voluntarily, and changes made for the Censor which I was to disregard [for the English edition].[85]

Maude sent Tolstoy twenty-three long letters with detailed queries as he worked his way painstakingly through the text, which was finally published in full in 1898. The socialist playwright George Bernard Shaw, a didactic writer like Tolstoy who would enter into correspondence with him in his last years, was almost the only critic to write an enthusiastic review in England. There was a certain degree of mutual admiration between the two, but Tolstoy later chided Shaw for a lack of seriousness.[86] In Russia most people shared the view about *What is Art?* expressed by the artist Isaak Levitan, who described it in a letter to his friend Chekhov in Nice as brilliant and ridiculous at the same time. Five thousand copies were sold in the first week.[87]

Tolstoy was glad to get aesthetics out of the way, as his major project in 1898 was to help persecuted sectarians. In 1897 some Molokans came from Samara to ask for his help and advice: police had raided their villages late at night and taken away their children in order to bring them up in the Orthodox faith at an orphanage. Tolstoy wrote a lengthy letter to Nicholas II, and then a few months later wrote again when there was no response. His second letter was also greeted with silence, as was the letter he published in the *St Petersburg Gazette* that October. The Molokan children were returned to their parents only after Tolstoy's daughter Tanya succeeded in gaining an audience with Pobedonostsev in January 1898.[88] That left Tolstoy free to concentrate all his energies on the mission to help the Dukhobors, who finally learned that month that they were going to be allowed to settle abroad. Tolstoy had been tinkering since 1889 with a new novel, and this news gave him the impetus to finish it. He now decided he would make an exception and sell the rights, so that he could raise money to help pay for the Dukhobors to emigrate. As it turned out later, the funds would go to pay their passage to Canada, the country which expressed a willingness to receive them.

Resurrection, as the novel came to be called, drew on a story Tolstoy had heard from a lawyer friend. A nobleman appointed as a jury member had recognised a defendant on trial for theft as a poor woman he had once seduced, and been overcome with remorse. When she was sentenced to exile in Siberia, he offered to marry her, but she had died before he could atone for his sins. Hearing the story aroused guilty feelings in Tolstoy, who could not help but remember having taken advantage of his sister's servant girl Gasha Trubetskaya when he was a young man. He now combined the story he had heard from his lawyer friend with that of his own spiritual journey. Accordingly, the central character Prince Nekhlyudov breaks with his former life once he recognises in court his aunt's former peasant girl Katyusha Maslova, whom he once callously seduced. After she is sentenced to hard labour in Siberia through a miscarriage of justice, Nekhlyudov gives his land away to his peasants and follows her to Siberia in the hope of expiating his sins. Sonya had found it hard enough to deal with her husband's sanctimonious advocacy of chastity in *The Kreutzer Sonata* back in 1889, while still being forced to satisfy his apparently unquenchable sexual appetite. A decade later, when it was finally beginning to subside (when Masha had married in 1897, Sonya had moved into her bedroom at Yasnaya Polyana),[89] she read with distaste her husband's sensual description of the ravishing of Katyusha Maslova. But *Resurrection* was more than a love story and Bildungsroman, as Tolstoy suppressed the dictates of his artistic conscience to exploit another opportunity for lambasting all his favourite targets, namely the government, the Church and the judicial system, as well as private property and upper-class mores. Not all his readers would find the resulting mixture of intense lyricism, biting satire and moralising demagoguery terribly appealing, even if it was a compulsively readable narrative, like everything else that Tolstoy wrote, with flashes of brilliance.

Tolstoy worked on *Resurrection* throughout 1898, even on 28 August, his seventieth birthday. The government had forbidden the press from publishing any celebratory articles, but he received over a hundred congratulatory telegrams, and his picture appeared in shop windows in cities and towns all over Russia.[90] By autumn, Tolstoy was ready to negotiate a contract for the publication of *Resurrection*, and in October he signed a record-breaking deal with Adolf Marx, a publishing magnate based in Petersburg. Marx was proprietor of the weekly illustrated family magazine *The Cornfield*, which was enormously popular. Tolstoy had been paid 500 roubles per printer's sheet for his last novel, *Anna Karenina*, which appeared in an elite literary journal with a readership of a few thousand. For *Resurrection*, published in instalments in *The Cornfield*, which had 200,000 subscribers, Tolstoy received twice that, and a 12,000-rouble advance. The novel appeared throughout 1899, illustrated by Leonid Pasternak, and was a runaway success, being the first novel by Russia's most famous writer in over twenty years. It was an exhausting year for Tolstoy, since it entailed checking weekly sets of proofs, dealing with savage cuts made by the censor and being in constant communication with Chertkov in England.

Since arriving in England in the spring of 1897, Chertkov's main interest had been in propagandising Tolstoy's works throughout the world. He had begun by collaborating with John Kenworthy's Brotherhood Publishing

Company, but very soon had set up his own Russian-language publishing operation which took up most of his time. The goal of the Free Word Press, which was established near to the house with the apple orchard he had rented for his family near Purleigh, was to publish everything by Tolstoy that was banned in Russia, as well as articles he and other Tolstoyans had written. Everything was primarily destined for readers in Russia.[91] There were nine publications in 1897 alone, one of which was Tolstoy's afterword to the earlier Tolstoyan brochure 'Help! A Public Appeal Regarding the Caucasian Dukhobors'.[92] Chertkov now expanded his activities to act as Tolstoy's literary agent by orchestrating the publication of *Resurrection* abroad, both in Russian and in translation. His authorised edition of the novel for the Free Word Press was also the only unexpurgated Russian version printed, and it was published in book form at the end of 1899 at the same time as the first separate edition issued by Adolf Marx in St Petersburg. The novel was reprinted five times in 1900,[93] and was smuggled into Russia in enormous quantities. Chertkov also coordinated the British and American publication of Louise Maude's English translation by the Brotherhood Publishing Company in 1900. The success of *Resurrection* was phenomenal and unprecedented. Once it had appeared in *The Cornfield*, all rights were waived, and there were soon forty different editions in print in Russia, while fifteen different editions appeared in France in 1900.[94] The novel was read by literally hundreds of thousands of readers in the first few years of its publication. The Slovak translation was produced by Albert Škarvan, whom Chertkov had invited to Russia, and taken to Yasnaya Polyana to meet Tolstoy back in 1896.[95]

Assisted by Tolstoy's royalties, handsome contributions from wealthy Moscow merchants, unstinting donations from members of Kenworthy's colony at Purleigh (which brought it to near bankruptcy)[96] and English Quakers, over 7,500 Dukhobors made it to Canada on several specially chartered ships between December 1898 and May 1899. It was an enormous enterprise, involving Arthur St John, who travelled out to the Caucasus and was arrested and deported from Tiflis in February 1898, and Dmitry Khilkov, who had now completed his term of exile and took one group of Dukhobors initially to Cyprus, where conditions did not prove to be satisfactory. Then in March 1898, Chertkov happened to read an article by the exiled anarchist Pyotr Kropotkin, who was living in London but had just been to Canada in his capacity as a geographer to lecture on the glacial deposits in Finland.

In his article, Kropotkin wrote about the Mennonites who had left Russia in the 1870s to avoid conscription. They had settled in Canada, where they were now farming prairie land with considerable success. Chertkov invited Kropotkin to come to Purleigh to meet with him and the two Dukhobor representatives who had come to discuss their situation. After Kropotkin had convinced them that Canada was indeed the best place for the Dukhobors to settle, Aylmer Maude and Khilkov went on ahead to make arrangements (as a Tolstoyan, the seasick Maude was embarrassed at having to travel in a first-class cabin).[97]

By October 1898 agreement had been reached with the Canadian authorities, and with the help of Kropotkin's friend James Mavor, a Scottish-born Professor of Political Economy at the University of Toronto and Pavel Biryukov in Geneva, who acted as intermediary in the communications between Russia and Canada, the *Lake Huron* was chartered to make the first of several month-long sailings between the port of Batumi on the Black Sea and Halifax, Nova Scotia. The future Bolshevik Vladimir Bonch-Bruevich accompanied one of the sailings. He had a deep interest in the oral tradition of Dukhobor hymns and psalms, and remained in Canada for a year in order to study their culture. Later, as secretary to Lenin, he would play a crucial role in protecting the Tolstoyans for a short while when they in turn became victims of persecution after the Bolshevik Revolution. Amongst the many other volunteers who also took part in the operation was Tolstoy's son Sergey who set off first for England in August 1898 to have discussions with Chertkov and the Quakers. During his stay in London, Sergey and the two Dukhobor representatives who had been visiting Chertkov were shown round the British Museum by Kropotkin. Wherever they went they were followed by a top-hatted Russian spy and curious glances aroused by the exotic clothes of the Dukhobors, who were dressed in traditional blue *beshmets* (the belted knee-length coats worn by the Caucasian Cossacks), baggy trousers and wool caps.[98] From London, Sergey went to Paris to help negotiate first French rights to *Resurrection*, and then in December he accompanied 2,140 Dukhobors on the first sailing to Canada.[99] Tolstoy was overjoyed by the rapprochement with his eldest son.[100]

The exertion involved in writing and publishing *Resurrection* in serial form took a heavy toll on Tolstoy's health, and news that he had fallen ill spread rapidly throughout Russia. One person who was greatly concerned was Anton Chekhov, who a year earlier had gone to live in exile in the Crimea in a

11. Dmitry Khilkov (left) and Sergey Lvovich Tolstoy (right) standing amongst a group of those accompanying the Dukhobors to Canada, 1899

desperate attempt to stem the rapid advance of tuberculosis. He had suffered his first serious haemorrhage in Moscow in March 1897, and been taken to a clinic near Tolstoy's house. After Tolstoy came to visit him and spent hours talking to him about immortality, he had suffered another haemorrhage.[101] Even though he was in faraway Yalta, Chekhov not only managed to procure a copy of *Resurrection* the minute it was published as a complete novel, but had already finished it by the end of January 1900, as he declared in a letter to the journalist Mikhail Menshikov: 'I read it straight through in one gulp, not in instalments or in fits and starts. It is a magnificent work of art.'[102] In this letter, Chekhov also confessed that Tolstoy's illness had alarmed him and kept him in a 'constant state of tension'. He went on to speak for no doubt millions of Russians when he explained why that was. It is a remarkable letter that deserves quoting at length:

> I fear the death of Tolstoy. If he were to die, a large empty space would appear in my life. In the first place, there is no other person whom I love as I love him; I am not a religious person, but of all faiths I find his the closest to me and the most congenial. Secondly, when literature possesses a Tolstoy, it is easy and pleasant to be a writer; even when you know that you have achieved nothing yourself and are still achieving nothing, this is not as terrible as it might otherwise be because Tolstoy achieves for everyone. What he does serves to justify all the hopes and aspirations invested in literature. Thirdly, Tolstoy stands proud, his authority is colossal, and so long as he lives, bad taste in literature, all vulgarity, insolence and snivelling, all crude, embittered vainglory, will stay banished into outer darkness. He is the one person whose moral authority is sufficient in itself to maintain so-called literary fashions and movements on an acceptable level. Were it not for him the world of literature would be a flock of sheep without a shepherd, a stew in which it would be hard for us to find our way.[103]

In fact, it was the much younger Chekhov who would die first.

It was just as Tolstoy fell ill in November 1899 that Orthodox hierarchs began to discuss seriously the question of what to do with the heretic in their midst. Some of the most scathing chapters in *Resurrection* had been directed at the Orthodox Church, and this was an acute problem for an institution whose prestige and moral authority were closely bound up with those of the Russian government, which felt threatened on several fronts by the end of the nineteenth century. The final instalment of *Resurrection* had yet to appear, but Tolstoy had already provided enough evidence of his blasphemy in the eyes of the Holy Synod, not least in his vicious satire of the thinly disguised Chief Procurator Toporov, and two infamous chapters describing a service held for convicts which subject Orthodox rites to merciless ridicule. Consider, for example, Tolstoy's infamous description of the Holy Eucharist in chapter 39 of Part One:

> The essence of the service consisted in the supposition that the bits [of bread] cut up by the priest and put by him into the wine, when manipulated and prayed over in a certain way, turned into the flesh and blood of God. These manipulations consisted in the priest's regularly lifting and holding up his arms, though hampered by the gold cloth sack he had on, then, sinking on to his knees and kissing the table and all that was on it, but chiefly in his taking a cloth by two of its corners and waving it regularly and softly over the silver saucer and golden cup. It was supposed that, at this point, the bread and the wine turned into flesh and blood; therefore, this part of the service was performed with the utmost solemnity.[104]

The publication of *Resurrection* brought the question of the excommunication of Tolstoy back to the top of the Holy Synod's agenda.

Tolstoy's rebellion against the Orthodox Church was driven by his perception of its supine position as the mainstay of Russian autocracy. 'The sanctification of political power by Christianity is blasphemy; it is the negation of Christianity,' he had thundered in his 1886 article 'Church and State'. Supporting the state when it went to war was tantamount to the direct sanction of violence, and this was completely untenable as far as he was concerned, for it was a flat contradiction of Christ's teaching, not to mention one of the Ten Commandments. The Orthodox Church *was* vulnerable to Tolstoy's charges, and for the root causes of its moribund state at the end of the nineteenth century we need to look back to the fundamental changes to its autonomous status wrought by Peter the Great. The Russian Orthodox Church was still a very powerful institution when Peter became tsar in 1682, but his determination to forestall any challenge to his autocratic powers led him to take the momentous decision not to replace Patriarch Adrian after his death in

1700. Instead he placed the Church under the jurisdiction of a newly created department of state, the 'Most Holy Synod', which was established in the secular capital of St Petersburg in 1721 to replace the Patriarchate in 'Holy Mother Moscow'. Overseen by a lay chief procurator, whose title in Russian – *Ober-prokurator* – betrays the German Protestant origins of Peter's reformist ideas, the Russian Orthodox Church now became for many simply a tool of the government. Peter introduced formal seminary training to Russia in order to raise standards, but he also reduced the large number of Orthodox clergy, only a third of whom were actually ordained and had received some form of education. Peter's organisation of the state into a hierarchy of service ranks effectively also created a caste system in Russia which separated the clergy from all other classes and made it more or less hereditary, because only the sons of priests were eligible to enter seminaries and train for the priesthood.[105]

Most clergy were very poor. They received no salary and were dependent for their livelihood (and that of their often numerous families) on the small sums offered by parishioners in return for the performance of church offices. This was only slightly augmented by the income from farming the small plot of land attached to their parish, so their standard of living was often scarcely better than the average peasant. Chekhov's story 'A Nightmare', written in 1886, describes the embarrassment of a conscientious young priest who is too poor even to be able to offer tea to a visitor. His church is as shabby as his ill-fitting, patched cassock and his house, which is described as being 'no different from the peasant izbas, except that the straw on the roof was a bit more even, and there were little white curtains in the windows'.[106] It is quite a different picture from the usual portrayal in English fiction of the country vicar in his comfortable parsonage, a respected and educated member of the community, and socially inferior only to the local squire. The status of most rural Russian priests, who depended on the peasantry for their basic income, remained very low.

The moral authority of the clergy had steadily eroded over the course of the nineteenth century for understandable reasons. Reliant on assistance from the local peasants in tilling their land, parish priests were understandably disinclined to offend them by refusing their hospitality during icon processions, or by proffering unwelcome moral reproof. The clergy often found themselves equally compromised, for different reasons, when it came to their relations with members of the nobility. Priests found themselves having to pander to the whims of despotic, lawless landowners by carrying out forced marriages or burials of serfs who had died in suspicious circumstances. The overall result of Peter the Great's 'reform' was a highly conservative Church with no interest in doctrinal development, and a demoralised and corrupt clergy which was little respected.[107] The publication abroad in 1858 of a frank exposure of the realities of Russian parish life written by a priest hopeful of change created a sensation when it was illicitly read in Russia on the eve of the Great Reforms.[108] Attempts were made in the late 1860s to improve the church education system (in 1863 seminary graduates were allowed for the first time to go to university, and in 1864 children of clergy were allowed the privilege of attending a state lycée), but the reforms went no further after the seminaries became hotbeds of revolutionary activity.[109] Against such a background, the rise in spiritual prestige of the Optina Pustyn Monastery becomes clearer: by reviving the Hesychast traditions of the Church Fathers, its elders were able to separate themselves from the tainted world of ecclesiastical officialdom.

At the end of the nineteenth century the Russian Orthodox Church certainly felt embattled. The legendary piety of the peasantry expressed itself more in ritual observance of fasts and processions than in attendance at church, its acquaintance with the Scriptures severely restricted by the archaic Church Slavonic which remained the ecclesiastical language of both the Bible and all services.[110] There were already about 180 fast days of differing severity in the Orthodox calendar, but it was quite common for peasants to observe extra fasting days. One old woman confessed to her priest that she had eaten forbidden food on a fast day: radishes whose seeds had been soaked in milk before planting. Many peasants regarded it as sinful to drink tea with sugar on fast days, as they not only regarded tea as 'semi-sinful', but thought that sugar was made of animal bones (dog bones, in fact). There were even some fiercely ascetic peasants who regarded mother's milk as sinful. The Church had also long before ceased to be looked up to as a spiritual authority by the intelligentsia, whose more radical members typically tended to see themselves as morally superior to the clergy, while the aristocracy tended to be apathetic, and their religious devotions merely notional. This is why Protestant Evangelists like Lord Radstock who championed private Bible study made great inroads in high-society circles frequented by people like Chertkov's mother,

Elizaveta Ivanovna. By resisting the production of modern Russian translations of the Bible for so long, the Church played its own part in sustaining the rich world of superstitions which the Russian people lived by. Fearing that ordinary believers might make their own erroneous interpretations, and challenge its authority, it was only in 1876 that the Synod officially approved a translation from Church Slavonic into the modern vernacular as mentioned earlier. Even then it tried to control access, but by the end of the nineteenth century about a million copies had been successfully distributed by Russian and foreign religious groups.[111]

The other main challenge to the Russian Orthodox Church came from religious dissenters. In order to dissuade the peasantry from being drawn to the Old Believers, who had been identified with popular rebellion by the authorities ever since the schism of the 1660s, clergy were exhorted in the 1880s to make their services as sumptuous as possible.[112] Most threatening of all to the Church and government, however, were the many newer sects which grew rapidly in popularity in the nineteenth century. The Old Believers, and to a lesser extent sects such as the Khlysty and the Skoptsy at least subscribed essentially to the same faith – their differences were over details of ritual. The so-called 'rational' sectarian faiths, however, dispensed fundamentally with religious ritual, along with priests, churches, icons and all other paraphernalia. Their adherents preached a Christian doctrine of love, equality and freedom which did not recognise governmental authority. On the one hand there were the descendants of German colonists known as 'Stundists', whose economic enterprise, teetotalism and devotion to personal Bible reading in the vernacular began to attract large numbers of Russian peasants in the nineteenth century, while on the other there were the indigenous Dukhobors and the Molokans.

Tolstoy's spiritual rebellion, then, did not arise in a vacuum, and should be seen in this important socio-religious context. Unceasing expansion had made Russia an enormous multi-ethnic empire, and by the time of the 1897 Missionary Congress thirty per cent of its population were Muslim, Jewish or belonged to other faiths. Nevertheless, only the Orthodox Church was allowed to engage in missionary activities within the borders of the empire. The first two Missionary Congresses, held in Moscow in 1887 and 1891, had mostly focused on ways to corral the Old Believers into coming back into the fold of Orthodoxy, but the third, held in Kazan, had focused on countering the influence in Russia of sects and Bible-based Protestant and Evangelist denominations. These, it found, were on the increase, despite missionary work and government initiatives. Metropolitan Melety of Ryazan won support at the Congress with his proposal that sectarians should be deported to special camps in the Siberian tundra. He also proposed that their property should be confiscated, and their children removed.[113] Only fear of widespread protests from Baptists abroad apparently prevented Nicholas II from making this official policy. Confident that the peasantry would never follow political revolutionaries, he was far more worried about evangelical Christians and figures like Tolstoy. The liberal newspaper *Russian Gazette* reported that the 200 bishops, priests and ecclesiastical figures at the 1897 Missionary Congress had classified Tolstoyanism as a sect like any other:

> The Congress placed the religious-moral views of Count Lev Tolstoy amongst the new sectarian faiths, asserting that his followers made up a 'fully formed sect'. Asserting also that this sect fully conformed to the definition of sects which were 'particularly dangerous to the Church and the state', the Congress resolved to ask the Holy Synod to propose to the government that the law established with regard to 'particularly dangerous' sects be applied to its adherents.[114]

Tolstoyanism was seen as all the more pernicious for its potential to appeal simultaneously to the educated elite and the peasantry, and the influence of Tolstoy's ideas on Pyotr Verigin and the Dukhobors shows the reality of this threat.

Konstantin Pobedonostsev, who had become Chief Procurator of the Holy Synod in 1880, a post which he held for twenty-five years, regarded Tolstoy as his arch-enemy. Tolstoy had first antagonised him by asking him to pass on the letter he wrote in 1881 to Alexander III, in which he asked for clemency for his father's assassins. Convinced from the time of reading that letter (which he had refused to pass on), that Tolstoy was intent on bringing down the government, Pobedonostsev had led a vigorous campaign to silence his opponent. This had resulted in Tolstoy's religious teachings being regularly denounced by Church figures, and the constant, and often intrusive, surveillance of his private life (even the Yasnaya Polyana priest was obliged to send reports to the Bishop of Tula).[115] The ambitious son of a

Moscow priest, who rose to become a professor of law before occupying the post of Procurator, Pobedonostsev was devoted to his duty. The wonderfully named Hermann von Samson-Himmelstierna provides a vivid thumbnail portrait of him in the history of Alexander III's reign which he published in 1893:

> There are two classes of fanatics, the cold and the hot – that is, fanatics from reflection and fanatics by temperament. It is easy to know to which Pobedonostsev belongs. His looks betray him. He is old and of a spare build, his nose is pointed, his eyes are keen and penetrating, he wears spectacles, his forehead is fringed with a few grey hairs, his face is clean-shaven, and his expression is keen.[116]

Both Pobedonostsev and Tolstoy, who were almost exact contemporaries, felt Russian society needed to be healed, but they certainly differed in their diagnosis of its ailments.

When Tolstoy fell ill at the end of 1899, while he was completing *Resurrection*, the Holy Synod decided first to ban all prayers in his memory after his death, anticipating that he might not have much longer to live. When he regained his health it then pressed on with its ill-conceived excommunication plan. In his zeal to shore up the foundations of the Orthodox Church, Pobedonostsev had long ago clamoured for Tolstoy to be excommunicated, but it was Metropolitan Antony of St Petersburg who now took the initiative, motivated by fears that even the clergy might succumb to Tolstoyanism. There was some justification for this. In 1898 Grigory Petrov, a charismatic young priest in St Petersburg, had published a book called *The Gospel as the Foundation of Life* which focused on the Tolstoyan idea of the practical application of Christianity in everyday living; it went into twenty editions. In early February 1901 Petrov was reprimanded by Metropolitan Antony for discussing Tolstoy in a positive light at a meeting of the Religious-Philosophical Society: he had declared that Tolstoy was doing for Russian society what Virgil had done for Dante, by leading people who had lost their way spiritually out of purgatory.[117] The process to excommunicate Tolstoy was initiated the next day, and was announced ten days later. Nicholas II was apparently angry not to have been asked for his approval beforehand, and Pobedonostsev was forced to apologise.[118]

Metropolitan Antony had actually been keen to act earlier, so that the Synod's edict could be announced on 18 February, which was the first Sunday of Great Lent. Until 1869 it had been traditional to pronounce an annual anathema in church against enemies of the state on the first Sunday of Lent, just before the 'Victory of Orthodoxy' week, and no doubt the Church would have liked to include Tolstoy in its roster of heretics at least in memory of the traditional proclamation:

> To those who do not believe that the Orthodox monarchs have been raised to the throne by virtue of a special grace of God – and that, at the moment the sacred oil is laid on them, the gifts of the Holy Ghost are infused into them anent the accomplishment of their exalted mission; and to those who dare to rise and rebel against them, such as Grisha Otrepev, Ivan Mazeppa, and others like them: Anathema! Anathema! Anathema![119]

Back in 1837 the German travel writer J. G. Kohl had the chance to witness the 'cursing of the heretics' first-hand at the Kazan Cathedral in St Petersburg, and so many believers wanted to attend, he claimed, that police had to be called to keep order. He described it as 'the most extraordinary, incomprehensible, and terrible service of the Eastern Church', the only one where cursing could be heard in a country where the people were generally more inclined to bless nearly everything:

> The anathematizing began with a long service, with singing, reading, opening and shutting of doors; lighting of tapers, and burning of incense; coming and going, &c … [The Venerable Metropolitan] stepped forward and called down anathemas upon a number of people; on the false Demetrius, on Boris Godunoff, Mazeppa, Stenka Razin and Pugatsheff; and after these political heretics followed the religious ones, but they were only mentioned in general terms. Each person or class was first characterized by a few introductory words, their names pronounced, and then followed two or three times, like thunder after lightning, the word: *anafema, anafema* …[120]

Tolstoy was in lofty company. In 1901, clergy in Russian churches had to make do with an anathema on Tolstoy's *Resurrection*, rather than on his person. Nonetheless it was a huge event of huge social and political significance.

The Church had historically only anathematised individuals after repeated efforts to bring about repentance. The edict about Tolstoy stressed that he had preached fanatically against Orthodox dogma, so could not be regarded as a member of the Church unless he repented, but it was all very measured. The words 'anathema' or 'excommunication' were not in fact explicitly mentioned in the edict, which was announced on the front page of the weekly *Church News* (the official publication of the Holy Synod since 1888), and followed by an explanatory letter.[121] Edict No. 577, dated 20–22 February, was signed by the three metropolitans, an archbishop and three bishops, none of whom was under any illusion that it would frighten Tolstoy, or even bring him to heel. But by having it published on the front page of every major Russian newspaper on 25 February, and issuing a government decree banning its discussion in the press, the Synod hoped it could undermine the public support for Tolstoy which was steadily growing in Russia amongst all sections of the population. The intention was to provoke a backlash of hostility towards him and diminish his authority at a critical time of social and political unrest, while simultaneously enhancing the profile of the Orthodox Church. The reality was the opposite – it was a dismal failure. No one except the ecclesiastical authorities took the excommunication seriously, and yet it proved to be an event whose repercussions would be far-reaching.

Tolstoy was in Moscow at the beginning of 1901. As usual, his preoccupations were intellectual. He had begun the year by reading *The Six Systems of Indian Philosophy* by Max Müller, and alongside his engagement with Hindu and Nietzschean philosophy, continued his study of Dutch. Sonya's concerns were, as usual, more worldly. She was as busy as ever. She travelled to Yasnaya Polyana to look after their daughter Tanya after she had a stillborn child, then came back to Moscow to help with the preparations for their son Misha's wedding to Alexandra Glebova on 31 January: she sewed little bags which would later be filled with sweets and given to the guests. The wedding was a high-society event attended by Grand Dukes (one of whom came specially from St Petersburg) but pointedly not by her husband. On 12 February she went back to Yasnaya Polyana when she heard that Masha had miscarried, and then came back to take care of the household in Moscow, and a gloomy husband who was expressing his fears of death. The seven weeks of the Great Lent began, and with it fasting, so on 16 February she went to the mushroom market with Semyon Nikolayevich the cook, and on to church. The next day she took herself off to buy toys for the children in the Moscow orphanage of which she had become patron.

On the day the excommunication became public, Tolstoy declared in a letter to his daughter Masha that the only thing he really wanted to write about now was people's lack of religion, which he believed was the cause of all the horrors in the world.[122] He was far more serious about living in accordance with Christian principles than the majority of those in his class, and he believed in God more than most, so there was an irony in the Church excommunicating someone with such deeply held, if unorthodox, Christian views. He had been oblivious to all the machinations earlier, and so he just carried on writing outspoken polemical articles and letters of protest attacking the corruption of the Church and the government whose militarist policies it supported. From Sonya's diary we learn that there was wonderful weather at the time of Tolstoy's excommunication – clear days and moonlit nights. She records how affectionate and passionate her husband suddenly became when the edict was published, and how his health and state of mind improved in the peculiarly festive atmosphere that prevailed at that time. She immediately wrote an impassioned letter to Pobedonostsev and Metropolitan Antony to protest against the edict, then went back to knitting woolly hats for the orphanage. Unusually, both Sonya's letter and the response from Metropolitan Antony were printed in *Church News*.

The Holy Synod marshalled its minions to send poison-pen letters and death threats to Tolstoy when the excommunication was announced, but there were far more demonstrations, petitions and ovations in his honour. The Tolstoy house in Moscow was immediately besieged with visitors wanting to take action, and mounted police had to intervene when Tolstoy was mobbed by enthusiastic students who spotted him walking in the centre of the city on the day the excommunication was made public. Far from diminishing Tolstoy's stature, the Holy Synod's edict only enhanced it, particularly in view of the government's ban on the publication of all telegrams and expressions of support. The excommunication also intensified interest in Tolstoy's writings. People who had never read him before started asking for his books in libraries, and Russians abroad were immediately questioned about him as soon as their nationality became known.[123] Employees at the Maltsev Glass Factory outside Moscow sent Tolstoy a lump of green glass with their message to him incised in gold:

12. Cartoon showing Tolstoy as a mighty giant next to the tiny figure of Tsar Nicholas II, 1901

> You have shared the fate of many great people ahead of their time,
> esteemed Lev Nikolayevich. They used to be burned at the stake, left to rot
> in jails and in exile. Let the hypocrite priests excommunicate you however
> they want. Russian people will always be proud, seeing you as their own
> great dearly beloved.

Tolstoy was the conscience of the nation, and the excommunication was the most eloquent expression of the abyss separating the Church from educated Russian society. In Moscow, as elsewhere, the intelligentsia saw the excommunication primarily as an act of political vengeance. Alexey Suvorin, editor of *New Times*, quipped that Russia now had two tsars. While Nicholas II was clearly unable to make Tolstoy's throne wobble, he observed, Tolstoy was destabilising the entire Romanov dynasty.[124] Tolstoy finally started drafting an article in response to the Holy Synod's edict on 24 March, which carried new denunciations. The letter was sent to Chertkov for publication in England. He was still hoping he might be one day be arrested.[125]

Repin had an important new portrait of Tolstoy on show at the 29th Wanderers Exhibition in Petersburg which had opened a week before the excommunication was announced. Ironically it depicted the writer at prayer, barefoot in the woods at Yasnaya Polyana. When the exhibition opened, the portrait was immediately surrounded with flowers, and naturally attracted more attention after the excommunication. Before the exhibition closed on 25 March a student stood on a chair and tied bouquets round the entire frame, as if it was a venerated popular icon, then gave an impromptu speech. A telegram of support signed by the 400 people present was sent to Tolstoy, and even more people festooned Repin's portrait with flowers.[126] This led to the painting being taken down, and it was not shown when the exhibition moved to Moscow and the provinces.

The excommunication caused a sensation amongst Russia's educated classes, but it is worth pointing out that many Russian rural priests had scant knowledge of Tolstoy beyond knowing that he was an aristocrat who wrote society novels. The majority of peasants, meanwhile, knew only that he was a count, and thus representative of the nobility who were hated and distrusted,[127] but there was nevertheless a significant number who followed Father Ioann of Kronstadt in believing that Tolstoy was the Antichrist. Father Ioann, an even more charismatic figure than Grigory Petrov (who ended up leaving the Church), was not a prominent bishop or theologian, but a parish priest who was seen by many as Russia's third 'tsar' in view of his extraordinary popularity.[128] Born one year after Tolstoy into an impoverished sacristan's family in Arkhangelsk province in 1829, he married in 1855 and was ordained that year in St Andrew's Cathedral in Kronstadt, where his father-in-law was the senior priest. During the fifty years in which Father Ioann served in the port of Kronstadt outside St Petersburg, home to the imperial navy's Baltic Fleet, he acquired renown for his Populist, informal style, and for the unusual mass confessions which were held at his church. Father Ioann encouraged charity and greater piety, and by the time he administered to Alexander III on his deathbed in 1894, he had become famous throughout Russia. Nicholas II and his wife Alexandra also revered Father Ioann: they had a picture of him on the wall behind their bed at the Livadia Palace in the Crimea.

In the 1890s Father Ioann began condemning Tolstoy for teaching that Christ was not divine, that Mary was simply an unmarried mother, and that the Orthodox Church was pagan and idolatrous. 'You ought to have a stone hung round your neck and be lowered with it into the depths of the sea; you ought not to have any place on earth' – it was in these terms that Father Ioann denounced Tolstoy, and a collection of his diatribes against Tolstoy was published in 1902.[129] Father Ioann was perhaps Tolstoy's most famous public opponent, and his polar opposite. Indeed, for the writer Nikolay Leskov,

Tolstoy and Father Ioann represented the opposing forces struggling for Russia's future.[130] Father Ioann was seen as the pastor of the people, whereas Tolstoy was worshipped more by the intelligentsia, and yet there were some striking similarities between them. Like Tolstoy, Father Ioann also aspired to an ascetic ideal. In maintaining a celibate marriage (his wife Elizaveta would have liked children), he was rather more successful in curbing his libido than Tolstoy. Father Ioann was also strict about food consumption, which, like Tolstoy, he linked to sensuality: 'Buckwheat kasha is good, cream bad'; 'No horseradish with vinegar!'; 'NEVER EAT SUPPER!' Father Ioann saw his wife's cooking as a threat to his spirituality.[131] Both Father Ioann and Tolstoy were puritans who attacked social inequality, excessive materialism and moral depravity, and both were the subject of a cult of personality – the Russian Post Office had to make special provision to deal with the huge volume of letters Father Ioann received from adoring parishioners.[132] Father Ioann also inspired the birth of a kind of sectarian religion, which was reported with alarm by Pobedonostsev in 1901, the year of Tolstoy's excommunication. His followers, who were called 'Ioannity', saw him variously as God, Jesus, or John the Baptist, and treated his photograph as an icon (he was particularly popular with women).[133] Control over its clergy was a priority for the Holy Synod, and there was some alarm when Father Ioann seemed to be becoming dangerously independent. Like Tolstoy, he enjoyed greater popularity at court than in the offices of state, but even some of his congregation found his tone a little too strident at times. One person wrote to him after becoming acquainted with his 'words of denunciation directed against Count Lev Tolstoy', and now could not find 'inner calm', nor knew how to reconcile his 'diatribes, so alien to the spirit of Christian gentleness, tolerance and forgiveness for all', with his earlier writing on spirituality.[134]

Tolstoy and Father Ioann were part of an extraordinary religious renaissance at the beginning of the twentieth century which affected all classes of Russian society, with huge numbers of pilgrims making visits to monasteries and taking part in processions such as the one immortalised in Repin's famous painting of the Kursk procession. There was also a religious revival amongst the intelligentsia which first began at around the time of the publication of Dostoyevsky's last novel, *The Brothers Karamazov* in 1880, which was inspired by the writer's meetings with the elders of Optina Pustyn. It is noteworthy that this was the book Tolstoy was reading when he finally left

Yasnaya Polyana at the end of his life and went on the last of his many visits to the monastery, which seems to have been a place which both repelled and drew him. Even before he was excommunicated Tolstoy was widely seen as 'the elder of Yasnaya Polyana', and in the last decades of his life received not only scores of visitors who came to seek his guidance, but thousands of letters from people who asked for his help. He tried diligently to respond to them with the help of secretaries, who functioned like the lay brothers who traditionally assisted the elders.[135] A further sign of the religious revival came in November 1901 with the launch of a series of historic meetings held in the hall of the Imperial Geographic Society in St Petersburg. These meetings brought about the first constructive contact between the intelligentsia and the clergy in Russia. Initiated by modernist writers like Dmitry Merezhkovsky, who wished to bridge the gulf separating the educated classes from the Church, the aim was to try to find some common ground, and a possible religious solution to the socio-political crisis in Russia. The name of Tolstoy loomed large and, not surprisingly, his conflict with the Church was the topic of the third of the Religious-Philosophical Society meetings held in early 1902.[136] Amongst the issues hotly debated was whether it had been the Church or the state which had been the driving force behind Tolstoy's excommunication.

Tolstoy remained a problem for the Church hierarchy even after he was excommunicated, as in June 1901 he fell seriously ill with malaria, necessitating the drawing up of a new strategy: governors and police chiefs were ordered not to allow any speeches or demonstrations in the event of his death.[137] Sergey was mortified to find out his brother was in a critical condition from the newspapers, whose editors regarded Tolstoy's state of health as a matter of public interest. Sergey now wrote his brother a heartfelt letter in which he told him how much he meant to him, and how there was no other person in the world to whom he could talk in the same way. Underneath his signature he added sadly: 'Apart from our closeness from childhood, I just need you, but you don't need me. You have a legion apart from me.'[138] Not for the first time, Tolstoy's strong constitution helped him recover, and Alexandrine's friend Countess Panina kindly offered her dacha outside Yalta for his convalescence. In September 1901, the family decamped to the Crimea. Contrary to his usual habit of travelling fourth class with fleas and cockroaches, as Sergey put it, this time the family was allotted a private compartment, which had been arranged with the help of a Tolstoyan who worked for the railways. Despite the ban on press coverage of his movements, there was a huge crowd of 3,000 supporters waiting at Kharkov station to cheer him. The Tolstoys would remain in the Crimea for the best part of ten months, during which time Sonya tended to her husband with her usual devotion.

Countess Panina's 'dacha' was in fact a gothic palace – a fairy-tale castle with two towers. Tolstoy had never lived in such luxury in all his life, and wrote to tell Sergey about the profusion of exotic flowers, the marble fountain in a pond with fish swimming in it, the manicured lawns, the luxuriant view of the sea past the cypress trees, and even the lavatories, a convenience he was not used to. Back in 1887 Tolstoy had written a long letter to the future pacifist writer Romain Rolland in which he declared that the first test of the sincerity of those who professed to live by Christian principles was to put an end to living parasitically off the manual work done by the poor and take care of one's own needs, which included emptying one's own chamber pot.[139] Tolstoy told his brother that the grand dukes and millionaires who lived nearby were surrounded by even greater luxury.[140]

As usual Tolstoy was thronged with visitors, but there were also pleasant meetings with Chekhov, who was a local telephone call away in Yalta, and with the young writer Gorky. Tolstoy also developed a friendship with the urbane and scholarly Grand Duke Nikolay Mikhailovich, an old friend of Chertkov who sought him out. Not only was he unflustered by Tolstoy's pariah-status in official circles, it turned out he was an avid reader of his virulently anti-government writings. His lofty position as a member of the Romanov family enabled him to receive uncensored all the editions Chertkov published in England.[141] Fearing this might be his last chance, Tolstoy seized the opportunity of this serendipitous acquaintance to write another lengthy letter to Nicholas II, which the Grand Duke gamely offered to deliver. Addressing the Tsar as 'Dear brother', Tolstoy dispensed with the niceties of protocol. After admonishing Nicholas II for increasing police surveillance, censorship and religious persecution to unacceptable levels, Tolstoy disputed the notion that Orthodoxy and autocracy were inherently Russian. First of all he pointed to the ever increasing numbers of those 'defecting' to other faiths, despite the dangers of persecution entailed. Next he declared that autocracy was outmoded and bankrupt as a form of government. Tsarist power might still have had prestige under Nicholas I, he admitted, but in the nearly fifty years since his death, it had completely disintegrated, to the point that people from all classes of society now openly criticised and ridiculed the Tsar himself (that is, Nicholas II, the person he was addressing):

> The fact that crowds of people run after you with shouts of 'Hurrah!' in Moscow and other cities has probably misled you about the people's love for autocracy and its representative, the Tsar. Don't believe that this is an expression of devotion to you – they are just a crowd of curious people who will go after any unusual spectacle.[142]

Only someone with the authority of a tsar would have the temerity to speak in such terms to a crowned head of state. The fact that Nicholas II pledged not to show this letter to anyone (as attested by Grand Duke Nikolay Mikhailovich's mistress, Princess Elena Baryatinskaya, who happened to be Chertkov's cousin) lends credence to the view that Tolstoy and Chertkov still enjoyed a certain amount of favour and protection at court.[143]

When Tolstoy fell seriously ill again in January 1902 there was a new flurry of despatches from the Holy Synod, the Ministry of Internal Affairs and the Censorship Committee, its officials all terrified of outbreaks of civil disobedience, or worse. Pobedonostsev hatched a plan to despatch a priest to the Tolstoy household and thus be able to announce a last-minute recantation, the Head of Censorship stipulated that pictures of Tolstoy in the press were only permissible after his death, and Metropolitan Antony sent a letter in which he implored Tolstoy to return to the Church.[144] Needless to say, Tolstoy was not interested. Under the care of numerous doctors and his wife and daughters, with constant visits from other family members and friends (who had all converged on Gaspra thinking they were coming to pay their last respects), Tolstoy slowly recovered. He returned home in June, cheered by an even bigger crowd at Kharkov station, and he and Sonya now took up permanent residence in Yasnaya Polyana. On the advice of doctors, and much to Tolstoy's own relief, there would be no more winters in Moscow. Also on the advice of doctors, he moved his study upstairs to the large, well-lit room with the balcony next to his bedroom, which caught the morning sun.

Tolstoy did not exactly mellow in old age. In the autumn of 1902 he wrote a fierce attack on Christian clergymen of all denominations, in the hope of showing them the harm they caused, as he put it in a letter to his brother. *To the Clergy*, which was sent to Chertkov and published by the Free Word Press in 1903, was another example of Tolstoy talking 'man to man' with clerics, regardless of their rank. It was a vintage Tolstoyan harangue:

> You know that what you teach about the creation of the world, about the inspiration of the Bible by God, and much else is not true. How then can you teach it to little children and to ignorant adults, who look to you for true enlightenment? ... Whoever you may be – popes, cardinals, archbishops, bishops, superintendents, priests, or pastors – think of this. If you belong to those of the clergy (of whom there are unfortunately very many, and continually more and more in our days) who see clearly how obsolete, irrational, and immoral the Church teaching is, but who, without believing in it, still continue to preach it from personal motives (for their salaries as priests or bishops), do not console yourselves with the supposition that your activity is justified by any utility it has for the masses of the people, who do not yet understand what you understand.[145]

Father Ioann of Kronstadt immediately fought back with a famous riposte. Journalists often likened Tolstoy to Ilya Muromets, the greatest of Russia's mythical medieval warriors (bogatyrs), who was famous for performing Herculean feats. To Father Ioann, however, Leo Tolstoy was a predatory lion akin to the devil (1 Peter, 5: 8), and since few of the Orthodox faithful would have been able to read Tolstoy's contraband article, he provided a summary of its contents for them:

> For Tolstoy there is no supreme spiritual perfection in the sense of the achievements of Christian virtues – simplicity, humility, purity of heart, chastity, repentance, faith, hope, love in the Christian sense; he does not recognise Christian endeavours; he laughs at holiness and sacred things – it is he himself he adores, and he bows down before himself, like an idol, like a superman; I, and no one else but me, muses Tolstoy. You are all wrong; I have revealed the truth and am teaching everyone the truth! The Gospel according to Tolstoy is an invention and a fairy tale. So, Orthodox people, who is Lev Tolstoy? He is a lion roaring [*Lev rykayushchy*], looking for someone to devour. And how many he has devoured with his flattering pages! Watch out for him.[146]

Tolstoy was certainly aware of Father Ioann, but he never paid him any attention.

It is perhaps indicative that the year in which Tolstoy published *To the Clergy*, was also the year of the canonisation of Serafim of Sarov (1759–1833), the first and greatest of Russia's elders. The celebrations were attended by Nicholas II and Empress Alexandra, and half a million pilgrims.[147] The fact that there were suddenly many more canonisations in the reign of Nicholas II lends credence to the theory that there was an agenda afoot to inspire patriotism and loyalty to the monarchy. This was also the year in which the Religious-Philosophical Society meetings were shut down, for the same reason. The Church and government were finding it difficult to unite the population amidst a growing discontent that was spreading throughout the country, and the philosophers, poets, literary critics and public figures who attended the Religious-Philosophical Society meetings had been entering into debates with members of the clergy that the authorities felt were too heated in such tense times.

The political situation in Russia had indeed become very volatile by 1904. In the 1890s radical Marxist groups committed to revolution had changed their tactics from spreading propaganda amongst the new population of oppressed factory workers to mass agitation, causing a wave of strikes, and then had united to form the Social Democratic Labour Party, which the police endeavoured but failed to destroy. When he reached the end of his term of Siberian exile in 1900, Vladimir Ulyanov had gone abroad. As well as founding a newspaper and adopting the name of Lenin, he had proposed the creation of a disciplined party of hard-line professional revolutionaries in his tract *What Is to Be Done?* (not to be confused with eponymous works by Tolstoy and Chernyshevsky). Publication of this tract contributed in 1903 to the Social Democratic Labour Party splitting into Bolsheviks and Mensheviks. Apart from the clamour for reform from liberal parties, in 1904 the Russian government found itself dealing with the constant threat of terrorist activities from the various revolutionary groups, as well as increasing peasant unrest and a rising number of mass strikes in urban factories. Discontent was only exacerbated by the government's heavy-handed pogroms against the Jews (Tolstoy spoke out against them too), its continued persecution of religious minorities and its obvious support for employers rather than employees. With the domestic situation so fraught, the sudden outbreak of war with Japan in January 1904 took everyone by surprise.

It was the disastrous Russo-Japanese War which finally brought an end to imperial hubris. The Foreign Ministry and the armed forces had stagnated under Nicholas II: the British ambassador to Russia knew he could safely go on leave from September to December, and ministry officials would habitually arrive for work at midday and leave again at four. The stagnation was born of an unmerited complacency. So great had been Russia's sense of superiority towards Japan that when it acquired a lease from China to expand into its north-eastern provinces in 1898, Foreign Minister Nikolay Muravyov declared that one flag and a sentry was all that was required to secure Port Arthur: Russian prestige would do the rest. But the ill-founded perception of Russian might was about to be challenged. Within weeks of Admiral Makarov arriving in Port Arthur, he perished with all his crew when the Russian flagship *Petropavlovsk* hit a Japanese mine. When war broke out, Tolstoy was distressed by feelings of patriotism which he did not feel able to suppress, and he started riding over to Tula several times a week to read the latest telegrams.[148] Naturally he soon put pen to paper.[149] In his article 'Bethink Yourselves!', Tolstoy exhorted his fellow-Russians to remember biblical texts like Luke 13: 5 ('If you do not bethink yourselves, you will all perish').[150] Insisting that the war contravened the teachings of both Christ and the Buddha, he deplored its wanton violence:

> We say that wars of today are not as those of yesterday, and that we are very far removed from that ancient cannibalism in Nation struggles, but it exists still under other forms. What other can be said of the destruction of the fleet and of the siege of Port Arthur? When did Humanity witness such horrors? What comparison can be found equal to those caused by this frightful carnage? More than 200,000 lives have been lost now in this insensate struggle …[151]

Chertkov translated this article into English, and arranged for its publication in newspapers throughout Europe, which provoked some people to write to Tolstoy in protest at his lack of patriotism, but expressions of sympathy were more common.[152]

Altogether, 1904 was a fairly bleak year for Tolstoy. Although he had little tolerance for those who espoused the Orthodox faith, he was nonetheless

13. Tolstoy photographed with his brother Sergey's widow Maria Mikhailovna, the former gypsy singer in 1906

greatly saddened to receive the news of the death of his old relative Alexandra Andreyevna Tolstaya in March 1904. After their frosty meeting back in 1897 there had been little contact between them, but they were reconciled the year before she died at the age of eighty-seven. In his last letter, in which he addressed her as 'Dear, kind, old friend Alexandrine', he thanked her for half a century's friendship.[153] In July Chekhov lost his fight against tuberculosis at the age of forty-four, and in August, a couple of weeks after Tolstoy's wayward son Andrey was posted to the front (it was already bad enough that he was serving in the army), his elder brother Sergey died of cancer. Sergey had led a secluded and quite unhappy life, disappointed by his four surviving children, and by his marriage to someone from such a different background, and he spent his last days in agony. Tolstoy went out to Pirogovo three times in the summer of 1904, and was instrumental in relaying his sister and sister-in-law's wish that Sergey receive communion before he died. To their surprise he agreed, despite his well-known religious indifference.[154]

When Port Arthur finally fell to the Japanese in December 1904, Tolstoy became very despondent. Meanwhile, the 18,000-mile voyage halfway round the world of the imperial Baltic Fleet under Admiral Rozhdestvensky was dogged by incompetence. Soon after leaving St Petersburg in October, one inebriated captain opened fire on British fishing trawlers in the North Sea, mistaking them for Japanese torpedo boats, while another frigate in what came to be known as the 'Russian mad-dog fleet' was eventually discovered to be travelling up the Thames due to a navigation error. The day after the fleet finally arrived in the Pacific in May 1905, Japanese forces summarily destroyed it in the Battle of Tsushima. This was the final humiliating defeat which brought the war to a close.[155] Tolstoy followed all these events with horror from Yasnaya Polyana, and was aghast when there was further violence closer to home. The extent of Russia's domestic problems meant that the war with Japan enjoyed no popular support, as expressed by the assassination in July 1904 of the Minister of Internal Affairs. Nicholas II's half-hearted response to calls for reform led to the outbreak of revolution on the infamous 'Bloody Sunday' of 9 January 1905, when tsarist troops fired on an unarmed procession of workers bringing a petition to the Winter Palace. The public outcry was followed by mass strikes all over Russia and the assassination on 22 January of the governor general of Moscow, Grand Duke Sergey Alexandrovich, who had received Sonya during the famine in 1892. Tolstoy was stunned, and confessed that the news had made him physically suffer.[156] Amongst the disturbances and uprisings which followed was a mutiny in June 1905 on the battleship *Potemkin* in Odessa. Perhaps regretting that he had not heeded Tolstoy's brazen personal appeal back in 1902, Nicholas II was forced now to retreat from autocratic rule. In October he issued the historic manifesto which promised civil rights, the creation of a national legislative assembly (the 'Duma'), the abolition of censorship, religious tolerance and permission to found political parties. There was also a general amnesty.

The 1905 Revolution directly affected Tolstoy, since it meant that all his banned writings could now suddenly be published, although it took a while for the reforms to take effect. His new article, 'Appeal to the Russian People', in which he predictably condemned both the government and the revolutionaries, was seized by the police before it could be distributed in March 1906, but it went on sale freely in St Petersburg at the end of the year when it was published by the Free Word Press, which Chertkov had just moved to St Petersburg.[157] Scores of Tolstoy's other previously banned writings followed, while he moved on to his next article: 'The Meaning of the Russian Revolution'. In March 1906 Chertkov received official notification that he could return to Russia, but he had already made one visit back home. In the midst of all the disturbances in 1905, Chertkov's influential mother had obtained permission from the Tsar for her son to make a three-week visit, not only to St Petersburg to see her, but also to Yasnaya Polyana. It was a joyous reunion, and even Sonya was glad to see Chertkov.[158] Moving back to Russia permanently was inhibited for Chertkov by his sick wife, the comfort of his surroundings in England and the extent of his publishing operations, and so it was a gradual process which took place over the next few years.

Since his illness in 1902, the situation at Yasnaya Polyana had been more or less peaceful. Tolstoy still hated having to live in the luxurious environment of his ancestral home. He still hated being served dinner by servants in white gloves, and he wanted to leave, but somehow he had stayed put. Despite his professed desire for a secluded life, there was little chance of that. Biryukov returned from exile in December 1904. He had been completing the first authorised biography of Tolstoy, and his subject now had the chance to read the manuscript and answer his questions before preparing it for publication.[159] The quiet Slovak doctor Dušan Makovický also arrived in December 1904, and settled at Yasnaya Polyana as Tolstoy's personal physician. Makovický's salary was paid by Chertkov, who now acquired a useful channel of communication about his friend's state of health, and much more besides.[160] A fervent Tolstoyan who had made his first visit to Yasnaya Polyana in 1894, Makovický worshipped the ground Tolstoy walked on, and took to keeping a pencil and notebook in his trouser pocket so he could surreptitiously scribble down everything he said. The gathering of Tolstoy's utterances was a project Chertkov was also fanatic about. He had started it in 1889, and continued with it until 1923, when his appointed compiler died, by which time there were about 25,000 diverse and sometimes very trivial thoughts recorded in an enormous file.[161]

With an eye to posterity, Sonya had meanwhile started writing what would prove to be an extremely long account of her own life as the spouse of an impossible genius. She also put together an inventory of the enormous library at Yasnaya Polyana, and started putting her husband's archive in order. In 1904 she was obliged to move everything from the Rumyantsev Library (where she had placed his manuscripts initially) to the History Museum next to Red Square, and so now on her trips to Moscow to take care of publishing business, she also spent her mornings copying out the material she needed.[162] Sonya was renowned for being short sighted (a photograph of her attending a photography lecture shows her sitting almost underneath the speaker), for lacking a sense of humour (a lot of Chekhov's early stories left her cold), and for being busy. Like her husband, she also never 'retired', and as well as becoming an accomplished photographer, she acquired skill in painting.[163] She also enjoyed being a grandmother. In 1905, after many miscarriages, Tanya gave birth to a daughter, also named Tatyana, who was affectionately given a 'matronymic' rather than the usual patronymic in deference to Tanya's heroic achievement in becoming a mother. 'Tatyana Tatyanovna' became the Tolstoys' fifteenth grandchild, and was particularly beloved.

The precarious harmony established after the Tolstoys returned home from the Crimea had disappeared by the end of 1906. A wonderful snapshot of life at Yasnaya Polyana just before everything began to disintegrate is provided by the Japanese writer Tokutomi Roka, who spent five days at the estate in June, and duly wrote an account of his visit. He arrived just before Sergey (now forty-three) married for the second time. Tokutomi had been Meiji Japan's most fervent Tolstoy devotee since the age of twenty-three, and having been brought up as a Protestant, was drawn as much to his religious philosophy as he was to his fiction. He took life just as seriously as Tolstoy, with whom he conversed in English. Apart from his hero, who was just as he expected, but 'looked all of his seventy-eight years', Tokutomi met most of the family: Sonya ('the look in her eyes was a little lacking in charm'), Masha ('sickly and thin'), her husband Nikolay ('gentle of voice and manner and typifies the effeminate Slavic male'), the 'fun-loving student' Sasha ('and her weight would be about 170 pounds'), as well as Lev and his Swedish wife Dora, plus Andrey, now estranged from his first wife, and Misha. Amongst the Tolstoy children, it was Sasha whom Tokutomi got to know best, and whom he obviously found a little overwhelming. He once encountered her 'zooming up on her bicycle, travelling like a cyclone' ('and with her physique I was sure she was certain to smash the machine'). Tokutomi also took care to describe the family's four dogs who were a presence at the outside dining table under the maple tree: a white Siberian, a brown pointer, a black setter and a black and white spaniel.

Tokutomi was accompanied on swims and walks by Tolstoy, and he noticed that he never forgot to attach the chain of his silver watch to his belt, and take with him a notebook with pencil thrust in it. During one walk in the woods, Tolstoy shared his thoughts on Russian writers such as Turgenev, whose works he described as 'remarkably beautiful, but not very deep'. Gorky, on the other hand, he declared had 'genius but no learning', while Merezhkovsky had 'learning and no genius, and Chekhov has a great genius, a great genius'. Towards the end of a sometimes rather awestruck account of his pilgrimage to Yasnaya Polyana, Tokutomi describes being taken to Tolstoy's study, and watching him breathe heavily as he wrote letters of reference for him with his goose-quill pen, his thick brows arched together: 'He is a prophet in his final years, his frame weakening day by day, but within him a raging fire burns ever brighter. Just to see him inspires you with a feeling of awe and makes you weep bitterly.' Tokutomi touches here on Tolstoy's extraordinary charisma, which affected even those immune to his religious message. Many were the sceptical Anglo-Saxon visitors to Yasnaya Polyana who found themselves in awe of Tolstoy's physical presence, and surprised by his deep sincerity. After replacing the quill in the rack, Tolstoy picked up a lamp to show Tokutomi the pictures on the wall of Henry George, his brother Sergey, William Lloyd Garrison, Syutayev, and a reproduction of Raphael's *Sistine Madonna*, divided into five panels, which had been given to him by his sister Maria.[164] Before they parted, Tolstoy showed Tokutomi his beloved *Circle of Reading* – an immense compendium of the thoughts of wise people he had compiled for every day of the year taken from an equally huge array of sources, including his own works.

The problems at Yasnaya Polyana began shortly after Tokutomi's departure. First Andrey and Lev told their father in no uncertain terms that they approved of capital punishment, which led to a dreadful row, with much slamming of doors. Tolstoy was upset for two days, and then became worked up again a few weeks later when Sonya insisted on taking to court the peasants who had chopped down some oak trees in their forest. Once again, Tolstoy threatened to leave home.[165] Then in August, having just turned sixty-two, Sonya fell seriously ill and almost died. On 2 September, attended by at least four doctors, she underwent an operation to remove the fibroid which had caused her to contract peritonitis. Remarkably, her constitution was as strong as that of her husband, and she recovered, but thirty-five-year-old Masha was not so fortunate. After catching a chill that November, she died in her father's

14. Tolstoy and Chertkov in his study at Yasnaya Polyana, 1907

arms.[166] Of all his children, it had been Masha who had been closest to him, and her death was a terrible loss.

Chertkov had spent several weeks near Yasnaya Polyana in the summer of 1906, and he returned with his family for the whole of the summer in 1907. This time Sonya was not as thrilled by the prospect as her husband was, and showed it. She caused further friction by insisting on employing guards for Yasnaya Polyana after some peasants had raided the vegetable garden one night and stolen some cabbages.[167] The armed Circassian hired to provide security proved to be very unpopular with the villagers, and Tolstoy was greatly pained. The autumn of 1907 was thus no happier than the autumn of 1906, and Sonya's estrangement from her husband increased still further when the businesslike Chertkov found an obliging twenty-five-year-old called Nikolay Gusev to become Tolstoy's secretary. Chertkov paid Gusev fifty roubles a month to help Tolstoy deal with his enormous correspondence, but for Sonya that meant another non-family member at Yasnaya Polyana who was privy to her husband's thoughts. Gusev arrived in September 1907, and took up residence in the upstairs room nicknamed the 'Remingtonnaya' for the Remington typewriter that had recently been installed there. A month later, he was arrested for spreading revolutionary propaganda, and spent two months in the Tula prison. The Russian government had resumed its previous tactics of targeting Tolstoy's followers, despite the fact it was Tolstoy himself authoring the anti-tsarist tracts.[168]

Another source of depression for Tolstoy that autumn was his son Andrey's second marriage. Andrey's first marriage, to Olga Diterikhs, the sister of Chertkov's wife, had broken down soon after the birth of their two children, but to his father's horror, he had then taken up with the wife of the Tula governor. Ekaterina Artsimovich abandoned six children as well as her husband to pursue her passion with Andrey, and was six months pregnant with his child when they married in November. They had difficulty enough in finding a priest who was prepared to marry them when Andrey's divorce finally came through, and then they had to rush through the night to an obscure rural parish so the ceremony could be conducted at the crack of dawn, before the start of the forty-day Christmas fast.[169] Andrey, who had not seen much of his father when he was growing up, was a serial philanderer, and was soon unfaithful to his second wife.

The cause of the greatest happiness in Tolstoy's last years – the return of Chertkov – was also the cause of great unhappiness for his wife. Chertkov had worked indefatigably during his time in England. In 1900 he had moved from Essex to Christchurch in Hampshire (now Dorset), a pleasant town on the River Stour. His mother owned a plush residence at nearby Southbourne (where she would die, penniless, in 1922, at the age of ninety),[170] and she now bought her son a spacious three-storey detached house with a large garden, together with a building on Iford Lane for his printing press. The Purleigh colony had fallen apart, partly due to Chertkov's autocratic ways (he fell out with Kenworthy, Maude and Khilkov). A few Tolstoyans moved to the Cotswolds to set up a new colony at Whiteway (which uniquely survives to this day),[171] but the main centre for Tolstoyanism in Britain now became Tuckton House, Chertkov's residence in Christchurch. Russian-language publication continued under the Free Word Press imprint, but Chertkov now also set up the Free Age Press to publish English translations of Tolstoy's writings. In the first three years, before he fell out with his manager, Arthur Fifield (who had been secretary at the Brotherhood Church), the Press produced forty-three publications, with a combined print run of over 200,000.[172] Russian-language productivity was also impressive: in 1902 Chertkov started publishing the first Russian edition of *Tolstoy's Complete Collected Works Banned in Russia* under the imprint of the Free Word Press.

Chertkov also built a state-of-the-art, temperature-controlled vault to store all the manuscripts Tolstoy had been sending him, which now included his precious diaries. One of its custodians was Ludwig Perno, an exiled Estonian revolutionary who lived in nearby Boscombe, and he was made to promise that he would never to leave the house without a guard.[173] Unlike so many other political exiles who were followed by swarms of spies, Chertkov led a life which was remarkably untrammelled by interference from the Russian government. He kept up an intense correspondence with Tolstoy during his years of exile, and was able to travel round England unhindered, giving lectures on Tolstoy and attending weekly 'Progress Meetings for the Consideration of the Problems of Life' in Bournemouth. He even played football for local teams in Christchurch.[174]

Before Chertkov moved back to Russia in 1908 he coordinated the publication, both in Russia and abroad, of one of Tolstoy's most important and influential articles. 'I Cannot Be Silent' was written immediately after Tolstoy heard the news that twenty peasants had been hanged for attempted robbery and is one of his most finely articulated and heartfelt pleas for the government to end its systematic programme of organised violence, which he defined as worse than revolutionary terrorism. When the article was published in July, Tolstoy immediately received sixty letters of support – it was still a novelty for people in Russia to be able to read his broadsides. Many newspapers were fined for printing it, however. The liberal *Russian Gazette* had to pay a penalty of 3,000 roubles and the editor of a Sebastopol newspaper was arrested for pasting it up all over the city.[175] Thoughts of capital punishment now led Tolstoy back to the events of 1866, when he had failed to prevent Private Shabunin from being executed. In the late 1880s, a former cadet in the regiment who had witnessed the events had come to see Tolstoy. He wanted to discuss an account he had written and hoped to publish.[176] Tolstoy had refused, which seems only to have served to increase his feeling of guilt. In 1908 he finally resolved to speak out when questioned by Biryukov in connection with his biography. Bursting into tears three times while dictating an account of what had happened in 1866 to his secretary Gusev, Tolstoy now

*15. Employees of the Free Word Press in the vault at Chertkov's house in Christchurch, 1906.
Evgeny Popov is seated second from left, Ludwig Perno, custodian of the Tolstoy archive,
is seated at the typewriter on the right, and Chertkov's wife is seated in the foreground.
Chertkov is standing behind the door.*

declared that Shabunin's execution had exerted far more influence on his life
than all those events conventionally regarded as significant, such as bereavement, impoverishment, career setbacks and so forth. He confessed to being
ashamed of his defence of Shabunin, which in retrospect he felt had been
perfunctory and more concerned with legal details than with moral impera-
tives. It certainly stands in marked contrast to the impassioned stand taken
in court by his fictional alter ego Nekhlyudov in *Resurrection*, which was
conceivably written in part to assuage his guilt over the Shabunin affair.[177]

A quarter of a century on from their first meeting, Chertkov's life was
still characterised by his unswerving devotion to Tolstoy, and in 1908 he and
his family took up permanent residence in a new house they built on land
inherited by Tolstoy's youngest daughter Sasha at Telyatinki, three miles
from Yasnaya Polyana. Shortly after Chertkov's return Tolstoy turned eighty.

Such was the groundswell of support for him across the country that the Church felt compelled to issue a plea to all true believers to refrain from celebrating the occasion. It also tried to take Tolstoy to court for blasphemy against the holy personality of Jesus Christ, and arranged for icons to be painted which depicted him as a sinner burning in hell. Father Ioann, Tolstoy's implacable foe, even wrote a prayer requesting that he die soon, but it was Father Ioann who died in 1908, not Tolstoy.[178] The few dissenting voices were anyway drowned out by the well-wishers who far outnumbered them. Two thousand telegrams wishing Tolstoy many happy returns were delivered to Yasnaya Polyana on 28 August, and Charles Wright, librarian at the British Museum, arrived at Yasnaya Polyana with birthday greetings signed by 800 English writers, artists and public figures, including George Bernard Shaw, H. G. Wells and Edmund Gosse.[179]

Tolstoy had halted the activities of a special celebratory committee established in January 1908, just as he received his first birthday present: a phonograph sent to him by Thomas Edison. There were thus no official undertakings, but that did not stop a flood of ecstatic articles appearing in the press. Journalists gushed that there had never been a cultural celebration in Russia like it ever before, and that while the Pushkin Statue festivities had captured the national imagination back in 1880, this was an event on an international scale. Merezhkovsky proclaimed the Tolstoy celebration as a 'celebration of the Russian revolution', and declared that Tolstoy had against his will 'turned out to be the radiant focal point of Russian freedom'.[180]

'Lev Nikolayevich' had long been a household name in Russia, and it had become quite common to overhear passengers on a train discussing him as if he were a close acquaintance. The labels accompanying the photographic chronology in the special supplement published by the newspaper *Russian Word* to mark Tolstoy's eightieth birthday said it all – from the earliest photographs, labelled 'Count L. N. Tolstoy' when he was an unknown author, to 'Lev Tolstoy', and finally the familiar 'Lev Nikolayevich'. There were only a few notes of criticism amongst the scores of birthday tributes published, and one of them was by Lenin, whose first and most famous article about Tolstoy, 'Lev Tolstoy as a Mirror of the Russian Revolution' appeared in *The Proletarian*. While praising his attacks on the tsarist regime, Lenin not surprisingly condemned Tolstoy's philosophy of non-violence which he held responsible for the failure of the 1905 Revolution.

In addition to all the greetings cards and telegrams, Tolstoy received gifts, some of which were rather ill-judged, such as the several thousand cigars in boxes with his picture on the front.[181] Having Chertkov living so near to him was undoubtedly the best birthday present as far as Tolstoy was concerned. The Chertkovs and all the local Tolstoyans, such as Maria Alexandrovna Schmidt and Ivan Gorbunov-Posadov, were invited to a festive dinner at Yasnaya Polyana along with family members, friends and relatives. It was the first and last such occasion, as in 1909 Sonya started to become increasingly paranoid, and also increasingly hostile to Chertkov. The battle with him revolved around Tolstoy's will and his late diaries. She was as obsessive as Chertkov about her husband's legacy, but not as powerful as he was. Much as it was rewarding to enter into correspondence with figures like Gandhi in 1909, and exciting to be filmed by some of Edison's colleagues, Tolstoy's desire to become a homeless wanderer became more and more intense.

In March 1909 Chertkov was ordered to leave Tula province. Politics and personnel had changed in St Petersburg, and suddenly he no longer had so many friends at court. Tolstoy was mortified, and even Sonya wrote to protest, but the Chertkovs were obliged to move from their new home. They took up residence at Vasily Pashkov's old estate Krekshino, about twenty miles outside Moscow. As the year went by, relations between Tolstoy and Sonya now sharply deteriorated. First she found the manuscript of Tolstoy's unpublished story 'The Devil', about a young nobleman's passion for a peasant girl, which opened up a lot of old wounds. Then, in July, she discovered that the power of attorney Tolstoy had given her to manage his property in 1883 did not give her any legal rights to them.[182] She was livid. During Tolstoy's illness in the Crimea, Masha had managed to procure her father's signature on a will which relinquished the copyright on all his works. Sonya had managed to reinstate her name as a beneficiary back then, wanting to ensure that her children and not publishers would benefit from royalties after her husband's death. Tolstoy, however, had other ideas, of course, and Chertkov fully supported his desire to waive all rights over his works. Sonya also faced a new problem as there was a new Tolstoyan in the midst of her family: her daughter Sasha, who had long resented her mother. Sasha turned twenty-five in 1909, and she now devoted herself to working for her father, and with Chertkov. She was determined to thwart her mother, and make sure a will was drawn up which denied her any rights to her father's works.

Tolstoy had been tipped for one of the recently introduced Nobel Prizes several times, and had published a letter in the *Stockholm Tageblatt* in 1897 suggesting the Dukhobors were more deserving recipients of the prize money, but the Swedish Academy had been repeatedly frightened off by his 'anarchism'.[183] In 1909, through the agency of Chertkov, he was invited to the Stockholm Peace Congress. Sonya suspected her husband was going to meet Chertkov behind her back and threatened to poison herself.[184] Tolstoy finally agreed not to go, and then in August the Congress was cancelled anyway. It was just at this time that Gusev was arrested for a second time, which was a further blow.[185] This time he was exiled to the Urals for two years. Chertkov began the search for a new secretary.

In September, Tolstoy went to visit Chertkov, stopping off on the way in Moscow, where he had not been for eight years. Before he left Krekshino towards the end of the month, he drew up a will handing over all his works written after 1881 into the public domain, and the manuscripts to Chertkov. A huge crowd gave him an ovation at the Kursk station as he set off back home to Yasnaya Polyana. He would never see Moscow again. In January Valentin Bulgakov, a young philosophy student originally from Siberia, arrived to become Tolstoy's new secretary. Like Gusev, he was instructed by Chertkov to take copious notes on Tolstoy's day-to-day life. He thus became witness to the worst few months in the Tolstoys' marriage, and after her husband's death it was to Bulgakov that Sonya confirmed what the root cause of all the problems had been. In a letter of June 1911 she told him that she could not tolerate being supplanted in her husband's affections by Chertkov. She had spent forty-eight years being married to Tolstoy, as the most important person in his life, and now to have her husband tell her that Chertkov was the closest person to him was unbearable.[186] Sonya did not behave well in the last few months of Tolstoy's life, and numerous doctors correctly diagnosed paranoia and hysteria, but she was not mentally ill. She was just felt out of control, usurped and desperate. She feared poverty, and she feared her name being blackened.

In June 1910, Tolstoy made another trip to visit Chertkov, and at the end of the month Chertkov was allowed to return to Telyatinki. Sonya now tried to stop her husband from seeing him, and when she discovered that Chertkov had his diaries from the last ten years, she demanded they be given to her, fearing they would expose her in a bad light. She felt she should have them, as her husband's rightful executor, but Tolstoy refused to accede to her demands. Finally, after bitter conflict, Tolstoy agreed to take back his latest diaries from Chertkov, in order to hand them to their daughter Tanya, who would deposit them in the Tula bank. Sonya and her husband had always read each other's diaries, but now Tolstoy began to keep a secret private journal. And in June he wrote another secret will, bequeathing the rights to his works to Sasha or, in the event of her death, to Tanya. Sonya was not made privy to its contents, but Tolstoy came to regret not having been open about it all.

Tolstoy was compelled to conduct his friendship with Chertkov by letter again, to avoid further hostilities with Sonya. In September she invited a priest to Yasnaya Polyana to conduct an exorcism to expel Chertkov's evil spirit. In late October, after discovering her rifling through his study, Tolstoy decided finally to leave. He had long yearned to leave home and set off on foot with nothing but the clothes on his back as a wanderer. In 1910 he finally did, leaving superstitiously at the age of 82 on 28 October in the middle of the night with Dr Makovický, so he would not be pursued by Sonya. Despite his antagonistic relations with the Orthodox Church, it is entirely in keeping with Tolstoy's contradictory character that his first destination was the Optina Pustyn Monastery. Finding he was unable to receive spiritual guidance from the elders at Optina Pustyn, he visited his sister at her convent, then boarded a train heading south towards the Caucasus. As soon as she found out her husband had left, Sonya tried to drown herself in the pond.

Tolstoy never reached his destination. On 31 October he boarded a train heading south to Rostov-on-Don with Dr Makovický and Sasha (who had joined them by this time), but had to get off at Astapovo when he fell ill. Tolstoy was put to bed in the station master's house. Sasha summoned Chertkov, who arrived with his secretary on 2 November, followed by Sergey, and then Sonya who had chartered a train with Tanya, Andrey and Misha. The next day Ilya arrived, as well as Gorbunov-Posadov and Goldenweiser, and on 5 November sixty army officers swelled the ranks of the secret police officers already stationed there. Once the news reached the press, the story made front page headlines. Soon the whole world knew what was happening at the remote railway station in Ryazan province. On 7 November 1910, amidst of a frenzy of international publicity, which included regular headlines in *The Times*, and the whirr of Pathé cameras, Tolstoy finally passed away. Sonya was allowed to see her husband only after he had lost consciousness. There was no reconciliation with the Church. By this time it was only too aware of the public relations disaster it had brought upon itself through the excommunication, but its increasingly frantic attempts to effect a deathbed recantation were an abject failure. Father Varsonofy came down from Optina Pustyn, but Sasha refused him access to her father, which she later felt bitter remorse about when she herself later came back to the Church. Tolstoy was not given Extreme Unction, and was buried very quickly, on 9 November.

There was only one place Tolstoy could be buried, and that was in the grounds of his ancestral home Yasnaya Polyana, where he had spent some seventy of his eighty years. He was interred where exactly as he had wished, at the spot in the woods a short walk from his house where the little green stick was buried – the little green stick on which his brother Nikolay had told him the secret to human happiness was written. Aware that mourners from all over Russia would want to attend the funeral, and that the quicker the burial, the fewer would have time to make the journey, the Russian government hastened with the arrangements. There were so many students attending the meetings organised at Moscow University the day following Tolstoy's death that even the corridors were full, and the 800 reserved seats on the train that their representatives managed to negotiate with the management of the Kursk station could have been filled many times over. Thousands besieged the station, but the government forbade the running of any extra trains. Nevertheless, thousands did manage to pay their last respects, having sat all night on a freezing train which brought them to Zaseka station (as Yasenki had been renamed) in the early hours of the morning. It was a clear November night, bonfires were burning, and students had to struggle to restrain the enormous crowd awaiting the arrival of the special train bearing Tolstoy's coffin. But as soon as the train's yellow lights emerged out of the fog on that cold morning, the crowd fell completely silent.

When it was removed from the carriage, which prompted the immediate removal of hats, the wooden coffin containing Tolstoy's body seemed somehow small and too short. The writer's sons passed the coffin over to peasants from Yasnaya Polyana, who would carry it on its final journey. With the exception of the police in attendance, the entire crowd started softly singing 'Eternal Memory', the sombre song which concludes every Orthodox funeral. Still singing, the crowd set off behind Sofya Andreyevna and her sons, to walk for three hours to reach Tolstoy's ancestral home – first down the slope and across the little wooden bridge over the stream, then through the birch and alder forest underneath frosted branches, and then along bare, frozen fields, lightly covered in snow, which were the same pale-white colour as the sky.

Ahead of the coffin village carts carried wreaths and fir-twigs, which were strewn along the path by students and old women. As many noted with amazement, the whole of Russian society had come together on that day to pay their last respects – peasants, aristocrats, intellectuals and factory workers, old and young, male and female – and this was something quite unprecedented. Two local peasants carried a banner as they walked on which they had painted 'Lev Nikolayevich! The Memory of Your Goodness Will not Die Amongst the Orphaned Peasants of Yasnaya Polyana'. No one in the village surrounding Tolstoy's estate had been to bed, and their houses remained lit throughout the night. One local peasant was heard to remark that it was just like at Easter, when everyone stayed up for the midnight service, before going home to break the long fast in the early hours and start celebrating.

When the procession arrived at Yasnaya Polyana, Tolstoy's coffin was brought into the house, so that the 5,000 mourners could file past and pay their last respects. Many people were shocked by the discrepancy between the Tolstoy they knew from all the portraits and photographs and the wax-like, wizened face of his corpse, and some fainted or had hysterics. Three and a half hours later the coffin was lifted up again and taken on its final journey into the wood, a short walk from the main house. At ten minutes to three in the afternoon, it was quietly lowered into the simple unmarked grave that had been prepared. Speeches had been banned, but everyone fell to their knees (even the policeman who had been despatched to monitor the proceedings). 'Eternal Memory' was sung softly again, but there was nothing Orthodox about this funeral rite, which was the first civil burial to take place in Russia. There were no priests, no icons, and no prayers, and no cross was erected at the head of the grave. Mourners continued to flock to Tolstoy's bare burial mound in the days and weeks following his funeral. Only the following spring did grass begin to grow over it. As the attention finally receded from Astapovo, where over 1,000 telegrams had been sent and received during the last week of Tolstoy's life, Yasnaya Polyana became once again a place of pilgrimage.

'Eternal Memory' was sung at memorial services held throughout Russia after the funeral, and also at demonstrations that had nothing ostensibly to do with Tolstoy. Tolstoy's death, in fact, acted as a catalyst for political action: there were widespread strikes in Moscow on the day of the funeral, as well as student demonstrations, marches and processions, and vociferous calls were made for the death penalty to be abolished. The Russian government was caught on the back foot. Unable to join in the eulogies flooding the media, having demonised Tolstoy for so long, and equally unable to denounce him now that his great significance as a writer and thinker was being celebrated around the world, it found itself in an intractable position, for it could not remain silent. Ministers debated how they should honour the memory of a writer who had condemned governments, monarchs and state authority, but they had already become irrelevant and impotent, and their efforts to contain public manifestations were ineffectual. The Russian population at large had seized the initiative and was now beginning to write the script: it was a defining moment. Schools and universities closed, and factories, offices and theatres shut their doors while Russians from all backgrounds united in grieving publicly for a great writer and mighty hero who had defiantly spoken up on behalf of a nation that had been maimed and muzzled for so long. The import of these unprecedented events was not lost on one exiled revolutionary in Switzerland – Vladimir Lenin, who wrote three new articles on Tolstoy in November 1910. Tolstoy was still just a mirror of diverse and contradictory impulses in Russia in his view, but the nation had moved on since 1905. Tolstoy had taken giant steps during his lifetime, and his death was one last giant step – on the road to Revolution.[187]

· Epilogue ·

PATRIARCH OF THE BOLSHEVIKS

I believe their example and their lives give an answer to the question which I have asked myself and my readers in my previous books: is it possible to withstand, and to preserve one's integrity intact while living in a Totalitarian regime? The Tolstoyans answered this question with their lives, both tragically and heroically.

Mark Popovsky, 1983[1]

THE NATION'S ATTENTION was focused on Yasnaya Polyana at the time of Tolstoy's burial, and initially his widow was kept busy. On 17 December, forty days after her husband's death, Sonya walked to his grave in order to commemorate his memory according to Orthodox custom, and was joined by the entire population of the village – men, women and children. The grave was tidied up, fresh fir branches laid on it, and those present took off their hats and sank to their knees three times to sing 'Eternal Memory'.[2] There were frequent visitors in the first weeks after Tolstoy's death. In her now brief diary entries Sonya recorded the arrival of various journalists, a group of fifty-two female students from St Petersburg, a Muslim visitor from the

Caucasus bearing a wreath, and her sister Tanya, who stayed on for a month. But as family and friends departed, Sonya was left alone to mourn. Yasnaya Polyana suddenly felt very empty.

Sonya had to get used to the idea of being a widow at the age of sixty-six, and she was inevitably racked by grief and guilt: her last years were ones of loneliness and self-recrimination. She feared with some justification what people would write – and were indeed already writing – about her, and at the same time she felt completely superfluous, as the curtain had now fallen on the drama in which she had starred. To some it seemed that she had at last become meek and acquiescent, as if she had undergone the spiritual trans-formation her husband had wished; to others it seemed she was the only one to have emerged from the trauma as a better person.[3] One of the few consolations for Sonya in the days following her husband's funeral was the beautiful wintry weather which at last descended after those bleak Novem-ber days, bringing sub-zero temperatures, clear blue skies and lots of snow. Just before Christmas in 1910 she walked out with her camera to take pho-tographs of Tolstoy's grave to send to her daughter Tanya, who was then in Rome, although, she confided to her diary, the beauty of the frost and the blue sky made her feel even more sad. Another consolation was the moral support of her sons, who had remained loyal to her throughout. She was still estranged from her daughter Sasha, and relations with her eldest daughter Tanya also remained quite tense.

In January 1911 the kind-hearted Dr Makovický left for good, and Sonya felt another precious link to her husband had been lost. It was difficult for Sonya not to feel embattled. Sasha was still on the side of the 'hateful' Chert-kov, despite a growing discord between them, while the profligate ways of three of her sons prompted them to bring up, with indecent haste, the uncomfortable question of their father's legacy and the future of Yasnaya Polyana. Since Vanechka Tolstoy's death, the estate had belonged to Sonya, Ilya, Misha, Andrey and Lev (Sergey having relinquished his share). They all wanted to be able to preserve Yasnaya Polyana as a cultural monument, but they did not have the necessary funds – indeed they seemed always to be short of cash, and dependent on handouts from their mother. Despite Sonya's unease, Ilya, Misha and Andrey hatched a plan to sell some of the land to a wealthy American (Lev was in Sweden at this point). This was not such a new idea, as Chertkov had been on the look-out for an American philanthropist to purchase Yasnaya Polyana back in 1908. The plan then had been for the land to be given to the local peasants, as Chertkov felt this would constitute the best possible eightieth birthday present for Lev Nikolayevich, but nothing had materialised. Alexander Kuzminsky, Sonya's nephew, was now deputised to move this project forward and he duly arrived in New York on 1 January 1911 armed with a list of American millionaires who had shown an interest in literature and the arts. Unfortunately, as he soon learned, Jews were still prohibited from buying land outside the Pale of Settlement in Russia, so most of the names on his list were ineligible. Tolstoy had made good copy during his lifetime, and American newspapers now pounced on the story of the disputes over this ill-conceived new proposal. Sonya persuaded her sons to give an interview to a Russian newspaper in order to explain that they had wanted to sell only the land, not the house.[4]

That was not the only scandal: journalists also had a field-day with the battle over Tolstoy's manuscripts, which were split between the two warring camps of Chertkov and Sasha on the one side, and Sonya on the other.[5] When the provisions of Tolstoy's will had come into effect a lawyer had promptly appeared at the Historical Museum, where Sonya had kept those Tolstoy's manuscripts in her possession, and ordered the archive to be sealed. Sonya was aghast, as she believed the manuscripts still belonged to her, and she used her connections at the Museum to refuse access to Chertkov and Sasha. Another edition of the Tolstoy collected works was underway, and she had invested large amounts of money already to have each of the twenty volumes typeset: she was not going to give up her rights easily. It was now open warfare. In January 1911 Chertkov published a very biased account of Tolstoy's last days, and he and Sasha published a joint letter shortly afterwards stating their grievances regarding the copyright issue. Tolstoy's name thus continued to appear frequently in the Russian press, and Tanya pleaded with her mother to give way and so restrain Sasha from engaging in an undignified and shameful public battle with her. The matter would not be resolved for another three years.[6]

In May 1911 Sonya went to Moscow to sort out what could be included in her latest edition of Tolstoy's collected works, since most of his later writings were still censored. She also began negotiations to sell the family's empty house to the City of Moscow for 125,000 roubles, planning to use the money to help her sons. She then travelled on to Petersburg for meetings at court and with Prime Minister Stolypin, in the hope of interesting the Tsar in purchasing Yasnaya Polyana for the nation. Initially the situation looked promising, and newspapers reported on 28 May that the government would buy Yasnaya Polyana for 500,000 roubles.[7] Sonya put together detailed inventories of each of the rooms when she returned home, in preparation for receiving government officials and surveyors, but everything was still very raw for her. The meeting that summer with her sister-in-law, who came on a visit from her convent, was a particularly emotional one, since it was to Masha that Tolstoy had first gone after leaving Yasnaya Polyana for the last time. Maria Nikolayena would die the following April of pneumonia aged eighty-two, the same age as her brother.

Fortunately Sonya was kept busy that first summer by the huge numbers of visitors who wanted to make the pilgrimage to Yasnaya Polyana. Biryukov brought 200 village schoolteachers on 6 June to inspect the Tolstoy memorial rooms, for example, and on one day in July Sonya noted in her diary that there had been 140 visitors. On Tolstoy's birthday on 28 August, as many as 300 people gathered at his grave.[8] Nevertheless, for Tolstoy's former secretary Nikolay Gusev, who returned after his two-year Siberian exile in the summer of 1911, Yasnaya Polyana felt deserted and empty.[9] In October, soon after Stolypin was assassinated, Sonya learned that the government had now decided against buying Yasnaya Polyana. In debates at the Duma there had been some Church figures who objected very strongly to the state honouring the memory of an apostate who had been excommunicated.[10] On 18 November, shortly after the first anniversary of Tolstoy's death, Sonya wrote to Nicholas II to warn him that her sons might soon have to sell Yasnaya Polyana, and she expressed the hope that he would not want to see 'the heart of the Russian nation' fall into private hands, but on 20 December Nicholas noted in a memo to his ministers that he regarded the purchase of Yasnaya Polyana by the government to be 'inadmissible'.[11]

The estate gradually started coming back to life in 1912. When Valentin Bulgakov came back that summer he sensed an air of liberation about the place – there were games of croquet and tennis again, and no longer any need to be preoccupied with questions of death and immortality, serving the people, and moral self-improvement. Bulgakov wound up the gramophone and played a record of Strauss waltzes which Tolstoy had particularly loved.[12] Tolstoy's birthday that August was almost an occasion for celebration, with nineteen sitting at table, but there were mixed feelings on 23 September, when Sonya marked her fiftieth wedding anniversary by dressing all in white. It was a festive occasion, she told Bulgakov when he came to visit that day, but her face was tear-stained. Bulgakov was living at Telyatinki with the Chertkovs at this time, and he was appalled by their continuing hostility towards Sonya. Bulgakov had not really noticed anyone else while Tolstoy was alive as his huge, magnetic personality had involuntarily commanded his full attention. Now, however, as he started the mammoth task of compiling a detailed inventory of the Yasnaya Polyana library, for use as a scholarly resource, he got to know Sonya better. He enjoyed listening to her tell stories about the happy days of her marriage, but found her continuing anger and bitterness over the last years hard-going. Faced with the choice of either criticising her husband severely or concluding she had never understood him, she told Bulgakov she preferred to opt for the latter.[13] A young priest brought Sonya a degree of peace in November 1912 when he arrived at Yasnaya Polyana soon after the second anniversary of Tolstoy's death, requesting permission to say prayers at Tolstoy's grave and perform a requiem in his room.[14] The following month the first Tolstoy Museum opened in Moscow under the aegis of the Tolstoy Society. With the support of Sonya and her children, Biryukov and Bulgakov had put together a permanent exhibition in a flat rented on Povarskaya Street on the proceeds of ticket sales and member subscriptions.

In December 1913 the dispute over the rights to Tolstoy's pre-1881 manuscripts was finally decided in Sonya's favour and she was at last free to proceed with publishing and selling her final edition of the collected works. She also sold to the Moscow publisher Ivan Sytin all remaining copies from previous editions for 100,000 roubles, which meant she could give another handout to her sons, as well as keep some money by for her beloved daughter Tanya. She was also, at last, getting on much better with her other daughter, Sasha, who, following a further deterioration in her relations with Chertkov, had sold her house at Telyatinki in order to buy a small farmhouse near Yasnaya Polyana (which she called New Polyana).[15] Sasha proposed using the proceeds of a three-volume edition of Tolstoy's works edited by Chertkov to buy from the family the most westerly part of the estate, closest to the Yasnaya Polyana village, which she would then immediately give to the peasants. Sonya and her sons readily agreed, and received 400,000 roubles. The peasants also agreed to Tolstoy's behest, namely that they would not sell or rent out their newly acquired land. From the total of 2,230 acres, 1,620 acres now belonged to the peasants. Sonya next sold what remained of the land to Sasha, so that it too could be handed over to the peasants, and then she bought out her sons' shares of the Yasnaya Polyana house.[16] Sonya now began to pass control of her publishing operation to Sasha, and took pleasure in celebrating her daughter's thirtieth birthday in June 1914. The peaceful co-existence did not last long, however, as on 1 August Russia entered World War I. Misha was drafted into the army, Lev went to work for the Red Cross, and Sasha went to the front as a nurse. Bulgakov and twenty-six other conscientious objectors were arrested and spent thirteen months in the Tula jail (they were eventually exonerated when their case was heard at the Moscow military court in 1916).[17]

Sonya spent her last years essentially copying out the past and endeavouring to provide for her descendants, as she always had. In preparation for publication, she made copies of Tolstoy's old diaries, and his letters to her, as well as various of his artistic works. She also carried on writing the story of her life, and showed visitors round the house (one summer's day, eleven bicyclists from St Petersburg had turned up), but there were few joys. When her sons pressed her again for money, she wrote a new letter to the Tsar about selling Yasnaya Polyana, but there were still many members of the Russian government who balked at the idea of the home of that notorious heretic Tolstoy becoming part of the national heritage. In the end, Nicholas II awarded Sonya a 10,000-rouble annual state pension, but held firm on his refusal to buy Yasnaya Polyana.[18] There were personal losses for Sonya to endure during her last years: the deaths of her sister-in-law Maria Nikolayevna, her son-in-law Mikhail Sukhotin and, most painfully of all, her son Andrey from pleurisy in February 1916. Lev accompanied his mother to Petrograd (as Petersburg became when the war began) on a packed train, and they arrived just before Andrey died. After she returned home, Sonya steadily lost interest in life; she took to sitting for hours in the old Voltaire chair that Tolstoy had particularly liked because it had been in his family since before he was born.

Where Sonya's life was now empty and static, Chertkov's was congested with activity. He was a man with a mission, and had become even busier after Tolstoy's death. It had been Chertkov who was in control of the situation during his friend's last days, and it was to him that people turned afterwards. There were interviews and lectures to give, and a mass of manuscripts to put into order and prepare for publication. Chertkov published his first book on Tolstoy's last days in 1911, and that was followed in 1912 by a volume of Tolstoy's diaries. Next came the editing of the three volumes of posthumous fiction, whose proceeds enabled Sasha to buy the Yasnaya Polyana farmland from her family to give to the peasants.[19] But Chertkov's main task now was to produce a canonical edition of Tolstoy's complete collected works, which he knew would be an enormous project. He had been entrusted with all of Tolstoy's late manuscripts, and in 1913 he brought them from storage in England and took them to the Academy of Sciences in St Petersburg for temporary safe-keeping.[20]

When Russia was drawn into World War I, the Tolstoyans were placed in a difficult position. Despite Tolstoy's baleful predictions about large-scale bloodshed and violence, and his warnings about the false allure of patriotism, Chertkov supported the war effort. He arranged for his 1909 article about pacifism to be republished in 1914 and 1917, but in this extreme situation, his pacifism could ultimately not stand up against his patriotism (he had, after all, once been an officer in the Imperial Guard). He also felt a deep allegiance to England, which he declared was his 'second fatherland', not least because he had spent about eleven years of his life there.[21] Biryukov was now in Switzerland, so it was left to Bulgakov to become the chief spokesman for the Tolstoyans. Bulgakov typed up and distributed copies of an article he wrote about the war in September 1914, after being released from jail, and the following month he started gathering signatures for a collective anti-war petition which was entitled 'Come to Your Senses, Brothers!' Russian soldiers at the front were exhorted to love all of their fellow human beings in uniform regardless of their nationality. The tsarist government moved swiftly to arrest those who signed the petition, three of whom were rounded up at Chertkov's house in Moscow at six in the morning one cold January day in 1915. Fortunately, Sasha and Tanya were able to step in to post bail for Bulgakov and Makovický, and Chertkov called on his influential British contacts to dissuade the Russian government from sending them to prison or to do hard labour along with other conscientious objectors. Most of the Tolstoyans were later acquitted.[22]

The atrocities of World War I served to make Tolstoy's ideas even more relevant and topical, and then suddenly, in 1917, it finally became possible to publish all of his banned writings in Russia. The collapse of the Romanov dynasty and the February Revolution brought the end of censorship, and

Tolstoy's followers lost no time. The board of the Tolstoy Society in Moscow could at last seriously discuss publishing a truly complete edition of the collected works, and in April 1917 Sergey and Sasha, as representatives of the Tolstoy family, became members of a new committee charged with overseeing editorial matters and raising the necessary funds for publication.[23] They were joined by Valentin Bulgakov and Nikolay Gusev. Between 1917 and 1918 the old Intermediary publishing house produced sixty-three editions of Tolstoy's writings, but a new publishing house called Zadruga was also set up now, to publish all those Tolstoy essays that had previously been banned. In the heady days of June 1917 a new Tolstoyan organisation was also formed. The Society of True Freedom quickly launched a journal, *Voice of Truth and Unity*, which had a print run of 10,000 and established a network of affiliated branches in cities across Russia.[24] It was estimated there were between 5,000 and 6,000 Tolstoyans active in Russia at this time.[25]

The situation was less optimistic in 1917 at Yasnaya Polyana. The February Revolution unleashed widespread looting, and in particular the indiscriminate destruction of former gentry estates. Chertkov later likened the situation to the bursting of a dam. After centuries in which the Russian people had existed 'under the heel of autocratic oppression', the pent-up water was now bearing down 'in a wild, irresistible torrent, relentlessly flooding and ruining all that it encounters'.[26] Blinded by the propaganda of class hatred unleashed by the Bolsheviks, the peasants and demobbed soldiers who went on the rampage did not see why Count Tolstoy's estate was deserving of exemption. And the aggressors were not all male. In September 1917 Sasha received a postcard from her sister Tanya informing her that hundreds of local women and children had broken into the extensive orchards at Yasnaya Polyana and stolen all the apples – around 16,500 kilograms' worth by her reckoning.[27] When Bulgakov read newspaper reports that autumn about marauding peasants breaking into Yasnaya Polyana and wreaking havoc not just in its orchards, but also in its apiaries and its fields of crops, he came down from Moscow straight away to meet with villagers to arrange the provision of some kind of security. Sonya meanwhile also appealed to the Ministry of Internal Affairs for help, and the writer Pyotr Sergeyenko, who had known Tolstoy and was also known to the local peasants, was appointed to help protect Yasnaya Polyana from future raids. When it became known that a group of young peasants and demobbed soldiers were inciting the locals to wreck Yasnaya Polyana at the end of 1917, a Red Army unit was eventually assigned to the estate to provide security. Bulgakov was soon able to report that a telephone had been installed for the first time at Yasnaya Polyana, so that there could be regular communication with local political organisations in Tula, who were aware this landed estate was not like the others, and needed special safeguarding.[28]

The Tolstoyans had welcomed the February Revolution, and they continued to feel a certain camaraderie with the Bolsheviks. This was not only because the Bolsheviks had attempted to sabotage the war effort by persuading rank-and-file soldiers that their real enemy was their own military hierarchy, but also because both groups rejoiced to see both Church and landowners being divested of their lands (albeit for completely different reasons).[29] The events of October 1917 and the violence of the ensuing weeks and months filled the Tolstoyans with horror, however. 'Stop the Fratricide!' was the title of the leaflet distributed on the streets in Moscow by the Tolstoyans three days after the Bolsheviks seized power. The desire to get their message across outweighed their fears of exposing themselves to mortal danger while doing so.[30] The Peace concluded with Germany in March 1918 was followed by yet more bloodshed. Despite his initial support of the imperial army, Chertkov was proud that Russian soldiers had eventually left the ranks in great numbers and returned home in 1917, 'disgusted and physically exhausted by the international carnage' and no longer willing to be treated as 'cannon fodder'. A similar idea was argued by émigré intellectuals in Paris, who saw the situation in a far less favourable light. In a 1918 article Nikolay Berdyaev argued that the Russian Revolution was in its way a victory for Tolstoyanism, while Dmitry Merezhkovsky declared that Bolshevism was the 'suicide' of Europe: 'Tolstoy began it, and Lenin finished it off.'[31] Berdyaev argued that spiritual regeneration would entail overcoming Tolstoyanism.[32]

It was not only Russians who associated Tolstoy directly with the Bolshevik Revolution immediately after it took place. Tolstoy's English translator and biographer Aylmer Maude was also under no doubt that Tolstoy's 'courage and intellectual force', his outspokenness and deep love of the people, had played a cardinal role in bringing about the fall of the Romanovs. An American article published in 1919 quoted Maude extensively:

Tolstoy's condemnation of the very foundations of civilized life and of all established government must be effectively met, or a growing spirit of anarchy, challenging, indicting and disparaging every effort to secure any definiteness in human relations or to establish any fixed law, will undermine the bases of all our social efforts, and sooner or later the whole structure will crash down as it has done in Russia. Merely to deny or deride Tolstoy's opinions will not do. His themes are too important, his statement of them is too masterly, and his sincerity is too apparent.

The article described Tolstoy as the 'Great Patriarch of the Bolsheviki Family'.[33]

Sasha came back from World War I with the rank of colonel, and two St George medals awarded for bravery (the decoration which had once eluded her father). She had served on the Western Front, and also in the Caucasus, where she set up orphanages and ran a field hospital, but the situation became dangerous after the February Revolution and she returned home.[34] It was Sasha, or Alexandra, as we should call her, since she was now stepping out of the role of daughter, who took over the running of Yasnaya Polyana from her ailing mother at the end of 1917. She took up residence in the old family home again along with her aunt Tanya, her sister Tanya (both now widowed) and her niece Tanya, and now began to turn her attention back to her father's legacy. It was now that Sonya finally handed over the keys to the twelve chests of Tolstoy's manuscripts under her jurisdiction to Alexandra, removing the last bone of contention between them. Sonya's eldest and youngest children (Sergey was now fifty-five, Alexandra was thirty-four) were thus at last able to start serious work on preparing their father's manuscripts for the projected complete scholarly edition.

It was thanks to Lenin's personal initiative that the gargantuan project of Tolstoy's collected works was moved to the top of the agenda in the cultural sphere and viewed as a matter of state importance. An article to this effect appeared in the Bolshevik newspaper *Sovetskaya pravda* at the end of January 1918, when the figure of sixty volumes was mentioned.[35] (It was also at Lenin's personal behest that Sonya's state pension was reinstated in March 1918, having been reduced in 1917.[36]) The archives in the Rumyantsev Museum, which had once again become the repository of Tolstoy's early manuscripts, became a hive of activity in the winter of 1918. Pashkov House, the elegant mansion that housed the Rumyantsev Museum, located a short walk from the Kremlin, was still the home of Moscow's most important library, and would later become the nucleus of the Lenin Library. In the harsh post-revolutionary conditions of 1918, however, no one cared much for well-appointed surroundings, particularly in the winter months when there was no heating. Alexandra, Sergey and their colleagues were forced to work in their overcoats and hats, with regular bursts of gymnastics in order to survive the freezing temperatures. They had formed a Society for the Study and Dissemination of the Works of L. N. Tolstoy, chaired by Alexandra, but it soon became clear to them that Chertkov and other key followers of their father would be instrumental in the preparation of any authoritative edition. Chertkov was not a member of their society, as he was preparing a rival edition. Having appointed himself as chief editor of the *Complete Collected Works*, he started negotiations with Lenin and Anatoly Lunacharsky, the new Commissar of People's Enlightenment, for the publication of an edition which he now projected would comprise ninety volumes. By December 1918 he had won assurances that 10 million roubles would be allocated by the Bolshevik government to fund the entire enterprise, but until the money became a reality, he paid the thirty-strong editorial team he assembled out of his own pocket.[37]

Bulgakov had been effective in setting up and running the Tolstoy Museum in Moscow, but the situation remained bleak at Yasnaya Polyana, which the family still owned and ran as an unofficial museum. Sovnarkom, the administrative arm of the new Soviet government, formally took over the estate in May 1918, and stipulated that Tolstoy's widow should be able to reside there for the rest of her life, but provided no money at this point for its upkeep. Pride disinclined the Tolstoys from asking the Bolsheviks for money, but the estate had begun to go into such decline that in February 1919 Tanya proposed handing it over to the local society which had been formed to provide security. In a letter to her brother Sergey in Moscow that April, Tanya described the desperate conditions she and the other thirteen members of the family had to endure at Yasnaya Polyana. They had so little to eat they were unable to provide for their staff, let alone the animals. For the staff the situation was even worse: some of them had to endure effluent from the next-door pigsty seeping into their accommodation and rotting the floorboards. Rooves leaked, the belt from the threshing machine had been stolen, books were disappearing from Tolstoy's library, and the furnishings in the house were becoming very worn. Tanya had to resort to knitting scarves, to sell along with Yasnaya Polyana honey in Tula. We have the KGB to thank for preserving Tanya's letter to her brother – it was confiscated and copied when their sister Alexandra was arrested the following year – and we have the stubborn efforts of the Moscow writer Vitaly Shentalinsky to thank for gaining access to its previously impregnable archive in the 1980s.[38]

In May 1919 the Soviet government approved the proposal for the Yasnaya Polyana Society to take over the running of the estate, with the family continuing to act as guides for visitors. The society would retain control until June 1921, when Yasnaya Polyana was finally nationalised and placed under the aegis of the Soviet government. By this time, the Tolstoy Museum in Moscow had also been nationalised and allotted a handsome mansion on the former Prechistenka, renamed Kropotkinskaya. It now became the central repository for the 2.5 million pages in Tolstoy's archive. The formal opening took place on the tenth anniversary of Tolstoy's death, which was now 20 November 1920 (Russia adopted the Gregorian calendar after the October Revolution).[39] Tolstoy's former Moscow house was also nationalised, and opened as a 'museum-estate' on 20 November 1921. Dolgo-Khamovnichesky Lane was also renamed Tolstoy Street.

In the meantime, the Tolstoy family decided to do something about Pyotr Sergeyenko, who had been appointed as the head of the Yasnaya Polyana Society. He had alienated them all with his rudeness and patronising manner, and they all loathed him; it was particularly upsetting for Sonya to be treated in such an offhand manner. Alexandra took matters into her own hands by going to Moscow to see Lunacharsky, who promptly appointed her Commissar of Yasnaya Polyana. Sergeyenko could now be given his marching orders.[40] It was a difficult year, and at the end of 1919, bruised by Sergeyenko's brusque and imperious manner, a shadow of her former self, Sonya died. In the touching letter she wrote to her children and sister Tanya before her death she said her farewells and asked her daughters to forgive her for the pain she had caused them. But she ended on a bright note of loving gratitude to her granddaughter Tanyushka for bringing her so much joy and affection.[41]

As well as being appointed Commissar of Yasnaya Polyana by Lunacharsky in 1919, Alexandra was also arrested for the first time in July of that year at her flat in Moscow. On this occasion her stay in the Lubyanka was short lived. Chertkov at this point wielded considerable power, and he immediately wrote to Felix Dzerzhinsky, the founder and head of the Cheka, the first incarnation of what eventually became the KGB. Presuming her detainment was surely due to a misunderstanding, Chertkov was successful in his impeccably polite request that Alexandra be released.[42] In February 1920 Alexandra shored up her position by formally confirming her appointment as Commissar with the Ministry of People's Enlightenment, and the following month, the Ministry of Agriculture also placed her in charge of farming at Yasnaya Polyana.[43] A few days later, however, she was arrested by the Cheka again, and this time accused of counter-revolutionary activities. Her father had foreseen the Russian Revolution back in 1905, and had been under no illusion about the violence which would be used to bring about this inevitable upheaval, while heartily deploring its application.[44] But even he could not have predicted that ten years after his death his beloved daughter and devoted follower Alexandra would be sitting in a rat-infested cell in the notorious Lubyanka awaiting interrogation by the secret police.[45]

Alexandra spent two months in the Lubyanka before her fellow Tolstoyans successfully petitioned for her to be released on bail until her case came to trial in August 1920. There is no doubt that her father would have been proud of her defiant final statement in court:

> I am not using my final statement to defend myself, because I do not consider myself guilty of anything. But I would just like to say to the citizens judging me that I do not recognise human judgement and consider that it is a misunderstanding that a person has the right to judge another. I consider that we are all free people, and that this freedom is within myself – no one can deprive me of it, neither the walls of the Special division, nor internment in a camp. This free spirit is not the freedom which is surrounded by bayonets in free Russia, but is the freedom of my spirit, and it will stay with me …[46]

For putting on the samovar for members of an alleged counter-revolutionary organisation, whom she had unwittingly allowed to meet in her flat, the Commissar of Yasnaya Polyana was sentenced to three years at the Novospassky Monastery in Moscow, which had recently been converted by the Bolsheviks into a concentration camp. From her cell, Alexandra drafted a letter to Lenin:

Vladimir Ilyich! If I am harmful to Russia, send me abroad. If I am harmful there, then in acknowledgement of the right of a person to deprive another of life, kill me as a harmful member of the Soviet republic. But do not force me to lead the miserable existence of a parasite, locked up in four walls with prostitutes, thieves and bandits …[47]

Alexandra was in fact released after two only months, on the proviso that she attended no public events, but was almost immediately arrested again after she was spotted at the lecture Bulgakov gave to mark the tenth anniversary of her father's death.[48] She was released a few months later in February 1921,[49] thanks partly again to the intervention of friends, but mostly due to a petition signed by the peasants at Yasnaya Polyana and neighbouring villages. She endured one further arrest in August 1921, but was detained only briefly.[50]

All the Tolstoyans began to encounter difficulties with the Soviet government in 1919. Back in 1917, the Provisional Government had granted the Tolstoyans an amnesty from conscription, but after the October Revolution the Bolsheviks started a new mobilisation offensive against them. They were determined to conscript Tolstoyans into the Red Army along with other conscientious objectors, some of whom were only now beginning to return home from serving their sentences. Chertkov was naturally implacably opposed to this idea, and neither would he accept the compromise suggested by the Bolshevik leadership, which would have seen Tolstoyans working in medical units. It is testament to Chertkov's authority at this point that he won this particular battle, and his impressive ability to give the Bolsheviks to understand that he was the figurehead of an enormous international organisation catapulted him into high-profile positions. In 1918 he became the head of a United Council aimed at protecting pacifist religious communities in Russia. This was the first time that Tolstoyans had been grouped together with sectarians and religious minority groups such as Baptists and Mennonites. Chertkov continued his opposition to the Bolsheviks, and only partially backed down after a meeting with Lenin forced another compromise, so that an official decree could be agreed in 1919.[51]

Chertkov found himself writing hundreds of testimonials for Tolstoyans at this time. He also longed for the Civil War to come to an end, and in October 1919 wrote an impassioned 'Letter to English Friends' in which he pleaded for foreign involvement in Russia, covert or otherwise, to stop, leaving the country to proceed with social reconstruction on its own. Tolstoy had a great role to play in this task, he argued, for in him 'the people find a clear and powerful expression of their own most sacred beliefs and highest aspirations'. Tolstoy's religious writings, accessible to the masses for the first time, were in enormous demand, he wrote. In the wake of World War I, which had confirmed all Tolstoy's predictions, Chertkov was sure that working people everywhere would draw inspiration from his writings, but it was the Russian people, he argued, 'as yet uncontaminated by European civilisation', who were pre-eminently in a position to understand and appreciate the teaching of Christ 'in the pure undefiled aspect in which it is expounded by Tolstoy'.[52]

In many ways, the Civil War period was actually the 'golden age of Tolstoyanism', when Tolstoyan ideas were put into practice at the new Tolstoyan communes that began to spring up, and also vigorously debated as a matter of life importance. The Tolstoyans entered into a series of passionate debates with Lunacharsky and other luminaries in front of huge audiences at the Polytechnical Museum in Moscow. On 5 March 1920, for example, Bulgakov appeared alongside the erudite Symbolist poet Vyacheslav Ivanov, a rabbi and an Orthodox priest.[53] In November 1920 an audience of 2,000 crowded the Great Hall of the Moscow Conservatoire to take part in an event commemorating the tenth anniversary of Tolstoy's death. Bulgakov, who was already highly critical of the Bolsheviks, was unable to finish his speech amidst the raucous applause and whistling.[54] Tolstoy's name was also still on everybody's lips in the huge émigré community which had formed in Paris immediately after the Revolution, and there were many who still wanted to pin the blame for the Bolshevik victory directly on his influence. In vain did the former statesman Vasily Maklakov insist that Tolstoy had nothing in common with Bolshevism in the speech that he gave in Paris to mark the tenth anniversary of Tolstoy's death – numerous others were ready to argue that Tolstoy's ideas about non-resistance to violence had exerted a profoundly pernicious effect, and should be opposed with a show of strength.[55]

A key figure during these years was Vladimir Bonch-Bruevich, who had worked with Tolstoy and Chertkov to help the Dukhobors emigrate before the Revolution. He now occupied a prominent position in the Bolshevik government, and it was he who helped Chertkov obtain meetings with Lenin in the early years.[56] Widespread famine during the Civil War caused the Bolsheviks to remember that the Dukhobors and other sectarians were good farmers, and in 1921 Lenin responded enthusiastically to a request from some Dukhobors in Canada who requested permission to return home to Russia so they could help revive the national economy. Taking heart from these developments, and reassured by the respect in which Chertkov was held, Tolstoyans began meeting in the cafeteria of the Vegetarian Society in Moscow and organising communes, too naïve to see the cynicism behind Bolshevik official policy. The Tolstoyans were mostly peasants from rural areas, but their numbers also included teachers, doctors and urban office workers who now consciously became peasants on the Tolstoyan model. The 'Life and Labour' commune, for example, which began life in December 1921 in the southern outskirts of Moscow (roughly where the metro station Belyaevo is located), was founded by a geologist called Boris Mazurin, who turned to Tolstoyanism after being sickened by the endless violence he saw around him. By 1925 the commune was totally self-sufficient. There were disagreements amongst the Tolstoyans who formed communes, as they did not all share the writer's aspirations to a spiritual life untainted by any intrusion from the state, but they did all agree on the importance and nobility of work in the fields as the prerequisite for their independence and autonomy.

On one level it seemed that the Tolstoyans were truly a force to be reckoned with. Chertkov was not only the coordinator of the Congress of Religious Sects held in June 1920, but also head of the largest delegation: twenty Tolstoyans took part in the congress. On another level, however, the Bolsheviks soon started to become more hard-line. When complaints that the decree on conscientious objection was already being frequently violated were investigated, it turned out that both armies, Red and White, were indeed flouting it. Indeed, the Bolsheviks were responsible for executing by firing squad more than 100 Tolstoyan objectors, the first eight by December 1919.[57] At the end of 1920 the Bolsheviks altered the 1919 decree, then they simply disbanded the council over which Chertkov presided. It had considered applications from some 40,000 conscious objectors. Finally, in November 1923, the People's Commissar for Justice decided to remove Tolstoyans from the list of bona fide conscientious objectors altogether, now deciding that they did not belong to a religious sect, and objected to military service on ethical grounds.[58] Fortunately pressure had already been eased on those who opposed military service, because by this time the Civil War had finally come to an end.

Opposition to military service was not the only problem Chertkov had to deal with, as he soon also started to clash with the Bolsheviks over the projected edition of Tolstoy's *Complete Collected Works*, which was taking a long time to get off the ground. In July 1919, when Alexandra's flat was being searched for evidence of sedition, the Bolsheviks had decided to nationalise the manuscripts of all Russian writers held in state libraries. That meant they also had a monopoly on publication, and since Tolstoy had famously surrendered the copyright on all his works, Chertkov naturally opposed this.[59] He argued that Tolstoy would never have agreed to his writings becoming the property of any person or institution, particularly a state, and rightly viewed the idea of a state monopoly as a form of censorship.[60] In September 1920 he was finally granted an audience with Lenin to discuss the matter, along with the issue about the Tolstoyans' refusal to serve in the Red Army, but the discussions ended in stalemate.

Chertkov found a way out of the copyright problem over the Tolstoy *Collected Works* when Lenin introduced the New Economic Policy (NEP) in March 1921. This allowed the temporary return of private enterprise in order to resuscitate the economy after the ravages of the Civil War, and the wily Chertkov turned the situation to his advantage. Alexandra had just been released from prison, and she renewed her association with Chertkov in an effort to move the *Collected Works* project along, but each still headed two distinct groups. As soon as it was legally possible, Chertkov and Alexandra formed a Co-operative Association for the Study and Dissemination of the Works of Lev Nikolayevich Tolstoy, and on 8 April the association invited Chertkov to become its chief editor.[61] Chertkov was also busy at this time writing his own magnum opus about the story of Tolstoy's final departure from Yasnaya Polyana. Sofya Andreyevna's death had been a liberation for him, as it meant he could finally speak his mind. Naturally vindicating himself, he apportioned blame for the tragedy of Tolstoy's last years to his 'marital problems'. The book was published in 1922, and greatly upset Tolstoy's children, even Alexandra.[62] Lev Lvovich, who particularly detested Chertkov, immediately retaliated against the slur on his mother by publishing a book of his own the following year in Prague, where he was now based. It was entitled *The Truth About My Father*, and painted Sonya in glowing terms.[63] Chertkov was undaunted, but whatever unease one might feel about his lack of tact in the years immediately following Tolstoy's death must eventually give way to respect for his single-minded refusal to compromise his beliefs in the increasingly hostile atmosphere of high Stalinism in the 1930s.

When she was released from prison in 1921, Alexandra settled once again at Yasnaya Polyana, where she was still Commissar, but in June she was summoned to a meeting with Mikhail Kalinin, head of the Central Committee. After disembarking from the train in Moscow, Alexandra set off for the Kremlin on her bicycle. At this important meeting it was agreed that Yasnaya Polyana would now become the property of the Russian Federation, and would be run as a commune under the jurisdiction of the Commissariat of People's Enlightenment. The commune would include a school, a library, and later a hospital. Alexandra's title was now changed from Commissar to 'Custodian', and she was given the duties of managing the estate as a museum, organising lectures and events and acting as head of the new school. The agricultural work was to be undertaken by Tolstoyans.[64] The commune lasted less than a year. The seventeen so-called Tolstoyans who took up residence at Yasnaya Polyana in March 1921 turned out to be a bunch of no-hopers, who either argued that they could not remove worms from the cabbages because they could not kill 'anything living', or were simply incapable of working. These 'faux Tolstoyans' thankfully soon left, some miraculously transforming themselves into devout Communist Party apparatchiks.[65] Alexandra then turned her energies to starting the village school at Yasnaya Polyana, and to restoring the estate to its pre-revolutionary condition.

Alexandra was not the only Tolstoyan to attract the attention of the secret police in the early 1920s. Despite his political clout, Chertkov himself was the subject of several denunciations between 1920 and 1922. As he became more vociferous about his opposition to the Bolsheviks, informers from the Cheka were despatched to report on him, and also what went on at the headquarters of the Society of True Freedom, whose vegetarian cafeteria and library were popular haunts for Tolstoyans and those of like mind. Unlike the Chekist and part-time Futurist with the flowing locks and velvet jacket who had come to arrest Alexandra, not all the Bolshevik spies were well informed. In one report which mentioned discussion of someone called 'Socrates', the hapless agent noted in parentheses that he did not know him, apparently unaware that Socrates had been dead for some time.[66]

Sixty Tolstoyans were arrested for 'anti-Soviet' activity in Vitebsk at the end of 1920, and it was only a matter of time before they caught up with

Chertkov and Bulgakov, whose homes were raided by the Cheka in December 1922. Both were summoned to the Lubyanka for questioning. Chertkov defiantly refused to participate, and coolly and calmly demanded the return of the papers which had been confiscated. The Bolsheviks decided to send both Chertkov and Bulgakov into exile for three years. Bulgakov had earlier interceded on Alexandra Lvovna's behalf, and this time it was her turn to plead for clemency. In February 1923 she wrote to Lev Kamenev, chairman of the new all-important Politburo (its other members were Lenin, Stalin, Trotsky and Krestinsky), requesting that Bulgakov be allowed to stay in Moscow so that he could continue his important work at the Tolstoy Museum, where he was director. Chertkov wrote a dignified and pedantic letter meanwhile to Avel Enukidze, a another prominent Bolshevik and close friend of Stalin who was a member of the Central Committee. In his letter he argued wearily that he was now in his late sixties, and so did not have much time left; he could not possibly proceed with the important project of producing Tolstoy's collected works if he was exiled abroad. Chertkov was allowed to stay, but it was in keeping with his nickname of 'Iron Felix' that Dzerzhinsky refused to relent in Bulgakov's case. A little more than a month later, Bulgakov left for Czechoslovakia with his family, and was only allowed to return to Russia twenty-six years later in 1949. When he came back he immediately resumed his job at the Tolstoy Museum in Moscow.

If Chertkov thought NEP was going to bring about greater freedom for the dissemination of Tolstoyan ideas, he was mistaken. In 1923 the Bolsheviks shut down the new independent Tolstoyan publishing house Zadruga as part of its drive to bring all publishing under state control. Lenin's wife Nadezhda Krupskaya also demanded that all of Tolstoy's religious writings be removed from municipal libraries.[67] Tolstoy's ideas had been considered heretical by the tsarist government, and within five years they had become also unacceptable to the regime which replaced it. The Bolsheviks now had the upper hand with nonconformists, but they clearly still saw Tolstoyanism as a threat. As a world-famous writer-turned-anarchist who preached non-resistance to violence, Tolstoy had exasperated the tsarist government during his lifetime, and the Bolsheviks found it no easier to deal with his legacy. On the one hand they revered him for attacking the Russian tsarist state and exposing the moral flaws of all its institutions, but on the other they could not countenance his uncompromising rejection of the state in any form. The problem was that Tolstoy was not just the 'greatest novelist of any age and of any country', as the prominent Belgian political writer Charles Sarolea commented after a sobering visit to the Soviet Union in 1923, but also 'one of the greatest teachers and preachers of modern times'.[68] Sarolea was, of course, not alone in coming to the apparently paradoxical conclusion that there was a direct connection between Tolstoy and Bolshevism. This was still a topic on the lips of many in the early 1920s, both in Russia and abroad.[69] The extent to which the Bolsheviks still regarded Tolstoyanism as one of the greatest threats facing the fledgling Communist state may be gauged by the fact that Lunacharsky gave a lengthy lecture on the subject in 1924, which was also disseminated in book form. The basic ideologies dividing Russians at that time, he stated categorically, were Marxism and Tolstoyanism.[70]

From the beginning, Russia's leading revolutionaries had disagreed about Tolstoy while acknowledging his seminal importance. Lenin had played a prominent role in the debate by writing seven articles on Tolstoy between 1908 and 1911. In 1908 he had directly attributed the failure of the 1905 Revolution to the influence of Tolstoy's ideas of non-violence. His article 'Lev Tolstoy as a Mirror of the Russian Revolution' was widely reprinted after his death, and became the Soviet blueprint for the official view of Tolstoy. Trotsky, who wrote on Tolstoy in 1908 and 1910, had shone a more positive light on Tolstoy's impact on the events of 1905, while Plekhanov had simply dismissed Tolstoy as a patriarchal, reactionary landowner with nothing to offer the revolutionary movement. Tolstoy's name was inevitably invoked again at the time of the 1917 Revolutions, and continued to figure in public discourse, as the Bolshevik government struggled to find a way of exploiting his legacy.

It was not until the centenary of Tolstoy's birth in 1928 that a clear policy was formulated, and twenty years of debate came to an abrupt end. What the Bolsheviks decided to do was separate Tolstoy from Tolstoyanism. Despite the 'contradictions' in his teachings, the Bolsheviks decided the centenary of Tolstoy's birth should be celebrated in grand style, and a government committee headed by Lunacharsky was formed in 1926, two years in advance of the anniversary.[71] Alexandra was pinning great hopes on the Tolstoy Jubilee, and on the fact that it was being officially sanctioned at the very highest level. For her it was a form of self-defence against the dozens of local communists whom she described as buzzing around Yasnaya Polyana like flies, hoping to find fault and denounce her.[72] Like Chertkov, she had calmly stuck to her apolitical Tolstoyan beliefs, and refused to capitulate to the anti-religious propaganda war being waged around her. In 1924 the Yasnaya Polyana school had become part of the revolutionary 'experimental station' schools network, which drew partly on Tolstoy's ideas about education.[73] But the situation grew increasingly hostile, with the local powers seeing Alexandra and her colleagues as representatives of the 'loathed bourgeoisie', and resenting their achievements. The hostility was not restricted to barbs from local officials: Alexandra was also publicly attacked in *Pravda* as a 'former countess' who continued to exploit the workers and live a life of luxury and depravity while disseminating religious propaganda to her pupils. Alexandra faced her critics by reiterating Lenin's declaration that 'Soviet power can afford the luxury of a Tolstoyan corner in the USSR'. She also responded by publishing a rebuttal of the criticisms on 2 July 1924 in *Pravda*, but she already felt extremely beleaguered.[74]

When the committee for the anniversary celebrations was formed in 1926, Alexandra submitted proposals for extensive renovation work at Yasnaya Polyana, including new buildings for the school and hospital there. She also proposed the reorganisation of the Tolstoy Museum in Moscow. Her sister Tanya had taken over the management of the Moscow museum from Bulgakov when he was sent into exile in 1923, but she herself had emigrated in 1925. Since Ilya, Lev and Mikhail were all already abroad, and Sergey had a job teaching at the Moscow Conservatoire, the seemingly indefatigable Alexandra now became Director of the Tolstoy Museum as well. Lunacharsky, Chertkov, Gusev and the other members of the committee were receptive to Alexandra's proposals, but were powerless to do anything, owing to the simple fact that there was no money: the Commissariat of People's Enlightenment was always the poorest of all the Soviet ministries. Alexandra showed her mettle at this point, and decided to go to the top, and after making several visits to Moscow from Yasnaya Polyana she eventually obtained an audience with Stalin, who had assumed power after Lenin's death in January 1924. The brief interview was chastening. Stalin flatly refused to pay the million roubles requested by the Jubilee Committee for its construction and renovation programme, and it quickly became apparent to Alexandra that he did not care about Tolstoy and the Tolstoy Jubilee at all. What he did care about was exploiting it as a felicitous opportunity for international propaganda, and doing so as cheaply as possible.[75]

The situation with the Tolstoy *Collected Works* was also bleak. In 1926, with just two years to go, there was still no contract signed for what was now pegged to the centenary year as the Jubilee Edition. Chertkov had also been having high-level meetings with the Soviet leadership. He had been forced to accept the idea of a 'temporary' state monopoly on Tolstoy's manuscripts, which would at least be lifted with publication, but found himself constantly lobbying for funds to pay the editorial team. His first meeting with Stalin, which took place in the autumn of 1924, had produced results. In November 1925 the Soviet government finally approved the release of a million roubles to pay for the cost of the project. The money was very slow in materialising, however, and in June 1926 Chertkov was forced to write to Stalin to tell him he could no longer afford to pay the forty-three members of the editorial staff working on the project (most of their wages were still coming from his own pocket). Alexandra was still very much involved with the project, but she and Chertkov did not see eye to eye. Finally, in 1925, they reached an agreement: her group would prepare Tolstoy's manuscripts written before 1880, and his team would work on the later writings. In December 1925 the two groups were united under Chertkov's leadership.[76]

The Central Committee now decided it should form a special commission to investigate and monitor the Tolstoy Jubilee Edition, and in September 1926 a 'troika' was appointed, headed by Stalin's deputy Vyacheslav Molotov. In March 1927 the state bank finally paid out a miserly 15,000 roubles, but meanwhile the contract had got lost in a morass of bureaucracy and ever-changing personnel at Gosizdat, the state publishing house. Chertkov wrote to Stalin again in March 1928 to protest that Gosizdat was refusing to sign the contract, despite the special commission having approved it. The contract was finally signed on 2 April 1928, but by then it was too late for even the first volume to appear in time for Tolstoy's centenary.[77] By this point, Alexandra had lost interest in an edition which was clearly going to be limited and expensive. There had been further disagreements with Chertkov over payment for editorial work, and Chertkov now took over as editor-in-chief.

The Jubilee Edition of Tolstoy's *Complete Collected Works* was to set the standard for Soviet scholarly editions. Artistic works were designated for the first forty-five volumes, with separate volumes for the different versions of major works (*War and Peace* takes up four volumes, for example). Editors had to work painstakingly through thousands and thousands of pages of

Tolstoy's often illegible handwriting before presenting their volume for discussion at one of the 156 committee meetings which were held over the course of edition's publication. More than 900 corrections were made to produce a definitive edition of *Anna Karenina* (although even that version was later superseded by the Academy of Sciences edition published in 1970). Tolstoy's artistic works were to be followed by thirteen volumes of diaries and notebooks. Finally there would be thirty-one volumes of letters. Tolstoy had written at least 8,500 letters during his lifetime, with Chertkov by far and away his most frequent correspondent.[78]

The hundreds of events marking the centenary of Tolstoy's birth in 1928 were the first to be undertaken by the Soviet government in honour of a pre-revolutionary writer on a nationwide scale. Because of the ambivalence surrounding the Jubilee, the Bolsheviks were concerned to use the occasion to educate Soviet citizens on how to approach Tolstoy. Thus, along with the issue of commemorative stamps, there were guides providing instructions on how the Tolstoy centenary should be celebrated. Pride of place in all writing on Tolstoy, from now until the end of the Soviet regime, was taken by Lenin's 1908 article.[79] The main centenary celebrations began on Tolstoy's birthday on 9 September (as 28 August had become according to the new calendar), and they lasted a week. According to Lunacharsky in the speech he made, such was the 'gigantic interest' in Tolstoy in the new Soviet state that the writer was not dead at all.[80] Tolstoy was, in fact, the most widely read author in Russia at this point according to data compiled by the Bolshevik journal *Red Librarian*, and the only writer to have maintained his pre-revolutionary popularity. Even in the countryside, readers often had to queue up for months to read the one copy of *War and Peace* held by their local library.[81]

As a fervent admirer of Tolstoy, the Austrian writer Stefan Zweig was one of the distinguished foreign visitors invited to Russia to take part in the centenary celebrations in 1928. The celebrations were launched with a commemorative evening at the Bolshoi Theatre in Moscow on 9 September. Like everything else at that time, it was held up by Soviet bureaucrats who fussed over memoranda and permits. 'The principal event which was announced for six o'clock began at 9.30,' Zweig later recollected. 'When I left the opera house exhausted at three in the morning, the speakers were still hard at it.'[82] The festivities then transferred to Yasnaya Polyana. At 7.00 a.m. on 12 September, in pouring rain, Alexandra made her way to the Yasnaya

Polyana railway station (as Zaseka was now called) along with journalists, photographers and curious locals. There they greeted the official delegation of eighty guests who had travelled down from Moscow, and included the actress Olga Knipper (Chekhov's widow), esteemed professors and foreign guests, who were easy to spot because they were not shabbily dressed.[83] On the train down, Zweig had chatted to Lunacharsky about whether Tolstoy was a revolutionary or a reactionary, and whether the great writer had even known himself. Lunacharsky suggested that in his eagerness to change the whole world 'in a flick of the wrist', Tolstoy was an ingrained Russian, just like the Bolsheviks who wanted to modernise their country overnight.[84]

As the minister responsible for Soviet culture in the 1920s, Lunacharsky played a key role in orchestrating the assimilation of Tolstoy into Bolshevik ideology in the early Stalinist years, and he published a volume of his writings on Tolstoy in 1928. A cultured and educated man, he did not always find his task easy, and since there was no place for even Lunacharsky's comparatively moderate views in the Soviet regime, he lost his job the following year. Both sides of his personality were on show on 12 September at Yasnaya Polyana. First he produced the standard official peroration, cutting off attempts by a Slovak guest and Alexandra to speak out about their harassment by Communist Party militants, but then gave an impassioned, personal and sincere speech about how much Tolstoy meant to him. After a day of speeches, a choir of 250 Yasnaya Polyana schoolchildren sang the 'Ode to Joy' from Beethoven's 9th Symphony (later condemned by a *Pravda* correspondent, who thought they had been singing a psalm), and village women dug out old embroidered blouses and coloured sarafans from their trunks and sang folksongs.[85]

There was a good deal of press coverage of the Tolstoy Jubilee. An unsigned editorial in *Pravda* published on 9 September may well have been written by Stalin himself. After questioning whether the Bolsheviks, who had 'chosen revolutionary violence', and regarded religion as the 'opium of the people', should honour a writer who 'did not understand' the proletarian movement, and to whom the revolution was alien, the conclusion was that they should.[86] Nevertheless, a list of twenty acceptable works of fiction by Tolstoy was now drawn up, Lenin's articles criticising Tolstoy were continually cited, and the writer's philosophical views were roundly condemned. Some important advances in Tolstoy scholarship had been made in the 1920s by literary scholars (such as the Formalists Boris Eikhenbaum and Viktor

Shklovsky), but the Russian Association of Proletarian Writers played safe by basing their interpretation of Tolstoy on Lenin's literary criticism, namely his famous 1908 characterisation of Tolstoy's method as the 'tearing off of masks', which was proffered as a good model for budding Soviet writers to follow. It was, in fact, political figures like Lenin and Rosa Luxemburg who dominated publications on Tolstoy around the time of the centenary. One volume published in 1929 may have included the very last Russian publication by Trotsky, who was expelled from the Soviet Union that year.[87] The chapter headings for one of the many centenary volumes about Tolstoy published in 1928 reflect the efforts that were made by the Soviet government to render the great writer acceptable to the regime:

> Part 1: The Jubilee and Our Tasks
> Part 2: Tolstoy as a Thinker
>   Tolstoy and his Epoch
>   The Lack of Synthesis; The Social Reasons for This
>   Dialectical Materialism and Religious Idealism
>   Class war/Struggle and Non-Resistance to Evil
>   Tolstoy's Criticism of Capitalism
>   Tolstoy's Criticism of Patriotism and Militarism
> Part 3: Tolstoy as Artist
> Part 4: Tolstoy and the Soviet Public[88]

In the face of this ideological onslaught, Alexandra's work at Yasnaya Polyana became more and more difficult. Once the Jubilee was over, she was once again subject to harassment by local Party officials when she refused to comply with their demands. Eventually she was forced to accept as her deputy at the estate-museum an anonymous Soviet writer who proposed using Tolstoy's teachings as a weapon in the anti-religious campaign. The requirement by the 'League of the Godless' that pupils at the Yasnaya Polyana school were to have lessons on Easter Sunday, in keeping with Stalin's calendar 'reforms', was the last straw. In the autumn of 1929 Alexandra got on a train for Vladivostok, en route for Japan, where she had been invited to lecture. She never returned to Russia.[89]

    By 1930, only two volumes of the Jubilee Edition had appeared, and there were still problems with obtaining funds to keep going. Chertkov was seventy-six and very ill by this time, but this was his life's work and he plodded resolutely on, despite having exhausted all his savings to fund the enterprise. In February 1934 he wrote about the lack of funds to Molotov, who had been head of Sovnarkom (Council of Ministers) since 1930, but he received no answer. On 27 May he wrote to Stalin:

> The situation of our editorial team is now completely hopeless as a result of the lack of funds to complete our work, the release of which, to the tune of 75,000 roubles, I requested from Sovnarkom. Meanwhile, my requests to accelerate the publication and fund the editing work to the end, as I have been informed by Sovnarkom, have not met with any objections in principle, and the entire delay is to do with the paperwork, which has been going on for four months already. I am not writing again to Comrade Molotov, because I have already written to him twice, and having not received a reply, I am not sure that he has the time to turn his personal attention to my appeal to him amongst many complex governmental affairs. But I am being so bold as to appeal to you, esteemed Iosif Vissarionovich, as the comrade on whose initiative this project was essentially launched following the lead of the late V. I. Lenin. I think that just one word from you would be enough to bring an immediate conclusion to the formal side of the protracted satisfaction of my requests, as set out in my letter of 23 February 1934 to Comrade Molotov …[90]

There was again no response, nor to a letter Chertkov wrote in July 1934, by which time he was so ill he was no longer in full control of his faculties, but in August that year the money started to trickle through at last.

Lenin had supposedly expressly stipulated that the edition should include everything ever written by Tolstoy, without any changes, and should restore cuts made by tsarist censors. His word was law, but the Stalinist government soon realised how subversive some of the material was. There was indeed a good deal of criticism by Tolstoy of the revolutionary movement in his late writings, and Chertkov, as chief editor, came in for criticism himself now from the Bolsheviks for not compiling the commentaries to Tolstoy's texts from a Marxist point of view.[91] Chertkov, of course, ever the aristocrat like Tolstoy, had never deigned to pay obeisance to contemptible Bolshevik ideology, and his persistently apolitical stance is all the more remarkable – and brave – given the militant rhetoric and coercive policies of the times. The Soviet government certainly came to regret giving Chertkov so much autonomy.

The great irony of the Tolstoy Jubilee Edition was that it made Tolstoy's works no more accessible than they had been during his lifetime. Not only was each volume extremely expensive, as Alexandra feared, but the print run was tiny: 5,000 or at the most 10,000. By the time that Nikolay Rodionov took over as chief editor when Chertkov died in 1936 at the age of eighty-two (the same age that Tolstoy had been when he died), seventy-two volumes were ready to be printed, but only twenty-nine had been published. They were appearing, moreover, in a strange order. Volume fifty-nine was published in 1935, for example, but it would not be until 1952 that volume thirty-four was published.[92] Eight volumes appeared in 1937, the year after Chertkov died, but this was the height of the purges, and Solomon Lozovsky, the new head of the state publishing house, now restyled as the acronym Goslitizdat, literally feared for his life. He had been appointed in 1936, having already been arrested once on Stalin's orders. The editorial team, whose office by a strange quirk of fate was located near the Lubyanka, now lost its independence, and were forced to take orders from Goslitizdat. In such fearful times there was no chance that Lozovsky could even contemplate approving the volumes in the Jubilee Edition which included Tolstoy's principal religious writings (volumes 23, 28, 48, 49, for example).

Between 1939 and 1949 publication ground to a complete halt, with staff working without a salary and Rodionov courageously seeking new ways to continue by trying to play the apparatchiks at their own game, and by emphasising Lenin's imprimatur on the whole enterprise. In the late thirties, under constant threat of arrest, the team doggedly prepared for publication more innocuous volumes, such as those containing Tolstoy's correspondence to his wife (83, 84), and they flagged up quotations by Lenin at the expense of their own commentary. The Tolstoy scholar Inessa Medzhibovskaya is right to liken Rodionov's dealings with Soviet bureaucracy during the purges to the literature of the absurd. In her review of a book published in 2002 by Lev Osterman, which has been one of the many important post-Soviet sources to explode the myth of Tolstoy's hallowed status after 1917, she gives an amusing abridged version of the transcript Osterman provides of Rodionov's encounter in 1939 with Pyotr Pospelov, deputy head of the Propaganda and Agitation Department of the Central Committee:

RODIONOV: I have been so insistently trying to gain a chance to see you in order to seek your advice, receive your guidance for action as to how we may resolve this painful situation without violating the will of L. N. Tolstoy and, at the same time, act in accordance with the current guidelines that the Central Committee of the Party has in mind.

POSPELOV: You have committed serious errors. The first one is your lengthy commentaries. Tolstoy's *Complete Works* are replaced with the complete works of his commentators. The second error is your method of commentary. You do not observe the contract and the contract stresses the need to be objective. Yet who could be more objective than Lenin? Why don't you enlist this most objective of sources? Why do you write long biographies about the most insignificant people, even about those who ended up being counter-revolutionary?[93]

The Jubilee Edition was only properly resuscitated after Stalin's death in 1953. The last volumes were eventually all published by 1958, by which time the heroic scholars of the original editorial team had been relegated to assistant status by Goslitizdat, and the names of Chertkov and Alexandra Tolstaya were no longer mentioned on the masthead. It had taken thirty years. The scholarship in the volumes published later inevitably suffered, and fresh rounds of 'editing' were so drastic that some volumes had to double up with others. The much-touted total of ninety volumes, in fact, comprises only seventy-eight separate books.[94] Once Tolstoy's religious works had appeared in the Jubilee Edition, they were banned from future publication. Nevertheless, in the 'official' history of the publication of the Jubilee Edition which Rodionov published in 1961, he could with justification point to it being compared to the 143 volumes of the benchmark Weimar Goethe edition, despite the necessary political accommodation with the regime.[95] Forty years later, in a very different political climate, Osterman's book *Srazhenie za Tolstogo* (*The Battle for Tolstoy*) would reveal the true story behind the publication of this extraordinary edition.

Over the course of the first few decades of Soviet power, Tolstoy was successfully transformed by the Bolsheviks from a 'socially alien' writer into one whose name was 'synonymous with Russia herself', as has been pointed out by Alexander Fodor in a valuable book which explores the history of Russia's relationship with Tolstoy.[96] A key role in this process of transformation was played by World War II. During the celebrations to mark the October Revolution in besieged Leningrad in 1941, Tolstoy's stories about the defence of Sebastopol were broadcast via loudspeaker in Palace Square. *War and Peace* also became a vitally important work while Russians fought to defend their country from the Nazi invasion. By this time, twenty-five trunks from the archive at the Tolstoy Museum in Moscow had been evacuated to Tomsk in Siberia, with other precious items directed to Tashkent. Tomsk was also the destination for the most valuable exhibits at Yasnaya Polyana, which was invaded by the Nazis on 30 October 1941, two days after the last party of tourists had been shown round its empty rooms.[97]

By the time the war was over, Tolstoy's entire corpus of anti-war writings had quietly been forgotten. In the 1950s Tolstoy was firmly entrenched in the Soviet imagination as a symbol of Russia, and as her most ardent patriot. Generations of Russian schoolchildren now grew up with the officially approved novels and stories that had become a fixture on the national curriculum, completely unaware of Tolstoy's enormous legacy of religious and political writings. Tolstoy's 'official' status was cemented by the number of new streets named after him in cities across the country, from Penza to Vladivostok, and in time his legacy was also tainted by the exigencies of the command economy which bred corruption and cynicism. Like all major Soviet literary museums, the Tolstoy Museum in Moscow was founded to be a centre for cutting-edge scholarship as much as a tourist destination, and it had been initially placed under the jurisdiction of the Academy of Sciences, along with the Tolstoy estate-museum. In 1953, however, that jurisdiction passed to the Soviet Ministry of Culture, and three years later there was a further 'demotion' to the Ministry of Culture of the Russian Federation, which placed more emphasis on meeting targets for visitor numbers. Scholars battled on valiantly, already hampered by the Soviet censorship, but standards inevitably slipped in some areas.[98]

In 1960 the fiftieth anniversary of Tolstoy's death was celebrated with official pomp by the Soviet establishment, which organised another, albeit more sedate, commemorative evening at the Bolshoi Theatre. And on 9 September 1978, to mark the 150th anniversary of Tolstoy's birth, the 'Museum-estate Yasnaya Polyana' was awarded the Order of Lenin by order of the Presidium of the Supreme Soviet of the USSR for 'major work in the aesthetic education of workers, and the study and propaganda of the creative legacy of the great Russian writer L. N. Tolstoy' (the Tolstoy Museum in Moscow was awarded the Order of the Red Banner). After she had left Russia in 1929 and become a vociferous critic of the Soviet regime, Alexandra's name had been erased from history as a 'traitor to the motherland', as Nikolay Rodionov had been forced to put it in his 1961 article about the Jubilee Edition, but at least he had mentioned her name. In an article about Yasnaya Polyana in the first years of the Revolution published in 1962, her name does not appear at all.[99] In 1977 Alexandra was partially rehabilitated and invited back to Russia to take part in the forthcoming celebrations, but by this time she was bedridden and gravely ill, and she died the following year in the United States, where she had been resident since the 1930s. The rehabilitation was partial, because even a book about the history of Yasnaya Polyana as a museum published as late as 1986 makes no mention of Alexandra; the fact that its author was Ilya Tolstoy, the grandson of her brother Ilya, is all the more dismaying.[100]

The almost total ignorance of Soviet citizens about the extent to which Tolstoy's ideas also continued to send powerful reverberations across Russia deep into the twentieth century is witness to the Communist Party's success in eliminating Tolstoyanism as a movement. At the same time that the Soviet regime firmly placed Tolstoy the novelist in its pantheon of model artists by reissuing his works with print runs running into the hundreds of thousands, it had unleashed a systematic campaign against his doctrines and all who followed them. The publication in the West in 1983 of a remarkable book about the Soviet followers of Tolstoy by a respected dissident writer and advocate of human rights based in Moscow called Mark Popovsky, however, pays tribute to the indomitable spirit of those who continued to be inspired by Tolstoy even in the face of unbelievable adversity and hardship. It was at the end of the 1970s when Popovsky, author of numerous books about Soviet scientists, both published and unpublished, was handed a copy of a letter from a peasant called Dmitry Morgachev. Writing at the age of eighty-four from the town of Przhevalsk in far-away Soviet Kirghizia to the USSR Public Prosecutor on 24 July 1976, Morgachev requested rehabilitation, and an acknowledgement from the Soviet government that he and his comrades had not committed any crime.

Popovsky discovered to his surprise that Morgachev was a follower of Tolstoy, who had been arrested along with other Tolstoyans at their commune in Siberia in 1936. Morgachev explained in his letter to the Public Prosecutor that the following year, the Soviet government had decided the three-year sentence was too mild, and in 1940 had increased it to seven years, with an additional three years of hard labour at the end of the term. Morgachev told the Public Prosecutor that he was one of the few who had survived, and counted himself lucky. Resolutely believing that he had never committed any crime, he explained that he had requested rehabilitation in 1963, by which time he was already seventy-one and an invalid, but had been flatly refused. Morgachev went on to explain in his letter that his Tolstoyan commune had transferred from central Russia to Siberia in 1930, in accordance with the decision of the All-Russian Central Executive Committee. Since it had operated as a model communist farm based on joint ownership, he argued that it should have been protected by law, but its few years of peaceful existence were instead paid for by many of its members with their lives. Morgachev stated that he still shared Tolstoy's views on life, and wished to be rehabilitated before he died. 'I don't need rehabilitation now,' he added in a handwritten postscript to his letter, 'but young prosecutors should learn what was done to the friends and followers of Lev Tolstoy.' Morgachev was officially rehabilitated in December 1976. As Popovsky noted drily, the Soviet Supreme Court had now effectively exonerated Tolstoy's followers from the earlier allegation that they were Tolstoyans.[101]

Popovsky was astonished to discover not only that Tolstoyans still existed in Russia, but that they had remained true to their beliefs through thick and thin. Like every Soviet citizen, he was reminded every day of the 'cult' of Tolstoy in his country – streets and squares were named after him, his fiction was permanently on the syllabus in schools and universities and there were several museums dedicated to him in different parts of the country. But also like every Soviet citizen, Popovsky had only ever had access to Tolstoy's literary works. As to forming an opinion about Tolstoy's philosophical views, he had, of course, been guided by Lenin's essay 'Lev Tolstoy as a Mirror of the Russian Revolution', which was required reading, even ahead of *Anna Karenina*. Thus Popovsky had grown up with the notion that Tolstoy had no talent as a thinker, and was certainly no prophet, that his philosophical ideas were actually harmful, that his followers were pathetic and that self-perfection and vegetarianism were ridiculous nonsense. All these ideas were reinforced in articles, commentaries and encyclopaedias. Days after Morgachev was rehabilitated, moreover, the Soviet President Leonid Brezhnev left a long rambling entry in the VIP guest book at Yasnaya Polyana, later reproduced in *Pravda*, which discussed Tolstoy exclusively as the author of *War and Peace*.[102]

When Popovsky canvassed some of his Moscow friends (who were all typical members of the Russian intelligentsia), he discovered that none of them knew anything about the Tolstoyans either. His curiosity piqued, he set out to do some research. This was not straightforward in the Cold War climate of phone-tapping, room-bugging and perlustration of personal correspondence. It was certainly not possible to talk about Tolstoyanism publicly, or write about it at that time. But with the help of the many sympathetic people who went out of their way to provide assistance, Popovsky eventually obtained addresses for thirty-two Tolstoyans scattered all over the Soviet Union, and along the way acquired an extensive archive of manuscripts by and about Tolstoyans. Some were self-penned memoirs by Tolstoyans, some were accounts of Tolstoyan communes, while others comprised correspondence, including with the Communist Party Central Committee regarding the Tolstoyans' aspiration to publish Tolstoy's philosophical and religious writings in the Soviet Union. These manuscripts had been carefully hidden from the authorities, and the threat of persecution was very real: a few months after the General Prosecutor officially exonerated Dmitry Morgachev, his flat was searched by the KGB, who threatened the now eighty-five-year-old invalid not to cause trouble. After successfully managing to bring out to the West 3,000 pages of materials covering the period from 1918 to 1977, Popovsky emigrated to the United States, and immediately got to work on putting together an extraordinary story of belief and survival. With the support of the Kennan Institute in Washington DC, his book about the Soviet peasant Tolstoyans was published in London in 1983.

By the time of the 150th anniversary of Tolstoy's birth in 1978, Popovsky concluded there were probably only about fifty original Tolstoyans left alive in Russia, all aged between seventy-five and ninety. Hundreds had been thrown into prisons, concentration camps and lunatic asylums, and more than 100 had been shot for the sake of their beliefs. It was the lives of the Tolstoyans above all which provided Popovsky with a positive answer to the question he had continually asked in his books about Soviet scientists, as to whether it was possible to preserve a clear conscience living in a totalitarian society.[103] The real problems had started for the Tolstoyans with the commencement of collectivisation and the first Five-Year Plan in the centenary year of 1928. Communes began to be shut down one after the other, and increasing numbers of Tolstoyans were arrested. The young members of the intelligentsia (including artists, writers and doctors) who had set up a Tolstoyan commune in the countryside west of Moscow in 1923 were informed that their commune would be merged with another farm to form the 'Red October' collective farm, and a subsequent act of arson was blamed on them. Some 15,000 Dukhobors and other sectarians had applied to re-emigrate by 1929, now bitterly regretting their decision to return home, but all their applications were turned down. Tolstoy's old peasant friend Mikhail Novikov ingenuously sent the Soviet government an open letter in February 1929 in which he proposed practical measures for increasing the harvest. He was arrested for his pains, despite being sixty-nine, and he ended his life in the camps. Five Tolstoyans were arrested in Moscow in 1929 and exiled to five years of hard labour at the notorious concentration camp on the Solovetsky islands. This was the former monastery-prison in the White Sea which had served as the place of exile of Tolstoy's great-great-great-grandfather in the eighteenth century. In February 1930 Chertkov sent a letter to Stalin, in which he tried to intercede on their behalf. He explained that the Tolstoyans were suffering from severe malnutrition due to being vegetarians, and also from hypothermia, since their winter clothes had been stolen by other prisoners.[104] In February 1929 the L. Tolstoy Moscow Vegetarian Society was forced to close when the authorities refused to prolong the lease on the premises it rented. There were by this time no other Tolstoyan organisations left.[105]

The Tolstoyans simply refused to be collectivised, and began to think about moving far away to the edge of the country, where they would be free from further acts of repression and could live peaceful lives on their own terms. There was a historic precedent here, as this had been the tactic of huge numbers of Cossacks, sectarians and Old Believers down the centuries during tsarist times. The Soviet Union was different: despite the vastness of its terrain, there were no quiet corners for the Tolstoyans to retreat to, but the Tolstoyans only discovered that after the fact. Chertkov encouraged members of the Life and Labour commune to ask the government for land in Siberia, and he petitioned on their behalf himself, thinking this was indeed a good solution. Amazingly, the Soviet government gave its official approval in February 1930, and in March 1931 about 1,000 Tolstoyans from three communes set off on a 2,000-mile journey east to the town of Novokuznetsk (soon to be renamed Stalinsk). The new commune worked well, and in 1931 Anna Malorod managed to found the first and only Tolstoyan school in the history of the Soviet Union. Even though the Tolstoyans were willing to make compromises in order to cooperate with state institutions, the local Party organisations ensured its lifespan was short: the school was closed down in 1934. The Life and Labour commune celebrated its fifth anniversary in 1936, but arrests were already being made, and the regional authorities began to treat it like a regular collective farm. By the time it held its last general meeting in January 1939, there were barely any men left.[106] The remaining commune members were transferred to state farms. They lived lives of great poverty, but that was of minor importance, as material prosperity had never been their priority.

During his research, Mark Popovsky discovered that the Tolstoyans were quite a disparate group: not all were vegetarians, some smoked, and some had even gone off to the front in 1941, some never to return. But even if their views and way of life diverged, he was struck by what they all shared: a deep ethical sense, a heightened sensitivity to injustice and a profound desire to do no evil. And they had remained loyal to Tolstoy, despite being unable to follow his ideas in a practical way. On 20 November 1960 the former schoolteacher Anna Malorod noted in her diary:

> Today it is fifty years since the death of L. N. Tolstoy, my dear father and teacher of life. He helped me purify Christ's teaching from superstitions accreted over the centuries, he helped me find dear friends, a spiritual family if not related by blood, which is better, stronger, and more genuine. Thanks to Tolstoy I moved from the city to the country, to be amongst those working the earth, and I started manual labour myself in the vegetable plot and in the garden, and learned to love it. Tolstoy helped me find true goodness in life. He showed the true way in love and unity for the whole world. He showed the shortcomings which divide people, and even sometimes destroy human life altogether. The great, still underrated Tolstoy![107]

The Soviet Tolstoyans had a great attachment to the written word: without it their stories would have never come to light. From the 1950s onwards they tried to donate their memoirs and correspondence to the Tolstoy Museum in Moscow, but archivists refused to accept them, through understandable fear of political reprisals.[108] The Tolstoyans also zealously defended Tolstoy from what they regarded as slander by Orthodox Soviet literary critics. Boris Mazurin followed publications on Tolstoy particularly closely, even from the remote Siberian village where he lived, and made it a point of principle to pen carefully written and robustly argued letters whenever he felt something needed to be corrected. He tackled Party member Boris Meilakh, for example, after the publication in 1961 of his book about Tolstoy's departure and death. 'You often talk in your book about the "weak" places in Tolstoy's worldview, calling them weak in view of their incompatibility with Marxist views, particularly as regards the possibility of changing life for the better through violence …', he wrote in his letter to Meilakh. To his credit, Meilakh replied, but Mazurin was still not satisfied, and wrote again to take issue with him about the idea that Tolstoy had been involved in any kind of political struggle to acquire power over people: 'It's impossible to imagine Tolstoy as a government figure leading and organising people by means of the necessary instruments of state power. And it is equally impossible to imagine Tolstoy remaining silent in such awful years as 1937 and 1938.'[109] It is indeed hard to imagine Tolstoy remaining silent, but it is harder still to imagine that he would have survived the Purges. It is more likely that he would simply have been shot at the first opportunity.

The Tolstoyans were disappointed to see Chertkov's name now blackened, both in Meilakh's book, and also in the new edition of Valentin Bulgakov's memoir of Tolstoy, which was published in 1964. But most painful of all to them was the speech given by the establishment writer Leonid Leonov to mark the fiftieth anniversary of Tolstoy's death at the Bolshoi Theatre on 19 November 1960. It was reprinted in all the major Soviet newspapers, and issued as a separate publication the following year. Leonov, recipient of Stalin and Lenin prizes, a Hero of Socialist Labour and a Deputy of the Supreme Soviet, parroted the standard view on Tolstoy, implying it was shortcomings in his philosophical and religious views which explained why there were no longer any apostles or ardent acolytes around to continue his ideas except for a few sectarians scattered about the globe. After much discussion with fellow Tolstoyans, who were understandably indignant, Mazurin wrote Leonov a lengthy riposte in February 1962, then travelled all the way to Moscow with it, only to be rebuffed by officials when seeking to find his address. Eventually he got his letter to Leonov, however, and in September 1962 he actually received a reply. Rather predictably, Leonov failed to answer any of Mazurin's criticisms.[110] Many other Tolstoyans vigorously proclaimed their existence, and challenged untruths. In 1975 Dmitry Morgachev sent an open letter to Alexander Klibanov, with copies to leading newspapers, after the latter published a book about religious sectarianism in which he alleged, for example, that the Tolstoyans had refused to join collective farms because they were essentially kulaks.[111]

When James Billington, the Librarian of Congress, asked Mark Popovsky in the early eighties why he had chosen to research the history of a small group whose influence had been negligible, he answered that he had been impressed with the intelligent way the Tolstoyans had protested against the status quo, by simply living individual lives in accordance with their moral principles.[112] Their patience and determination to bear witness was finally rewarded a few years later. Russian scholarship on Tolstoy entered a new phase with the publication in May 1988 of Vladimir Lakshin's article 'The Return of Tolstoy the Thinker'. It was obvious that Tolstoy could no longer be seen as just a mirror reflecting the contradictions of the 1905 Revolution, he wrote, since Tolstoy was a laser – a laser of humanity.[113] With the onset of perestroika and glasnost, the story of the Tolstoyans' tenacious struggle to establish communes and till the land in the communist Eden of the Soviet Union could finally be told in Russia as well as in the West. Everything changed in Russia in the late 1980s with the arrival of Gorbachev's reforms and the lifting of censorship. Mazurin, at the age of eighty-seven years, lived to witness the sensation produced by the publication of his memoirs in Russia's most prestigious literary magazine *Novy mir*, which in 1988 had a subscription of well over a million.[114] Many other articles and books followed.

Tolstoy did not believe in the idea of an afterlife in the Christian sense; indeed, the prospect of death summarily curtailing his existence, at a time which he had no control over, was the biggest problem he ever wrestled with. He did not believe his works would be remembered for very long after his death, nor did he believe he had all that many followers. Since the collapse of the Soviet Union in 1991, and the final liberation of literary and cultural historians from the shackles of ideology, an important position in the wealth of new publications about Tolstoy's legacy in Russia has been occupied by materials shedding light on the lives of those who sought to put his ideas into practice after his death. Not only have they made it possible to piece together the complex and fascinating story of Tolstoy's 'afterlife', but they have shown how just how deeply Tolstoy's ideas continued to resonate well into the twentieth century.

In April 1990 an application was made by a group of scholars to the Tula educational authorities to found an L. N. Tolstoy School research institute, with the aim of reintroducing Tolstoy's pedagogical ideas into teaching and learning in contemporary Russian education.[115] In 1998 its achievements in developing a three-stage educational programme from kindergarten to university entrance were recognised when the Russian government awarded it the status of a 'Federal Experimental Platform', and by 2010 there were already hundreds in Russia and abroad using Tolstoy's methods.[116] The revival of Tolstoyan schools was the brainchild of Vitaly Remizov, who became director of the Tolstoy Museum in Moscow in 2001. In an interview in 2005 he explained that the schools aimed to nurture independence in their pupils above all, in an atmosphere of freedom, using at the primary level the texts developed by Tolstoy in the 1870s.[117]

In November 1991, shortly after the fall of the Soviet Union, the religious association 'Spiritual Unity (the Church of Lev Tolstoy)' was registered in Moscow with the Russian Ministry of Justice, a step that would have been unthinkable in the Soviet era. Its statutes proclaimed its goal to be the dissemination of a Tolstoyan understanding of religion and spiritual life.[118] Its umbrella organisation was named as the Unity Church, which was initially founded by Charles and Myrtle Fillmore in Kansas City in 1889 under the inspiration of Tolstoy's teachings. The Unity Church describes itself as 'a positive, practical, progressive approach to Christianity based on the teachings of Jesus and the power of prayer' which honours 'the universal truths in all religions and respects each individual's right to choose a spiritual path'.[119] In 1996 a new Department of Tolstoy's Spiritual Heritage with eight faculty members opened its doors at the L. N. Tolstoy Tula State Pedagogical Institute.

In 2000, three years before she died at the age of seventy-eight, the distinguished Tolstoy scholar Lidiya Gromova-Opulskaya published the first volume in the new Academy of Sciences edition of Tolstoy's *Complete Collected Works*. Drawing on the many new materials which have come to light since the publication of the Jubilee Edition, this edition will run to 100 volumes, and, as the editors take pains to note, will be the first to be *truly* complete; it will not be marred by 'omissions or constraints', unlike the Jubilee Edition.

When the project was first conceived in the late 1980s, Gromova-Opulskaya commented on its aims:

> Tolstoy is published and re-published in our country with print runs running into the millions. The 90-volume *Complete Collected Works*, published between 1928 and 1958, is so significant and monumental a publication that we continue to be proud of it. Nevertheless, Russian textual scholarship has not completely fulfilled its duty. The texts of many of the works of this great world writer remain unverified, manuscripts have been published incomplete and unsystematically. These are the main tasks in the new, probably 100-volume, genuinely academic edition on which work has now begun.[120]

While Tolstoy scholarship may no longer be hostage to political mandates, the harsh realities of the market economy in contemporary Russia dictate that the progress of the new edition may well be slow.

It seems the only institution in Russia still refusing to open its doors as far as Tolstoy is concerned is the Orthodox Church. In 1994 Tolstoy's great-great-grandson Vladimir Ilyich Tolstoy was appointed as the new director of Yasnaya Polyana, which is still one of the most famous museums in Russia. In early January 2001 he wrote to the Moscow Patriarch with a suggestion that the Church reflect on the significance of the excommunication which had taken place 100 years earlier. Patriarch Alexy's refusal to discuss the issue created a stir. Vladimir Tolstoy certainly never doubted the importance of the excommunication. 'I am deeply convinced,' he declared in an interview at the time, 'that it was one of the most important historical events in the history of the Russian state, which either obliquely or directly affected future developments, and divided Russian society along both vertical and horizontal axes.'

Just how great the reverberations of Tolstoy's excommunication were with regards to Russian national life is perhaps most eloquently expressed by the fact that the first official meeting between the Orthodox Church and the Tolstoy estate took place in 2006 – 105 years after the event. The occasion was a special conference held in March 2006 at Yasnaya Polyana, when scholars met representatives from the Orthodox Church to debate the significance of the excommunication. As well as re-examining the sources of the original conflict and the legal aspects of the Holy Synod's decree, delegates discussed its moral, spiritual and social dimensions and consequences, including its continuing public resonance today. The conference was widely reported in the Russian press, which noted that the unprecedented debate between the Church and literary community was 'heated, to say the least'. As the writer Alexey Varlamov remarked in one paper, the conflict between Tolstoy and the church was one of the most painful points of the twentieth century, and crucial to the cause of the Russian Revolution. Another delegate, Father Georgy Orekhanov, who spoke on the spiritual aspect of Tolstoy's death, defended the Church's actions in 1901, but acknowledged that it was important to understand why so many people had immediately supported the writer at this 'significant moment' in Russian history. In the light of the collapse of communism and the subsequent resurgence of Christianity, he added, the question of the relationship between the Russian people and the Orthodox Church was just as topical now.[121] Father Orekhanov gave another conference paper on Tolstoy in January 2009 at a panel devoted to topical problems in the history of the Orthodox Church,[122] but it is unlikely that discussion will move beyond the academic sphere. To a church and state once again forging close bonds in today's authoritarian Russia, Tolstoy's teachings must seem as problematic and as dangerous as ever.

NOTES

Abbreviations Used in Notes

References to V. G. Chertkov's 'Jubilee Edition' of Tolstoy's complete collected works are indicated by 'JE', followed by volume number and page reference (e.g. JE 68, 49). The six volumes of *L. N. Tolstoi: materialy k biografii* are distinguished by author and volume (e.g. 'Gusev 1', 'Opul'skaya 2'). The two volumes of the *Letopis' zhizni i tvorchestva* are indicated as '*Letopis'* 1' and '*Letopis'* 2'.

Introduction

1. R. M. Meiendorf, 'Stranichka vospominanii o L've Nikolaeviche Tolstom', in *Letopisi Gosudarstvennogo literaturnogo muzeya*, vol. 12: *L. N. Tolstoi: K 120-letiyu so dnya rozhdeniya (1828–1848)*, ed. N. N. Gusev, Moscow, 1948, 369.

2. Henry Norman, *All the Russias*, London, 1902, 47; cited in Alexander Fodor, *Tolstoy and the Russians: Reflections on a Relationship*, Ann Arbor, 1984, 15.

3. Stefan Zweig, *Adepts in Self-Portraiture: Casanova, Stendhal, Tolstoy*, New York, 1928 (a translation of his *Drei Dichter ihres Lebens: Casanova, Stendhal, Tolstoi*, Leipzig, 1928), 218–219, cited in Fodor, *Tolstoy and the Russians*, 15.

4. N. Berdyaev, *The Origin of Russian Communism*, tr. R. M. French (first published 1937), Ann Arbor, 1960, 8.

5. E. D. Meleshko, *Khristianskaya etika L. N. Tolstogo*, Moscow, 2006, 272.

6. Sjeng Scheijen, *Diaghilev: A Life*, London, 2009, 47–48.

7. T. A. Sukhotina-Tolstaya, *Dnevnik*, ed. T. Volkova, Moscow, 1984, 526–527.

8. S. A. Tolstaya, Pis'ma K L. N. Tolstomu, Moscow, 1936, 496.

9. Sophia Kishkovsky, 'Chechnya's Favorite Russian', *International Herald Tribune*, 29 December 2009, 10.

10. T. V. Komarova, ed., *Druz'ya i gosti Yasnoi Polyane: materialy nauchnoi konferentsee posvyashchennoi 160-letiyu S. A. Tolstoi*, Tula, 2006; N. Nikitina, *Sof'ya Tolstaya*, Moscow, 2010.

11. Alexander Boot, *God and Man According to Tolstoy*, New York, 2009, 11–12.

12. Irina Paperno, 'Tolstoy's Diaries: The Inaccessible Self', *Self and Story in Russian History*, ed. Laura Engelstein and Stephanie Sandler, Ithaca, 2000, 242–65.

13. See N. I. Burnasheva, ed., *'Tolstoi – eto tselyi mir': stat'i i issledovaniya*, Moscow, 2004, which is dedicated to the memory of Lidiya Gromova-Opul'skaya.

14. V. Bulgakov, *O Tolstom*, Tula, 1964, 237–8.

1 Ancestors: The Tolstoys and the Volkonskys

1. L. N. Tolstoi, *Polnoe sobranie sochinenii*, ed. V. G. Chertkov, 90 vols, Moscow, 1928–1958, vol. 84, 281.

2. Il'ya L. Tolstoi, *Moi vospominaniya*, Moscow, 1969, 57–58.

3. James Mavor, *My Windows on the Street of the World*, 2 vols, London, 1923, vol. 1, 68.

4. Isabel Hapgood, *Russian Rambles*, London, 1895, 149.

5. Nina Nikitina, *Povsednevnaya zhizn' L'va Tolstogo v Yasnoi polyane*, Moscow, 2007, 9–10.

6. Count Leon L. Tolstoi, *The Truth about my Father*, London, 1924, 1. See also L. L. Tolstoi, *V Yasnoi polyane. Pravda ob otse i ego zhizni*, Prague, 1923.

7. L. N. Tolstoi, *Polnoe sobranie sochinenii v sta tomakh*, ed. L. D. Gromova-Opul'skaya et al.; *Khudozhestvennye proizvedeniya v vosemnadtsati tomakh*, vol. 3, Moscow, 2000, 400.

8. P. V. Dolgorukov, *Russkaya rodoslovnaya kniga*, 4 vols, St Petersburg, 1855–1857.

9. See N. N. Gusev, *Lev Nikolaevich Tolstoi. Materialy k biografii s 1828 po 1855 god* [Gusev 1], Moscow, 1954, 616.

10. See L. M. Kulaeva, 'Gost' yasnoi polyany R. Levenfel'd', in *Druz'ya i gosti Yasnoi Polyany: materialy nauchnoi konferentsii posvyashchennoi 160-letiyu S. A. Tolstoi*, ed. T. V. Komarova, Tula, 2006, 166.

11. Evgenii Solov'ev, *L. N. Tolstoi: ego zhizn' i literaturnaya deyatel'nost'*, St Petersburg, 1894, 9.

12. M. N. Nazimova, 'Iz semeinoi khroniki Tolstykh', *Istoricheskii vestnik*, 10 (1902), 104.

13. Gusev 1, 615.

14. S. M. Tolstoi, *Tolstoi i Tolstye. Ocherki iz istorii roda*, Moscow, 1990, 15.

15. Gusev 1, 614.

16. For further details on Pyotr Tolstoy's biography see N. I. Pavlenko, *Ptentsy gnezda Petrova*, Moscow, 1984, and Max J. Okenfuss, ed. and tr., *The Travel Diary of Peter Tolstoi: a Muscovite in Early Modern Europe*, DeKalb, Ill., 1987.

17. Gusev 1, 12.

18. Roy Robson, 'Transforming Solovki: Pilgrim Narratives, Modernization and Late Imperial Monastic Life', *Sacred Stories: Religion and Spirituality in Modern Russia*, ed. Mark Steinberg and Heather Coleman, Bloomington, 2008, 49.

19. A. Izmailov, 'U L'va Tolstogo', *Birzhevye vedomosti*, 3–5 July, 1907; cited in V. Lakshin, ed., *Interv'yu i besedy s L'vom Tolstym*, Moscow, 1986.

20. S. A. Papkov, 'Zalozhniki sovesti (Tolstovtsy na Solovkakh)', *Vozvrashchenie pamyati. Istoriko-arkhivnyi al'manakh*, vol. 3, ed. I. V. Pavlova, Novosibirsk, 1997, 176–180.

21. Tolstoi, *Tolstoi i Tolstye*, 25.

22. JE 34, 394.

23. Tolstoi, *Tolstoi i Tolstye*, 31.

24. T. V. Komarova, 'Gerb roda grafov Tolstykh', *Yasnopolyanskii sbornik*, Tula, 1992, 188–190.

25. JE 34, 359.

26. Gusev 1, 21.

27. JE 34, 359.

28. Gusev 1, 39.

29. Gusev 1, 27–28.

30. Gusev 1, 29.

31. Nikitina, *Povsednevnaya zhizn' L'va Tolstogo*, 30.

32. JE 34, 352.

33. N. A. Nikitina and V. P. Nikitin, 'Yasnaya Polyana vremen detstva i yunosti Tolstogo', *Yasnopolyanskii sbornik*, Tula, 1982, 135–150.

34. See Richard Stites, *Serfdom, Society and the Arts in Imperial Russia: The Pleasure and the Power*, New Haven, 2005.

35. Gusev 1, 631.

36. JE 34, 351.

37. Gusev 1, 634–635.

38. Nikitina, *Povsednevnaya zhizn' L'va Tolstogo*, 33.

39. Tolstoi, *Tolstoi i Tolstye*, 57–58.

40. Gusev 1, 634, 638–640.

2 Aristocratic Childhood

1. S. L. Tolstoi, 'Ob otrazhenii zhizni v 'Anne Kareninoi': Iz vospominanii', *Literaturnoe nasledstvo*, 37/38 (1939), vol 2, 574.

2. Il'ya Tolstoi, *Moi vospominaniya*, Moscow, 1933, 32.

3. Nina Nikitina, *Yasnaya Polyana: puteshestvie s L'vom Tolstym*, Tula, 2002, 58; N. N. Gusev, *Lev Nikolaevich Tolstoi. Materialy k biografii s 1828 po 1855 god* [Gusev 1], Moscow, 1954, 71.

4. Gusev 1, 60.

5. Gusev 1, 60–61.

6. Gusev 1, 48–51; 34, 350.

7. JE 34, 353.

8. '5 marta – den' svyatogo L'va Katanskogo'; www.kulina.ru/articles/29740/

9. A. N. Varlamov, 'Lev Tolstoi, Stolypin and ieromonakh Iliodor', *Yasnopolyanskii sbornik*, Tula, 2008, 419–426.

10. Nikitina, *Yasnaya Polyana: puteshestvie s L'vom Tolstym*, 345–346.

11. Il'ya Tolstoi, *Moi Vospominaniya*, 32.

12. Gusev 1, 64.

13. S. M. Tolstoi, *Tolstoi i Tolstye. Ocherki iz istorii roda*, Moscow, 1990, 90.

14. Nikitina, *Yasnaya Polyana: puteshestvie s L'vom Tolstym*, 43–44.

15. JE 34, 355–357.

16. JE 34, 356.

17. Tolstoi, *Tolstoi i Tolstye*, 2.

18. JE 34, 357.

19. Gusev 1, 79.

20. JE 34, 357.

21. JE 34, 358.

22. JE 34, 371.

23. JE 34, 360.

24. JE 34, 389–390.

25. JE 34, 359–361.

26. Nikitina, *Yasnaya Polyana: puteshestvie s L'vom Tolstym*, 45.

27. JE 34, 361–364.

28. JE 34, 364–366.

29. JE 34, 382.

30. JE 34, 370–371.

31. JE 34, 372–373.

32. JE 34, 374–378.

33. JE 34, 378.

34. JE 34, 357.

35. JE 34, 375–377.

36. Gusev 1, 82.

37. JE 34, 391.

38. JE 34, 393.

39. JE 8, 25; cited in Gusev 1, 18.

40. JE 61, 123.

41. *Perepiska L. N. Tolstogo s Gr. A. A. Tolstoi, 1857–1903*, St Petersburg, 1911, 44, 217.

42. *Anna Karenina*, part 1, chapter 10.

43. Eugene Schuyler, 'Count Leo Tolstoy Twenty Years Ago', *Scribner's Magazine*, May 1889, 537–552, June 1889, 733–747, 540.

44. See S. L. Tolstoi, *Fedor Tolstoi Amerikanets*, Moscow, 1926.

45. See Peter Henry Buck, *Explorers of the Pacific: European and American Discoveries in Polynesia*, Honolulu, 1953.

46. S. L. Tolstoi, *Fedor Tolstoi-Amerikanets*.

47. JE 34, 393.

48. JE 34, 385–387.

3 Orphanhood

1. I. N. A. Kalinina, *Perepiska L. N. Tolstogo c sestroi i brat'yami*, Moscow, 1990, 23.

2. JE 34, 347.

3. N. N. Gusev, *Lev Nikolaevich Tolstoi. Materialy k biografii s 1828 po 1855 god* [Gusev 1], Moscow, 1954, 98.

4. JE 34, 401.

5. JE 34, 393.

6. S. M. Tolstoi, *Tolstoi i Tolstye. Ocherki iz istorii roda*, Moscow, 1990, 91.

7. Gusev 1, 102.

8. Gusev 1, 104.

9. Gusev 1, 106–108.

10. Gusev 1, 110; JE 34, 402.

11. Gusev 1, 112–113.

12. Gusev 1, 115.

13. Gusev 1, 116–117.

14. JE 34, 396; Gusev 1, 120.

15. Gusev 1, 124.

16. Gusev 1, 125.

17. Gusev 1, 127.

18. Gusev 1, 128–129.

19. JE 34, 403.

20. N. A. Kalinina et al., *Perepiska L. N. Tolstogo s sestroi i brat'yami*, Moscow, 1990, 20–21.

21. Gusev 1, 130.

22. Alexander I's manifesto. See V. G. Sirotkin, *Napoleon i Rossiya*, Moscow, 2000.

23. Sirotkin, *Napoleon i Rossiya*, 229.

24. Gusev 1, 132.

25. Sirotkin, *Napoleon i Rossiya*, 251.

26. N. N. Gusev, *Letopis' zhizni i tvorchestva L. N. Tolstogo, 1828–1890*, Moscow, 1958 [*Letopis'* 1], 18.

27. JE 34, 356.

28. Gusev 1, 146–147.

29. Gusev 1, 135–136.

30. Gusev 1, 143–144.

31. Gusev 1, 145.

32. Letter of 25 October 1891, cited in *Letopis'* 1, 21.

33. Gusev 1, 77.

34. Count Alexey Konstantinovich Tolstoy (1817–1875) was descended from Tolstoy's great uncle Pyotr Andreyevich (1746–1820).

35. See, for example, Neil Cornwell, ed., *The Reference Guide to Russian Literature*, London, 1998, 818.

36. See 'Il'ya Muromets v russkom epose', *Il'ya Muromets*, ed. A. M. Astakhova, Moscow, 1958, 393–419.

37. Quotation from the poet and scholar Guido Mazzoni in P. Sergeenko, *O Tolstom*, Moscow, 1911, 135.

38. See caricatures reproduced in *Gr. Lev Tolstoi: velikii pisatel' zemli russkoi v portretakh, grayurakh, zhivopisi, skul'pture, karikaturakh i t d.*, ed. P. N. Krasnov and L. M. Vol'f, Moscow, 1903.

39. See Alexander Fodor, *Tolstoy and the Russians*, Ann Arbor, 1984, 20.

40. Gusev 1, 154.

4 Youth

1. Pavel Biryukov, *Biografiya L'va Nikolaevicha Tolstogo*, Moscow, 1923, vol. 1, 124.

2. JE 34, 347.

3. N. N. Gusev, *Lev Nikolaevich Tolstoi. Materialy k biografii s 1828 po 1855 god* [Gusev 1], Moscow, 1954, 157.

4. N. N. Gusev, *Letopis' zhizni i tvorchestva L. N. Tolstogo, 1828–1890*, Moscow, 1958 [*Letopis'* 1], 20.

5. N. A. Kalinina et al., *Perepiska L. N. Tolstogo s sestroi i brat'yami*, Moscow, 1990, 30.

6. Gusev 1, 158.

7. JE 34, 380.

8. JE 34, 381.

9. JE 34, 380.

10. Leo Tolstoy, *A Confession and Other Religious Writings*, tr. Jane Kentish, London, 1987, 19.

11. JE 34, 382–383.

12. S. M. Tolstoi, *Tolstoi i Tolstye: Ocherki iz istorii roda*, Moscow, 1990, 178.

13. Gusev 1, 168–169.

14. Gusev 1, 169.

15. Gusev 1, 179.

16. JE 34, 387.

17. JE 34, 387–388.

18. JE 34, 379.

19. David Schimmelpenninck van der Oye, *Russian Orientalism: Asia in the Russian Mind from Peter the Great to the Emigration*, New Haven, 2010, 106.

20. Gusev 1, 160.

21. Gusev 1, 181.

22. JE 34, 397.

23. JE 59, 10.

24. Gusev 1, 162.

25. *Letopis'* 1, 28.

26. Gusev 1, 237.

27. Robert Wokler, *Rousseau: A Very Short Introduction*, Oxford, 2001, 1.

28. Gusev 1, 197.

29. *Letopis'* 1, 25; Gusev 1, 198.

30. *Letopis'* 1, 26; Gusev 1, 199.

31. Aleksei Zverev, Vladimir Tunimanov, *Lev Tolstoi*, Moscow, 2007, 41; Gusev 1, 159.

32. Gusev 1, 161.

33. Gusev 1, 193.

34. JE 59, 10.

35. *Letopis'* 1, 27; Gusev 1, 202.

36. Nicholas Berdyaev, *The Origin of Russian Communism*, tr. R. M. French, London, 1937, 1.

37. JE 46, 245–255.

38. JE 46, 262.

39. JE 46, 265.

40. JE 46, 263–272.

41. Marthe Blinoff, *Life and Thought in Old Russia*, University Park, 1961, 86.

42. JE 46, 3–4.

43. JE 46, 4–28.

44. JE 46, 12, 21.

45. JE 34, 383; JE 46, 19.

46. Gusev 1, 232–233.

5 Landowner, Gambler, Officer, Writer

1. JE 46, 45.

2. JE 46, 31–33.

3. N. A. Kalinina et al., *Perepiska L. N. Tolstogo s sestroi i brat'yami*, Moscow, 1990, 33.

4. N. N. Gusev, *Lev Nikolaevich Tolstoi. Materialy k biografii s 1828 po 1855 god* [Gusev 1], Moscow, 1954, 236–237.

5. S. M. Tolstoi, *Tolstoi i Tolstye. Ocherki iz istorii roda*, Moscow, 1990, 166.

6. Tolstoi, *Tolstoi i Tolstye*, 188.

7. Tolstoi, *Tolstoi i Tolstye*, 177.

8. Kalinina et al., *Perepiska*, 44.

9. Astolphe, Marquis de Custine, *La Russie en 1839*, 4 vols, Brussels, 1843.

10. Marquis de Custine, *Letters from Russia*, tr. and intro. Robin Buss, London, 1991, 63.

11. Gusev 1, 238.

12. Ivan Turgenev, 'Instead of an Introduction', *Turgenev's Literary Reminiscences and Autobiographical Fragments*, tr. David Magarshack, with an essay by Edmund Wilson, London, 1984, 92–93.

13. Gusev 1, 237.

14. For further details see Donna Tussing Orwin, *Tolstoy's Art and Thought, 1847–1880*, Princeton, 1993.
15. See Y. M. Lotman, 'Kartochnaya igra', *Besedy o russkoi kul'ture*, St Petersburg, 1997, 136–163; Ian M. Helfant, *The High Stakes of Identity: Gambling in the Life and Literature of Nineteenth-Century Russia*, Evanston, 2002.
16. See Ian M. Helfant, 'Pushkin's Ironic Performance as a Gambler', *Slavic Review*, 58 (1999), 378–92; 373.
17. JE 59, 25.
18. Kalinina et al., *Perepiska*, 39–41.
19. Kalinina et al., *Perepiska*, 44.
20. Kalinina et al., *Perepiska*, 37, 47.
21. Kalinina et al., *Perepiska*, 50–51.
22. Kalinina et al., *Perepiska*, 51–52.
23. Kalinina et al., *Perepiska*, 54.
24. Kalinina et al., *Perepiska*, 55–56.
25. Geir Kjetsaa, *Dostoyevsky: A Writer's Life*, tr. Siri Hustvedt and David McDuff, London 1987, 91.
26. Gusev 1, 262.
27. JE 59, 98.
28. See G. S. Demeter, ed., *Istoriya tsygan: novyi vzglyad*, Voronezh, 2000.
29. Marquis de Custine, *Empire of the Czar: The Social, Political, and Religious State and Prospects of Russia, Made During a Journey Through That Empire*, 3 vols, London, 1843, vol. 3, 97–98, 248–249.
30. 'Svyatochnaya noch", L. N. Tolstoi, *Polnoe sobranie sochinenii v 100 tomakh*, vol. 2, Moscow, 2000, 209–232.
31. JE 46, 36–37.
32. S. A. Tolstaya, *Dnevniki v dvukh tomakh*, ed. V. E. Vatsuro et al., 2 vols, Moscow, 1978, vol. 1, 410.
33. Gusev 1, 268.
34. Gusev 1, 271.
35. JE 59, 42.
36. JE 59, 45.
37. JE 59, 65, 81.
38. JE 59, 92.
39. JE 59, 87–88.
40. JE 59, 39.
41. JE 59, 49. See Barbara W. Maggs, 'The Franklin-Tolstoy Influence Controversy', *Proceedings of the American Philosophical Society*, 129 (1985), pp. 268–277. Tolstoy's 'Franklin Journal' has not survived.
42. See Tom Cain, 'Tolstoy's Use of David Copperfield', *Tolstoi in Britain*, ed. W. Gareth Jones, Oxford, 1995, 67–78.

43. Richard Gustafson, *Leo Tolstoy: Resident and Stranger: A Study in Fiction and Theology*, Princeton, 1986, 27.

44. B. Eikhenbaum, *Lev Tolstoi v semidesyatie gody*, Leningrad, 1974, 254.

45. JE 59, 91; Gusev 1, 283.

46. JE 46, 60.

47. See Charles King, *The Ghost of Freedom*, Oxford, 2008 for a full overview of Russia's conquest of the Caucasus.

48. See L. B. Zasedateleva, *Terskie kazaki (seredina XVI – nachalo XX v.). Istoriko-etnograficheskie ocherki*, Moscow, 1974.

49. See V. Astalov, S. Gapurov, 'Tersko-grebenski kazaki i chechentsy v XVI-XIX vekakh', *L. N. Tolstoi i Sheikh Kunta-Khadzhi Kishnev: problemy mira i gumanizma*, Tula, 2006, 17–38.

50. Gusev 1, 310–311.

51. N. N. Gusev, *Letopis' zhizni i tvorchestva L. N. Tolstogo, 1828–1890 [Letopis' 1]*, Moscow, 1958, 46.

52. For a lively travel guide aimed at British tourists a few decades later, see Oliver Wardrop, *The Kingdom of Georgia: Travel in a Land of Women, Wine and Song*, London, 1888.

53. See King, *The Ghost of Freedom*, 84–90.

54. See King, *The Ghost of Freedom*, 74–75.

55. Gusev 1, 328.

56. Gusev 1, 333–339.

57. Gusev 1, 392.

58. Gusev 1, 394–396.

59. Kalinina et al., *Perepiska*, 124.

60. *Letopis'* 1, 65.

61. Kalinina et al., *Perepiska*, 145.

62. Kalinina et al., *Perepiska*, 148; Gusev 1, 501.

63. Gusev 1, 444–449.

64. Gusev 1, 480.

65. Gusev 1, 491.

66. *Letopis'* 1 79.

67. Gusev 1, 505.

68. Gusev 1, 501.

69. *Letopis'* 1, 81.

70. JE 47, 29.

71. *Letopis'* 1, 83.

72. Gusev 1, 508.

73. For an overview of the war see Trevor Royle, *Crimea: the Great Crimean War 1854–1856*, London, 1999.

74. JE 47, 31.

75. *Letopis'* 1, 85.

76. *Letopis'* 1, 84.

77. Gusev 1, 518.

78. Kalinina et al., *Perepiska*, 183.

79. Kalinina et al., *Perepiska*, 179.

80. JE 4, 284–285; Gusev 1, 529–531.

81. JE 47, 37–38.

82. Gustafson, *Leo Tolstoy: Resident and Stranger*, xi–xii.

83. Gusev 1, 537.

84. Leo Tolstoy, *The Sebastopol Sketches*, tr. and intro. David McDuff, 1986, 51. See McDuff's excellent introduction for an overview of the siege of Sebastopol, and of Tolstoy's reportage.

85. Gusev 1, 548.

86. JE 47, 46.

87. Tolstoy, *Sebastopol Sketches*, 108.

88. Gusev 1, 590.

89. Gusev 1, 586.

6 Literary Duellist and Repentant Nobleman

1. N. N. Gusev, *Letopis' zhizni i tvorchestva L. N. Tolstogo, 1828–1890*, Moscow, 1958 [*Letopis'* 1], 69.

2. N. N. Gusev, *Lev Nikolaevich Tolstoi. Materialy k biografii s 1828 po 1855 god* [Gusev 1], Moscow, 1954, 430.

3. N. A. Kalinina et al., *Perepiska L. N. Tolstogo s sestroi i brat'yami*, Moscow, 1990, 186–187.

4. Kalinina et al., *Perepiska*, 187.

5. N. N. Gusev, *Lev Nikolaevich Tolstoi. Materialy k biografii s 1855 po 1869 god* [Gusev 2], Moscow, 1957, 4.

6. R. Bartlett and Anna Benn, *Literary Russia: A Guide*, London, 2007, 207.

7. Gusev 2, 10.

8. Gusev 2, 5.

9. Gusev 2, 15.

10. JE 34, 385.

11. Kalinina et al., *Perepiska*, 171.

12. JE 47, 65.

13. Gusev 2, 17.

14. Gusev 2, 33.

15. Gusev 2, 30.

16. Gusev 2, 25.

17. Gusev 2, 36.

18. William Coxe, *Travels into Poland, Russian, Sweden and Denmark*, London, 1784, cited in *St Petersburg: A Traveller's Companion*, ed. Laurence Kelly, London, 1981, 70–71.

19. Aleksandr Radishchev, *A Journey from St Petersburg to Moscow*, tr. Leo Wiener, ed. Roderick Page Thaler, Cambridge, Mass., 1958, 188.

20. Gusev 2, 18.

21. *Letopis'* 1, 113.

22. *Letopis'* 1, 117.

23. Gusev 2, 54.

24. Kalinina et al., *Perepiska*, 186, 199.

25. S. M. Tolstoi, *Tolstoi i Tolstye. Ocherki iz istorii roda*, Moscow, 1990, 188.

26. Gusev 2, 80–83.

27. JE 47, 90–91.

28. *Letopis'* 1, 124, 126, 130.

29. Gusev 2, 93.

30. JE 60, 149.

31. JE 60, 151.

32. Andrzej Walicki, *A History of Russian Thought from the Enlightenment to Marxism*, tr. Hilda Andrews-Rusiecka, Oxford, 1980, 200.

33. N. G. Chernyshevsky, 'Tolstoy's Military Tales', tr. Michael R. Katz, in *Tolstoy's Short Fiction*, ed. and tr. Michael Katz, New York, 1991, 368.

34. JE 47, 118.

35. Kalinina et al., *Perepiska*, 206.

36. Kalinina et al., *Perepiska*, 206.

37. Gusev 2, 196.

38. JE 60, 189.

39. In the autumn of 2004 the monastery had to shut the kennels as it could no longer afford to run them.

40. JE 47, 136.

41. *Letopis'* 1, 158.

42. JE 47, 140.

43. Gusev 2, 213.

44. Gusev 2, 226.

45. *Letopis'* 1, 163.

46. JE 47, 149.

47. JE 60, 222.

48. Gusev 2, 237.

49. Gusev 2, 250.

50. *Letopis'* 1, 180.

51. Gusev 2, 286.

52. Gusev 2, 276.

53. Richard Stites, *Serfdom, Society and the Arts in Imperial Russia*, New Haven, 2005, 317.

54. Gusev 2, 265.

55. Gusev 2, 269.

56. JE 57, 112.

57. Gusev 2, 300.

58. Valeriya Abrosimova, 'Syn velikogo Tolstogo. Voina i Amerika', *Toronto Slavic Quarterly*, 24 (2008): www.utoronto.ca/tsq/24/ambrosimova24.shtml

59. Vladimir Zhdanov, *Lyubov' v zhizni Tolstogo* (first published 1928), Moscow, 2005, 43.

60. Gusev 2, 320.

61. L. Sabaneev, *Russkaya okhota* (first published 1892), Moscow, 2003, 482.

62. Gusev 2, 317.

63. See Hugh McLean, 'Buried as a Writer and as a Man', *In Quest of Tolstoy*, Brighton, Mass., 2008, 3–20.

64. Gusev 2, 331.

65. Jeffrey Brooks, *When Russia Learned to Read: Literacy and Popular Literature 1861–1917*, Princeton, 1985, 4.

66. Gusev 2, 351.

67. Gusev 2, 367.

68. Gusev 2, 374.

69. Gusev 2, 392.

70. I am grateful to Jennie de Protani, Archivist at the Athenaeum, for supplying me with this information.

71. *Letopis'* 1, 225.

72. Victor Lucas, *Tolstoy in London*, London, 1979.

73. Gusev 2, 403.

74. Gusev 2, 409.

75. *Letopis'* 1, 231.

76. *Letopis'* 1, 233.

77. Eugene Schuyler, *Selected Essays*, New York, 1901, 274–275.

78. Gusev 2, 431.

79. Gusev 2, 445.

80. *Letopis'* 1, 237.

81. Gusev 2, 445–447.

82. Gusev 2, 459, 484.

83. L. Tolstoi, 'Yasno-Polyanskaya shkola za Noyabr' i Dekabr' mesyatsy', *Yasnaya Polyana*, 1 (1862), cited in Aylmer Maude, *The Life of Tolstoy* (first published in 1930), Ware, 2008, 239–241.

84. Gusev 2, 510.

85. Gusev 2, 481.

86. Eugene Schuyler, 'Preface' to Ivan Turgenev, *Fathers and Sons*, tr. Eugene Schuyler, New York, 1867, vii.

87. Gusev 2, 478.

88. JE 60, 438.

89. JE 60, 436.

7 Husband, Beekeeper and Epic Poet

1. JE 48, 48.

2. S. A. Tolstaya, 'Moya zhizn", *Novy mir*, 8 (1978), 360.

3. Eugene Schuyler, *Selected Essays*, New York, 1901, 216.

4. JE 48, 40.

5. S. L. Tolstoy, *Ocherki bylogo*, 3rd rev. edn, Tula, 1965, 15.

6. N. N. Gusev, *Lev Nikolaevich Tolstoi. Materialy k biografii s 1855 po 1869 god* [Gusev 2], Moscow, 1957, 641.

7. *The Autobiography of Countess Sophie Tolstoi*, preface and notes by Vasilii Spiridonov, tr. S. S. Koteliansky and Leonard Woolf, Richmond, 1922, 10.

8. T. A. Kuzminskaya, *Moya zhizn' doma i v Yasnoi Poliane*, ed. T. N. Volkova, Tula, 1973, 58.

9. S. A. Tolstaya, *Dnevniki v dvukh tomakh*, ed. V. E. Vatsuro et al., 2 vols, Moscow, 1978, vol. 1, 476.

10. Tolstaya, *Dnevniki*, vol. 1, 480.

11. JE 60, 441–442.

12. N. A. Kalinina et al., *Perepiska L. N. Tolstogo s sestroi i brat'yami*, Moscow, 1990, 242.

13. Gusev 2, 578.

14. Tolstaya, *Dnevniki*, vol. 1, 491.

15. JE 48, 41.

16. Tolstaya, *Dnevniki*, vol. 1, 490.

17. Kuzminskaya, *Moya zhizn'*, 143.

18. Kuzminskaya, *Moya zhizn'*, 138.

19. Tolstaya, *Dnevniki*, vol. 1, 492.

20. Kuzminskaya, *Moya zhizn'*, 139.

21. JE 48, 46.

22. Tolstaya, *Dnevniki*, vol. 1, 40, 54.

23. Tolstaya, *Dnevniki*, vol. 1, 495.

24. Kuzminskaya, *Moya zhizn'*, 197.

25. Tolstaya, 'Moya zhizn", *Novy mir*, 44.

26. Kuzminskaya, *Moya zhizn'*, 196.

27. Tolstaya, 'Moya zhizn", *Novy mir*, 35.

28. N. Nikitina, *Povsednevnaya zhizn L'va Tolstogo v Yasnoi polyane*, Moscow, 2007, 94.

29. *Povarennaya kniga S. A. Tolstoi*, Tula, 1991.

30. Tolstaya, 'Moya zhizn", *Novy mir*, 35.

31. JE 60, 448.

32. JE 48, 46.

33. JE 48, 47.

34. Tolstaya, *Dnevniki*, vol. 1, 44.

35. *Autobiography of Countess Sophie Tolstoi*, 86.

36. The story is about an alcoholic, renegade peasant bearing this nickname who is so mortified after failing, through no fault of his own, to carry out a task he has been entrusted with by his mistress, who has given him a chance to redeem himself, that he ends up committing suicide.

37. Georgy Lesskis, *Lev Tolstoi (1852–1869)*, Moscow, 2000, 310.

38. Lesskis, *Lev Tolstoi*, 344 (Gnedich's 1829 translation).

39. Gusev 2, 584.

40. JE 61, 23–24.

41. Gusev 2, 594.

42. Tolstaya, 'Moya zhizn", *Novy mir*, 36.

43. JE 60, 455.

44. N. N. Gusev, *Letopis' zhizni i tvorchestva L. N. Tolstogo, 1828–1890*, Moscow, 1958 [*Letopis'* 1], 287.

45. JE 60, 451.

46. S. Stakhovich, 'Kak pisalsya "Kholstomer"', *L. N. Tolstoi*, vol. 1, Moscow, 1938, 332–336.

47. Tolstaya, 'Moya zhizn", *Novy mir*, 36.

48. Gusev 2, 603.

49. Kuzminskaya, *Moya zhizn'*, 201.

50. JE 61, 15.

51. Nikitina, *Povsednevnaya zhizn L'va Tolstogo*, 92, 95.

52. *Letopis'* 1, 285.

53. Tolstaya, *Dnevniki*, vol. 1, 54.

54. I. I. Mints and S. A. Tolstaya-Esenina, eds., *Yasnaya Polyana: stat'i, dokumenty*, Moscow, 1942, 105.

55. Tolstaya, 'Moya zhizn", *Novy mir*, 39.

56. Nikitina, *Povsednevnaya zhizn L'va Tolstogo*, 98–99.

57. S. A. Tolstaya, 'Moya zhizn", *Oktyabr'*, 9 (1998), 148.

58. I am grateful to Thomas Newlin for letting me read his unpublished article '"Swarm Life" and the Biology of *War and Peace*', and for his help with Russian beekeeping terminology.

59. Kuzminskaya, *Moya zhizn'*, 162.

60. Kuzminskaya, *Moya zhizn'*, 217–218.

61. Tolstaya, 'Moya zhizn", *Novy mir*, 41.

62. JE 48, 59.

63. JE 48, 58.

64. For a detailed account see Kathryn B. Feuer, *Tolstoy and the Genesis of 'War and Peace'*, ed. Robin Feuer Miller and Donna Tussing Orwin, Ithaca, 1996.

65. JE 61, 23–24.

66. JE 48, 63; Gusev 2, 641.

67. N. Gusev, 'Gde iskat' kanonicheskii tekst "Voiny i mira"', in *Tolstoi i o Tolstom: Novye materialy*, ed. N. Gusev, vol. 1, Moscow, 1926, 132–135.

68. I. N. Sukikh, *Voina iz-za 'Voiny i mira': Roman L. N. Tolstogo 'Voina i mir' v russkoi kritike i literaturovedenii*, St Petersburg, 2002, 34.

69. Vladimir Zhdanov, *Lyubov' v zhizni Tolstogo* (1928), Moscow, 2005, 106.

70. M. A. Tsyavlovsky, 'Kak pisalsya i pechatalsya roman "Voina i mir"', in *Tolstoi i o Tolstom: Novye materialy*, ed. N. Gusev, vol. 3, Moscow, 1927, 142.

71. *Letopis'* 1, 295; Tolstaya, 'Moya zhizn", *Oktyabr'*, 157.

72. Tsyavlovsky, 'Kak pisalsya i pechatalsya roman "Voina i mir"', 131.

73. Gusev 2, 633.

74. *Letopis'* 1, 303.

75. Tsyavlovsky, 'Kak pisalsya i pechatalsya roman "Voina i mir"', 151.

76. Tolstaya, 'Moya zhizn", *Oktyabr'*, 139.

77. Tolstaya, 'Moya zhizn", *Oktyabr'*, 149.

78. Tsyavlovsky, 'Kak pisalsya i pechatalsya roman "Voina i mir"', 135–138.

79. Tsyavlovsky, 'Kak pisalsya i pechatalsya roman "Voina i mir"', 149.

80. Alexander Fodor, *Tolstoy and the Russians: Reflections on a Relationship*, Ann Arbor, 1984, 105.

81. JE 61, 139; *Letopis'* 1 320.

82. L. N. Tolstoi, *Voina i mir*, Moscow, 2000.

83. E. Zaidenshnur, 'Poiski nachala romana "Voina i mir: Pyatnadtsat" nabroskov (1863–1864)', *Literaturnoe nasledstvo*, 69 (1961), vol. 1, 291–324, and *Polnoe sobranie sochinenii*, ed. V. G. Chertkov, 90 vols, Moscow, 1928–1958, vols. 13–16.

84. See Elena Klepikova, 'Novaya staraya "Voina i mir"', *Russkii bazar*, 27 March 2003.

85. *War and Peace: Original Version*, tr. Andrew Bromfield, London, 2007.

86. A. V. Gulin, *Lev Tolstoi i puti russkoi istorii*, Moscow, 2004, 219.

87. Lesskis, *Lev Tolstoi*, 391.

88. Tsyavlovsky, 'Kak pisalsya i pechatalsya roman "Voina i mir"', 154.

89. JE 61, 174; Tsyavlovsky, 'Kak pisalsya i pechatalsya roman "Voina i mir"', 156.

90. Or 26 August, by the old Russian calendar.

91. *War and Peace*, part 2, vol. 3.

92. For an authoritative account of what actually happened in 1812 see Dominic Lieven, *Russia Against Napoleon: The Battle for Europe, 1807 to 1814*, London, 2009.

93. JE 61, 180; Tsyavlovsky, 'Kak pisalsya i pechatalsya roman "Voina i mir"', 158.

94. Tsyavlovsky, 'Kak pisalsya i pechatalsya roman "Voina i mir"', 160.

95. Tsyavlovsky, 'Kak pisalsya i pechatalsya roman "Voina i mir"', 164.

96. *Letopis'* 1, 346.

97. Tolstoy's preface was published in *Russkii arkhiv* in March 1868, and reprinted in *Polnoe sobranie sochinenii*, ed. Chertkov, vol. 16.

98. *Autobiography of Countess Sophie Tolstoi*, 35.

99. Gusev 2, 665.

100. *Letopis'* 1, 320.

101. *Letopis'* 1, 315.

102. *Letopis'* 1, 320.

103. For Schuyler's biography see Peter Bridges, 'Eugene Schuyler, The Only Diplomatist', *Diplomacy and Statecraft*, 16 (2005), 13–22.

104. E. Schuyler, 'Count Leo Tolstoy Twenty Years Ago', *Scribner's Magazine*, May and June 1889, reprinted in Schuyler, *Selected Essays*.

105. Schuyler's translation of *The Cossacks* was published in London in 1878 by Sampson, Low.

106. Tolstaya, 'Moya zhizn'', *Oktyabr'*, 156.

107. Tolstaya, 'Moya zhizn'', *Oktyabr'*, 155.

108. *Letopis'* 1, 337.

109. See I. N. Sukhikh, ed., *Voina iz-za 'Voiny i mira': Roman L. N. Tolstogo 'Voina i mir' v russkoi kritike i literaturovedenii*, St Petersburg, 2002.

110. *Letopis'* 1, 346.

111. A. F. Rogalev, '"Une russe" – pervyi perevodchik romana L. N. Tolstogo "Voina i mir" na frantsuzskii yazyk', *Vestnik VGU*, 2003, 4–9. Pashkevich's translation was later used to produce English, Hungarian, Dutch, Polish and Turkish editions.

112. Sukhikh, *Voina iz-za 'Voiny i mira'*, 353–354.

8 Student, Teacher, Father

1. JE 48, 129.

2. N. N. Gusev, *Letopis' zhizni i tvorchestva L. N. Tolstogo, 1828–1890*, Moscow, 1958 [*Letopis'* 1], 362.

3. JE 61, 225, 228, 231; *Letopis'* 1, 368.

4. *Letopis'* 1, 373.

5. JE 61, 237. Urusov retired from the army at the rank of general at the end of the Crimean War in order to concentrate on his chess-playing career (he was ranked fifth in the world in 1866). His main interests therefore remained cerebral, so he may not have empathised with this feeling of happiness, even if Tolstoy had been able to describe it. After he gave up competitive chess in the late 1870s, Urusov gave his considerable collection of books about chess to Tolstoy's son Ilya. He burned most of Tolstoy's letters to him after he renounced the Church. He was godfather to Lev, Maria and Pyotr Tolstoy.

6. *Letopis'* 1, 374, 382–383.

7. JE 61, 220.

8. *Letopis'* 1, 370.

9. A. A. Donskov, *L. N. Tolstoi i S. A. Tolstaya: Perepiska s N. N. Strakhovym*, Ottawa, 2000, 2.

10. *Letopis'* 1, 369.

11. JE 61, 242.

12. JE 61, 240.

13. JE 61, 228.

14. JE 61, 252.

15. JE 61, 253.

16. T. A. Kuzminskaya, *Moya zhizn' doma i v Yasnoi Poliane*, ed. T. N. Volkova, Tula, 1973, 404.

17. This account draws on Walter Kerr, *The Shabunin Affair: An Episode in the Life of Leo Tolstoy*, Ithaca, 1982.

18. S. A. Tolstaya, *Dnevniki v dvukh tomakh*, ed. V. E. Vatsuro et al., 2 vols, Moscow, 1978, vol. 1, 80.

19. Kerr, *The Shabunin Affair*, 182; JE 37, 75.

20. Vladimir Zhdanov, *Lyubov' v zhizni Tolstogo* (1928), Moscow, 2005, 118; JE 61, 167.

21. JE 61, 221.

22. *Letopis'* 1, 363.

23. Tolstaya, *Dnevniki*, vol. 1, 84; 1884 diary entry, cited by Zhdanov, *Lyubov' v zhizni Tolstogo*, 128.

24. 'O brake i prizvanii zhenshchiny', in JE 7, 134.

25. An incomplete translation of only the first three volumes was published in 1870.

26. Tolstaya, *Dnevniki*, vol. 1, 497.

27. N. A. Kalinina et al., *Perepiska L. N. Tolstogo s sestroi i brat'yami*, Moscow, 1990, 358–359. Sergey complained in April 1877 that his brother was not keeping to his side of the bargain and sending on issues of the *Russian Messenger* which contained instalments of *Anna Karenina* and was therefore disgruntled to be paying twenty roubles for *Messenger of Europe*.

28. Tolstaya, *Dnevniki*, vol. 1, 497.

29. JE 21, 409–410.

30. JE 61, 233.

31. Tolstaya, *Dnevniki*, vol. 1, 83.

32. N. N. Gusev, *Lev Nikolaevich Tolstoi. Materialy k biografii s 1870 po 1881 god* [Gusev 3], Moscow, 1963, 54.

33. S. A. Tolstaya, 'Moya zhizn'', *Prometei*, 12 (1980), 159.

34. Tolstaya, 'Moya zhizn'', *Prometei*, 153. Sonya cites Auber's *La Muette de Portici*, Donizetti's *Lucia* and Bellini's *La somnambula*, and Tolstoy's favourite opera as *Don Giovanni*.

35. Gusev 3, 54.

36. *Letopis'* 1, 365.

37. Zhdanov, *Lyubov' v zhizni Tolstogo*, 140.

38. JE 48, 167.

39. Eugene Schuyler, *Selected Essays*, New York, 1901, 274–275.

40. *The Autobiography of Countess Sophie Tolstoi*, preface and notes by Vasilii Spiridonov, tr. S. S. Koteliansky and Leonard Woolf, Richmond, 1922, 46.

41. JE 21, 410.

42. *Letopis'* 1, 377–378.

43. *Letopis'* 1, 379.

44. *Letopis'*1, 380.

45. JE 61, 381.

46. S. A. Tolstaya, *Pis'ma k L. N. Tolstomu, 1862–1910*, Moscow, 1936, 96.

47. Tolstaya, *Dnevniki*, vol. 1, 498.

48. Tolstaya, *Dnevniki*, vol. 1, 499.

49. A. Grodetskaya, *Otvety predaniya: zhitiya svyatikh v dukhovnom poiske L'va Tolstogo*, St Petersburg, 2000, 5.

50. Tolstaya, *Dnevniki*, vol. 1, 499.

51. Grodetskaya, *Otvety predaniya*, 4.

52. Tolstaya, *Dnevniki*, vol. 1, 499.

53. See Grodetskaya, *Otvety predaniya*.

54. Kirsha Danilov's collection, first published in *Drevnye russkie stikhotvoreniya*, ed. A. F. Yakubovich, St Petersburg, 1804, was used in Tolstoy's *ABC*.

55. *Pesni, sobrannye P. N. Rybnikovym*, 4 vols, St Petersburg, 1861–1867.

56. JE 61, 269; Gusev 3, 46.

57. Pavel Golokhvastov, *Alesha Popovich, predstavlenie v 5 deistviykah, sochinennoe po starym russkim bylinam*, Moscow, 1869; *Zakony stikha russkogo i nashego literaturnogo*, St Petersburg, 1883.

58. *Russkie narodnye skazki*, 8 vols, St Petersburg, 1855–1863.

59. Tolstaya, 'Moya zhizn'', *Prometei*, 164.

60. Tolstaya, *Dnevniki*, vol. 1, 496.

61. *Letopis'* 1, 389; Gusev 3, 46.

62. *Letopis'* 1, 386; Gusev 3, 46 (48, 92–93, 130–162).

63. JE 7, 395.

64. *Aesop's Fables*, tr. Laura Gibbs, Oxford, 2002. The Greek original reads: Λέων καὶ βάτραχος'. Λέων ἀκούσας βατράχου κεκραγότος ἐπεστράφη πρὸς τὴν φωνήν, οἰόμενος μέγα τι ζῷον εἶναι. Προσμείνας δὲ μικρὸν χρόνον, ὡς ἐθεάσατο αὐτὸν ἀπὸ τῆς λίμνης ἐξελθόντα, προσελθὼν καταπάτησεν εἰπών· Εἶτα τηλικοῦτος ὢν τηλικαῦτα βοᾷς;' Πρὸς ἄνδρα γλωσσαλγίαν οὐδὲν πλέον τοῦ λαλεῖν δυνάμενον ὁ λόγος εὔκαιρος.

65. JE 21, 628.

66. JE 22, 77.

67. JE 22, 89–90.

68. JE 61, 277–278.

69. Letter of 28 November 1871, cited in Gusev 3, 40.

70. JE 61, 269.

71. In his letter to Strakhov, December 1871, Tolstoy writes that he is convinced 'I have raised myself a monument': JE 61, 349.

72. E. G. Babaev, 'Bol'shaya azbuka ili oshchushchenie shchast'ya', *Knizhnye sokrovishcha knigi. Iz fondov Gosudarstvennoi biblioteki im. V. I. Lenina*, Moscow, 1989, 94–109.

73. JE 61, 283.

74. T. L. Sukhotina-Tolstaya, *Vospominaniya*, Moscow, 1976, 100–102.

75. Gusev 3, 41.

76. Gusev 3, 42.

77. See Elliott Mossman, 'Tolstoi and Peasant Learning in the Era of the Great Reforms', *School and Society in Tsarist and Soviet Russia*, ed. Ben Eklof, Basingstoke, 1993, 36–69.

78. *Letopis'* 1, 390.

79. Gusev 3, 48.

80. JE 22, 576.

81. Gusev 3, 57.

82. JE 22, 578.

83. JE 62, 42.

84. *Letopis'* 1, 413.

85. *Letopis'* 1, 425.

86. JE 17, 100.

87. Daniel Murphy, *Tolstoy and Education*, Blackrock, 1992, 69.

88. JE 21, 583.

89. Gusev 3, 205.

90. Gusev 3, 207.

91. Gusev 3, 208.

92. Gusev 3, 209.

93. JE 61, 333–334.

94. Tolstaya, 'Moya zhizn", *Prometei*, 158.

95. S. L. Tolstoi, *Ocherki bylogo*, Moscow, 1949; T. L. Sukhotina-Tolstaya, *Vospominaniya*, Moscow, 1976; I. L. Tolstoi, *Moi vospominaniya*, Moscow, 1914.

96. S. A. Tolstaya, *Pis'ma k L. N. Tolstomu, 1862–1910*, Moscow, 1936, 70.

97. Tolstaya, *Pis'ma*, 69.

98. *Letopis'* 1, 384.

99. Zhdanov, *Lyubov' v zhizni Tolstogo*, 144–146; Tolstaya, 'Moya zhizn", *Prometei*, 165.

100. Tolstaya, 'Moya zhizn", *Prometei*, 161.

101. This was the servant given to Dmitry; he transferred to Tolstoy and went to the Caucasus with him in 1851.

102. JE 83, 179.

103. Andreas Kappeler, *The Russian Empire: A Multiethnic History*, tr. Alfred Clayton, London, 2001, 39–41.

104. JE 83, 190–192.

105. Tolstoy's American visitor Eugene Schuyler had made the journey from Samara to Orenburg via Buzuluk in the spring of 1868, having stopped off in Kazan to meet his ageing uncle Vladimir, and published a colourful account entitled 'On the Steppe' in *Hours at Home: A Popular Monthly Journal of Instruction and Recreation*, vol. 4 (1869), issue 4, 319–330.

106. JE 83, 210.

107. Tolstaya, 'Moya zhizn", *Prometei*, 165.

108. JE 62, 47.

109. JE 62, 37.

110. JE 62, 38–39.

9 Novelist

1. S. L. Tolstoi, 'Ob otrazhenii zhizni v "Anne Kareninoi": Iz vospominanii', *Literaturnoe nasledstvo*, 37/38, vol. 2 (Moscow, 1939), 567.

2. N. N. Gusev, *Lev Nikolaevich Tolstoi. Materialy k biografii s 1870 po 1881 god* [Gusev 3], Moscow, 1963, 124.

3. See Nicholas V. Riasanovsky, *The Image of Peter the Great in Russian History and Thought*, Oxford, 1985, 200.

4. S. Solov'ev, *Petrovskie chteniya*, St Petersburg, 1872.

5. Gusev 3, 17.

6. JE 61, 342–343, for example.

7. Musorgsky, letter to Stasov, June 1872, *M. P. Musorgskii: pis'ma*, Moscow, 1984, 100.

8. Gusev 3, 131.

9. JE 61, 349.

10. Gusev 3, 118.

11. E. Schuyler, *Peter the Great: Emperor of Russia*, 2 vols, New York, 1884.

12. See Peter Bridges, 'Eugene Schuyler: The Only Diplomatist', *Diplomacy and Statecraft*, 16 (2005), 13–22.

13. N. N. Gusev, *Letopis' zhizni i tvorchestva L. N. Tolstogo, 1828–1890*, Moscow, 1958 [*Letopis* 1], 404.

14. See Barbara Alpern Engel, 'Women, the Family and Public Life', *The Cambridge History of Russia*, vol. 2: *Imperial Russia, 1689–1917*, ed. Dominic Lieven, Cambridge, 2006, 306–325.

15. S. A. Tolstaya, *Dnevniki v dvukh tomakh*, ed. V. E. Vatsuro et al., 2 vols, Moscow, 1978, vol. 1, 508.

16. Gusev 3, 134–135.

17. Alexandre Dumas, *L'Homme-femme*, Paris, 1872.

18. Roderick Phillips, *Putting Asunder: A History of Divorce in Western Society*, Cambridge, 1988, 422.

19. JE 62, 11.

20. See Priscilla Meyer, *How the Russians Read the French: Lermontov, Dostoevsky, Tolstoy*, Madison, 2008, 152–248.

21. JE 59, 64.

22. JE 34, 368.

23. JE 62, 16.

24. *Letopis'* 1, 403.

25. V. A. Zhdanov, 'K istorii sozdaniya "Anna Karenina": dva rannikh nabroska romana', *Literaturnoe nasledstvo*, 69 (1961), vol. 1, 404.

26. Zhdanov, 'K istorii sozdaniya "Anna Karenina"', 423.

27. V. A. Zhdanov and E. E. Zaidenshnur, 'Tekstologicheskie poyasneniya', in L. N. Tolstoi, *Anna Karenina*, Literaturnye Pamyatniki, ed. Zhdanov and Zaidenshnur, Moscow, 1970, 687.

28. Gusev 3, 280.

29. Zhdanov and Zaidenshnur, 'Tekstologicheskie poyasneniya', 810.

30. JE 62, 25.

31. JE 62, 15.

32. JE 62, 27.

33. *Letopis'* 1, 408.

34. JE 17, 704.

35. JE 61, 315–316.

36. JE 17, 702–708.

37. JE 62, 29.

38. Oleg Neverov, *Great Private Collections of Imperial Russia*, London, 2004, 165–166; Irina Nenarkomova, *Pavel Tret'yakov i ego galereya*, Moscow, 1998.

39. David Jackson, *The Wanderers and Critical Realism in Nineteenth-Century Russian Painting*, Manchester, 2006, 26.

40. Gusev 3, 150–151.

41. See Irina Paperno, *Suicide as a Cultural Institution in Dostoevsky's Russia*, Ithaca, 1997.

42. JE 62, 50.

43. Paperno, *Suicide as a Cultural Institution*.

44. *Letopis'* 1, 413.

45. JE 62, 56.

46. JE 62, 69.

47. JE 62, 55.

48. JE 62, 72.

49. JE 62, 56.

50. Vladimir Zhdanov, *Lyubov' v zhizni Tolstogo* (1928), Moscow, 2005, 161–162.

51. JE 62, 40.

52. Gusev 3, 154–155.

53. Gusev 3, 296.

54. *Letopis'* 1, 418.

55. JE 62, 95.

56. JE 62, 78.

57. JE 62, 81.

58. JE 62, 89.

59. JE 62, 92.

60. JE 34, 367–368.

61. JE 62, 95.

62. JE 62, 103.

63. JE 62, 100.

64. JE 62, 107.

65. JE 62, 117. See also Boris Eikhenbaum, *Lev Tolstoi: semidesyatye gody*, Leningrad, 1974.

66. JE 62, 112.

67. *Letopis'* 1, 435.

68. JE 62, 130.

69. JE 62, 185.

70. Zhdanov, *Lyubov' v zhizni Tolstogo*, 164–165.

71. Chapters 1–14 in the journal; chapters 1–23 in the final version.

72. *Letopis'* 1, 434.

73. Part One, chapter 22.

74. Zhdanov and Zaidenshnur, 'Tekstologicheskie poyasneniya', 840.

75. In the final version the chapter was split, with the two lines of dots coming at the end of chapter 10 of Part Two.

76. JE 62, 139.

77. JE 62, 149.

78. Zhdanov, *Lyubov' v zhizni Tolstogo*, 166–167.

79. S. A. Tolstaya, *Pis'ma k L. N. Tolstomu, 1862–1910*, Moscow, 1936, 135.

80. S. L. Tolstoi, *Ocherki bylogo*, Moscow, 1949, 43.

81. Ten laps according to Gusev, who claims the winner boasted a time of one hour thirty-nine minutes, which seems somehow unlikely. See Gusev 3, 212.

82. I. L. Tolstoi, *Moi vospominaniya*, Moscow, 1914, 86–88.

83. JE 62, 199.

84. Tolstaya, *Dnevniki*, vol. 1, 88–89.

85. *Letopis'* 1, 448.

86. JE 62, 216.

87. JE 62, 216.

88. JE 62, 226–228.

89. JE 62, 218.

90. JE 62, 248.

91. N. A. Kalinina et al., *Perepiska L. N. Tolstogo s sestroi i brat'yami*, Moscow, 1990, 349.

92. Zhdanov, *Lyubov' v zhizni Tolstogo*, 168–169.

93. JE 62, 256–257.

94. Part Five, chapter 20 (chapter 19 in the journal).

95. JE 62, 248.

96. Kalinina et al., *Perepiska*, 352–353.

97. Kalinina et al., *Perepiska*, 272.

98. She is the only one of Tolstoy's siblings not to be made the subject of a separate chapter in the expanded Russian version of the 1980 book about the Tolstoy family by

Sergey Mikhailovich, the writer's grandson (S. M. Tolstoi, *Tolstoï et les Tolstoï: Essais de l'histoire de la famille*, Paris, 1980; *Tolstoi i Tolstye: Ocherki iz istorii roda*, Moscow, 1990), although he published her biography in Russian elsewhere (S. M. Tolstoi, 'Edinstvennaya sestra', *Prometei*, 12 (1980), 269–287).

99. Kalinina et al., *Perepiska*, 272.

100. Tolstoi, 'Edinstvennaya sestra', 274–275.

101. G. L. Freeze, 'Bringing Order to the Russian Family: Marriage and Divorce in Imperial Russia, 1760–1860', *Journal of Modern History*, 62, 4 (1990), 709–746.

102. Michelle Lamarche Marrese, 'Gender and the Legal Order in Imperial Russia', *The Cambridge History of Russia*, vol. 2: *Imperial Russia, 1689–1917*, ed. Dominic Lieven, Cambridge, 2006, 326–343.

103. William G. Wagner, *Marriage, Property and Law in Late Imperial Russia*, Oxford, 1994, 70.

104. Elena Belyakova, *Tserkovnyi sud i problemy tserkovnoi zhizni*, Moscow, 2004.

105. Belyakova, *Tserkovnyi sud*, 215.

106. Barbara Alpern Engel, 'In the Name of the Tsar: Competing Legalities and Marital Conflict in Late Imperial Russia', *Journal of Modern History*, 77, 1 (2005), 70–95.

107. V. Shklovskii, *Lev Tolstoi*, Moscow, 1967, 388; A. Bers, 'Otryvki vospominanii o L. N. Tolstom', in *Tolstoi i o Tolstom: Novye materialy*, ed. V. G. Chertkov and N. N. Gusev, vol. 2, Moscow, 1926, 131.

108. S. L. Tolstoi, 'Ob otrazhenie zhizni v "Anne Kareninoi": iz vospominanii', *Literaturnoe nasledstvo*, 37/38, Moscow, 1939, vol. 2, 568; N. M. Chernov, 'Novosil'skie druz'ya Turgeneva', www.turgenev.org.ru/e-book/chernov/novosil-drug.htm

109. Kalinina et al., *Perepiska*, 353.

110. T. A. Kuzminskaya, *Moya zhizn' doma i v Yasnoi Poliane*, ed. T. N. Volkova, Tula, 1973, 354.

111. Kalinina et al., *Perepiska*, 292.

112. JE 62, 332.

113. Tolstaya, *Pis'ma k L. N. Tolstomu, 1862–1910*, 11.

114. Zhdanov, *Lyubov' v zhizni Tolstogo*, 180–181.

115. JE 62, 302.

116. A. D. Obolensky, 'Dve vstrechi s L. N. Tolstym', *Tolstoi. Pamyatniki tvorchestva i zhizni*, vol. 3, Moscow, 1923, 34.

117. Edwina Cruise ('Tracking the English Novel in *Anna Karenina*: Who Wrote the English Novel that Anna reads?', *Anniversary Essays on Tolstoy*, ed. Donna Tussing Orwin, Cambridge, 2010, 159–182), also puts forward novels by Mrs Henry Wood as a candidate.

118. Obolensky, 'Dve vstrechi', 27.

119. Gusev 3, 255.

120. JE 62, 326.

121. Anna Aksakova (Tyutcheva), *Pri dvore dvukh imperatorov*, Moscow, 2008, diary entry 28 October 1876.

122. JE 62, 288.

123. See David MacKenzie, *The Serbs and Russian Pan-Slavism, 1875–1878*, Ithaca, 1967.

124. Obolensky, 'Dve vstrechi', 29–37.

125. *Russkii vestnik*, 5 (1877), 472.

126. JE 53, 331.

127. *Letopis'* 1, 475.

128. Joseph Frank, *Dostoevsky: The Mantle of the Prophet, 1871–1881*, Princeton, 2002, 332.

10 Pilgrim, Nihilist, Muzhik

1. JE 62, 347

2. JE 83, 445 (letter of 28 October 1884).

3. N. N. Gusev, *Letopis' zhizni i tvorchestva L. N. Tolstogo, 1828–1890*, Moscow, 1958 [*Letopis'* 1], 661.

4. JE 62, 311.

5. S. A. Tolstaya, *Dnevniki v dvukh tomakh*, ed. V. E. Vatsuro et al., 2 vols, Moscow, 1978, vol. 1, 503.

6. *Letopis'* 1, 472.

7. JE 62, 419.

8. S. A. Tolstaya, 'Iz zapisok Grafini Sofii Andreevny Tolstoi pod zaglaviem "Moya Zhizn"', *Tolstovskii ezhegodnik*, St Petersburg, 1913, 3.

9. Chris Chulos, 'Russian Piety and Culture from Peter the Great to 1917', *Cambridge History of Christianity*, vol. 5: *Eastern Christianity*, ed. Michael Angold, Cambridge, 2006, 338.

10. See Robert L. Nichols, 'The Orthodox Elders (Staretsy) of Imperial Russia', *Modern Greek Studies Yearbook*, 1 (1985), 1–30.

11. See Sergii Chetverikov, *Optina Pustyn'*, Paris, 1926; Leonard J. Stanton, *The Optina Pustyn Monastery in the Russian Literary Imagination: Iconic Vision in Works by Dostoevsky, Gogol, Tolstoy, and others*, New York, 1995.

12. P. Matveev, 'L. N. Tolstoi i N. N. Strakhov v Optinoi Pustyni', *Istoricheskii vestnik*, 2 (1907), 151–157.

13. www.optina.ru/starets/amvrosiy_life_full/

14. JE 62, 335; N. N. Gusev, *Lev Nikolaevich Tolstoi. Materialy k biografii s 1870 po 1881 god* [Gusev 3], Moscow, 1963, 442.

15. Matveev, 'L. N. Tolstoi i N. N. Strakhov v Optinoi Pustyni', 153–154.

16. Gusev 3, 441.

17. Gusev 3, 442.

18. JE 62, 334.

19. Gusev 3, 436.

20. JE 62, 353.

21. Matveev, 'L. N. Tolstoi i N. N. Strakhov v Optinoi Pustyni', 155.

22. Tolstaya, *Dnevniki*, vol. 1, 505.

23. S. L. Tolstoi, *Ocherki bylogo*, Moscow, 1949, 59.

24. *Letopis'* 1, 481.

25. V. I. Alekseev, 'Vospominaniya', *L. N. Tolstoi: K 120-letiyu so dnya rozhdeniya (1828–1948)*, 2 vols, ed. N. N. Gusev, Moscow, 1948, vol. 2, 232–330.

26. JE 62, 422, 509.

27. S. L. Tolstoi, *Ocherki bylogo*, 57.

28. Mark Aldanov, 'A Russian Commune in Kansas', *Russian Review*, 1 (1944), 30–44.

29. N. Nikitina, *Povsednevnaya zhizn L'va Tolstogo v Yasnoi polyane*, Moscow, 2007, 286.

30. Tolstaya, *Dnevniki*, vol. 1, 191, 239, 384.

31. M. Zabylin, *Russkii narod: obychai, predaniya, obryady i sueveriya*, Moscow, 2003, 74; O. G. Baranova et al., *Russkii prazdnik. Prazdniki i obryady narodnogo zemledel'cheskogo kalendarya: illyustrirovannaya entsiklopediya*, St Petersburg, 2002, 570–578; Andrei Sinyavsky, *Ivan the Fool: Russian Folk Belief, A Cultural History*, tr. Joanne Turnbull and Nikolai Formozov, Moscow, 2007, 245–247.

32. Alekseev, 'Vospominaniya', 250.

33. T. L. Sukhotina-Tolstaya, *Vospominaniya*, Moscow, 1976, 437.

34. Edward Spencer Beesly, *The Life and Death of William Frey*, London, 1888, 3.

35. Gusev 3, 504.

36. S. A. Tolstaya, *Pis'ma k L. N. Tolstomu, 1862–1910*, Moscow, 1936, 146.

37. Alekseev, 'Vospominaniya', 250–263. See also, 85, 80.

38. Tolstaya, *Pis'ma k L. N. Tolstomu*, 150.

39. Gusev 3, 476.

40. Gusev 3, 476–467.

41. *Letopis'* 1, 491.

42. Gusev 3, 476.

43. JE 83, 249.

44. S. M. Tolstoi, 'Edinstvennaya sestra', *Prometei*, 12 (1980), 273.

45. *Letopis'* 1, 493, 497.

46. *Letopis'* 1, 492, 495.

47. It was estimated that there were between 20 and 35 million Old Believers and sectarians in Russia at the beginning of the twentieth century, and that as much as a third of the population was sectarian by 1917: see A. Etkind, *Khlyst: sekty, literatura i revolyutsiya*, Moscow, 1998, 34.

48. Robin Milner-Gulland, *The Russians*, Oxford, 1997, 123.

49. N. Berdyaev, 'Dukhovnoe khristianstvo i sektantstvo v Rossii', *Russkaya mysl'*, 11 (1916).

50. *Khlysty* also means 'flagellants', but they did not as a rule practise flagellation.

51. Malcolm V. Jones, 'A Note on Mr. J. G. Blissmer and the Society for the Encouragement of Spiritual and Ethical Reading', *Slavonic and East European Review*, 130 (January 1975), 93.

52. See E. Heier, *Religious Schism in the Russian Aristocracy 1860–1900: Radstockism and Pashkovism*, The Hague, 1970.

53. N. A. Kalinina et al., *Perepiska L. N. Tolstogo s sestroi i brat'yami*, Moscow, 1990, 266–268, 284.

54. S. A. Behrs, *Recollections of Count Leo Tolstoy*, tr. Charles Edward Turner, London, 1893, 95.

55. Donald Mackenzie Wallace, *Russia*, London, 1877, 294.

56. Mackenzie Wallace, *Russia*, 331.

57. Gusev 3, 509.

58. Sukhotina-Tolstaya, *Vospominaniya*, 245.

59. Gusev 3, 512–514.

60. Gusev 3, 533, 536.

61. *Letopis'* 1, 488.

62. Jules Montels, 'L'État d'âme de Tolstoï en 1878–1880', *Les Temps Nouveaux*, 10 December 1910, 5–6.

63. Gusev 3, 538.

64. Tolstaya, *Dnevniki*, vol. 1, 100.

65. JE 62, 477.

66. Gusev 3, 564.

67. Gusev 3, 566.

68. JE 62, 487.

69. Gusev 3, 567.

70. Gusev 3, 570.

71. See Christine Worobec, 'The Unintended Consequences of a Surge in Orthodox Pilgrimages in Late Imperial Russia', *Russian History*, 36 (2009), 62–76.

72. Gusev 3, 584.

73. Gusev 3, 585.

74. 2 Peter, 2: 22: 'Of [False Teachers] the proverbs are true: "A dog returns to its vomit".' Proverbs 26: 11 reads: 'As a dog returns to its vomit, so a fool returns to its folly.'

75. Gusev 3, 603.

76. Gusev 3, 609.

77. Gusev 3, 610.

78. S. A. Tolstaya, 'Moya zhizn'', *Prometei*, 12 (1980), 168.

79. Gusev 3, 506.

80. Gusev 3, 644.

81. Gusev 3, 625.

82. JE 83, 270.

83. Count N. [sic] Tolstoi, *Childhood and Youth*, tr. M. von Meysenbug, London, 1862.

84. See Will Ryan, 'W. R. S. Ralston and the Russian Folktale', *Folklore*, 120 (2009), 2, 123–132.

85. JE 62, 448.

86. W. R. S. Ralston, 'Count Leo Tolstoy's Novels', *The Nineteenth Century*, 4 (1879), 651.

87. Konstantin Mochulsky, *Dostoevsky: His Life and Work*, tr. Michael A. Minihan, Princeton, 1967, 639.

88. Gusev 3, 639.

89. *Letopis'* 1, 531.

90. *Letopis'* 1, 526–527.

91. Gusev 3, 641.

92. Gusev 3, 653.

93. Gusev 3, 637.

94. Gusev 3, 640.

95. Gusev 3, 612.

96. See Pål Kolstø, 'Leo Tolstoy, a Church Critic Influenced by Orthodox Thought', in *Church, Nation and State in Russia and Ukraine*, ed. Geoffrey Hosking, London, 1991, 148–66.

97. Gusev 3, 619–625.

98. JE 23, 541.

99. Gusev 3, 613.

100. Tolstaya, *Dnevniki*, vol. 1, 507–508.

101. Gusev 3, 667.

102. *Novum Testamentum Graece. Textum ad fidem codicum, versionum, et patrum recensuit et lectionis varietatem adjecit D. Jo. Jac. Griesbach*, Jena, 1818; Edouard Reuss, *La Bible. Traduction nouvelle avec introduction et commentaires*, 17 vols, Paris, 1764–1881.

103. Ernest J. Simmons, *Tolstoy*, London, 1973, 107.

104. See David Matual, *Tolstoy's Translation of the Gospels: A Critical Study*, Lewiston, 1992.

105. I. I. Ivakin, 'Vospominaniya o Tolstom', *Literaturnoe nasledtsvo*, 69 (1961), vol. 2, 40.

106. Ivakin, 'Vospominaniya o Tolstom', 40.

107. JE 24, 25.

108. Gusev 3, 670.

109. Vladimir Zhdanov, *Lyubov' v zhizni Tolstogo* (1928), Moscow, 2005, 214.

110. Gusev 3, 18.

111. Ray Monk, *Wittgenstein: The Duty of Genius*, Oxford, 1990, 116.

112. Gusev 3, 28.

113. *Letopis'* 1, 537.

114. *L. N. Tolstoi v vospominaniyakh sovremennikov*, 2 vols, Moscow, 1978, vol. 1, 293–315; S. Tolstaya. 'Iz zapisok Grafini Sofii Andreevny Tolstoi pod zaglaviem 'Moya zhizn'. 'Chetyre poseshcheniya gr. L'va Nikolaevicha Tolstogo monastyrya "Optina Pustyn'", *Tolstovskii ezhegodnik,* Moscow, 1913, 4–6.

115. JE 83, 300, 304–305.

116. Gusev 3, 67.

117. Gusev 3, 73.

118. Zhdanov, *Lyubov' v zhizni Tolstogo*, 217.

11 Sectarian, Anarchist, Holy Fool

1. JE 63, 194.
2. JE 25, 173–181.
3. Matthew, 25: 31, 35–36.
4. 'Dopolnitel'nye voprosy k lichnym kartam statisticheskoi perepisi predlagaemye Antoshei Chekhonte', *Budil'nik*, 5 (1882), 65; A. P. Chekhov, *Polnoe sobranie sochinenii i pisem v tridtsati tomakh*, ed. N. F. Bel'chikov et al., Moscow, 1974–83, Sochineniya, vol. 1, 116.
5. N. N. Gusev, *Materialy k biografii L. N. Tolstogo s 1881 po 1886 god*, Moscow, 1970 [Gusev 4], 124.
6. Gusev 4, 149.
7. S. A. Tolstaya, *Pis'ma k L. N. Tolstomu, 1862–1910*, Moscow, 1936, 179.
8. Gusev 4, 125.
9. N. A. Kalinina et al., *Perepiska L. N. Tolstogo s sestroi i brat'yami*, Moscow, 1990, 377.
10. Gusev 4, 126.
11. Leonid Kavelin, *Istoricheskoe opisanie Korennoi Rozhdestvo-Bogoroditskoi Pustyni*, Moscow, 1876.
12. David Jackson, *The Wanderers and Critical Realism in Nineteenth-Century Russian Painting*, Manchester, 2006, 44.
13. *The Autobiography of Countess Sophie Tolstoi*, preface and notes by Vasilii Spiridonov, tr. S. S. Koteliansky and Leonard Woolf, Richmond, 1922, 50.
14. 'Shlissel'burgskaya krepost'', 12 (1880), 'Znachenie sektantstva v russkoi narodnoi zhizni', 1 (1881), 'Raskol i ego issledovateli', 2 (1881), 'Alchuchshie i zhazhdushchie pravdy', 10, 12 (1881), 1 (1882).
15. Gusev 4, 155.
16. Gusev 4, 171.
17. Gusev 4, 159–160.
18. N. Nikitina, *Sof'ya Tolstaya*, Moscow, 2010, 126.
19. Gusev 4, 150.
20. Gusev 4, 165.
21. JE 83, 378.
22. JE 83, 384.
23. JE 83, 382.
24. Gusev 4, 172.
25. Gusev 4, 173.
26. N. N. Gusev, *Letopis' zhizni L. N. Tolstogo, 1828–1890*, Moscow, 1958 [*Letopis'* 1], 559–560.
27. See *Letopis'* 1, 566, for example.
28. Gusev 4, 207–208.
29. Gusev 4, 209.
30. Gusev 4, 217.

31. Gusev 4, 156.

32. Gusev 4, 217. Prince Leonid Urusov is not to be confused with Tolstoy's other friend Prince Sergey Urusov.

33. Gusev 4, 218.

34. Gusev 4, 217.

35. JE 63, 124.

36. Georgy Orekhanov, *V. G. Chertkov v zhizni L. N. Tolstogo*, Moscow, 2009, 17.

37. Orekhanov, *V. G. Chertkov v zhizni Tolstogo*, 25–27.

38. Alexander Fodor, *A Quest for a Non-Violent Russia: The Partnership of Leo Tolstoy and Vladimir Chertkov*, Lanham, Md, 1989, 44.

39. Orekhanov, *V. G. Chertkov v zhizni Tolstogo*, 26. Orekhanov claims that Chertkov met the 'pastor John Kenworthy', who was 'sympathetic to Tolstoy's views' during this period, but this is unlikely as Kenworthy (see ch. 12) was only sixteen in 1879.

40. Gusev 4, 224.

41. Orekhanov, *V. G. Chertkov v zhizni Tolstogo*, 25–26.

42. Fodor, *A Quest for a Non-Violent Russia*, 47.

43. Orekhanov, *V. G. Chertkov v zhizni Tolstogo*, 31.

44. Letter to S. A. Tolstaya, 29 January 1884; *Letopis'* 1, 8, 570.

45. Peter Brang, *Ein Unbekanntes Russland: Kulturgeshichte vegetarischer Lebensweisen von den Anfängen biz zur Gegenwart*, Cologne, 2002, 151–152.

46. Gusev 4, 249.

47. Gusev 4, 254.

48. Gusev 4, 256.

49. L. N. Tolstoy, *V chem moya vera*, in JE 23, 304–465.

50. N. Berdyaev, 'Vetkhii i Novyi Zavet v religioznom soznanii L. Tolstogo', *O religii L'va Tolstogo*, Moscow, 1912, reprinted in *Russkie mysliteli o L've Tolstom*, ed. V. I. Tolstoi, Tula, 2002, 366.

51. JE 63, 242. See also Henry Gifford, *Tolstoy*, Oxford, 1982, 46.

52. M. Arnold, 'Count Leo Tolstoi', *Fortnightly Review*, 48 (1887), 783–99, reprinted in *Tolstoi and Britain*, ed. W. Gareth Jones, Oxford, 1995, 105–124.

53. Gusev 4, 228.

54. JE 23, 368.

55. Gusev 4, 262–263.

56. Gusev 4, 270. Sonya omitted the latter, and most critical, part of this letter when quoting it later in her autobiography.

57. Gusev 4, 323.

58. Gusev 4, 325.

59. Gusev 4, 331.

60. Gusev 4, 333–334.

61. *Letopis'* 1, 583.

62. Vladimir Zhdanov, *Lyubov' v zhizni L. N. Tolstogo* (1928), Moscow, 2005, 243.

63. Gusev 4, 334.

64. Gusev 4, 337–338.

65. S. A. Tolstaya, 'Moya zhizn', *Novy mir*, 8 (1978), 62.

66. Tolstaya, *Pis'ma*, 158, 199.

67. Gusev 4, 351.

68. T. L. Sukhotina-Tolstaya, *Dnevnik*, ed. T. Volkova, Moscow, 1984, 10.

69. JE 83, 433, 437, 441, 446.

70. Fodor, *A Quest for a Non-Violent Russia*, 50.

71. Fodor, *A Quest for a Non-Violent Russia*, 52–53.

72. Fodor, *A Quest for a Non-Violent Russia*, 63.

73. Fodor, *A Quest for a Non-Violent Russia*, 57.

74. *Letopis'* 1, 601.

75. 'How Much Land Does a Man Need?', for example, was published in *Russian Wealth* in April 1886.

76. Gusev 4, 419.

77. Tolstaya, *Pis'ma*, 297.

78. *Letopis'* 1, 619.

79. *Letopis'* 1, 646, 670, 723.

80. Tolstoy, *What Then Must We Do?*, tr. Aylmer Maude, Oxford, 1935.

81. See T. L. Motyleva, *Khudozhestvennye proizvedeniya L. N. Tolstogo v perevodakh na inostrannye yazyki: otdel'nye zarubezhnye izdaniya: bibliografiia*, Moscow, 1961.

82. *Letopis'* 1, 595.

83. Gusev 4, 385.

84. *Letopis'* 1, 597.

85. JE 63, 338.

86. JE 63, 334.

87. See Andrew Donskov, *L. N. Tolstoi i T. M. Bondarev: perepiska*, Munich, 1996.

88. JE 25, 386. In 1958, the village of Iyudino, where Bondarev was exiled, was renamed Bondarevo, and a statue of him was erected in 2005. In 2008, the regional capital of Abakan hosted a conference entitled 'Lev Tolstoy and the Siberian peasant philosopher and lover of truth Timofey Bondarev'.

89. A. S. Skorokhodova, '"Russkii" religioznyi pozitivist V. Frei', *Sotsiologicheskie issledovaniya*, 9 (1997), 93–98.

90. S. A. Tolstaya, *Povarennaya kniga S. A. Tolstoi*, Tula, 1991, 45.

91. Tolstaya, *Povarennaya kniga*, 51.

92. *Letopis'* 1, 699.

93. *Letopis'* 1, 615.

94. Zhdanov, *Lyubov' v zhizn Tolstogo*, 258.

95. Zhdanov, *Lyubov' v zhizn Tolstogo*, 260.

96. Tolstaya, *Pis'ma*, 376.

97. JE 83, 576.

98. JE 85, 392–396; N. N. Gusev, *Letopis' zhizni i tvorchestva L'va Nikolaevicha Tolstogo, 1891–1910 [Letopis' 2]*, Moscow, 1960, 91.

99. L. D. Opul'skaya, *Materialy k biografii L. N. Tolstogo, 1886–1892*, Moscow, 1979 [Opul'skaya 1], 91.

100. S. A. Tolstaya, *Dnevniki v dvukh tomakh*, ed. V. E. Vatsuro et al., 2 vols, Moscow, 1978, vol. 1, 115.

101. Opul'skaya 1, 110; *Letopis' 2*, 713.

102. Opul'skaya 1, 27–28.

103. Opul'skaya 1, 62–63.

104. *Letopis' 2*, 659–661.

105. Opul'skaya 1, 117.

106. S. L. Tolstoi, 'Muzykal'nye proizvedeniya, lyubimye L. N. Tolstym (po vospominaniyam S. L. Tolstogo)', *Tolstovskii ezhegodnik*, St Petersburg, 1913, 161–162.

107. Tolstaya, *Dnevniki*, vol. 1, 121; Opul'skaya 1, 120–121.

108. Opul'skaya 1, 131–132.

109. Opul'skaya 1, 123.

110. Fodor, *A Quest for a Non-Violent Russia*, 57–58.

111. Nikitina, *Sof'ya Tolstaya*, 176.

112. A. N. Wilson (*Tolstoy*, London, 1988, 375) seems to confuse the religious principles of the Shakers with the ideas put forward by Stockham, who did not advocate complete celibacy, or that men and women should live platonically.

113. JE 63, 202.

114. JE 86, 188.

115. JE 63, 312.

116. See William Nickell, 'The Twain Shall Be of One Mind: Tolstoy in "Leag" with Eliza Burnz and Henry Parkhurst', *Tolstoy Studies Journal*, 6 (1993), 130.

117. 'Stockham on the Ethics of Marriage', *American Naturalist*, 30, 355 (1896), 569–570.

118. Opul'skaya 1, 175.

119. Opul'skaya 1, 173.

120. Opul'skaya 1, 182.

121. R. Bartlett, ed., *Chekhov: A Life in Letters*, tr. R. Bartlett and A. Phillips, London, 2004, 197–198.

122. Chekhov, *Polnoe sobranie sochinenii i pisem*, Pis'ma, vol. 4, 270.

123. See Fodor, *A Quest for a Non-Violent Russia*, 42.

124. See Tolstaya, *Dnevniki*, vol. 1, 168–179 for Sonya's detailed account of her visit.

125. Opul'skaya 1, 229.

126. *Letopis' 2*, 51.

127. Opul'skaya 1, 231.

128. *Letopis' 2*, 42.

129. Opul'skaya 1, 229.

130. William Stead, *The Truth About Russia*, London, 1888, 453.

131. www.attackingthedevil.co.uk/bio.php

132. Ewa M. Thompson, *Understanding Russia; The Holy Fool in Russian Culture*, Lanham, Md, 1987, 136–139.

133. See E. D. Meleshko, *Khristianskaya etika L. N. Tolstogo*, Moscow, 2006, 226–229.

134. Opul'skaya 1, 172.

135. Opul'skaya 1, 204.

136. Thompson, *Understanding Russia*, 127.

137. JE 85, 270.

138. JE 25, 717.

139. Opul'skaya 1, 238.

140. See Ronald D. LeBlanc, 'Tolstoy's Way of No Flesh: Abstinence, Vegetarianism, and Christian Physiology', *Food in Russian History and Culture*, ed. Musya Glants and Joyce Toomre, Bloomington, 1997, 87.

141. Tolstoy, 'The First Step', *Essays and Letters*, tr. Aylmer Maude, New York, 1909, pp. 82–91.

142. See, for example, Eric Schlosser, *Fast Food Nation* (New York, 2001) and Jonathan Safran Foer, *Eating Animals* (New York, 2009).

143. Letter to Georgy Chekhov, December 1890, in Bartlett, *Chekhov: A Life in Letters*, 257.

144. Letter to Evgraf Egorov, 11 December 1891, in Bartlett, *Chekhov: A Life in Letters*, 289.

145. *Letopis'* 2, 34.

146. Tolstaya, 'Moya zhizn", *Novy mir*, 80; Opul'skaya 1, 256.

147. Tolstaya, 'Moya zhizn", *Novy mir*, 192.

148. *Letopis'* 2, 52.

149. Tolstaya, 'Moya zhizn", *Novy mir*, 84–5.

150. *Autobiography of Countess Sophie Tolstoi*, 62.

151. Tolstaya, 'Moya zhizn", *Novy mir*, 86.

152. *Letopis'* 2, 61, 63.

153. Opul'skaya 1, 251.

154. R. Vittaker, 'Posleslovie', in I. Borisova, ed., *Neizvestnyi Tolstoi v arkhivakh Rossii i SShA*, Moscow, 1994, 240.

155. *Letopis'* 2, 61.

156. See Ewa M. Thompson, 'Holy Foolishness, Mental Illness and Mental Normalcy in Russia', in *Understanding Russia*, 25–50.

157. Jonas Stadling, 'With Tolstoy in the Russian Famine', *The Century*, 2 (June 1893), 249.

158. Tolstaya, 'Moya zhizn", *Novy mir*, 98.

159. Opul'skaya 1, 252–254.

160. Tolstaya, 'Moya zhizn", *Novy mir*, 98.

161. *Letopis'* 2, 70.

162. Opul'skaya 1, 257.

163. Tolstaya, 'Moya zhizn", *Novy mir*, 99–100.

164. Jonas Stadling and Will Reason, *In the Land of Tolstoi: Experiences of Famine and Misrule in Russia*, London, 1897.

165. Opul'skaya 1, 267.

166. Robert Edwards, 'Tolstoy and Alice B. Stockham: The Influence of "Tokology" on *The Kreutzer Sonata*', *Tolstoy Studies Journal*, 6 (1993), 90.

167. Opul'skaya 1, 164.

168. K. Kallaur, 'L. N. Tolstoi i Edin Ballu: dukhovnoe rodstvo', in Borisova, ed., *Neizvestnyi Tolstoi v arkivakh Rossii i SShA*, 276.

169. Stadling and Reason, *In the Land of Tolstoi*, 71.

170. Opul'skaya 1, 212–213.

171. *Letopis'* 2, 83.

172. JE 68, 235–236.

173. L. D. Opul'skaya, *Lev Nikolaevich Tolstoi: materialy k biografii s 1892 po 1899 god* [Opul'skaya 2], 45.

174. Opul'skaya 2, 44–47.

175. *Letopis'* 2, 149.

12 Elder, Apostate and Tsar

1. V. Bulgakov, *L. N. Tolstoi v poslednii god ego zhizni*, Moscow, 1989, 71–72.

2. Roza Lyuksemburg, 'Lev Tolstoi', *O Tolstom*, ed. V. Friche, Moscow, 1928, 125. First published in *Die Gleichheit*, 3 December 1910.

3. T. V. Komarova, ed., *Druz'ya i gosti Yasnoi Polyane: materialy nauchnoi konferentsee posvyashchennoi 160-letiyu S. A. Tolstoi*, Tula, 2006, 104.

4. W. T. Stead, *The Truth About Russia*, London, 1888, 393.

5. The book was published in 1889. See *Literaturnoe nasledstvo*, 75 (1965), vol. 1, 123.

6. Eugène-Melchior de Vogüé, *Le Roman russe*, Paris, 1886.

7. 'T. W. H.', 'The Russian School of Writers', *Harper's Bazaar*, 20, 38 (1887), 642.

8. R. Löwenfeld, *Leo N. Tolstoj. Sein Leben, seine Werke, seine Weltanschauung*, Berlin, 1892; Evgeny Solov'ev, *L. N. Tolstoi, ego zhizn' i literaturnaya deyatel'nost'. Biograficheskii ocherk*, St Petersburg, 1894.

9. George Kennan, 'A Visit to Count Tolstoy', *The Century*, 34 (1887), 252–265; reprinted in *Americans in Conversation with Tolstoy: Selected Accounts, 1887–1923*, ed. Peter Sekirin, Jefferson, NC, 2006. This often valuable book is seriously undermined by its title. Apart from the obvious problem with the dates (Tolstoy died in 1910), many of the conversations are with people are who clearly not American, including Aylmer Maude, whose first name is misspelled 'Aymler' throughout.

10. Darra Goldstein, 'Is Hay Only for Horses? Highlights of Russian Vegetarianism at the Turn of the Century', *Food in Russian History and Culture*, ed. Musya Glants and Joyce Toomre, Bloomington, 1997, 103–123.

11. S. A. Tolstaya, *Dnevniki v dvukh tomakh*, ed. V. E. Vatsuro et al., 2 vols, Moscow, 1978, vol. 1, 122.

12. Tolstaya, *Dnevniki*, vol. 1, 224.

13. E. E. Gorbunova-Posadova, *Drug Tolstogo Mariya Aleksandrovna Shmidt*, Moscow, 1929, 13.

14. Tolstaya, *Dnevniki*, vol. 1, 245.

15. Gorbunova-Posadova, *Drug Tolstogo Mariya Aleksandrovna Shmidt*, 73.

16. L. D. Opul'skaya, *Lev Nikolaevich Tolstoi: materialy k biografii s 1892 po 1899 god* [Opul'skaya 2], 11.

17. Graham Camfield, 'From Tolstoyan to Terrorist: The Revolutionary Career of Prince D. A. Khilkov, 1900–1905', *Revolutionary Russia*, 12, 1 (1999), 2–3.

18. Aylmer Maude, *The Life of Tolstoy* (rev. edn, Oxford, 1930), Ware, 2008, 626.

19. N. N. Gusev, *Letopis' zhizni i tvorchestva L'va Nikolaevicha Tolstogo, 1891–1910* [*Letopis'* 2], Moscow, 1960, 683.

20. *Letopisi Gosudarstvennogo literaturnogo muzeya*, vol. 12: *L. N. Tolstoi*, vol. 1, Moscow, 1938, 114.

21. V. A. Mazur, 'Khozhdenie po mukam knyazya Dmitriya Aleksandrovicha Khilkova', *Izvestiya Ural'skogo gosudarstvennogo universiteta*, 15 (2000); http://proceedings.usu.ru/?base=mag/0015(03_08–2000)&xsln=showArticle.xslt&id=a07&doc=../content.jsp

22. *Letopis'* 2, 111.

23. *Letopis'* 2, 155.

24. E. Popov, *Zhizn' i smert' Evdokima Nikiticha Drozhzhina, 1866–1894*, Berlin, 1895.

25. Opul'skaya 2, 66–67.

26. Lao Tzu, *Tao Te Ching: A Book About the Way and the Power of the Way*, a new English version by Ursula K. Le Guin, with the collaboration of J. P. Seaton, Boston, 1998, 68.

27. See, for example, N. Berdyaev, 'Vetkhii i novii zavet v religioznom soznanii L. Tolstogo', *O religii L'va Tolstogo*, Moscow, 1912, 172–195.

28. M. V. Muratov, *L. N. Tolstoi i V. G. Chertkov*, Moscow, 1934, 231.

29. For further details, see Andrew Donskov, ed., *Sergej Tolstoy and the Doukhobors: A Journey to Canada*, Ottawa, 1998, 3–8.

30. See Andrew Donskov, ed., *Leo Tolstoy-Peter Verigin: Correspondence*, tr. John Woodsworth, Ottawa, 1995.

31. Tolstaya, *Dnevniki*, vol. 1, 245.

32. Tolstaya, *Dnevniki*, vol. 1, 227, 229.

33. Leah Bendavid-Val, *Song Without Words: The Photographs and Diaries of Countess Sophia Tolstoy*, Washington DC, 2007, 78.

34. Tolstaya, *Dnevniki*, vol. 1, 236.

35. Opul'skaya 2, 135.

36. Vladimir Zhdanov, *Lyubov' v zhizni L. N. Tolstogo* (1928), Moscow, 2005, 200.

37. Opul'skaya 2, 139.

38. Komarova, *Druz'ya i gosti*, 173.

39. *Letopis'* 2, 173.

40. *Letopis'* 2, 177.

41. T. Polyakova, 'Velosiped No. 97011', *Prometei*, 12 (1980), 415–418.

42. Opul'skaya 2, 189.

43. N. Nikitina, *Sof'ya Tolstaya*, Moscow, 2010, 201.

44. See Ul'rikh Lina, *Opasnyi yazyk*, Moscow, 1998.

45. L. L. Sabaneev, 'Moi vospominaniya o S. I. Taneeve', *Sergei Ivanovich Taneev: lichnost', tvorchestvo i dokumenty ego zhizni: k 10-ti letiyu so dnya ego smerti, 1915–1925*, Moscow, 1925, 101.

46. L. L. Sabaneev, *S. I. Taneev: Mysli o tvorchestve i vospominaniya o zhizni*, Paris, 1930, 121–122.

47. See Tolstoy's diary entry, November 1851 (JE 46, 237): 'I have never been in love with a woman – I felt one strong feeling similar to love when I was 13 or 14; but I don't want to believe that this was love; because the object was a fat maid (although she did have a pretty little face), and from 13–15 years is the most disorganised time for a boy (adolescence); you don't know what to throw yourself at, and lust, at that time acts with extraordinary force. I have often fallen in love with men … I fell in love with men before I had any idea about the possibility of pederasty, but when I did, the idea of the possibility of coitus never entered my head …'

48. See Alexander Fodor, *A Quest for a Non-Violent Russia: the Partnership of Leo Tolstoy and Vladimir Chertkov*, Lanham, Md, 1989, 146–147.

49. Opul'skaya 2, 92.

50. JE 67, 62.

51. M. J. de K. Holman, 'The Purleigh Colony: Tolstoyan Togetherness in the Late 1890s', in *Tolstoi and Britain*, ed. W. Gareth Jones, Oxford, 1995, 155.

52. A. G. Rose, 'Some Influences on English Penal Reform, 1895–1921', in *Tolstoi and Britain*, 262.

53. See Peter Brock, tr. and ed., *Life in an Austro-Hungarian Military Prison: the Slovak Tolstoyan Dr. Albert Škarvan's Story*, Syracuse, 2002.

54. www.kirjasto.sci.fi/arvidj.htm

55. JE 68, 23.

56. Muratov, *L. N. Tolstoi i V. G. Chertkov*, 232.

57. Opul'skaya 2, 155–156.

58. Georgy Orekhanov, *V. G. Chertkov v zhizni L. N. Tolstogo*, Moscow, 2009, 43.

59. Opul'skaya 2, 199–200.

60. Apostolov, *Tolstoi i russkoe samoderzhavie*, Moscow, 1928, 125–126.

61. Orekhanov, *V. G. Chertkov v zhizni L. N. Tolstogo*, 31.

62. Opul'skaya 2, 234; Fodor, *A Quest for a Non-Violent Russia*, 88–89.

63. See Fodor, *A Quest for a Non-Violent Russia*, 67–68.

64. T. L. Sukhotina-Tolstaya, *Dnevnik*, ed. T. Volkova, Moscow, 1984, 163.

65. Sukhotina-Tolstaya, *Dnevnik*, 132.

66. Fodor, *A Quest for a Non-Violent Russia*, 67.

67. Sukhotina-Tolstaya, *Dnevnik*, 300.

68. Muratov, *L. N. Tolstoi i V. G. Chertkov*, 248.

69. S. M. Tolstoi, *Deti Tolstogo*, Tula, 1993, 77.

70. Tolstoi, *Deti Tolstogo*, 175.

71. N. A. Kalinina et al., *Perepiska L. N. Tolstogo s sestroi i brat'yami*, Moscow, 1990, 419, 431.

72. Opul'skaya 2, 252.

73. Tolstoy, *What is Art?*, tr. A. Maude, ed. W. Gareth Jones, Bristol, 1994, 184.

74. Opul'skaya 2, 158.

75. See Gary Adelman, *Anna Karenina: The Bitterness of Ecstasy*, Boston, 1990, 124–125.

76. A. B. Gol'denveizer, 'Tolstoi i muzyka: iz vospominanii', *Literaturnoe nasledstvo*, 37/38, (1939), vol. 2, 591–594.

77. Gol'denveizer, 'Tolstoi i muzyka: iz vospominanii', 591–594.

78. S. L. Tolstoi, 'Muzykal'nye proizvedeniya, lyubimye L. N. Tolstym (po vospominaniyam S. L. Tolstogo)', *Tolstovskii ezhegodnik*, St Petersburg, 1913, 161–162.

79. Alexandra Orlova, *Tchaikovsky: A Self Portrait*, tr. R. M. Davison, Oxford, 1990, 62.

80. Orlova, *Tchaikovsky: A Self Portrait*, 253.

81. S. A. Tolstaya, 'Moya zhizn'', *Prometei*, 12 (1980), 191.

82. See R. Bartlett, *Wagner and Russia*, Cambridge, 1995, 48.

83. 'The Theology of Redemptive Love' is the sub-title of a chapter in Richard F. Gustafson's *Leo Tolstoy: Resident and Stranger*, which should be consulted for an in-depth discussion of this topic. For a brief overview of the importance of redemption in Wagner's works, see Robert Donington, 'The Search for Redemption in Wagner', *Musical Times*, vol. 130, no. 1751 (Jan. 1989), 20–22.

84. Thomas Mann, 'The Sorrows and Grandeur of Richard Wagner', April 1933, in *Pro and Contra Wagner*, tr. Allan Blunden, introd. Erich Heller, London, 1985, 94.

85. Maude, *The Life of Tolstoy*, 757; Muratov, *L. N. Tolstoi i V. G. Chertkov*, 257–266.

86. See Tolstoy, *What is Art?*, v, x.

87. *Letopis'* 2, 268, 270.

88. Opul'skaya 2, 248–250.

89. N. Puzin, *Dom-muzei L. N. Tolstogo v Yasnoi Polyane*, Tula, 2001, 67.

90. Opul'skaya 2, 318.

91. Fodor, *A Quest for a Non-Violent Russia*, 98.

92. *Letopis'* 2, 263.

93. L. Tolstoi, *Voskresen'e: roman v trekh chastyakh: polnaya neiskazhennaya tsensur'yu versiya*, 5th edn, Purleigh, 1900.

94. Orekhanov, *V. G. Chertkov v zhizni L. N. Tolstogo*, 48.

95. Fodor, *A Quest for a Non-Violent Russia*, 136.

96. Fodor, *A Quest for a Non-Violent Russia*, 91.

97. Holman, 'The Purleigh Colony', 173.

98. S. L. Tolstoi, *Ocherki Bylogo*, 3rd rev. edn, Tula, 1965, 197–218.

99. *Letopis'* 2, 306.

100. Opul'skaya 2, 326.

101. R. Bartlett, ed., *Anton Chekhov: A Life in Letters*, tr. R. Bartlett and A. Phillips, London, 2004, 366.

102. Bartlett, *Anton Chekhov: A Life in Letters*, 434.

103. Bartlett, *Anton Chekhov: A Life in Letters*, 434.

104. Tolstoy, *Resurrection*, tr. Louise Maude, Oxford World's Classics edn, New York, 2000, 147.

105. See Gregory L. Freeze, *The Parish Clergy in Nineteenth-Century Russia: Crisis, Reform, Counter-Reform*, Princeton, 1983.

106. Anton Chekhov, *The Exclamation Mark*, tr. Rosamund Bartlett, London, 2008, 56.

107. I. S. Belliustin, *Description of the Clergy in Rural Russia: The Memoir of a Nineteenth-Century Parish Priest*, tr. with an interpretive essay by Gregory L. Freeze, Ithaca, 1985.

108. See Chris J. Chulos, 'Russian Piety and Culture from Peter the Great to 1917', *Cambridge History of Christianity*, vol. 5: *Eastern Christianity*, ed. Michael Angold, Cambridge, 2006, 348–70.

109. See Leonid Heretz, *Russia on the Eve of Modernity: Popular Religion and Traditional Culture Under the Last Tsars*, Cambridge, 2008, 39.

110. See Simon Dixon, 'Superstition in Imperial Russia', *Past and Present*, 3 (2008), 207–228.

111. Chulos, 'Russian Piety and Culture from Peter the Great to 1917', 360.

112. V. Fedorov, *Russkaya pravoslavnaya tserkov' i gosudarstvo: sinodal'nyi period, 1700–1917*, Moscow, 2003, 228.

113. S. Mel'gunov, *Tserkov' i gosudarstvo v Rossii: k voprosu o svobode sovesti*, Moscow, 1907, 136.

114. I. M. Gromoglasov, *Tretii vserossiiskii missionerskii s'ezd*, Sergiev Posad, 1898, 4.

115. See John Shelton Curtiss, *Church and State in Russia: The Last Years of the Empire, 1900–1917*, New York, 1940, 76, regarding the 235 pages of sermons given by Archbishop Nikanor of Kherson.

116. Hermann von Samson-Himmelstierna, *Russia under Alexander III*, tr. J. Morrison, ed. Felix Volkhovsky, London, 1893.

117. Pål Kolstø, 'The Demonized Double: The Image of Lev Tolstoi in Russian Orthodox Polemics', *Slavic Review*, 65, 2 (2006), 310.

118. Curtiss, *Church and State in Russia*, 41.

119. Curtiss, *Church and State in Russia*, 87.

120. J. G. Kohl, *Russia*, London, 1842, 256–257.

121. See Georgy Orekhanov, 'Poslednyaya ispoved' L'va Tolstogo', *Sovetskaya rossiya*; www.samara.orthodoxy.ru/Smi/Npg/053_10.html

122. JE 73, 44–45.

123. V. I. Sreznevskii, *Tolstoi: Pamyatniki tvorchestva i zhizni*, vol. 3, Moscow, 1923, 124, 131.

124. Apostolov, *L. Tolstoi i russkoe samoderzhavie*, 147.

125. *Letopis'* 2, 376.

126. Sreznevskii, *Tolstoi: Pamyatniki tvorchestva i zhizni*, vol. 3, 114.

127. See Heretz, *Russia on the Eve of Modernity*, 143.

128. Diakon Filipp Il'iashenko, 'L. N. Tolstoi i svyatoi pravednyi Ioann Kronshtadtskii: nekotorye aspekty vospryatiya konflikta sovremmenikami', *Yasnopolyanskii sbornik*, ed. V. I. Tolstoy et al, Tula, 2008, 343.

129. Nadieszda Kizenko, *A Prodigal Saint: Father John of Kronstadt and the Russian People*, University Park, 2000, 250.

130. Kizenko, *A Prodigal Saint*, 259.

131. Kizenko, *A Prodigal Saint*, 25, 35.

132. N. Kizenko, 'Ioann of Kronstadt and the Reception of Sanctity', *Russian Review*, 57 (July 1998), 338.

133. J. Eugene Clay, 'Orthodox Missionaries and "Orthodox Heretics" in Russia, 1886–1917', in *Of Religion and Empire: Missions, Conversion, and Tolerance in Tsarist Russia*, ed. Robert P. Geraci and Michael Khodarkovsky, Ithaca, 2001, 55.

134. Kizenko, *A Prodigal Saint*, 258.

135. See Pål Kolstø, 'The Elder at Iasnaia Poliana: Lev Tolstoi and the Orthodox *Starets* Tradition', *Kritika*, 9, 3 (2008), 533–554.

136. Religious-Philosophical Society, third meeting, 'Lev Tolstoi i russkaya tserkov'', in *Zapiski peterburgskikh Religiozno-filosofskikh sobranii (1901–1903)*, ed. S. M. Polovinkin, Moscow, 2005, 45–70.

137. *Letopis'* 2, 382.

138. Kalinina et al., *Perepiska*, 438.

139. JE 69, 84.

140. Kalinina et al., *Perepiska*, 442–443.

141. Orekhanov, *V. G. Chertkov v zhizni L. N. Tolstogo*, 53.

142. JE 73, 184–187.

143. Orekhanov, *V. G. Chertkov v zhizni L. N. Tolstogo*, 55.

144. *Letopis'* 2, 407–410.

145. www.nonresistance.org/tolstoy.html

146. http://pravlib.narod.ru/ioann_kronchtadt_otvet_lvu_tolstomu.html

147. Robert L. Nichols, 'The Friends of God: Nicholas II and Alexandra at the Canonization of Serafim of Sarov, July 1903', in *Religious and Secular Forces in Late Tsarist Russia*, ed. Charles E. Timberlake, Seattle, 1992, 206–230.

148. JE 55, 111.

149. *Letopis'* 2, 477.

150. Tolstoy, 'Bethink Yourselves!', tr. V. Tchertkoff and I. F. M. London, 1906, p. 27.

151. Tolstoi, 'Bethink Yourselves!', 8.

152. Muratov, *L. N. Tolstoi i V. G. Chertkov*, 326.

153. JE 74, 264.

154. Kalinina et al., *Perepiska*, 501.

155. See R. Bartlett, 'Japonisme and Japanophobia: The Russo-Japanese War in Russian Cultural Consciousness', *Russian Review*, 1 (2008), 1–38.

156. *Letopis'* 2, 503.

157. Fodor, *A Quest for a Non-Violent Russia*, 111.

158. Muratov, *L. N. Tolstoi i V. G. Chertkov*, 336.

159. *Letopis'* 2, 496–497.

160. Fodor, *A Quest for a Non-Violent Russia*, 141.

161. Fodor, *A Quest for a Non-Violent Russia*, 119.

162. *The Autobiography of Countess Sophie Tolstoi*, preface and notes by Vasilii Spiridonov, tr. S. S. Koteliansky and Leonard Woolf, Richmond, 1922, 67.

163. See Leah Bendavid-Val, *Songs Without Words: The Photographs and Diaries of Countess Sophia Tolstoy*, Washington DC, 2007.

164. All information about the visit is taken from Laurence Kominz, 'Pilgrimage to Tolstoy: Tokutomi Roka's Junrei Kiko', *Monumenta Japonica*, 41, 1 (1986), 51–101.

165. *Letopis'* 2, 559.

166. Nikitina, *Sof'ya Tolstaya*, 224–226.

167. *Letopis'* 2, 596.

168. Orekhanov, *V. G. Chertkov v zhizni L. N. Tolstogo*, 53; Puzin, *Dom-muzei*, 76; Muratov, *L. N. Tolstoi i V. G. Chertkov*, 365.

169. T. N. Volkova, *Tolstoi i ego blizkie*, Moscow, 1986, 262.

170. Fodor, *A Quest for a Non-Violent Russia*, 165.

171. See Joy Thacker, *Whiteway Colony: The Social History of a Tolstoyan Community*, Stroud, 1993.

172. W. Gareth Jones, ed., *Tolstoi and Britain*, 14.

173. Orekhanov, *V. G. Chertkov v zhizni L. N. Tolstogo*, 64.

174. Fodor, *A Quest for a Non-Violent Russia*, 95–96.

175. *Letopis'* 2, 635.

176. N. V. Ovsyannikov, 'Epizod iz zhizni L. N. Tolstogo', *Russkoe obozrenie*, 11 (1896).

177. Walter Kerr, *The Shabunin Affair: An Episode in the Life of Leo Tolstoy*, Ithaca, 1982, 182.

178. Father Ioann was canonised in 1990.

179. *Letopis'* 2, 644; Tolstaya, *Dnevniki*, vol 2, 109.

180. I. V. Petrovitskaya, "Tolstovskii s'ezd russkikh zhurnalistov. 1908 god', *Iz istorii russkoi literatury i zhurnalistiki: Ezhgodnik*, ed. I. V. Petrovitskaya and I. E. Prokhorov, Moscow, 2009, 243–245.

181. Tolstaya, *Dnevniki*, vol. 2, 110.

182. *Letopis'* 2, 700.

183. Opul'skaya 2, 261.

184. *Letopis'* 2, 701.

185. *Letopis'* 2, 705.

186. V. Bulgakov, *O Tolstom*, Tula, 1964, 283.

187. The above account of Tolstoy's departure from Yasnaya Polyana, death and burial draws on V. I. Nevskii, ed., *Smert' Tolstogo: po novym materialam*, Moscow, 1929, B. Meilakh, *Ukhod i smert' L'va Tolstogo*, Moscow, 1960, Uil'yam Nikell, 'Smert' Tolstogo', *Novoe literaturnoe obozrenie*, 44 (2000), 43–61, Pål Kolstø, 'Mass for a

Heretic? The Controversy over Lev Tolstoi's Burial', *Slavic Review*, 60, 1 (2001), 75–95, and *William Nickell*, 'Transfigurations of Tolstoy's Final Journey: The Church and the Media in 1910', *Tolstoy Studies Journal*, 17 (2006), 32–51.

Epilogue: Patriarch of the Bolsheviks

1. Mark Popovsky, *Russkie muzhiki rasskazyvayut: posledovateli L. N. Tolstogo v Sovetskom Soyuze*, London, 1983.
2. S. A. Tolstaya, *Dnevniki v dvukh tomakh*, ed. V. E. Vatsuro et al., 2 vols, Moscow, 1978, vol. 2, 330.
3. Aleksei Zverev and Vladimir Tunimanov, *Lev Tolstoi*, Moscow, 2007, 758.
4. N. Nikitina, *Sof'ya Tolstaya*, Moscow, 2010, 239.
5. Herman Bernstein, 'The Scandal Surrounding the Tolstoy Legacy', *New York Times*, 26 February 1911.
6. Nikitina, *Sof'ya Tolstaya*, 245.
7. Nikitina, *Sof'ya Tolstaya*, 240.
8. Tolstaya, *Dnevniki*, vol. 2, 355.
9. Zverev and Tunimanov, *Tolstoi*, 756.
10. Nikitina, *Sof'ya Tolstaya*, 241.
11. Nikitina, *Sof'ya Tolstaya*, 241.
12. V. F. Bulgakov, *O Tolstom*, Tula 1964, 233.
13. Bulgakov, *O Tolstom*, 234–240.
14. Tolstaya, *Dnevniki*, vol. 2, 383. See also Pål Kolstø, 'A Mass for a Heretic? The Controversy over Lev Tolstoi's Burial', *Slavic Review*, 60, 1 (2001), 75–95.
15. Nikitina, *Sof'ya Tolstaya*, 245.
16. Nikitina, *Sof'ya Tolstaya*, 243.
17. Bulgakov, *O Tolstom*, 314.
18. Alexander Fodor, *A Quest for a Non-Violent Russia: The Partnership of Leo Tolstoy and Vladimir Chertkov*, Lanham, Md, 1989, 175.
19. Fodor, *A Quest for a Non-Violent Russia*, 157.
20. Lev Osterman, *Srazhenie za Tolstogo*, Moscow, 2002.
21. V. Tchertkoff [Chertkov], *Save Russia*, London, 1920.
22. Fodor, *A Quest for a Non-Violent Russia*, 162.
23. Tolstaya, *Dnevniki*, vol. 2, 593.
24. Fodor, *A Quest for a Non-Violent Russia*, 163.
25. *Memoirs of Peasant Tolstoyans in Soviet Russia*, tr., ed. and intro. William Edgerton, Bloomington, 1993, 11.
26. Tchertkoff, *Save Russia*, 2.
27. A. Khechinov, *Krutye dorogi Aleksandry Tolstoi*, Moscow, 1995, 206.
28. Tolstaya, *Dnevniki*, vol. 2, 591.
29. Fodor, *A Quest for a Non-Violent Russia*, 167.
30. Popovsky, *Russkie muzhiki rasskazyvayut*, 56.

31. N. Berdyaev, 'Dukhi russkoi revolyutsii', *Iz glubiny*, Paris, 1918; D. Merezhkovskii, 'L. Tolstoi i bol'shevizm', *Tsarstvo antikhrista*, Paris, 1923.

32. Y. Lur'e, *Posle L'va Tolstogo*, St Petersburg, 1993, 70.

33. 'Literary Progenitors of Bolshevist Russia', *Current Opinion*, 66, 1 (January 1919), 49.

34. Robert Croskey, *The Legacy of Tolstoy: Alexandra Tolstoy and the Soviet Regime in the 1920s*, Seattle, 2008, 11.

35. Tolstaya, *Dnevniki*, vol. 2, 594.

36. Fodor, *A Quest for a Non-Violent Russia*, 175.

37. L. A. Osterman, *Srazhenie za Tolstogo*, Moscow, 2002, 8.

38. V. Shentalinsky, *Donos na Sokrata*, *Novy mir*, 11 (1996); reprinted in *Donos na Sokrata*,, Moscow, 2001, 34–5.

39. www.tolstoymuseum.ru/history/

40. A. Tolstaya, *Probleski v t'me*, Washington DC, 1965, 30–31.

41. S. L. Tolstoi, *Ocherki bylogo*, 3rd rev. edn, Tula, 1965, 270.

42. Shentalinsky, *Donos na sokrata*, 38.

43. Croskey, *The Legacy of Tolstoy*, 26.

44. Lur'e, *Posle L'va Tolstogo*, 36, 479–480, 487–488, 667.

45. Tolstaya, *Probleski v t'me*; Lur'e, *Posle L'va Tolstogo*, 90.

46. Shentalinsky, *Donos na sokrata*, 51.

47. Yury Khechinov, *Krutye dorogi Aleksandry Tolstoi*, Moscow, 1995, 252.

48. Croskey, *The Legacy of Tolstoy*, 13.

49. Khechinov, *Krutye dorogi Aleksandry Tolstoi*, 253.

50. Tolstaya, *Probleski v t'me*, 121.

51. Fodor, *A Quest for a Non-Violent Russia*, 168.

52. Tchertkoff, *Save Russia*, 5.

53. Popovsky, *Russkie muzhiki rasskazyvayut*, 64.

54. Popovsky, *Russkie muzhiki rasskazyvayut*, 60–61.

55. Lur'e, *Posle L'va Tolstogo*, 72.

56. Osterman, *Srazhenie za Tolstogo*, 10.

57. Lur'e, *Posle L'va Tolstogo*, 95.

58. Fodor, *A Quest for a Non-Violent Russia*, 171.

59. Osterman, *Srazhenie za Tolstogo*, 10.

60. Fodor, *A Quest for a Non-Violent Russia*, 181.

61. Osterman, *Srazhenie za Tolstogo*, 12.

62. Fodor, *A Quest for a Non-Violent Russia*, 178.

63. L. Tolstoi, *Pravda o moem otse*, Prague, 1923.

64. Tolstaya, *Probleski v t'me*, 131.

65. Tolstaya, *Probleski v t'me*, 135–136; Croskey, *The Legacy of Tolstoy*, 37.

66. Shentalinsky, *Donos na Sokrata*, 54–5.

67. Lur'e, *Posle L'va Tolstogo*, 90.

68. Charles Sarolea, 'Was Tolstoy the Spiritual Father of Bolshevism?', *English Review*, January 1925, 156.

69. See, for example, V. A. Maklakov, *Tolstoi i Bol'shevizm*, Paris, 1921.

70. A. Lunacharskii, 'Tolstoi i Marks', *Sobranie sochinenii v vos'mi tomakh*, vol. 1, Moscow, 1963, 290.

71. Tolstaya, *Probleski v t'me*, 207.

72. Tolstaya, *Probleski v t'me*, 206.

73. Tolstaya, *Probleski v t'me*, 160.

74. Tolstaya, *Probleski v t'me*, 164, 183.

75. Tolstaya, *Probleski v t'me*, 208.

76. Croskey, *The Legacy of Tolstoy*, 64.

77. Osterman, *Srazhenie za Tolstogo*, 14.

78. Fodor, *A Quest for a Non-Violent Russia*.

79. William Nickell, 'Tolstoi in 1928: In the Mirror of the Revolution', in *Epic Revisionism: Russian History and Literature as Stalinist Propaganda*, ed. Kevin M. F. Platt and David Brandenberger, Madison, 2006, 17–18.

80. A. V. Lunacharskii, 'Tolstoi i nasha sovremennost'', – *Literaturnoe nasledstvo*, 69 (1961), vol. 2, 407.

81. D. A. Bondarev, *Tolstoi i sovremennost'*, Moscow, 1928, 6–7.

82. Stefan Zweig, *The World of Yesterday: An Autobiography*, English translation of *Die Welt vom Gestern* (1943), London, 1987, 252.

83. Tolstaya, *Probleski v t'me*, 214.

84. Zweig, *The World of Yesterday* (1943 edn), 253.

85. Tolstaya, *Probleski v t'me*, 217.

86. Alexander Fodor, *Tolstoy and the Russians: Reflections on a Relationship*, Ann Arbor, 1984, 71. Fodor observes how close the style of the editorial is to that of Stalin.

87. See V. M. Friche, ed., *L. N. Tolstoi v svete marksistskoi kritiki*, Moscow, 1929. See also V. M. Friche, ed., *O Tolstom: literaturno-kriticheskii sbornik*, Moscow, 1928.

88. Table of contents, Bondarev, *Tolstoi i sovremennost'*.

89. Tolstaya, *Probleski v t'me*, 235.

90. Osterman, *Srazhenie za Tolstogo*, 32–3.

91. Fodor, *A Quest for a Non-Violent Russia*, 183.

92. Osterman, *Srazhenie za Tolstogo*, 32–33.

93. Innessa Medzhibovskaya, 'Every Man in His Tolstoy Humor: On Lev Osterman, Questions of Method and More', *Tolstoy Studies Journal*, 19, 2007, 111–112.

94. See Fodor, *A Quest for a Non-Violent Russia*, 188.

95. N. Rodionov, 'Istoriya i organizatsiya [yubileinogo sobraniya sochinenii L. N. Tolstogo]', *Literaturnoe nasledstvo*, 69, vol. 2, 429.

96. Fodor, *Tolstoy and the Russians*, 11–12.

97. I. I. Mints and S. A. Tolstaya-Esenina, *Yasnaya Polyana: Stat'i i dokumenty*, Moscow, 1942, 173.

98. Al'bert Opul'skii, *Vokrug imeni L'va Tolstogo*, San Francisco, 1981, 120.

99. V. A. Zhdanov, 'Yasnaya Polyana v pervye gody revolyutsii (1917–1919)', *Yasnopolyanskii sbornik*, Tula, 1962, 23.

100. I. V. Tolstoi, *Svet Yasnoi Polyany*, Moscow, 1986.

101. Popovsky, *Russkie muzhiki rasskazyvayut*, 15.

102. Popovsky, *Russkie muzhiki rasskazyvayut*, 18.

103. Popovsky, *Russkie muzhiki rasskazyvayut*, 22.

104. Papkov, 'Zalozhniki sovesti (Tolstovtsy na Solovkakh)', in *Vozvrashchenie pamyati: istoriko-publitsisticheskii al'manakh*, vol. 3, Novosibirsk, 1997, 178–180.

105. Popovsky, *Russkie muzhiki rasskazyvayut*, 105, 111, 123, 127.

106. Popovsky, *Russkie muzhiki rasskazyvayut*, 129, 133–134, 222.

107. Popovsky, *Russkie muzhiki rasskazyvayut*, 176–177.

108. Popovsky, *Russkie muzhiki rasskazyvayut*, 278.

109. Popovsky, *Russkie muzhiki rasskazyvayut*, 282, 283.

110. Popovsky, *Russkie muzhiki rasskazyvayut*, 286–290.

111. Popovsky, *Russkie muzhiki rasskazyvayut*, 291–292; A. Klibanov, *Iz mira religioznogo sektantstva: vstrechi, besedy, nablyuzdeniya*, Moscow, 1974.

112. Popovsky, *Russkie muzhiki rasskazyvayut*, 304.

113. V. Lakshin, 'Vozvrashchenie Tolstogo-myslitelya', *Voprosy literatury*, 5 (1988), 104–117.

114. B. Mazurin, 'O kommune 'Zhizn' i trud'', *Novy mir*, 9 (1988), 180–226.

115. http://tolstoy-school.ru/

116. Ol'ga Bugrova, 'Vitaly Remizov: "Ya sluzhu Tolstomu vsyu zhizn"', *Golos Rossii*, 14 December 2009; http://rus.ruvr.ru/2009/12/14/3021120.html

117. Elena Novoselova, 'Obrazovanie. Ne plyuite na mertvogo l'va', *Rossiiskaya gazeta*, 22 November 2005; www.rg.ru/2005/11/22/shkola.html

118. S. A. Skiba, 'Sovremennoe Tolstovstvo (Tserkov' L'va Tolstogo)', *Vestnik Moskovskogo universiteta*, seriya 7: *Filosofiya*, 5 (1998), 65–73.

119. http://unity.org/aboutunity/visionMissionValues/index.html

120. www.imli.ru/tolstoy/sherbakova.php

121. Pavel Basinskii, 'Vernut' nel'zya pomilovat': Sto pyat let nazad L'va Tolstogo otluchili ot pravoslavnoi tservki', 3 March 2006. See also the proceedings of the conference in *Yasnopolyanskii sbornik*, Tula, 2008.

122. A. Kostryukov, 'Pervyi den' raboty sektsii "Aktual'nye problemy istorii Russkoi Pravoslavnoi Tserkvi v XX veke"', http://pstgu.ru/scientific/conference/xix/winter/chronik/xxcentury_1

FURTHER READING IN ENGLISH

In addition to *War and Peace*, *Anna Karenina* and *Resurrection*, all of which are widely available in English translation, two anthologies of Tolstoy's shorter works can be recommended: *Great Short Works of Leo Tolstoy*, tr. Louise and Aylmer Maude (1969), and *Tolstoy's Short Fiction*, ed. and tr. Michael R. Katz, 2nd edn (2008), which is accompanied by a selection of critical articles. Also valuable are the Penguin editions of *Childhood, Boyhood and Youth*, translated by Rosemary Edmonds (1973), *The Sebastopol Sketches*, translated and introduced by David McDuff (1986), and *How Much Land Does a Man Need?*, translated by Ronald Wilks with an introduction by A. N. Wilson (1993)

English translations of Tolstoy's religious works include *A Confession and Other Religious Writings*, ed. and tr. Jane Kentish (1987), and *Last Steps: The Late Writings of Leo Tolstoy*, ed. and tr. Jay Parini (2009). *A Calendar of Wisdom: Daily Thoughts to Nourish the Soul*, ed. and tr. Peter Sekirin (1997), is a translation of Tolstoy's last major religious compilation *Put' zhizni* (*The Path of Life*).

Two essential biographical sources are *Tolstoy's Diaries*, ed. and tr. R. F. Christian (1985), and *The Diaries of Sofia Tolstoy*, tr. Cathy Porter (2009). Also recommended is Leah Bendavid-Val, *Song Without Words: The Photographs and Diaries of Sophia Tolstoy* (2007). Amongst biographies, the most dependable are Aylmer Maude, *The Life of Tolstoy* (1930), and A. N. Wilson, *Tolstoy* (1988).

For critical literature on Tolstoy, *The Cambridge Companion to Tolstoy*, ed. Donna Tussing Orwin (2002), and Richard F. Gustafson's *Leo Tolstoy: Resident and Stranger – A Study in Fiction and Theology* (1986) are a good place to start.

SELECT BIBLIOGRAPHY

Primary Sources

EDITIONS OF TOLSTOY'S WORKS

L. N. Tolstoi, *Polnoe sobranie sochinenii*, ed. V. G Chertkov, 90 vols, Moscow, 1928–1958

L. N. Tolstoi, *Polnoe sobranie sochinenii v sta tomakh*, ed. L. D. Gromova- Opul'skaya et al.; *Khudozhestvennye proizvedeniya v vosemnadtsati tomakh*, Moscow, 2000

CORRESPONDENCE

B. L. Modzalevsky, ed., *Perepiska L. N. Tolstogo s Gr. A. A. Tolstoi, 1857–1903*, St Petersburg, 1911

A. A. Donskov, ed., *L. N. Tolstoi i T. M. Bondarev: perepiska*, Munich, 1996

A. A. Donskov, ed., *L. N. Tolstoi i S. A. Tolstaya: Perepiska s N. N. Strakhovym*, Ottawa, 2000

N. A. Kalinina et al., eds, *Perepiska L. N. Tolstogo s sestroi i brat'yami*, Moscow, 1990

A. T. Tolstaya, S. A. Tolstaya and P. S. Popov eds., *Pis'ma k L. N. Tolstomu, 1862–1910*, Moscow, 1936

FAMILY MEMOIRS AND DIARIES

S. A. Behrs, *Recollections of Count Leo Tolstoy*, tr. Charles Edward Turner, London, 1893

A. Bers, 'Otryvki vospominanii o L. N. Tolstom', in *Tolstoi i o Tolstom: Novye materialy*, ed. V. G. Chertkov and N. N. Gusev, vol. 2, Moscow, 1926, 124–132

T. A. Kuzminskaya, *Moya zhizn' doma i v Yasnoi Poliane*, ed. T. N. Volkova, Tula, 1973

T. L. Sukhotina-Tolstaya, *Vospominaniya*, Moscow, 1976

T. L. Sukhotina-Tolstaya, *Dnevnik*, ed. T. Volkova, Moscow, 1984

A. L. Tolstaya, *Otets*, 2 vols, New York, 1953

A. L. Tolstaya, *Probleski v t'me*, Washington DC, 1965

S. A. Tolstaya, 'Iz zapisok Grafini Sofii Andreevny Tolstoi pod zaglaviem "Moya Zhizn"', in *Tolstovskii ezhegodnik*, St Petersburg, 1913

S. A. Tolstaya, *The Autobiography of Countess Sophie Tolstoi*, preface and notes by Vasilii Spiridonov, tr. S.S. Koteliansky and Leonard Woolf, Richmond, 1922

S. A. Tolstaya, *Dnevniki v dvukh tomakh*, ed. V. E. Vatsuro et al., 2 vols, Moscow, 1978

S. A. Tolstaya, 'Moya zhizn", *Novyi mir*, 8 (1978), 34–134

S. A. Tolstaya, 'Moya zhizn", *Prometei: istoriko-biograficheskii al'manakh serii "Zhizn' zamechatel'nykh lyudei"*, 12 (1980), 148–198

S. A. Tolstaya, *Povarennaya kniga S. A. Tolstoi*, Tula, 1991

S. A. Tolstaya, 'Moya zhizn", *Oktyabr'*, 9 (1998), 136–177

I. L. Tolstoi, *Moi vospominaniya* (1933), Moscow, 1969

L. L. Tolstoi, *V Yasnoi Polyane. Pravda ob otse i ego zhizni*, Prague, 1923

L. L. Tolstoi, *The Truth about My Father*, London, 1924

S. L. Tolstoi, *Ocherki Bylogo*, 3rd rev. edn, Tula, 1965

S. L. Tolstoy, *Sergej Tolstoy and the Doukhobors: A Journey to Canada*, ed. Andrew Donskov, Ottawa, 1998 [Sergey's 1898–1899 diary and unpublished letters]

Secondary Sources

Anna Aksakova (Tyutcheva), *Pri dvore dvukh imperatorov*, Moscow, 2008

Mark Aldanov, 'A Russian Commune in Kansas', *Russian Review*, 1 (1944), 30–44

M. P. Alekseev et al., eds., *Prometei, 12: Tolstovskii vypusk. Istoriko-biograficheskii al'manakh, posviashchennyi 150-letiiu so dnia rozhdeniia L.N. Tolstogo*, Moscow, 1980

N. N. Apostolov, *Tolstoi i russkoe samoderzhavie*, Moscow, 1928, 125–126

W. H. G. Armytage, *Heavens Below: Utopian Experiments in England, 1560–1960*, London, 1961

W. H. G. Armytage, 'J. C. Kenworthy and the Tolstoyan Communities in England', *Tolstoy and Britain* (1995), 135–152

A. M. Astakhova, ed., *Il'ya Muromets*, Moscow, 1958

V. Astalov and S. Gapurov, 'Tersko-grebenski kazaki i chechentsy v XVI–XIX vekakh', in *L. N. Tolstoi i Sheikh Kunta-Khadzhi Kishnev: problemy mira i gumanizma*, Tula, 2006, 17–38

E. G. Babaev, 'Bol'shaya azbuka ili oshchushchenie shchast'ya', *Knizhnye sokrovishcha knigi. Iz fondov Gosudarstvennoi biblioteki im. V. I. Lenina*, Moscow, 1989, 94–109

O. G. Baranova et al., *Russkii prazdnik. Prazdniki i obryady narodnogo zemledel'cheskogo kalendarya: illyustrirovannaya entsiklopediya*, St Petersburg, 2002

R. Bartlett, 'Japonisme and Japanophobia: The Russo-Japanese War in Russian Cultural Consciousness', *Russian Review*, 1 (2008), 1–38

Edward Spencer Beesly, *The Life and Death of William Frey*, London, 1888

I. S. Belliustin, *Description of the Clergy in Rural Russia: The Memoir of a Nineteenth-Century Parish Priest*; tr. with an interpretive essay by Gregory L. Freeze, Ithaca, 1985

Elena Belyakova, *Tserkovnyi sud i problemy tserkovnoi zhizni*, Moscow, 2004

Leah Bendavid-Val, *Song Without Words: The Photographs and Diaries of Countess Sophia Tolstoy*, Washington DC, 2007

N. Berdyaev, 'Vetkhii i novii zavet v religioznom soznanii L. Tolstogo', in *O religii L'va Tolstogo*, Moscow, 1912, 172–195

N. Berdyaev, *The Origin of Russian Communism*, tr. R. M. French, London, 1937

N. Berdyaev, *The Russian Idea*, London, 1947

N. Berdyaev, 'Dukhovnoe khristianstvo i sektantstvo v Rossii', *Russkaya mysl'*, 11 (1916), reproduced in N. Berdyaev, *Sobranie sochinenii*, vol. 3, Paris, 1989, 441–462

N. Berdyaev, 'Dukhi russkoi revolyutsii', in *Iz glubiny*, Paris, 1918

Pavel Biryukov, *Lev Nikolaevich Tolstoi: Biografiya*, 4 vols, Moscow, 1906–1910, rev. edn 1911–1923

Y. Bitovt, ed., *Graf L. N. Tolstoi v karrikaturakh i anekdotakh*, Moscow, 1908

V. Bonch-Bruevich, ed., *Letopisi Gosudarstvennogo literaturnogo muzeya*, vol. 12: *L. N. Tolstoi*, Moscow, 1938

D. A. Bondarev, *Tolstoi i sovremennost'*, Moscow, 1928

Alexander Boot, *God and Man According to Tolstoy*, New York, 2009

I. Borisova, ed., *Neizvestnyi Tolstoi v arkhivakh Rossii i SShA*, Moscow, 1994

Peter Brang, *Ein Unbekanntes Russland: Kulturgeschichte vegetarischer Lebensweisen von den Anfängen bis zur Gegenwart*, Cologne, 2002

Nicholas Breyfogle, *Heretics and Colonizers: Forging Russia's Empire in the South Caucasus*, Ithaca, 2005

Jeffrey Brooks, *When Russia Learned to Read: Literacy and Popular Literature, 1861–1917*, Princeton, 1985

V. Bulgakov, *O Tolstom*, Tula, 1964

V. Bulgakov, *L. N. Tolstoi v poslednii god ego zhizni*, Moscow, 1989

N. I. Burnasheva, ed., *'Tolstoi – eto tselyi mir': stat'i i issledovaniya*, Moscow, 2004

Graham Camfield, 'From Tolstoyan to Terrorist: The Revolutionary Career of Prince D. A. Khilkov, 1900–1905', *Revolutionary Russia*, 12, 1 (1999), 1–43

Vladimir Chertkov, *Ukhod Tolstogo*, Moscow, 1922

Sergii Chetverikov, *Optina Pustyn'*, Paris, 1926

R. F. Christian, 'The Road to Yasnaya Polyana: Some Pilgrims from Britain and their Reminiscences', *Slavonic and East European Review*, 66, 4 (1988), 526–552; reproduced in W. Gareth Jones, ed., *Tolstoy and Britain*, Oxford, 1995

Chris J. Chulos, 'Russian Piety and Culture from Peter the Great to 1917', in *Cambridge History of Christianity*, vol. 5: *Eastern Christianity*, ed. Michael Angold, Cambridge, 2006, 348–70

J. Eugene Clay, 'Orthodox Missionaries and "Orthodox Heretics" in Russia, 1886–1917', in *Of Religion and Empire: Missions, Conversion, and Tolerance in Tsarist Russia*, ed. Robert P. Geraci and Michael Khodarkovsky, Ithaca, 2001

Robert Croskey, *The Legacy of Tolstoy: Alexandra Tolstoy and the Soviet Regime in the 1920s*, Seattle, 2008

Edwina Cruise, 'Tracking the English Novel in *Anna Karenina*: Who Wrote the English Novel that Anna reads?', in *Anniversay Essays on Tolstoy*, ed. Donna Tussing Orwin, Cambridge, 2010, 159–182

John Shelton Curtiss, *Church and State in Russia: The Last Years of the Empire, 1900–1917*, New York, 1940

Marquis de Custine, *Empire of the Czar: The Social, Political, and Religious State and Prospects of Russia, Made During a Journey Through That Empire*, 3 vols, London, 1843

G. S. Demeter, ed., *Istoriya tsygan: novyi vzglyad*, Voronezh, 2000

Michael Denner, '"Be Not Afraid of Greatness", Leo Tolstoy and Celebrity', *Journal of Popular Culture*, vol. 42, 4 (2009), 614–45

Simon Dixon, 'Superstition in Imperial Russia', *Past and Present*, 3 (2008), 207–228

Alexandre Dumas, *L'Homme-femme*, Paris, 1872

William Edgerton, tr. and ed., *Memoirs of Peasant Tolstoyans in Soviet Russia*, Bloomington, 1993

Robert Edwards, 'Tolstoy and Alice B. Stockham: The Influence of "Tokology" on *The Kreutzer Sonata*', *Tolstoy Studies Journal*, 6 (1993), 87–104

Boris Eikhenbaum, *Lev Tolstoi: semidesyatye gody*, Leningrad, 1960

Ben Eklof, *Russian Peasant Schools: Officialdom, Village Culture, and Popular Pedagogy, 1861–1914*, Berkeley, 1986

Barbara Alpern Engel, 'In the Name of the Tsar: Competing Legalities and Marital Conflict in Late Imperial Russia', *Journal of Modern History*, 77, 1 (2005), 70–95

Barbara Alpern Engel, 'Women, the Family and Public Life', *The Cambridge History of Russia*, vol. 2: *Imperial Russia, 1689–1917*, ed. Dominic Lieven, Cambridge, 2006, 306–325

V. Fedorov, *Russkaya pravoslavnaya tserkov' i gosudarstvo: sinodal'nyi period, 1700–1917*, Moscow, 2003

Kathryn B. Feuer, *Tolstoy and the Genesis of 'War and Peace'*, ed. Robin Feuer Miller and Donna Tussing Orwin, Ithaca, 1996

Alexander Fodor, *Tolstoy and the Russians: Reflections on a Relationship*, Ann Arbor, 1984

Alexander Fodor, *A Quest for a Non-Violent Russia: The Partnership of Leo Tolstoy and Vladimir Chertkov*, Lanham, Md, 1989

G. L. Freeze, *The Parish Clergy in Nineteenth-Century Russia: Crisis, Reform, Counter-Reform*, Princeton, 1983

G. L. Freeze, 'Bringing Order to the Russian Family: Marriage and Divorce in Imperial Russia, 1760–1860', *Journal of Modern History*, 62, 4 (1990), 709–746

V. M. Friche, ed., *O Tolstom: literaturno-kriticheskii sbornik*, Moscow, 1928

V. M. Friche, ed., *L. N. Tolstoi v svete marksistskoi kritiki*, Moscow, 1929

Henry Gifford, *Tolstoy*, Oxford, 1982

E. E. Gorbunova-Posadova, *Drug Tolstogo Mariya Aleksandrovna Schmidt*, Moscow, 1929

A. Grodetskaya, *Otvety predaniya: zhitiya svyatikh v dukhovnom poiske L'va Tolstogo*, St Petersburg, 2000

I. M. Gromoglasov, *Tretii vserossiiskii missionerskii s'ezd*, Sergiev Posad, 1898

A. V. Gulin, *Lev Tolstoi i puti russkoi istorii*, Moscow, 2004

N. N. Gusev, *Lev Nikolaevich Tolstoi. Materialy k biografii s 1828 po 1855 god*, Moscow, 1954

N. N. Gusev, *Lev Nikolaevich Tolstoi. Materialy k biografii s 1855 po 1869 god*, Moscow, 1957

N. N. Gusev, *Letopis' zhizni i tvorchestva L. N. Tolstogo, 1828–1890*, Moscow, 1958

N. N. Gusev, *Letopis' zhizni i tvorchestva L'va Nikolaevicha Tolstogo, 1891–1910*, Moscow, 1960

N. N. Gusev, *Lev Nikolaevich Tolstoi. Materialy k biografii s 1870 po 1881 god*, Moscow, 1963

N. N. Gusev, *Lev Nikolaevich Tolstoi. Materialy k biografii s 1881 po 1885 god*, Moscow, 1970

N. N. Gusev, ed., *Tolstoi i o Tolstom: Novye materialy*, 4 vols, Moscow, 1924–1928

N. N. Gusev, ed., *L. N. Tolstoi: K 120-letiyu so dnya rozhdeniya (1828–1948)*, 2 vols, Moscow, 1948

N. N. Gusev et al., eds., *L. N. Tolstoi v vospominaniyakh sovremennikov*, 2 vols, rev. edn, Moscow, 1978

Richard Gustafson, *Leo Tolstoy: Resident and Stranger: A Study in Fiction and Theology*, Princeton, 1986

Isabel Hapgood, *Russian Rambles*, London, 1895

E. Heier, *Religious Schism in the Russian Aristocracy, 1860–1900: Radstockism and Pashkovism*, The Hague, 1970

Ian M. Helfant, *The High Stakes of Identity: Gambling in the Life and Literature of Nineteenth-Century Russia*, Evanston, 2002

Leonid Heretz, *Russia on the Eve of Modernity: Popular Religion and Traditional Culture Under the Last Tsars*, Cambridge, 2008

M. J. de K. Holman, 'The Purleigh Colony: Tolstoyan Togetherness in the Late 1890s', in *New Essays on Tolstoy*, ed. Malcolm Jones, Cambridge, 1978, 194–222

M. J. de K. Holman, 'Half a Life's Work: Aylmer Maude Brings Tolstoy to Britain', *Scottish Slavonic Review*, 1 (1985), 39–53

David Jackson, *The Wanderers and Critical Realism in Nineteenth-Century Russian Painting*, Manchester, 2006

W. Gareth Jones, ed., *Tolstoi and Britain*, Oxford, 1995

Malcolm V. Jones, 'A Note on Mr. J. G. Blissmer and the Society for the Encouragement of Spiritual and Ethical Reading', *Slavonic and East European Review*, 130 (January 1975), 92–96

K. Kallaur, 'L. N. Tolstoi i Edin Ballu: dukhovnoe rodstvo', *Neizvestnyi Tolstoi v arkhivakh Rossii i SShA*, ed. I. Borisova, Moscow, 1994

Andreas Kappeler, *The Russian Empire: A Multiethnic History*, tr. Alfred Clayton, London, 2001

Leonid Kavelin, *Istoricheskoe opisanie Korennoi Rozhdestvo-Bogoroditskoi Pustyni*, Moscow, 1876.

Walter Kerr, *The Shabunin Affair: An Episode in the Life of Leo Tolstoy*, Ithaca, 1982

Yury Khechinov, *Krutye dorogi Aleksandry Tolstoi*, Moscow, 1995

Charles King, *Ghost of Freedom: A History of the Caucasus*, Oxford, 2008

Nadieszda Kizenko, 'Ioann of Kronstadt and the Reception of Sanctity', *Russian Review*, 57 (July 1998), 325–344

Nadieszda Kizenko, *A Prodigal Saint: Father John of Kronstadt and the Russian People*, University Park, 2000

Geir Kjetsaa, *Dostoyevsky: A Writer's Life*, tr. Siri Hustvedt and David McDuff, London, 1987

A. Klibanov, *Iz mira religioznogo sektantstva: vstrechi, besedy, nablyudeniya*, Moscow, 1974

J. G. Kohl, *Russia*, London, 1842

Pål Kolstø, 'Leo Tolstoy, a Church Critic Influenced by Orthodox Thought,' *Church, Nation and State in Russia and Ukraine*, Geoffrey Hosking, ed., London, 1991, 148–166

Pål Kolstø, 'A Mass for a Heretic? The Controversy over Lev Tolstoi's Burial', *Slavic Review*, 60, 1 (2001), 75–95

Pål Kolstø, 'The Demonized Double: The Image of Lev Tolstoi in Russian Orthodox Polemics', *Slavic Review*, 65, 2 (2006), 304–324

Pål Kolstø, 'The Elder at Iasnaia Poliana: Lev Tolstoi and the Orthodox *Starets* Tradition', *Kritika*, 9, 3 (2008), 533–554

T. V. Komarova, ed., *Druz'ya i gosti Yasnoi Polyane: materialy nauchnoi konferentsee posvyashchennoi 160-letiyu S. A. Tolstoi*, Tula, 2006

Laurence Kominz, 'Pilgrimage to Tolstoy: Tokutomi Roka's Junrei Kiko', *Monumenta Japonica*, 41, 1 (1986), 51–101

P. N. Krasnov and L. M. Vol'f, eds., *Gr. Lev Tolstoi: velikii pisatel' zemli russkoi v portretakh, grayurakh, zhivopisi, skul'pture, karikaturakh i t d.*, Moscow, 1903

V. Lakshin, 'Vozvrashchenie Tolstogo-myslitelya', *Voprosy literatury*, 5 (1988), 104–117

V. Lakshin, ed., *Interv'yu i besedy s L'vom Tolstym*, Moscow, 1986

Ronald D. LeBlanc, 'Tolstoy's Way of No Flesh: Abstinence, Vegetarianism, and Christian Physiology', in *Food in Russian History and Culture*, ed. Musya Glants and Joyce Toomre, Bloomington, 1997

Georgii Lesskis, *Lev Tolstoi (1852–1869)*, Moscow, 2000

Dominic Lieven, *Russia Against Napoleon: The Battle for Europe, 1807 to 1814*, London, 2009

Literaturnoe nasledstvo, 35/36, 37/38, Moscow, 1939; 69, 2 vols, Moscow 1961; 75, 2 vols, Moscow, 1965 [all volumes dedicated to the publication of materials about Tolstoy]

Y. M. Lotman, *Besedy o russkoi kul'ture*, St Petersburg, 1997

Victor Lucas, *Tolstoy in London*, London, 1979

A. V. Lunacharskii, 'Tolstoi i Marks', *Sobranie sochinenii v vos'mi tomakh*, vol. 1, Moscow, 1963

Y. Lur'e, *Posle L'va Tolstogo*, St Petersburg, 1993

David MacKenzie, *The Serbs and Russian Pan-Slavism, 1875–1878*, Ithaca, 1967

David Magarshack, ed. and tr., *Turgenev's Literary Reminiscences and Autobiographical Fragments*, London, 1984

Barbara W. Maggs, 'The Franklin–Tolstoy Influence Controversy', *Proceedings of the American Philosophical Society*, 129 (1985), 268–277

V. A. Maklakov, *Tolstoi i Bol'shevizm*, Paris, 1921

Michelle Lamarche Marrese, 'Gender and the Legal Order in Imperial Russia', in *The Cambridge History of Russia*, vol. 2: *Imperial Russia, 1689–1917*, ed. Dominic Lieven, Cambridge, 2006, 326–343

David Matual, *Tolstoy's Translation of the Gospels: A Critical Study*, Lewiston, 1992

P. Matveev, 'L. N. Tolstoi i N. N. Strakhov v Optinoi Pustyni', *Istoricheskii vestnik*, 2 (1907), 151–157

Aylmer Maude, *The Life of Tolstoy* (1930), Ware, 2008

James Mavor, *My Windows on the Street of the World*, 2 vols, London, 1923

B. Mazurin, 'O kommune "Zhizn' i trud"', *Novyi mir*, 9 (1988), 180–226

Hugh McLean, *In Quest of Tolstoy*, Brighton, Mass., 2008

Inessa Medzhibovskaya, 'Every Man in His Tolstoy Humor: On Lev Osterman, Questions of Method and More', *Tolstoy Studies Journal*, 19 (2007), 108–118

Inessa Medzhibovskaya, *Tolstoy and the Religious Culture of his Time: A Biography of a Long Conversation*, Lanham, MD, 2008

B. Meilakh, *Ukhod i smert' L'va Tolstogo*, Moscow, 1960

E. D. Meleshko, *Khristianskaya etika L. N. Tolstogo*, Moscow, 2006

S. Mel'gunov, *Tserkov' i gosudarstvo v Rossii: k voprosu o svobode sovesti*, Moscow, 1907

D. Merezhkovskii, *Tsarstvo antikhrista*, Paris, 1923

Priscilla Meyer, *How the Russians Read the French: Lermontov, Dostoevsky, Tolstoy*, Madison, 2008

I. I. Mints and S. A. Tolstaya-Esenina, eds., *Yasnaya Polyana: Stat'i i dokumenty*, Moscow, 1942

Elliott Mossman, 'Tolstoi and Peasant Learning in the Era of the Great Reforms', in Ben Eklof, ed., *School and Society in Tsarist and Soviet Russia*, Basingstoke, 1993, 36–69

T. L. Motyleva, *Khudozhestvennye proizvedeniya L. N. Tolstogo v perevodakh na inostrannye yazyki: otdel'nye zarubezhnye izdaniya: bibliografiia*, Moscow, 1961

M. V. Muratov, *L. N. Tolstoi i V. G. Chertkov*, Moscow, 1934

Daniel Murphy, *Tolstoy and Education*, Blackrock, 1992

M. N. Nazimova, 'Iz semeinoi khroniki Tolstykh', *Istoricheskii vestnik*, 10 (1902), 104–132

Irina Nenarkomova, *Pavel Tret'yakov i ego galereya*, Moscow, 1998

V. I. Nevskii, ed., *Smert' Tolstogo po novym materialam*, Moscow, 1929

Robert L. Nichols, 'The Orthodox Elders (Startesy) of Imperial Russia', *Modern Greek Studies Yearbook*, 1 (1985), 1–30

Robert L. Nichols, 'The Friends of God: Nicholas II and Alexandra at the Canonization of Serafim of Sarov, July 1903', in *Religious and Secular Forces in Late Tsarist Russia*, ed. Charles E. Timberlake, Seattle, 1992, 206–230

Uil'yam Nikell, 'Smert' Tolstogo', *Novoe literaturnoe obozrenie*, 44 (2000) 43–61

William Nickell, 'The Twain Shall Be of One Mind: Tolstoy in "Leag" with Eliza Burnz and Henry Parkhurst', *Tolstoy Studies Journal*, 6 (1993), 123–151

William Nickell, 'Transfigurations of Tolstoy's Final Journey: The Church and the Media in 1910'; *Tolstoy Studies Journal*, 17 (2006), 32–51

William Nickell, 'Tolstoi in 1928: In the Mirror of the Revolution', in *Epic Revisionism: Russian History and Literature as Stalinist Propaganda*, ed. Kevin M. F. Platt and David Brandenberger, Madison, 2006

Nina Nikitina, *Yasnaya Polyana: puteshestvie s L'vom Tolstym*, Tula, 2002

Nina Nikitina, *Povsednevnaya zhizn L'va Tolstogo v Yasnoi polyane*, Moscow, 2007

Nina Nikitina, *Sof'ya Tolstaya*, Moscow, 2010

N. A. Nikitina and V. P. Nikitin, 'Yasnaya Polyana vremen detstva i yunosti Tolstogo', in *Yasnopolyanskii sbornik*, Tula, 1982, 135–150

A. D. Obolenskii, 'Dve vstrechi s L. N. Tolstym', in *Tolstoi. Pamyatniki tvorchestva i zhizni*, vol. 3, Moscow, 1923

Max J. Okenfuss, ed. and tr., *The Travel Diary of Peter Tolstoi: A Muscovite in Early Modern Europe*, DeKalb, 1987

L. D. Opul'skaya, *Lev Nikolaevich Tolstoi: materialy k biografii s 1886 po 1892*, Moscow, 1979

L. D. Opul'skaya, *Lev Nikolaevich Tolstoi: materialy k biografii s 1892 po 1899 god*, Moscow, 1998

Al'bert Opul'skii, *Vokrug imeni L'va Tolstogo*, San Francisco, 1981

Georgii Orekhanov, *Zhestokii sud Rossii: V. G. Chertkov v zhizni L. N. Tolstogo*, Moscow, 2009

Alexandra Orlova, *Tchaikovsky: A Self Portrait*, tr. R. M. Davison, Oxford, 1990

Lev Osterman, *Srazhenie za Tolstogo*, Moscow, 2002

Donna Tussing Orwin, *Tolstoy's Art and Thought, 1847–1880*, Princeton, 1993

Irina Paperno, *Suicide as a Cultural Institution in Dostoevsky's Russia*, Ithaca, 1997

Irina Paperno, 'Tolstoy's Diaries: The Inacessible Self', *Self and Story in Russian History*, ed. Laura Engelstein and Stephanie Sandler, Ithaca, 2000, 242–265

S. A. Papkov, 'Zalozhniki sovesti (Tolstovtsy na Solovkakh)', in *Vozvrashchenie pamyati. Istoriko-arkhivnyi al'manakh*, vol. 3, ed. I. V. Pavlova, Novosibirsk, 1997

N. I. Pavlenko, *Ptentsy gnezda Petrova*, Moscow, 1984

I. V. Petrovitskaya, "Tolstovskii s'ezd russkikh zhurnalistov. 1908 god", in *Iz istorii russkoi literatury i zhurnalistiki: Ezhgodnik*, ed. I. V. Petrovitskaya and I. E. Prokhorov, Moscow, 2009, 243–245

S. M. Polovinkin, ed., *Zapiski peterburgskikh Religiozno-filosofskikh sobranii (1901–1903)*, Moscow, 2005, 45–70

T. Polyakova, 'Velosiped No. 97011', *Prometei*, 12 (1980), 415–418

Mark Popovsky, *Russkie muzhiki rasskazyvayut: posledovateli L. N. Tolstogo v Sovetskom Soyuze*, London, 1983

N. Puzin, *Dom-muzei L. N. Tolstogo v Yasnoi Polyane*, Tula, 2001

Nicholas V. Riasanovsky, *The Image of Peter the Great in Russian History and Thought*, Oxford, 1985

Roy Robson, 'Transforming Solovki: Pilgrim Narratives, Modernization and Late Imperial Monastic Life', in *Sacred Stories: Religion and Spirituality in Modern Russia*, ed. Mark Steinberg and Heather Coleman, Bloomington, 2008

Will Ryan, 'W. R. S. Ralston and the Russian Folktale', *Folklore*, 120 (2009), 2, 123–132.

L. Sabaneev, *Russkaya okhota* (1892), Moscow, 2003

L. L. Sabaneev, *Sergei Ivanovich Taneev: lichnost', tvorchestvo i dokumenty ego zhizni: k 10-ti letiyu so dnya smerti, 1915–1925*, Moscow, 1925

L. L. Sabaneev, *S. I. Taneev: Mysli o tvorchestve i vospominaniya o zhizni*, Paris, 1930

Hermann von Samson-Himmelstierna, *Russia under Alexander III*, tr. J. Morrison, ed. Felix Volkhovsky, London, 1893

L. I. Saraskina, 'Neverie i nedoverie kak etapy dukhovnogo poiska russkikh pisatelei XIX veka', in *Yasnopolyanskii sbornik*, Tula, 2008, 343–365

Eugene Schuyler, 'Count Leo Tolstoy Twenty Years Ago,' *Scribner's Magazine*, May 1889, 537–552, June 1889, 733–747

P. Sergeenko, ed., *O Tolstom*, Moscow, 1911

Vitaly Shentalinskii, *Donos na sokrata*, Moscow, 2001

V. Shklovskii, *Lev Tolstoi*, Moscow, 1963

Ernest J. Simmons, *Tolstoy*, London, 1973

Andrei Sinyavsky, *Ivan the Fool: Russian Folk Belief: A Cultural History*, tr. Joanne Turnbull and Nikolai Formozov, Moscow, 2007

V. G. Sirotkin, *Napoleon i Rossiya*, Moscow, 2000

A. S. Skorokhodova, '"Russkii" religioznyi pozitivist V. Frei', *Sotsiologicheskie issledovaniya*, 9 (1997), 93–98

V. I. Sreznevskii and I. L. Bem, *Tolstoi: Pamyatniki tvorchestva i zhizni*, 4 vols, Moscow, 1917–1923

S. Stakhovich, 'Kak pisalsya "Kholstomer"', in *L. N. Tolstoi*, vol. 1, Moscow, 1938, 332–336

Jonas Stadling and Will Reason, *In the Land of Tolstoi: Experiences of Famine and Misrule in Russia*, London, 1897

Leonard J. Stanton, *The Optina Pustyn Monastery in the Russian Literary Imagination: Iconic Vision in Works by Dostoevsky, Gogol, Tolstoy, and Others*, New York, 1995

William Stead, *The Truth About Russia*, London, 1888

Richard Stites, *Serfdom, Society and the Arts in Imperial Russia: The Pleasure and the Power*, New Haven, 2005

I. N. Sukikh, *Voina iz-za 'Voiny i mira': Roman L. N. Tolstogo 'Voina i mir' v russkoi kritike i literaturovedenii*, St Petersburg, 2002

Joy Thacker, *Whiteway Colony: The Social History of a Tolstoyan Community*, Stroud, 1993

Ewa M. Thompson, *Understanding Russia: The Holy Fool in Russian Culture*, Lanham Md, 1987

I. V. Tolstoi, *Svet Yasnoi Polyany*, Moscow, 1986

S. L. Tolstoi, 'Muzykal'nye proizvedeniya, lyubimye L. N. Tolstym (po vospominaniyam S. L. Tolstogo)', in *Tolstovskii ezhegodnik*, St Petersburg, 1913, 161–162

S. L. Tolstoi, *Fedor Tolstoi Amerikanets*, Moscow, 1926

S. M. Tolstoi, *Tolstoï et les Tolstoï: Essais de l'histoire de la famille*, Paris, 1980

S. M. Tolstoi, 'Edinstvennnaya sestra', *Prometei*, 12 (1980), 269–287

S. M. Tolstoi, *Tolstoi i Tolstye. Ocherki iz istorii roda*, Moscow, 1990

V. I. Tolstoi, ed., *Russkie mysliteli o L've Tolstom*, Tula, 2002

M. A. Tsyavlovsky, 'Kak pisalsya i pechatalsya roman "Voina i mir"', in *Tolstoi i o Tolstom: Novye materialy*, ed. N. Gusev, vol. 3, Moscow, 1927, 120–174

A. N. Varlamov, 'Lev Tolstoi, Stolypin and Ieromonakh Iliodor', in *Yasnopolyanskii sbornik*, ed. V. I. Tolstoi et al., Tula, 2008, 419–426

T. N. Volkova, ed., *Tolstoi i ego blizkie*, Moscow, 1986

William G. Wagner, *Marriage, Property and Law in Late Imperial Russia*, Oxford, 1994

Andrzej Walicki, *A History of Russian Thought from the Enlightenment to Marxism*, tr. Hilda Andrews-Rusiecka, Oxford, 1980

Donald Mackenzie Wallace, *Russia*, London, 1877

A. N. Wilson, *Tolstoy*, London, 1988

George Woodcock, 'James Mavor, Peter Kropotkin, Lev Tolstoy and the Doukhobors', *From Russia with Love: the Doukhobors*, special issue of *Canadian Ethnic Studies*, 27, 3 (1995), 95–101

Christine Worobec, 'The Unintended Consequences of a Surge in Orthodox Pilgrimages in Late Imperial Russia', *Russian History*, 36 (2009), 62–76

M. Zabylin, *Russkii narod: obychai, predaniya, obryady i sueveriya*, Moscow, 2003

L. B. Zasedateleva, *Terskie kazaki (seredina XVI – nachalo XX v.). Istoriko-etnograficheskie ocherki*, Moscow, 1974

Vladimir Zhdanov, *Lyubov' v zhizni Tolstogo* (1928), Moscow, 2005

V. A. Zhdanov, 'K istorii sozdaniya "Anna Karenina": dva rannikh nabroska romana', in *Literaturnoe nasledstvo*, 69, vol. 1, Moscow, 1961

V. A. Zhdanov, 'Yasnaya Polyana v pervye gody revolyutsii (1917–1919)', *Yasnopolyanskii sbornik*, Tula, 1962

V. A. Zhdanov and E. E. Zaidenshnur, eds., L. N. Tolstoi, *Anna Karenina*, Literaturnye Pamyatniki, Moscow, 1970

Aleksei Zverev and Vladimir Tunimanov, *Lev Tolstoi*, Moscow, 2007

Stefan Zweig, *The World of Yesterday: An Autobiography* [translation of *Die Welt vom Gestern*, 1943], London, 1987

LIST OF ILLUSTRATIONS

Plates

1. Tolstoy as a newly promoted ensign, 1854.
2. Tolstoy with his brother Nikolay, 1851.
3. Sergey, Nikolay, Dmitry and Lev Tolstoy, February 1854.
4. The writers associated with the journal *The Contemporary*, St Petersburg, 1856. From left to right: Goncharov, Turgenev, Tolstoy, Grigorovich, Druzhinin and Ostrovsky.
5. Tolstoy in Brussels, 1861.
6. Alexandra Andreyevna Tolstaya (Alexandrine), 1860s.
7. Sofya (Sonya) Tolstaya and her younger sister Tatyana (Tanya) Bers, 1861.
8. Sonya in the drawing room at Yasnaya Polyana, 1902.
9. The old Yasnaya Polyana mansion where Tolstoy was born in 1828, and which he later sold to a neighbouring landowner.
10. Tolstoy's house at Yasnaya Polyana before the addition of a final extension in the 1890s.
11. Tolstoy by Kramskoy (1873).
12. Tolstoy ploughing with horses, 1887 by Repin.
13. Repin, Tolstoy in his study at Yasnaya Polyana, 1891.
14. Repin's first portrait of Tolstoy, 1887.
15. Sonya standing by a portrait of her deceased son Ivan (Vanechka), Yasnaya Polyana, 1897.
16. Tolstoy and his Starley Rover bicycle, 1895.
17. Tolstoy and Sonya, August 1895.
18. The Tolstoy children with their mother in Gaspra, Crimea, 1902.
19. Tolstoy and his sister Maria (Masha), 1908.
20. Tolstoy on horseback in the environs of Yasnaya Polyana, 1908.
21. Tolstoy at the opening of the People's Library in Yasnaya Polyana village, 31 January 1910.
22. Repin, Tolstoy barefoot, 1901.

Illustrations in the text

1. Tolstoy's maternal grandfather, Nikolay Sergeyevich Volkonsky.
2. The house in Moscow, to which Nikolay Ilyich Tolstoy brought his mother, sister and five children in 1837.
3. Page from the first edition of Tolstoy's *ABC* book, 1872.
4. The fourth draft of the opening of *Anna Karenina*, 1873.
5. Father Ambrosy, the Elder at Optina Pustyn Monastery.
6. Konstantin Pobedonostsev.
7. Vladimir Chertkov as a young man, 1880s.
8. Pencil drawing by Repin of Tolstoy reading in his favourite chair, 1887.
9. Cartoon showing 'Tolstoy at work'.
10. Tolstoy skating in the back garden of his Moscow house in 1898.
11. Dmitry Khilkov and Sergey Lvovich Tolstoy with a group of those accompanying the Dukhobors to Canada, 1899.
12. Cartoon showing Tolstoy as a giant next to the tiny Tsar, 1901.
13. Tolstoy photographed with his brother Sergey's widow, the former gypsy singer, 1906.
14. Tolstoy and Chertkov, Yasnaya Polyana, 1907.
15. Chertkov and employees of the Free Word Press at his house in Christchurch, 1906.

Picture credits

PLATES

Russian Museum, St Petersburg, / The Bridgeman Art Library: 22; Tretyakov Gallery, Moscow / The Bridgeman Art Library: 11, 12, 14; Leah Bendavid-Val, *Song Without Words: The Photographs & Diaries of Countess Sophia Tolstoy*, Washington, DC, 2007: 15; M. Loginova et al, *L. N. Tolstoi: Dokumenty. Rukopisi. Fotografii*, Moscow, 1995: 1–7, 10, 16–18, 20, 21; S. M. Tolstoi, *Tolstoi i Tolstye: ocherki iz istorii roda*, Moscow, 1990: 9, 19

ILLUSTRATIONS IN THE TEXT

L. N. Tolstoi, *Polnoe sobranie sochinenii*, ed. V. G Chertkov, 90 vols, Moscow, 1928–58, vol 20: 4; vol. 22: 3; M. Loginova et al, *L. N. Tolstoi: Dokumenty. Rukopisi. Fotografii*, Moscow, 1995: 2, 5, 6, 7, 11, 15; S. M. Tolstoi, *Tolstoi i Tolstye: ocherki iz istorii roda*, Moscow, 1990, : 1, 8, 13; Yury Bitovt, *Graf L. N. Tolstoi v karrikaturakh i anekdotakh*, Moscow, 1908: 9; P. N. Krasnov and L. M. Vol'f, eds., *Gr. Lev Tolstoi: velikii pisatel' zemli russkoi v portretakh, grayurakh, zhivopisi, skul'pture, karikaturakh i t d.*, Moscow, 1903: 12

ACKNOWLEDGEMENTS

Many people have helped me in various ways during the writing of this book, and I should like to thank: Catherine Clarke; Peter Carson, Penny Daniel, Trevor Horwood and Valentina Zanca; everyone at the Taylor Bodleian Slavonic Library in Oxford, in particular Jenny Griffiths; Gabriel Amherst, Paul and Hilary Bartlett, Clem Cecil, Olga Dubova, Jane Eagan, Michael Earley, Roberta di Giorgi, Candida Ghidini, Monika Greenleaf, Peter Greenleaf, Alexander Hoare, Lara Lamb, Inessa Medzhibovskaya, Nina Lobanov-Rostovsky, Judith Luna, Quentin Newark, Tom Newlin, Janet Phillips, Jennie de Protani, Damiano Rebecchini, Laura Rossi, Zoya Serebrennikova, Nick Stargardt, Vladimir Tarnopolsky, Lucy and Tom Walker and Nana Zhvitiashvili. Special thanks to David Tietjen.

INDEX

Figures in *italics* indicate captions.